The Book of

Useless Information

Publications International, Ltd.

Cover Illustration: Images.com/Corbis

Interior Illustrations: Hye Lim An, Art Explosion, Linda Howard Bittner, Erin Burke, Daisy De Puthod, Dan Grant, iStockphoto, Jupiterimages, Nicole H. Lee, Robert Schoolcraft, Shutterstock.com, Shavan R. Spears, Elizabeth Traynor, John Zielinski

ISBN: 978-1-4508-0746-3

Manufactured in U.S.A.

8 7 6 5 4 3 2 1

Contents

✳ ✳ ✳ ✳

Fill Your Head with Useless Information!

✳ ✳ ✳ ✳

WHAT EXACTLY MAKES INFORMATION "useless"? Certainly, if you're ever in the hot seat on a quiz show, you'll be thankful for every tiny bit of knowledge you've ever managed to commit to memory. But honestly, how often do you have to recall extraordinary facts in such a way? Still, just because something isn't practical, doesn't mean it can't be interesting or fun.

Whether you're looking for odd facts and trivia to share with friends at your next cocktail party, or if you simply love learning about the stranger facets of life, *The Book of Useless Information* is bound to entertain and enlighten. From the horrifying to the hilarious, there is more than enough stuff in this book to keep you occupied for hours.

Here's a small sample of what's in store for you:

✳ The link between rocket science and the occult

✳ An inventory of some famous Marilyn Monroe copycats

✳ Tips for surviving shark and bear attacks

✳ The origins of amazing things: from the Internet to ice cream cones

✳ Stories of bloodthirsty criminals and murderers

✳ And much, much more!

Useless or not, the contents of this book will help you to better know the world we live in and, in a small way, why things are the way they are. After all, when you are able to understand the small details, you can more easily see the big picture. Hey, maybe this information isn't so useless, after all!

Chapter 1

The Unexplained

The Kecksburg Incident

*Did visitors from outer space once land
in a western Pennsylvania thicket?*

✳ ✳ ✳ ✳

Dropping in for a Visit

O N DECEMBER 9, 1965, an unidentified flying object (UFO) streaked through the late-afternoon sky and landed in Kecksburg—a rural Pennsylvania community about 40 miles southeast of Pittsburgh. This much is not disputed. However, specific accounts vary widely from person to person. Even after closely examining the facts, many people remain undecided about exactly what happened. "Roswell" type incidents— ultra-mysterious in nature and reeking of a governmental cover-up—have an uncanny way of causing confusion.

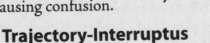

Trajectory-Interruptus

A meteor on a collision course with Earth will generally "bounce" as it enters the atmosphere. This occurs due to friction, which forcefully slows the average space rock from 6 to 45 miles per second to a few hundred miles per hour, the speed at which it strikes Earth and officially becomes a meteorite. According to the official explanation offered by the U.S. Air

Force, it was a meteorite that landed in Kecksburg. However, witnesses reported that the object completed back and forth maneuvers before landing at a very low speed—moves that an unpowered chunk of earthbound rock simply cannot perform. Strike one against the meteor theory.

An Acorn-Shape Meteorite?

When a meteor manages to pierce Earth's atmosphere, it has the physical properties of exactly what it is: a space rock. That is to say, it will generally be unevenly shaped, rough, and darkish in color, much like rocks found on Earth. But at Kecksburg, eyewitnesses reported seeing something far, far different. The unusual object they described was bronze to golden in color, acorn-shape, and as large as a Volkswagen Beetle automobile. Unless the universe has started to produce uniformly shaped and colored meteorites, the official explanation seems highly unlikely. Strike two for the meteor theory.

Markedly Different

Then there's the baffling issue of markings. A meteorite can be chock-full of holes, cracks, and other such surface imperfections. It can also vary somewhat in color. But it should never, ever have markings that seem intelligently designed. Witnesses at Kecksburg describe intricate writings similar to Egyptian hieroglyphics located near the base of the object. A cursory examination of space rocks at any natural history museum reveals that such a thing doesn't occur naturally. Strike three for the meteor theory. Logically following such a trail, could an unnatural force have been responsible for the item witnessed at Kecksburg? At least one man thought so.

Reportis Rigor Mortis

Just after the Kecksburg UFO landed, reporter John Murphy arrived at the scene. Like any seasoned pro, the newsman immediately snapped photos and gathered eyewitness accounts of the event. Strangely, FBI agents arrived, cordoned off the area, and confiscated all but one roll of his film. Undaunted,

Murphy assembled a radio documentary entitled *Object in the Woods* to describe his experience. Just before the special was to air, the reporter received an unexpected visit by two men. According to a fellow employee, a dark-suited pair identified themselves as government agents and subsequently confiscated a portion of Murphy's audiotapes. A week later, a clearly perturbed Murphy aired a watered-down version of his documentary. In it, he claimed that certain interviewees requested their accounts be removed for fear of retribution at the hands of police, military, and government officials. In 1969, John Murphy was struck dead by an unidentified car while crossing the street.

Resurrected by Robert Stack

In all likelihood the Kecksburg incident would have remained dormant and under-explored had it not been for the television show *Unsolved Mysteries*. In a 1990 segment, narrator Robert Stack took an in-depth look at what occurred in Kecksburg, feeding a firestorm of interest that eventually brought forth two new witnesses. The first, a U.S. Air Force officer stationed at Lockbourne AFB (near Columbus, Ohio), claimed to have seen a flatbed truck carrying a mysterious object as it arrived on base on December 10, 1965. The military man told of a tarpaulin-covered conical object that he couldn't identify and a "shoot to kill" order given to him for anyone who ventured too close. He was told that the truck was bound for Wright-Patterson AFB in Dayton, Ohio, an installation that's alleged to contain downed flying saucers. The other witness was a building contractor who claimed to have delivered 6,500 special bricks to a hanger inside Wright-Patterson AFB on December 12, 1965. Curious, he peeked inside the hanger and saw a "bell-shaped" device, 12-feet high, surrounded by several men wearing anti-radiation style suits. Upon leaving, he was told that he had just witnessed an object that would become "common knowledge" in the next 20 years.

Will We Ever Know the Truth?

Like Roswell before it, we will probably never know for certain what occurred in western Pennsylvania back in 1965. The more that's learned about the case, the more confusing and contradictory it becomes. For instance, the official 1965 meteorite explanation contains more holes than Bonnie and Clyde's death car, and other explanations, such as orbiting space debris (from past U.S. and Russian missions) reentering Earth's atmosphere, seem equally preposterous. In 2005, as the result of a new investigation launched by the Sci-Fi Television Network, NASA asserted that the object was a Russian satellite. According to a NASA spokesperson, documents of this investigation were somehow misplaced in the 1990s. Mysteriously, this finding directly contradicts the official air force version that nothing at all was found at the Kecksburg site. It also runs counter to a 2003 report made by NASA's own Nicholas L. Johnson, Chief Scientist for Orbital Debris. That document shows no missing satellites at the time of the incident. This includes a missing Russian Venus Probe (since accounted for)—the very item once considered a prime crash candidate.

Brave New World

These days, visitors to Kecksburg will be hard-pressed to find any trace of the encounter—perhaps that's how it should be. Since speculation comes to an abrupt halt whenever a concrete answer is provided, Kecksburg's reputation as "Roswell of the East" looks secure, at least for the foreseeable future. But if one longs for proof that something mysterious occurred there, they need look no further than the backyard of the Kecksburg Volunteer Fire Department. There, in all of its acorn-shape glory, stands an full-scale mock-up of the spacecraft reportedly found in this peaceful town on December 9, 1965. There too rests the mystery, intrigue, and romance that have accompanied this alleged space traveler for more than 40 years.

The Curse of the Boy King

The discovery of King Tut's tomb in 1922 is said to be the most important find ever in the field of Egyptology. But was there really a curse upon the interlopers who dared disturb the resting place of the boy king? Or was that just an urban legend?

❋ ❋ ❋ ❋

IN NOVEMBER 1922, English archaeologist Howard Carter announced one of the world's greatest archaeological finds: the resting place of Tutankhamen, Egypt's fabled boy king. At nine years old, he was the youngest pharaoh ever. The tomb, discovered in the Valley of the Kings, was amazingly intact; it was one of the few Egyptian tombs to have escaped grave robbers. The furnishings and treasures were dazzling. In fact, the golden death mask that adorned the sarcophagus is purported to be the most renowned example of Egyptian art.

The boy king, who reigned from 1355 to 1344 B.C., was only 19 years old when he died. Until recently, the cause of his death was a mystery to historians. Many believed Tut had been murdered, but a recent CT scan of the mummy conducted by a team of researchers dispelled that possibility. According to experts, his death may have been from an infection that occurred as the result of a broken leg.

The Curse That Won't Die

Another mystery surrounding the boy king is the alleged curse on anyone disturbing his resting place. That rumor can be traced back to the press. In 1923, shortly after the tomb was discovered, the man who endowed the expedition to locate Tut's tomb, Lord Carnarvon, was bitten on the cheek by a mosquito and died from a resulting infection. This was not an ominous event in itself, but when the lights of Cairo went out at the exact moment of his death, the press had a field day, and an urban legend was born. The legend continues to this day, especially each time Tut goes on tour.

The Mystery of Montauk

Montauk is a beach community at the eastern tip of Long Island in New York State. Conspiracy theorists, however, tell another tale. Has the U.S. government been hiding a secret at the former Camp Hero military base there?

* * * *

I N THE LATE 1950S, Montauk was not the paradise-style resort it is today. It was an isolated seaside community boasting a lighthouse commissioned by George Washington in 1792, an abandoned military base called Camp Hero, and a huge radar tower. This tower, still standing, is the last semiautomatic ground environment radar tower still in existence and features an antenna called AN/FPS-35. During its time of air force use, AN/FPS-35 was capable of detecting airborne objects at a distance of more than 200 miles. One of its uses was detecting potential Soviet long-distance bombers, as the Cold War was in full swing. According to conspiracy theorists, however, the antenna and Camp Hero had other purposes, namely human mind control and electro-magnetic field manipulation.

Vanishing Act

On October 24, 1943, the USS *Eldridge* was allegedly made invisible to human sight for a brief moment as it sat in a naval shipyard in Philadelphia. The event, which has never been factually substantiated but has been sworn as true by eyewitnesses and other believers for decades, is said to have been part of a U.S. military endeavor called the Philadelphia Experiment, or Project Rainbow. Studies in electromagnetic radiation had evidenced that manipulating energy fields and bending light around objects in certain ways could render them invisible. Since the benefits to the armed forces would be incredible, the navy supposedly forged ahead with the first experiment.

There are many offshoots to the conspiracy theory surrounding the alleged event. The crew onboard the USS *Eldridge* at the time in question are said to have suffered various mental illnesses, physical ailments, and, most notably, schizophrenia, which has been medically linked to exposure to electromagnetic radiation. Some of them supposedly disappeared along with the ship and relocated through teleportation to the naval base in Norfolk, Virginia, for a moment. Despite severely conflicting eyewitness reports and the navy's assertion that the *Eldridge* wasn't even in Philadelphia that day, many Web sites, books, a video game, and a 1984 science fiction film detail the event.

But what does this have to do with Montauk right now?

What's in the Basement?

Camp Hero was closed as a U.S. Army base in November 1957, although the air force continued to use its radar facilities. After the air force left in 1980, the surrounding grounds were ultimately turned into a state park, which opened to the public in September 2002. Yet the camp's vast underground facility remains under tight government jurisdiction, and the AN/FPS-35 radar tower still stands. Many say there is a government lab on-site that continues the alleged teleportation, magnetic field manipulation, and mind-control experiments of Project Rainbow. One reason for this belief is that two of the sailors onboard the *Eldridge* on October 24, 1943—Al Bielek and Duncan Cameron—claimed to have jumped from the ship while it was in "hyperspace" between Philadelphia and Norfolk, and landed at Camp Hero, severely disoriented.

Though Project Rainbow was branded a hoax, an urban legend continues to surround its "legacy," which is commonly known as the Montauk Project. Theorists cite experiments in electromagnetic radiation designed to produce mass schizophrenia over time and reduce a populace's resistance to governmental control, which, they believe, would explain the continual presence of the antenna. According to these suspicions, a large number of orphans, loners, and homeless people are subjected to testing in Camp Hero's basement; most supposedly die as a result.

Behind the Seal

The secret's out: A legendary fraternal organization is not quite as mysterious as people have been led to believe.

❋ ❋ ❋ ❋

CONSPIRACY THEORISTS DELIGHT in telling how the Freemasons rose from the ashes of the Knights Templar (an earlier secret society that protected Christians on the road to Jerusalem and supposedly guarded the location of the Holy Grail), founded the United States of America, and continue to shape world politics under the guise of their sister organization, the Illuminati. The truth, however, is much more sedate and much less "Hollywood."

Freemasonry is a fraternal organization—originally comprised of stonemasons and craftsmen—that now admits anyone who believes in a Supreme Being, is invited by an existing member, and enacts several secretive rituals. Before it became a gentlemen's society in the 1600s, Freemasonry was a guild of stonemasons working in and around England and Scotland. The "free" part of the name refers to the fact that they were not tied to the land, unlike most European people of that time.

Secretive or Just Undocumented?

Although Freemasonry practices secrecy, its murky origins are due more to the lack of reliable historical records than to any conspiracy. Freemasons pass down a story called the "Key of Solomon" as an allegorical creation myth. This story says Freemasonry originated during the building of Solomon's Temple in the 10th century B.C. Sources point to meetings at Masonic lodges in England as early as 1390, but it wasn't until the 1800s that the group made an impact. The first Grand Master was elected in 1717 at London's Goose and Gridiron alehouse. This new Mother Grand Lodge of the World ushered in the founding of Grand Lodges around Europe and North America and began the society's most influential period.

The principles of Freemasonry echoed those of the Enlightenment, such as charity and religious and political tolerance. The symbols on the seal of the Freemasons—a crossed square and compasses—are an architect's tools and represent the Masonic belief in a "Great Architect"—God. The three central tenets of Freemasonry are brotherly love, relief (charity), and truth.

During the 18th century, the Age of Enlightenment ushered in reform in Europe and North America. Freemasonry subscribed to these principles and helped shape the American and French revolutions, although—contrary to conspiracy theorists' claims—it did not foment these events alone. It should instead be seen as part of the intellectual framework that countered the tyranny and superstition still dominating Europe.

Because of their nondenominational religious beliefs and criticism of the role of the Church, Freemasons were first condemned by the 1738 Papal Bull, *In Eminenti*, which charged Church authorities to pursue and punish people involved in Freemasonry. Later pronouncements contained similar censure. During the mid-20th century, Nazi Germany and Stalinist Russia sent Freemasons to concentration camps.

The abject secrecy propagated by members has fostered legends about their origins. Some of these myths have become fodder for novelists like Dan Brown and Umberto Eco. Still, links between the Freemasons and the Knights Templar, the Catholic Church, or the Illuminati are only speculative.

Fun and Fellowship

What *is* known is that the Freemasons act to help each other by providing social contacts and resources. Purported members include almost every British king, Voltaire, Mozart, Benjamin Franklin, and presidents George Washington and Franklin Delano Roosevelt. The Shriners (the guys with the red fez hats and tiny cars) are also Masons. Primarily a charitable organization, the Shriners, or Shrine Masons, began in 1872 to promote "fun and fellowship." Not so mysterious anymore, is it?

Pope Joan: Was She or Wasn't He?

Posing as a man, a scholarly German woman of English descent entered the Catholic Church hierarchy, rising to become pope in A.D. 855. Her secret emerged, literally, when she gave birth to a son while riding in a papal procession through the streets of Rome. The populace, which just couldn't take a joke, tied her to a horse's tail and dragged her to death while stoning her.

✳ ✳ ✳ ✳

S o HERE'S THE question: Is this story fact or fiction?

What does the Holy See say?

Not a chance. They list Pope Benedict III, A.D. 855–858, with no suggestion that the Holy Father might have been a Holy Mother. The Church has long blamed anti-Catholic writers and saboteurs said to have doctored the evidence.

Surely that's plausible, given the avalanches of anti-Catholic hatred since the Reformation.

Up to a point, yes. Catholic-bashers pummelled the papacy with Pope Joan taunts. However, that cannot explain the pre-Reformation references.

An example, please.

Jan Hus, the Czech heretic burned at the stake in 1415 (a century before Luther picked up steam). In the trial record, Hus rebukes the papacy for letting a woman become pope.

That indicates only that the Inquisitors believed the legend at the time, not that it's true.

Good point. But then there's Martin of Poland, a Dominican who wrote his history of the papacy in 1265. He's the primary source for Pope Joan, the hardest to dismiss. He didn't hate the church; he held high rank as papal chaplain. Did someone doctor our oldest copy of his account (circa 1300s)? Hard to say.

Could a woman have pulled it off?

Possibly. Medical checkups were even rarer than baths. The clergy shaved, solving the dilemma of facial hair. Papal garments were heavy and hanging. Every reference to Joan attests to her great intellect, a necessary aspect since no idiot could have been elected pope in drag. It wouldn't be easy, but it's possible.

Okay: If Joan was so smart, she knew she was pregnant. How did she plan to dispose of the child?

That's a big weakness in the pro-Joan theory. You can cover up your body and tonsure your head, but ask anyone who's ever flown commercially: You can't keep a baby quiet. How would she care for the infant if she managed to give birth in secret? If it's possible to insult a mythical figure's legacy, suggesting that she might abandon the infant would be that insult. She'd have had to know this pregnancy wouldn't end well.

So, historian, what of this? Legend or covered-up truth?

Stoning a pope to death in the streets would have been a big event, which should have spawned at least a few contemporary accounts. Where are they? There isn't enough strong evidence to say, "Pope Joan existed." There is just enough to make us wonder if the legend has some basis in reality.

How could that be?

Stories morph and change. About 700 years span the time between Joan and the Protestant Reformation—nearly the lifespan of the Roman Republic and Empire combined. The story could have changed greatly in that time.

But we do not know.

Without compelling new evidence, we never will.

Unexplained Phenomena

If a phenomenon can't be readily explained, does that make it any less true to those who witnessed it?

✳ ✳ ✳ ✳

Moodus Noises

The Moodus Noises are thunderlike sounds that emanate from caves near East Haddam, Connecticut. The name itself is derived from the Native American word *machemoodus*, which means "place of noises." When European settlers came to the late 1600s, the Wangunk tribe warned them about the odd, supernatural sounds. In 1979, seismologists showed that the noises were always accompanied by small earthquakes spread over a small area. But no known faultline exists at Moodus. Nor does this describe how small tremors generate booms.

Rock Concert

Visitors to Pennsylvania's Ringing Rocks Park often show up toting hammers. Seems odd, but they're necessary for the proper tone. Ringing Rocks is a seven-acre boulder field that runs about ten feet deep. For unknown reasons, some of these rocks ring like bells when struck lightly by a hammer or other object. Because igneous diabase rocks don't usually do this, the boulder field has caused quite a stir through the years. In 1890, Dr. J. J. Ott assembled rocks of different pitches, enlisted the aid of a brass band, and held his own "rock concert."

Cry Me a Red River

A Mother Mary statue cries "tears of blood" at the Vietnamese Catholic Martyrs Church in Sacramento. It began crying in November 2005 when parishioners discovered a dark reddish substance flowing from her left eye. A priest wiped it away only to see it miraculously reappear a moment later. News of the incident spread quickly. Skeptics say that black paint used as eyeliner on the statue is the true culprit and that her "tears" are closer to this color than red.

Who Shot JFK?
Conspiracy Theories

*Conspiracy theories are a favorite
American pastime, right up there with
alien abductions and Elvis sightings.
Perhaps no conspiracy theories
are more popular than the ones
involving that afternoon in Dallas—November 22, 1963—when
the United States lost a president. John F. Kennedy's life and
death have reached out to encompass everyone from Marilyn
Monroe to Fidel Castro, Sam Giancana to J. Edgar Hoover.*

* * * *

* **The single-shooter theory:** This is the one the Warren
  Commission settled on—that Lee Harvey Oswald (and only
  Lee Harvey Oswald) fired his Mannlicher-Carcano rifle
  from the window of the Texas Book Depository and killed
  the president in Dealey Plaza. But this is the official finding,
  and where's the excitement in that?

* **The two-shooter theory:** A second shooter on the nearby
  grassy knoll fired at the same time as Oswald. His bullets
  hit Texas Governor John Connally and struck President
  Kennedy from the front. This theory arose after U.S. Marine
  sharpshooters at Quantico tried to duplicate the single-
  shooter theory but found it was impossible for all the shots
  to have come from the Book Depository.

* **The LBJ theory:** Lyndon Johnson's mistress, Madeleine
  Brown, said that the vice president met with powerful
  Texans the night before the killing. She claimed he told
  her, "After tomorrow those goddamn Kennedys will never
  embarrass me again—that's no threat—that's a promise."
  Jack Ruby also implicated LBJ, as did E. Howard Hunt, just
  before his death.

* **The CIA theory:** After Kennedy forced Allen Dulles to resign as head of the CIA following the Bay of Pigs fiasco, the CIA, resenting Kennedy's interference, took its revenge on the president. They'd had plenty of practice helping plotters take out Patrice Lumumba of the Congo, Rafael Trujillo of the Dominican Republic, and President Ngo Dinh Diem of Vietnam.

* **The Cuban exiles theory:** Reflecting more bitterness over the Bay of Pigs, the powerful Cuban exile community in the United States was eager to see Kennedy dead and said so. However, this probably played no part in the assassination.

* **The J. Edgar Hoover and the Mafia theory:** The Mafia was said to have been blackmailing Hoover about his homosexuality for ages. The theory goes that when Attorney General Robert Kennedy began to legally pursue Jimmy Hoffa and Mafia bosses in Chicago, Tampa, and New Orleans, they sent Hoover after JFK as payback.

* **The organized crime theory:** Chicago Mafia boss Sam Giancana, who supposedly shared the affections of Marilyn Monroe with both JFK and RFK—using Frank Sinatra as a go-between—felt betrayed when RFK went after the mob. After all, hadn't they fixed JFK's 1960 election? This theory is a tabloid favorite.

* **The Soviet theory:** High-ranking Soviet defector Ion Pacepa said that Soviet intelligence chiefs believed that the KGB had orchestrated the Dallas killing. But they were probably just bragging.

* **The Castro theory:** Supposedly the Cuban government contracted Oswald to kill Kennedy, telling him that there was an escape plan. There wasn't.

People will probably still be spinning these theories in a hundred years. But then, everyone needs a hobby.

The Black Dahlia Murder Mystery

On the morning of January 15, 1947, Betty Bersinger was walking with her young daughter in the Leimert Park area of Los Angeles, when she spotted something lying in a vacant lot that caused her blood to run cold. She ran to a nearby house and called the police. Officers Wayne Fitzgerald and Frank Perkins arrived on the scene shortly after 11:00 A.M.

✳   ✳   ✳   ✳

A Grisly Discovery

LYING ONLY SEVERAL feet from the road, in plain sight, was the naked body of a young woman. Her body had numerous cuts and abrasions, including a knife wound from ear to ear that resembled a ghoulish grin. Even more horrific was that her body had been completely severed at the midsection, and the two halves had been placed as if they were part of some morbid display. That's what disturbed officers the most: The killer appeared to have carefully posed the victim close to the street because he wanted people to find his grotesque handiwork.

Something else that troubled the officers was that even though the body had been brutally violated and desecrated, there was very little blood found at the scene. The only blood evidence recovered was a possible bloody footprint and an empty cement package with a spot of blood on it. In fact, the body was so clean that it appeared to have just been washed.

Shortly before removing the body, officers scoured the area for a possible murder weapon, but none was recovered. A coroner later determined that the cause of death was from hemorrhage and shock due to a concussion of the brain and lacerations of the face, probably from a very large knife.

Positive Identification

After a brief investigation, police were able to identify the deceased as Elizabeth Short, who was born in Hyde Park,

Massachusetts, on July 29, 1924. At age 19, Short had moved to California to live with her father, but she moved out and spent the next few years moving back and forth between California, Florida, and Massachusetts. In July 1946, Short returned to California to see Lt. Gordon Fickling, a former boyfriend, who was stationed in Long Beach. For the last six months of her life, Short lived in an assortment of hotels, rooming houses, and private homes. She was last seen a week before her body was found, which made police very interested in finding out where and with whom she spent her final days.

The Black Dahlia Is Born

As police continued their investigation, reporters jumped all over the story and began referring to the unknown killer by names such as "sex-crazed maniac" and even "werewolf." Short herself was also given a nickname: the Black Dahlia. Reporters said it was a name friends had called her as a play on the movie *The Blue Dahlia*, which had recently been released. However, others contend Short was never called the Black Dahlia while she was alive; it was just something reporters made up for a better story. Either way, it wasn't long before newspapers around the globe were splashing front-page headlines about the horrific murder of the Black Dahlia.

The Killer Is Still Out There

As time wore on, hundreds of police officers were assigned to the Black Dahlia investigation. They combed the streets, interviewing people and following leads. Although police interviewed thousands of potential suspects—and dozens even confessed to the murder—to this day, no one has ever officially been charged with the crime. More than 60 years and several books and movies after the crime, the Elizabeth Short murder case is still listed as "open." We are no closer to knowing who killed Short or why than when her body was first discovered.

Mythical Creatures

From the time man first began telling tales, every human culture has described creatures with characteristics quite different from average animals. The legends of horses and snakes with wings, behemoths with horns in odd places, or other conglomerations live on to tease us with questions of their existence.

✳ ✳ ✳ ✳

Dragons: Real Scorchers

ONE OF THE oldest and most universal mythical creatures is the dragon. Huge, winged lizards or serpents with greenish scales and flaming breath are found in tales from ancient China to medieval Europe.

In China, the dragon originally represented the rising sun, happiness, and fertility. Sumerians included dragons in their religious art as early as 4000 B.C. The ancient Greeks called their dragon *Draco* and pictured it as a massive, winged snake emitting light and squeezing victims to death in its coils.

In the British Isles, dragons were associated with the legendary King Arthur and St. George, and though it is generally accepted that dragons do not exist, some think ancient man's glimpses of giant sea snakes may have inspired dragon myths.

People Acting Fishy: Mermaids and Mermen

The ancient Babylonians worshipped a half-human/half-fish creature named Oannes who gave them the gift of civilization. The contemporary mermaid, a beautiful woman with the lower body of a fish, may have been popularized by Danish writer Hans Christian Andersen's tale *The Little Mermaid*. Some think that mermaids spotted at sea by lonesome sailors are nothing more than manatees—large flat-tailed mammals.

Unicorns: Creatures that Make a Point

Variations of the unicorn, a horse with a single, long horn growing out of its forehead, appear in myths worldwide. It is possible that a similar, actual creature may have appeared at one time to inspire these myths. In the 1800s, a French woman grew a single, ten-inch horn from her forehead. A wax casting of the horn is preserved in Philadelphia's Mütter Museum. More recently, in 2003, a 95-year-old Chinese woman began growing a similar horn. By May

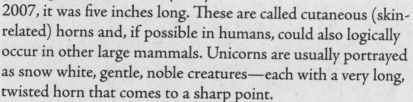

2007, it was five inches long. These are called cutaneous (skin-related) horns and, if possible in humans, could also logically occur in other large mammals. Unicorns are usually portrayed as snow white, gentle, noble creatures—each with a very long, twisted horn that comes to a sharp point.

Pegasus: Cloud Galloper

Greek legend has it that when Poseidon, god of the sea, got together with Medusa, the gorgon with the snake-infested hair, their offspring was Pegasus, a great white horse with wings. Pegasus became the mount of the hero Bellerophon, and together they slew the bizarre Chimera (a fire-breathing monster with the head of a lion, body of a goat, and tail of a snake). Pride in the great deed made Bellerophon think he could ride Pegasus to Mt. Olympus, home of the gods, so he sprang away for the heavens. But the mortal Bellerophon was thrown back to Earth by Zeus, who kept the winged horse for himself. There is a constellation named for Pegasus.

Cyclops: Keeping an Eye Out

They were not pretty, according to Greek legend. The small group of grotesque, one-eyed giants called Cyclopes (in the plural) was warlike and given to eating human flesh. Their one skill was an astonishing talent for creating weapons for the gods, such as swords and arrows. Could such people ever have existed? Humans inflicted with an endocrine disorder known as gigantism have been known to reach a height of eight feet, and very rarely humans may also be born with a birth defect that gives them a single eye, so perhaps this monster has roots in a long-forgotten, actual human being.

Having a Lot of Faun

Very similar to goat-man creatures called satyrs but not at all related to baby deer (fawns), fauns looked like men from the navel up, except for the goat horns sprouting from their temples. They also bounded about on goat legs and hooves. Fathered by the Greek god Faunus, fauns protected the natural world, especially fields and woods. They were also similar in appearance to Pan, Greek god of nature, who gave us the word panic for the fright he could inspire by blowing on his magical conch shell. Mr. Tumnus from C. S. Lewis's *The Lion, the Witch, and the Wardrobe* was a faun.

Centaurs: When Horse and Rider are Truly One

A skilled rider will often appear as one with his or her galloping steed, so it isn't hard to see how ancient Greeks may have envisioned a creature that was humanlike from the trunk up but with the legs and body of a stallion—it makes for truly seamless horsemanship. Centaurs were meat-eating revelers who loved to drink, according to Greek legend, except for one gentle man-horse named Chiron known for his wisdom and teaching abilities. Chiron lives on as the centaur constellation Sagittarius, and centaurs are still seen on the coats of arms of many old European families.

Trolls: Mammoth Mountain Men

Although the descriptions of these ugly, manlike beings vary from country to country, trolls originated in Scandinavian lands, where they were said to be gigantic, grotesque humanoids who lived in the hills or mountains, mined ore, and became wondrous metalsmiths. Trolls could turn to stone if caught in the sun, and Norway's ancient rock pillars are said to be evidence of this belief. But perhaps legends of trolls are based on a few individuals with a disorder that would not have been understood in ancient times. A rare hormonal disorder called gigantism causes excessive growth of the long bones and, thus, greatly increased height.

Griffins: In the Cat-Bird Seat?

Depictions of these folk monsters can be found in artwork from ancient Egypt and other cradles of civilization as early as 3300 B.C. Mainly a lion-eagle combo, griffins featured a lion's body and an eagle's wings, head, and legs. But they also sported big ears and fierce, ruby-colored eyes. Griffins often guarded rich treasure troves and viciously defended their turf with their sharp beaks and talons. They have survived in modern fantasy fiction, making an appearance in Lewis Carroll's *Alice's Adventures in Wonderland*.

Fairies: Not Always Tinkerbell

Fairies, also known as wood nymphs, sprites, pixies, and many other names in cultures around the world, are usually thought of as attractive little spirit beings, proportioned like humans and charmingly dressed in wildflowers and acorns. In modern times, they are often depicted as sweet little beings with translucent wings. But in medieval times, the *fée* or *fay*, as they were called in Old French or English, could be naughty or nice.

One Irish tradition maintains that fairies often stole babies, substituting an old, wrinkled fairy or even a bundled log in place of the infant. Some European folk traditions believed fairies were descended from an old, superior race of humanoid creatures, and others thought they were fallen angels that had landed in woods or meadows. Shakespeare's play, *A Midsummer Night's Dream*, with its royal fairies Oberon and Titania, helped popularize the notion of fairies as small, magical people living in their own kingdom among humans. And folk belief worldwide still insists that these little people must be treated respectfully and given offerings and gifts to keep them from pulling nasty tricks on their human neighbors.

Unexplained Mysteries of the Universe

Unidentified flying objects are old hat compared with these popular supernatural mysteries, unexplained phenomena, and unsolved puzzles. Read on and see if we can make a believer out of you.

✳ ✳ ✳ ✳

Bermuda Triangle

THIS AREA IN the Atlantic Ocean between Bermuda, Miami, and San Juan is legendary as the site from which an astoundingly high number of ships, small boats, and airplanes have allegedly disappeared. Although the United States Coast Guard does not officially recognize the Bermuda Triangle or maintain any data on the area, conspiracy theorists have spent countless hours documenting the mysteries of the region. Some researchers estimate that more than 2,000 boats and 125 planes have been lost there, including the famous Flight 19, and five Navy bombers that disappeared in 1945, followed by their search-and-rescue seaplane. Explanations for the disappearances include extraterrestrials that captured the boats and planes, deep-water earthquakes that caused freak waves, and time warps that took vessels to a different time or dimension.

Easter Island

One of the most remote areas on Earth, Easter Island is in the southern Pacific Ocean, 1,400 miles from any other island. So how is it that more than 800 giant, centuries-old stone statues line the island's coast? Who built them? How did they get there? These questions have baffled enthusiasts for decades. The island was discovered in 1722 by a Dutch explorer who found it uninhabited, except for the numerous *moai*, as the statues are known. The most popular explanation for the statues suggests that Polynesian seafarers arrived on the island between A.D. 400 and 1600 in canoes carried by ocean currents. Unable to paddle against the currents to leave the island, the new inhabitants carved the statues out of a volcanic wall and placed them around the island using simple machines. But when the island's resources began to give out, the people resorted to cannibalism, wiping out the population by the time the Dutch landed.

Area 51

Officially, Area 51 is a remote strip of land about 90 miles north of Las Vegas that the Air Force uses to test new military aircraft. Unofficially, it's a storage and examination site for crashed alien spaceships, a meeting spot for extraterrestrials, a breeding ground for weather control and time travel technology, and possibly the home of a one-world political group. Because the U.S. government won't discuss what goes on at Area 51, inquiring minds have had to develop their own theories. In 1989, Bob Lazar, a former government scientist, told a Las Vegas TV station that he worked on alien technology at a facility near Area 51. Millions believed Lazar's story, and Area 51's mysterious reputation was sealed.

Nostradamus

Whether you believe his predictions or not, 16th-century French philosopher Nostradamus was an impressive guy. After all, how many authors' books are still in print 450 years after their first editions? *Les Prophéties*, first published in 1555, is a series of poems that predict major world events in a vague, timeless manner that leaves much room for interpretation. Nostradamus's followers credit him with predicting the rise of both Napoleon and Hitler, the French Revolution, the Great Fire of London, both World Wars, the death of Princess Diana, the Apollo moon landings, and the terrorist attacks of September 11, 2001, among other things. Skeptics say the links between his prophecies and world events are the result of misinterpretations or mistranslations, or are so vague that they are laughable.

Stonehenge

Situated near Amesbury, England, Stonehenge is a collection of giant stones standing in a circular formation. Archaeologists estimate that the stones were erected between 3000 and 1600 B.C. in three separate phases.

Visitors to the site have been hypothesizing as to its origins for centuries, but various academics have credited the Danes, the Druids, the Romans, the Greeks, and the Egyptians, among others. Just as many theories  exist regarding its purpose: a predictor of solar phenomena, a means of communicating with heaven, a pre-historic computer, a sacred place of worship, and more. Some people even believe it's an extraterrestrial landing site and claim to have seen UFOs in the area.

Crop Circles

Art exhibit, practical joke, or universal mystery, crop circles have been captivating observers for decades. They occur when crops are flattened to form geometric patterns most visible from the sky. Crop circles are usually found in England but have also been spotted in Australia, South Africa, China, Russia, and other countries. In 1991, two men admitted they had created a number of the crop circles identified in England since 1978 by marking out circles with a length of rope and flattening the crops with iron bars and wooden planks. But "croppies," a group of scientists and paranormal enthusiasts, argue that some of the designs are far too complex for humans to create with simple tools. Croppies believe that some of the circles are the result of flying saucers that land in fields, freak wind vortexes, or ball lightning—a brief flash of light usually the size and shape of a basketball that's not always associated with a thunderstorm.

Benjamin Franklin: Secret Agent Man?

Benjamin Franklin was a man of many roles: inventor, scientist, publisher, philosopher, diplomat, and one of America's founding fathers. But could he also have been a spy?

✳ ✳ ✳ ✳

French Connection

RUMORS ABOUND THAT Franklin was involved in French espionage activities during the American Revolution. While most say that he was spying for the Americans, some claim that Franklin was in league with the British.

In September 1776, Congress appointed Franklin, Silas Deane, and Thomas Jefferson commissioners to France to plead the American cause in its war against Great Britain. Jefferson declined, but Franklin (despite the fact that he was 70 years old) and Deane agreed.

One of the most celebrated people on the planet, Franklin could hardly slip into France unnoticed. Almost from the moment he arrived, he was involved in a web of intrigue. Spies surrounded Franklin at every turn. French police chief Jean-Charles Lenoir ran an organized and efficient spying operation in Paris, which was so riddled with spies that it was said when two Parisians talked, a third inevitably listened. In addition to being tailed by the French, the British ambassador to France was also following Franklin's every move.

The Spy Who Stayed Cold

Every week, like clockwork, secret messages were sent from Franklin's residence to British intelligence, keeping them abreast of everything Franklin was planning, doing, or talking about. While Franklin was certainly involved in this undercover war, was he aware of these notes? Was he the source of them? Or was this all part of Franklin's master plan?

Franklin could hardly have been unaware of the situation. Soon after he arrived in France, a Philadelphian living in Paris had warned Franklin to be wary. In a letter she wrote, "You are surrounded with spies who watch your every movement."

His reply has become legendary. "I have long observed one rule . . . to be concerned in no affairs I should blush to have made public, and to do nothing but what spies may see and welcome." He did nothing to tighten security, which led John Adams to believe that Franklin was, at best, senile, and at worst, criminally careless. Franklin even claimed that he would not dismiss his valet, Edward Bancroft, even if he were "a spy, as probably he is."

Double-Aught-Seven

If Franklin wasn't a British spy, was he spying for America? Biographer James Srodes calls this a more plausible scenario, and notes that mid-20th century CIA director Allen Dulles concluded that Franklin had set up a spy network inside the British government. However, his assumption lacks documentation. As Srodes notes, Franklin hardly needed a ring of secret informants in London; he had many friends inside the British government, any of whom could feed him valuable information.

"The important thing about intelligence is not how it is obtained but how it is used," says Srodes. Franklin used information obtained from England to force the French to move quickly to the aid of American rebel forces. He then turned around and casually let it be known how much France was aiding America, which disturbed the British.

This much we know: Franklin had indeed been close to someone who was a spy. Decades later it was revealed that Edward Bancroft was indeed spying for America—and for England.

We may never know if Bancroft's boss, Benjamin Franklin, was also a spy, or even for what side. However, what we do know is that Benjamin Franklin was certainly a cagey American.

Now You See Them, or Maybe You Don't

Reports of UFOs have been around since the pyramids and the Inca temples, both of which were allegedly constructed by visitors from outer space needing navigational aids. Judging from the following accounts, perhaps aliens were just doing a little celebrity watching.

✳ ✳ ✳ ✳

JOHN LENNON'S SONG "Nobody Told Me" touches on his experience with a UFO. In 1974, the former Beatle reported seeing a UFO outside his apartment in New York City. As he and a friend watched, the UFO drifted away, changing its shape with each rotation. Lennon took photos of the craft, but when he attempted to develop the film, it turned out blank. Lennon's friend called the police, who had received two other calls on the incident, and the *New York Daily News*, which had received five calls reporting a UFO on the East Side that night. *The New York Times* allegedly hung up on him.

Astronaut Gordon Cooper participated in a United Nations panel discussion on UFOs in New York in 1985. During the discussion, Cooper said, "I believe that these extraterrestrial vehicles and their crews are visiting this planet from other planets, which obviously are a little more technically advanced than we are here on Earth. I feel that we need to have a top-level, coordinated program to scientifically collect and analyze data from all over the Earth concerning any type of encounter, and to determine how best to interface with these visitors in a friendly fashion."

Heavyweight boxing champ Muhammad Ali has also claimed to have seen UFOs hovering over New York City. The occurrence was said to have taken place early in his career while he was working with his trainer, Angelo Dundee, in Central Park.

Just before dawn, the two men observed a large, round UFO as it came out from behind the city skyline and moved slowly across the sky, a sighting that lasted about 15 minutes. Ali claimed at least 16 sightings. In one, he was a passenger in a car motoring along the New Jersey Turnpike when a cigar-shape craft hovered briefly over his vehicle.

Ronald Reagan is considered the first president to talk about the possibility of an alien invasion. He believed that if such a situation occurred, all the nations of the world should unite to fight off the attackers. Reagan even discussed this scenario with General Secretary Mikhail Gorbachev during their first summit meeting in Geneva in 1985.

Guitarist Jimi Hendrix often claimed to have been followed around by UFOs and frequently referred to them in his lyrics. In addition, Hendrix allegedly was saved from freezing to death in 1965 by an eight-foot-tall angel-like alien who thawed the snowdrift in which the musician's van was stuck. He also once told a *New York Times* reporter that he was actually from Mars.

During Jimmy Carter's presidential election campaign of 1976, he told reporters that he once saw what could have been a UFO in 1969, before he was governor of Georgia. "It was the darndest thing I've ever seen," he said of the incident. He claimed that the object that he and a group of others had watched for ten minutes was as bright as the moon. Because he filed a report on the matter, Carter was often referred to as "the UFO president" after being elected.

✳ **The Roswell Incident spurred widespread controversy over the July 1947 recovery of materials thought to be debris from a crashed alien craft near Roswell, New Mexico. Proponents of this theory continue to believe in a U.S. military cover-up.**

It's a Bird! It's a Plane! It's ... Avrocar?!?

Not all UFOs are alien spaceships.

✳ ✳ ✳ ✳

O H, THE 1950S—A time of sock hops, drive-in movies, and the Cold War between America and the Soviet Union, when each superpower waged war against the other in the arenas of science, astronomy, and politics. It was also a time when discussion of life on other planets was rampant, after the alleged alien ship crash near Roswell, New Mexico, in 1947.

Watch the Skies

Speculation abounded about the unidentified flying objects (UFOs) spotted nearly every week by everyone from farmers to airplane pilots. As time passed, government authorities began to wonder if the flying saucers were, in fact, part of a secret Russian program to create a new type of air force. Fearful that such a craft would upset the existing balance of power, the U.S. Air Force decided to produce its own saucer-shape ship.

In 1953, the military contacted Avro Aircraft Limited of Canada, an aircraft manufacturing company that operated in Malton, Ontario, between 1945 and 1962. Project Silverbug was initially proposed because the government wanted to find out if UFOs could be manufactured by humans. Before long, both the military and the scientific community speculated about its potential. Intrigued by the idea, designers at Avro—led by British aeronautical engineer John Frost—began working on the VZ-9-AV Avrocar. The round craft would have been right at home in a scene from a science fiction film.

Security for the project was so tight that it probably generated rumors that America was actually testing a captured alien spacecraft—speculation that remains alive and well even today.

Of This Earth

By 1958, the company had produced two prototypes, which were 18 feet in diameter and 3.5 feet tall. The Avrocar was shaped like a disk, with a curved upper surface. It included an enclosed 124-blade turbo-rotor at the center, which provided lift for the craft through an opening in the bottom. The Avrocar was operated with a single control stick, which activated different panels around the ship. The turbo also powered the craft's controls. It was designed for two passengers, but in reality a single pilot could barely fit inside.

The military envisioned using the craft as "flying Jeeps" that would hover close to the ground and move at a maximum speed of 40 mph. But that, apparently, was only going to be the beginning. Avro had its own plans, which included not just commercial Avrocars, but also a family-size Avrowagon, an Avrotruck for larger loads, Avroangel to rush people to the hospital, and a military Avropelican, which, like a pelican hunting for fish, would conduct surveillance for submarines.

But Does It Fly?

The prototypes impressed the U.S. Army enough to award Avro a $2 million contract. Unfortunately, the Avrocar project was canceled when an economic downturn forced the company to temporarily close and restructure. When Avro Aircraft reopened, the original team of designers had dispersed. Further efforts to revive the project were unsuccessful, and repeated testing proved that the craft was inherently unstable. It soon became apparent that whatever UFOs were spotted overhead, it was unlikely that they came from this planet. Project Silverbug was abandoned when funding ran out in March 1961, but one of the two Avrocar prototypes is housed at the U.S. Army Transportation Museum in Fort Eustis, Virginia.

Atlantis

Although it's often re-created as a popular theme resort for vacationers, the lost city of Atlantis is rich in historical lore.

✳   ✳   ✳   ✳

✳ Plato claimed in his dialogues *Timaeus* and *Critias* that on a single night around 9400 B.C., the great island civilization Atlantis (named for the ocean in which it was situated) sank into the sea. Most historians believe that Plato created the myth of Atlantis to support his political theories.

✳ A volcanic eruption occurred about 3,600 years ago on the Santorini archipelago, located in the Aegean Sea about 125 miles southeast of Greece. The massive explosion likely didn't sink a fake city called Atlantis, but it may well have destroyed the very real Minoan civilization on the nearby island of Crete.

✳ Dan Brown's blockbuster novel *The Da Vinci Code* reignited public interest in Atlantis in a roundabout way. Brown's story referenced the Knights Templar, an early Christian military order with a dramatic history that involved bloodshed, exile, and secrets—one of which was that they were carriers of ancient wisdom from the lost city of Atlantis.

✳ Ulf Erlingsson, a Swedish geographer, believes that the lost city of Atlantis is actually Ireland. Erlingsson claims that Plato's measurements, geography, and landscape reports of Atlantis perfectly match those of Ireland. He claims that somewhere around 6100 B.C., Dogger Bank (an isolated shoal in the North Sea connecting Britain and Denmark) flooded, and over the centuries, the Irish have confused the sinking of the shoal with the sinking of Atlantis.

✳ The name Atlantis derives from Atlas, the Greek god who is said to have supported the world on his back. In Greek, Atlantis means "Daughter of Atlas."

Chapter 2

Science and Technology

Modern Rocketry and the Moonchild

American rocket scientist Jack Parsons wielded the power to bring mass devastation to the world— though not in the way he anticipated.

※　※　※　※

A Flight of Fancy

IN 1936, 22-YEAR-OLD Jack Parsons was the epitome of "tall, dark, and handsome." Parsons's natural charisma and fierce intellect, however, did not prevent him from leaving his chemistry studies at Caltech, where he drew criticism for his abiding interest in rocketry, specifically the quest to develop a workable rocket fuel. In Depression-era America, rocketry was seen as nothing more than a flight of fancy. Exiled from campus for their explosive experiments, Parsons and his fellow enthusiasts trekked out to the isolated Arroyo Seco Canyon. On October 31, they conducted a test that, instead of resulting in an explosion, led to a successful launch. Soon thereafter, they formed the Jet Propulsion Laboratory (JPL).

So Far, So...Bad

With the arrival of the Second World War, Parsons's talents were suddenly very much in demand. Thanks to Parsons's intuitive understanding of chemistry, the company was able to produce a working jet-assisted take-off (JATO) rocket for aircraft. The military found the JATO particularly useful on the short runways that dotted South Pacific islands.

Parsons soon started another successful enterprise—AeroJet Corporation. The founding of AeroJet seemed like just another chapter in Parsons's successful life. But then everything seemed to take a much darker turn. Jack sold his AeroJet shares to finance his other abiding interest—the occult.

British writer, hedonist, and self-proclaimed master of the occult Aleister Crowley led a religious organization called Ordo Templi Orientis, through which he spread his mystical life philosophy of Thelema, dictating "Do what thou wilt." This pagan, power-based religion of the individual appealed to Parsons, who had regularly invoked the Greek god Pan when conducting rocket tests for JPL. Jack joined the West Coast chapter in 1941 and was quickly recognized as a likely successor to Crowley himself. A year later, Parsons was made the leader of the West Coast church and began conducting "sex magick" rituals intended to bring about the end of the world.

Then things got really weird.

Enter (and Exit) L. Ron Hubbard

Parsons's first wife, Helen Parsons Smith, left him shortly after he joined Crowley's church. And no wonder—Parsons and his new friend, fellow church member L. Ron Hubbard, were busy conducting lewd rituals intended to call forth an "elemental" partner to sire a "moonchild," who was to be the harbinger of the apocalypse. After a particularly vigorous ritual, a young woman knocked on the door. Redheaded (a prerequisite for the elemental), she was willing to carry Parsons's moonchild. Despite many attempts at conception, it was to no avail. Finally, Hubbard absconded with all of Parsons's money, as well as his girlfriend. Soon thereafter, Hubbard used the money to finance his first book, and lo, Scientology was born.

But, Getting Back to Jack

Parsons's life began to unravel. The moonchild didn't materialize, his friend had stolen his money, and he was under investigation by the FBI. For a time he worked at a gas station; later he remarried and began making special effects for movies. He was reportedly hard at work on a new kind of artificial fog when an explosion in his apartment took his life on June 17, 1952.

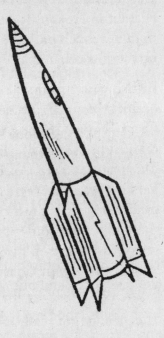

By then, the Cold War was new and fear was rampant. Soon both the Soviet Union and the United States developed intercontinental ballistic missiles, and the threat of global nuclear apocalypse grew increasingly real. Parsons may not have conceived a magical moonchild to bring about the apocalypse, but he had created the technology needed to hurl atomic weapons through space—enabling a possible apocalypse in itself.

* Jack Parsons wrote a series of essays about occult rituals and practices.

* Simple rockets originated in China, but nobody is sure exactly when. However, it is likely that they appeared just over 1,000 years ago.

* The word rocket is based on the Italian word *rocchetta,* which means "little fuse." This was the name for an old firecracker.

* During World War II, Nazi Germany fired rockets armed with warheads into France, Belgium, and England.

IBM Before It Was IBM

IBM has cast a long shadow on American life and industry since the 1920s, but its ancestor companies were bound up with workplace automation from the concept's earliest days.

✳ ✳ ✳ ✳

Roots

IN 1896, HERMAN Hollerith formed the Tabulating Machine Company (TMC) to market a punch-card tabulating device that had revolutionized the U.S. Census. Held once per decade, the Census took about eight years to tabulate. Hollerith's system required less than two years. Yet, the brilliant inventor was a lousy businessman. By 1911, TMC needed a bailout.

Meanwhile, in 1891, the also creatively named Computing Scale Company (CSC) began making sophisticated computing scales—essential to all businesses that measured product by weight. CSC acquired several competitors in the early 1900s and was successful but not dominant in its niche.

Late 1800s labor law was minimal, and companies went to great lengths to wring maximum work from their wage dimes. In 1889, the Bundy Manufacturing Company (BMC) cashed in with the first industrial time clock. For slackers who showed up late and/or left early, the party was over. By 1911, BMC had bought several competitors and had grown into International Time Recording Company (ITRC), a leader in the field.

Consolidation

In 1911, financier Charles Flint arranged to merge ITRC, CSC, and TMC as the Computing-Tabulating-Recording Company (C-T-R). C-T-R's time clock and data tabulation businesses thrived. In 1914, Flint hired Thomas J. Watson Sr. to manage C-T-R. Watson was a veteran of National Cash Register (NCR) and had done a year in jail for NCR's antitrust violations—his conviction was overturned on a technicality.

Whatever his past, Watson established key elements of IBM's future corporate culture. Everyone (even Watson) punched in and out on a time clock. The marketing uniform was a dark suit and white shirt: no exceptions. Within a year of his hire, Watson was named president; within four years, C-T-R's revenues had doubled. The company was going places.

Expansion

In 1917, C-T-R set up shop in Canada as International Business Machines Company, Ltd., though the U.S.-based parent didn't change its name. Watson emphasized leasing rather than sales, which had several advantages. It meant steady, predictable cash flow for C-T-R. It tied up less of customers' capital. And when C-T-R developed new products, clients weren't stuck with the old ones; they could lease C-T-R's new gear.

By 1924, C-T-R produced an array of equipment. Some, like electric keypunch adding machines, survive today in advanced form. With European and Canadian offices, C-T-R had truly gone international, so Watson renamed it International Business Machines Corporation (IBM). Under his savvy leadership, IBM actually grew through the Depression. It also became somewhat cultlike, introducing its own hymnal for employees with songs celebrating Watson's leadership.

Explosion

World War II enhanced IBM's prestige tremendously, even as two-thirds of its facilities shifted production to the war effort. Watson continued the salaries of employees called to war, a generous and patriotic step. And IBM's equipment was essential enough to the navy that its enlisted crewmen had their own rating—"IBM Operator."

Most important for IBM, WWII drove demand for its information processing technology. Thomas Watson Jr. took over IBM in 1952 and steered the company into computing, a field it owned for 30 years. He retired in 1971. In 1981, IBM introduced the IBM Personal Computer.

Groundbreaking Scientific Theories

Many of these scientific breakthroughs may seem glaringly obvious to modern people, but they show the fascinating evolution of knowledge. Take a trip back to when Earth was believed to be flat, and try to imagine the contemporary reactions to these cutting-edge theories.

✳   ✳   ✳   ✳

Mineral Cures

PHILIPPUS THEOPHRASTUS AUREOLUS Bombastus von Hohenheim: Try saying that ten times fast! Better yet, don't: Use the name his parents gave him upon his birth in 1493, Phillip von Hohenheim, or the name he assumed for himself, which most historians now use: Paracelsus. No matter what you call him, Paracelsus pioneered the world of therapeutic medicine by treating diseases with chemical and mineral remedies—something that was virtually unheard of at the time. Back then, most physicians created their remedies from organic compounds ranging from tree bark to animal organs, from plants or plant extracts to dung. Depending on the physician, you could find any number of cures in different dosages for the same illness!

With a father who was a physician and chemist, it's no wonder that Paracelsus began studying medicine and chemistry at age 16 at the University of Basel in Switzerland. He discovered that minerals and metals could be used to treat gout and lithiasis (common diseases contracted by miners). This led him to formulate new ideas on the use of certain minerals as medicine for other ailments. One such mineral, zinc (whose name comes from the German *zink*, meaning "pointed," due to its sharp crystalline structure), is now a common mineral found in many cold, cough, and flu remedies.

Paracelsus' knowledge of remedies came primarily from his travels to far-off places such as Russia and the Middle East. Despite this, his arrogance, his eccentric ways, and his insistence on the correctness of his theories often incurred the anger of physicians throughout Europe. In 1526, while serving as the chair of medicine at the University of Basel, Paracelsus publicly burned the school's traditional medical textbooks. Yes, he did get fired.

Before his death in 1541, Paracelsus proposed that the cause of all contagious diseases fell into two categories—natural and spiritual. He believed that the body and spirit required a balance of certain minerals and could therefore be cured of many diseases through the proper administration of minerals and chemicals in correct dosages. Paracelsus' theories paved the way for new research into cures and remedies. He is generally considered the father of toxicology.

Blood Circulation

Let's say you're a young British doctor at the turn of the 17th century, and you want to take your career to the next level. Do you (a) marry the daughter of the most important physician in the land, or (b) pioneer research and make one of the most important discoveries in human physiology? Well, if you're William Harvey, you do both!

Born in 1578, Harvey was educated at the King's College in Canterbury, Cambridge University, and the University of Padua in Italy. He returned to England around 1602 and married Elizabeth Browne in 1604. Browne just happened to be the daughter of the court physician to Queen Elizabeth I, Lancelot Browne. Not one to rest on his social achievements, Harvey soon began researching the flow of blood through the human body. What he found, the circulatory system, would change the way people understood human physiology.

Prior to Harvey's discovery, most people believed that food was converted into blood by the liver and then consumed as fuel by the body, more specifically, the heart. Through dissections of animals and human cadavers, Harvey quickly realized that the heart and body did not "feed" on blood, nor was blood converted from food by the liver. He discovered a series of ventricles that essentially push blood through the body with contractions (heartbeats), pumping the blood in one direction through a closed circuit of veins and arteries.

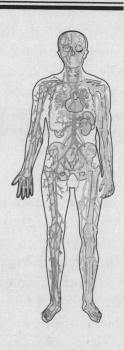

Harvey also theorized, correctly, that veins and arteries were somehow connected, but he couldn't prove it. Modern doctors now know that they're connected by capillaries, but without a compound microscope, the capillaries were too tiny to see.

In Harvey's time, claiming anything other than the commonly accepted "science" of the day was considered career suicide for any doctor. This is probably why, despite his discoveries, he waited until 1628—when he had reached the age of 50—to publish his work.

Vaccination

Remember getting vaccination shots at the doctor's office with hypodermic needles larger than you ever wanted to see? Well, you can thank an English country doctor by the name of Edward Jenner for your pain. And yes, you should thank him! Without Jenner, the world might not have vaccines—medicines that help your body produce its own antibodies against such diseases as polio, mumps, and smallpox. Never heard of these diseases? Good. That probably means you never caught them—more than likely because of vaccinations you received.

Jenner was born in Gloucestershire, England, in 1749, when smallpox was a common disease that often resulted in death. With a natural interest in medicine, Jenner served as a surgeon's apprentice for nine years and later studied at St. George's Hospital in London. After his training, Jenner returned to the Gloucestershire countryside to practice medicine. After noticing that milkmaids who had caught cowpox—a milder, less dangerous disease—did not catch smallpox, he theorized that cowpox would prevent people from contracting the deadly smallpox disease.

When a milkmaid with cowpox came to him seeking medical attention, Jenner took a big gamble with his career and the life of a young boy named James Phipps. With consent from the boy's father, Jenner took liquid from the milkmaid's sores and infected Phipps with cowpox. After the boy recovered, Jenner then exposed the boy to smallpox to prove his theory. Thankfully, Phipps failed to contract the disease. His body had developed antibodies against smallpox thanks to Jenner's cowpox vaccination.

Jenner continued experimenting successfully for several years and published his findings in 1798 under the title *An Inquiry into the Causes and Effects of the Variolae Vaccinae, a Disease Known by the Name of Cow Pox*. Despite resistance to his findings, Jenner's book was soon translated into several different languages and quickly distributed all over the world. So, why did Jenner call it a vaccine? That's simple—the Latin word for cow is *vacca*, and the suffix *-ine* or *-inus* translates to "of," creating vaccine, "of cows." Jenner died in 1823 at age 74—but not from smallpox.

Who Invented the Printing Press?

Johannes Gutenberg's development of the printing press in 15th-century Germany led to mass-market publishing. But innovations in printing technology were around long before Gutenberg.

✳   ✳   ✳   ✳

The Stamp of Uniformity

ALTHOUGH PRINTING IS usually associated with making reading materials, the original impetus behind printing technology was the need to create identical copies of the same thing. Printing actually began with coining, when centralized states branded their coins with uniform decorations. In those days, written manuscripts were copied the old-fashioned way—by hand. Only the upper classes were literate, books were costly, and the laborious method of copying meant books were rare.

The first major innovation in printing came with the Chinese invention of block printing by the eighth century A.D. Block printing involved carving letters or images into a surface, inking that surface, and pressing it on to paper, parchment, or cloth. The method was used for a variety of purposes, from decorating clothes to copying religious scrolls. The blocks were usually made of wood, which posed a problem as the wood eventually decayed or cracked. Oftentimes entire pages of a manuscript, complete with illustrations, were carved into a single block that could be used again and again.

The Chinese also invented movable type—the key to efficient printing. Movable type is faster than block printing because individual characters, such as letters or punctuation, are created by being cast into molds. Once the characters are made, they can then be reused and rearranged infinitely by changing the typeset. Movable type characters are also more uniform than block printing's carved letters. Pi-Sheng invented this method in 1045 using clay molds. The method spread to Korea and Japan, and metal movable type was created in Korea by 1230.

Supply and Demand

The Chinese didn't use movable type extensively because their language consists of thousands of characters, and movable type makes printing efficient only in a language with fewer letters, like the English alphabet's 26. Meanwhile, Europeans used the imported concept of block printing to make popular objects like playing cards or illustrated children's books. During the Middle Ages, serious secular scholarship had all but disappeared in Europe, and the reproduction of new and classical texts was mostly confined to the Asian and Arab worlds.

That is, until literacy began to spread among the middle classes, and lay people, especially in Germany, showed an interest in reading religious texts for themselves. Thus, German entrepreneur Johannes Gutenberg, the son of a coin minter, began to experiment with metal movable type pieces. It's believed Gutenberg was unfamiliar with the earlier Chinese method, but at any rate, several other Europeans were experimenting with similar methods at the same time as Gutenberg.

By the 1440s, Gutenberg had set up a printing shop in Mainz, Germany, and in 1450, he set out to produce a Bible. Gutenberg perfected several printing methods, such as right justification, and preferred alloys in the production of metal types. By 1455, Gutenberg's press had produced 200 copies of his Bible—quite the feat at the time, considering one Bible could take years to copy by hand. These Bibles were sold for less than hand-copied ones yet were still expensive enough for profit margins equivalent to modern-day millions.

Presses soon popped up all across Europe. By 1499, an estimated 15 million books had been produced by at least 1,000 printing presses, mostly in Germany and then throughout Italy. For the first time, ideas were efficiently reproduced and spread over long distances. The proliferation of these first German printing presses is commonly credited with the end of the Middle Ages and the dawn of the Renaissance.

ARPANET: The Grandfather of the Internet

Rumors abound that ARPANET was designed as a communications network that would withstand nuclear attacks. That is simply not true. The creators of ARPANET weren't seeking invulnerability, but reliability—in order to fulfill one man's vision of an "inter-galactic" computer network. It was a crude beginning to the Internet, but it led to important technical developments that made today's Internet a reality.

✳   ✳   ✳   ✳

ON OCTOBER 4, 1957, the Soviet Union launched the world's first human-made satellite, Sputnik I, into space. It was a clear message that Russian technology was more advanced than American technology. To amend this oversight, the Advanced Research Projects Agency (ARPA) was formed to fund technical research. The United States already had a substantial financial investment in computer tech—the initial purpose of ARPA was to figure out the best way to put that to use. Though it fell under the auspices of the U.S. Department of Defense (and was renamed DARPA), the research was never intended to be used solely for military purposes. Instead, the agency's purpose was to develop technology that would benefit civilization and the world in general.

Not Connected to Other Galaxies—Yet

The expert chosen to head ARPA's initial effort was Joseph "Lick" Licklider, a leading computer scientist. Lick had a vision of a worldwide communications network connected by computers, which he referred to as the "inter-galactic computer network." Lick departed ARPA in 1965, before his plan could be implemented, but he left a lasting impression on his successor, Bob Taylor.

Taylor selected a new leader for the system design team that would make Lick's vision a reality: Dr. Lawrence "Larry" G. Roberts, an MIT researcher. He became one of the four people most closely associated with the birth of the Internet. (The other three are Vinton Cerf, Leonard Kleinrock, and Robert Kahn.) Roberts had gained experience in computer linking while at MIT, having linked computers using the old-fashioned telephone method of circuit switching. The concept of packet switching was at first controversial, but it proved to be one of the key factors in linking multiple computers to form a network. The other important technical achievement was the use of small computers, known as interface message processors (IMPs), to store and handle the data packets.

By 1968, the concept for ARPANET was in place, and invitations to bid on the project were sent to 140 institutions; only 12 actually replied. The others apparently believed the concept to be impractical, even bizarre, and never bothered to bid. In the end, BBN Technologies—Licklider's former employer—got the nod.

A Hesitant Start

The first piece went to UCLA, thanks to the reputation of Professor Kleinrock, an expert in computer statistical analysis and measurement. The first IMP link was with Stanford Research Institute (SRI). The first message was sent on October 29, 1969, and was supervised by Kleinrock—it was an omen of things to come. The message was supposed to be "login," but after two letters, the system crashed, and only "lo" was sent. About an hour later, the system was up and running again, and the full message was transmitted. By December 5, 1969, four IMPs were linked: UCLA, SRI, University of California at Santa Barbara, and the University of Utah. These IMP sites were chosen on the basis of their ability to research and implement the protocol that would allow for the continued growth of ARPANET.

ARPANET was no longer just a vision—it was a reality. The growth of ARPANET during the 1970s was phenomenal, as newer and better protocols were designed. In 1971, e-mail was born; in 1972, telnet was developed; and in 1973, file transfer protocol came into play.

By 1986, ARPANET had serious competition from the National Science Foundation Network (NSFNET), which became the true backbone of the Internet. ARPANET closed up shop in 1990. In 1991, NSFNET opened to the public, introducing the Internet we know today. Within four years, more than 50 million people had traveled the information superhighway. As of March 2008, worldwide Internet usage stood at 1.4 billion—and that's only the beginning. The Internet may not have solved all of the problems of the world, but it has managed to connect people around the world in ways they'd never previously imagined.

* By 2009, it was believed that 25 percent of the world's population used the Internet.

* Amazon.com began as an online bookstore in 1995, but today sells a wide variety of goods—from clothes to electronics.

* The first online bank opened in 1994.

* In 1971, the first electronic message to use the @ symbol in the address was sent over ARPANET.

Calling for Help

The 911 emergency system was modeled after the United Kingdom's 999.

✳ ✳ ✳ ✳

FOR AMERICANS BORN after 1968, reaching emergency aid—police, fire department, or ambulance—has always been as easy as dialing 911. Before then, people had to dial services directly or reach an operator who could place the call. The 911 system is a great achievement in public safety and has saved countless lives—but it's not an American invention.

Some historians believe that the first telephone call ever made—by Alexander Graham Bell to his assistant, Thomas A. Watson, on March 10, 1876—was also the first emergency call. Bell and Watson were in separate rooms testing a new transmitter when Bell supposedly spilled battery acid on his clothing. Watson heard Bell say "Mr. Watson, come here. I want you!" over the transmitter and rushed to his aid.

999

Great Britain introduced the first universal emergency number in 1937. Citizens calling 999 reached a central operator who would dispatch the police, fire department, or ambulance, as needed. According to records, the wife of John Stanley Beard of 33 Elsworthy Road, London, made the first 999 call to report a burglar outside her home. The police arrived promptly, and the intruder was arrested. The British system proved so successful that other countries ultimately followed. Today, most industrialized nations have some sort of universal emergency number.

911

In the United States, the idea of a universal emergency number was introduced in 1967 at the urging of the Presidential Commission on Law Enforcement. Congress quickly established a series of committees to determine how to make the system a reality. The committees had to work out several issues, foremost being the selection of a three-digit number that was not already a United States area code or an international prefix. Another consideration was ease of dialing on a rotary telephone. After much discussion, they finally decided on 911.

On January 12, 1968, AT&T, the nation's primary telephone carrier at the time, announced the designation of 911 as the universal emergency number during a press conference in the office of Indiana Representative Ed Roush, who had championed the cause before Congress. The AT&T plan initially involved only the Bell companies, not the small number of independent telephone companies across the country.

On February 16, 1968, the first 911 call was placed in Haleyville, Alabama. But it wasn't made through AT&T. Instead, the Alabama Telephone Company (a subsidiary of Continental Telephone) holds that honor. Its president had read about AT&T's plan in *The Wall Street Journal* and decided to beat the telecommunications giant to the punch. Haleyville was determined to be the best place to roll out the program, and the company set to work on the local system, with a scheduled activation date of February 16. Interestingly, that first call wasn't an emergency. It was a test call placed by Alabama Speaker of the House Rankin Fite from Haleyville City Hall to U.S. Representative Tom Bevill at the town's police station.

The first 911 systems sent callers to a predetermined emergency response agency, where an operator would dispatch services based on what the caller reported. This was occasionally problematic, especially when the caller was panicked, disoriented, or lacked the necessary information, such as an address.

A more sophisticated system, called "Enhanced 911," eliminated much of the confusion by providing operators with a caller's location and telephone number through special computers and displays. It also allows for selective routing and transfer of 911 calls to multiple emergency response jurisdictions.

Birth of the Magic Pill

Before 1960, activist Margaret Sanger dreamt of a "magic pill" for birth control that women could take as easily as an aspirin. This dream became a reality.

✳   ✳   ✳   ✳

IN THE 1950S, American women were having babies in unprecedented numbers. A big family was the perceived ideal. However, many women longed for inexpensive, reliable, and simple contraception. Diaphragms were costly. Condoms and other contraceptives were unreliable. None were easy to use.

Fortunately, history brought together Margaret Sanger, Katharine McCormick, Gregory Pincus, and John Rock.

The Players

Born in 1879, Margaret Sanger was 19 when her mother, who had given birth to 11 children and suffered 7 miscarriages, died from tuberculosis. In 1916, as a nurse in New York treating poor women recovering from botched illegal abortions, Sanger began defying the law by distributing contraceptives. In 1921, she founded the American Birth Control League, a precursor to the Planned Parenthood Federation, and in 1923 opened the first legal birth control clinic in the United States. For the next 30 years, Sanger advocated for safe and effective birth control while dreaming of a "magic pill" that would usher in an era of female-controlled contraception.

Katharine Dexter McCormick was born in 1875, to a prominent Chicago family. In 1904, she married Stanley McCormick, heir to the International Harvester Corporation fortune. Her life changed when Stanley developed schizophrenia. Believing the condition to be hereditary, she vowed to remain childless. In 1917, she met Sanger at a suffragette rally and took up her cause. After her husband's death in 1947, she dedicated his $15 million estate to the discovery of Sanger's "magic pill."

In January 1951, Sanger met Dr. Gregory Pincus, a former Harvard University biologist, now called "Dr. Frankenstein" after developing in-vitro fertilization in rabbits in 1934. Booted from Harvard, Pincus was working in obscurity at a Clark University lab when he met Sanger. He told Sanger her "magic pill" was possible, using hormones as a contraceptive. Sanger quickly arranged a grant for Pincus to research using progesterone to inhibit ovulation and prevent pregnancy. Within a year, Pincus confirmed that the drug was effective in lab animals.

A Bitter Pill

Pincus set out to invent a progesterone pill, unaware that both Syntex and G.D. Searle pharmaceutical companies had done so. (Neither company pursued its use as an oral contraceptive for fear of a public backlash.) Worse for Pincus, Planned Parenthood halted funding, saying his research was too risky.

Things turned for Pincus in late 1952 following a chance encounter with Dr. John Rock, a renowned fertility expert and birth control advocate from Harvard. Rock was a devout Catholic who reconciled the Vatican's rigid stance against artificial birth control with his personal conviction that planned parenting and contraception promoted healthy marriages. Rock floored Pincus when he explained that his tests using progesterone injections on female patients (ironically, he was attempting to stimulate pregnancy) worked as a contraceptive.

A New Era

Then in June 1953, Sanger introduced Pincus to McCormick. Sold on Pincus's research, McCormick donated $40,000 to restart the project. Pincus recruited Rock, and in 1954, using progesterone pills provided by Searle, they conducted the first human trials of the drug with 50 women, successfully establishing the 21-day administering cycle still used today.

In May 1960, Searle received FDA approval to sell the progesterone pill, Enovid, for birth control purposes. Within five years, six million American women were using the "magic pill."

The Floppy Disk Story

Two engineers walk into a bar...

* * * *

THE PERSONAL COMPUTER was made possible by two crucial developments: the microprocessor and the floppy disk. The first provided the PC with its brains. The second gave it long-term memory—lasting after the computer was turned off.

But who invented the floppy disk? Dr. Yoshiro Nakamatsu claims he developed the basic technology—a piece of plastic coated with magnetic iron oxide—back in 1950 and later licensed the technology to IBM. IBM has never acknowledged these claims, but it does own up to an "ongoing relationship" with Dr. Nakamatsu, who holds more than 3,000 patents and also claims to have invented the CD, DVD, and digital watch.

IBM made the first floppy disks, which were eight inches in diameter, encased in a paper jacket, and held 80 kilobytes of memory. But these disks were too big for personal computers, so in 1976 two engineers sat down in a Boston bar with An Wang of Wang Labs to discuss a new format. When they asked Dr. Wang how big the new floppies should be, he pointed to a cocktail napkin and said, "About that size." The engineers took the napkin back to California and made the floppies exactly the same size as the napkin: 5¼ inches.

The 5¼-inch floppy became standard in early personal computers, but they were easy to damage or get dirty, and as PCs got smaller, the disks were too large. Various companies released smaller formats, but it wasn't until Apple Computer added a 3½-inch floppy drive in its Macintosh computer that things began to change. The new disks had a stiff plastic case and a sliding metal cover to protect the data surface, and they stored 360K, 720K, and later 1.44 megabytes. The writing was on the disk, and these days, the original floppies are long gone.

Dino Mix-Ups

The field of paleontology, once the realm of dusty fossils displayed in museums, has in recent years become a hot field of study. New methods of testing, using DNA analysis, CAT scans, and MRI imaging, allow researchers to study fossil findings in new ways. However, one result of this current wave of research is the unearthing of mixed-up fossils, scientific wrong turns, and mistaken identities.

✳   ✳   ✳   ✳

You Say *Brontosaurus*, I say *Apatosaurus*

ONE OF THE first dino-bloopers was the case of the *Brontosaurus*. In 1877, paleontologist O. C. Marsh identified a specimen as being of the species type, *Apatosaurus ajax*. A few years later, he found a more complete sample of the same dinosaur. In the paper following this find, Marsh called the beast a Brontosaurus, setting off decades of confusion. The two names mean the same thing, but over time they began to be thought of as two different dinos. According to the rules for naming new species, the older name takes precedence; to put a halt to the confusion, Brontosaurus was officially dropped as the dino's name. Despite this, the Brontosaurus is still one of the most recognized dinosaur names.

Big, Bigger, Much Bigger

At an estimated 90 feet long and weighing 11 tons, the long-necked, plant-eating *Diplodocus* was considered to be the largest animal ever to have lived. It enjoyed that distinction for nearly a century until someone discovered the 100- to 130-foot-long *Supersaurus* in 1972. Then the *Seismosaurus*, at 150 feet long and weighing 85 tons, was uncovered in 1979. As more research emerges, museums around the world continue to rewrite identification cards for these long-necked beasts. It is now thought that while the Seismosaurus probably made tremor-like sounds when stamping through the forest, and the Supersaurus was very, very big, they were not separate species. In fact, both were just large specimens of the Diplodocus.

Plateosaurus Puzzler

It is remarkable that scientists can make any sense out of the jumble of bones that they discover. It's something like putting together a puzzle—one that is sure to have missing pieces, broken parts, and no picture to show how it should look in the end. It is not surprising that the pieces would get mixed up at times, as in the case of the *Plateosaurus*. In the late 1800s, German fossil hunters found the skeleton of a dinosaur that had the razor teeth of a meat eater. This was named *Teratosaurus* ("monster reptile") and was thought of as a slow-moving, long-necked carnivore. It took almost 100 years for paleontologists to sort out the fact that the Teratosaurus was actually the remains of a plant-eating Plateosaurus, whose skull was mixed up with that of the crocodile-like creature that ate it. This beast, one of the top predators of the time, was not a dinosaur at all. Even so, it got to keep the name Teratosaurus.

Oviraptor: Falsely Accused

The first *Oviraptor* specimens discovered in Mongolia, were found near fossilized eggs. It was assumed at the time that the eggs were from the *Protoceratops*, and since the new dinosaur was toothless, it made sense to assume the eggs were a part of its diet. This theory led to its name: Oviraptor ("egg thief"). However, it was not until the 1990s when excavations in China cleared the Oviraptor's name. At the site, Oviraptor specimens were found, as they had been in the past, near eggs. Thanks to new technologies, this time scientists were able to examine the inside of the fossilized eggs. What they found was the embryo of an Oviraptor—the "egg thieves" were actually very good parents, protecting their nests and their young with their lives.

Beam Me Up

Star Trek fans who watch as the crew are "beamed" across space want to believe that such instantaneous transport of matter—called "teleportation"—is actually possible. But is it?

✳   ✳   ✳   ✳

What is teleportation?

SINCE 1998, SCIENTISTS have been applying Einstein's term for teleporting, *spukhafte Fernwirkung*, or "spooky action at a distance," to atoms and beams of light, sending their replicas across space. These experiments in physics are done through a bizarre process called "quantum entanglement."

Laboratory researchers create three charged atoms of an element such as beryllium—let's call them A, B, and C. Like all atoms, atom A has certain unique properties, such as its spin, motion, and magnetic field. Atoms B and C have their own properties. In teleportation, scientists move the properties of atom A to atom C, in essence re-creating atom A.

Yet physicists face a big obstacle in moving atom A's unique characteristics: It's called Heisenberg's Uncertainty Principle: The scientific theorem that one cannot know with certainty the properties of a particle, including its location and speed.

To fix this, scientists "entangle" atom B and atom C. Through the magic of quantum physics, researchers can measure the properties of an atom without changing it. Next they transmit the properties of atom A, via atom B, to atom C. Atom C takes on the properties of atom A, in effect "becoming" atom A.

Great! When do we leave?

Photons of light and atoms can be transmitted. Atoms can be sent about a foot and a half, and photons launched about 20 miles. Even so, this experiment can't yet be done with people. To duplicate a person, you'd need machines smart enough to copy and position the trillions of atoms in the human body.

Beatrix Potter's Scientific Side

This iconic children's author was much more than just the creator of Flopsy, Mopsy, Cottontail, and Peter Rabbit.

✳   ✳   ✳   ✳

A Victorian Upbringing

Cᴀʟʟ ɪᴛ ᴀ case of living in the wrong place at the wrong time. If not for her strict Victorian upbringing, Beatrix Potter might have been too busy with scientific research to introduce readers to the tale of Peter Rabbit. Born in 1866 to a wealthy family in London, her parents left her upbringing to a string of tutors and governesses. Potter was so sharp that most of her teachers could not keep up with her. Once, she learned six of Shakespeare's plays by heart in less than a year.

Potter the Scientific Illustrator

In the Victorian era, it was not considered necessary, or even appropriate, to send girls away for a proper education. Instead, Potter's teachers were to instruct her in so-called "womanly" subjects such as French and drawing. Certainly, the study of mushrooms and lichens was not part of Potter's curriculum.

But Potter had been fascinated by nature since childhood. She kept all sorts of animals as pets, and she drew beautiful and accurate pictures of them. This interest continued to manifest itself in her botanical drawings, particularly of mushrooms. In her late 20s, unmarried and increasingly at odds with her parents who expected their daughter to take on the domestic responsibilities of their household, Potter found a much-needed escape in her drawings and nature studies.

Potter began visiting the Royal Botanical Gardens at Kew to learn more about the fungi that were being researched there. In a journal she wrote in code to keep her studies a secret from her mother, Potter expressed her excitement over recent scientific findings such as that of scientist Louis Pasteur. She grew her own spores, observed them under a microscope, and carefully recorded her findings. Entirely self-taught, Potter began developing theories of her own.

A Dream Denied

At the time, the British scientific community deemed the notion that lichens could actually be made up of two organisms—an algae and a fungus—absurd. However, Potter's readings of recent findings from Continental Europe contradicted this. In her studies, she had observed firsthand how the algae and fungus found in lichens did, in fact, need each other to survive. She wrote her findings in an 1897 paper, *On the Germination of the Spores of Agaricineae*. Unfortunately, because she was a woman, she was not allowed to be present when it was read at a meeting of a society of naturalists. Her work had little impact on the biologists of her time; decades later, however, her findings would be accepted as pioneering work in the understanding of symbiotic relationships in biology.

Potter tried to gain acceptance as a student at the Kew Gardens in order to formalize her research and gain credentials as a scientist. When she went to meet the director, however, botanical drawings in hand, it was immediately clear that he did not take her application seriously. The director would not even look at her drawings. This was great humiliation for the shy Potter; afterward, she gave up what she called "grown-up science."

The Birth of a Bunny

The same year her paper was rejected, Potter began writing and illustrating children's books. With her 25 books, she eventually achieved what few women of her era managed: financial and intellectual independence. She may have given up formal study, but she never stopped drawing with scientific accuracy. After all, even if her rabbits are wearing sweaters, the trees and flowers in the background are drawn with a biologist's eye for detail.

Space Is the Place: Astronaut Facts

Think being an astronaut is all glamour, weird tubes of food, and putting flags into moonscapes? Read on to get a further glimpse into what it's like to travel in outer space.

✳ ✳ ✳ ✳

I T'S THE FINAL frontier, so it may come as no surprise that life in space is strange. Astronauts have all sorts of unusual procedures in their day-to-day life amid the stars; everything from their dinners to their digs has fascinating facts behind them.

Cleanliness Concerns

Sloppy bachelors would feel right at home in orbit. Because of the lack of laundry facilities, astronauts on missions change their socks, shirts, and underwear just every two days and their pants once a week. After that, the worn garments are sealed in airtight plastic bags. (That might be a good policy for some guys on Earth, come to think of it.)

As for showering, it's sponge-baths only for space crews. Water droplets could escape, posing a danger to expensive electronics. To be safe, the astronauts step in a cylindrical stall, where they have about a one-gallon ration of water to use. The dirty water is sucked up by a vacuum and stored in special trash tanks.

Water isn't part of the tooth-brushing regime at all. NASA developed a unique kind of toothpaste that astronauts swish around without the need for liquid.

Waste Not

Contrary to common perception, most garbage is sealed in bags to be brought back to Earth for disposal—it isn't just tossed into orbit. As for the other, shall we say, "waste" produced onboard, astronauts use toilets similar to those back home. Their facilities, though, have no water; instead, the space toilet uses a constant vacuum-like airflow in the bowl to keep things from floating back up in the zero gravity. Crew members also have to strap in their feet and thighs to keep themselves from floating away mid-act.

Slumber Situation

Sleeping takes a different turn in space. Astronauts zip themselves into specially designed sleeping bags that attach to their lockers. They can sleep either in the normal horizontal position or in a bat-like vertical stance—the two poses are indistinguishable when gravity isn't a factor. Some crew members may also rest in removable bunk beds.

Magnetic Attraction

Because of objects' tendency to float in space, magnets are a common commodity. Meal trays are magnetic and designed to keep forks, spoons, and knives stuck down, which can make eating a slight challenge. The food packages are also adhered to the trays with strips of Velcro.

Space in Space

At the International Space Station, it becomes a lot less crowded. Once finished, the station's set of solar panels will be big enough to cover the entire U.S. Senate Chamber three times. The whole facility will be about the size of a large five-bedroom house, with eight miles of electrical wire snaking through the walls. And get this: The completed station will weigh a whopping one million pounds—about the weight of 67 fully grown male elephants.

✳ The finished International Space Station will be 361 feet long. It'd take 57 Bob Saget clones stacked on top of each other to fill that much space.

✳ The station's robotic arm can lift 220,000 pounds—or nearly 900 American Gladiators—in a single swipe.

✳ By the time the space station is done, astronauts will have spent 800 hours on spacewalks working on the facility.

On the Airwaves: Frequency Modulation (FM Radio)

An innovator's marvelous invention is tarnished by betrayal.

✳   ✳   ✳   ✳

FAME AND RICHES are supposed to go to those visionaries that build the better mousetraps. But with the invention of frequency modulation (FM radio), things didn't quite work out that way. Edwin H. Armstrong (1890–1954) invented a new transmission medium that left the former giant, amplitude modulation (AM radio), quivering in its wake. For most people, such a lofty achievement would bring a degree of satisfaction—not to mention a stack of cash. For Armstrong, it would bring mostly heartache.

Before this underappreciated genius found his way to FM, he made other worthy contributions. Two of Armstrong's inventions, the regenerative circuit of 1912 and the superheterodyne circuit of 1917, would set the broadcasting world on its ear. When combined, they would produce an affordable tube radio that would become an American staple.

Soon afterward, the inventor turned his attentions to the removal of radio static, an inherent problem in the AM circuit. After witnessing a demonstration of Armstrong's superheterodyne receiver, David Sarnoff, the head of the Radio Corporation of America (RCA) and founder of the National Broadcasting Company (NBC), challenged the inventor to develop "a little black box" to remove the static. Armstrong spent the late 1920s through the early 1930s tackling the problem. Sarnoff backed the genius by allowing him use of a laboratory at the top of the Empire State Building. This was no small offering—in the broadcasting game, height equals might, and none came taller than this 1,250-foot giant, which has since been named one of the seven wonders of the modern world.

In 1933, Armstrong made a bold announcement. He had cracked the noise problem using frequency modulation. With a wider frequency response than AM and no background noise, the new technology was a revolutionary step in broadcasting.

Armstrong's upgraded system had the ability to relay programming from city to city by direct off-air pickup by 1936. Without knowing it, the inventor had effectively boxed himself in. NBC, and by extension Sarnoff, was the dominant force in conventional radio during this time. With America mired in an economic depression, NBC wasn't interested in tooling up for a new system. Even worse for Armstrong, television loomed on the horizon, and NBC was pouring most of its resources into the new technology. Instead of receiving the recognition and financial rewards that he so rightly deserved, Armstrong was fired unceremoniously by his "friend" Sarnoff. It seemed like the end of the line, but Armstrong's battle was only just beginning.

In 1937, a determined Armstrong erected a 400-foot tower and transmitter in Alpine, New Jersey. Here, he worked to perfect his inventions. Unfortunately, without Sarnoff's backing, his operation was severely underfunded. To make matters worse, Armstrong became embroiled in a patent battle with RCA, which claimed the invention of FM radio. The broadcasting giant ultimately won the fight and shut Armstrong down. The ruling was so lopsided that it robbed Armstrong of his ability to claim royalties on FM radios sold in the United States.

To fully appreciate Armstrong's contribution, compare AM and FM radio stations: The difference in sound is pronounced, with FM sounding wonderfully alive and AM noticeably flat in comparison. Even "dead air" sounds better on FM because the band lacks the static that plagues the AM medium. Clearly, FM technology is a tremendous breakthrough. But it came at a terrible cost. On January 31, 1954, Armstrong—distraught over his lack of recognition and dwindling finances—flung himself from a 13th-floor window of his New York City apartment.

Science vs. Séance

*In which we examine the curious nature of ectoplasm
and the story of famed medium and ectoplasm producer
Margery Crandon's examination by a scientific committee.*

✳   ✳   ✳   ✳

The Essence of Ectoplasm

TODAY MOST PEOPLE associate the term "ectoplasm" with
the film *Ghostbusters* in which Bill Murray's character gets
slimed by a slovenly ghost. To spiritualists of the late 18th and
early 19th centuries, however, ectoplasm was an essential substance produced by mediums during a séance.

Ectoplasm was typically white and often luminescent, and it
appeared to have the consistency of cheesecloth (which, skeptics wryly observed, was because it was cheesecloth). While
many regarded ectoplasm as a physical manifestation of spirits,
to others it was part of the 19th-century spiritualism craze.

The first use of the word *ectoplasm* is credited to French scientist and 1913 Nobel Prize winner Charles Richet, who used
it to describe the substance produced by a European medium
during a séance in 1894. That a highly regarded scientist such
as Richet should have a deep and abiding interest in spiritualism did not strike his contemporaries as a contradiction. In fact,
the idea that the spiritual world could transfer messages and
substances into the world of the living was an appealing notion
to Victorians. It was, after all, an era that bridged widespread
beliefs in the metaphysical with the emerging fields of quantum
theory and technological experimentation.

Enter Margery, Mistress of Ectoplasm

In 1924, Mina "Margery" Crandon, wife of a Boston surgeon,
was on her way to becoming the world's foremost medium.
With the alleged help of Walter, her long-dead brother and
spirit-world contact, Crandon had been able to levitate objects,

manifest writing, and produce auditory emanations. She traveled to Europe and submitted to scientific tests in Paris and London to prove her talents. Upon her return to the United States, she perfected the art of producing ectoplasm in the form of glowing strands, hands, rods, and, in one instance, the figure of a tiny girl. At different times the ectoplasm streamed from all of her orifices—mouth, nose, ears, and vagina.

Put to the Test

In 1923, *Scientific American* magazine offered $2,500 to any medium that could conduct a successful séance while under professional scientific scrutiny. Several amateur mediums tried and were proven frauds. Finally, the magazine's associate editor, J. Malcolm Bird, convinced Crandon to sit for the committee.

Those who observed Crandon in Boston in 1924 included Dr. William McDougall, psychology professor at Harvard; Dr. Daniel Comstock, former Massachusetts Institute of Technology professor; professional magician and spiritualist skeptic Harry Houdini; Dr. Walter Prince, researcher at the American Society of Psychical Research; and amateur magician and author Hereward Carrington.

Although Crandon was able to provide many examples of her intimacy with the spirit world, including the production of ectoplasm, Houdini became convinced that Crandon was a fraud. He delivered a series of lectures denouncing her and accusing Bird of incompetence and collaboration.

Mired in mistrust, the observers published their disparate findings separately in November 1924. Their inability to disprove Crandon's abilities, however, catapulted her into national prominence. Her career peaked years later when she manifested her deceased brother's fingerprint in dental wax. Later examination showed the fingerprint was that of her living dentist. This episode, coupled with Bird's admission that Crandon's husband had asked him to collaborate in fooling the *Scientific American* committee, thoroughly debunked her abilities.

Strange But True Inventions

And to think, we didn't even know we needed all this stuff.

✳ ✳ ✳ ✳

Pierced Glasses

TIRED OF YOUR glasses slipping down your nose? Try pierced glasses—spectacles that connect to a piercing surgically implanted into the nose. Invented by James Sooy in 2004, these glasses should appeal to body modification artists.

The Bulletproof Bed

Are you consumed with fearful thoughts when you go to bed? Perhaps you'll rest more peacefully in a bulletproof bed. The Quantum Sleeper's coffinlike design protects from attacks, fires, and natural disasters with its airtight and waterproof interior. The bed features an air filtration system and can be fitted with DVD screens, a refrigerator, and even a microwave!

The Portable Crosswalk

There never seems to be a crosswalk when you need one, and nobody wants to break the law by jaywalking. Instead, use a portable crosswalk, a vinyl sheet that can be spread across a busy street to ensure your safety as you make your way through traffic. Though its legality may be in question, it will certainly stop traffic . . . we hope.

Sauce-Dispensing Chopsticks

Need to shave time from your daily schedule? Try sauce-dispensing chopsticks for the sushi eater in a rush. No longer do you have to waste valuable seconds dipping your food into the soy sauce—just squeeze the end of the stick and the liquid flows right onto your food! The utensils cost about $20, but can you really put a price on time-saving of this magnitude?

The Drymobile

In this day and age, everyone is looking for ways to save time and energy. Now you can do both with the Japanese

Drymobile. Hang your clothes from a rack that fits on top of your car and your clothes will be dry in no time as you run your daily errands . . . unless, of course, it starts to rain.

One-Cut Nail Clippers

Staying well groomed can be quite time-consuming. But now one task can be shortened with one-cut nail clippers. A series of five clippers are positioned over the toes or fingernails, allowing the user to cut all five nails at once.

The Gas Grabber

Sometimes you just can't blame the dog. For those occasions, turn to the Gas Grabber, a charcoal filter that slips into your underwear to cover up those social faux pas. The filter was originally developed by the British to guard against nerve agents.

The Grin Grabber

Some people just don't smile enough, so it's the Grin Grabber to the rescue! Attach a hook to each side of your mouth, grasp the string, and yank. The pulley system will lift the corners and soon you'll be beaming from ear to ear!

The Snot Sucker

No tissue? No problem! The WIVA-VAC Nasal Aspirator uses vacuum power to clean up a runny nose. Perfect for children on the go, just slip the tapered end into a nostril and suck the snot right out of 'em!

The Daddy Nurser

Since the beginning of time, men have been accused of not pulling their weight in the baby department. Now men can truly experience the joy of motherhood with the Daddy Nurser, a pair of milk-filled orbs that connect to a man's chest to mimic the act of breast-feeding. Now if they could only invent a way for men to give birth!

A Weapon for Peace

*How an eccentric genius caused a stir over
ray guns—30 years after his death.*

✳   ✳   ✳   ✳

Tech Dissention

THE U.S. GOVERNMENT never throws away a good idea—it
might come in handy someday. In a May 1977 issue of
Aviation Week & Space Technology, Major General George J.
Keegan, retired head of Air Force intelligence, asserted in an
article that the Soviet Union was in the final stages of developing a particle beam weapon capable of neutralizing intercontinental ballistic missiles. Yet soon afterward another article
appeared in the *Baltimore Sun* entitled, "Moscow Yet to Develop
Laser Weapon, [President] Carter Says." It seemed U.S. intelligence needed to get their story straight.

The United States had experimented with developing a particle
beam weapon as early as 1958, but they eventually abandoned
the device, deeming it unfeasible. Why then, nearly 20 years
later, was there a need to deny the existence of such a weapon
in the enemy's hands? What possible edge could the Soviets
have over the United States that might lend a semblance of
credibility to Keegan's claims? The edge lay in the work of
Nikola Tesla, the brilliant scientist and inventor who claimed to
have developed the plans for a "teleforce" weapon against which
there could be no defense.

Enter Nikola Tesla

Tesla's particular area of specialty was electricity, but unlike
Thomas Edison—his contemporary, rival, and onetime
employer—Tesla's knowledge of the medium seemed more akin
to sorcery than science. He claimed his discoveries and inventions came to him in hallucinatory flashes. In his laboratory,
he entertained luminaries such as Mark Twain and president
Theodore Roosevelt with displays of electrical wonder.

As Tesla grew older, his claims and concepts for inventions became more bizarre. Many of these were born from his hatred of warfare. He was convinced that future peace and prosperity lay in the development of weapons so terrible, yet so universally available, that all nations would cease to consider warfare a practical means of settling disputes.

Death Rays for Peace

In 1931, Tesla conceived of an invention he later termed a "New Art of Projecting Concentrated Non-Dispersive Energy through Natural Media"—what we now call a particle accelerator. The press chose to call the invention a "Death Beam." In a 1934 article in the *New York Times*, Tesla said his invention would make war impossible because every nation would be able to send bursts of energy through the air with enough power to destroy "10,000 enemy airplanes at a distance of 250 miles."

Tesla sought funding for the device. With World War II imminent, Tesla sent his proposal to all the Allied nations. Only the Soviets took interest and provided Tesla with $25,000 for plans to develop the weapon. Tesla's increasingly bold assertions led many to consider him a crackpot. After his death in 1943, certain items, including a notebook, were removed from his belongings by an unknown agent (possibly Russian). The U.S. government quickly moved to confiscate his remaining papers.

From Stalingrad to Star Wars

When reports of Soviet experiments in high-velocity particle beam weapons began to proliferate in the 1970s, the U.S. government definitely paid attention. Many experts already believed that the Soviets, capitalizing on their dealings with Tesla in the '30s, had successfully tested such a weapon as early as 1968. The furor reinvigorated U.S. interest in particle beam weapons, which gave rise to the Strategic Defense Initiative, or "Star Wars," program of the Reagan administration.

The Truth About Space Travel

Like nature, humans abhor a vacuum, and we've been filling the void of scientific knowledge with near-truths and outright falsehoods ever since we broke the grip of Earth's gravity. Here are a few.

✳ ✳ ✳ ✳

There is no gravity in space. There is a difference between "weightlessness" and "zero-g" force. Astronauts may effortlessly float inside a space shuttle, but they are still under the grasp of approximately 10 percent of Earth's gravity. Essentially, gravity will decrease as the distance from its source increases, but it never just vanishes.

Gravitational forces are powerful enough to distort a person's features. This popular notion can be traced to the fertile minds of Hollywood filmmakers, who quickly learned the value of "artistic license" when dealing with the subject of outer space. In 1955's *Conquest of Space*, director Byron Haskin portrayed space travelers stunned and frozen by the forces of liftoff, pressed deep into their seats with their faces grotesquely distorted. When humankind actually reached space in 1961, the truth became known: Although gravitational forces press against the astronauts, they are perfectly capable of performing routine tasks, and their faces do not resemble Halloween masks.

An ill-suited astronaut will explode. Filmmakers would have you believe that an astronaut who is exposed to the vacuum of space without the protection of a spacesuit would expand like a parade float. With eyes bulging and the body swelling like a big balloon, the poor soul would soon blow up. It would be a gruesome sight, indeed, but that's not the way it would happen. The human body is too tough to distort in a complete vacuum. The astronaut would double over in pain and eventually suffocate, but that unfortunate occurrence would likely not make the movie highlight reel.

Stranded space travelers will be asphyxiated. The film world's take on space dangers has occasionally spilled into reality. In movies such as *Marooned*, astronauts are stuck in space as their oxygen supply runs out. Although the danger of being stranded in space is very real (*Apollo 13* comes to mind), astronauts in such a situation would not die from lack of oxygen. Carbon dioxide in a disabled spacecraft could build up to life-threatening levels long before the oxygen ran out.

The world watched as the *Challenger* "exploded." Myth even lies in one of the most tragic spaceflights in U.S. history—the *Challenger* disaster of January 1986. Stories tell of the millions of horrified viewers who watched as the spacecraft and its solid-rocket boosters broke apart on live television. Except for cable network CNN, however, the major networks had ceased their coverage of the launch. Because crew member Christa McAuliffe was to be the first teacher in space, NASA had arranged for public schools to show the launch on live TV. Consequently, many of those who actually saw it happen were schoolchildren. It was only when videotaped replays filled the breaking newscasts that "millions" of people were able to view the catastrophe. Another misconception about the *Challenger* is that it actually "exploded." It didn't, at least not in the way most people assume. The shuttle's fuel tank ripped apart, but there was no blast or detonation.

We even have the quote wrong. History has attributed this famous quote to Neil Armstrong as he stepped from the lunar module and became the first man on the moon in July 1969: "That's one small step for man, one giant leap for mankind." But Armstrong was misquoted. He never intended to speak on behalf of thousands of years of human development by declaring it "one small step for man." An innocent "a" got lost in the clipped electronic transmission of nearly 250,000 miles. According to Armstrong himself (and upon further review of the recording), he said, "That's one small step for a man, one giant leap for mankind," giving a much more humble tone to his statement.

On a Roll

Toilet paper is one invention that has been flushed with success.

✳ ✳ ✳ ✳

L IKE PASTA AND gunpowder, toilet paper was invented in China. Paper made from pulped bamboo and cotton rags was also invented by the Chinese, although Egyptians had already been using papyrus plants for thousands of years to make writing surfaces. Still, it wasn't until 1391, almost 1,600 years after the invention of paper, that the Ming Dynasty Emperor first used toilet paper. The government made 2×3 foot sheets, which either says something about the manufacturing limitations of the day or the Emperor's diet!

Toilet paper didn't reach the United States until 1857 when the Gayetty Firm introduced "Medicated Paper." Prior to the industrial revolution, many amenities were available only to the wealthy. But in 1890, Scott Paper Company brought toilet paper to the masses. The company employed new manufacturing techniques to introduce perforated sheets. In 1942, Britain's St. Andrew's Paper Mill invented two-ply sheets (the civilized world owes a great debt to the Royal Air Force for protecting this London factory during The Blitz!). Two-ply sheets are not just two single-ply sheets stuck together; each ply in a two-ply sheet is thinner than a single-ply sheet. The first "moist" toilet paper—Cottonelle Fresh Rollwipes—appeared in 2001.

What was the rest of the world doing? Some pretty creative stuff! Romans soaked sponges in saltwater and attached them to the end of sticks. Medieval farmers used balls of hay. American pioneers used corncobs. Leaves have always been a popular alternative to toilet paper but are rare in certain climates, so Inuit people favor Tundra moss. Of all people, the Vikings seemed the most sensible, using wool. It's not easy being a sheep.

America's First Skyscraper

Chicago's Home Insurance Building certainly earned the grandiose nickname "the father of the skyscraper" when its creation set off a building trend.

✳   ✳   ✳   ✳

COMPLETED IN 1885, William LeBaron Jenney's architectural innovation was the first building with a structural steel frame. It was initially erected at ten stories tall, or about 138 feet. Even with two additional stories tacked on five years later, the structure known as "America's First Skyscraper" would, at 180 feet, still be tiny next to Chicago's current giant, the Willis Tower (formerly the Sears Tower), which boasts a rooftop height of approximately 1,450 feet.

Vertical Construction

Modeled in classic Chicago School architectural styling, the Home Insurance Building led the burgeoning trend toward the upward urban sprawl that now defines major U.S. cities: Prior to its creation, architects had only plotted building growth in a horizontal fashion. But with this new breed of building, the future of business architecture was all upward. After all, why rely on mere land, when the sky's the limit?

Torn down in 1931, the Home Insurance Building was replaced just three years later by the still-standing, 45-story LaSalle National Bank Building (originally called the Field Building). The Home Insurance Building had served its purpose, and the city was ready for the next round of architectural advancements. Just as the Home Insurance Building initiated a new era in architecture, its replacement was significant: It capitalized on the architectural trend of the time by capturing the magniloquence of the Art Deco movement. But as significant as the Field Building may have been, it didn't break new ground in the same way as the Home Insurance Building had.

Chapter 3

Games People Play

Great Golf Courses from Around the World

What differentiates golf from most other sports is that the average person can play a round where Palmer, Nicklaus, Hogan, Trevino, and Woods have played. Here are some hallowed golf temples.

✳　✳　✳　✳

St. Andrews Old Course (1400s), public, Scotland: St. Andrews represents six centuries of golf on six courses, of which the Old Course is the most famous. Storied hole: number 17, the famous Road Hole (par 4, 455 yards from the black tees), with the hungering Road Bunker awaiting anyone who overshoots the green. Stays in the Road Bunker can be so long the golfer needs to find a motel.

Carnoustie Championship (1842), public, Scotland: Tour players often call this "Car-nasty," mainly for its unpredictable weather. Storied hole: number 6 (par 5, 578), which is likely to involve a driver from the fairway on the second shot.

Royal County Down Championship (1889), public, Northern Ireland: This is where the famous David Feherty honed his slice. Your first three holes take you along Dundrum Bay. Storied hole: number 9 (par 4, 486 from the blacks), a blind tee shot threaded down a narrow fairway toward an undulating green.

Lahinch (1892), public, Ireland: Lahinch is up close and personal with the North Atlantic. Storied hole: number 5 (par 3, 154 from the blues), aka The Dell, a blind shot at a foot-shape green tucked completely behind a dune.

Oakmont (1903), private, Pennsylvania: Golfers wallow in the pain this course inflicts. If you want to get a feel for its greens, hit some practice putts on a gently sloped basketball court. Storied hole: number 3 (par 4, 428 from the green tees), where a hooked tee shot sends you to pray in the vast Church Pews—a bunker complex nearly the size of a football field.

Pinehurst No. 2 (1907), resort, North Carolina: Of Pinehurst Resort's eight courses, this is the most famous. Long, tree-lined dogleg fairways make for jungle safaris if you miss off the tee. Storied hole: number 11 (par 4, 434 from the blues), one of Ben Hogan's favorites, encouraging a slight fade off the tee.

Pine Valley (1918), private, New Jersey: Pine Valley is that rare course with no dull holes. The designer felt that a course should require every club in the bag, and Pine Valley does. Some call it the world's best. Storied hole: number 18 (par 4, 483 from the back tees), descending from an elevated tee into a steep second shot firing at a huge green flanked by perilous bunkers.

Pebble Beach (1919), public, California: If you golf, you've heard of Pebble. One of four courses clustered in the area, much of Pebble plays along the Pacific Ocean's stony shores. Storied hole: number 7 (par 3, 106 from the blues), where you hit down onto a well—a bunkered peninsular green with flaky wind gusts. If the wind gets hold, "on the beach" has a literal meaning.

Royal Melbourne West (1931), semiprivate, Australia: You'll have to have a letter of introduction and a respectable handicap to make a reservation here. The West Course is the highest rated of three. Storied hole: number 18 (par 4, 433), a boomerang-shape dogleg right requiring a precise 230-yarder off the tee and a great long iron or hybrid to get home in two.

Cypress Point (1928), private, California: This Pebble Beach neighbor is known chiefly for its beauty. It has three holes that string together along the Pacific Ocean. Storied hole: number 16 (par 3, 220 yards), the second of the three oceanfront holes, where timid tee shots end up in a jumble of vines or skitter back down into the ocean inlet.

Pine Needles (1928), resort, North Carolina: This course is rated excellent for women because of its emphasis on finesse and strategy rather than cannon shots off the tee. Call it the anti-Augusta National. Often hosts the U.S. Women's Open. Storied hole: number 3 (par 3, 145 from the medal tees), a middle iron over a pond where the penalty for overshooting will likely be a three-putt.

Augusta National (1933), private and exclusive, Georgia: It hosts the annual Masters Tournament and has thus seen some of the most dramatic moments in championship golf history. Augusta's refusal to allow women to join makes it controversial. Storied hole: number 13 (par 5, 510), the Azalea Hole, with its psyche-testing drive followed by a water-hazard clearance and a tough green.

Highland Links (1939), public, Nova Scotia: A contender for Canada's best golfing honors, this course has the natural beauty you'd expect in a national park. Storied hole: number 15 (par 4, 540 from the blues), where the prevailing winds and downhill play encourage you to break out your driver and hit it at the Atlantic with a fair chance to reach in two strokes.

Bandon Dunes (1999), public, Oregon: One of three fantastic courses, it's far from urbanity but worth the long trip. Old school golf—no carts. Sometimes Bandon and its sibling Pacific Dunes will make the same top ten lists—that's how great the place is. Storied hole: number 16 (par 4, 363 from the blacks), bisected by an ocean inlet and with numerous options on the way home.

Whip It!: Roller Derby Names

Roller derby is back on the scene in a big way. Check out this fun list of derby girls' nom de skate.

✳ ✳ ✳ ✳

IN 2004, the Women's Flat Track Roller Derby Association was founded, bringing women's competitive roller derby back to the masses. With roots in the 1930s, derby bouts are rowdy, risky, fun, and imbued with a special brand of humor, as evidenced by the names of players, referees, and support staff.

Name and League

Tequila Mockingbird—Windy City Rollers

Bone Crawford—Jersey Shore Roller Girls

Gefilte Fists—Philly Roller Girls

Midwife Crisis—Arch Rival Roller Girls

Genghis Connie—Assassination City Roller Derby

Grrrilla—Sonoma County Roller Derby

Graceless Kelly—Maine Roller Derby

Doris Day of the Dead (referee)—Windy City Rollers

Skatie Couric—Boston Derby Dames

Cruisin' B. Anthony—Ithaca Roller Derby

Grudge Judy—Texas Rollergirls

Abbey Rogue—Denver Roller Dolls

Raggedy Animal—Gotham Girls Roller Derby

Tall Drinka Slaughter—Windy City Rollers

Ella Mental—Rollers Syndicate

Count Smacula—Pikes Peak Derby Dames

Bill Bleeping Buckner

Put "Red Sox" and "1986 World Series" in the same sentence, and the name "Bill Buckner" is only a few words away. Despite popular belief, though, the team's collapse wasn't entirely his fault.

* * * *

URING BOSTON'S 85 consecutive seasons without a World Series championship, the word *bleeping* assumed a prominent place in the lexicon of Red Sox Nation. Commonly inserted between the first and last names of players who separated the Sox from the prize, its use reached an alliterative zenith in 1986, when Bill bleeping Buckner let that bleeping ball roll through his bleeping legs. Had the first baseman stabbed the easy grounder for the final out of Game 6, the Series could have ended in Boston's favor, but it is just as true that the Sox had the chance to take care of business numerous times before and after the miscue.

By the time the contest had snaked to the bottom of the tenth inning, the Red Sox already had given back two other leads and left 14 runners on base. Even before the New York Mets' Mookie Wilson trickled the game-winning bouncer, it was timorous young pitcher Calvin Schiraldi who surrendered three singles to establish the precarious scenario. It was Schiraldi's replacement, Bob Stanley, who allowed the tying run to score by zipping an errant pitch past backstop Rich Gedman.

Then there's manager John McNamara, who had two chances to replace the hobbled 36-year-old Buckner before the game reached critical mass. Three innings earlier, Mac allowed the left-handed hitter to pop out with the bases loaded against a tough lefty pitcher, despite having powerful right-hander Don Baylor available. Protecting a lead in the tenth, the skipper's obvious move would have been to insert the more mobile Dave Stapleton at first base. By that time, however, strategic rigor bleeping mortis had set in.

Grapple and Grind

From body slams to all-out glam, female grapplers have long been a featured part of the pro wrestling game.

✳ ✳ ✳ ✳

Rejecting the Status Quo

IN THE MID-1950S, women's roles were as clearly defined as they were limited. For many women in the United States, the burgeoning "baby boom" spelled out their fate: They would become housewives. It was also an era of high femininity and manners, where popular culture dictated what was "ladylike."

Still, amid this model, fringe elements were flowering. In professional wrestling, a new women's division took these accepted roles of femininity and stood them flat on their cauliflower ears. Under this entertaining banner, tough, self-assured women were suddenly tossed into the white-hot spotlight. Literally. Among the standout acts was a woman named Moolah.

Meet Moolah

Lillian Ellison hit the wrestling game at the perfect time. Women were screaming for excitement, and men were eager for the next gimmick. But this didn't concern Ellison. She moved to her own beat and set her own goals. In the early 1950s, she married and became a very young mother as a teenager. The union would last only two years, but it reinforced Ellison's free-spirit outlook on life. Despite having a baby to raise, Ellison, an ardent wrestling fan, decided to suit up and give the professional ranks a shot. History was about to be made.

As the "Fabulous Moolah" Ellison gave both genders what they wanted. With her signature moves, such as the "Big Punch," the "School Girl Roll Up," and the "Spiral

Backbreaker," Moolah was unlike any wrestler fans had seen. In 1956, she became the World Wide Wrestling Federation Women's Champion. It's a title she would hold until 1984. She recaptured it again in 1985, 1986, and 1999. She went on to wrestle in Japan, Mexico, Canada, and throughout Europe.

While Moolah was adept at delivering pile-drivers and subjecting opponents to painful half-nelsons, her appearance was one of pure utility. With her tough-as-nails grimace and strong, stocky shape, Moolah was as hard as she looked, and she didn't mind playing the villain. "I loved when they got mad at me," she said. "They called me all kinds of names. I said: 'Call me anything you want. You don't write my check.'"

Changing Roles

Women have had other roles in wrestling. Some weren't wrestlers at all, but the supposed *girlfriends* of wrestlers. Perhaps the most famous of the girlfriend archetype was Miss Elizabeth, the gorgeous companion/manager of wrestler "Macho Man" Randy Savage during the late 1980s and early '90s. Often rival wrestlers would develop crushes on Elizabeth, but she fawned over her belligerent man, snaring the hearts of wrestling fans everywhere. Wrestling honchos seized on this sexpot phenomenon and filed it for future reference: They would eventually create a composite wrestling figure that coupled the athleticism of Moolah with the sex appeal of Miss Elizabeth.

While part of wrestling's draw had always included the allure of attractive women in skimpy clothing, today's women are more *va-va-voom* than ever. Nowadays, a wrestler like the tan, blonde Michelle McCool is as much a pinup diva as she is an athlete. Some might argue that women's wrestling has taken a step back from Moolah's day. Ultra-sexy stars make it seem as though a woman's cheesecake factor matters at least as much as her wrestling skills. On the other hand, the popularity of female wrestling has reached new heights. Perhaps it's time to give wrestling's newest stars credit for being both sexy *and* capable.

Hockey's Other Hat Trick

One might logically assume that NHL great Gordie Howe invented the "Gordie Howe Hat Trick." Then again, when you assume...

* * * *

MR. HOCKEY DID not invent the three-pronged feat that bears his name. In fact, the term used to describe the art of recording a goal, an assist, and a fight in a single hockey match didn't enter the sport's lexicon until 1991. That's a full ten years after the game's longest-serving veteran hung up his blades.

Honoring a Hockey Great

Make no mistake: Gordie Howe was more than capable of achieving all three elements necessary to complete the celebrated triple play. He was a wizard at putting the biscuit in the basket, a magician at deftly slipping a pass through myriad sticks and skates and putting the disc on the tape of a teammate's stick, and he wasn't opposed to delivering a knuckle sandwich to a deserving adversary. However, the tattered pages of the NHL record books show that he recorded only one Howe Hat Trick in his 32-year career in the NHL and the World Hockey Association. On December 22, 1955, in a game against the Boston Bruins, Howe (playing for the Detroit Red Wings) scored the tying goal, set up the winning 3–2 tally, and bested Beantown left winger Lionel Heinrich in a spirited tussle.

The Record Holder

The Gordie Howe Hat Trick isn't an official statistic—in fact, the only franchise that lists the achievement in its media guide is the San Jose Sharks—but it is a widely acknowledged measurement of a skater's ability to play the game with both physical skill and artistic grace. The New York Rangers' Brendan Shanahan is the NHL's all-time leader in "Howe Hats." According to *The Hockey News*, Shanny scored a goal, recorded an assist, and had a fight nine times in the same game.

Greatest Sports Nicknames

The banter-filled atmosphere of the locker room, the media's fertile imagination, and fans' wisecracks give professional sports an inexhaustible source of interesting nicknames for teams, coaches, and players. Here are some of the most apt, colorful, and amusing.

❋ ❋ ❋ ❋

Hockey

Stu "The Grim Reaper" Grimson (1988–2002; eight different NHL teams): One of hockey's tougher pugilists, six-foot-five Grimson earned more than 2,100 penalty minutes during his 729-game NHL career—with only 17 career goals. When asked how he reconciled his frequent fighting with his born-again-Christian faith, Grimson replied: "I don't think that Christ would be shy to shake off his gloves and protect his teammates."

André "Red Light" Racicot (1989–1994; Montreal Canadiens): For you non-hockey fans, the red light behind the net signals a goal—usually accompanied by a blaring siren or horn. For a goalie, being referred to as "Red Light" is like being called "Swiss Cheese" or "Sieve." But Racicot was nowhere near as lousy as his unfortunate nickname suggests. He won 26 games, lost 23, and tied 8 for the Canadiens, averaging 3.5 goals against per game—not All-Star stuff, but no reason for Racicot to hang his head.

Dave "Cementhead" Semenko (1977–1988; WHA and NHL Edmonton Oilers, NHL Hartford Whalers and Toronto Maple Leafs): During Wayne Gretzky's heyday with the great Edmonton teams, Dave had one job: Keep Wayne safe. Most players didn't rough up Gretzky, preferring to avoid being punched out by someone who once acquitted himself respectably in an exhibition bout with Muhammad Ali, as Semenko had.

Football

Dick "Night Train" Lane (1952–1965; Los Angeles Rams, Chicago Cardinals, Detroit Lions): Though this defensive wizard's tackles indeed felt like locomotive hits arriving out of the night, Night Train got the odd nickname from associating with fellow Hall of Famer Tom Fears, who constantly played the record "Night Train" on his phonograph. The name became so associated with Lane that today hardly anyone remembers his first name.

William "The Refrigerator" Perry (1985–1994; Chicago Bears, Philadelphia Eagles): The 326-pound "Fridge" took up a lot of space on the defensive line. But what brought him the most attention was Chicago coach Mike Ditka's willingness to use him at fullback on goal-line plays. Although he was considered quite formidable, this reputation was mostly media hype—Perry had only eight regular-season NFL carries for five yards and two touchdowns. Still, it was great fun for fans while it lasted.

Baseball

Burleigh "Ol' Stubblebeard" Grimes (1916–1934; seven NL/ AL teams): The last pitcher legally allowed to throw the spitball under the grandfather clause when baseball outlawed any ball-doctoring, Burleigh always showed up with a faceful of scruffy whiskers. On the hill, he was meaner than a bag of bobcats, and he handily admitted this while wondering about all the "nice" guys in baseball.

Mike "The Human Rain Delay" Hargrove (1974–1985; Texas Rangers, San Diego Padres, Cleveland Indians): A lifetime .290 hitter, Hargrove got his nickname by fooling around in the batter's box: He would adjust his helmet, adjust his batting glove, pull on his sleeves, and wipe his hands on his pants before every pitch. If the pitcher instead threw to a base, Hargrove started screwing around all over again. Most pitchers like to get on with an at-bat, and it's probably no coincidence that Hargrove drew so many walks, intentional walks, and hits-by-pitch.

Pepper "The Wild Horse of the Osage" Martin (1928–1944; St. Louis Cardinals): According to teammate Leo Durocher, Oklahoman Martin played commando-style ball on more than one level: He wore no underwear, much less a protective cup. His rather wild, free-spirited base-running got him the nickname, though it also probably referred to his love of practical jokes. Baseball historian Lee Allen summed up Pepper: "A chunky, unshaven hobo who ran the bases like a berserk locomotive, slept in the raw, and swore at pitchers in his sleep." ("Pepper" was a nickname too. He was born Johnny Leonard Roosevelt Martin.)

Basketball

Darrell "Dr. Dunkenstein" Griffith (1980–1991; Utah Jazz): This doctor was six-foot-four and could jump as though grafted to a pogo stick. Griffith grew up in the era of George Clinton's Parliament and Funkadelic bands, and his brother and friends gave him a nickname that rhymed with Clinton's Dr. Funkenstein character—hardly knowing it would become a household name when Griffith became a pro.

Vinnie "The Microwave" Johnson (1979–1992; Seattle Supersonics, Detroit Pistons, San Antonio Spurs): Basketball fans know how important the "sixth man" can be, and Vinnie was one of the best off the bench. Boston Celtic Danny Ainge hung the tag on him in 1985 after Johnson's brilliant 34-point outing off the bench: "If that guy in Chicago is 'The Refrigerator,' then Vinnie Johnson is 'The Microwave.' He sure heats up in a hurry."

"Pistol Pete" Maravich (1970–1980; Atlanta Hawks, New Orleans Jazz, Utah Jazz, Boston Celtics): Had he played his full career in the three-point era, there's no telling how many this deadly long-range gunner might have racked up. Pistol Pete's nickname evoked his quick-draw shooting, but he was also a lot of fun to watch. He used his eerie peripheral vision to pull off hotdog passes and circus shots like one of the Harlem Globetrotters. The former gym rat died playing the sport he loved, suffering a heart attack when he was just 40 years old.

Pinstripes and Babe Ruth

Did the New York Yankees add pinstripes to conceal Babe Ruth's expanding barrel gut?

* * * *

Pinstripes

THE YANKEES FIRST wore pinstriped uniforms on Opening Day 1912, when George Herman Ruth was 17 years old. Baseball has its own fashion trends, and other teams were copying the flashy new look, so the Yanks abandoned the design for a couple of years. Only in 1915 did Yankee pinstripes return for good, by which time about half the teams in both leagues had tried some variation of them.

Babe's Career

Nineteen-year-old Babe broke into the bigs in 1914 with the Boston Red Sox. Until 1918, he was simply a great pitcher who could also hit. But pitchers didn't play every day, and Babe's bat was too helpful to keep on the rack three games out of four. In 1918 and 1919, the Sox increasingly put him in the outfield or at first base. When Boston sold Ruth to the Yanks before the 1920 season, New York made him a full-time outfielder, and he became the most feared slugger in the game.

Weighty Issues

Ruth undoubtedly lived large, but his gut didn't become large until he was about washed up. This is best revealed in reliably dated photographs. In 1914, he hadn't yet filled out. By 1918, the 6'2" Babe just looked like a big, strong guy. In 1923, he was still looking solidly fit, but by 1930, he probably should have been cutting back on the beer. When he finished with the Boston Braves in 1935, Babe was pretty chubby. His statistics bear out the visuals: From 1920 to 1930, he stole an average of nine bases per season, sometimes ranking among the team leaders. Fat guys don't do that. From 1931 to 1935, he swiped just over two per year. Fat guys do that.

Bowls of Confusion

Since the first college "bowl" game in 1902 almost every conceivable mishap and happenstance has occurred. Consider this trifecta of turmoil involving a player, a coach, and—in keeping with the spirit of the endeavor—a mascot.

✳ ✳ ✳ ✳

Wrong-Way Riegels—Rose Bowl, 1929: Perhaps the most infamous play to ever to take place during a bowl game occurred during the Rose Bowl between Georgia Tech and the University of California. Midway through the second quarter, Golden Bear center Roy Riegels recovered a Georgia fumble and immediately tore down the sidelines toward the end zone. There was only one problem: In his confusion after snagging the loose pigskin, Riegels ran the wrong way! The end zone he was about to reach was his own. Teammate Benny Lom, the bounciest Bear of the bunch, ran his errant buddy down, caught Wrong-Way, and tackled him on the three-yard line. Things deteriorated after that. After failing to advance the ball, California tried to punt the pill from their own end zone. A surging Georgia scrum blocked the kick and recovered the ball for a two-point safety, which proved to be the margin of victory in Tech's 8–7 win.

Hothead Hayes—Gator Bowl, 1978: One of the most celebrated college coaches of all time, Woody Hayes led his Ohio State charges to 16 championships, including 13 Big Ten crowns in the 28 seasons he spent strolling the sidelines for the Buckeyes. Revered for his innovative teaching techniques, Hayes was equally renowned for his volatile temper, and it was a tantrum that eventually ended his tenure in Columbus. In the closing minutes of the 1978 Gator Bowl, the Buckeyes were trailing the Clemson Tigers by a slim 17–15 margin. A last-ditch Ohio State drive was nullified when Clemson's Charlie Bauman intercepted a pass near the Buckeye bench. Bauman was forced out of bounds and into a melee of Ohio State sideline personnel.

Hayes wandered into the throng and sucker-punched Bauman in the throat, instigating a free-for-all that tarnished the reputation of both the school and its coach. The following day Hayes was dismissed by the university, bringing to an inglorious end one of the game's most illustrious careers.

Prancing Ponies—Orange Bowl, 1985: Since 1964, tradition at Oklahoma has been that every home-field score by the Sooners is commemorated with a victory lap by the Sooner Schooner, a covered wagon pulled by a pair of Shetland ponies dubbed Boomer and Sooner. However, in the 1985 Orange Bowl, it was a case of "too soon to Schooner" that proved to be the downfall of Oklahoma's bid to wipe out the University of Washington and win the Orange Bowl. With the score tied at 14–14, the Sooners drove down the field and kicked a field goal that appeared to give them a three-point cushion. In customary fashion, it was wagons-ho as Boomer and Sooner rumbled onto the field to signify the score. Unfortunately, the ponies' prance was premature, because a penalty had been called, thereby nullifying the play. Adding insult to error, the wagon's wheels became stuck in the soggy turf, and another penalty was flagged against the Oklahoma team. The Sooners missed the ensuing field goal attempt and played the remainder of the match in a lackluster slumber, eventually losing what would become known as the Sooner Schooner Game by a score of 28–17.

Limit: One Bowl, Please

* Aluminum Bowl—Little Rock, Arkansas (1956)
* Aviation Bowl—Dayton, Ohio (1961)
* Bluegrass Bowl—Louisville, Kentucky (1958)
* Boys Bowl—Houston, Texas (1946)
* Cement Bowl—Allentown, Pennsylvania (1962)
* Glass Bowl—Toledo, Ohio (1946)

How the Marathon Didn't Get Started

The primary connection between the modern race and the ancient messenger lies in a 19th-century poem that gets the details wrong.

✳ ✳ ✳ ✳

The Basic Legend

ALMOST EVERYONE HAS heard it: The Athenians paddled the Persians in the Battle of Marathon (490 B.C.), saving Greece from becoming a Persian province. Afterward, Pheidippides the messenger ran all the way to Athens to announce the elating news, then fell dead. Thereafter, a distance race called the Pheidippidaion became popular.

Okay, that wasn't its name. Can you imagine the "Boston Pheidippidaion"? It sounds like a tongue twister. And "Pheidippi-de-doo-dah" would never have caught on.

Did the run happen? We can't know for sure; it isn't impossible. Did the run inspire an ancient sport? No. Evidently, distance running was already an ancient sport if we believe Herodotus, since he clearly calls Pheidippides a professional distance runner. The longest race at the ancient Olympics was the well-documented *dolichos*, which literally means "long race" and was anywhere from 7 to 24 stades, or 1,400 to 4,800 meters. Pheidippides probably ran this race.

Ancient Sources

For those not steeped in the ancient world, Herodotus is revered as the "father of history"; antiquarians do not casually dismiss him. The story about Pheidippides usually gets pinned on Herodotus, but people garble what the great man actually wrote. Pheidippides (others name him "Philippides" or "Phidippides") was a professional distance runner sent to Sparta (which was also in for a stomping if Persia won) to ask for help.

Pheidippides returned, saying that the god Pan had waylaid him. "How come you ungrateful Athenians never worship Me? After all I do for you, too. I hear you have a battle coming up; planned to pitch in there as well. The least you could do is throw Me a decent bash now and then," whined the deity. (Herodotus digresses that the Athenians responded to this come-to-Pan meeting by initiating annual ceremonies and a torch-race honoring him, mindful of his help in the battle.)

As for Spartan aid, Pheidippides relayed their lame excuse: Spartan law forbade them to march until the moon was full. That's a heck of a note for someone who purportedly just ran 135 miles in two days, then returned at the same pace. Gods only knew how quickly Pheidippides might have arrived had he not stopped to listen to Pan complain.

Herodotus says nothing of a messenger to Athens after the battle. (One wonders just how the Athenians had managed to reach 490 B.C. without acquiring a horse.) A few later Greek sources refer to the event, but none ever met living witnesses to this Marathon. Herodotus may well have met some elderly survivors, writing nearly half a century after the events.

More Recently...

As with numerous popular legends, this one owes its modern currency to a poet. In 1879, Robert Browning published "Pheidippides," in which the runner makes the run to Sparta and back *á la* Herodotus' histories, then the run to Athens where he announces Athens' salvation before keeling over.

People believed this, as they are apt to believe nearly any legend embellished by a poet. What's more, a philhellenic era was about to revive the ancient Olympics in modern form, minus the prostitutes and blood sports. In 1896, the modern Olympics restarted and included a marathon for men. It took 88 more years to include one for women. Marathon lengths have varied over the years but not by much: 40–43 kilometers (25–26.5 miles) was typical. The modern distance is 26.22 miles.

Stretching the Truth

In a time-honored tradition, baseball fans rise from their seats between the top and bottom of the seventh inning to sing a hearty rendition of "Take Me Out to the Ball Game." Was this custom really started as a nod of respect to President William Howard Taft?

✳   ✳   ✳   ✳

RATHER THAN BEING remembered for his one-term residency in the White House and for being the only man to serve as both president and chief justice of the Supreme Court, Taft is probably best known as the fattest man ever to serve as commander in chief. Indeed, Taft's girth was impressive, and it sometimes restricted his movements, especially when he attended Washington Senators baseball games (a pastime pursuit that was his preferred method of relaxation). After sitting through a few innings of action, Taft would extract himself from the compressed confines of his chair, stand, stretch, and waddle off to the men's room. The denizens sitting near him would also rise, showing a measure of respect for their honored guest. This presidential pause for the cause was rumored to have occurred in the seventh-inning break.

However, there's no proof that the president was responsible for instituting or influencing the tradition. Taft attended many ball games, but he rarely stayed as late as the seventh inning. It's been said he had more pressing matters on his home plate— running the country, for instance.

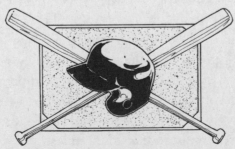

Heavenly Heaves

Football fans are occasionally blessed with clutch celestial conclusions of biblical proportions. Here are a couple.

❋　❋　❋　❋

Franco Harris—The Immaculate Reception: The outcome looked blacker than bleak for the Pittsburgh Steelers as the clock wound down on their 1972 AFC divisional playoff clash with the Oakland Raiders. Sequestered on their own 40-yard line, down by a single point, bereft of time-outs, and facing a seemingly insurmountable fourth and ten, the supernatural was required and a miracle was delivered. With 22 seconds left, Steelers pivot Terry Bradshaw evaded an onslaught of Oakland pass rushers, twisted, turned, and tossed a pass toward receiver Frenchy Fuqua, who was just about to haul in the ball when he was blindsided from behind by Raiders safety Jack Tatum. The ball sailed over the flattened Fuqua, plunked Tatum on the top of his shoulder pads, and caromed wildly into the air, actually moving backward as it plunged toward the pitch. Incredibly, it was caught by Pittsburgh running back Franco Harris, who scooped up the cascading ball just before it hit the ground and trotted untouched the length of the field for the touchdown that gave the Steelers a 12–7 lead. After considerable debate, including a call from the field to the press box for a rule clarification, the play was allowed to stand, sealing a Steelers win. Since Bradshaw's pass was thrown on a wing and a prayer, Franco's catch was enshrined in the lexicon of legends under the heading, "The Immaculate Reception."

Doug Flutie—Hail Mary: Although it is widely believed that former Dallas Cowboy quarterback Roger Staubach was responsible for concocting the catchphrase "Hail Mary," it was a stick of diminutive dynamite named Doug Flutie who put a face on Mary's grace. At five-foot-ten, Flutie looked more like a jockey than a jock, though his slight stature could hardly contain his competitiveness. In his final season with the Boston College Eagles, Flutie was leading the nation in a bevy of offensive categories and was a considered a top contender for the Heisman Trophy. In 1984, in a nationally televised game against the University of Miami, Flutie captured the attention of scribes and spectators around the country. After Miami marched down the field to take a 45–41 lead in the closing moments of the game, Flutie consulted his celestial playbook and pulled out a passing prayer that would forever be dubbed the Hail Mary. Smothered deep in his own territory with only six seconds remaining on the play clock, Flutie avoided a horde of Hurricanes, scrambled to his right, and heaved a pass toward the end zone. The missile sailed through a maze of outstretched arms before settling in the grasp of Boston receiver Gerard Phelan, who fell to the field clutching the game-winning pass that delivered a 47–45 victory to the enthroned Eagles.

* On November 17, 1968, in a game referred to as the Heidi Bowl, the New York Jets had the lead over the Oakland Raiders 32–29. With 1:05 left on the clock, television network NBC cut away to the classic children's movie *Heidi,* preventing millions of viewers from seeing Oakland's comeback, 43–32.

* Linebacker Chuck Howley was the first player voted Super Bowl MVP after playing on the losing team. It was Super Bowl V (1970), when Howley was with the Dallas Cowboys.

* The first regular season overtime game ever played ended in a tie. On September 22, 1974, the Steelers and Broncos played to a 35–35 tie. Oddly, the NFL instituted overtime in order to reduce the number of tied games.

* In 1980, Green Bay Packers kicker Chester Marcol ran in his own blocked field-goal attempt for a touchdown to beat the Chicago Bears 12–6.

* Early in the 1968 season, the Baltimore Colts lost Johnny Unitas to an injury. Quarterback Earl Morrall stepped up and eventually led the Colts to a 13–1 record. Morrall led the league in passing, with 2,909 yards and 26 touchdowns.

Saving Face: The Hockey Goalie Mask

Gruesome facial injuries to two legendary hockey goalies spurred the invention and acceptance of the goalie mask. Yet despite the hazards posed by playing without a mask, the face-saving innovation took a long time to catch on.

✳ ✳ ✳ ✳

ON APRIL 7, 1974, the Pittsburgh Penguins faced off against the Atlanta Flames as the 1973–74 National Hockey League regular season drew to a close. Playing in goal for the Penguins was a 30-year-old journeyman named Andy Brown.

Brown turned in a sievelike performance, and the sad-sack Penguins were thrashed 6–3. Worse yet, the loss turned out to be the last game of Brown's NHL career. But as he braved pucks whizzing past his head, Brown staked his place in hockey history: He would be the last goalie to play in an NHL game without a mask.

Today, it's hard to fathom a hockey goalie playing without a mask. Indeed, all pro and amateur hockey leagues now require the mask to be part of a goalie's equipment. But for the first nine decades of hockey's existence, the goalie mask was an object as odd and rare as the U.S. two-dollar bill.

As crazy as it sounds, goalies actually chose not to wear masks despite obvious occupational hazards. Not surprisingly, then, the introduction and popularization of the goalie mask only came about after a near-tragedy involving two of the game's greatest netminders.

Clint Benedict played 18 pro seasons with the Ottawa Senators and Montreal Maroons, backstopping the Senators to Stanley

Cup titles in 1920, 1921, and 1923, as well as helping lead the Maroons to their first Cup win in 1926. Arguably the best goalie of his era, Benedict revolutionized how the position was played. He earned the nickname "Praying Benny" due to his habit of falling to his knees in the era of the stand-up goaltender. As a result, the NHL eventually abandoned its rule prohibiting goalies to leave their feet.

In 1930, Benedict inadvertently led to yet another innovation to the goaltending profession. That year, in a game between the Maroons and the Montreal Canadiens, the Canadiens' Howie Morenz nailed Benedict in the face with a shot that knocked him unconscious, shattered his cheekbone and nose, and hospitalized him for a month. When Benedict returned to the ice to face the New York Americans, he surprised the crowd by sporting a leather mask, making history as the first goalie to wear face protection in an NHL game.

After five games, Benedict fatefully discarded the mask, saying its oversize nosepiece hindered his vision. Shortly after, another Morenz shot struck Benedict in the throat and ended his NHL career. Amazingly, for the next 29 years, the first man to wear a mask in a game would also be the last.

The mask reappeared in 1959 in a game between the Montreal Canadiens and the New York Rangers. Three minutes into the game, Rangers star Andy Bathgate drilled the Canadiens' goalie Jacques Plante in the nose and cheek with a hard shot, sending a badly bleeding Plante to the dressing room. Plante had used a fiberglass mask in practices since the mid-1950s, but Montreal coach Toe Blake forbade him to don it in games. Now, as Plante was being stitched up, he told the coach he wouldn't go back on the ice without his mask. Blake had no suitable backup goalie, so was forced to relent. Plante returned to the game wearing his mask and led the Canadiens to a 3–1 victory. Montreal followed with an 18-game unbeaten streak, with a masked Plante in net every game. The goalie mask was here to stay.

Going on About Golf

Stuff you really don't need to know about life on the links…

✳ ✳ ✳ ✳

✳ King James II of Scotland banned golf in 1457 because golfers spent too much time on the game instead of improving their archery skills.

✳ The first golf course in England was the Royal Blackheath Golf Club, founded in 1608.

✳ The first golf course constructed in the United States was Oakhurst Links Golf Club in White Sulfur Springs, West Virginia, in 1884. It was restored in 1994.

✳ The oldest continuously existing golf club in the United States is St. Andrews Golf Club in New York. It was formed by the Apple Tree Gang in 1888.

✳ The first golf balls were made of wood. Next were leather balls filled with goose feathers, followed by rubber balls, gutta-percha balls (made of a leathery substance from tropical trees), and then modern wound balls.

✳ The first sudden-death playoff in a major championship was in 1979, when Fuzzy Zoeller beat Tom Watson and Ed Sneed in the Masters.

✳ The longest sudden-death playoff in PGA Tour history was an 11-hole playoff between Cary Middlecoff and Lloyd Mangrum in the 1949 Motor City Open. They were declared cowinners.

✳ Beth Daniel is the oldest winner of the LPGA Tour. She was 46 years, 8 months, and 29 days old when she won the 2003 BMO Financial Group Canadian Women's Open.

✳ Most golf courses in Japan have two putting greens on every hole—one for summer and another for winter.

* Tiger Woods has won ten PGA Player of the Year Awards as of the 2009 season, the most won by any PGA Tour player. Tom Watson is second, with six awards.

* The youngest player to win a major championship was Tom Morris Jr. (known as "Young" Tom), who was 17 years old when he won the 1868 British Open.

* The PGA Tour ranks Sam Snead as the best golfer in its history. Snead has 82 victories, followed by Jack Nicklaus with 73 wins, Ben Hogan with 64, Arnold Palmer with 62, and Tiger Woods with 71 wins through the 2009 season.

* The LPGA Hall of Fame is a tough one to make. Among other qualifications, players must be active on the tour for ten years, have won an LPGA major championship, and have secured a significant number of trophies. It is considered one of the most difficult accomplishments in golf.

* The shortest hole played in a major championship is the 106-yard, par-3 seventh hole at Pebble Beach.

* The longest hole in the United States is the 841-yard, par-6 twelfth hole at Meadows Farms Golf Club Course in Locust Grove, Virginia.

* In 1899, Dr. George Grant, a New Jersey dentist, invented and patented the first wooden tee. Before tees were invented, golfers elevated balls on a tiny wet-sand mound.

* The oldest player to win a major championship was 48-year-old Julius Boros at the 1968 PGA Championship.

* The youngest golfer to shoot a hole-in-one was five-year-old Coby Orr. It happened in Littleton, Colorado, in 1975.

* The chances of making two holes-in-one in a single round of golf are 1 in 67 million.

* There are more than 11,000 golf courses in North America.

Baseball: They Used to Be the...

What and where were some of today's major-league baseball teams? Some borrowed the names of defunct teams but have no other continuity with the ghosts of old.

✻ ✻ ✻ ✻

Atlanta Braves (National Association/National League): Formerly the Boston Red Caps and Red Stockings (1876–1882), then the Bean-eaters (until 1906), then Doves (to 1910), then Rustlers (for 1911). In 1912, they stopped the insanity, becoming the Boston Braves. After a 38–115 season in 1935, they played as the Boston Bees from 1936 to 1940. Just before the 1953 season, they lit out for Milwaukee and stayed 12 years, moving to Atlanta in 1966.

Boston Red Sox (American League): Founded as the Boston Americans in 1901, unconnected with the Boston Red Stockings, who became the modern Atlanta Braves. They've been playing as the Boston Red Sox since 1908. Other early names, such as Pilgrims, were in fact rarely used and not official.

Baltimore Orioles (AL): Started play as the Milwaukee Brewers in 1901 (finishing last), then became the St. Louis Browns. Deciding that 52 years of bad baseball in one place would suffice, the team became the Baltimore Orioles in 1954—honoring a rough-and-tumble 1890s team by that name, though without direct succession.

Chicago Cubs (NA/NL): Once the Chicago White Stockings (1876–1889), then Colts (1890–1897), then Orphans (1898–1901). In 1902, they finally settled on the current name.

Chicago White Sox (AL): Grabbed the Cubs' old nickname (White Stockings) in 1901 on their founding, then took the official abbreviation of White Sox in 1904. If you want to have fun with Sox fans, just point out that their name is actually an old Cubs nickname.

Cincinnati Reds (American Association/NL): Formerly the Red Stockings (1882–1889), then the Reds. During the McCarthy years (1954–1958), they quietly became the Cincinnati Redlegs, lest a team playing the American national pastime hint at a Bolshevik takeover. They soon resumed the nickname "Reds."

Cleveland Indians (AL): Born the Cleveland Blues in 1901, called Broncos in 1902, then became the Naps in 1903 to honor star Nap Lajoie. After trading Lajoie in 1914, the team took its current name.

Los Angeles Angels (AL): Began play in 1961, but in 1965 they became the California Angels, now playing in Anaheim. Thirty years later, they became the Anaheim Angels. Since 2005, the team has officially been the Los Angeles Angels of Anaheim.

Los Angeles Dodgers (AA/NL): Began as the Brooklyn Atlantics in 1884 and were often called the Trolley Dodgers. They would play as the Grays, Bridegrooms, Grooms, Superbas, Infants, and Dodgers—all before World War I! In 1914, they became the Robins (after manager Wilbert Robinson), then went back to Dodgers in 1932. After the 1957 season, their owner moved them to Los Angeles.

Milwaukee Brewers (AL/NL): Started as the Seattle Pilots in 1969. After giving Emerald City ball fans a season of futile baseball in Sicks Stadium (today the spot is a hardware store), they fled to Milwaukee in haste for the 1970 season. When major-league baseball expanded in 1998, a team had to switch leagues, and the Brew Crew moved to the National League.

Minnesota Twins (AL): Began in the District of Columbia as the Washington Senators but were also periodically called the Nationals—from 1905 to 1906 the name even appeared on their jerseys. How could this nebulous situation be? In 1961, the Senators/sometime Nationals moved to their current Minneapolis home.

New York Yankees (AL): Began (in 1901) as one of several Baltimore Orioles franchises. Moving to the Bronx in 1903, they became the New York Highlanders. The name Yankees gradually supplanted Highlanders, becoming official in 1913.

Oakland Athletics (AL): Started play as the Philadelphia Athletics in 1901, and in 1955 they became the Kansas City Athletics, an informal Yankee farm team sending promising players to the Bronx in exchange for declining veterans. They moved to Oakland in 1968. They've also been called A's since they began.

Philadelphia Phillies (NL): Started as the Philadelphia Quakers in 1883, but by 1890 the popular Phillies nickname was official. However, between 1943 and 1944, they were called the Blue Jays.

Pittsburgh Pirates (AA/NL): Go Alleghenys! In 1882, that's how they were born—just Alleghenys, spelled thus, not Pittsburgh anything. Soon the Pittsburgh designation took over. Briefly called Innocents in 1890, they were then called Pirates for supposedly stealing a player from another team. That name stuck.

St. Louis Cardinals (AA/NL): Used to be the Brown Stockings (1882). The team quickly became the Browns. In 1899, someone decided to rename them the Perfectos, but that was too dumb to stick. The next year they became Cardinals.

Texas Rangers (AL): Started in 1961 as the new Washington Senators (the old Sens having run off to Minnesota) and underwhelmed the baseball world throughout the decade. The team left for Arlington, Texas in 1972 and became the Rangers.

Washington Nationals (NL): Started in 1969 as the Expos de Montréal but never quite seemed to fit there. In 1977, they took bad baseball locations to the next level by moving to Stade Olympique, with its dysfunctional retractable roof. Local interest got so bad that from 2003 to 2004, they played some home games in Puerto Rico. The ownership disconnected the Expos from the Montreal respirator for the 2005 season, moving to D.C. and reviving the old Nationals name.

The Lowdown on Hockey Fights

The old joke is, "I went to a fight and a hockey game broke out." A typical pro football game has regular skirmishes, and major league baseball teams clear the benches to brawl over a hangnail. And people call hockey ultraviolent?

✳ ✳ ✳ ✳

Y OU'VE HEARD IT before: "I love hockey! It's the only team sport that allows fighting." In fact, it doesn't. Hockey officials measure penalties in minutes: two-minute minors, five-minute majors, ten-minute misconducts, and ejection for a game misconduct or match penalty. Fighting is a five-minute major penalty.

Can't You Play Nice?

Let's compare some of the other hockey crimes, many of which merit less sin-bin time than fighting. You can't shove with the shaft of the stick, hook someone with it, or slash with it like a broadsword. These minor penalties usually merit only two minutes in the hockey hoosegow. Major penalties (besides fighting) include stabbing with the stick's blade or butt, ramming someone too hard into the boards (how subjective is that?), and any flagrant version of a minor penalty (e.g., you shove someone aside with the stick shaft in his face).

That's Some Sport

If you join a fight in progress or get your third fighting major in the game, you'll be charged with automatic game misconduct. Breaking your stick in frustration, grossly disrespecting officials, and flipping the bird or a puck at the fans: misconduct. Leaving the penalty box early: game misconduct. Pulling hair: match penalty. You can also get the heave-ho for kicking with your skate blade, spitting on someone, head-butting, throwing the stick like a javelin, face-masking, biting, or any act seen as a deliberate attempt to injure. On second thought, maybe the game *is* ultraviolent.

If You Build It, They Will Play

It's safe to say that the inventor of miniature golf hit a hole in one!

✳   ✳   ✳   ✳

MINIATURE GOLF HAS been described as a novelty game, but it requires the same steady hands, analytical observation, and maneuvering as regular golf.

In their infancy, miniature golf courses were designed the same as full-size courses but were built at one-tenth the size, much like the popular par-3 courses of today. In 1916, James Barber of Pinehurst, North Carolina, created a miniature golf course that resembles the game played today. He dubbed his design "Thistle Dhu," supposedly a twist on the phrase "This'll do." Barber's course was an intricate maze of geometric shapes coupled with symmetric walkways, fountains, and planters. Until 1922, mini-golf courses used live grass—just like the real game—and were subject to the same grooming needs and growing woes. That all changed when a man named Thomas McCulloch Fairbairn prepared a mixture of cottonseed hull—or mulch, sand, oil, and green dye—and used the concoction to resurface the miniature golf course he was designing. The first artificial putting green was born.

The game boomed for the next few years, with hundreds of miniature golf outlets opening around the country, including 150 rooftop courses in New York City alone. The arrival of the Great Depression severed the popularity of the pastime, and its growth remained stagnant until 1938 when brothers Joseph and Robert R. Taylor Sr. revitalized the game. The Taylors redesigned the sport by adding complicated obstacles such as windmills, castles, and wishing wells to increase the competitive enjoyment. Today, miniature golf tournaments are held around the world.

Slots O' Luck

Do slot machines, or "one-armed bandits," have predetermined pay cycles? Don't bet on it. The money you lose may be your own.

✳ ✳ ✳ ✳

S JAKE WEARILY feeds quarters into a humming slot machine, a thought occurs to him: "I think this machine is dead. I'd like to try a different one, but I've heard they all have fixed pay cycles. I've been on this one for two hours, so it should be about ready to cough it up. I guess I'll stay put."

The fact is that many such thoughts steer gamblers into repetitive or superstitious habits that have little to no bearing on reality. A modern slot machine just generates numbers. It can't discern between its first spin and its twenty-thousandth, so Jake could easily spend weeks "babysitting" it, hoping for the big payoff. Slot machines do have certain payout percentages, but these are based on millions of spins to reach a jackpot.

Frustrated by its stinginess, Jake finally walks away from his slot machine. An instant later another patron takes Jake's seat, plops in a coin, and hits the super jackpot. If Jake had simply stuck it out, would he be the rich one? Not unless he had pushed the spin button or yanked the handle at precisely the same microsecond as the winner had. The reason is that changes in timing yield completely different results—a phenomenon referred to as the "hero or zero" rule.

Disgusted, Jake decides to rely on another tactic: He'll come back when the place is jam-packed, knowing that more jackpots are won when the casino is crowded. At this point it would be easy to again call Jake a loser, but we won't go there. The reason a casino gives up more jackpots when it's busy is obvious: More people are playing, so more spins are taking place—which means more jackpots will be hit. In the end, Jake might want to stick to scratch-offs.

Abner Strikes Out!

Generations of baseball fans have been led to believe that the game was invented by Civil War hero Abner Doubleday in Cooperstown, New York, in 1839. Historians tell a different story.

✳ ✳ ✳ ✳

THE DOUBLEDAY MYTH can be traced to the Mills Commission, which was appointed in 1905 by baseball promoter Albert Spalding to determine the true origins of the game. Henry Chadwick, one of Spalding's contemporaries, contended that the sport had its beginnings in a British game called rounders, in which a batter hits a ball and runs around the bases. Spalding, on the other hand, insisted that baseball was as American as apple pie.

Can We Get a Witness?

The seven-member Mills Commission placed ads in several newspapers soliciting testimony from anyone who had knowledge of the beginnings of the game. A 71-year-old gent named Abner Graves of Denver, Colorado, saw the ad and wrote a detailed response, saying that he'd been present when Doubleday outlined the basics of modern baseball in bucolic Cooperstown, New York, where the two had gone to school together. In his account, which was published by the *Beacon Journal* in Akron, Ohio, under the headline "Abner Doubleday Invented Baseball," Graves alleged to have seen crude drawings of a baseball diamond produced by Doubleday both in the dirt and on paper.

The members of the Mills Commission took Graves at his word and closed their investigation, confident that they had finally solved the mystery of how baseball was invented. The commission released its final report in December 1907, never mentioning Graves by name, and a great American legend was born.

Sadly, Graves's story was more whimsy than fact. For one thing, he was only five years old in 1839, when he claimed to have seen Doubleday's drawings. But even more important, Doubleday wasn't even in Cooperstown in 1839—he was a cadet attending the military academy at West Point. In addition, Doubleday, a renowned diarist, never once mentioned baseball in any of his writings, nor did he ever claim to have invented the game.

Nonetheless, the Doubleday myth received a boost in 1934 when a moldy old baseball was discovered in an attic in Fly Creek, New York, just outside Cooperstown. It was believed to have been owned by Graves and as such was also believed to have been used by Abner Doubleday. The "historic" ball was purchased for five dollars by a wealthy Cooperstown businessman named Stephen Clark, who intended to display it along with a variety of other baseball memorabilia. Five years later, Cooperstown became the official home of the Baseball Hall of Fame.

Who Was Baseball's Daddy?

If anyone can lay claim to being the father of American baseball, it's Alexander Cartwright. He organized the first official baseball club in New York in 1845, called the Knickerbocker Base Ball Club, and published a set of 20 rules for the game. These rules, which included the designation of a nine-player team and a playing field with a home plate and three additional bases at specific distances, formed the basis for baseball as we know the sport today. Cartwright's Hall of Fame plaque in Cooperstown honors him as the "Father of Modern Base Ball," and in 1953, Congress officially credited him with inventing the game.

Babe Ruth's "Called" Shot

Most of Babe Ruth's achievements can be appraised by statistics, but a prominent one is stuck in the vortex between fact and fantasy.

✳   ✳   ✳   ✳

LIKE THE CONUNDRUM about whether those flailing arms in the distant ocean signal waving or drowning, Babe Ruth's finger to the sky in Game 3 of the 1932 World Series must be interpreted by the eye of the beholder.

The Bambino hated the Chicago Cubs, whose fans had been pelting him with trash and whose players' taunts infuriated him. So when Ruth came to the plate in the fifth inning with the score tied 4–4, he seemed to mock his nemeses when he lifted his index finger and pointed ... somewhere.

Although conventional wisdom credits the great slugger with indicating that Charlie Root's next pitch was destined for Wrigley Field's centerfield bleachers, most onlookers later recounted that Ruth appeared to point to the pitcher ... or to the Cubs' dugout ... or perhaps that he was simply indicating the count. There's no debating what happened next: Ruth hammered a 440-foot laser over the wall, getting his Yankees back into the game and propelling them to a four-game sweep.

Subsequent news stories nurtured the notion that the Babe "called" his shot. Many of the principals begged to differ. "He [just] indicated he had one more strike remaining," assessed Frank Crosetti, Babe's teammate. Former major leaguer Babe Herman even claimed to have overheard a conversation between Root and Ruth years later in which the hitter said, "I know I didn't [call it]. But it made a hell of a story, didn't it?"

In 2000, ESPN aired a newly unearthed 16-mm film of the episode, which, though not definitive, indicated that Ruth was merely gesturing to Chicago's bench.

The Truth About Monopoly

Monopoly is as American as apple pie. Yet, the story of how the most commercially successful board game came to be is a rather sordid tale. Despite information perpetuated for some 40 years by the game's manufacturer, "creator" Charles Darrow was not it's true inventor at all.

✳   ✳   ✳   ✳

O N JANUARY 5, 1904, Lizzie J. Magie, received a patent for The Landlord's Game. It was based on economist Henry George's belief that landowners should be charged a single federal tax to extend equality to renters, from whom landlords were, in George's opinion, disproportionately profiting. Magie created an educational game, demonstrating how a single tax would control land speculation.

Except for the fact that properties were rented rather than purchased, The Landlord's Game was suspiciously identical to Parker Brothers' Monopoly, which premiered almost 30 years later. Through the years, The Landlord's Game was passed through communities, evolving along the way. It picked up the name Monopoly despite Magie's intention for the game to be a teaching tool against the very idea of monopolies. The Atlantic City-inspired properties were also incorporated. This well-documented chain of events led to Charles Darrow, who learned the game at a hotel in Pennsylvania.

Enthralled, Darrow produced his own copies of the game and subsequently patented and sold "his" idea to Parker Brothers. The company conveniently forgot its refusal to buy the same game (under its old name) from Magie years earlier but promptly covered those tracks. It slyly bought out Magie's patent for a paltry $500, paid off at least three other "inventors" who had versions circulating, and cranked up its propaganda machine. Monopoly has sold in excess of 250 million copies.

Chapter 4

The Wild

The Never-Ending Story of the Hibernating Bear

It's a myth that bears hibernate. It's also a myth that bears don't hibernate. Where does this story end?

✳ ✳ ✳ ✳

Once Upon a Time

IN THE UNITED STATES circa 1950, the story of the hibernating bear was told with confidence and abandon. Schoolchildren from coast to coast knew of the sleepy bear that, come cold temperatures and snow, escaped into a cave for months of deep slumber. With the arrival of spring and warmer weather, the bear would emerge from the cave to search for food and frolic in a nearby stream.

And then came the scientists with their sophisticated shiny metal objects, which they used to measure the bears' metabolism, temperature, and oxidation. In the 1960s, '70s, and '80s, many of these scientists concluded that bears do not hibernate. The logic went something like this: When animals hibernate, their body temperature drops. Smaller mammals that hibernate can drop their body temperature below freezing. Bears, however, drop their body temperature by only 10 to 15 degrees. Further, whereas some smaller mammals cannot be easily awakened during hibernation, a hibernating bear can be stirred from its sleep with relatively little effort. The conclusion was that bears do not hibernate.

Catastrophes of Classification

This created quite a stir in the scientific community. If bears aren't hibernating, what exactly are they doing? A replacement theory was the concept of "torpor," a biological state in which animals lower their metabolic rates, but generally for shorter periods of time. Torpor is considered to be less of a "deep sleep" than hibernation and is observed in birds, rodents, insectivores, and marsupials.

Yet the torpor argument came with its own set of problems. In many respects, the hibernation period of a bear is actually deeper than that of other hibernating species. Although rodents and other small mammals drastically reduce their body temperatures during hibernation, they wake every few days in order to eat and urinate. Some species of bears are able to go six to eight months without eating, urinating, defecating, or fully waking. Further, it is because of their large size that bears do not drastically reduce their body temperatures during hibernation. In the face of this confusion, words such as denning and dormancy were coined to describe the habits of bears.

The Essence of Hibernation

Whether the physical inactivity of an animal is labeled hibernation, torpor, or denning, the purpose of these prolonged states is to conserve energy in the face of food scarcity or uncomfortable temperatures. Metabolism is reduced when an animal lowers its body temperature, slows its breathing and heart rate, and reduces its movements. The particular strategy a species takes in these endeavors varies greatly and depends on its environment. In the colder northern regions of North America, where food is unavailable for the long stretch of winter, black bears hibernate for several months. In the Arctic Circle, where food supplies are unpredictable, polar bears can go into hibernation at any time of year. Only female polar bears hibernate, no doubt because of the elevated energy requirements of pregnancy, birth, and feeding the young.

The Shift in Consensus

Scientists moved back into the "pro-hibernation" camp after the discovery of a lemur that hibernates in the tropics, apparently to save energy in the face of heat and food scarcity (the word estivation refers to species that hibernate in warm temperatures). It was traditionally thought that hibernation served as an "escape" from the cold, but the energy-saving behavior of the lemur's hibernation demonstrated that the process is about lowering metabolism in the face of environmental stressors that vary from species to species. "Hibernate" is now accepted as a broader phrase that refers to a reduction in metabolism for prolonged periods of time—meaning it is once again safe to tell the tale of the hibernating bear.

Odd Animal Facts

* The sleepiest mammals are armadillos, sloths, and opossums. They spend 80 percent of their lives sleeping or dozing.

* Vultures sometimes eat so much they can't take off in flight.

Freaky Frog Facts

Kermit, Jeremiah the Bullfrog, Prince Charming—
frogs are clearly special creatures with many talents.
They're also sort of gross. Check out these freaky
frog facts that are sure to delight and disgust.

✳   ✳   ✳   ✳

✳ At about four weeks old, tadpoles get a bunch of very tiny teeth, which help them turn their food into mushy, oxygenated particles.

✳ Horned lizards are often called horny toads, though they're not actually amphibians. Horny toads can squirt blood from their eyeballs to attack predators. This only happens in extreme cases, but they can shoot it up to three feet, so watch out.

✳ The Goliath frog of West Africa is the largest frog in the world. When fully stretched out, this sucker often measures more than $2\frac{1}{2}$ feet long!

✳ When frogs aren't near water, they will often secrete mucus to keep their skin moist.

✳ Frogs typically eat their old skin once it's been shed.

✳ One European common toad lived to be 40 years old, making it the oldest known toad on record.

✳ While swallowing, a frog's eyeballs retreat into its head, applying pressure that helps push food down its throat.

✳ A frog's ear is connected to its lungs. When a frog's eardrum vibrates, its lungs do, too. This pressure system keeps frogs from hurting themselves when they blast their mating calls.

✳ The earliest known frog fossils were found in Arizona and are thought to be about 190 million years old.

Animals that Taste Bad to Predators

Many animals have a bad taste that protects them from predators. Here are a few crummy-tasting critters.

✳   ✳   ✳   ✳

Slow Loris

THIS PRIMATE, WHICH lives in China and Southeast Asia, has a special gland in its elbow that secretes a toxin that it mixes with saliva. Before leaving to search for food, a mother applies this toxin to her babies to protect them from predators.

Poison Dart Frog

This species of frog is native to Central and South America, and one variety has been introduced to the Hawaiian Islands. The name originates from South American tribes that smear the poison from the skin of the frog on their arrows or blow-gun darts. Just touching the skin of the golden poison dart frog species with your tongue can be fatal. Evidence suggests that the toxin in poison dart frogs comes from their diet, primarily ants, mites, and beetles, which also contain the poison, but in much smaller doses.

Eurasian Water Shrew

This shrew is highly territorial and can be found from Great Britain to North Korea. It has venomous saliva that can quickly kill its natural enemy, the vole.

Platypus

Native to eastern Australia and Tasmania, the platypus is one of the few species of mammals that lay eggs. It's also one of the few venomous mammals. The male platypus has spurs on his hind feet that deliver a poison that isn't powerful enough to kill other animals but does cause severe pain. Scientists believe the platypus uses this poison to assert dominance over rival males during the mating season.

Cane Toad

This large toad is native to Central and South America. An adult cane toad averages four to six inches in length; however, the largest recorded specimen measured 15 inches long and weighed nearly six pounds. The cane toad has large poison glands behind its eyes that make it highly toxic to predators.

Puffer Fish

The puffer fish, also called the blowfish, gets its name from its ability to inflate itself to several times its normal size by swallowing water or air when threatened. Some puffer fish produce a powerful neurotoxin in their internal organs, making them an unpleasant and possibly lethal meal for any predator, including humans. In Japan and Korea, specially trained chefs prepare puffer fish for adventurous diners who consider it a delicacy.

Monarch Butterfly

The monarch butterfly is foul-tasting and poisonous due to the toxic chemicals it ingests when feeding on milkweed during the caterpillar stage. The monarch shares this defense mechanism with the even more unpleasant-tasting viceroy butterfly, which resembles the monarch.

Ladybugs

Most people like ladybugs, but the same can't be said of the predators that swallow them. Adult ladybugs are able to force themselves to bleed from their leg joints, releasing an oily yellow toxin with a strong repellent smell that's poisonous to small birds and lizards. Don't worry if you accidentally swallow one, because humans have to ingest several hundred before feeling any effects of the poison.

Skunk

The best-known feature of the skunk is its anal scent glands, which produce a mixture of sulfur-containing chemicals that give off an offensive smell strong enough to ward off bears, wolves, foxes, badgers, and other potential attackers. Skunks also use their spray during mating season.

Animals by the Bunch

Everyone is familiar with the saying "It's more fun than a barrel of monkeys." But how many times have you heard, "You're as loud as a murder of magpies"? Here are the official collective names for various groups of critters.

✳ ✳ ✳ ✳

a congregation of alligators

a shoal of bass

a smack of jellyfish

a gaze of raccoons

a clowder of cats

a cackle of hyenas

a troop of kangaroos

a leap of leopards

a fall of woodcocks

a romp of otters

a prickle of porcupines

a crash of rhinoceroses

a troubling of goldfish

a pod of whales

a charm of finches

an exaltation of larks

a murder of magpies

a watch of nightingales

a parliament of owls

a covey of partridges

an ostentation of peacocks

a colony of penguins

a bevy of quails

a business of ferrets

a wisdom of wombats

a flamboyance of flamingoes

a rhumba of rattlesnakes

a gang of elk

a tower of giraffes

a tribe of goats

a band of gorillas

a bloat of hippopotamuses

a richness of martens

a labor of moles

a pod of seals

a drove of sheep

a dray of squirrels

an ambush of tigers

Strange Doings Beneath the Sea

Most sea creatures are quite comfortable with habitats and relationships that human land-dwellers find rather odd. Here is a sample of some odd sea creature behavior.

✳ ✳ ✳ ✳

No-Brainers

SEA SQUIRTS—SO NAMED because they squirt water at whatever annoys them—are small, blobby creatures that live in all oceans and seas. Many are short and fat, while others are elongated. Sea squirts can grow to the size of an egg, though most are much smaller. Some live alone and some form colorful colonies that look like flowers blooming on the ocean floor. Although usually found in shallow water, sea squirts also turn up as deep as 28,000 feet.

Sea squirts are categorized as *chordates*, the same phylum as humans. That's because the larval stage has a notochord (a flexible skeletal rod) and a simple nervous system. With a head, mouth, sucker, and tail, the young sea squirt looks and moves like a tadpole. But this adolescent goes through some major changes as it grows up—more than a human teen.

Attaching itself to a piling, a seashell, a sandy bottom, gravel, algae, or even the back of a big crab, the youngster absorbs its own tail and nervous system. The mature sea squirt is a spineless, sedentary, immobile glob. Tufts University science philosopher Daniel C. Dennett put it this way: "When it finds its spot and takes root, it doesn't need its brain anymore, so it eats it! (It's rather like getting tenure.)"

Sex-Shifters

Worldwide, the oceans' coral reefs harbor about 1,500 species of fish, including some with adaptable sexual identities. Wrasses, parrotfish, and other reef fish start out female and eventually become male. However, other types of reef fish change sex according to the needs of the group. If there aren't enough males or females, the problem is easily taken care of.

Gobies that live in Japan's coral reefs can change back and forth as need dictates. If the dominant male dies or leaves, a female will become male, changing gender in about four days. If a larger male shows up, the gobie that changed simply switches back to female. Many fish that change sex do so quickly. A particular variety of sea bass found in reefs from North Carolina to Florida and in the northern Gulf of Mexico are both female when they meet for mating. One switches to male, they mate, then both switch sex and they mate again. This toggling between sexes is accompanied by color changes; the female is blue, and the male is orange with a white stripe.

Dual Sexuality

The belted sandfish (a coastal sea bass) is a hermaphrodite, with active male and female organs. It can theoretically self-fertilize, meaning that a single individual can release eggs, then shift to its male self (in about 30 seconds) and release sperm. More often, two fish take turns fertilizing each other's eggs. Hermaphroditic sea slugs are underwater snails without shells. The *Navanax inermis* variety, found off the coast of California and Mexico and in the Gulf of Mexico, have male sex organs on one end and female sex organs on the other. They sometimes mate in chains of three or more, with suitable ends attached. The slugs in the middle of the line serve as both male and female simultaneously.

The Perfect Couple?

Seahorses, those bony little fish that swim upright, live in sea grasses, mangrove roots, corals, and muddy bottoms in both tropical and temperate oceans and lagoons. They keep the sex they were born with, and seahorse couples tend to remain monogamous throughout a mating season. Couples perform a little dance when they meet, joining tails, swimming around together, and circling each other. It's the male seahorse that gets pregnant. After he opens a special pouch in his body, the female aligns with the opening and lays her eggs. The male fertilizes the eggs, his pouch swells, and two weeks later he gives birth to as many as 1,500 live offspring. Male seahorses sometimes experience false pregnancies; the pouch swells but no eggs or babies are present. Males can even die of postpartum complications such as infections caused by dead, unborn young.

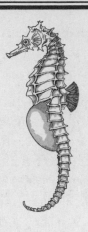

Partners Forever

Far down in the ocean, between 3,000 and 10,000 feet, is a cold, dark world of sharp-toothed hunters. There, many fish use built-in lights to confuse pursuers, to signal a mate, or to bait a trap. Among these deep-sea hunters are anglerfish that grow a "fishing rod" with deceptive "bait" dangling from it. They move about slowly, waving their glowing lures to attract potential meals toward their big toothy mouths. However, only the female anglerfish grows a lure—the male doesn't need one. He's also born without a digestive system, because he isn't going to need that either.

When a young male anglerfish is just a few inches long, he searches out a (much larger) female and sinks his teeth into her. His jaws begin to grow into her skin, and after a few weeks he is unable to let go. The male's eyes get smaller and eventually disappear. Most of his internal organs also disappear. His blood vessels connect to those of the female, so he gets nutrition from whatever she eats. The male grows a little larger, but the gain is all in testes. Finally, he's the sex object he was destined to be— a producer of sperm and little else. The female gains a mate that's literally attached to her forever. Sometimes she doesn't settle for just one but drags several males along through life.

Who Says Dinosaurs Are Extinct?

*Dinosaurs vanished from Earth 65 million years ago…
or did they? Don't get nervous—you won't see a
Tyrannosaurus rex stomping down your street.*

✳ ✳ ✳ ✳

ECENT FINDINGS HAVE turned the field of paleontology
on its head. Scientists now believe that there is a group of
dinosaurs that are not extinct. In fact, they could be flapping
around your neighborhood right now!

Look…Up in the Sky!

The dinosaurs that exist today are descendants of theropod
dinosaurs, a group that includes such popularly known creatures as velociraptor and T. rex, as well as myriad smaller
dinosaurs. These living relics are avian dinosaurs, also known
as birds.

For hundreds of years, scientists had observed similarities
between birds and the fossils of theropod dinosaurs—features
such as hollow bones and birdlike feet. The conceptual leap
from "birdlike" to "bird" was cemented in 1996, when an
extraordinary finding was reported from China's Liaoning
Province. Paleontologist Chen Pei Ji presented a fossilized skeleton of a small theropod surrounded by impressions of fuzzy
down, or feathers, on the perimeter of its body. Since then,
hundreds more of these feathered dinosaur specimens have
been found all over the world.

Jurassic Zoo

Our understanding of dinosaurs has always been limited by what
we can glean from dusty fossilized remains. If you want to learn
about how theropod dinosaurs moved, how their bodies were
shaped, and even how they cared for their young, you can skip
the trip to a natural history museum and go to the zoo instead.
An afternoon with an emu could be your day with a dinosaur.

Ant-ics: The Doings of an Industrious Insect

Considered more of a pest than a pet, getting positive PR is no picnic for an ant. But despite their perceived lowly status, ants are anything but common.

✳ ✳ ✳ ✳

ANTS OUTNUMBER HUMANS a million to one. Their combined weight outweighs the combined weight of all the humans in the world. Possessing the largest of insect brains, an ant's intellect reportedly rivals the processing power of a Macintosh II computer. Yet, despite these distinctions, ants are stepped on the world over. Respect is due!

Long Live the Queen

In the ant world, males are superfluous. During the queen's brief courtship, she mates with several "kings," extracting and storing enough sperm to last her 10- to 30-year reign. No longer necessary, the male ants soon die. The queen then gives birth to thousands of subjects, populating her empire. Her fertilized eggs become females; unfertilized eggs become males. Most females are born sterile, consigned to be workers.

Ants pass through four life stages: egg, larvae, pupae, and adult. The tiny ant eggs are sticky, allowing them to bond together for ease of care. Since eggs and larvae are susceptible to cold temperatures, worker ants must ferry them from deep within the nest to the nest's surface to control their climate.

Models of Civility

Most ants live in organized, industrious harmony. Young workers care for their queen mother and larvae, then graduate to nest duties such as engineering, digging, and sanitation. Finally, when they are older (and closer to death), they advance to the dangerous jobs of foraging and security. By frequently switching jobs, ants remain cross-trained and ready for emergencies.

However, such civility is not universal. Members of the barbarous *Polyergus rufescens* species, or slave-maker ants, raid neighboring nests to steal their young. Sir John Lubbock, an acclaimed chronicler of ant behavior, reported that certain slave-making ants were so dependent on their minions that they would starve to death if the slaves failed to feed them.

Agricultural Innovators

Only four of the world's species engage in agriculture: humans, termites, bark beetles, and ants. Leaf-cutter ants carefully cultivate subterranean fungus gardens by spraying their crops with self-produced antibiotics to ward off disease, then fertilizing them with their protease-laced anal secretions. Ants also engage in livestock farming. They domesticate and raise aphids, which they milk for honeydew like a farmer would a cow for its milk. The honeydew provides important nourishment for ants, which are incapable of chewing or swallowing solids.

Some ants are also accomplished hunters. Marching in long processions while carrying their eggs and larvae on their backs, nomadic South American army ants attack everything in their path. Though blind, they fearlessly swarm on reptiles, birds, small mammals, and other insects (which they kill but don't eat). Up to 700,000 members strong, an army ant colony can make thousands of kills each day.

15 Tips for Surviving a Shark Attack

In 2005, there were 58 unprovoked shark attacks reported worldwide. Fewer than ten of those attacks, which occurred off the coasts of California, Hawaii, and Brazil, proved fatal. Below are some tips for staying out of the way of a hungry shark and what to do if you happen to cross paths with one.

✳ ✳ ✳ ✳

1. **Check with the Locals:** If you don't want to tangle with a shark, don't go where sharks hang out. If you plan to vacation near the ocean, contact local tourism offices and ask for shark stats in the area.

2. **Skip the Bling:** Sharks see contrast well, so wearing bright colors like yellow and orange is not a great idea. Also avoid shiny jewelry as sharks may mistake it for fish scales.

3. **Know Your Sharks:** Three species of shark are responsible for most human attacks: great white, tiger, and bull sharks. A hammerhead might freak you out, but it probably won't bite you.

4. **Be Adventurous, but Don't Be Ridiculous:** Who knows why you might choose to swim in murky waters, around harbor entrances or steep drop-offs, or among rocky, underwater cliffs, but if you do choose to swim in these dangerous places, don't be surprised if you come face-to-face with a shark.

5. **Swim Smart:** Always swim with a buddy, and don't swim at dusk or at night. Sharks don't have the best vision, so when it's dark, you look like dinner to them.

6. **Check with the Turtles:** Creatures of the sea know much more about the waters than you ever will. So, if turtles and fish start freaking out, there's probably a reason. If you

witness erratic behavior from other animals, there might be a very large, toothy beast approaching. Take a cue from those who have seen it before and take off.

7. **For the Ladies:** If you're menstruating, stick to the sand. Blood attracts sharks. Think of it as a great excuse to stay out of the water and work on your tan! Female or male, if you cut yourself on a reef or a rock while swimming, it's best to get out right away—the smell of blood to a shark is like the smell of fresh doughnuts to humans.

8. **Keep Fido on the Beach:** Allowing dogs to swim in the ocean can be dangerous if you're in shark territory. Animals swim erratically, attracting the attention of sharks. Don't let pets stay in the water for long periods of time.

9. **See a Shark? Shout!:** If there's a dorsal fin on the horizon, letting people know is a good idea. The more people know what's going on, the better off you are if the situation worsens. Then quickly swim toward shore as if your life depends on it . . . because it just might.

10. **Shark Approaching: Stay Silent and Immobile:** If you aren't able to get to shore and a shark approaches you, try to stay still and be quiet to avoid an attack.

11. **Shark Zigzagging: Find Something Solid:**
The zigzagging shark is looking for angles, so if you can back up against a reef, a piling, or some other kind of outcropping, do so. This reduces the number of angles the shark has to come at you. If you're in open water, 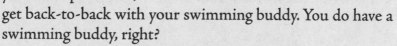 get back-to-back with your swimming buddy. You do have a swimming buddy, right?

12. Shark Circling: Uh-Oh: This is not a good sign for swimmers. If a shark is circling you, that means it's about to strike. Time to fight back!

13. Shark Attacking: The Eyes Have It: It might sound ridiculous, but try to stay calm. If you're being attacked by a shark, go for the eyes and gills, the most vulnerable parts of the shark. If you can wound the eyes, you've got a chance.

14. Go for the Nose (or Not...):
Although opinions differ, the general consensus seems to be that if you can get a clear shot, hitting the shark on the nose can be highly effective at ending the attack. Trouble is, when you're being attacked, hitting a specific target becomes challenging at best.

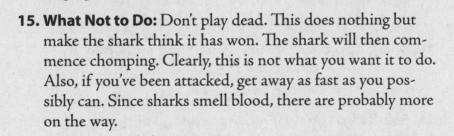

15. What Not to Do: Don't play dead. This does nothing but make the shark think it has won. The shark will then commence chomping. Clearly, this is not what you want it to do. Also, if you've been attacked, get away as fast as you possibly can. Since sharks smell blood, there are probably more on the way.

✳ Whale sharks are the largest fish in the sea, reaching lengths of more than 40 feet. Even with their large size, they are no danger to humans, as they feed on mostly plankton and small fish.

✳ Even with the odd placement of their eyes, hammerhead sharks have a better visual range than most other kinds of sharks.

✳ Great white sharks can swim at speeds of up to 15 miles per hour.

Spiders: They're Everywhere

Studies have shown that you're never more than ten feet away from a spider, and one estimate puts you as close as three feet. To be truly "spider-free" you'd have to go into space in a fumigated capsule. Rather than flee, read these facts and appreciate the amazing arachnid.

✳   ✳   ✳   ✳

✳ Unlike insects, spiders cannot fly—but they can balloon! Young spiderlings pull out silk until the breeze can lift them into the sky. Most don't travel high or far, but some have been seen at altitudes of 10,000 feet and on ships more than 200 miles from land. Most ballooners are small spiderlings, but adult spiders have been captured by planes with nets.

✳ Jumping spiders are smart. Studies have shown that they can solve simple 3-D puzzles; they also learn the behavior patterns of other spiders in order to capture them.

✳ Female wolf spiders carry their egg sacs behind them, attached to their spinnerets. After the spiders emerge, they crawl onto the mother's abdomen and hold on while she actively runs and hunts. After about a week, the spiderlings molt to a larger size and then take off to live on their own.

✳ While most spiders live for one year, a few may have more than one generation each year. Some spiders can live 3 to 4 years, and certain tarantulas are known to live for 25 years or longer.

✳ Male spiders are almost always smaller than the females and are often much more colorful. Some males are so small that they actually look like they're newly hatched.

✳ Male spiders are unique among all animals in having a secondary copulatory organ. While most animals spread their sperm in water or insert them into the female, mature male spiders weave a small "sperm" web. They place a drop of semen on the web, suck it up with their pedipalps (special structures on their first "arm"), and then use the pedipalp to insert the sperm into a female.

* It is estimated that up to 1 million spiders live in one acre of land—in the tropics, that the number might be closer to 3 million.

* Some spiders live underwater all of their lives. They surface to collect a bubble of air, which acts as an underwater lung. An underwater spider fills its bell-shape web with air bubbles and derives oxygen from them.

* The fisher or raft spider is able to walk across the surface of a pond or other body of water by skating like a water strider. When it detects prey (insects or tiny fish) under the surface, it can quickly dive to capture its dinner.

* Spiders are not only predators, they are often prey. Many birds and animals love to feed on them. The coatimundi, relatives of the raccoon, are fond of eating large tarantulas.

* Hummingbirds use the silk from spider webs to weave together the sticks that form their nests.

* A few species of trapdoor spiders use their abdomens to "plug" their burrows to protect themselves from wasps. The abdomen is flat on the back end and tough enough that a wasp's stinger can't penetrate it.

* Spiders eat more insects than birds and bats combined, so they should be considered another of humans' best friends. They play a big role in controlling insect populations.

* The decoration in the web of some orb-weaving spiders serves a variety of purposes: It can be a warning so birds don't fly into the web, an attractor so prey flies in on purpose, or an "umbrella" to shade the spider from the hot sun.

Animals that Keep Harems

When we hear the word "harem," we envision an exotic den that housed the concubines of a wealthy sultan. In the animal kingdom, however, harems are so common that some scientists believe monogamy to be unusual. Here are a few animals that keep harems.

✳   ✳   ✳   ✳

Elephant Seals

MALE ELEPHANT SEALS, found in the Antarctic and along the California coast, are enormous creatures that can reach up to 18 feet long. Their harems start off as a form of female bonding; toward the end of their 11-month pregnancies, females go ashore to give birth in groups. The males follow, fighting among themselves for the right to mate with the females once they've given birth.

Elk

Elk live in the Rocky Mountain region of the western United States and Canada, as well as in the Appalachian region of the eastern United States. Each fall, male elk fight with one another to win the females that will form their harems, which usually consist of six females. The females leave the harems in the spring and form small groups to care for their young before rejoining other elk in herds of up to 400 for the summer. This time, however, the tables are turned, with herds structured as a matriarchy, with one female leader.

Hamadryas Baboons

Most species of baboon form harems, though these are generally informal groupings. By contrast, male hamadryas baboons, which live in Africa, guard their harems fiercely and will attack any female that appears to be wandering away from the group. Males will also attempt to raid another male's harem to capture his females.

Shrimp

These crustaceans are found in most seas of the world, and they all form harems, usually consisting of one male and as many as ten females. The interesting thing about shrimp harems is that when the male dies, he may be replaced by a young female shrimp that is able to change her gender to take his place.

American Buffalo

American buffalo, or bison, live on plains, on prairies, in river valleys, and sometimes in forests. During breeding season males will fight for control of harems by charging at each other until one of them gives up. Harems generally include only three or four females, but during breeding season they keep the males so busy that they have little time to even eat.

Sperm Whales

A harem is just one option for the sperm whale, which will take part in a number of social groupings over its lifetime. Young whales often form coed pods that gradually split up as dominant males drive off smaller ones until just one male is left with as many as 25 females.

Lions

All species of lion form harems (commonly known as prides), usually consisting of one or two adult males, plus six to eight females and their cubs. Because they are smaller, quicker, and more agile than males, females do the hunting. While the lionesses are at work, the males patrol the area and protect the pride from predators.

Bats

Depending on the species, a male bat may have as many as 30 females in its harem. Female bats seek out males, drawn by their scents or, in some cases, their mating calls. Male African hammer-headed fruit bats can produce a symphony of loud, low-frequency honks by banding together in groups. When a female approaches, the calls become more frantic as each male battles to outdo the others.

You're Such an Animal

It would take lifetimes to uncover every odd detail of the animal world, but from our human perspective, the following creatures stand out.

* The fish tapeworm reaches lengths of up to 60 feet and can infect humans as well as fish.

* The torpedo ray builds up an electric charge in its head, then grabs a small fish and zaps it with 200 volts.

* Unborn crocodiles make noises inside their eggs to alert the mother that it's time for them to hatch.

* The alacran tartarus scorpion has been found in caves as far as 2,600 feet below ground—that's more than eight football fields deep.

* Eggs of the sand tiger shark hatch within one of two womb chambers. The embryos then eat each other until only one shark survives in each chamber. Only those two remaining sharks are actually born.

* The killer whale, or orca, will actually beach itself to feast on baby seals. It then worms its way back to the water.

* A mere .002 ounce (about the volume of a very small rain-drop) of venom from the Australian small-scaled snake can kill several adult humans.

* The imperial scorpion, one of Africa's many charming insects, grows up to seven inches long. It looks dangerous, but its venom isn't very toxic.

* The African honey badger will fight anything or anyone at any time. Its tough hide can resist penetration and most poisons, a great help when the badger's dinner includes puff adders or beehive honey.

* The male starling will line a nesting area with vegetation that helps the baby birds resist the impact of bloodthirsty lice.

* In the Galapagos, the woodpecker finch digs bug larvae out of wood with a stick, twig, or cactus spine.

* The skin of some toads contains poison, thus few creatures prey upon them. The skunk is an exception: It rolls the toads in wet grass to get the poison off.

* The large-eared pika, essentially a mini squirrel, can make its home at an altitude of 20,000 feet.

* The shingleback lizard of Australia has a thick, short, rounded tail that's shaped just like its head. This characteristic confuses predators and gives this slow, sleepy reptile a better chance to escape.

* The Japanese macaque is a rare monkey that likes cold weather. When temperatures in its mountain habitat drop below freezing (which they do regularly), the macaque lounges in natural hot springs.

* Amorous great gray slug couples hang from a rope of their slime as they twist around each other in the throes of slug passion.

* The red deer on the island of Rhum (in Scotland) kill seabird chicks and gnaw the bones to get nutrients otherwise unavailable on the isle.

* The rabbit-size mouse deer of Asia has long upper incisors that make it look like a miniature vampire deer. When these timid creatures encounter people, however, they quickly flee.

* An echidna is a spiny anteater of Australia and New Guinea that can grow to three feet long. The echidna and the duck-billed platypus are the only egg-laying mammals on earth.

Six Animals That Are Extinct Because of Humans

Shame on us. If not for our actions, these critters would still be around.

✳ ✳ ✳ ✳

Dodo

PROBABLY THE MOST famous species eradicated by people, the dodo was a three-foot-tall flightless bird that lived on the island of Mauritius in the Indian Ocean. The dodo had no natural predators, so it was able to nest on the ground in perfect safety until Dutch settlers arrived in the 16th century. Having never before been bothered, the dodo had no fear of people, nor of the sheep, dogs, pigs, and rats that accompanied them. The animals attacked the birds, the settlers destroyed their habitat, and the species disappeared in less than a century.

European Lion

Until the first century A.D., thousands of wild lions roamed modern-day Spain, Portugal, southern France, Italy, and the Balkans. This was the species pitted against the gladiators in Roman arenas. In addition, lions were hunted by the Macedonians and Greeks (among others), and it wasn't long before the Romans were forced to import lions from North Africa and the Middle East for their entertainment.

Passenger Pigeon

At one point there were an estimated 5 billion passenger pigeons in the United States. They gathered in enormous flocks, sometimes consisting of as many as 2 billion birds. When European settlers began to colonize North America in the 17th century, they hunted the birds, mainly for food. By 1896, almost all of the flocks had been killed for sport by hunters, and in 1914, the last remaining passenger pigeon, known as Martha, died in the Cincinnati Zoo.

Bluebuck or Blue Antelope

This species of antelope lived on the southwestern coast of South Africa. It was widespread during the last ice age (though its numbers dwindled as the planet heated up again) and survived until the 17th century. Europeans began to hunt the bluebuck obsessively—though purely for sport, because they didn't like the taste of its meat—until it became extinct at the beginning of the 19th century.

Alaskan Prehistoric Horse

Until recently, it was believed that these animals had died out because of climate changes long before the first people settled in Alaska. However, recent discoveries of fossil remains suggest that the horses may have been around when humans began to cross the Bering Land Bridge from Asia around 12,000 B.C. So it is likely that ancient humankind had something to do with their extinction.

Great Auk

Similar in appearance to the penguin, the flightless great auk was found in great numbers in eastern Canada, Greenland, Iceland, Norway, Ireland, and Great Britain. Although it couldn't use its wings to fly, the great auk used them to swim underwater, and its main food was fish. In the 18th century, great auks began to be hunted extensively for their meat and feathers, and they became extinct in 1844.

* Many people equate "extinction" with obliteration, but the process of extinction follows a simple rule: A species becomes extinct when its death rate is continually greater than its birthrate. The species mentioned here are goners, but there is great hope for a lot of others.

* Of all species that have existed on Earth, 99.9 percent are now extinct. According to a recent poll, seven out of ten biologists think we are currently experiencing another mass extinction, though many other researchers dispute this.

Setting the Record Straight on the Ostrich

The ancient Roman encyclopedist and philosopher Pliny the Elder once wrote that the ostrich, being profoundly stupid, sticks its head into a bush at the first sign of danger and considers itself invisible. Here's the truth about this magnificent, maligned bird.

✳   ✳   ✳   ✳

✳ To dispel the ancient libel, ostriches do not bury their heads when faced with danger—a species that did so would hardly be able to survive for more than 120 million years. They do, however, stretch their long necks flat on the ground when they sleep; from a distance, it can look as though their heads are buried.

✳ Ostriches cannot fly, but don't feel too sorry for them. The ostrich is the fastest bipedal runner in the world, capable of reaching speeds up to 45 miles per hour—about twice what the fastest human can achieve. What's more, an ostrich can maintain this speed for up to half an hour.

✳ Of the three main varieties of ostriches, only the African black ostrich (*Struthio camelus domesticus*) is found in captivity. They are farmed for meat, leather, and feathers in at least 50 countries and just about all climatic conditions, from Alaska to equatorial Africa. Ostriches have the best feed-to-weight ratio gain of any farmed land animal in the world and produce the strongest commercially available leather.

✳ The ostrich's eyes are about the size of billiard balls. They take up so much room in the skull that the ostrich's brain is actually smaller than either one of its eyeballs. This may be why the ostrich, despite its tremendous running speed, is not very good at eluding predators: It tends to run in circles.

* The ostrich's intestines are 46 feet long—about twice as long as those of a human. This enables the bird to get the most out of the tough plants it eats. To help with digestion, it also swallows sand and small stones to break down food in its gizzard. Ostriches in captivity have been known to swallow just about anything that can fit down their gullet, including coins, bicycle valves, alarm clocks, and even small bottles.

* The ostrich is the largest living bird in the world. An ostrich chick grows one foot taller each month until it is seven or eight months old. Adult ostrich roosters are six to ten feet in height and can weigh as much as 340 pounds. Because of their prodigious size, ostriches were occasionally used for riding or pulling chariots in ancient Egypt; the practice never really took off, because ostriches have a nasty temper.

* This great bird has only two toes; all other birds have three or four. Ostriches kick forward, not backward, because that's the direction in which their knees bend. Ostriches never need to drink water—some of it they make internally, and the rest is derived from the vegetation they eat.

* Although the ostrich egg is the largest of all eggs, it is the smallest egg in relation to the size of the bird. A three-pound egg is only about 1 percent as heavy as the ostrich hen; by contrast, a kiwi's egg—the largest in comparison to the mother—is 15 to 20 percent of the mother bird's mass. An ostrich egg is still equivalent in volume to two dozen chicken eggs.

* Male ostriches are polygamous, but they tend the nest with a single favored mate. This hen lays about a half dozen eggs in a shallow depression in the sand, which takes her about two weeks. Other hens then add their own eggs to the nest, and once they are finished, the favored mate chases them off. The nest owners then incubate all the eggs: The female sits on them during the day, and the male takes a turn at night.

Those Poor Piranha!

One of the most popular myths in the animal kingdom is that of the ferocious piranha, a fish so mean that it has stricken terror in the hearts of South American explorers for nearly a century.

❋ ❋ ❋ ❋

THESE FISH CERTAINLY look menacing, with their beady eyes and mouthful of razor-sharp teeth. But piranha aren't the Amazonian killing machines everyone thinks they are. In fact, experts say that piranha are quite timid and fear humans more than we fear them.

Teddy Tells a Tale

You can thank President Theodore Roosevelt for his help in spreading the myth of the piranha as a relentless, bloodthirsty carnivore. During a trip through Brazil in 1913, Roosevelt witnessed a piranha feeding frenzy that caused him to label the fish "the embodiment of evil ferocity." But according to historians, Roosevelt was the victim of a setup. Because his hosts wanted to give him a good show, Brazilian ichthyologist (a scientist who studies fish) Miranda Ribeiro had a small section of a local river blocked off with nets and stocked with thousands of pole-caught piranha, which were left unfed for several days.

When Roosevelt and his entourage arrived by boat, they were warned not to stick their hands in the water because of the vicious fish that lived there. Skeptical, Roosevelt and the journalists who were with him demanded proof, so an ailing cow was driven into the water, where it was immediately devoured by the starving piranha. Roosevelt was awestruck by what he had seen, and he went home with a tale of aquatic terror that remains popular to this day.

Chicken Fish

Most people assume there is only one kind of piranha. However, the fish come in a variety of colors and sizes, ranging from six inches to two feet. They swim in schools, but this is more for protection—safety in numbers, after all—than to help them hunt prey.

Although piranha wouldn't turn down a steak dinner if presented with one, they are actually scavengers rather than aggressive hunters. If there happens to be flesh in the water, such as a dead animal, they will happily graze on it, but they're just as content to dine on insects, smaller fish, and plantlife. Feeding frenzies do occur, but usually only when food is scarce. Attacks on humans are relatively uncommon and are generally attributed to an intrusion into the piranha's breeding grounds. In other words, we should watch where we're sticking our toes.

It's interesting to note that while humans are fearful of piranha because of their nasty reputation, the fish are actually much more frightened of us and will flee rather than attack if given the opportunity. In fact, one scientist who was studying wild-caught piranha in a tank had to erect a special screen around the aquarium because the fish became terrified and dangerously stressed every time she and her colleagues got too close.

The Real Stone-Cold Killer

Biologists warn that though the piranha is (erroneously) considered in a league with the great white shark as a natural killing machine, there are many other fish that are much more dangerous to humans. The stonefish, for example, carries in its dorsal fins a venom that can cause excruciating pain, swelling, and tissue death that can require amputation. In severe cases, the venom of the stonefish can even result in death if the victim is not treated promptly.

Most troubling about the stonefish, however, is its highly effective camouflage. It looks just like a rock on the ocean floor—until you step on it. And its dorsal fins are so sharp that they can pierce a shoe. So the next time you see a piranha, remember: There are far more terrible creatures in the water.

Celebrities and Their Pets

"Make me the person my dog thinks I am," goes the famous quip. And for those living under the constant scrutiny of the public eye, that plea is likely invoked with an extra grain of truth. Dogs—and for that matter cats, pigs, and the occasional kinkajou—prove loyal companions to the famous and infamous in a sometimes less-than-friendly world.

✳ ✳ ✳ ✳

1. **Martha Stewart:** The woman who twice landed on *Forbes* magazine's list of the 50 Most Powerful Women may be a tough cookie in business, but she's a softie about her pets. Her brood has included at least six chow chows: Zu Zu, Paw Paw, Chin Chin, Empress Woo, Max, and Ghengis Khan; and seven Himalayan cats: Teeny, Weeny, Mozart, Vivaldi, Verdi, Berlioz, and Bartok.

2. **Edgar Allan Poe:** Edgar Allan Poe wrote essays, short stories, and long poems, most of them more than a little macabre. Poe's short story, "The Black Cat," was inspired by his own tortoiseshell cat, Catarina, who curled up in bed with the writer's wife to keep her warm while she was dying of tuberculosis.

3. **Bill Clinton:** Famous for his foreign diplomacy, former president Bill Clinton was even able to persuade a cat and dog to peacefully coexist in the White House. Socks the cat came with Clinton when he moved into the executive mansion in 1993. Buddy, a chocolate Labrador retriever, arrived in 1997 as a gift. Socks and Buddy achieved national fame with the publishing of *Dear Socks, Dear Buddy: Kids' Letters to the First Pets*, by Hillary Rodham Clinton. Upon leaving office, Clinton gave Socks to secretary Betty Currie and took Buddy with him to New York. Sadly, Buddy was struck and killed by a car in 2002 near the Clintons' New York home.

4. John Lennon: John Lennon's mother, Julia, had a cat named Elvis (after Elvis Presley), which fostered John's feline fascination. Growing up in Liverpool, the Beatle-to-be had three cats: Tich, Tim, and Sam. With wife Cynthia, he had a tabby named Mimi. With girlfriend May Pang, he had a white cat and a black cat—Major and Minor. John and Yoko Ono shared their New York home with another black and white pair—Salt and Pepper. You can see his sketches of his cats at play in the books *A Spaniard in the Works* and *Real Love: The Drawings for Sean.*

5. Oprah Winfrey: Named World's Best Celebrity Dog Owner by the readers of *The New York Dog* and *The Hollywood Dog* magazines, Oprah Winfrey plays mommy to cocker spaniels Sophie and Solomon and golden retrievers Luke, Layla, and Gracie. The five canines live with Winfrey in a super-condo (formerly four separate units) in Chicago, where the talk show host has defended her pets against noise complaints and the building's pesky one-pet-per-unit rule. Oprah also gets props from pet lovers for introducing her audience to Cesar Millan, aka "The Dog Whisperer," and his revolutionary dog-training methods.

6. Jessica Simpson: What a difference a year makes. Back in 2004, when Jessica Simpson and Nick Lachey were happily married and starring in the MTV reality series *The Newlyweds*, they acquired Daisy, a Maltipoo (a Maltese-poodle mix). The dog's every scratch, sniff, and wag were dutifully recorded by the ever-present cameras: Daisy being toted around in Jessica's handbag, Daisy on *The Dukes of Hazzard* set, Daisy accompanying Jess to the tanning salon. In 2005, Nick and Jessica split up, but Daisy remains a loyal companion to the blonde bombshell.

7. Franklin Delano Roosevelt: Dogs in the White House are nothing out of the ordinary, but a dog at the signing of a war declaration? That would be Fala, Franklin Roosevelt's black Scottish terrier, who was a constant companion to the president—even in December 1941, when the nation entered World War II. In 1944, Fala traveled with the president to the Aleutian Islands, a trip that would live on in presidential infamy. Rumors swirled that Fala was somehow left behind, and Roosevelt sent a destroyer back for him, costing taxpayers millions of dollars. FDR answered critics with the famous "Fala speech" on September 23, 1944, in which he vehemently denied the rumors.

8. **Britney Spears:** Call her the anti-Oprah: Britney Spears was named World's Worst Celebrity Dog Owner in the same poll by the readers of *The New York Dog* and *The Hollywood Dog* magazines. In 2004, Brit was the proud owner of three Chihuahuas: Lacy, Lucky, and Bit-Bit. But one K-Fed and two kids later, and the pop diva appears to be dogless. Apparently she gave them away to friends.

9. **George Clooney:** George Clooney may be an eternal bachelor, but the former winner of *People* magazine's Sexiest Man Alive had no trouble committing to Max, the beloved potbellied pig he owned for 18 years. The Oscar-winning actor received Max in 1989 as a gift and often brought the 300-pound porker to movie sets with him. When Max died of natural causes in December 2006, Clooney told *USA Today* that he didn't plan to replace his porcine companion.

10. **Adam Sandler:** The best man at Adam Sandler's 2003 wedding was not a man at all, but an English bulldog named Meatball, dressed in a tux and yarmulke. Sandler, the comedian known for his goofball roles in films such as *Happy Gilmore* and *Billy Madison*, originally worked with Meatball's dad, Mr. Beefy, in the 2000 film *Little Nicky*. Sandler doted on Meatball, going so far as to film a comedy short with the pooch titled *A Day with the Meatball*, about a typical day in the dog's life. Meatball died of a heart attack at age four, but Sandler and his wife, Jackie, continue to enjoy the company of their other bulldog, Matzoball.

11. **Tori Spelling:** A pregnant Tori Spelling caused a bit of a tabloid frenzy in December 2006 when she was photographed in Beverly Hills pushing her famous pug, Mimi La Rue, in a baby stroller. But kindness to animals comes naturally to the *Beverly Hills 90210* star and daughter of late TV producer Aaron Spelling. Tori helps run Much Love, an animal rescue foundation that finds families for homeless pets. Tori purchased Mimi La Rue from a pet store seven years ago, but she adopted her other dog, Leah, a wire-haired terrier mix, from Much Love. She also has two cats, Madison and Laurel.

12. **Paris Hilton:** Paris Hilton's best friends change about as frequently as the weather, but she's held on to her Chihuahua, Tinkerbell, since 2002. Tinkerbell achieved fame through her costarring role in all four seasons of *The Simple Life* and her memoir entitled *The Tinkerbell Hilton Diaries*. Tinkerbell went missing briefly in 2004 after Paris' apartment was burglarized, but the hotel heiress ponied up a $5,000 reward and the dog was soon returned. For a brief spell, Tinkerbell took a backseat to a pet kinkajou, Baby Luv, until the exotic animal bit Paris on the arm, sending the starlet to the emergency room in August 2006. The kinkajou hasn't been spotted publicly with Paris since.

"Until one has loved an animal, a part of one's soul remains unawakened."

—ANATOLE FRANCE

Curious Habits of Birds

Approximately 10,000 species of birds make up the class Aves—a diverse group that has long fascinated the human race with peculiar behaviors and adaptations.

✳ ✳ ✳ ✳

Home invader: The kea (New Zealand), the world's only cold-weather parrot, loves to swing on car antennas and sled down the snowy roofs of ski lodges. The bird's favorite sport, though, is to get inside a lodge through its chimney and then trash the joint in search of food.

Neighborhood lookout: Bright-beaked puffins (northern seacoasts) adopt a low-profile walk to tell other puffins they are just passing through. The other puffins adopt a sentry pose to warn the tourists not to get any bright ideas.

Garbage disposal: The gull-like sheathbill (Antarctic) eats dead fish, other birds' eggs and babies, and seal and bird droppings.

Mugger: Skuas (various cold aquatic climes) are gull-like seabirds that chase other birds and force them to drop or cough up their food.

Aussie storm chaser: Huge, flightless emus (Australia) run after rain clouds, hoping for water.

Poacher: The world's smallest owl (about five inches), the elf owl (Mexico and southwestern United States), moves into abandoned gila woodpecker holes in cacti.

Family planner: Similar to the cockatoo, the galah (Australia) raises a larger or smaller clutch of chicks, depending on food availability.

Sponge dad: A male sand grouse (Asian and African deserts) soaks himself in water, then flies back to the nest so his chicks can drink from his feathers.

Mach 0.13 in level flight: The spine-tailed swift (Asia) can fly 106 miles per hour—without benefit of a dive.

The Stuka: These Arctic terns know little fear and will dive-bomb larger predators, often in squadrons.

Deep-sea diver: The common loon (northern North America and Greenland) can dive more than 250 feet underwater.

Vermonter at heart: The widespread sapsucker bores holes in trees, then slurps up the sweet sap.

Captain Ahab: The wetlands-dwelling anhinga spears fish with a long, sharp, slightly barbed beak that keeps food from sliding off.

Detox dieter: The stunning scarlet macaw (South America) eats clay from riverside deposits, which may help it process the toxic seeds it consumes.

Busy mom: A gray partridge hen (Europe) can lay up to 20 eggs. She has to, because many partridge chicks don't survive.

Lazy mom: A paradise whydah hen (equatorial and southern Africa) lays her eggs in a finch nest. This fools the finch, which raises the chicks as its own.

Fears nothing: The two-and-a-half-foot-tall great gray owl (northern forests) has a wingspan of five feet and fiercely attacks anything that gets too close to its nest and owlets.

Preventive measures: The southern carmine bee-eater (Africa) rubs a bee's "butt" against a tree branch to break off its stinger.

Bone-breaker: European and Asian mountains are home to the lammergeier, a high-flying vulture that drops bones repeatedly to get at the tasty marrow.

Sanitary engineer: A malleefowl (Australia) lays eggs in a nest full of rotting vegetation. The decay gives off heat to keep the eggs warm; the male bird checks the temperature often and adjusts the pile as necessary.

Stuff About Sharks

Here are some fascinating facts about nature's greatest predator.

✳   ✳   ✳   ✳

✳ Sharks have been around for nearly 400 million years. It's believed that larger, now extinct species used to eat dinosaurs.

✳ Sharks have no tongues. Their taste buds are in their teeth.

✳ Bull sharks, one of the most dangerous, aggressive shark species, have the highest testosterone levels of any animal in the world. They are also the only species of shark that can survive in both saltwater and freshwater.

✳ Sharks are well known for their "sixth sense"—the ability to sense electromagnetic pulses sent out by creatures and objects in the water. The sensors in their snouts are small pores called the Ampullae of Lorenzini.

✳ Scientists have discovered that a shark can be put into a catatonic state called "tonic immobility" when it's flipped onto its back or when the Ampullae of Lorenzini are appropriately stimulated. When the contact is stopped or the animal is righted, the shark typically snaps out of the "trance" very quickly.

✳ Several types of sharks have demonstrated an affinity for being touched or for being put into a state of tonic immobility. Scientists have seen Caribbean reef sharks compete with each other for a diver's attention, sometimes ignoring food in favor of being touched. Some great whites have even shown positive responses to being touched and have allowed divers to ride along on their dorsal fins. (This is, of course, very dangerous, even for professionals.)

✳ Humans are significantly more dangerous to sharks than sharks are to humans. People kill as many as 100 million sharks every year, often when the sharks are accidentally caught in fishing nets. Many other sharks are caught only for their fins, which are cut off (to be used in shark-fin soup) before the sharks are thrown back into the sea to drown.

* The largest known shark litter was discovered in a blue shark. When examined, she carried 135 pups in her uterus.

* Tiger sharks are often called the "garbage cans of the sea" because they will eat nearly anything. They favor sea turtles, but the contents of their stomachs have revealed tires, baseballs, and license plates.

* Although short-fin mako sharks are renowned for their ability to jump out of the water, the great white shark also makes spectacular aerial breaches, particularly when hunting seals off the coast of South Africa. Occasionally, they land in passing boats, much to the surprise of passengers.

* Sharks are not the mindless killers of lore. Many species have shown extraordinary curiosity and intelligence. They migrate to new feeding grounds at the times when their prey is most plentiful there, and they adapt their hunting techniques depending on their prey. Some have even been trained to push a bell to receive food.

* Great whites are frightening enough, but they have an extinct relative that makes the biggest of them look unimposing. Carcharodon megalodon was a huge shark that grew to 50 feet long and could easily swallow an entire person. They died out around a million years ago.

* Short-finned makos are the fastest sharks. They have been clocked at 36 miles per hour and have been estimated to swim up to 60 miles per hour. They need this extreme speed to chase down their favorite food—the lightning-fast yellowfin tuna.

✳ Most sharks are solitary hunters, but others are quite social. Greater hammerheads are known to group into large schools of 100 or more off the Island of Cacos near Mexico, and blacktip reef sharks frequently hunt in packs the way wolves do, helping one another grab fish and crabs out of the coral.

✳ The reportedly voracious great white shark can actually go nearly three months without eating.

✳ Scientists have identified more than 400 species of sharks in the world, ranging from less than a foot long to 40-foot behemoths. Approximately 30 of those species are considered dangerous to humans.

✳ The pygmy ribbontail catshark is the smallest shark in the world, with a maximum length of seven inches.

✳ Movies such as *Jaws* may make us think otherwise, but shark bites are uncommon, and fatal attacks rarely occur. A person is 1,000 times more likely to be bitten by a dog than by a shark, and dogs kill more people every year than sharks do.

✳ If you happen to be attacked by a shark, try to gouge its eyes and gills, its most sensitive areas. Sharks are opportunistic feeders and generally don't pursue prey that puts up a fight in which they could be injured.

✳ Gansbaii, South Africa, touts itself as the "Great White Capital of the World," and for good reason. Its shores host the greatest concentration of great white sharks in any ocean.

✳ Great white attacks are usually caused by the animals' curiosity about an unfamiliar object. Indeed, they are extremely curious, and lacking hands, they "feel out" the new object with their teeth, usually in a gentle bite. Unfortunately, the sharks are so large that even a nibble can do a lot of damage. The common belief that great white bites are a case of mistaken identity is false. Great whites have sharp eyesight, and they are often placid when interacting with humans—behavior that differs greatly when they are hunting seals.

Where Are Shark Attacks Most Common?

Most shark attacks occur in North American waters. In the United States, attacks happen most often in:

1. Florida

2. California

3. Texas

4. Hawaii

5. North Carolina

In other places around the world, most shark attacks occur in:

1. Australia

2. Brazil

3. South Africa

4. Reunion Island (Indian Ocean)

Roughly tied are the Bahamas, Cuba, Egypt, Fiji, New Zealand, and Venezuela.

Tips for Surviving a Bear Encounter

In North America, there are two species of bear—black and brown (which includes subspecies grizzly and Kodiak bears)—but it is often difficult to distinguish between the two. Both types are known to attack humans, and, in the past century, approximately 100 people have died in North America due to bear attacks. In the interest of not becoming part of that "grizzly" statistic, the following list offers a few tips to avoid or survive a bear attack.

✻   ✻   ✻   ✻

1. **Why Are You Here?:** Avoid investigating dark, unknown caves or hollow logs, where bears make their dens, and avoid areas identified by scavengers, such as raccoons, as there may be a feeding bear nearby.

2. **You're Kidding with the Camera, Right?:** Leave pictures of bears to professional wildlife photographers. Many attacks have occurred because someone decided to try to snap a photo in bear territory. Bears don't like you, and they don't want their picture taken.

3. **Whoa, Mama!:** If you see a bear with a cub, leave quickly. A mother bear with her cubs is not open to negotiation. She will attack if she thinks she or her cubs are in danger.

4. **Leave No Trace:** If you're camping, pick up all garbage, cooking supplies, and other materials. Clean up thoroughly after meals, and secure food overnight high above the ground (by hanging it from a tree branch) to prevent it from attracting bears. Not only do sloppy campers damage the area's ecosystem, they're also more likely to come face-to-face with a bear that has followed their gravy train.

5. Keep a Lookout: As you hike through bear country, keep an eye out for claw marks or droppings, and note any scratched up trees or fresh kills, such as deer.

6. Raise a Ruckus, Ring a Bell: Some experts recommend tying a bell to your foot or backpack to make noise as you travel. You can also sing or holler at your hiking buddies. Just don't be a ninja. Bears don't like to be surprised.

7. Freeze! Stick 'Em Up!: Okay, so you've spotted a bear, and the bear has spotted you. Stop right there, and don't move. Speak to the bear in a low, calm voice, and slowly raise your arms up above your head. This makes you appear larger.

8. Back Off: Clearly, you should try to leave now. Do it slowly and go back from whence you came. Don't cross the path of the bear (or any cubs, if present). Just rewind, slowly, and don't come back.

9. Don't Run!: The worst thing you could do at this point would be to get out your camera or try to feed the bear a snack. The second worst thing you could do would be to run. Bears run faster than humans, and they think chasing prey is fun.

10. Hello, Tree: "But bears can climb trees," you say. You're right: Some bears, like black bears, can climb trees. But others, like grizzly bears, cannot. Either way, if you can get more than 12 feet up into a tree, you should be okay. But that's pretty far up, so this is not your best option.

11. Grizzly Bear? Play Dead!: If a bear is charging you, you've got a couple of less-than-desirable options. The first thing you might try is going into the fetal position and playing dead. This might make you seem vulnerable to the grizzly bear and he or she will sniff you, growl at you, and hopefully leave you alone. Being in the fetal position will also protect your vital organs. IMPORTANT: If you're dealing with a black bear, do NOT play dead. They'll be thrilled that the work's been done for them and will commence lunch. If you can't tell what kind of bear you're dealing with, don't try it!

12. Go Undercover: While you're in the fetal position, try to put your backpack up on top of you to give you an extra layer of protection.

13. Bang, Bang: If a bear is charging you and you've got a gun, now might be the time to use it. Make sure you've got a clean shot because it usually takes more than one bullet to kill a bear and bad aim will only make it angrier. This should only be used as a last resort—wrongful killing of a bear in the United States incurs a hefty fine up to $20,000.

14. Spray, Spray: Many camping and national park areas don't allow firearms, so some recommend bear spray or pepper spray. But beware: If you spray halfheartedly, it will only make the bear angrier.

15. The Fight of Your Life: Your last option is to fight back with everything you've got. There's really no need to tell you that, at this point, you're in big trouble. Kick, scream, flail your arms, go for the eyes—do whatever you can because you're in for the fight of your life.

"Bears are made of the same dust as we, and breathe the same winds and drink of the same waters. A bear's days are warmed by the same sun, his dwellings are overdomed by the same blue sky, and his life turns and ebbs with heart-pulsings like ours and was poured from the same fountain."

—JOHN MUIR, AMERICAN AUTHOR AND ENVIRONMENTALIST

The Wacky World of Ant Farms

They invade our homes, ruin our picnics, and make a general nuisance of themselves. Ask most people what they think of ants, and they'll tell you these insects are nothing but irritating pests. But Milton Levine wouldn't agree. To him, ants are amazingly industrious workers who are fascinating to watch.

✳   ✳   ✳   ✳

IN 1956, LEVINE was at a Fourth of July picnic when he was struck with the idea for the ant farm. At one point, he reached for a sandwich and found it covered with ants, but rather then being repulsed, Levine thought back to his youthful fascination with insects. "I'd fill a jar with sand, put in some ants and watch them cavort," he said in a 2002 interview. "So at the picnic I thought, why not make a toy that would let kids watch the ants?"

The Ants Go Marching One by One...

Within a few months, Levine had designed the first plastic Ant Farm, and a remarkable new toy was born. Levine—known fondly to millions as Uncle Milton—fell into the toy game after leaving the army in 1946. Along with his brother-in-law, Joe Cossman, he formed a mail-order novelty company that sold things such as plastic soldiers and circus animals for a dollar. The company did well, and Levine eventually packed up his family and moved to California, where he continued to sell children's novelties. The ant farm, however, would ultimately prove to be his legacy.

A Few Bugs in the System

In the early days, the enterprise posed some unique challenges. Levine had to develop and refine the two-step process in which customers would first buy a farm and then mail in a certificate to get the ants. But that's not all. Before he could send live ants through the mail, Levine had to secure authorization on a state-by-state basis. (If you live in Hawaii, you're out of luck—

ants are labeled a nuisance there, so the company can't ship its product to that state.) Another issue was the sand. Levine first used beach sand, but it was the same color as the ants, so he switched to a whiter volcanic soil for better contrast.

Levine found that red harvester ants, which are found in the Mojave desert, worked best. Unlike other types of ants, red harvester ants work all the time. As a side benefit, their slippery feet made them unable to crawl out of the plastic container.

Crawling with Success

Levine first advertised the ant farm in a small notice in the *Los Angeles Times* Sunday magazine and was soon overwhelmed with orders. This was good in that it proved he had hit on something big, but bad in that he didn't have enough ants to fill the requests. He advertised for ant pickers, offering one cent per ant, but had trouble finding someone who was reliable.

Eventually, Levine signed a contract with the Gidney family, who created a special vacuum to gently collect the insects and delivered them to Levine on Sunday for Monday mailing to customers. The Gidneys provided Levine with ants for many years. When they were no longer able to do so, the job was given to another family, whose name is a company secret.

Levine bought out Cossman in 1965 and renamed the company Uncle Milton Industries. He kept the ant farm in the public eye through shrewd promotion, including appearances on *The Merv Griffin Show* and *The Shari Lewis Show*. Levine also planted his son, Steve, on children's television shows, where the host would inevitably notice him holding an ant farm and ask about the unusual toy.

The continued success of the ant farm never failed to amaze Levine. "I thought it would sell for maybe two years," he once said. But he couldn't have been more wrong. Uncle Milton Industries has sold more than 20 million Ant Farms over the decades and continues to sell approximately 30,000 a month.

Chapter 5

Hollywood

Hollywood's Warped Sense of History

Many writers consider it "creative license." The simple truth is that sometimes facts get in the way of a good story.

✳ ✳ ✳ ✳

✳ *Alexander* (2004): The big flaws in this biography are its omissions: The pivotal battles of Alexander's military career—the sieges of Thebes, Tyre, and Gaza—go completely unnoticed. The disastrous trek through the Gedrosian desert is barely touched on, even though it killed more of Alexander's soldiers than all of the onscreen battles combined. The three-hour epic presents a series of bloody exchanges between Greeks and Macedonians, but the audience is subjected to Irish, Scottish, and American accents.

✳ *Anna and the King* (1999): This film depicts a close relationship between British governess Anna Leonowens and King Mongkut, even hinting at a romance. In truth, they hardly knew each other, having had only a handful of exchanges. The film also depicts Anna playing a leading role in the reform and development of the Thai nation. This so offended Thai people that the movie is banned in Thailand.

✳ *Apocalypto* (2006): Mel Gibson's epic adventure portrays the ancient Mayan world as an ultraviolent, religiously void

civilization with few redeeming qualities. Finally, white missionaries
come to save the heathens from
themselves. Such a view, however, has been thoroughly
discounted by historians
who point to the scientific,
astronomical, spiritual,
agricultural, and artistic achievements of the Mayas.

* *Braveheart* (1995): The major fabrication here revolves
  around the relationship between William Wallace and
  Isabella of France, who was around ten years old when
  Wallace died. The two never even met, let alone had an affair
  or a child. Wallace's wardrobe also had historians shaking
  their heads: He wears a kilt even though they weren't introduced to Scotland for another 300 years.

* *Elizabeth* (1998): This movie's characters and time sequences
  are all over the place. Bishop Stephen Gardiner, who led the
  opposition to the queen in the movie, actually died three
  years before she was crowned. Also, the real Elizabeth was
  well aware that Lord Robert Dudley was married. It was
  only when his wife died in suspicious circumstances that the
  queen distanced herself from him.

* *Gladiator* (2000): Marcus and Commodus Aurelius were,
  of course, father and son. However, Commodus did not
  smother his father to death because his father wasn't
  going to make him emperor—the truth is he already was
  emperor! On November 27, 176, Marcus gave his son the
  rank of Imperator, which conveyed equal ruling power upon
  Commodus, then 15 years old. Three years later Marcus
  died (of natural causes), and Commodus continued his rule.

* *JFK* (1991): This film is guilty of both hyperbole and fantasy: There were 20 people (not 51) who heard shots from
  the grassy knoll, the mayor of Dallas did not change the

motorcade route, and David Ferrie never claimed to have inside knowledge of the killing. In addition, the "mysterious" deaths of such witnesses as Lee Bowers, David Ferrie, and "Jada" indicated no evidence of foul play.

* *The Patriot* (2000): The character of William Tavington is based on British lieutenant colonel Banastre Tarleton, who gets a bad rap in the film. In truth, he never set fire to churches full of people, nor did he die in the climactic Battle of Cowpens. Rather than the dour wallflower depicted in the film, Tarleton was a fun-loving extrovert who died in his sleep when he was 78.

* *Tombstone* (1993): In reality, Johnny Behan was not the sheriff when Wyatt Earp arrived in Tombstone, Arizona. John Ringo was not the leader of the cowboys, who, by the way, did not wear red sashes to identify themselves. Nor did Deputy Billy Breakenridge and outlaw Curly Bill Brocius have a homosexual relationship. Regarding the famous shoot-out: In the film, there are 51 shots fired in 128 seconds in a 30-foot-wide lot. In reality, there were 30 shots fired in 30 seconds in a space just 18 feet wide.

* The first motion picture to be shot in Hollywood was filmed in 1911. Hollywood's first movie studio also opened that year.

* Hollywood was annexed into the City of Los Angeles in 1910. The main reason for annexation was to gain access to Los Angeles' water and sewer systems.

* The Hollywood Walk of Fame was created in 1958, but ground was not broken until 1960.

Early Roles of Nine Hollywood Stars

The hair is big, and the script is bad, but everyone has to start somewhere. In showbiz, a job is a job and young actors take what they can get. These stars might be famous today, but they weren't born on the A-list. They worked their way up through bit parts and the strange, often painfully mediocre jungle of Hollywood. Here are some of the early films of today's red-carpet royalty.

✳   ✳   ✳   ✳

1. **Julia Roberts in *Firehouse* (1987):** Julia Roberts got super famous relatively early in her career, so there wasn't too much time for clunkers. But there were a few. *Firehouse* is a raunchy comedy à la *Police Academy* that used the tagline, "When the fire's out ... the heat is on!" Roberts plays a character named Babs, but doesn't do enough in the film to even get a screen credit. Roberts filmed another movie entitled *Blood Red* before *Firehouse*, but it wasn't released until 1989, making this lowbrow farce her big-screen debut.

2. **Keanu Reeves in *One Step Away* (1985):** The man who cracked *The Matrix* and was half of the cultural phenomenon known as *Bill and Ted's Excellent Adventure* (he was Ted), Reeves did some TV work before his role in this troubled teen flick produced by the National Film Board of Canada. He plays a kid with tough choices to make in a world that has stacked the odds against him. *One Step Away* is a couple steps away from being a good movie, but the future *Speed* star showed promise.

3. **Tom Cruise in *Endless Love* (1981):** The only people to benefit commercially from this story of two star-crossed lovers (played by Brooke Shields and Martin Hewitt) were Diana Ross and Lionel Richie, who sang the hit song of the same name. The movie itself, directed by Franco Zefferelli,

was pretty much a disaster. Tom Cruise makes a quick appearance as Billy—he auditioned for the lead but was beat out by Hewitt. Not only did Cruise, the future *Top Gun* hunk/Oscar nominee/media magnet, make his big-screen debut in this sappy teen flick, James Spader, Jamie Gertz, and Ian Ziering were also rookies in *Endless Love*.

4. **Nicole Kidman in *BMX Bandits* (1983):** Before the Chanel campaign, even before Tom, there was *BMX Bandits*. Nicole Kidman filmed several movies in 1983, but this one stands out. Hilarity ensues when two BMX bikers and their friend (Kidman) become entangled with a group of bank robbers. The Aussie has said this is one of her favorite films from the early days, and while it's no *Moulin Rouge*, the reviews weren't that bad.

5. **Chris Rock in *Beverly Hills Cop II* (1987):** Surely no one on the set of *Beverly Hills Cop II* looked at the young actor playing "Playboy Mansion valet" and thought, "That kid's going to be hosting the Academy Awards someday!" Chris Rock has made a name for himself as one of the most brilliant voices in stand-up comedy, but before his own original material opened doors at HBO and network television, Rock was opening car doors for Eddie Murphy in this classic '80s comedy.

6. **Courtney Cox in *Masters of the Universe* (1987):** Life was pretty sweet while playing Monica in NBC's megahit sitcom, *Friends*, but in 1987 Courtney Cox was running for her life from characters named Gildor and Karg. Cox had done a Bruce Springsteen video and television work before this He-Man movie, and she completed other film projects in 1987, but this role made her a favorite among the sci-fi set and possibly foretold her future work in kitschy movies such as the 1996 thriller *Scream*.

7. **Jack Nicholson in *The Cry Baby Killer* (1958):** One of the better-known and most-respected screen actors of our time,

Jack Nicholson has won three Oscars and has been nominated for many more. But before that he had to pay the rent. At age 21, Nicholson got a part in *The Cry Baby Killer*, a super low-budget, not-yet-ready-for-prime-time movie about an unstable young man who finds  himself in dire circumstances. Nicholson plays Jimmy, the "cry baby killer," and does a good job with a weak script. But if you want to see Jack at his best, check out *One Flew Over the Cuckoo's Nest*, *The Shining*, or *The Departed*.

8. **Madonna in *A Certain Sacrifice* (1985):** In 1985, when it was clear the world had a pop icon on its hands, the creators of *A Certain Sacrifice* released this low-budget movie, much to Madonna's chagrin. In the movie, filmed in New York in the late '70s, Madonna portrays a streetwise teen who gets in over her head with some unsavory characters. Madonna may not be known as a great actor, but *A Certain Sacrifice* shows she had star appeal long before she ruled the airwaves of MTV.

9. **Tom Hanks in *He Knows You're Alone* (1980):** Long before he made us laugh in *Big*, before he made us cry in *Forrest Gump*, and way before he made mega-blockbusters like *The Da Vinci Code*, Tom Hanks was in a simple teen horror flick called *He Knows You're Alone*. The tagline of the movie was: "Every girl is frightened the night before her wedding, but this time... there's good reason!" A young bride-to-be is being stalked while her future husband is out of town. Hanks plays the grieving boyfriend of another victim. Maybe the promise of a shelf full of Oscars would have cheered him up.

Truth or Blair?

Although legend says that the town of Burkittsville, Maryland, has suffered from a vengeful witch's curse since 1785, residents say the curse began in 1999—with The Blair Witch Project.

✳ ✳ ✳ ✳

"In October of 1994, three student filmmakers disappeared in the woods near Burkittsville, Maryland, while shooting a documentary called *The Blair Witch Project*. A year later their footage was found." These words began the movie *The Blair Witch Project* and touched off one of the biggest media controversies since the 1938 radio broadcast of *War of the Worlds*.

The Myth

Local legend tells the tale of Elly Kedward, who lived in Blair Township, Maryland, in 1785. Accused of preying upon neighborhood children, she was tried as a witch and banished. Over the next 150 years, the cursed town (later renamed Burkittsville) was the site of numerous murders, mutilations, and disappearances, all blamed on the so-called "Blair Witch."

Hearing these tales, film students Heather Donahue, Joshua Leonard, and Michael Williams went to Burkittsville in 1994 to film a documentary about the Blair Witch. They entered the woods on October 21 and never came out. A year later, a duffel bag holding their cameras, film, and journals was found buried under the foundation of a 100-year-old cabin.

The Movie

The Blair Witch Project opened to general release on July 16, 1999, and was touted as a compilation of the missing students' footage. The completely fictional work was the brainchild of struggling filmmakers Daniel Myrick and Eduardo Sánchez, who created the backstory, wrote the 35-page script, and directed the mostly improvised film. They hired three unknown actors and told them only that they would be involved in a movie project about fear and that "safety is our concern . . . your comfort is not." They took the actors to Maryland's Black Hills State Park, gave them cameras, and used GPS navigators to guide the trio through the movie's narrative, gradually depriving them of food, sleep, and comfortable shelter.

Unlike other contemporary horror movies, *The Blair Witch Project* has no onscreen bogeyman but instead relies on piles of rocks, the infamous "stickman" figures, and babies' cries to strike fear in the hearts of its protagonists (and audiences). The film's video vérité style and the actors' seemingly real fear and frustration heighten the movie's tension. What really snagged imaginations, however, was the overlap between the movie and the real world, helped by its documentary style, extensive mythology, and familiar locations. The preponderance of "evidence" forced even savvy viewers to question their assumptions.

The Mess

Myrick and Sánchez didn't foresee the problems that they would create with their crossover into reality. Even the Internet Movie Database had, rather ominously, listed the three actors as "missing, presumed dead" prior to the film's release. This was changed when post-release media interviews showed the trio to be alive and thriving, a fact that still didn't convince everyone.

Gawkers and vandals besieged Burkittsville, looking for truth about the Blair Witch. A group of townspeople posted an online statement that refuted the legend, the film's geography, and other "facts." When locals started to harass the sheriff's department about a purported 33,000-hour search to find the filmmakers, it also published an online rebuttal.

The Reality

To be clear, Myrick and Sánchez made up *The Blair Witch Project* and readily admit it. There is no legend of the Blair Witch; Elly Kedward is a fictional character. Blair Township, Maryland, never existed. Despite these facts, there are some who continue to insist that the story is true.

What the Heck Is a Gaffer?

You watch a movie and are thoroughly entertained for two hours. But as the closing credits roll, you have just one question: "What the heck is a gaffer?"

＊　＊　＊　＊

The world of professional filmmaking employs thousands of people in highly skilled positions—many of which are a mystery to the general moviegoing public. Here's a cheat sheet:

Gaffer: This is the chief lighting person—the man or woman who follows the design drawings from the lighting director—placing all lights, colored gels, and other rigging gear.

Production Designer: This role is key in developing the overall appearance of the picture. The production designer usually has a background in art. He or she works with the director, cinematographer, set designer, costume designer, and anyone else involved with creating the visual "look" of a film.

Key Grip: People who move and arrange major set pieces, cameras, dollies, and who work with the lighting crew are called grips. The key grip is the supervisor of the grips and works with the cinematographer to make the set look like it should.

Best Boy: This role (which can belong to a man or woman) belongs to the second-in-command for the key grip, helping to get the movie set in shape for shooting.

Set Dresser: A living room set, for example, might have a ceiling and three walls, two doors, and two windows. But what about the drapes? What about the chairs, sofa, end tables, lamps, pictures on the walls, doorknobs, or the 1,001 other things that make a movie set believable? The set dresser makes sure all of those items are in their proper places.

Armorer: Any film with guns needs an armorer. This person ensures that all prop weapons are historically accurate. More important, the armorer is charged with the duty of ensuring the guns and weapons are safely stored and handled.

Second Unit Director: Every film includes scenes that don't require the main performers or main action. Crowd scenes and shots that introduce a location or show travel are usually filmed by a secondary crew, or the "second unit." The second unit director manages the shooting of these elements.

Boom Operator: Ever since the silent era ended, sound has been an important part of the film industry. And if you've got sound, you need to have someone operating the microphones. The boom refers to the boom microphone, which is often at the end of a long pole. It can pick up sounds by hanging above the actors, just out of camera range.

Foley Artist: A young woman walks down a dark alley, followed by a sinister stranger—all to the sound of crackling footsteps. These sounds, and many others, often need to be enhanced or re-created. The Foley artist watches the finished scene on a screen and mimics the footsteps to make sounds that are recorded to replace the original sounds. This process gets its name from James Foley, an early filmmaker who used this technique.

Craft Service: This group is responsible for providing beverages and snacks on a movie set or location. They also clean up after the crew has gone home.

ADR Editor: Among the alphabet soup of film jargon is ADR—Automatic Dialogue Replacement (which isn't really automatic). Many factors can make the recorded sound from a scene unusable. The performers record their lines again while watching the completed action on a screen—a process called looping—and then the ADR editor splices the new audio into the scenes.

Unit Publicist: This person is part of the publicity department that goes out on location during the filming. The unit publicist assembles press kits, sets up media interviews, and works to keep peace with the local residents.

And the Award of Merit Goes to...

The Academy Awards were almost an afterthought for the Academy of Motion Picture Arts and Sciences.

✳ ✳ ✳ ✳

WHEN THE ACADEMY of Motion Picture Arts and Sciences (AMPAS) was created, bestowing "awards of merit" for distinctive achievement was not their first priority. The Academy was the brainchild of director Fred Niblo, actor Conrad Nagel, and producers Louis B. Mayer and Fred Beetson, who were concerned that the film industry had no official voice to counter criticism that it was a bad influence on society. In addition, Mayer hoped to prevent the various craft groups (directors, writers, actors, etc.) from unionizing by forming one large professional organization for all. Thus, AMPAS, which received its official charter on May 4, 1927, was intended to encourage the improvement and advancement of the film industry, promote a harmonious working relationship among the different groups, counter criticism, and sponsor technical research.

The Academy is made up of five branches representing different creative groups—producers, directors, writers, actors, and technicians—with each group receiving equal representation. At a banquet to recruit additional members on May 11, 1927, newly elected president Douglas Fairbanks mentioned in passing that the Academy might also bestow "awards of merit."

The Committee for the Award of Merits was formed shortly after to develop the voting process. In the meantime, Mayer asked MGM art director Cedric Gibbons to come up with an award statue. Gibbons designed the familiar figure, nicknamed Oscar, which holds a sword while standing on a film reel with five spokes, each of which represents one of the five branches of the Academy.

The First Academy Awards

In July 1928, the Committee announced a voting system for the awards. Each Academy member nominated a film for his/her branch. Then a Board of Judges counted the votes to determine the nominations, turning over the results to a Central Board of Judges. The Central Board, consisting of one representative from each branch, selected the winners. The films eligible for the first Academy Awards were released between August 1, 1927, and July 31, 1928. The Central Board met to decide the final winners on February 15, 1929. Part of the reason for the long, drawn-out nomination process was that many Academy members either forgot or ignored the eligibility dates and nominated films from as far back as 1925, so the voting had to be done all over again. Nominations were made in 12 categories.

Winners were announced on February 18, 1929, with the awards banquet scheduled for May 16. Since the winners had already been announced, there was no sense of anticipation. Consequently, few of the losing nominees, such as Gloria Swanson and Charlie Chaplin, attended. In the time between the announcement of the winners and the banquet, excitement had waned, and several of the winners, including Best Actor Emil Jannings, did not show up either. *Wings* won for Production and *Sunrise* for Artistic Quality of Production, but the distinction between the two categories was never clear.

The following year, the Artistic Quality of Production category was dropped, as were Comedy Direction, Title Writing, and Engineering Effects. Also, the winners were announced at the banquet, which made the ceremony a more highly anticipated event. Over the years, more changes were made in the categories and the voting rules as the awards process and ceremony evolved into their now-familiar forms. Currently, members of each branch nominate films in their field, while the entire Academy votes for the winner in each major category, including Best Picture.

The Last Movies of Nine Noteworthy Stars

There's something eerily gripping about watching a late movie star in his or her final role. Whether it's a comedy or a drama, a flop or a smash, that last glimpse is always worth savoring. Below are the last movies of nine notable stars.

✳ ✳ ✳ ✳

1. **James Dean:** Rising star James Dean was just 24 years old, with a mere three starring roles under his belt, when he was killed in a car accident in 1955. The astonishingly talented actor became an enduring cult icon with his roles in *East of Eden* and *Rebel Without a Cause*. But *Giant*, released in 1956, was Dean's farewell picture. In the movie, Dean plays Jett Rink, a nonconforming ranch hand who becomes a rich oil tycoon. Dean's character ages about 30 years in the film, so his hair was dyed gray. When Dean was killed on September 30, 1955, while driving his Porsche Spyder to an auto race in Salinas, California, he eerily appeared much older, due to his hair. Dean received Oscar nominations for Best Actor for his roles in *Giant* and *East of Eden*, the first person to receive a posthumous nod from the Academy.

2. **Katharine Hepburn:** On the American Film Institute's list of Top 100 U.S. Love Stories, six of the movies star Katharine Hepburn, more than any other actress on the list. Her final movie, 1994's *Love Affair*, tells the tale of a budding romance, and stars famous lovebirds Warren Beatty and Annette Bening. In addition to her immense talent, Hepburn was known for a razor-sharp wit, a willingness to speak her mind freely, and a decades-long love affair with costar Spencer Tracy. The actress, who earned four Oscars

(a record for any actress), starred on the big screen for more than 60 years before retiring in the mid-1990s. *Love Affair*, in fact, was the only big-screen project she embarked on in the '90s. Hepburn died at home in 2003, at age 96.

3. Jayne Mansfield: Jayne Mansfield's career had taken a nosedive by the time she died at age 34. Her notoriety reached its peak in 1963 when she starred in *Promises! Promises!*, in which she appeared nude. The film was banned in some areas, but enjoyed box office success where it was shown. Once a highly sought-after actress, by the early 1960s the blonde bombshell had resorted to tacky roles that relied on her sex appeal. But she gave an honest, clear-eyed performance in what would prove to be her last movie, *Single Room Furnished*, released in 1968 after her death. In the film, she portrays a woman who turns to prostitution after her husband and later her fiancé both desert her. Mansfield was killed on June 29, 1967, when the car she and three of her children were riding in crashed into a tractor-trailer. The children survived with minor injuries.

4. Christopher Reeve: Christopher Reeve is best remembered as Superman after portraying Clark Kent in the 1978 box office smash *Superman*. After he was paralyzed during a horse-riding accident in 1995, his grace, courage, and devotion to furthering the cause of paralysis victims earned him worldwide respect and adoration. Reeve devoted the majority of his time after the accident to advocacy work, but he continued to act and dabbled in directing, as well. He appeared on several TV shows, including *The Practice* and *Smallville*, and directed a number of made-for-TV movies, including 1997's *In the Gloaming*, which was nominated for five Emmys. His final role was in *Rear Window* (1998), a remake of the Alfred Hitchcock classic, in which he portrayed a paralyzed architect who thinks he witnessed a murder from his apartment window. Reeve won a Screen Actors Guild Award for his performance.

The courageous actor died in 2004 of cardiac arrest from a reaction to antibiotics. He was 52 years old.

5. **John Belushi:** You'd think John Belushi's last role would be as some wild-eyed, ranting lunatic. Instead Belushi played the victim of a crazy neighbor in 1981's *Neighbors*, his third film with *Saturday Night Live* partner Dan Aykroyd. Belushi portrayed straight-laced Earl to Aykroyd's wacky Vic in the dark comedy about suburban life. Belushi's fame came on *SNL* and with *Animal House* in 1978. And when he left *SNL* in 1979, he quickly churned out *1941* and *The Blues Brothers*. Three months after *Neighbors* was released, he died of a cocaine and heroin overdose on March 5, 1982, at age 33.

6. **Chris Farley:** As a child, Chris Farley idolized comedian John Belushi. In his own career, Farley was known for playing portly misfits who'd stop at nothing for a laugh, and his last role was no exception. In 1998's *Almost Heroes*, Farley and Matthew Perry starred as two early American explorers who set out to beat Lewis and Clark. Offscreen, Farley, who got his start at Chicago's Second City and broke into Hollywood via *Saturday Night Live*, had battled drug and alcohol addiction and chronic obesity for years. Still, he completed a string of successful comedies, including *Tommy Boy* in 1995. But by the time he began work on *Almost Heroes*, his addictions were out of control, and filming reportedly had to be stopped several times while he was in rehab. Shortly after completing the movie, Farley died on December 18, 1997, ironically, of a cocaine and heroin overdose at age 33, just as his idol John Belushi had.

7. **Henry Fonda:** You know you've had a stellar acting career when your greatest film is a toss-up between *The Grapes of Wrath* and *12 Angry Men*. Or was it *The Ox-Bow Incident* or *Mister Roberts?* Some critics pass over those classics altogether and declare Henry Fonda's best film to be his last,

On Golden Pond. The actor received numerous Oscar nods during a career that spanned five decades, but by the 1980s, he had limited most of his work to television, with the exception of 1981's *On Golden Pond.* The film, which also starred his daughter Jane and Katharine Hepburn, tells the story of an aging couple who spend a life-changing summer at their vacation home. It earned 11 Academy Award nominations and a Best Actor win for Fonda, his first and only Oscar. He died of heart disease at age 77, just eight months after the film was released.

8. **Audrey Hepburn:** As a child, Audrey Hepburn grew up in Nazi-occupied Amsterdam and carried secret messages to the Resistance. After World War II ended, Audrey trained as a ballerina and worked as a model before embarking on an award-winning acting career. The graceful and elegant brunette was an instant success, winning a Best Actress Oscar for her first major film role as Princess Ann in *Roman Holiday* (1953). But she is best remembered for her roles in *Breakfast at Tiffany's* and *My Fair Lady,* two roles that garnered her nods from the Academy, but no Oscars. One of only a handful of performers to win a Tony, an Emmy, an Oscar, and a Grammy Award, Hepburn portrayed an angel in her final film role in Steven Spielberg's *Always* (1989). She died of cancer in January 1993 at age 63.

9. **Marilyn Monroe:** Marilyn Monroe packed a number of memorable roles into her tragically short career, but her final completed film, *The Misfits,* is remembered for its offscreen turmoil as much as its big-screen success. Written by Monroe's third husband, playwright Arthur Miller, the 1961 movie was plagued by Monroe's chronic tardiness. Ironically, costar Clark Gable suffered a massive heart attack the day after filming wrapped and died 11 days later. Meanwhile, Monroe's marriage to Miller was about to end in divorce, and she was battling substance abuse. She died at age 36 from barbiturate poisoning on August 5, 1962.

The Spanish *Dracula*

Bela Lugosi has indelibly made his stamp on the character Dracula. But another version of the story was shot alongside the classic film.

✳ ✳ ✳ ✳

IN DIRECTOR TOD Browning's *Dracula*, Bela Lugosi masterfully captured the fiendish essence of the count, a role he reprised from Broadway. Often described as the definitive *Dracula*, the film is considered a classic largely due to Lugosi's unnerving portrayal of the renowned vampire. Many of its fans, however, have likely missed the Spanish-language version, shot by night on the very same set.

Parallel Pictures

Studios of the time believed international filmgoers would be cheated if English-language films were dubbed into other languages. Instead, alternative-language editions were often filmed alongside their English-language counterparts. Traditionally, the resulting films were of lesser quality, due to small budgets, short shooting schedules, and lack of big-name talent. Yet many devotees have dubbed George Melford's Spanish *Dracula* more artistically sound than Browning's film.

The Spanish *Dracula*, also released in 1931, featured Latin actor Carlos Villarías and voluptuous Lupita Tovar in the female lead. The acting chops of these actors have been questioned, but the eye-popping expressiveness of the cast makes up for in passion what might be lacking in technique. Also, while Browning was said to have run a rather chaotic set, Melford had access to Browning's dailies and could smooth over the bumps that plagued the daytime *Dracula* set.

The Spanish version of *Dracula* ran nearly 30 minutes longer than the English version due to elements Melford added at night to perfect the concepts put forth by Browning during the day.

Nine Outrageous Hollywood Publicity Stunts

The movie industry isn't exactly shy about self-promotion. Well-orchestrated PR campaigns designed to get people into theaters have helped many films' box office success. Here are some of the wildest feats in the long history of movie publicity.

✳   ✳   ✳   ✳

1. ***The Prisoner of Zenda* (1937):** Legendary Hollywood publicist Russell Birdwell created a buzz for this swashbuckling movie by arranging for an airplane to bring a dozen residents from Zenda, Ontario, to the world premiere in New York City. The publicity apparently worked because the film received two Oscar nominations.

2. ***Gone With the Wind* (1939):** Birdwell was also involved in one of the industry's most famous PR efforts: The search for the actress to play Scarlett O'Hara in the screen version of Margaret Mitchell's novel created much hoopla as the casting director traveled the country holding open auditions. After three years of interviews and auditions with stars such as Katharine Hepburn, Paulette Goddard, and Lana Turner, the role went to Vivien Leigh, who had appeared in a few films, but was largely unknown outside of Great Britain. Frankly, the public didn't seem to give a damn, because they made *Gone With the Wind* the highest grossing film in movie history (adjusted for inflation). Its original release and seven rereleases over the years have raked in nearly $2.7 billion in today's figures.

3. ***Down Missouri Way* (1946):** This musical features an agriculture professor who secures a movie role for her trained mule, Shirley. To promote the film, a studio publicity

man led Shirley, with an ad for the movie on her back, down Fifth Avenue and into the restaurant overlooking Rockefeller Plaza's ice rink. Managers naturally refused to seat the animal. The press showed up to record the event, so it accomplished the publicist's mission . . . but it didn't do much for the movie, which was not a box office smash.

4. *Teacher's Pet* (1958): Clark Gable and Doris Day star in this comedy about a newspaper editor. For publicity purposes, Paramount filmed 50 Hollywood newsmen sitting at desks and gave a few of them lines in the film. What better way to get reporters to focus on your movie than to put them in it? The buzz may have worked; *The New York Times* placed *Teacher's Pet* in its top ten of 1958, and the movie received two Oscar nominations.

5. *Mr. Sardonicus* (1961): Colombia Pictures executives told director William Castle to film an alternate, happy ending for this dark movie. Castle turned the episode into a publicity opportunity, giving audience members cards with thumbs-up and thumbs-down to "vote" for the main character's fate. Castle apparently understood human nature well—there are no accounts of audiences wanting a happy ending. He may not have known their movie desires quite as well—they gave their thumbs-down to the movie.

6. *The Blair Witch Project* (1999): Producers intimated that this thriller's documentary style was authentic and implied that the footage making up the entire movie had been discovered after three student filmmakers searching for the so-called "Blair Witch" disappeared in the woods of rural Maryland. They even listed the film's lead actors (the supposed filmmakers) as "missing, presumed dead" on the Internet Movie Database before the movie's release. The stunt seemed to work: The movie made *The Guinness Book of World Records* for the highest box-office-proceeds-to-budget ratio in film history. It cost only around $35,000 to

make but pulled in more than $140 million in the United States and more than $248 million worldwide.

7. **Office Space (1999):** The corporate "cube farm" is the target of both this cult classic—which follows three company workers who rebel against their less-than-rewarding work environment—as well as its publicity stunt. For a week, the studio had a man sit inside a Plexiglas work cubicle on top of an office building overlooking Times Square. Everyone from Howard Stern to nearby office workers expressed sympathy. The publicity seemed to help the film, which ranked number 65 on Bravo's 2006 list of the 100 funniest movies of all time.

8. **House of Wax (2005):** Producers often use a celebrity's star power to draw audiences to their films. But Joel Silver took things in a darker direction for this horror flick by advertising the death of Paris Hilton's character in the movie. Turning her notoriety to his advantage, he sold shirts reading "See Paris Die May 6." The publicity may have been for naught. *House of Wax* was almost universally panned, and U.S. ticket sales came a few million dollars short of covering the movie's $35 million production costs. But it made up for its weak domestic performance overseas, grossing more than $70 million worldwide.

9. **Borat (2006):** As the title character, British actor Sacha Baron Cohen played a misspeaking journalist from Kazakhstan. In September 2006, Secret Service officers prevented Cohen (dressed in character, as he often does for his stunts) from entering the White House where he hoped to invite "Premier George Walter Bush" to a screening of the film. His antics even prompted the Kazakh government to remind audiences that the obnoxious character does not properly represent the country's values. Whether due to Cohen's antics, generally positive reviews, or word-of-mouth, the film made more than $248 million worldwide.

Booze, Broads, and Busted Careers: Hollywood's Bundy Drive Boys

Amid the glitz and glamour of Hollywood's Gilded Age, the Bundy Drive Boys lived hard, drank hard, and died hard.

❋ ❋ ❋ ❋

Six Degrees of Barrymore

THE CENTER OF the Bundy Drive Boys was legendary stage and screen actor John Barrymore. Already an established star in the 1920s and '30s—when the other Boys were just beginning their careers in New York—Barrymore befriended bulbous-nosed comedian W. C. Fields; writer Sadakichi Hartmann; writer Gene Fowler; and John Decker, a caricature artist who sketched actors for the *New York Evening World*.

In Hollywood, Barrymore partied with Errol Flynn and John Carradine who, as a college student, had shown up unannounced at Barrymore's house just to meet the actor. Barrymore also ran with Anthony Quinn, who got his start spoofing Barrymore in a Hollywood play (while Barrymore sat in the audience); and screenwriter Ben Hecht, who famously boycotted the first Academy Awards in 1929—and used his award for Best Original Screenplay as a doorstop. But the Bundy Drive Boys had more than Barrymore in common. They also battled the same demons.

The Drinking

When Barrymore died in 1942 at age 60, doctors estimated the actor had drunk hundreds of gallons of alcohol. One estimate puts the number at about 640 gallons over a 40-year period—about 16 gallons of booze each year.

To keep Barrymore from drinking on film productions, his managers often hired prostitutes to keep him company. His drinking got him fired from the 1933 film *Romeo and Juliet*, but the director hired him back on one condition: Barrymore must spend each night in an insane asylum to keep from drinking. But the Boys had Barrymore's back: One night, Fowler and Decker visited the asylum, distracted a guard, and hoisted booze up to Barrymore's window.

Barrymore wasn't the only one with alcohol problems. Decker arrived in New York in 1921 and made a name for himself with his witty caricatures and portraits—most notably a painting of Fields as Queen Victoria. But for all of his success as a painter (and sometimes art forger), he would immediately blow his money on parties and alcohol. Hartmann won a role opposite Douglas Fairbanks in the 1924 film *The Thief of Baghdad*—for a rumored fee of $250 a week and a case of whiskey. Several weeks into the project, Hartmann abandoned the set. As legend has it, he complained that the whiskey was "inferior." And Flynn was allegedly so drunk on the 1958 set of *Too Much, Too Soon* (in which he portrayed his late friend Barrymore) that it required 17 takes for him to say "parole" instead of "patrol."

Barrymore, Decker, and Flynn, as well as W. C. Fields, would all die from cirrhosis of the liver, caused by chronic alcoholism. Fields would be the oldest at 66 years old, although Flynn, who died at age 50, was said to have had the "body of a 75-year-old."

The Dames

Barrymore and Carradine each had four wives, while Hecht had two. Fowler had only one wife, and so did Fields, but only because his Catholic wife wouldn't divorce him. Instead, Fields had a mistress for most of his adult life. Hartmann also married only once, but fathered children (as many as 12 or 13) with other women. Flynn, Decker, and Quinn had three wives apiece.

Divorced from his first wife, Flynn was acquitted of statutory rape in 1943. During the trial, he fell for the teenage girl working the cigar stand at the courthouse, whom he soon married (and divorced). He remarried again in 1950, but died in the arms of his 15-year-old mistress in 1959. Decker also went to court over a woman—namely his first wife, whom he forgot to divorce before marrying the other two.

Quinn left his first wife of 27 years when his mistress (and later wife) gave birth to their son. Thirty years later, the nearly 80-year-old Quinn fathered a daughter with his secretary (50 years his junior) and divorced wife number two to marry her. Quinn's last child was born just after the actor's 81st birthday in 1996. All in all, he fathered 13 children with a rumored five women.

The Distant Dads

Beyond the drinks and the dames, many of the Bundy Drive Boys were haunted by a darker secret: their fathers. Barrymore feared going insane, as his father had. Decker was abandoned by his parents when he was a teenager, and Hartmann was left by his father when he was just an infant. Fowler's father left his family; Quinn's died when the actor was nine years old. Fields had been physically abused by his father, while Flynn, on the other hand, suffered from a verbally abusive mother.

The Clubhouse

If Barrymore was the president of this self-destructive club, in 1940, Decker's new Bundy Drive home became its official hangout. Group members regularly arrived unannounced to drink, smoke, sword fight, trade insults, and deliver monologues. Hartmann occasionally wet his pants as he sat drinking at the bar. But the good times were short lived: In less than a decade, most of the club's founding fathers would be dead.

In January 1944, shortly after Barrymore's death, Hartmann gathered with the remaining men at Decker's home and gave an ominous prediction: He himself would be dead in less than a year; Decker in three; Fields in two; Fowler in four—although Hartmann jokingly agreed to give him 16 years if Fowler would pay for his trip to the East Coast. On all counts, Hartmann was right. Quinn, the youngest of the Boys, outlived them all—dying at the age of 86 in 2001.

Memorable Movie Misquotes

People love to recite memorable lines from their favorite movies, TV shows, and books. But many of the most famous lines are misquoted or attributed to the wrong character. In some cases they were never uttered by anyone.

✳ ✳ ✳ ✳

"Play it again, Sam," from the classic 1942 movie *Casablanca*, is perhaps the most frequently misquoted movie line of all time. In fact, it was never spoken by anyone in the film. Ingrid Bergman's character comes closest when she says, "Play it, Sam." The nearest Humphrey Bogart's character gets is when he says, "If she can stand it, I can. Play it!" The line "Play it again, Sam" was used in the Marx Brothers' 1946 movie *A Night in Casablanca*, however, and Woody Allen used it as the title for his 1972 comedy.

"I think this is the start of a beautiful friendship" is the famous last line of *Casablanca*—and it's a misquote. As Rick and Renault walk off together into the night, Rick's final line is, "Louis, I think this is the beginning of a beautiful friendship."

"You dirty rat!" Cagney never uttered this line in a movie or in any recorded interview. The closest he came was in the 1931 movie *Blonde Crazy*, when he said, "Mmm, that dirty, double-crossin' rat." It is believed that one of Cagney's professional impersonators coined the phrase, and others went on to copy it.

"Elementary, my dear Watson!" is surely the most famous line attributed to the world's greatest detective, Sherlock Holmes. The problem is that at no point in any of the Sherlock Holmes novels from Sir Arthur Conan Doyle does the sleuth utter the line. The phrase first appeared in a *New York Times* film review and was then coined in the 1929 movie *The Return of Sherlock Holmes*.

How Does It End?: Real Alternate Movie Endings

Think you know everything about your favorite films? Think again.

❋   ❋   ❋   ❋

MOVIE STUDIOS OFTEN preview new movies with test audiences who can help producers and directors predict whether or not they've got a hit on their hands. After getting feedback, changes to the film are made—anything from small tweaks to total overhauls. Read on for some cases of big changes that were made at the eleventh hour. Consider this your official spoiler alert.

Little Shop of Horrors

The Broadway version of this story goes something like this: Boy meets girl, boy and girl fall in love, boy and girl get eaten by carnivorous plant. Audiences were traumatized by Frank Oz's movie version of *Little Shop*, however, so the boy and girl live happily ever after on the big screen.

I Am Legend

This film adaptation, starring Will Smith in Richard Matheson's classic horror novella, is all about role reversals. Well, that and vampirelike beings. In the book, the mean, nasty creatures are actually revealed to be compassionate beings that are only out to protect their own. It becomes clear that Smith's character is *their* enemy, just as much as they seem to be *his*. Well, this cautionary tale didn't fly with test audiences, so the main theme of Matheson's book was scrapped. Instead, Smith's character in the movie pretty much just blows everybody up.

The Wizard of Oz

The first audiences for this ultra-classic film thought Dorothy's classic "Over the Rainbow" number slowed down the story. It was kept in at the last minute.

Blade Runner

Ridley Scott, the Oscar-winning director who adapted Philip K. Dick's *Do Androids Dream of Electric Sheep* to film, loved the dark tone of the story. The studio, however, didn't love it as much. In the original version of the film, the intense protagonist (played by heartthrob Harrison Ford) decides to harbor the renegade android he loves, even though she's doomed to short-circuit any second. Throughout the film, there are also allusions to the notion that Ford's character himself might be an android. The studio thought all this was a little too bleak, though, and decided to let the man and his android live happily ever after.

Pretty Woman

In the original version, Vivian, the prostitute with a heart of gold and legs for miles (played by Julia Roberts), rejects Richard Gere's character and goes on to seek her fortune. Test audiences cried foul and the film ends with the couple together.

Fatal Attraction

Crazy Alex Forrest, the jilted lover brilliantly played by Glenn Close, was originally supposed to commit suicide and frame Michael Douglas's character for it. Test audiences didn't want the nasty lady to get off so easy, though; instead, Close's character was shot by Douglas's wife.

E.T.: The Extra-Terrestrial

In the original script, the lovable alien E.T. dies. This didn't sit well with children, so director Steven Spielberg gave in and allowed the little guy to make it home.

Butch Cassidy and the Sundance Kid

At the end of this timeless western, Butch and Sundance are surrounded by what seems to be the entire Bolivian army. The film ends before the final gunfight, a clever way to leave it up to the audience to decide if the duo dies or manages to survive. The original version of the film showed their death, but test audiences preferred the alternate, more ambiguous ending.

Marilyn Monroe Copycats

Depending on your age, when you think of a Marilyn Monroe imitator, you may picture a drag queen or even an early-1990s Anna Nicole Smith. But Marilyn copycats go back to the 1950s, when the actress was still alive and working.

✳   ✳   ✳   ✳

DURING MARILYN MONROE'S heyday, men and women alike couldn't get enough of the star. Her movies entertained, her personal life made headlines, and her sex appeal shook a modest America to its core.

Monroe had a production contract with 20th Century Fox, and the company struck gold with her. There was certainly an unmet demand for more sexy starlets like her—so much so, in fact, that other studios took notice, scrambling to sign the next Marilyn Monroe. The bustier, the better—performing talent wasn't always a deciding factor.

Monroe may quickly have been typecast as a sexpot or a good-time gal, but she was no idiot. She was fully aware of the copy-cat phenomenon surrounding her. "These girls who try to be me, I guess the studios put them up to it, or they get the ideas themselves. But gee, they haven't got it. You can make a lot of gags about it like they haven't got the foreground or else they haven't the background."

Of course, none of the copycats had the same success as Monroe, and many faded into obscurity after B-movie stardom. Marilyn Monroe's real story is pretty hard to beat, but here are the stories of some of the more notable Marilyn knockoffs.

Jayne Mansfield

Probably the most successful blonde in the faux-Marilyn bunch, Jayne Mansfield was credited as not only being a buxom beauty but also as having actual acting chops. One thing she definitely had a knack for was PR, and undoubtedly, if she were still alive today, she would be no stranger to *Entertainment Tonight* or TMZ.com.

Born Vera Jayne Palmer, Mansfield kept the last name from her first marriage—to Paul Mansfield at age 16—because she liked the sound of it. Throughout her career, she claimed that her IQ was an impressive 163, but that was hardly a selling point—she was more famous for being the first big-name actress to appear nude on the silver screen. Obviously comfortable with her body, Mansfield had more than one public "wardrobe malfunction." Those, along with her much-publicized love life, led to an amazing 2,500 photographs in newspapers during a few months in 1956 and 1957.

Of her three marriages, her most famous was to Mr. Universe 1955, Mickey Hargitay. The couple enjoyed sharing the spotlight and making babies—they had three children, including daughter Mariska, star of the popular TV show *Law and Order: Special Victims Unit*.

Press came easy to Mansfield, but movie roles did not. She found much success working the nightclub circuit, making $35,000 a week at her peak. En route to one gig, however, Mansfield, her manager (and lover), and the three Hargitay kids were in a terrible accident. Their car slammed into the back of a semitrailer, peeling the top off and instantly killing the adults in the front seat. The children survived with little physical harm, and Mansfield again made headlines, as pictures of the gruesome crash scene made their way into newspapers around the country.

Mamie Van Doren

Along with Monroe and Mansfield, Mamie Van Doren rounded out what was affectionately called the "Three Ms." What she lacked in fame and IQ, Van Doren made up in sheer sex appeal. Born Joan Lucille Olander, she seemed fully aware of her copycat status—her stage name, taken from the noted intellectual Van Doren family, was a stab at Mansfield's claimed IQ. She milked the role, signing a contract with Universal Studios to star in typecast roles as the thrill-seeking bad girl. And Van Doren didn't let something as trivial as a meaningful acting career stop her from having fun. She oozed sexuality; in the 1980s, a book detailing trysts with many Hollywood leading men brought her back into the spotlight.

Keeping up with the times and technology, Van Doren keeps her (admittedly, mostly geriatric) fans on the edge of their computer seats via her Web site, which features vintage and modern photos of the star and her blog. She's also got a MySpace page. One recent venture is Mamietage, a custom-blend red wine.

Sheree North

While considered a talented actress and an even more talented dancer, Sheree North's potential was never fully realized, as 20th Century Fox used her mostly to threaten Marilyn Monroe when she got out of line (although Monroe was hardly moved). North's biggest break came when Monroe turned down a part in *How to Be Very, Very Popular*. When the heyday of the blonde bombshell began to fade, North slipped into obscurity and resurfaced years later in numerous television roles on shows including *The Golden Girls* and *Magnum, P.I.* Her most famous modern gig, undoubtedly, was as Babs Kramer, Kramer's mother on *Seinfeld*. She revealed his first name, Cosmo, to fans. In 2005, she died of unspecified complications from surgery.

Diana Dors

Known as the "English Marilyn Monroe," Diana Dors was the curvaceous leading lady of the UK in the '50s and '60s. Despite being overshadowed by the living legend that was Monroe, Dors actually appeared in her first film in 1947, the same year Marilyn first flitted across the silver screen.

Born Diana Mary Fluck, Dors changed her surname to that of her maternal grandmother at the suggestion of her first director, who feared that Fluck would lend itself to crude suggestions. An early bloomer, she first appeared as a pinup at age 13. Dors signed her first film contract at 17 and later found herself in the limelight as the sexy siren in films such as *Yield to the Night* and *Lady Godiva Rides Again*.

As a rising star, she flitted from man to man until she married Dennis Hamilton in 1951. With a focus on PR, he helped propel her to stardom; he may have been the impetus behind her purchase of a Rolls-Royce, a prop that allegedly enabled her to raise her fee for appearing in a review from £25 to £40 a week. The couple was already separated when Hamilton died in 1959. Dors married twice more, to Richard Dawson and Alan Lake, who committed suicide months after Dors's 1984 death from cancer.

"Hollywood is a place where they'll pay you a thousand dollars for a kiss and fifty cents for your soul."

—Marilyn Monroe

"Many a small thing has been made large by the right kind of advertising."

—Mark Twain

Sound Secrets

Take a Hollywood movie scene: A leather-jacketed hero scuffles with a bad guy and then walks through the snow before driving into the night. Sounds good, right? But what you really heard was a Foley artist punching a roasted chicken with a rubber kitchen glove and squeezing two balloons together while walking in a sandbox filled with cornstarch.

✳   ✳   ✳   ✳

Things Are Not What They Seem

WHETHER YOU NOTICE it or not, the sounds of a movie can be as entertaining as the visual experience. But unbeknownst to many viewers, most sounds and special effects are not captured at the time of filming. Instead, they're either recorded in the studio by Foley artists or pulled from a library of prerecorded sound bites that are stored on computers until the sound is mixed for the movie.

The term "Foley artist" was used as early as 1927 when Al Jolson's movie *The Jazz Singer* became the first "talkie," or movie recorded with sound. In those days, recording the actors' dialogue superseded virtually all other sound or music recorded for the film. It wasn't until the early 1950s that producers discovered they could enhance the overall quality of the moviegoers' experience by adding specialized sounds that were purposely stripped away during filming in favor of spoken lines.

The profession's namesake, Jack Foley, was asked by his sound engineer to improve the quality of the audio tracks by introducing a series of "studio clips." Setting the industry standard, he discovered that in order to enhance the sound, three categories of sound were required, starting with "footsteps." Each actor executing a scene in a movie walks or runs with their own unique gait, on a variety of surfaces. By watching raw footage of the film, a Foley artist attempts to replicate and record the actor's pace and sound by walking on the most suitable surface.

The second sound category that must be captured is the "moves." Moves accompany footsteps and include the sounds of skirts swishing, pants rustling, or leather jackets squeaking. Finally, all of the other sounds required to make the experience more believable must be either pulled from thousands of computer-generated archives or made especially for the film.

The Life of a Foley Artist

Foley artists are natural-born scavengers. When they're not actively involved in producing sound effects for films and television, you'll often find them scrounging around garage sales and piles of trash looking for anything that will generate a particular sound. A fertile imagination is key: What may sound like a couple passionately kissing in a movie may actually be a Foley artist sucking on his or her own forearm.

When Foley artist Marko Costanzo began freelancing for C5, Inc., he needed to come up with a variety of new sounds to use on his projects. Since most clips weren't available, he invented the following ingenious additions to his audio library:

* For a two-minute sequence of a dragonfly in *Men in Black*, Costanzo clipped off the ends of the blades of a plastic fan and replaced them with duct tape. When the fan was turned on, he could control the quality of the resulting flapping sound by brushing his fingers against the duct-taped blades.

* For a knifing scene in *Goodfellas*, Costanzo tried stabbing raw chickens, beef, and pork roasts with the bones intact.

* To achieve the sound of walking on freshly fallen snow, he walked on sea salt covered with a thick layer of cornstarch.

The motion picture industry thrives on creating fantasies. From the moment that the actor steps onto the soundstage, nothing is what it seems. Without Foley artists, our movie-going experience would be a lackluster one.

A Lion in Your Lap

Hollywood embraced 3-D technology in the 1950s to counter a decline at the box office.

✳   ✳   ✳   ✳

IMAGERY IN 3-D existed as far back as the late 19th century, when stereoscopic photographs were popular parlor items. Hollywood dabbled with 3-D movies as early as the 1920s. However, 3-D is most frequently associated with the 1950s, when Hollywood embraced this process to counter a loss of revenue due to competition from television and a change in the makeup of the moviegoing audience. Studios were determined to give audiences spectacle and novelty—to offer something they couldn't get from television.

Studios exploited the 3-D technique by producing films that featured spears, rocks, animals, and human fists flying toward the audience. In 1953, during the publicity for *Bwana Devil*—the film that jump-started the 3-D craze—Gulu Productions promised viewers "A lion in your lap!" Unfortunately, audiences didn't necessarily want lions in their laps, and they grew weary of having projectiles tossed toward them. Exploitative rather than imaginative, the 3-D effects often got in the way of storytelling and character development.

The stereoscopic process of the 1950s used polarized lenses to create the 3-D effect, and audiences wore polarized eyepieces to experience the binocular vision. The glasses caused headaches and eye strain. Between these negative effects and the lackluster moviemaking, 3-D waned in popularity after 18 months.

Periodically, the film industry introduces an improved 3-D process, generally at a time when box office revenues are in decline. Yet 3-D is a filmmaking technology rather than a filmmaking technique; it interferes with standard filmmaking practices such as editing and setting, dooming it to novelty.

Hitchcock's *Rope:*
A Reel-to-Reel Murder

When filmmaker Alfred Hitchcock set out to adapt Patrick Hamilton's play Rope, *he provided audiences with such a carefully crafted movie that some filmgoers might not be able to perceive its genius. Sure,* Rope *stands as one of Hitchcock's least-successful theatrical releases, but it remains a technical triumph.*

✳ ✳ ✳ ✳

A Man with a Plan

ALFRED HITCHCOCK SET out to create a cinematic exper-ence that would allow viewers to feel as if they were watching Patrick Hamilton's original play, *Rope,* up on the silver screen. Since the play takes place in real time, viewers, like the theater audiences, traveled with the performers while they unraveled a murder mystery at a dinner party.

The story begins in a darkened apartment, with the gruesome strangulation of a young man, David, by two other young men, Brandon and Philip. The killers then prepare for a planned dinner party—setting up the buffet on a chest, which secretly holds David's lifeless body. The party begins; the guests include David's fiancée, her ex-boyfriend, David's father and aunt, and the boys' prep school teacher and mentor, Rupert Cadell (played in the movie by James Stewart).

Viewers discover that Brandon and Philip planned this murder—of one of their prep school friends, no less—as nothing more than an experiment in murder. Though many cite the infamous 1924 Leopold and Loeb murder case as having influenced the plot, screenwriter Arthur Laurents remarked in an interview that Hitchcock and the film crew "never discussed that it was based [on the case] ... of two rich boys in a Chicago school who decided to kill another boy" [in the spirit of adventure]. "They ignored it. I couldn't understand that."

A "Bewildering Technique"

Hitchcock wanted it to seem as if the camera were an invisible presence in the room. In doing so, he had to make several modifications to standard moviemaking. First, he wanted there to be no jarring edits or conspicuous camera jumps, but because reels of film at the time were only ten minutes long, each take had to be bookended by a zoom into a character's back.

Each take had to be absolutely perfect. The fluid camera movements were due to a specially built dolly—a remarkable feat, considering that the Technicolor movie cameras of the day were 1,000-pound machines that were not easily slipped through the set of a Manhattan penthouse. To this end, the set was equipped with movable walls. In order to coordinate the delicate dance of actors, sets, and characters, 15 days of rehearsals were required before filming started. Hitchcock even reported that Stewart "couldn't sleep nights because of the picture ... It was the bewildering technique that made him worry."

A Trick of Light

Another technical problem was that the story takes place at sunset. Since the back wall—seen in almost every shot—is a row of windows, the New York skyline had to reflect the subtle changes in light. This passage of time was accomplished, as the publicity material for the film put it, by a "magical ... cyclorama—an exact miniature reproduction of nearly 35 miles of New York skyline lighted by 6,000 incandescent bulbs and 200 neon signs." Even Hitch's tradition of slipping himself into the film's action proved a challenge. Hitchcock contemplated showing his profile on the neon sign of a building seen over the shoulders of two actors. But he scrapped the idea as too gimmicky. Later, Hitchcock added himself strolling outside the building during the opening credits.

Six Stars Who Turned Down Memorable Roles

It seems that the actors cast in our favorite movies are perfect for the part, but they're often not the director's first choice. Most celebs have turned down more roles than they've taken, some with regrets but many with thanks to their lucky stars.

✳ ✳ ✳ ✳

1. **Brad Pitt:** Brad Pitt has had roles in many films including *Troy* (2004), *Legends of the Fall* (1994), and *Thelma & Louise* (1991). But he turned down a role in *Apollo 13* (1995) to make the movie *Se7en* (1995), which won an MTV Movie Award for Best Movie, beating out *Apollo 13*. But *Apollo 13* received nine Academy Award nominations and won two Oscars, leaving *Se7en* in the dust.

2. **Mel Gibson:** Mel Gibson has had a blockbuster career as an actor, starring in both the *Mad Max* and *Lethal Weapon* series, and as a director, winning an Academy Award for *Braveheart* (1995), in which he also starred. Gibson turned down the lead role in *The Terminator* (1984) which went to Arnold Schwarzenegger. Gibson was also offered the lead in the first *Batman* movie (1989) (which went to Michael Keaton), but he was committed to *Lethal Weapon 2* (1989). Later, he turned down the part of villain Two-Face in *Batman Forever* (1995), which went to Tommy Lee Jones.

3. **Sean Connery:** A star with a career as long as Sean Connery's is bound to make a few bad decisions. The good ones include *Indiana Jones and the Last Crusade* (1989), *The Hunt for Red October* (1990), seven James Bond movies, and his Academy Award–winning role in *The Untouchables* (1987). But one questionable decision was turning down the 007 role in *Live and Let Die* (1973), which became a great career move for Roger Moore. Connery later turned

down the role of Gandalf in the *Lord of the Rings* trilogy, which went to Ian McKellen, and the role of Morpheus in *The Matrix* films, which went to Laurence Fishburne—two decisions that he admitted regretting.

4. **Al Pacino:** Al Pacino rose to fame playing Michael Corleone in *The Godfather* movies and has since starred in many great movies, including *Scarface* (1983), *Donnie Brasco* (1997), and *Scent of a Woman* (1992), for which he won an Oscar. But can you imagine Big Al as Han Solo in *Star Wars* (1977) instead of Harrison Ford? Pacino also turned down the lead role in *Close Encounters of the Third Kind* (1977), which instead went to Richard Dreyfuss. Pacino turned down starring roles in *Midnight Cowboy* (1969), *Marathon Man* (1976), and *Kramer vs. Kramer* (1979), all of which went to Dustin Hoffman.

5. **Rock Hudson:** Rock Hudson, a favorite leading man of the 1950s and 1960s, starred in films such as *Come September* (1961), *Send Me No Flowers* (1964), and *Pillow Talk* (1959), the first of several films that costarred Doris Day. He signed on to play the lead in *Ben Hur* (1959), but when contract negotiations broke down, the part went to Charlton Heston instead, an outcome that would ultimately be Hudson's only career regret.

6. **Will Smith:** Smith began his showbiz career as half of the hip-hop duo DJ Jazzy Jeff & the Fresh Prince, who won the first ever Grammy for Rap in 1988. Smith was nearly bankrupt by 1990, when he was hired to star in the sitcom *The Fresh Prince of Bel-Air*, which became a huge success. His movies include *Independence Day* (1996), *Men in Black* (1997), and *Ali* (2001). He was also offered the lead role in *The Matrix* (1999). Despite the film's success, Smith later said that he didn't regret turning down the role because Keanu Reeves "was brilliant as Neo." He also passed on *Men in Black*, but his wife convinced him to reconsider.

Artists United! The History of United Artists Corporation

It was a curious quartet of Hollywood superstars: One was a swashbuckling leading man, another was known as "America's Sweetheart," a third called himself the "Little Tramp," and the fourth was considered the father of epic filmmaking. Together, they formed the first production company run by creative talent rather than by studio moneymakers.

✳ ✳ ✳ ✳

Bucking the System

HOLLYWOOD STARS Douglas Fairbanks, Mary Pickford, Charlie Chaplin, and William S. Hart did their part for the World War I effort by traveling the country and selling Liberty Bonds. They also discussed how much they disliked studio executives ruling their lives. Even though they were big stars, the four felt they were slaves to the decisions of others.

Mary Pickford

Douglas Fairbanks

Charlie Chaplin

D. W. Griffith

The idea of forming their own distribution company developed, and in 1919, they founded United Artists. Although Hart declined to join, groundbreaking director D. W. Griffith took his place. The team's ambitious plan was to release five top-quality films every year. These pioneers were unique in Hollywood: They had no actual shooting studio, nor did they maintain any performers under contract.

Fairbanks and Pickford: United Artists, Indeed

Douglas Fairbanks was a successful star in romantic comedies when he met the diminutive Mary Pickford at a party in 1916. At age 24, she had already starred in nearly 200 films. Although married to others, the couple began an affair that eventually culminated in their marriage in 1920. Fairbanks and Pickford separated in 1933 and divorced three years later.

Charlie Chaplin: Genius at Work

The derbied comic came to Hollywood in 1913, having established himself at Chicago's Essanay Film Studios. He had near-complete creative control in making his films, per the terms of a contract with Mutual Films worth nearly $700,000 per year, but he still sought more independence. His greatest silent comedies, including *The Gold Rush*, were made for United Artists.

D. W. Griffith: Master Storyteller

David Wark Griffith began making short films in 1908—and within five years, he had directed more than 450! This laid the foundation for his first masterpiece in 1915, *Birth of a Nation*. At more than three hours, the film set a new standard for feature films. United Artists produced his biggest films including *Way Down East* and *Orphans of the Storm*.

Coming Together

The first years were difficult, as United Artists' plan to produce five films a year was overambitious and resulted in low-quality product. Producer Joseph Schenck was tapped to run United Artists in 1924, and he brought top-notch stars with him, including his wife, Norma Talmadge, and comedian Buster Keaton. Soon, Schenck was able to attract Rudolph Valentino and John Barrymore as well. He also started a separate company to build movie theaters to show United Artists films.

Falling Apart

By the 1930s, United Artists had established itself as a major player in Hollywood. But internal dissension and a shortage of good films resulted in the loss of an amazing $65,000 per week for the corporation by the end of the 1940s. Two enterprising attorneys salvaged the fading film company in the 1950s, leading to banner decades in the '60s and '70s with fan favorites such as the James Bond and Rocky series.

Landmark Movie Locations

Lots of people plan trips to visit the sites where their favorite movies were shot. But sometimes the "location" is computer generated, or it's just a movie set that's on two different continents.

✳ ✳ ✳ ✳

***The Godfather* (1972):** The Corleone mansion where Connie's wedding is held isn't on plush Long Island, New York, but rather on blue-collar Staten Island.

***Jaws* (1975):** The beach on fictitious Amity Island where sunbathers and waders get a scare is actually Joseph A. Sylvia State Beach on Martha's Vineyard in Massachusetts.

***Star Wars* (1977):** Several desert locales on Luke Skywalker's home planet of Tattoine are in Death Valley National Park, California. Several other Tattoine locations—including Luke's home—are in Tunisia.

***Pulp Fiction* (1994):** The spot where Vince and Jules eat Big Kahuna burgers before their morning hit is on Van Ness Avenue, north of Hollywood Boulevard, in Los Angeles.

***Fargo* (1996):** As depicted in the movie, the Coen brothers shot mainly in and around Brainerd, Minnesota, but a particularly mild winter there forced them to film a number of scenes in Grand Forks, North Dakota.

***North by Northwest* (1959):** One of Alfred Hitchcock's crowning directorial achievements, *North by Northwest* was shot largely on locations scattered across the United States. At the beginning of the film, Cary Grant's character is abducted from the Plaza Hotel in New York City. Later, he is attacked by a crop duster in a field in Wasco, California.

***Thelma and Louise* (1991):** The climactic car-over-the-cliff scene in this Ridley Scott film was shot at the dramatic Shafer

Overlook at Gooseneck State Park in southeastern Utah. The movie's plot begins in Arkansas, but Southern California fills in for the authentic South in the film.

***Dead Poets Society* (1989):** Welton Academy is actually St. Andrew's School in Middletown, Delaware. The Dead Poets Society meets in Wolf Cave, also in Delaware, though the cave scenes were shot in a faux cavern in a nearby warehouse.

***Taxi Driver* (1976):** Martin Scorsese's misanthropic classic was shot on location in New York City. Unhinged cabbie Travis Bickle works for a taxi company at 57th Street and 11th Avenue in Manhattan.

***Planet of the Apes* (1968):** Although most locations on the ape-controlled planet are near the Grand Canyon in northern Arizona, the seashore where Charlton Heston's character realizes he's been on Earth all along is actually Westward Beach in Malibu, California.

***Raiders of the Lost Ark* (1981):** The story for Steven Spielberg's reinvention of the pulp serial opens in what appears to be a South American jungle, but its scenes were shot in and around the Huleia River in Kauai, Hawaii.

***The Shining* (1980):** Though author Stephen King's Overlook Hotel was inspired by the Stanley Park Hotel in Estes Park, Colorado, Stanley Kubrick's film adaptation opens with exterior images of the Timberline Lodge atop Mount Hood in Oregon. Interiors were shot in a studio in England but drew upon the Ahwanee Hotel in Yosemite National Park, California.

***Forrest Gump* (1994):** The bus-stop bench where Forrest tells commuters his stories was in Chippewa Square in Savannah, Georgia. However, the bench was installed for the movie's production and removed afterward.

***Frankenstein* (1931):** The classic monster movie was shot almost entirely on the Universal Studios lot in Hollywood.

A notable exception is the scene that was cut from the original version in which Frankenstein's monster throws the little girl into the lake: That's Sherwood Lake in Sherwood Forest, northwest of Los Angeles.

***Do the Right Thing* (1989):** In Spike Lee's groundbreaking film, Sal's Famous Pizzeria is on Stuyvesant Street between Quincy and Lexington in Brooklyn, New York.

***Butch Cassidy and the Sundance Kid* (1969):** The scene in which Butch and Sundance escape their pursuers by jumping off a cliff into the rapids far below was shot at Trimble Bridge over the Animas River, near Durango, Colorado. However, the leap was not as death-defying as depicted: Robert Redford and Paul Newman's fall was cut short by a platform a mere six feet below the bridge itself.

***Apocalypse Now* (1979):** Francis Ford Coppola shot his war epic in the Philippines instead of Vietnam. The Philippine government allowed him to use its military helicopters, only to divert them to fight insurgents several times during the shoot.

***The Matrix* (1999):** The Wachowski brothers, the minds behind *The Matrix*, set this science-fiction classic in their hometown of Chicago, but the futuristic metropolis was actually filmed halfway across the world in Sydney, Australia.

***Gladiator* (2000):** Russell Crowe's character is sold into slavery in a scene shot in Aït Ben Haddou, a village in Morocco. Before Gladiator, the town had starring roles in other Hollywood movies, including *Lawrence of Arabia* and *Jewel of the Nile*.

***Good Will Hunting* (1997):** In the film that won Matt Damon and Ben Affleck Oscars for Best Original Screenplay, Toronto replaced Boston for much of the shoot. Damon's character, Will Hunting, works as a janitor at MIT, but most of the classroom interiors were shot on the campus of the University of Toronto.

Big Screen Blunders

When filmmakers set out to make "movie magic," these obvious errors probably aren't what they meant.

✳   ✳   ✳   ✳

✳ One of the most popular movie mistakes occurred when a stormtrooper in *Star Wars: A New Hope* hit his head on a too-short door while walking into the Death Star's control room. The digitally remastered DVDs even highlighted this goof by adding a "thunk" sound.

✳ In Rodgers and Hammerstein's *The King and I*, Yul Brenner's song about not being certain is consistent, but his wardrobe isn't. Pay attention to his earring: It disappears and reappears between shots.

✳ In *Raiders of the Lost Ark*, Harrison Ford faces off against a sword-wielding enemy in a busy marketplace. While the swordsman performs some showy maneuvers, Ford just raises his gun and shoots the man. Originally, Ford was supposed to snatch the guy's sword with his trademark whip, but he just couldn't perform the maneuver. Frustrated after many tries, he ad-libbed the shooting, and director Steven Spielberg liked it so much he used it.

✳ The *Star Wars* series seems to have more than its fair share of famous goofs. In the final Luke-versus-Vader battle sequence of *The Empire Strikes Back*, Luke kicks the Sith lord off a ledge in a carbonite chamber, then jumps down after him. Just before the scene cuts, Luke's head reappears as the actor bounces back up from the trampoline he landed on.

✳ In *The Wizard of Oz*, when the wicked witch confronts Dorothy in the apple orchard, you can clearly see a few ostriches lounging around in the background. Apparently, they had wandered away from the set of a nature film being shot next door.

* Movie vehicles seem to have a mystical ability to instantly repair themselves. In *Twister*, a tornado knocks the tailgate off Bill Paxton's pickup truck, but it's right back on in subsequent scenes. The yellow Porsche in *Commando* also seems to have an instant-fix function—its side gets completely trashed at one point, but as soon as Arnold Schwarzenegger hops in and drives off, it's pristine and shiny again.

* Other objects apparently have quick-fix skills too. When Mary Jane is being mugged in *Spider-Man*, Spidey tosses two bad guys through the windows behind her. The camera pans away for a moment, and when it pans back, the windows are magically repaired.

* Blame it on a Matrix glitch? When Agent Smith seals Neo's mouth shut, Neo jumps up and walks away while trying to get it open. However, the reflection in Smith's glasses shows Neo still sitting calmly in his chair. A later glitch involves Trinity and Neo killing a bunch of soldiers on a roof while rescuing Morpheus, but moments later the bodies are gone.

* Where did that come from? When the killer shark in *Jaws* gets into the pond, the man it attacks is barefoot when he is knocked from his boat. However, when we see his severed leg sink to the bottom of the pond, it's sporting a shoe.

* James Bond always has the best toys, including what appears to be a color-changing mask. During a diving scene in *Thunderball*, 007 rips a black mask off another diver's face, but when he puts it on himself, it's suddenly bright blue.

* In another Bond movie, *Diamonds Are Forever*, tires seem to spontaneously appear out of sand dunes. Bond's car rolls during a chase, and even though all four tires are clearly still on the car, a loose tire rolls through the foreground.

A Sign of the Times

The famed Hollywood sign has had its ups and downs.

*　*　*　*

THE MASSIVE HOLLYWOOD sign that overlooks America's movie-making mecca is one of the most famous landmarks in California. It has been featured in countless movies, television shows, and books and is instantly recognizable the world over. Like the countless aspiring movie stars who arrive in Hollywood each day, the sign demands to be seen. Perched atop the Hollywood Hills, it stands four stories high, with each letter measuring 30 feet across. And yet, most people are unaware of its origin—not to mention its intriguing history.

Hooray for Hollywood!

It was a unique combination of show business and real estate development that led to the sign's creation in 1923. Los Angeles was undergoing tremendous expansion, and the region around the Hollywood Hills was ripe for growth. *Los Angeles Times* publisher Harry Chandler saw opportunity there and joined forces with film producer Mack Sennett, who oversaw the investment company that sought to develop the region.

To promote the area, Chandler erected a huge sign in the Hollywood Hills reading "Hollywoodland." It was illuminated with 4,000 lightbulbs, and a cabin was erected nearby to house a maintenance man whose sole job was to change the bulbs.

A Tragic Turn

The sign shone down from the hills without incident until 1932, when its image was tarnished by scandal. A young woman named Peg Entwistle had come to Hollywood in the late 1920s hoping to become a movie star. A stage actress in New York, Entwistle believed motion pictures would be her key to fame, but things didn't work out as she had planned.

Though she managed to land some minor roles in a handful of movies, stardom eluded Entwistle. One day, she made her way up the hills to the Hollywoodland sign, found a maintenance ladder by the letter *H*, and climbed to the top. Then, with the city that had shattered her dreams laid out before her in the distance, she stepped off and plunged to her death.

Entwistle's suicide wasn't the only incident to take the shine off the Hollywoodland sign. The stock market crash of 1929 and the economic depression that followed took a heavy toll on the region's housing market. By the early 1940s, the developers were no longer able to pay for the sign's routine maintenance, so they sold it, along with the land it was on, to the city in 1944.

The Hollywoodland sign stood ignored and unattended until 1949, when a heavy wind knocked down the *H*. The Hollywood Chamber of Commerce, realizing the sign's promotional value, offered to remove the last four letters and restore the sign to its former glory.

But regular maintenance continued to prove difficult, and the sign eventually fell back into disrepair. By the late 1970s, it had become a termite-infested eyesore; an *O* had fallen down the hill, and arsonists set fire to the bottom of an *L*. Hollywood city officials determined that the sign would have to be completely rebuilt at a cost of $250,000.

Can I Buy a Vowel?

Playboy Magazine publisher Hugh Hefner immediately stepped in to help. He organized a fund-raising party at the Playboy Mansion, offering would-be donors the chance to "adopt" the letters of the new sign for $27,500 each. The campaign was a huge success, and people lined up for the opportunity to help bring the famous landmark back to its former glory. Hefner adopted the *Y*, cowboy actor Gene Autry bought an *L*, and rock star Alice Cooper kicked in to save an *O*. The new sign was unveiled in November 1978.

Chapter 6

The Arts

Twelve Best-Selling Books Repeatedly Rejected by Publishers

Novelists spend years developing their craft, editing and reediting their work, agonizing over the smallest word, often to be rejected by publisher after publisher. The following famous books and authors were turned down by publishers at least 15 times before they became household names.

✳ ✳ ✳ ✳

1. *Auntie Mame* **by Patrick Dennis:** Based on his party-throwing, out-of-control aunt, Patrick Dennis's story defined in 1955 what Americans now know as "camp." However, before Vanguard Press picked it up, 15 other publishers rejected it. Within years, *Auntie Mame* would not only become a hit on Broadway, but a popular film as well. Dennis became a millionaire and, in 1956, was the first author in history to have three books simultaneously ranked on *The New York Times* best-seller list.

2. *Jonathan Livingston Seagull* **by Richard Bach:** Richard Bach has always said that this story, told from the point of view of a young seagull, wasn't written but channeled. When he sent out the story, Bach received 18 rejection letters. Nobody thought a story about a seagull that flew not for survival but for the joy of flying itself would have an audience. Boy, were they wrong! Macmillan Publishers

finally picked up *Jonathan Livingston Seagull* in 1972, and that year the book sold more than a million copies. A movie followed in 1973, with a sound track by Neil Diamond.

3. ***Chicken Soup for the Soul* by Jack Canfield and Mark Victor Hansen:** Within a month of submitting the first manuscript to publishing houses, the creative team behind this multimillion-dollar series got turned down 33 consecutive times. Publishers claimed that "anthologies don't sell" and the book was "too positive." Total number of rejections? 140. Then, in 1993, the president of Health Communications took a chance on the collection of poems, stories, and tidbits of encouragement. Today, the 65-title series has sold more than 80 million copies in 37 languages.

4. ***Kon-Tiki* by Thor Heyerdahl:** With a name like Thor, adventure on the high seas is sort of a given, isn't it? In 1947, Heyerdahl took a crew of six men on a 4,300-mile journey across the Pacific Ocean. But not on a cruise ship—their vessel was a reproduction of a prehistoric balsawood raft, and the only modern equipment they carried was a radio. Heyerdahl wrote the true story of his journey from Peru to Polynesia, but when he tried to get it published, he couldn't. One publisher asked him if anyone had drowned. When Heyerdahl said no, they rejected him on the grounds that the story wouldn't be very interesting. In 1953, after 20 rejections, *Kon-Tiki* finally found a publisher—and an audience. The book is now available in 66 languages.

5. ***The Peter Principle* by Laurence Peter:** In 1969, after 16 reported rejections, Canadian professor Laurence Peter's business book about bad management finally got a green light from Bantam Books. Within one year, the hardcover version of *The Peter Principle* was in its 15th reprint. Peter went on to write *The Peter Prescription, The Peter Plan,* and the unintentionally amusing *The Peter Pyramid: Will*

We Ever Get to the Point? None of Peter's follow-up books did as well as the original, but no one can deny the book's impact on business publishing.

6. *Dubliners* **by James Joyce:** It took 22 rejections before a publisher took a chance on a young James Joyce in 1914. They didn't take too big of a chance—only 1,250 copies of *Dubliners* were initially published. Joyce's popularity didn't hit right away; out of the 379 copies that sold in the first year, Joyce himself purchased 120 of them. Joyce would go on to be regarded as one of the most influential writers of the 20th century. *Dubliners*, a collection of short stories, is still among the most popular of Joyce's titles, which include *A Portrait of the Artist as a Young Man, Finnegans Wake*, and *Ulysses*.

7. *Lorna Doone* **by Richard Doddridge Blackmore:** You know you've done well when you've got a cookie named after your novel's heroine. Not only does Nabisco's Lorna Doone cookie remind us of Blackmore's classic, there are nearly a dozen big-screen or TV versions of the story, as well. This Devonshire-set romance of rivalry and revenge was turned down 18 times before being published in 1889. Today, Blackmore is considered one of the greatest British authors of the 19th century, though his popularity has waned over time.

8. *Zen and the Art of Motorcycle Maintenance* **by Robert Pirsig:** Pirsig's manuscript attempts to understand the true meaning of life. By the time it was finally published in 1974, the book had been turned down 121 times. The editor who finally published *Zen and the Art of Motorcycle Maintenance* said of Pirsig's book, "It forced me to decide what I was in publishing for." Indeed, *Zen* has given millions of readers an accessible, enjoyable book for seeking insight into their own lives.

9. **M*A*S*H by Richard Hooker:** Before the television series, there was the film. Before the film, there was the novel. Richard Hooker's unforgettable book about a medical unit serving in the Korean War was rejected by 21 publishers before eventually seeing the light of day. It remains a story of courage and friendship that connects with audiences around the world in times of war and peace.

10. **Carrie by Stephen King:** If it hadn't been for Stephen King's wife Tabitha, the iconic image of a young girl in a prom dress covered in pig's blood would not exist. King received 30 rejections for his story of a tormented girl with telekinetic powers, and then he threw it in the trash. Tabitha fished it out. King sent his story around again and, eventually, *Carrie* was published. The novel became a classic in the horror genre and has enjoyed film and TV adaptations as well. Sometimes all it takes is a little encouragement from someone who believes in you.

11. **Gone With the Wind by Margaret Mitchell:** The only book that Margaret Mitchell ever published, *Gone With the Wind* won her a Pulitzer Prize in 1937. The story of Scarlett O'Hara and Rhett Butler, set in the South during the Civil War, was rejected by 38 publishers before it was printed. The 1939 movie made of Mitchell's love story, which starred Clark Gable and Vivien Leigh, is the highest grossing Hollywood film of all time (adjusted for inflation).

12. **A Wrinkle in Time by Madeleine L'Engle:** The publishing house of Farrar, Straus and Giroux was smart enough to recognize the genius in L'Engle's tale for people of all ages. Published in 1962, the story was awarded the prestigious Newbery Medal the following year. *Wrinkle* remains one of the best-selling children's books of all time, and the story of precocious children and the magical world they discover was adapted for television in 2001. Still, L'Engle amassed 26 rejections before this success came her way.

More than You Ever Wanted to Know About Mimes

Mimes—you know them as the silent, white-faced, black-clad street performers who pretend to be trapped in boxes or walk against the wind. In case you want to know a little more...

✳ ✳ ✳ ✳

Greco-Roman Tradition

✳ "Pantomime" means "an imitator of nature"—from *Pan*, the Greek god of nature, and *mimos*, meaning "an imitator."

✳ The first record of pantomime performed as entertainment comes from ancient Greece, where mimes performed at religious festivals honoring Greek gods. As early as 581 B.C., Aristotle wrote of seeing mimes perform.

✳ Greek mime made its way to the stage: Actors performed panto-mimic scenes as "overtures" to the tragedies depicting the moral lesson of the play to follow.

✳ Greek settlers brought mime to Italy, where it flourished during the Roman Empire and spread throughout Europe as the empire expanded.

✳ Today, "pantomime" and "mime" are used interchangeably to refer to a mute performer, but the ancient Romans distinguished between the two: Pantomimes were tragic actors who performed in complete silence, while mimes were comedic and often used speech in their acts.

The Rebirth of European Mime

✳ The Roman Empire brought pantomime and mime to England around 52 B.C., but with the fall of the Empire in the fifth century and the progress of Christianity, both were banished as forms of paganism.

* Pantomime and mime weren't really gone, though: The sacred religious dramas of the Middle Ages were acted as "dumb shows" (no words were used), and historians believe that comedic mime was used by court jesters, who included humorous imitations in their acts.

* After the Middle Ages, mime resurged during the Renaissance and swept through Europe as part of the Italian theater called *Commedia dell'arte*, in which comedic characters performed in masks and incorporated mime, pantomime, music, and dance.

* The first silent mime appeared on the English stage in 1702, in John Weaver's *Tavern Bilkers* at the Drury Lane Theatre. It was really more of a "silent ballet" than silent acting.

* British actor John Rich is credited with adapting pantomime as an acting style for the English stage in 1717. His "Italian Mimic Scenes" combined elements of both *Commedia dell'arte* and John Weaver's ballet.

* Meanwhile, mime flourished as a silent art in 18th-century France, when Napoleon forbade the use of dialogue in stage performance for fear something slanderous might be said.

* The classic white-faced/black-dressed mime was introduced and popularized in the 19th-century French circus by Jean-Gaspard Deburau, who was deemed too clumsy to participate in his family's aerial and acrobatics act.

Mime in the 20th Century

* Mime started to fade in popularity at the beginning of the 1900s but was revitalized with the birth of silent films, in which stars such as Charlie Chaplin and Buster Keaton relied on elements of pantomime.

* In the 1920s, French performer Etienne Decroux declared mime an independent art form—different from the circus form of Deburau—and launched the era of modern mime.

* In 1952, French-trained American mime Paul Curtis founded the American Mime Theatre in New York.

* In 1957, Etienne Decroux traveled to New York to teach a workshop at the Actors Studio, which inspired him to open a mime school in the city.

* Decroux's most famous student, Marcel Marceau, expanded modern mime's influence in the 1960s by touring the United States and inviting mimes to train with him.

* While growing up, Marceau had been greatly influenced by Charlie Chaplin. In fact, Marceau's alter ego, "Bip" the clown, was inspired by Chaplin's "Little Tramp" character.

* The San Francisco Mime Troupe (SFMT), one of the most powerful political theaters in the United States, began as a silent mime company in 1959. The founder, Ronnie Davis, had performed with the American Mime Theatre.

* Future concert promoter Bill Graham was so moved by an SFMT performance in 1965 that he left his corporate job to manage the group. That led to his career as the legendary promoter of The Rolling Stones, the Grateful Dead, and Janis Joplin, among others, in the 1960s and 1970s.

* Robert Shields, a former student of Marceau's, developed the "street mime" form in the 1970s. Performing in San Francisco's Union Square, he sometimes received traffic citations, landed in jail, or was beaten up for imitating people!

* Shields and his wife, fellow mime Lorene Yarnell (they married in a mime wedding in Union Square), brought Marceau's mime technique to TV in the late 1970s with the Emmy-Award-winning show *Shields and Yarnell.*

* Though the popularity of mime in the United States declined after the 1970s, it still influences aspects of current culture. Urban street dances, including break dancing, incorporate aspects of mime.

Whose Way?

Frank Sinatra's signature number "My Way" is one of the most popular songs of all time. Paul Anka wrote the lyrics to the song with Sinatra specifically in mind, but he did not write the tune.

✳ ✳ ✳ ✳

THE FRENCH SONG *"Comme d'habitude,"* composed by Claude Francois and Jacques Rivaux is the basis for "My Way." Known as CloClo, Francois was one of the most successful pop stars in France during the 1960s and '70s.

In 1967, Rivaux, an aspiring songwriter, presented Francois with a ballad called "For Me." CloClo adjusted the melody, rewrote the lyrics, and released the song as *"Comme d'habitude,"* a requiem to fading love. Paul Anka heard CloClo's original version while on vacation in Paris and subsequently acquired the publishing rights. He made subtle changes to the melody and completely rewrote the lyrics, tailoring them for Sinatra and, unwittingly, for tone-deaf karaoke crooners the world over.

Sinatra included "My Way" on his 1969 album of the same name, and versions of the song have since been released by artists as diverse as Dorothy Squires, Sid Vicious, and Jay-Z. In the Philippines, the song has caused incidents of violence among drunken karaoke fans, and in Britain it has become the most popular contemporary song played at funerals.

CloClo became a ruthless business tycoon who owned a record label and an erotic magazine, among other successful ventures. Although his greatest love was singing, he never had a hit outside of the French-speaking world, a fact that tortured him until his death in 1978. One cool spring evening, while taking a bath, Francois decided to change a flickering lightbulb above the tub and was electrocuted. It was certainly a foolish act, and some speculated suicide. What's more likely is that CloClo was just doing things as he always did—his way.

John Kennedy Toole and *A Confederacy of Dunces*

When John Kennedy Toole committed suicide on March 26, 1969, he believed himself a failure. Only 31 years old, Toole was depressed and frustrated over his lack of success in the world of publishing. No one was interested in his novel, A Confederacy of Dunces. *Not yet, anyway.*

✳   ✳   ✳   ✳

WHO WANTED TO read about a fat glutton ranting and raving in the streets of New Orleans? That was the question Toole had set for himself by making such a figure the focus of his tour de force novel. He was afraid that he knew the answer, and it wasn't a good one. Despondent, Toole asphyxiated himself by running a garden hose from the exhaust pipe through the window of his car. But Toole's biggest fan, his mother, refused to give up on him, even after he'd given up on himself.

Gimme Shelter

Thelma Agnes Ducoing Toole had always coddled and spoiled her son. From the moment he was born on December 17, 1937, she wrapped him in a cocoon of Southern domesticity and Roman Catholicism. She kept John indoors, discouraged him from playing with other kids, and told everyone who would listen that he was a literary genius who would make it big. Indeed, her son showed a great deal of intellectual promise: At only 16 years old, he wrote a novel called *The Neon Bible*. It seems that Toole made no attempt at the time to find a publisher for this work, but the seeds of his ambition had been sown.

After graduating from Tulane University, he earned a master's degree at Columbia University and began preparing for his doctoral studies. His plans were rudely interrupted by the draft in 1961, however, and Toole spent two years in the U.S. Army, teaching English in Puerto Rico.

Upon leaving the army, Toole went to live with his parents in New Orleans, but he was no longer the sheltered child he'd once been. When not busy with his day job teaching at Dominican College, he socialized with the colorful characters who hung around the French Quarter. These musicians, strippers, drunks, and food vendors inspired him to write his second novel, *A Confederacy of Dunces*.

An Unforgettable Protagonist

The main character in *A Confederacy of Dunces* is Ignatius J. Reilly, a man in some ways like Toole. Ignatius is obese and gluttonous, yet his intellectual genius leads him to feel superior to nearly everyone around him. Still living with his mother at age 30, he finds a way to blame all of his weaknesses and screw-ups on the fickle finger of fate. He is happy—as happy as someone like Ignatius can be—to spend his days writing a never-ending treatise about the evils of modernity, emotionally abusing his mother, and masturbating to memories of his dead dog. His lethargic bliss comes to an end when his mother crashes their car and Ignatius is forced to find employment.

A Confederacy of Dunces is also filled with a cast of memorable supporting characters: Irene Reilly, Ignatius's wine-swigging, long-suffering mother; Myrna "The Minx" Minkoff, a bohemian Jewish woman who antagonistically corresponds with Ignatius from New York; Angelo Mancuso, the incompetent police officer who tries to arrest Ignatius for vagrancy; and Darlene, a dumb-but-sweet stripper at Night of Joy, a nightclub in the French Quarter. These characters wind their way through the novel's many subplots, which are all masterfully tied together at the end of the book.

The Long, Sad Road to Publication

In 1966, *A Confederacy of Dunces* was rejected by Simon & Schuster. It's impossible to know just how much effort Toole put into getting it published or how many publishers he queried, but it's certain that his lack of success led to a deepening depression, severe migraine problems, and a crippling dependence on alcohol. Toole may also have been conflicted about his sexuality; friends and relatives disagree over whether he was gay. Toole left a note when he committed suicide, but his mother destroyed it and was later, at various times, either evasive or misleading as to what it said.

After Toole's suicide in 1969, the handwritten *Confederacy* manuscript sat, collecting dust in his mother's home as she tried unsuccessfully to find a publisher. Finally, in 1976, she persuaded Walker Percy, an acclaimed author and a professor at Loyola University New Orleans, to read her son's work. Percy was not enthused by the idea, but he ultimately acquiesced if only to get Mrs. Toole off his back. Yet, he fell in love with the novel and his endorsement led to its publication by Louisiana State University Press. The first printing consisted of only 800 copies, but Thelma Toole had lived to see her son's fragile creation published. Shortly thereafter, to the surprise of virtually everyone, she also saw her son posthumously awarded the Pulitzer Prize for Fiction in 1981. She died three years later.

Is There a Curse on Confederacy?

A Confederacy of Dunces has sold more than 1.5 million copies in 18 languages, and first edition copies now sell for thousands of dollars. When it comes to being adapted for film, however, some think the novel is cursed. When *Confederacy* was still in galleys, someone at Louisiana State University Press sent it to Scott Kramer, a young executive at 20th Century Fox. Nearly three decades later, Kramer is still trying to get the picture made. Millions of dollars have been spent on development, and through the years such big names as John Belushi, Drew Barrymore, Will Ferrell, Stephen Fry, Richard Pryor, Harold Ramis, Scott Rudin, and Steven Soderbergh have been attached to it. Currently optioned by Paramount, the film is on hold once again.

Functional Art: The American Quilt

Whether you curl up for a nap under your grandmother's quilt or do a little quilting yourself, rest assured, your interest in this beloved bedding is steeped in tradition.

✳   ✳   ✳   ✳

The First Few Stitches: Quilting is the process of sewing together layers of fabric and filler. The bottom layer is called the "backing," the middle layer is the filling or "batting," and the top layer is called, well, the "top." The layers are sewn together to create cozy bedding or clothing.

People have been quilting—but not necessarily making quilted blankets—for a long time. An ivory carving from around 3600 B.C. depicts a king in a quilted cloak. Excavation of a Mongolian cave revealed a quilted linen carpet, and a pair of quilted slippers found near the Russia/China border was probably from the eighth or ninth century.

Patchwork, the process of piecing together scraps of fabric to make a larger whole, was widely practiced in Europe through the 1600s because it was economical. Old clothes and blankets were often recycled into something entirely new.

Early Amish Influence: The roots of the traditional quilt began to take hold in Europe and the United States in the 18th century. The oldest existing piece is the Saltonstall quilt. It was made in Massachusetts in 1704 and, though tattered, provides a window to the quilt-making styles of the era.

Amish settlers arrived in Pennsylvania in the early 1700s, and their quilts, known for jewel-tone fabrics and bold geometric patterns, surfaced in the 1800s. Our concept of patchwork quilts has been greatly influenced by the Amish.

An Industrial Revolution: By the end of the 18th century, the textile industry in England had been fully mechanized, and the

French were coming up with better, faster, and cleaner ways to dye fabric. Large quantities of colorfast, printed cottons became readily available, much to the delight of people everywhere.

By the time the War of Independence rolled around, the vast English textile industry was exporting thousands of tons of cotton to America. These fabrics made up the majority of the clothes and quilts of the era.

Social Hour: It's a misconception that people made quilts just for practical purposes. In fact, most quilters engaged in the hobby because they loved the craft—not because they needed a blanket. By 1820, sewing groups were widespread, allowing people to work together to sew quilts pulled across large frames. Many of the close-knit community sewing bees (or "sewing circles") of yesterday still function as quilting guilds and clubs today.

Patterns and Designs: Though some quilters specialize in whole-cloth quilts, most of the quilts made today are of the patchwork variety. Pieces of fabric are sewn together to make a single block; multiple blocks are then stitched to each other, creating the quilt top.

One of the most admired quilt styles comes from Hawaii. These quilts incorporate just two colors—usually red and white—and one large cutout design sewn directly onto the quilt top. The striking geometric shapes and intricate stitching have made Hawaiian quilts popular among quilters and quilt admirers for two centuries.

Modern-Day Quilts: Quilting in the United States experienced a revival in the 1970s, largely due to the country's 200th birthday. As part of the celebration, women and men alike took a renewed interest in quilting and in folk art and crafts in general.

The surge in the popularity of quilting turned this humble pastime into the $3.3-billion-a-year industry it is today. The current movement toward more simple, eco-friendly lifestyles will likely keep quilting alive for years to come.

Canada's Musical Greats

Anne Murray, Gordon Lightfoot, Avril Lavigne, Rush, and Celine Dion are Canadian. In fact, a number of popular acts over the years have either come from Canada or have a Canadian connection.

✳ ✳ ✳ ✳

Individual Artists

Paul Anka, born in Ottawa, Ontario: When he got started in music (1955), Canada was still flying the Red Ensign. You've heard this renowned songwriter's music in dozens of movies, and he wrote "My Way" for Frank Sinatra.

Maynard Ferguson, born in Verdun, Quebec. Ferguson was one of the most incredible trumpet players ever, performing with a charisma that made jazz fun even for non-jazz buffs. It's his horn you hear in the song "Gonna Fly Now" (from the movie *Rocky*, 1976).

Terry Jacks, born in Winnipeg, Manitoba. For a few years in the early 1970s, you heard this pop singer on the radio day and night, usually singing "Seasons in the Sun." He has since become a record producer in Vancouver.

Guy Lombardo, born in London, Ontario. This bandleader's rendition of "Auld Lang Syne" emblematizes New Year's Eve. If you take the word of Louis Armstrong, you know this: "The man gets the melody right."

Sarah McLachlan, from Halifax, Nova Scotia. The winner of three Grammys and eight Junos might be most famous for starting Lilith Fair, a popular all-female tour that featured both aspiring artists and established stars and ran from 1997 through 1999.

Joni Mitchell, born in Ft. MacLeod, Alberta. She started singing while laid up with polio as a child and became a big name in folk music during the 1960s. She's also an accomplished photographer and painter who designed many of her album covers.

Alanis Morissette, born in Ottawa. This rock artist was first popular in her native land before breaking into the U.S. market in 1995. She won an impressive number of awards in 1996 for her breakthrough album, *Jagged Little Pill.*

Neil Young, born in Toronto, Ontario, but considers himself a Manitoban. With his wife, Pegi, he founded the Bridge School, which assists emotionally and physically handicapped children.

Groups

April Wine, formed in Halifax in 1969. Despite a few hiatuses, they're still rocking, touring often in Canada and enjoying a devoted following.

Bachman Turner Overdrive, formed in Winnipeg in 1970. These rockers owned mid-1970s airplay but never glorified wild living—Randy Bachman was an observant member of the Church of Jesus Christ of Latter-day Saints.

Barenaked Ladies, formed in 1988 in Scarborough, Ontario. This major force in alternative rock has never had a woman in the band. They enjoyed years of success in Canada before achieving global fame.

Crash Test Dummies, formed in Winnipeg in 1989. This folk-rock band won wide acclaim through the 1990s. Their second album, *God Shuffled His Feet* (1993), earned them international praise.

Irish Rovers, an Irish-Canadian group, has been a heavy hitter in the Irish folk genre since 1963. Their lively stage banter makes their performances purely entertaining.

Propagandhi is another Winnipeg act (1986), this one in progressive punk. Their unabashed activism—including long onstage sociopolitical rants—hasn't hurt their popularity. Their album *Less Talk, More Rock* (1996) reflects their sense of humor about reactions to the rants.

The Eye of the Beholder: The Guggenheim Museum

*What happens when you need a distinctive,
uncompromising design for a groundbreaking museum?
In the 1940s, you called Frank Lloyd Wright.*

✳   ✳   ✳   ✳

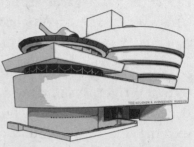

MODERN ART IS an acquired
taste. Not everyone is
comfortable with the free flow of
vibrant colors and abstract swirls
or the stark, featureless sculptures that dominate the genre.
But there's a lot more to abstract
art than just splattering paint on a canvas or carving chunks out
of stone. It's about personal style and vision—creating something that may not please everyone but is still unforgettable.

Setting the Stage

When the Guggenheim Foundation in New York City decided
that it needed an architectural maestro to create a new home
for its collection of modern masterpieces, only one man was
considered equal to the challenge: architect Frank Lloyd
Wright, whose unique vision had produced some of the most
distinctive buildings in the United States in the 20th century.
The result was his final triumph, the Solomon R. Guggenheim
Museum, a building with unusual lines that make it instantly
identifiable, even in New York's ever-changing landscape.

Solomon Guggenheim was an industrialist who made his fortune in copper mining. An avid art lover, he donated his vast art
collection to the foundation that bore his name before his death
in 1949. His collection included paintings by Vasily Kandinsky,
Pablo Picasso, and Georges Braque, who were noted for their
daring use of color and modern style. Together with the work

of sculptors including Constantin Brancusi, these works formed the heart of a multimillion-dollar collection that continued to grow as the years passed.

Two years after its 1937 incorporation, the Guggenheim Foundation opened the Museum of Non-Objective Painting on 54th Street to house the collection. But the trustees dreamed of constructing a building whose exterior and interior would reflect the avant-garde art better than such a traditional site. They commissioned Wright for the job in 1943, but more than a decade passed before the dream became a reality.

Wright Makes Himself Comfortable

While Wright was initially not pleased with the Guggenheim's decision to locate the new building in New York City, he traveled the area until he found what he considered to be the most appropriate location—the museum's site on Fifth Avenue between 88th and 89th streets. The architect drew on nearby Central Park as a source of inspiration to create what he felt was an appropriately organic design.

An Astonishing Work

Although Wright did not live to see the project finished, the Guggenheim fulfilled his plan to create a radical new setting for the artwork. When the museum opened in 1959, visitors were invited to start at the top of the building and follow a gently sloping curve downward. Gone were the boxlike rooms of an average museum. Instead, Wright's spiral of concrete, described by some as an inverted ziggurat or a nautilus shell, drew the crowds from one space to the next. The open rotunda provided a dazzling view of different paintings on several levels at once.

Some critics dismissed Wright's work as overpowering, but the architect was pleased with the design—he felt it was an extension of the artwork itself. Unfortunately, financial constraints did not allow the building to be built according to Wright's original concept. Recently, a tower containing four exhibit galleries was added that more accurately reflects Wright's plan.

Rock Around the Block

The sound of pop-rock music has always been influenced by certain regions of the country. Major music centers such as New York, Los Angeles, Philadelphia, San Francisco, Chicago, and Nashville have always been primary influences for the distinct sounds associated with the pop-rock culture. From time to time, however, savvy record producers and music promoters cast their eyes toward areas not normally associated with music influence.

✳   ✳   ✳   ✳

I T'S BEEN WELL established that rock music began with the Memphis sound—a combination of blues, country, and gospel first known as rockabilly, then rock 'n' roll, and finally simply as rock. It was Memphis that spawned the career of the King of Rock 'n' Roll and set the stage for the emergence and acceptance of just about every musical genre that followed, from R&B to grunge. Elvis popularized rock 'n' roll, and his importance in pop culture should never be underestimated. Still, it's important not to forget the designers of his sound—the people behind the scenes, such as Sam Phillips and Chips Moman, who revived the sagging career of the King. Almost every musical genre since the advent of rock is reflective of a certain regional style and sound.

Detroit, Michigan

The Motown sound, prevalent from 1960 to the mid-'70s, was a designer sound orchestrated by Detroit record shop owner Berry Gordy Jr., but executed by some of the most technically adept musicians, songwriters, and arrangers ever assembled. Motown was a unique blending of pop, R&B, and gospel-style call-and-response harmony supported by strings, brass, tambourines, and the innovative percussion sound of two drummers. The Motown sound produced the most consistent number of chart-topping records until the disco craze of the mid-'70s. (More than two-thirds of all Motown records produced during that period ended up on the top 50 best-seller charts.) The Motown sound faded from the pop scene when Gordy became interested in producing films and moved his operation west. In 1988, Gordy sold Motown to MCA for $61 million. Though the Motown sound has been frequently referred to as the Detroit sound, in reality there was another distinct style with that name that included performers the likes of Mitch Ryder, Bob Seger, the Amboy Dukes, and Grand Funk Railroad.

Asheville, North Carolina

When people think of Asheville, North Carolina, what usually comes to mind are the Great Smoky Mountains and the scenic Blue Ridge Parkway, but Asheville is also a major player in influencing certain pop-rock sounds. Once an economically depressed area, Asheville has risen from the ashes to earn the title "Soho of the South," after the trendy Manhattan art district, thanks to its lively, flashy cultural arts community. Asheville is a regional stronghold of live music venues, recording facilities, and exceptionally talented regional music groups and performers, including Warren Haynes (23rd on *Rolling Stone*'s list of the 100 Top Guitarists and a member of the Allman Brothers Band), Grammy-winner David Holt, Toubab Krewe, and Afromotive. The scene in Asheville is quite diverse, ranging from West African rock rhythms popular in the mid-'70s to moog-heavy techno to punk, indie-rock, classic Southern rock, and bluegrass. It's also one of the largest and friendliest gay and lesbian areas outside of San Francisco.

Athens, Georgia

A vibrant music scene has been thriving in Athens since the early 1900s, when the historic Morton Theatre was a haven for traveling musicians playing a new type of music called jazz. The more recent Athens style, a combination of new wave, pop-rock, and alternative rock, went national in the late '70s with the launching of the B-52s, whose quirky, sometimes spoken-word style made them a national favorite. In the '80s, R.E.M.

became one of the world's most popular rock bands. Athens, much like Asheville, has an active live music scene; two hot spots even made *Paste Magazine*'s list of America's 40 top live music venues.

Seattle, Washington

The name *grunge* quickly became associated with the music coming out of Seattle in the late '80s and early '90s. That was due to the "grungy" discordant and distorted guitar sounds, not to mention the unkempt appearance and thrift store duds of most band members. Grunge musicians scorned theatrics to concentrate instead on straight-ahead, high-energy music performances. Regional groups such as Nirvana, Soundgarden, Pearl Jam, and Alice in Chains—many of which recorded for local label Sub Pop—burst on the national scene making grunge the most popular alternative-rock sound in the country. By the mid-'90s, grunge was beginning to fade, and many of the groups were disbanding. The suicide of Nirvana's Kurt Cobain hastened the process, though Nirvana's albums continue to enjoy brisk sales today.

Minneapolis, Minnesota

Minneapolis's influence goes back to the early '60s when the first recording studio in the state, Kay Bank, started producing hit records such as "Surfin' Bird" by the Trashmen. The Minneapolis sound, per se, is a funky mix of disco and R&B, in the manner of its most prominent exponent, Prince, the architect of the Minneapolis sound. But what really makes the Twin Cities area unique is its diversity of musical genre, from the folk rock sounds of Bob Dylan and the Jayhawks to the hip-hop sounds of Atmosphere, with a side trip into post-punk with the Replacements, Hüsker Dü, and Soul Asylum. And there's been everything in between, including a fast-growing, live electronic dance music scene, a nationally renowned symphony orchestra, some of the nation's most talented and innovative studio musicians, and even *A Prairie Home Companion*.

William Shakespeare, Screenwriter

Does that big-screen storyline seem familiar?
You may have actually read it in a book.
The following movies are all based on plays
from the original storyteller himself, William Shakespeare.

✳   ✳   ✳   ✳

She's the Man (Twelfth Night): This version of Shakespeare's cross-dressing comedy stars Amanda Bynes as Viola.

Forbidden Planet (The Tempest): Many fans draw parallels between Shakespeare's classic story and this 1956 sci-fi flick, which features a stranded spaceship, a giant robot, and Oscar-nominated special effects.

O (Othello): Set in a high school, this adaptation is about a black basketball star in a mostly white world who is driven to murder his girlfriend Desi after being deceived by a jealous teammate.

Scotland, PA (MacBeth): This dark comedy transports the tragedy to 1975 as Joe and Pat McBeth scheme to take over the hamburger stand where they work.

My Own Private Idaho (Henry IV, Part 1): Directed by Gus Van Sant, this indie film about a pair of young male hustlers features sections of Shakespeare's script.

Ran (King Lear): A 1985 Japanese film with a $12 million budget, *Ran* follows the demise of Lord Hidetora Ichimonji and his three sons who are battling for power.

10 Things I Hate About You (The Taming of the Shrew): This late-'90s adaptation features a twisted plot in which teenage sisters Bianca and Kat face the tribulations of dating.

West Side Story (Romeo and Juliet): This musical retells the classic love story on the streets of New York City.

The Golden Age of New York Publishing

The 1940s, 1950s, and 1960s were the golden years of America's publishing industry, and New York was the vital center of the book world. The great New York houses— Random House, Simon & Schuster, Doubleday, and Alfred A. Knopf—rose like temples of art in Manhattan.

＊　＊　＊　＊

SHORTLY AFTER WORLD War II, American readers entered a wonderland of books and literature. Back from the battlefields and factories of the war streamed writers eager to make their mark. Robert Penn Warren earned the 1947 Pulitzer Prize for Literature for *All the King's Men*. Also in 1946, John Hersey published *Hiroshima*, and Dr. Benjamin Spock invaded the nursery with *Baby and Child Care*.

The Postwar Boom

Readers haunted libraries and bookstores to see what new pronouncements of taste came from the giant publishers. Hopeful writers, like pilgrims, flocked to New York to try to join their congregations. Radio was pedestrian, television was in its infancy, and movies tried too hard to appeal to everyone—but books brought art and the craft of storytelling into every home.

Fresh from combat in the Philippines came a 25-year-old soldier named Norman Mailer, who became the enfant terrible of the book world with the 1948 release of his novel *The Naked and the Dead*. Mailer was a boozer, brawler, and wild man; yet, he pioneered new forms of both fiction and nonfiction. In the profanity-shy world of American letters, he stayed true to the gritty world of GIs by coining the word "fug."

Other novels that sprung forth from the war experience included James A. Michener's Pulitzer Prize-winning *Tales of the South Pacific*, Irwin Shaw's *The Young Lions*, John Hersey's

The Wall, and Herman Wouk's *The Caine Mutiny*. On the non-fiction shelf were Dwight Eisenhower's *Crusade in Europe* and Samuel Eliot Morison's monumental 15-volume *United States Naval Operations in World War II*.

Changes in the 1950s

With the 1951 publication of J. D. Salinger's *The Catcher in the Rye* came the "Years of the Disaffected." Ray Bradbury's *The Martian Chronicles* and *Fahrenheit 451* heralded the birth of new forms of science fiction that replaced rockets and ray guns with troubling questions about human nature. The Beats—Jack Kerouac, Lawrence Ferlinghetti, Allen Ginsberg, William S. Burroughs—arrived, and in 1955 Mailer cofounded the newspaper *The Village Voice*.

By 1955, the United States had 8,420 public libraries, and the "Pyramids of Park Avenue" did their best to keep them stocked. Emerging literary titans, including Truman Capote, Gore Vidal, Grace Metalious, and Ayn Rand, were feted at lavish New York parties and had their exploits detailed in the newspapers. From Vidal's *A Visit to a Small Planet* to Neville Shute's chilling *On the Beach* (both 1957), the Cold War infected writers, and science fiction flew high with the voices of Isaac Asimov, Philip K. Dick, Harlan Ellison, and Kurt Vonnegut.

Readers Become Distracted

By 1960, disparate forces began to put the squeeze on Park Avenue publishing. Television developed into a force for change and drew people away from reading. A resurgence of European publishing snatched up new authors and sent their works directly to American bookstores. In Russia, the complete works of Tolstoy were released in 90 volumes, and Boris Pasternak's *Dr. Zhivago* took the West by storm. In New York and throughout the country, authors could—and did—appear on television. Mailer carried out an entertaining feud with Vidal on the talk shows. Mailer also made the news by stabbing (almost fatally) his then-wife at a drunken party in 1960.

Mailer was the poster child for unpredictable self-promotion. He had something to say about everything. He called poetry "a natural activity" and said that a poem is not written, but "a poem comes to one." Technology, on the other hand, was "insidious, debilitating, depressing." He never owned a type-writer, let alone a computer, and wrote 1,500 words a day with a pen. But in the 1960s, he pioneered a new form of nonfiction that combined events, autobiography, and commentary with his books *Presidential Papers, An American Dream, Why Are We in Vietnam?, Armies of the Night* (1969 Pulitzer Prize and National Book Award winner), and *Miami and the Siege of Chicago*. He won a second Pulitzer for *The Executioner's Song* and died in 2007, an unrepentant bad boy.

Southern Gothic novelist and journalist Capote, fresh from the success of *Breakfast at Tiffany's* (1958), created the nonfiction novel with 1966's *In Cold Blood*, a success of monumental pro-portions. He planned the party of the century, the Black-and-White Ball, at the Plaza Hotel. He observed his many friends, then wrote about their lives in the nonfiction *Answered Prayers*. When the first chapter appeared in *Esquire*, many close friends shut him off. Devastated, he went into a spiral induced by drugs and alcohol and died at age 59, forgetting his own advice: "Failure is the condiment that gives success its flavor."

During the Nixon years, the new writer was epitomized by Joan Didion. A journalist, essayist, and novelist with a B.A. in English from Berkeley, she wrote of life in 1960s California, a land of conspiracy theorists, paranoiacs, and sociopaths. By the time her nonfiction *Slouching Toward Bethlehem* came out in 1968, the great publishing houses were being quietly bought up by the same television networks and European publishers that had appeared at the beginning of the 1960s.

New York remains home to great publishers, editors, and writ-ers, but the Golden Years shone with a radiance that will likely never be seen again.

The Girls Are Writin' It for Themselves

Throughout history, the literary landscape has been dominated by male authors—but not because the female writers haven't been bringing their A-game. Read on for some fascinating "chick-lit" trivia.

✳   ✳   ✳   ✳

LITERARY ESSENTIALS SUCH AS *Uncle Tom's Cabin*, *Ethan Frome*, and *Frankenstein* are all classic novels with universal appeal that happen to be written by women. Still, the exposure female writers receive has often been paltry compared to the attention bestowed upon their male counterparts. Need an example? The Nobel Prize for Literature was first handed out in 1901, but so far, only 11 women have received the award.

✳ Barbara Cartland is the world's top-selling author, with more than 500 million copies of her books sold. Her career in romance novels began in 1923; when it ended with her death at age 98, it was estimated that she wrote 723 titles.

✳ *Gone With the Wind* by Margaret Mitchell (for which she won the 1937 Pulitzer Prize) still stands as one of the world's most popular books. Published in 1936 amid the Great Depression, *GWTW* sold more than a million copies in the first six months. More than 30 million copies of the novel have been sold worldwide, and it is estimated that 250,000 copies are still sold each year.

✳ *The Mouse Trap* by mystery novelist Agatha Christie is the longest-running play in history.

✳ Willa Cather, one of America's premier "frontier" authors, wrote such classics as *O Pioneers!* and *My Antonia*. Cather was openly attacked in the 1930s for her conservative politics and dodged rumors about her suspected homosexuality, as she often dressed in men's clothes and wore her hair short. Discouraged by negative criticism of her work, Cather became reclusive and burned most of her letters, destroying many of the details of her celebrated life.

* Harriet Beecher Stowe's *Uncle Tom's Cabin* was published March 20, 1852. It was the first American novel to sell one million copies.

* Louisa May Alcott wrote nonstop for two-and-a-half months. The result of her labor was *Little Women*, a novel based on her own experiences. Published September 30, 1868, *Little Women* immediately sold more than 2,000 copies.

* Lady Murasaki Shikibu, a Japanese noblewoman who was born in A.D. 970 and died in 1031, wrote the earliest novel on record, *The Tale of Genji*.

* Famous for her prolific prose including the book *I Know Why the Caged Bird Sings*, Maya Angelou is also a poet, playwright, editor, actress, director, and teacher. President Bill Clinton commissioned her to write a poem for his 1993 inauguration. The poem, "On the Pulse of Morning," garnered as much attention for its content as for Angelou's reading at the inaugural ceremony.

* Jane Austen is one popular lady. In addition to being the author of classics such as *Emma* and *Sense and Sensibility* as well as her role as the patron saint of book clubs (or so it seems), Austen is the source for an amazing number of adaptations. In fact, it is estimated that more than 600 of her adaptations are being produced worldwide at any given time.

* Anna Katharine Green wrote the first American detective novel, *The Leavenworth Case*, in 1878.

* The three Brontë Sisters (Charlotte, Emily, and Anne) broke onto the literary scene with a book of poetry written under the pen names Currer, Ellis, and Acton Bell. The book sold only two copies. Still, Charlotte went on to write the megablockbuster *Jane Eyre*, Emily penned *Wuthering Heights*, and Anne churned out critically acclaimed but slightly less popular works such as *Agnes Grey* before her untimely death at age 29.

* Erma Bombeck, the comedy writer and newspaper columnist who wrote of the joyful (and not-so-joyful) work of the typical American housewife, earned between $500,000 to $1 million a year at the height of her success. Still, Ohio-born Bombeck didn't hire a maid to clean, grocery shop, or cook dinner. "If I didn't do my own housework, then I have no business writing about it," she said. "I spend 90 percent of my time living scripts and 10 percent writing them."

* Virginia Woolf wrote all her books standing at her desk.

* In 1901, poet and avant-garde artist Gertrude Stein dropped out of medical school at Johns Hopkins University. She said it was "boring" and decided to move to Europe. Known for her wit and inventive, often circuitous style of writing, Stein quickly became an integral figure in the hotbed of artistic activity that occurred in Paris in the early years of the 20th century. Some of her friends and colleagues included Spanish artist Pablo Picasso, French artist Henri Matisse, and American writers Ernest Hemingway and F. Scott Fitzgerald. Despite criticism regarding her (sometimes confusing) work, Stein refused to back down. "It is always a mistake to be plain-spoken," she said.

* Emily Dickinson never married, and after age 30, was a bona fide hermit. Her preference for seclusion surely contributed to her work output: She penned more than 1,700 poems. Only ten of these were published in her lifetime—all without her permission.

The Music of Metal

The roots of heavy metal music are based in the hard rock sounds developed in the late 1960s and early 1970s by bands such as The Who, Led Zeppelin, and Deep Purple. These bands created a guitar- and drum-heavy sound and layered it with distortion behind a lead male vocalist. Eventually, metal itself split into some of these genres.

✳ ✳ ✳ ✳

Thrash Metal

Notable Purveyors: Overkill, Megadeath, Metallica

This genre features lightning-fast tempos, complex guitar riffs, and a style known as "shredding," in which the guitarist shows off his or her technical skills by playing intricate compositions really fast. Black Sabbath and Judas Priest are a couple of the bands credited with influencing thrash metal. Punk music from the 1970s also influenced thrash, because it usually featured the same quick rhythms and heavy guitar sound.

Goth Metal

Notable Purveyors: Candlemaas, Cathedral, Type O Negative

Sad, despondent tempos and melodies and a generally gloomy mood provide the soundscape of goth metal and its unholy brother, doom metal. Like most metal-offshoot genres, goth metal appeared in the 1980s. Legendary metal group Black Sabbath inspired the sound, and the hard-to-categorize group The Melvins are associated with the genre as well.

Death Metal

Notable Purveyors: Slayer, Possessed, Napalm Death

Marking the death metal genre are rapid percussion, basic chord progression from rhythm guitars, a ferocious vocal style, oft-changing time signatures, and lyrics about death, Satanism, and destruction. Death metal has its roots in thrash metal, with the majority of it coming out of Florida in the mid-1980s. A lot of death metal was also created in Sweden at the same time.

Power Metal

Notable Purveyors: Manowar, Queensrÿche

Power metal employs more melody and less-intense lyrics than most metal genres, while keeping the fast-paced, chord-heavy structural basis of metal music (don't be surprised if you hear an opera singer providing backup vocals). Power metal evolved as a response to the death metal and black metal music that came before it. Emerging mostly in Europe in the mid-1990s, power metal took the energy and drive of death metal and made it more appealing to the masses.

Christian Metal

Notable Purveyors: Stryper, Theocracy, Extol

For almost every metal genre that exists, there is a Christian counterpart, including Christian thrash metal and Christian death metal. Everything is the same except the lyrics, of course; rather than singing about Satan, Christian metal bands sing about Jesus. Metal musicians who also identified as Christians took what they liked about metal (chords, rhythm, and vocal style) and made it work with their ideology. Resurrection Band and Jerusalem are credited with being first on the scene in the 1970s, but it was Stryper who put Christian metal on the map with their platinum 1986 album *To Hell with the Devil.*

"Nu" Metal

Notable Purveyors: Marilyn Manson, Korn, Slipknot

Anything goes in "nu" or "alternative" metal: Hip-hop, punk, and funk sounds have all been incorporated. Metal's mainstream success in the 1980s was blasted away by grunge and "alternative" rock in the 1990s. Metal has been creeping back ever since, but it sounds different: Funkier bass lines, rap-inspired lyrical rhythms, and more complex production contribute to the mainstream metal of today.

The Wacky World of Car Art

Recycling isn't just for plastics. Say hello to car art.

✳ ✳ ✳ ✳

Carhenge

CRAFTED IN 1987, *Carhenge* stands as an exact proportional replica to the famed Stonehenge in England. Car for car to stone for stone, the measurements match up with precision. A total of 38 automobiles make up this tributary structure near Alliance, Nebraska. With some cars positioned upright, their trunks buried deep underground, and others settled into various contorted angles, this Stonehenge clone is complete with its coating of stone-gray paint.

Cadillac Ranch

Cadillac Ranch, located just off Route 66 in Amarillo, Texas, features a row of ten Golden Age Cadillacs buried in the ground with only their back halves sticking up. What can be seen of the cars is spray-painted in various shades of graffiti. The cars are periodically repainted by the sculpture's keepers, but visitor contributions of paint are strongly encouraged.

The Spindle

In 1989, a 40-foot spike was erected in a parking lot in Berwyn, Illinois, onto which eight cars were threaded in a towering vertical row. The *Spindle*, sometimes referred to as the car-kabob, was dismantled in May 2008 to make way for the construction of a new building, but it was reported that negotiations began almost immediately to rebuild it in a new location.

Cartopia

For those lovers of car art who want function with their form, there are also annual celebrations of art cars. One such event, *Cartopia*, held in Berwyn, Illinois, provides a showcase for the country's coolest art cars, complete with a parade. Hundreds of art cars come to town to show off the talents of their owners.

High Art in Low Places: The Work of Banksy

Armed with spray paint and stencils, a mysterious graffiti artist named Banksy is hard at work right now, offering incendiary street art to the people of the urban world.

✳ ✳ ✳ ✳

Graffiti Art and the Rise of Banksy

THE EARLY 1990s saw a boom in both hip-hop music and graffiti. In L.A., New York, and England especially, young men (and a few women) were expressing themselves through dance moves, record scratching, and spray-painting "tags," or embellished graffiti signatures. The first two modes of self-expression weren't illegal—but graffiti was.

City officials didn't see graffiti as a new art form: They felt it undermined authority and lowered property values. Others saw the artistry inherent in the work of taggers and graffiti artists, and felt the art represented people living in "the real world."

In Bristol, England (which has been referred to as the graffiti capital of the world), a rising star in the tagging scene emerged. His tag name was Banksy, and in 1998, he decided to organize some of the best taggers from the UK and America at an event called "Walls on Fire." Ideally, it was a meeting of the minds, a collaborative project, and a way to legitimize the art form to outsiders. The event was a huge success. Across the world, people increasingly saw graffiti artists as serious artists. As for Banksy, he gained a reputation for not only being a tremendously talented tagger but a voice for the community.

Found Art

The projects Banksy organized were really only side projects—his main work has always been the art. And the art definitely gives one pause, whether it ought to be on the wall of a government building or not.

Utilizing stencils and often incorporating slogans or pithy phrases, Banksy mostly paints children, adults, or animals engaged in activity—and always with a clever, unexpected twist. Some of the work is political, and some is just fun: A child might be fishing out of a bucket, but there's a syringe on the end of his line. A young girl hugs a bomb like she would hug a puppy. A pair of English policemen hold each other in a passionate embrace. A cat launches a caped rat into the air via a spoon catapult.

These scenes are depicted on concrete walls, under highway overpasses, high on city buildings, next to sewer grates, and everywhere in between. Fans of Bansky go on "treasure hunts" to find works by the artist. One gallery in Bristol does offer some Banksy works for sale, but since the artist paints murals on immovable surfaces and has chosen to remain totally off the media grid, the buying and selling of his art doesn't come easily. And that's just the way he likes it.

The Hunt for Banksy

The fact that no one truly knows Banksy's real identity drives theorists batty. Reporters who have spoken with Banksy usually do so via e-mail. Some speculators believe Banksy to be a male of about 30 years of age. One reporter claimed he met the artist and that he was scruffy and grimy and sported a silver tooth. Others believe that he's not really a single person but is a collaboration of artists. Still others think he could be the man who runs the gallery where some of Banksy's work is sold.

In mid-July 2008, the British tabloid *Mail on Sunday* reported that they had unmasked the elusive Banksy. According to the paper, they identified a man in a photograph taken four years prior as Robin Gunningham. A spokeswoman for Banksy commented to the BBC: "We get these calls all the time. I'll say what I always say: I never confirm or deny these stories."

Six Strings of Electricity

What if Chuck Berry's "Johnny B. Goode" hadn't been so good? Or if David Bowie's "Ziggy Stardust" actually played violin? What if Jimi Hendrix had to play an acoustic set at Woodstock? Certainly, life would have been different had it not been for the advent of the electric guitar.

❊　❊　❊　❊

Rock 'n' roll may never have evolved had it not been for early jazz guitarists in the 1930s who began to "mic" their hollow-bodied instruments to get a louder sound while playing in larger bands. Eventually, instead of merely placing a microphone next to the guitar, the musicians would place smaller microphones, called "pickups," within the guitar. And this is how traditional "acoustic" instruments got electrified.

The earliest electric guitars were designed by a variety of musical instrument manufacturers, musicians, and even electricians. Several major guitar makers that exist today were born of the same innovation. Adolph Rickenbacker and George Beauchamp helped devise the first Rickenbacker guitars, which were essentially hollow-bodied acoustic instruments.

One of the first solid guitars was a cast aluminum electric steel guitar nicknamed the "Frying Pan" or the "Pancake Guitar," but its sound was far from ideal. Another substance was needed to create a better sound, and thus, the solid wood guitar was born.

Jazz guitarist and musical innovator Les Paul successfully invented a solid-body electric guitar in the early 1940s, but Leo Fender can take credit for introducing the first commercially successful guitar in 1946. Originally known as the Broadcaster, the guitar became legendary as the Fender Telecaster. Les Paul's legend lives on in the Gibson Les Paul, a solid-body guitar designed by Ted McCarty but endorsed and used by Paul. Today, these are among the most popular guitars in rock music.

Eighteen Memorable Character Names from the Works of Charles Dickens

Born near London in 1812, Charles Dickens suffered many hardships throughout his life. Like many of the characters he would later create, Dickens stayed for a time in a workhouse, witnessed the death of several family members, and fell in and out of love a few times. All of this went into classic stories such as Oliver Twist, A Christmas Carol, *and* Great Expectations. *Dickens's characters typically had colorful names; the following list offers a sampling of these unusual and unique character names.*

✳   ✳   ✳   ✳

1. **Harold Skimpole (*Bleak House*):** This cheapskate claims he knows nothing about money management and uses that as an excuse to never pay for anything. Some claim Dickens modeled Skimpole after Leigh Hunt, another writer of the time, which, not surprisingly, caused a bit of animosity.

2. **Sloppy (*Our Mutual Friend*):** One of Dickens's many orphan characters, Sloppy lives with Betty Higden and is taken in by the Boffin family. The noble Sloppy later has a hand in exposing nasty Silas Wegg.

3. **Wopsle (*Great Expectations*):** Wopsle is a parish clerk at the start of this story, but chooses to become an actor and changes his name to Waldengarver.

4. **Polly Toodle (*Dombey and Son*):** Polly Toodle is Little Paul Dombey's nurse who gets fired after taking him to visit her dingy apartment in London's poorest area. Jolly and plump, Polly is a ray of hope in the face of poverty and hardship.

5. The Squeers (*Nicholas Nickleby*): Wackford Squeers is the patriarch of this conniving, weaselly pack. The Squeers run Dotheboys Hall, an orphanage for unwanted boys whom they mistreat horribly. Daughter Fanny, son Wackford Jr., and the missus are each more cruel than the last.

6. Luke Honeythunder (*The Mystery of Edwin Drood*): As with most of Dickens's characters, Luke Honeythunder's name fits him well. Described as boisterous and overbearing, this philanthropist is the guardian of Neville and Helena Landless.

7. Tulkinghorn (*Bleak House*): This unscrupulous lawyer to the Dedlock family learns of Lady Dedlock's secret past and tries to take advantage of it. It doesn't end well for him—he is eventually murdered by her maid.

8. Bumble (*Oliver Twist*): A petty officer in the workhouse where Oliver spends much of his time, Bumble symbolizes Dickens's contempt for the workhouse system.

9. Silas Wegg (*Our Mutual Friend*): This street vendor is a gold digger after the Boffin family fortune. He tries to swindle the family when he's hired to read to Mr. Boffin, but Sloppy later exposes Wegg's ulterior motives.

10. Dick Swiveller (*The Old Curiosity Shop*): Though the name sounds a little on the sinister side, this character is not a villain. Swiveller wants to marry the sweet and pretty Nell Trent but ends up with the Marchioness instead. He and the Marchioness expose the evil Brasses, Swiveller inherits money from his aunt, and the couple lives happily ever after.

11. Paul Sweedlepipe (*Martin Chuzzlewit*): An eccentric barber, landlord, and bird lover, this character later inspired *A Christmas Carol*. Themes of greed and false honor run through Martin Chuzzlewit and also appear in the tale of Ebenezer Scrooge, published the following year.

12. **Caroline "Caddy" Jellyby (*Bleak House*):** This sympathetic young woman is neglected by her mother, claiming, "I'm pen and ink to ma." Caddy ends up leaving home and marrying Prince Turveydrop.

13. **Smike (*Nicholas Nickleby*):** The title character in this story rescues Smike from the evil Squeers. Nicholas later learns Smike is his cousin. Unfortunately, this is discovered after Smike has died from the Squeers' cruelty.

14. **Mr. Sowerberry (*Oliver Twist*):** Oliver Twist runs away to London after being mistreated and abused by this ugly, cruel undertaker.

15. **Uriah Heep (*David Copperfield*):** Uriah Heep, the antagonist of this novel, is one of literature's most wicked villains. Scheming and hypocritical, he plans to ruin Copperfield's friend Agnes Wickfield but is ultimately undone by Mr. Micawber.

16. **Pumblechook (*Great Expectations*):** The great expectations of Pip, the main character and another Dickensian orphan, come from this rotund, loud-breathing guardian who takes Pip to wealthy and eccentric spinster Miss Havisham.

17. **John Podsnap (*Our Mutual Friend*):** Dickens coined the term podsnappery to describe middle-class pomp and complacency. John Podsnap embodied this undesirable trait. Apparently, he was modeled after Dickens's first biographer, John Forster.

18. **Lucretia Tox (*Dombey and Son*):** Described as tall, lean, and sad, Lucretia is friends with Mrs. Louisa Chick. Mrs. Chick has a brother named Paul. Lucretia is in love with Paul. Paul has a wife. Paul's wife dies. Lucretia hopes to marry Paul. Paul doesn't want Lucretia. Lucretia remains loyal, despite her broken heart. Classic Dickens.

Different Kinds of Funny

*With this helpful guide to humor, you'll never again
be left asking, "Wait, was that a joke?"*

✳ ✳ ✳ ✳

Absurdism

What it is: humor based on a belief that the universe is ridiculously unreasonable and meaningless. Contradictory sayings, one-liners, and paradoxes are all forms of absurdism.

Where you've seen it: Irish writer Oscar Wilde's famous absurdism: "Always forgive your enemies—nothing annoys them so much."

Caricature

What it is: an exaggerated portrayal of a person, often with distorted distinguishing features that might include mannerisms, speech patterns, styles of dress, or hairdo.

Where you've seen it: Comedians love to do caricatures of Hollywood personalities and politicians. Will Ferrell's caricature of George W. Bush on *Saturday Night Live* played up the president's malaprops and other verbal blunders.

Farce

What it is: comedy based on mockery, with broad exaggerations and stereotypes.

Where you've seen it: It's common in Mel Brooks's films, such as *Spaceballs* (a take on *Star Wars*), and the movie *Blades of Glory* (a mockery of competitive ice skating).

Hyperbole

What it is: conscious overstatement of facts for comedic effect.

Where you've seen it: It's often used in everyday speech, such as when we refer to someone as "older than dirt" or say, "this box weighs a ton." Any time we exaggerate to make something seem worse or better than it really is, we're using hyperbole.

Irony

What it is: an incongruity between cause and effect or between what you mean and what you say. It's similar to sarcasm and is typically cutting or biting.

Where you've seen it: Science-fiction writer Robert Heinlein summed up irony nicely when he said, "The supreme irony of life is that hardly anyone gets out of it alive."

Lampoon

What it is: to ridicule or mock someone or something.

Where you've seen it: Watch Chevy Chase's film *National Lampoon's Vacation*, which makes fun of the supposed "great family vacation," and NBC's hit show *30 Rock*, which pokes fun at producing a television show at a major network.

Malaprop

What it is: a slip of the tongue that involves the substitution of a word that sounds like the one intended but means something ridiculously different.

Where you've seen it: Recall when President George W. Bush spoke of finding "weapons of mass production," or when boxer Mike Tyson said, "I just might fade into Bolivian, you know what I mean?"

Parody

What it is: a literary or musical work mimicking the style of the original.

Where you've seen it: "Weird Al" Yankovic's renditions of popular rock songs, such as "Fat," a parody of Michael Jackson's "Bad." Comedy Central's *The Daily Show* parodies a news broadcast to satirize political and social trends and events.

Pun

What it is: a play on words, based either on different meanings of the same word or on similar meanings of different words.

Where you've seen it: Wannabe jokesters like to tell them just for the "pun" of it. And someone once said, "A pun is a short quip followed by a long groan."

Repartee

What it is: comedy based on one-upmanship, verbal sparring between two people who are typically trading clever insults.

Where you've seen it: The Algonquin Round Table, or "The Vicious Circle," was a group of writers, artists, and actors that included the likes of Dorothy Parker, Robert Benchley, and Alexander Woollcott. They were notorious for this.

Satire

What it is: humor with a point, usually exposing some kind of social or political issue for the purpose of reform.

Where you've seen it: Comedy Central's *The Colbert Report*. Stephen Colbert is the self-righteous host who ridicules the actions of politicians and other public figures by taking all of their beliefs and statements as gospel, revealing their hypocrisy.

Understatement

What it is: Also called "low exaggeration," understatement treats a topic as less important than it is.

Where you've seen it: British humor is often said to be understated, while American humor is not. Comedic legend Bob Newhart is a fine example, as well as the TV series *The Office*.

Wit

What it is: humor that depends on intellectual play.

Where you've seen it: Television gems *M*A*S*H* and *Sex and the City* got laughs from the quick-witted dialogue between its main characters.

Hooray for Bollywood

Since the mid-20th century, the Mumbai-based industry has made a "reel" mark on the world of film.

✳   ✳   ✳   ✳

IN AMERICAN CINEMA, it is usually only musicals—or comedies satirizing musicals—that feature characters breaking out in grand song and dance numbers. Not so in Bollywood. In fact, these musical montages are a standard element of popular films from India, no matter the subject or story line.

Today, the Mumbai-based, Hindi-language film industry is one of the largest producers of movies in the entire world. But when and how did Bollywood originate? The name "Bollywood" is semiofficial and comes from the combination of Bombay (the former name for Mumbai) and Hollywood. But unlike its American cousin, there is no Bollywood sign and no epicenter of studios. And while the name "Bollywood" is often used (incorrectly) to identify all Indian-made films, it actually describes just one very popular subset.

The roots of the Indian movie industry date to 1913 with the release of *Raja Harishchandra*, but it was the 1931 release of *Alam Ara* that took Bollywood filmmakers in a new direction with the advent of talkies. Prior to independence from Great Britain in 1947, India produced films centered on social issues, including the Indian independence movement. By the 1960s, the films were lavish romantic musicals and melodramas that incorporated the epic musical numbers still popular to this day.

While many films became grittier, more violent, and less lavish throughout the 1970s and 1980s, the familiar song-and-dance sequences remained. By the 1990s, romantic love stories were back in vogue. Several actors and actresses from this period became very famous in India, even surpassing some of Hollywood's brightest stars.

Dalí's Muse

What makes an artist create? Different artists have different responses, but in Salvador Dalí's case, the answer is very simple.

✳ ✳ ✳ ✳

A SURREALIST WITH A surreally long name, Salvador Domingo Felipe Jacinto Dalí y Domènech was born in 1904 in Figueres, Spain. He claimed that his given name, Salvador, indicated that he was "destined to rescue and save painting from the mediocre catastrophes of modern art." A versatile visionary, he also collaborated with other famous artists, including Man Ray, Alfred Hitchcock, Coco Chanel, Roy Disney, and Christian Dior.

Young Dalí Shows His Colors

Heavily influenced by art at an early age, Dalí attended the San Fernando Academy of Fine Arts, a private painting school in Madrid. He began to follow closely former Dadaist André Breton, who headed up the surrealist movement. When he was 22, Dalí was expelled from the San Fernando Academy for proclaiming that his teachers were idiots and that he was more qualified than those who examined him.

After his expulsion, Dalí traveled to Paris and met Pablo Picasso, whom he revered. Picasso had already heard good things about Dalí from his friend, Joan Miró, another artist who influenced Dalí's early works. Dalí showed his respect by telling Picasso, "I have come to see you before visiting the Louvre." Picasso's response: "You have done right, indeed."

After several successful one-man shows, Dalí joined the surrealist movement, quickly establishing himself as its principal figure. During his time in Paris, he collaborated with Spanish-born filmmaker Luis Buñuel on the surrealist movie *Un chien andalou* (*An Andalusian Dog*), further developing his leading role in the movement.

Enter the Muse

In 1929, Dalí met and became infatuated with a Russian immigrant ten years his senior, Helena Dmitrievna Diakonova, also known as Gala. At that time, she was married to surrealist poet Paul Éluard. It is reported that Dalí repeatedly tried to capture Gala's attention in a number of offbeat ways: He smeared himself with goat dung, waxed the hair from his armpits and colored them blue, wore flowers on his head. How could he go wrong? She responded by becoming his lover, wife, business manager, and muse for the rest of his life.

A Surrealist Clash

In 1931, Dalí painted one of his most famous works, *The Persistence of Memory*, whose soft or melting watches debunk the assumption that time is unchangeable. It is still noted as one of the world's best-known surrealist works. As World War II approached, however, politics brought Dalí into conflict with some of the other predominately Marxist surrealists. In 1934, he was forced out of the surrealist group during a "trial."

This didn't deter Dalí or Gala, who continued to create a buzz wherever they went. Dalí became an international sensation, and his antics were the stuff of legend. At the 1934 New York exhibition of his works and the social "Dalí Ball," the artist arrived wearing a brassiere enclosed in a glass case. During the London International Surrealist Exhibition, he delivered his lecture wearing a deep-sea diving suit.

Political Controversy

The 1936 outbreak of the Spanish Civil War caused upheaval throughout Spanish society, but it deeply affected the predominantly left-wing art scene. Although Dalí's lifelong friend surrealist poet Federico García Lorca was murdered by right-wing forces shortly after the civil war began, Dalí later broke with the majority of the nation's artists to ally himself with General Francisco Franco. He was among the few members of Spain's cultural elite who chose to stay in the new fascist state after the

Nationalist victory in 1939; others, including Pablo Picasso, chose exile over Franco's regime. Despite criticism of his political statements—which applauded Franco for bringing "clarity, truth and order" to Spain—Dalí continued to paint and followed his habit of flamboyant public appearances.

Classical Dalí

After World War II broke out, Dalí and Gala moved to the United States, where they lived for eight years. During these years, Dalí began inching away from surrealism into what is known as his classical period.

Behind his famous waxed moustache, Dalí was insecure and unhappy. Gala protected him. With her tough demeanor, she was the intermediary between Dalí and the rest of the world. Dalí thanked her by making her the model for his most sensual and beautiful paintings. Critics note that Dalí's depictions of Gala are perhaps some of the most affectionate and best-loved portrayals of a middle-aged woman in Western art.

In 1948, Dalí and Gala moved back to Europe, where he continued his work, this time focusing on science and religion. Additionally, he and Gala embarked on their largest project, the Dalí Theatre and Museum in his hometown. The museum was built on the ruins of the Figueres theater, destroyed in the Spanish Civil War. Dalí helped envision not only exhibits of his work, but also the reconstruction of the building, resulting in a surreal structure topped with a glittering geodesic dome.

The Persistence of Dalí

In 1982, Gala passed away, and in 1983, Dalí finished his last painting, *The Swallow's Tail*. After Gala's death, Dalí lost much of his vitality and died of heart failure in 1989. His body was interred in the Dalí Theatre and Museum. Dalí's legacy, like his life, has been one of controversy. Criticized in later years for his conservative politics, over-the-top shenanigans, and willingness to endorse almost any product, Dalí remains a recognizable force in the art world.

The National Film Board of Canada

In Canada, it's a cherished institution. In the United States, it's a name that's usually mentioned only during broadcasts of the Academy Awards. But either way, it can affect the movies we see.

✳   ✳   ✳   ✳

CANADIANS BELIEVE THAT the government should proudly support the arts. That's precisely the role of the National Film Board of Canada (NFB). Its mandate is "to produce and distribute audio-visual works which provoke discussion and debate on subjects of interest to Canadian audiences and foreign markets; which explore the creative potential of the audio-visual media; and which achieve recognition by Canadians and others for excellence, relevance, and innovation."

Early Canadian Films

Founded in 1918, the Canadian Government Motion Picture Bureau was the major Canadian film producer, but in 1938, the government invited noted British documentary filmmaker John Grierson to study Canadian production. The results of his report were included in the National Film Act of 1939, which established the National Film Board. Its initial thrust was to create propaganda films for World War II.

Getting Animated

When Norman McLaren joined the NFB in 1941, the board started to produce animated films. Working with American companies such as Disney, the NFB produced effective propaganda cartoons for the Allied war effort. McLaren, a pioneer in experimental animation, won an Oscar in 1952 for *Neighbours*, an antiwar cartoon short that popularized a new form of character movement known as pixilation. In 2006, the 65th anniversary of NFB animation was marked with the release of a DVD boxed set of restored classics in tribute to the pioneer: *Norman McLaren—The Master's Edition*.

Dogged by Controversy

McLaren's antiwar stance was only the beginning of a tradition of controversy for the NFB. In line with the NFB's independence, a 1950 revision of the Film Act removed any direct government interference into the board's operation. However, the government found other ways to stifle controversy: In 1996, the board lost one-third of its operating budget.

American conservatives have also had a long-standing beef with the NFB that began after a number of productions rankled their sensibilities. *If You Love This Planet* (1982), which won the Academy Award for Best Documentary (Short Subject), was labeled "political propaganda" in the United States.

But not all controversy was outside of Canada. Paul Cowan's *The Kid Who Couldn't Miss* (1982), a film that stripped away some of the mystique of Canadian World War I flying hero Billy Bishop, caused a firestorm of anger and calls to cut NFB funding. Originally released as a documentary (and currently listed as a docudrama), the film provoked an answering movie, H. Clifford Chadderton's *The Billy Bishop Controversy*, to counter bias that Chadderton felt Cowan had included in his film.

But the NFB continued to embrace controversy. *Abortion: Stories from North and South* (1984) and *Out: Stories of Lesbian and Gay Youth in Canada* (1994) drew fire from social critics.

Quality Wins the Day

NFB productions have been consistently recognized for their quality. Stuart Legg's 1941 *Churchill's Island* won the first-ever Best Documentary Academy Award. Eleven other NFB productions have won Oscars, including one in 2007 for *The Danish Poet*. In 1989, the NFB won an honorary Oscar in recognition of its 50th anniversary and excellent filmmaking. In fact, the NFB has received more than 5,000 film awards.

Riots at *Rite of Spring*

Ah, the ballet. The grace. The beauty. The fistfights?

✳ ✳ ✳ ✳

WHEN IGOR STRAVINSKY'S *Rite of Spring* premiered at the Théâtre des Champs-Élysées in Paris on May 29, 1913, spectators—so displeased with the discordant nature of the music, the experimental choreography, and the nontraditional costume of the cast—exploded into a full-blown riot.

Although Stravinsky was well-known for his diverse styling, the pre-Modernist audience apparently didn't have any hint of what was to come. Classical ballet, which most people were accustomed to, is tulle and temperance, not sexuality, barbarism, and bassoon. From the start, the audience in attendance at *Rite of Spring* was turned off by the innovations of all the major components: music, dance, story, and costume. The catcalls that erupted moments after the ballet began were a testament to their hatred of the whole darned thing!

What Part Did They Like?

The music, composed by Stravinsky, was riddled with a cacophony of new sounds and rhythms. Where typical scores felt light and even springlike themselves, the music in *Rite of Spring* was bumpy, angular, and full of haphazard staccatos.

Reflecting the music, the dance moves, choreographed by Vaslav Nijinsky, featured jerky twists and pelvic thrusts more indicative of Elvis than of a graceful ballet. The dancers' arms and legs flailed wildly in angles depicting the primitive movements of fertility rites in pagan Russia. Struck by the incongruity between this performance and ordinary ballet, the audience hissed so loudly that the performers couldn't hear one another. The story of *Rite of Spring* includes, in addition to the dance of fertility, an abduction, a virgin sacrifice, and paganism—an overload to the genteel sensibilities of the audience.

In the spirit of the story, the costumes reflected the tribal culture in which it was set. Thus, the dancers were adorned in heavy woolen smocks, decorated with geometrics, which created a furnacelike effect for the mocked, now sweating, performers. Their elaborately painted faces peering out at the audience topped off the atrocity of the sacrificial ritual to the god of spring uncomfortably unfolding before them.

Intermission at Last

Even with the intermission intervention of the Paris police, the spectators were still so overloaded by the ballet's brashness that their rioting carried on through the entire performance.

Stravinsky hid backstage embarrassed, perplexed, and angered by the reception. In later reflection, Stravinsky would blame the premiere's failure, in part, on Nijinsky's mistranslation of the music, suggesting he was a fine dancer but had been overwhelmed by the choreographic task he'd been handed.

Over the Years

Rite of Spring ran through its scheduled performances without further uproar. The Nijinsky choreography has since been lost, but similar angular dance moves have replaced them in the continued versions performed as a mainstay by troupes worldwide. In addition, the music was used in the Disney classic *Fantasia* to enhance the depiction of the cosmos creation, a true homage to Stravinsky's intent for the music to portray life in its most primitive form.

Stravinsky never attempted such audience-accosting innovation again, continuing his career without evidence of such bizarre scandal. Though Stravinsky might have given up his visionary take on the future of music, his *Rite of Spring* score had already done its magic. Musicologists consider it one of the great masterpieces of the 20th century. Stravinsky successfully achieved his goal of a harmonious juxtaposition of rhythm, pitch, and—somehow—dissonance.

Name That Tune

Murder, suicide, and corruption—the stuff of a good night's entertainment for lovers of opera. Here are some of the most frequently performed operas in the world.

✳   ✳   ✳   ✳

Tosca by Giacomo Puccini, premiered in 1900

Floria Tosca is a celebrated singer whose lover is arrested by a corrupt police chief. She kills the police chief, but her lover is executed, and she commits suicide.

La Bohème by Puccini, 1896

This opera deals with life in the Latin Quarter of Paris and focuses on the love affair between Rodolfo, a poet, and Mimi, a seamstress. The couple tragically separates, but they reunite shortly before Mimi dies of tuberculosis.

The Magic Flute by Wolfgang Amadeus Mozart, 1791

The complicated plot of this opera tells the story of Sarastro, a wise priest who takes a woman named Pamina to his temple to remove her from the influence of her mother, the Queen of the Night. The queen persuades the young Prince Tamino to search for her daughter, and in doing so, he both comes to admire Sarastro and falls in love with Pamina.

Madame Butterfly by Puccini, 1904

The first performance of this opera, in Milan, was a flop, but Puccini revised it the same year to great acclaim. *Madame Butterfly* tells of the love affair between Cio-Cio-San, a Japanese girl, and Lieutenant B. F. Pinkerton, a U.S. naval officer. The couple has a child together, but Pinkerton subsequently marries an American woman, and Cio-Cio-San commits suicide.

Don Giovanni by Mozart, 1787

The full title of Mozart's comic opera translates as "The Rake Punished, or Don Juan." It is the story of a nobleman with an eye for the ladies, who is ultimately punished for his ways by being sent to hell.

Otello by Giuseppe Verdi, 1887

Based on Shakespeare's play of the same name (spelled *Othello*), this opera tells the story of Otello, a Moor, who is convinced that his wife, Desdemona, has been unfaithful. Otello kills Desdemona in a jealous rage, then commits suicide in grief when he discovers that he was lied to and she was faithful to him all along.

The Barber of Seville by Gioachino Rossini, 1816

This comic opera tells the story of the love affair between Count Almaviva and Rosina, and how the barber Figaro helps them defeat Rosina's guardian's attempts to separate them.

La Traviata by Verdi, 1853

After a little light relief, we're back in tragic territory with *La Traviata* (which translates as "the woman who was led astray"), the tale of a courtesan who is spurned by her respectable lover before dying in his arms.

"Opera is where a guy gets stabbed in the back, and instead of dying, he sings."

ROBERT BENCHLEY

"People are wrong when they say opera is not what it used to be. It is what it used to be. That's what's wrong with it."

NOËL COWARD

"Of all the noises known to man, opera is the most expensive."

MOLIÈRE

Chapter 7

Health and the Human Body

Exposed to Poison

Long a favorite of mystery novel writers and opportunistic bad guys, poison has an ancient and infamous relationship with people. Some poisons occur naturally and others are manufactured, but all of them spell bad news if you're the unlucky recipient of a dose.

✳   ✳   ✳   ✳

Poison Plants

Deadly Nightshade, aka belladonna: Every part of this perennial herb is poisonous, but the berries are especially dangerous. The poison attacks the nervous system instantly, causing a rapid pulse, hallucinations, convulsions, ataxia, and coma.

Wolfsbane: This deadly plant was used as an arrow poison by the ancient Chinese, and its name comes from the Greek word meaning "dart." Wolfsbane takes a while to work, but when it does, it causes extreme anxiety, chest pain, and death from respiratory arrest.

Meadow Saffron: This tough little plant can be boiled and dried, and it still retains all of its poisonous power. As little as seven milligrams of this stuff could cause colic, paralysis, and heart failure.

Hemlock: This plant is probably the best known of the herbaceous poisons: It was used to knock off the Greek philosopher Socrates. Hemlock is poisonous down to the last leaf and will often send you into a coma before it finishes you for good.

Plans of Attack

There are five ways a person can be exposed to poison: ingestion (through the mouth), inhalation (breathed in through the nose or mouth), ocular (in the eyes), dermal (on the skin), and parenteral (from bites or stings).

Helpful Poison Stats

More than half of poison exposures occur in children under the age of six, and most poisonings involve medications and vitamins, household and chemical personal-care products, and plants. Eighty-nine percent of all poisonings occur at home. If you or someone in your house ingests something poisonous, you should stay calm and call 911 (if the person has collapsed or is not breathing) or your local poison control center (three-quarters of exposures can be treated over the phone with guidance from an expert).

Good Old Arsenic

Mystery novels are filled with stories of characters choosing to off their enemies with arsenic. Colorless and odorless, this close relative of phosphorous exists in a variety of compounds, not all of which are poisonous. Women in Victorian times used to rub a diluted arsenic compound into their skin to improve their complexions, and some modern medications used to treat cancer actually contain arsenic. When certain arsenic compounds are concentrated, however, they're deadly; arsenic has been blamed for widespread death through groundwater contamination.

The Dubiously Poisoned

Napoleon Bonaparte: Many historians believe that Napoleon died of arsenic poisoning while imprisoned, because significant traces of arsenic were found in his body by forensics experts 200 years after his death. It has been argued, however, that at that time in history, wallpaper and paint often contained arsenic-laced pigments, and that Napoleon was simply exposed to the poison in his everyday surroundings.

Vincent Van Gogh: Emerald green, a color of paint used by impressionist painters, contained an arsenic-based pigment. Some historians suggest that Van Gogh's neurological problems had a great deal to do with his use of large quantities of emerald green paint.

Yasser Arafat: Founder of the Palestinian liberation movement, Nobel Peace Prize winner, and politically controversial figure, Yasser Arafat died in 2004 from unknown causes. Leaders of the Islamic Resistance Movement, or Hamas, still accuse Israel of poisoning Arafat with an undetectable toxin, but there's no proof of that so far.

Food Poisoning

Unfortunately, this is a form of poisoning most of us know something about. When food is spoiled or contaminated, bacteria such as salmonella breed quickly. Because we can't see or taste these bacteria, we chomp happily away and don't realize we're about to become really sick. The Centers for Disease Control and Prevention estimates that in the United States alone, food poisoning causes about 76 million illnesses, 325,000 hospitalizations, and up to 5,000 deaths each year.

Blood Poisoning

This form of poisoning occurs when an infectious agent or its toxin spreads through the bloodstream. People actually have a low level of bacteria in their blood most of the time, but if nasty bacteria are introduced, they can cause sepsis, a life-threatening condition. The bacteria can enter the bloodstream through open wounds or from the bite of a parasite.

Snakebites

Because snakes' venom is injected, snakes themselves are considered "venomous" rather than "poisonous." Still, an estimated 8,000 snakebites occur in the United States  every year. Venomous snakes found in North America include rattlesnakes, copperheads, cottonmouths, and coral snakes. While most of these reptiles won't bite unless provoked, if you are bitten you have to take the antivenin fast.

Skull and Crossbones

When pirates sailed the high seas, they flew a flag emblazoned with a skull-and-crossbones symbol. When seafarers saw this Jolly Roger flag, they knew trouble was on its way. Bottles that contain poisons or other toxic substances often bear this symbol to warn anyone against drinking or even touching the contents with bare hands.

"I would prefer to suffer from the clean incision of an honest lancet than from a sweetened poison."

—MARK TWAIN

Who's Afraid of the Dark?

Well, Keanu Reeves is, for one. But he's not the only celebrity with a phobia. Read on to find out what scares the stars.

✳   ✳   ✳   ✳

Acrophobia (fear of heights): Sure, he scaled tall buildings in the *Spider-Man* movies, but Tobey Maguire would rather keep his feet on the ground.

Ataxophobia (fear of disorder): Soccer pro David Beckham likes to have things in order, matching, and in even numbers. In fact, his wife, Victoria, told *People* magazine, "If there are three cans of Diet Coke he'd throw one away rather than having three because it's uneven."

Aviophobia (fear of flying): This common fear keeps many stars on the ground, including John Madden, Colin Farrell, Aretha Franklin, and Jennifer Aniston.

Claustrophobia (fear of enclosed spaces): Uma Thurman can handle a lot of things, but tight spaces aren't among them. "There was no acting required. Real screams available," said the actress about a scene in *Kill Bill: Vol. 2* where she is buried alive.

Clourophobia (fear of clowns): Though he's a natural-born entertainer, you're not likely to find actor Johnny Depp anywhere near a circus. "Something must have happened when I was a kid," he told *Entertainment Weekly*.

Coimetrophobia (fear of graveyards): When filming the TV show *Buffy the Vampire Slayer*, Sarah Michelle Geller requested a fake cemetery be built because of her phobia.

Hoblophobia (fear of guns): Although he has played super spy James Bond, Roger Moore is not a fan of guns, fake or not.

Hydrophobia (fear of water): Even with all the time she spent in the water on *Baywatch*, Carmen Electra has a fear of it.

Camelot 9-1-1: JFK's Secret Ailments

The universal image of President John F. Kennedy is a young, athletic one: playing touch football, swimming a great distance after his PT boat was attacked, and rough-housing on the White House lawn with his children. But the popular image is false—in reality, Kennedy was a very sick man.

❋ ❋ ❋ ❋

State Secrets

THE STATUS OF presidential health is as zealously guarded as the formula for Coca-Cola. The image of a vigorous president is considered vital to the health of the nation, even if in reality he is incapacitated (Woodrow Wilson's debilitating stroke), seriously ill (Grover Cleveland had cancer surgery on his mouth), or just plain unhealthy (William Howard Taft weighed in at more than 300 pounds). To this day, many people still don't know that Franklin Roosevelt needed leg braces to stand because he and his staff hid his disability so well.

Kennedy was different. The youngest man ever elected a U.S. president, he projected an image of strength and vitality. Yet the further one gets from the idealistic facade of Camelot, the more one learns about it.

A Lifetime of Medicating

Kennedy was a sickly child. He suffered from scarlet fever, bronchitis, measles, whooping cough, chicken pox, and ear infections—all before age 13. He had an operation for appendicitis in the early 1930s, and he was rushed to the hospital in the winter of 1936 where doctors feared he had leukemia. He also repeatedly complained of abdominal pain and went to the Mayo Clinic that year to be treated for colitis.

Kennedy took steroids for his ailments, possibly as early as 1937. When he ran for a seat in the House of Representatives in 1946, he was described as looking "like a skeleton." Due to his many and varied illnesses, he received the Last Rites twice between 1947 and 1955. Robert Kennedy later said, "When we were growing up together we used to laugh about the great risk a mosquito took in biting Jack Kennedy—with some of his blood the mosquito was almost sure to die."

When Kennedy ran for president in 1960, an aide carrying a bag filled with medical supplies always followed him. Once the bag was misplaced in Connecticut. Kennedy frantically telephoned the state's governor to find the bag.

Patient-in-Chief

After he was elected president, Kennedy felt it more important than ever to maintain the fiction that he was in good, robust health. Reporters who tried to pursue stories of his Addison's disease (a rare disorder that affects the adrenal gland's production of steroid hormones) were told that he had a mild adrenal deficiency, which was being handled by oral medication.

As Chief Executive, Kennedy outwardly portrayed a picture of tanned vitality. However, the truth was that he had numerous doctors available at any given time. Among the physicians caring for the president were an allergist, an endocrinologist, a gastroenterologist, an orthopedist, a urologist, and an internist.

Kennedy's medical problems during his first six months in office read like the script for a melodramatic medical movie: high fevers; problems with his colon, stomach, and prostate; abscesses; back troubles; adrenal ailments; periodic dehydration; high cholesterol; and sleeplessness. During this time, Kennedy took so many medications that Dr. Janet Travell, the internist, kept a list called the "Medicine Administration Record" to keep straight all the drugs he was receiving.

In addition, Kennedy also kept Dr. Max Jacobson close at hand. A German doctor known as "Dr. Feelgood" and "Miracle Max," Jacobson treated celebrities for depression and fatigue with injections laced with amphetamines, steroids, multivitamins, and other substances. In 1961, Jacobson accompanied the president on a trip to France, so that he could continue treating him. Kennedy dismissed questions about Jacobson's dubious injections with a curt, "I don't care if it's horse piss. It works."

Long-term Effects

One long-term effect of steroids (unknown when Kennedy began taking them) is that they cause osteoporosis in the lower backbones. That, and several back surgeries, kept Kennedy in almost constant back pain for years. In the autumn of 1961, one of Kennedy's physicians, Admiral George Burkley, decided that the injections the president had been getting for his back, along with braces and other devices that he wore, were hurting rather than helping him. Burkley feared that Kennedy would soon be wheelchair-bound. He brought in orthopedic surgeon Hans Kraus, who warned Kennedy that he must begin immediate exercise to strengthen the muscles. Kennedy began exercising three times a week. By the spring of 1962, the president was doing better than he had in several years.

The million-dollar question is whether or not Kennedy's many medications affected his work. Historians agree that it doesn't seem to be the case. While president, Kennedy was taking antibiotics (urinary tract infections), anti-spasmodics (colitis), steroids (Addison's disease), antihistamines (allergies), and painkillers (back pain). Yet these medications probably helped him function at times when he otherwise could not have.

The Great What-If

There is an intriguing theory concerning the stiff back brace Kennedy was wearing the day of his assassination in Dallas, Texas, on November 22, 1963. If he had not been wearing the brace, which was designed to hold him upright, he might have moved sideways when the first shot hit him. Perhaps he would have been able to avoid the fatal second shot. But that's the funny thing about theories: We'll never know for sure.

The Ears Have It

An industrious boy earned a fortune by keeping his ears warm.

✳   ✳   ✳   ✳

CHESTER GREENWOOD was a hard-working boy from Farmington, Maine, who endured a typical hardscrabble childhood in rural New England. Disciplined and diligent, he dropped out of school to help his large family by working on the farm and trekking eight miles to deliver eggs and fudge to his neighbors. This was one of the few occasions when he had the opportunity to indulge in the fun that led to his fortune.

A Cool Idea

In the winter of 1873, the 15-year-old headed to a nearby pond to try out a new pair of ice skates. Before he reached his destination, he had to turn back because the bitter cold was hurting his ears. Determined to go skating, Greenwood took a piece of baling wire he found around the farm and formed a loop at each end. He brought the wire and some beaver fur to his grandmother and asked her to sew the material onto the loops. Then he slipped the device over his head.

Getting Warmer

Young Chester never had to worry about cold ears—or making money—again. His "Greenwood Champion Ear Protector" eventually became what we call earmuffs—but only after a few more years of tinkering. Unsatisfied with the loose fit of the original, Greenwood improved his invention by using a wide steel band instead of wire. This allowed him to add hinges where the band connected to the muff, so the fabric could fit snugly against the ears and the device could be folded when not in use.

Chester patented the revised design in 1877 at the age of 18 and then opened a factory near his hometown. His business became a central part of Farmington's economy, and it remains the largest producer of earmuffs in the world.

Twelve Deadly Diseases Cured in the 20th Century

According to the U.S. Census Bureau, the average life expectancy at the beginning of the 20th century was 47.3 years. A century later, that number had increased to 77.85 years, due largely to the development of vaccinations and other treatments for deadly diseases. Of course, vaccines and treatments only work if they're given, which is why many of these diseases still persist in poorer, developing countries. Despite the success of vaccines, only one of these diseases—smallpox—has been erased from the globe. Here are 12 diseases that could be completely eradicated from the world if vaccines were made available to all.

1. **Chicken Pox:** Before 1995, a case of the chicken pox was a rite of passage for kids. The disease, caused by the *varicella-zoster* virus, creates an itchy rash of small red bumps on the skin. The virus spreads when someone who has the disease coughs or sneezes, and a nonimmune person inhales the viral particles. The virus can also be passed through contact with the fluid of chicken pox blisters. Most cases are minor but in more serious instances, chicken pox can trigger bacterial infections, viral pneumonia, and encephalitis (inflammation of the brain). According to the Centers for Disease Control and Prevention (CDC), before the chicken pox vaccine was approved for use in the United States in 1995, there were 11,000 hospitalizations and 100 deaths from the disease every year. Many countries do not require the vaccination because chicken pox doesn't cause that many deaths. They'd rather focus on vaccinating against the really serious afflictions, so the disease is still common.

2. **Diphtheria:** Diphtheria is an infection of the bacteria *Corynebacterium diphtheriae* and mainly affects the nose and throat. The bacteria spreads through airborne droplets

and shared personal items. *C. diphtheriae* creates a toxin in the body that produces a thick, gray or black coating in the nose, throat, or airway, which can also affect the heart and nervous system. Even with proper antibiotic treatment, diphtheria kills about 10 percent of the people who contract it. The first diphtheria vaccine was unveiled in 1913, and although vaccination has made a major dent in mortality rates, the disease still exists in developing countries and other areas where people are not regularly vaccinated. The World Health Organization (WHO) estimates that worldwide there are about 5,000 deaths from diphtheria annually, but the disease is quite rare in the United States, with fewer than five cases reported each year.

3. **Invasive H. Flu:** Invasive H. flu, or Hib disease, is an infection caused by the *Haemophilus influenzae* type b (Hib) bacteria, which spreads when an infected person coughs, sneezes, or speaks. Invasive Hib is a bit of a misnomer because it is not related to any form of the influenza virus. However, it can lead to bacterial meningitis (a potentially fatal brain infection), pneumonia, epiglottitis (severe swelling above the voice box that makes breathing difficult), and infections of the blood, joints, bones, and pericardium (the covering of the heart). Children younger than five years old are particularly susceptible to the Hib bacteria because they have not had the chance to develop immunity to it. The first Hib vaccine was licensed in 1985, but despite its success in the developed world, the disease is still prevalent in the developing world. WHO estimates that each year Hib disease causes two to three million cases of serious illness worldwide, mostly pneumonia and meningitis, and 450,000 deaths of young children.

4. **Malaria:** This disease is a parasitic infection of the liver and red blood cells. In its mildest forms it can produce flu-like symptoms and nausea, and in its severest forms it can cause seizures, coma, fluid buildup in the lungs, kidney failure,

and death. The disease is transmitted by female mosquitoes of the genus *Anopheles*. When the mosquito bites, the parasites enter a person's body, invading red blood cells and causing the cells to rupture. As the cells burst, they release chemicals that cause malaria's symptoms. About 350 million to 500 million cases of malaria occur worldwide every year. About one million are fatal, with children in sub-Saharan Africa accounting for most of the deaths. Other high-risk areas include Central and South America, India, and the Middle East. Malaria is treated with a variety of drugs, some of which kill the parasites once they're in the blood and others that prevent infection in the first place. Of course, if you can avoid the parasite-carrying mosquitoes, you can avoid malaria, so the disease is often controlled using mosquito repellent and bed netting, especially in poor countries that cannot afford medications.

5. **Measles:** Measles is a highly contagious viral illness of the respiratory system that spreads through airborne droplets when an infected person coughs or sneezes. Although the first symptoms of measles mimic a simple cold, with a cough, runny nose, and red watery eyes, this disease is more serious. As measles progresses, the infected person develops a fever and a red or brownish-red skin rash. Complications can include diarrhea, pneumonia, brain infection, and even death, although these are seen more commonly in malnourished or immunodeficient people. Measles has historically been a devastating disease, but WHO reported in 2006 that measles mortality rates dropped from 871,000 to 454,000 between 1999 and 2004, thanks to a global immunization drive. Until 1963, when the first measles vaccine was used in the United States, almost everyone got the measles by age 20. There has been a 99 percent reduction

in measles since then, but outbreaks have occurred when the disease is brought over from other countries or when children don't get the vaccine or all the required doses. Most children today receive the measles  vaccine as part of the MMR vaccination, which protects against measles, mumps, and rubella (German measles).

6. **Pertussis:** If you suspect someone has whooping cough, move away. Pertussis, better known as whooping cough, is a highly contagious respiratory infection caused by the Bordetella pertussis bacteria. The descriptive nickname comes from the "whooping" sounds that infected children make after one of the disease's coughing spells. The coughing fits spread the bacteria and can last a minute or longer, causing a child to turn purple or red and sometimes vomit. Severe episodes can cause a lack of oxygen to the brain. Adults who contract pertussis usually have a hacking cough rather than a whooping one. Although the disease can strike anyone, it is most prevalent in infants under age one because they haven't received the entire course of pertussis vaccinations. The pertussis vaccine was first used in 1933, but adolescents and adults become susceptible when the immunity from childhood vaccinations wanes and they don't get booster shots. According to the CDC, pertussis causes 10 to 20 deaths each year in the United States, and there were 25,000 cases reported in 2004. Worldwide, the disease causes far more damage—about 50 million people around the world are infected annually, and WHO estimates around 294,000 deaths each year. However, 78 percent of the world's infants received three doses of the vaccine in 2004.

7. **Pneumococcal Disease:** Pneumococcal disease is the collective name for the infections caused by *Streptococcus*

pneumoniae bacteria, also known as *pneumococcus*. This bacteria finds a home all over the human body. The most common types of infections caused by S. *pneumoniae* are middle ear infections, pneumonia, bacteremia (blood stream infections), sinus infections, and bacterial meningitis. There are more than 90 types of pneumococcus, with the ten most common types responsible for 62 percent of the world's invasive diseases. Those infected carry the bacteria in their throats and expel it when they cough or sneeze. Like any other germ, S. *pneumoniae* can infect anyone, but certain population groups are more at risk, such as the elderly, people with cancer or AIDS, and people with a chronic illness such as diabetes. The CDC blames pneumococcal disease for the deaths of 200 children under the age of five each year in the United States. WHO estimates that annually pneumococcal disease is responsible for one million fatal cases of respiratory illness alone; most of these cases occur in developing countries. There are two types of vaccines available to prevent pneumococcal disease, which the CDC recommends that children and adults older than age 65 receive.

8. **Polio:** Of the deadly infectious diseases for which science has developed vaccines and treatments, people are most familiar with the victory over polio. The disease is caused by a virus that enters the body through the mouth, usually from hands contaminated with the stool of an infected person. In about 95 percent of cases, polio produces no symptoms at all (asymptomatic polio), but in the remaining cases of polio, the disease can take three forms. Abortive polio creates flu-like symptoms, such as upper respiratory infection, fever, sore throat, and general malaise. Nonparalytic polio is more severe and produces symptoms similar to mild meningitis, including sensitivity to light and neck stiffness. Finally, paralytic polio produces the symptoms with which most people associate the disease, even

though paralytic polio accounts for less than 1 percent of all cases. Paralytic polio causes loss of control and paralysis of limbs, reflexes, and the muscles that control breathing. Today, polio is under control in the developed world, and world health authorities are close to controlling the disease in developing countries, as well. Dr. Jonas Salk's inactivated polio vaccine (IPV) first appeared in 1955, and Dr. Albert Sabin's oral polio vaccine (OPV) first appeared in 1961. Children in the United States receive IPV, but most children in developing areas of the world receive OPV, which is cheaper and doesn't have to be administered by a health-care professional; however, in rare instances, OPV can cause polio.

9. **Tetanus:** Reproductive cells (spores) of *Clostridium tetani* are found in the soil and enter the body through a skin wound. Once the spores develop into mature bacteria, the bacteria produce tetanospasmin, a neurotoxin (a protein that poisons the body's nervous system) that causes muscle spasms. In fact, tetanus gets its nickname—lockjaw— because the toxin often attacks the muscles that control the jaw. Lockjaw is accompanied by difficulty swallowing and painful stiffness in the neck, shoulders, and back. The spasms can then spread to the muscles of the abdomen, upper arms, and thighs. According to the CDC, tetanus is fatal in about 11 percent of cases, but fortunately, it can't be spread from person to person—you need direct contact with C. *tetani* to contract the disease. Today, tetanus immunization is standard in the United States, but if you are injured in a way that increases tetanus risk (i.e. stepping on a rusty nail, cutting your hand with a knife, or getting bitten by a dog), a booster shot may be necessary if it's been several years since your last tetanus shot. According to the CDC, since the 1970s, only about 50 to 100 cases of tetanus are reported in the United States each year, mostly among people who have never been vaccinated or who did

not get a booster shot. And WHO says that globally there were about 15,500 cases of tetanus in 2005.

10. **Typhoid Fever:** Typhoid is usually spread when food or water has been infected with *Salmonella typhi*, most often through contact with the feces of an infected person. Once the typhoid bacteria enter the bloodstream, the body mounts a defense that causes a high fever, headache, stomach pains, weakness, and decreased appetite. Occasionally, people who have typhoid get a rash of flat red spots. Because sewage treatment in the United States is quite good, the disease is very rare, and the CDC reports only about 400 cases of it annually. However, people who live in developing countries where there is little water and sewage treatment, or where hand washing is not a common practice, are at high risk. Prime typhoid fever areas are in Africa, Asia, the Caribbean, India, and Central and South America. WHO estimates 17 million cases occur globally with 600,000 deaths each year. Despite these daunting statistics, typhoid fever vaccination is available for people who travel to high-risk areas, and the disease can be effectively treated with antibiotics. Without treatment, the fever can continue for weeks or even months, and the infection can lead to death.

11. **Yellow Fever:** Yellow fever is spread by mosquitoes infected with the yellow fever virus. Jaundice, or yellowing of the skin and eyes, is the hallmark of the infection and gives it its name. Most cases of yellow fever are mild and require only three or four days to recover, but severe cases can cause bleeding, heart problems, liver or kidney failure, brain dysfunction, or death. People with the disease can ease their symptoms, but there is no specific treatment, so prevention via the yellow fever vaccine is key. The vaccine provides immunity from the disease for ten years or more and is generally safe for everyone older than nine months. Yellow fever occurs only in Africa, South America, and some areas

of the Caribbean, so only travelers who are destined for these regions need to be concerned about it. WHO estimates that there are 200,000 cases of yellow fever every year, and 30,000 of them are fatal. The elderly are at highest risk of developing the most severe symptoms. Although vaccination and mosquito-eradication efforts have made a great difference, WHO says yellow fever cases are on the rise again.

12. **Smallpox:** Unlike other diseases on this list, which can still appear in outbreaks when vaccination vigilance weakens, smallpox has been wiped off the face of the earth, except for samples of the virus held in labs in the United States and Russia for research purposes. Symptoms of smallpox included a high fever, head and body aches, malaise, vomiting, and a rash of small red bumps that progressed into sores that could break open and spread the virus (the virus could also be spread via contact with shared items, clothing, and bedding). Smallpox was an entirely human disease—it did not infect any other animal or insect on the planet. Thus, once vaccination eliminated the chances of the virus spreading among the human population, the disease disappeared; in fact, the United States has not vaccinated for smallpox since 1972. Although smallpox was one of the most devastating illnesses in human history, killing more than 300 million people worldwide during the 20th century alone, scientists declared the world free of smallpox in 1979. The naturally occurring disease has been eradicated, but fears remain about the remaining smallpox samples being used as bioweapons.

"The art of medicine consists in amusing the patient while nature cures the disease."

—Voltaire

Becoming Fluent in Body Language

What does your body language convey about your thoughts? Learning to read the effects of nonverbal communication can help you better convey your own motivation—and understand that of others.

✳   ✳   ✳   ✳

Y OU CAN SAY a lot without ever opening your mouth. The science of body language theorizes that everything from hand placement to eye activity speaks volumes about our true intentions. Learn the dialect and you can gain a whole new kind of communication power.

Power of the Palms

Psychologists say the palms are among the most telling signs of body language—and not in the fortune-telling sense, either. Subconsciously, people tend to hold their palms out and open, facing another person, when they are being honest. In contrast, hiding one's palms is usually associated with lying or trying to conceal something. Some other palm moves to pick up include:

✳ Rubbing the palms together: shows excitement or expectation

✳ Hands clenched together: indicates an unspoken feeling of anxiety or negativity

✳ Palms up and flat against each other in a steeplelike position: shows a feeling of superiority and confidence

✳ Hands held together behind the back: shows a position of authority

✳ Stacking the hands on top of each other and resting the face on it: a sign of courtship, most often used by women to unwittingly indicate interest in a potential partner

All About the Arms

You may have heard that arms crossed in front of the chest indicate discomfort. Scientists agree: Studies have found that taking on the standard crossed-armed position actually leads others to develop a more negative impression of you. It is interpreted as being disagreeable or even hostile, particularly if the fists are also clenched.

Conversely, not crossing one's arms indicates a sense of confidence and superiority. It's theorized to be a function of evolution, as this would have shown an open and vulnerable body to potential predators.

Another common variation (limited to men) involves leaving their arms hanging down in front with their hands clasped together in the middle, directly over their, uh, nether region. Observers see this most frequently when a man is standing in front of a large group or when he is otherwise intimidated or dejected. It's considered a protective position (think about it) and is also thought to have an evolutionary function.

I Spy Your Eyes

A person's eyes can also tell you a lot. Lowering the eyebrows indicates dominance, while raising them shows submission. Widening the eyes, particularly in women, creates a babylike image that fosters men's protective instincts. Also, a woman tilting her head down and looking upward shows submission for the same reason—it's thought to increase a man's attraction. Researchers say the ultimate ammo a woman can use is tilting her head down, lowering her eyelids, looking up, raising her eyebrows, and slightly parting her lips—all at the same time.

Liar, Liar

While not foolproof, psychologists have found some common body language signs that often indicate a lie. Touching your nose, rubbing your eye, placing your hand over your mouth, scratching your neck, or pulling at your collar are all signs.

Here a Germ, There a Germ

Here's a rundown of the most germ-infested areas on the body and in the home, workplace, and around town.

✳ ✳ ✳ ✳

The Body is a Temple—for Germs

WHILE MOST OF the body is germ-free, the skin, intestines, mouth, respiratory tract, and other areas may be really germy. The mouth often contains more than 100 million bacteria, the skin more than 300 million, and the large intestine 200 trillion to 300 trillion! Most of these are "good bacteria" because they help protect the body from harmful bugs and improve the immune system.

Even Good Bacteria Can Be Bad

While most of the good bacteria in the large intestine keep the digestive system running, some can cause problems. People who are lactose intolerant cannot digest milk sugar in their small intestine, so the lactose moves into the large intestine. There, bacteria are able to break down the lactose, but the process creates a lot of acid and gas. Alcoholic sugars (the sugar found in "sugar free" products), Olestra (fake fat), and even starch from legumes may cause a person to have painful gas and diarrhea.

Germs that Cause Food Poisoning

Salmonella are bacteria usually associated with chicken and eggs. These organisms, which can cause severe food poisoning and even death, are found in the majority of kitchen sinks and often on sponges and dishcloths (items that contain the most germs in the home). Salmonella is also common on, and in, dogs, cats, turtles, lizards, and nearly every domesticated pet.

The Most Dangerous Germs

"Bad" bacteria can cause a variety of necrotic (dead-tissue) skin lesions. Community-Acquired-Methicillin-Resistant Staphylococcus, known as CA-MRSA, not only damage the skin but are also resistant to most antibiotics. *Staphylococcus aureus* are common and dangerous bacteria that cause pimples, boils, food poisoning, and toxic shock syndrome. They are a major cause of hospital-acquired infections.

Workplace Germs

Where is the germiest place at work? Not communal lunch tables or bathrooms—these are cleaned frequently. The most germ-infested areas are your desktop and phone: They're probably not washed often, and your hands, which touch a lot of other germy things, are all over them.

Breathe Deep?

Is a deep breath of fresh air good for us? In fact, people breathe in at least 100,000 bacteria every day. The air that presents the greatest hazard is near a toilet (flushing causes droplets to float into the air) or sink (splashing water has the same effect), or within six feet of anyone who sneezes or coughs. Some cold and flu viruses can survive for more than 72 hours on dust.

Man's Best Friend Has a Dirty Mouth

Many people claim that the canine mouth is cleaner than the human mouth. In reality, both contain billions of similar or identical bacteria and disease-causing agents. Moreover, many dogs eat fecal matter or rotten meat and therefore carry a variety of diseases and parasites.

Wash and Dry the Right Way

Most people believe that washing their hands with hot water will make them clean or even sterile. However, studies show that hot water causes the hands to sweat slightly, which brings more germs to the skin surface. Washing hands in cool or warm water is best. Another misconception is that hot-air hand dryers are more sanitary than towels. Studies have shown that hand dryers actually blow bacteria off the floor and shoot them into the air, increasing the number of bacteria on the hands by up to 162 percent. The spread of bacteria isn't limited to our hands—the germs are now everywhere.

The Evolution of the Cesarean Section

Today the cesarean section is considered a fairly routine surgery. But there was a time when it was a tragic procedure of last resort.

✳ ✳ ✳ ✳

What's in a Name?

THE HISTORY OF the cesarean section is shrouded in mystery. Legend has it that Julius Caesar was born by cesarean section in an era when the procedure was only done as a last-ditch effort to save the infant if its mother was dead or dying. However, historians debate whether Caesar was born via cesarean. There are references to his mother, Aurelia, being alive during his life, which would probably have been impossible had she undergone a cesarean. The procedure's name might alternatively derive from a Roman law called "Lex Caesarea," which dictated that if a woman in labor died or was dying, the baby must be saved so the population of the state would grow.

A Look Back

The cesarean's history is difficult to trace because two lives are at stake during the procedure, so the exact circumstances were either intentionally kept hush-hush or were mixed up with religious birthing and funereal ceremonies. In ancient times, cesareans were usually postmortem procedures: Deceased babies were removed from deceased mothers so that both could have a proper funeral. It was probably pretty rare for an emergency cesarean operation to be done on a dying woman during labor, since few would want to be responsible for determining when and if the mother's chance of survival was hopeless.

References to cesareans can be found in ancient pictures and texts the world over. There is some evidence that the surgery was performed on living women; scattered accounts indicate that some women may even have survived the procedure.

Cesareans have also been reported in hunter-gatherer and tribal cultures. In fact, one Western report dated to 1879 describes a Ugandan tribal healer who used banana wine to sanitize his hands and the woman's abdomen as well as to intoxicate the woman before practicing a strategy to massage the uterus and make it contract. The woman survived, and the Western observer concluded the procedure was old and well established.

The cesarean's Western rise to popularity began with the Renaissance, when anatomical studies improved all surgeries. The development of anesthesia in the 19th century made the cesarean possible as a procedure to preserve the mother's life during a difficult labor: If the mother was not conscious, the risk of her dying of shock was removed. Additionally, the development of antiseptics lowered the risk of infection. The cesarean slowly began to replace a tragic procedure called a *craniotomy*. During long and painful childbirths—or when it was clear that the infant had died in the womb—the baby had to be removed without killing the mother. A blunt object would be inserted through the woman's vagina in an effort to crush the baby's skull. The infant was then removed, piecemeal. This was dangerous, and the woman often did not survive.

At Last, Success

Although the cesarean ultimately replaced the craniotomy, maternal mortality remained high. A groundbreaking change came with the realization that the uterine suture—stitching up the uterus—which had been considered dangerous, was actually the key to a successful cesarean. This, combined with other advances, made the cesarean a feasible option. In fact, the cesarean has become so common that women sometimes choose a cesarean, even if there is no difficulty with their labor. This modern practice has led to a peculiar problem: Assuming there is no medical reason for the cesarean, it is safer for a woman to stick with a vaginal birth. The cesarean has thus completed its amazing transformation from an almost impossible option to one that, if anything, is used too frequently.

Hair Today

Nearly 80 percent of people in the United States say they spend more money on hair products than any other grooming goods. But no matter what that bottle of expensive shampoo says about nourishing your hair, it can't feed something that isn't alive.

* * * *

DESPITE ALL THE effort we put into coifing and pampering our locks, the hair we see is biologically dead. Hair is alive only in the roots, which are fed by small blood vessels beneath the skin's surface. Hair cells travel up the shaft and are eventually cut off from the blood supply that is their nourishment. The cells die before being pushed out of the follicle onto the head—or back, or arm, or anywhere else.

Even though it's dead, hair is incredibly strong. The average head of hair can support roughly 12 tons of weight—much more than the scalp it's attached to. The tough stuff grows in cycles: During the first phase, hair is actively growing. In the second phase, it rests in the follicle until it is pushed out of the root. Healthy hair grows about .39 inch in a month.

Each hair is completely independent from the others. When a hair falls out (the average person loses between 50 and 100 resting hairs each day), another one may not grow directly in its place. We are born with every hair follicle we'll ever have, though the composition, color, and pattern of the hair changes over the years. A characteristic full head of hair averages about 120,000 to 150,000 individual hairs (about 250 hairs on each square centimeter of scalp).

Eating a healthful diet that contains sufficient protein (hair is made of protein), vitamins, minerals, and water is the best way to ensure healthy hair. A better investment is on nutrient-dense foods rather than hair products. Lathering, rinsing, and repeating will only wash a lot of money down the drain.

Cutting the Fat

Americans are striving to overcome an epidemic of obesity—sometimes with humorous consequences.

✳   ✳   ✳   ✳

The National Crises

WHETHER YOU BLAME fast food, video games, or automobiles, the simple fact is that Americans are consuming more while doing less, and it's starting to show. In fact, two of every three Americans are now overweight, and nearly 70 million Americans are considered obese; that is, they have exceeded their optimal body mass by more than 30 percent. It's estimated that the resulting health crises will lower the national life-expectancy average, possibly by as much as five years, for the first time in American history.

Certainly the obesity crisis in America is a serious matter; but given the increased media coverage and resulting awareness in recent years there is good cause for hope. In the meantime, consider two illustrative events in the quest for good health that are, if not cause for laughter, then perhaps a polite smile.

Mississippi Leads the Way (to the Buffet)

West Virginia, Indiana, Alabama, and Mississippi have consistently ranked among the states with the highest rates of obesity in the United States, with Alabama and Mississippi usually within a hairsbreadth of each other for first place. Recently, Mississippi received the dubious honor of being the fattest state in the nation for three years in a row.

This was not lost on Mississippi State Representatives Ted Mayhall, John Read, and Bobby Shows, who decided to take action. In 2008, the three reps cosponsored House Bill 282, making it illegal for a restaurant to serve an obese person.

Besides pointing out the impossibility of enforcing the proposed law, critics claimed that the measure amounted to cruel punishment of obese individuals. The executive director of the Obesity Society called the proposed law "the most ill-conceived plan to address public health crisis ever proposed," and the chairman of the state House Public Health and Human Services Committee publicly announced that he would veto the measure when it reached his desk.

Chew on This: Rep. John Read claimed that the measure was simply meant to raise public awareness of the obesity crises. He succeeded: House Bill 282 received national attention, and it reminded everyone that Mississippi was still the fattest state.

Chew on This: At the time he introduced the bill, the 5'11" Read weighed 230 pounds—if his own bill had passed, he would have been unable to eat in restaurants.

It's a Not-So-Small World

In 2007, representatives of the Disneyland resort in Anaheim, California announced that the popular "It's a Small World" ride would close for the first time. The boats, which carried groups through a singsong tour of the world's cultures, were bottoming out and getting stuck in Canada and Scandinavia. Disney blamed the problem on "fiberglass buildup," but most observers saw it as simply the result of the average national weight increasing by 25 pounds since the ride was built in 1964.

The ride reopened on February 5, 2009, with channels an inch deeper and more buoyant boats. Certainly the cast members who work on the ride must be relieved, as they were often put in the awkward position of having to leave empty seats on boats containing larger people or faced the task of retrieving stranded patrons after their boats ran aground.

Chew on This: As the stoppages became more frequent, passengers whose rides were cut short by a grounded boat were compensated with a ticket for free food.

Picture Perfect: Making Wax Sculptures

Making a wax likeness of a person may be a centuries-old art, but this sort of portraiture is still a complicated process.

✳ ✳ ✳ ✳

The First Stages

AH, THE WAX SCULPTURE—PERHAPS the most obvious sign that someone has made it as a cultural icon. The art of wax sculpting has been around since the 1700s, when the now well-known Madame Tussaud made her first figures. These days, before the statue slides its way into a museum, it has to make a long journey that begins with weeks of research.

Once a museum decides to commission a particular person's model, a team of artists begins to collect piles of photographs and measurements of the soon-to-be-immortalized person. But before they even think about building the separate parts and putting the pieces together, the museum must decide exactly how the end product should appear.

Curators consider every last detail, ranging from the facial expression and posture to the wardrobe and setting. They'll even go as far as interviewing barbers and dentists to get a better feel of the person's most intimate details. Once those decisions have been made and the data has been collected, it's time to start sculpting.

Building the Face

Using a combination of photos and measurements and sometimes even a real-life impression, the artists work on creating a plaster mold of the head using regular clay. Next, they pour hot wax into this mold. Beeswax is often used along with manufactured petroleum-based waxes, mixed together with artificial coloring and chemicals to help the goo stay strong and resist heat. After everything is in place, it's time to let the magic happen.

The Fine Details

Once the mold has cooled, the wax is removed and the assembly begins. Prosthetic eyes are selected to best match the person's gaze.

Porcelain teeth, similar to dentures, are used to fill the kisser. And real human hair is brought in to be inserted, one strand at a time, into every spot where it's needed: the head, the eyebrows and eyelashes, and even the arms and chest. Specially trained workers use a tiny needle to painstakingly place every last hair perfectly. This process alone takes up to 60 hours. One can imagine that, in the case of hirsute comedian Robin Williams's model, it could take 60 days.

Next, painters use translucent paint to even out the skin tone and add in any blemishes or distinguishing features. The paint is put on in thin layers, allowing the wax to shine through and look more lifelike. The crew then puts all the pieces together and passes the final figure off to the next team.

The Big Picture

Now that the model is done, the rest of the work begins. Seamstresses and costuming consultants come in to create the figure's wardrobe and fit it onto the body. Designers then assemble the full set, including backgrounds, props, and furnishings to match the moment frozen in time. At long last, the model is ready to be placed. After final touch-ups, engineers are hired to design lighting that will play up the sculpture's features. Finally, the journey is done, and the show can open.

All together, the entire process usually takes a minimum of six months. Some cases have been more extreme: Royal London Wax Museum's model of former U.S. President Bill Clinton took eight months, and its sculpture of former Canadian Prime Minister Jean Chretien took just over a year. Museums say the creations can cost anywhere from $10,000 to $25,000, not including the various furnishings. Kind of makes the salon's $25 wax special seem a little more reasonable, doesn't it?

Chapter 8

History

Amazing Facts About the United States

Bet you didn't know these things about the good old red, white, and blue.

✳   ✳   ✳   ✳

✳ When the London Bridge (the version built in 1831) started to disintegrate, it was taken apart stone by stone, shipped to the United States, and lovingly reconstructed in Lake Havasu City, Arizona.

✳ Pittsburgh has more city-maintained steps than any other city in the world. If stacked up, they would reach a height of 26,000 feet.

✳ Denver is the only city in history to turn down the Olympic Games. The 1976 Winter Games were scheduled to be held there, but residents voted against it.

✳ Michigan can claim the only floating post office in the world. The *J. W. Westcott II* mail ship delivers freight and correspondence to boats ferrying on the Detroit River.

✳ The Rockville Bridge in Harrisburg, Pennsylvania, is the longest stone arch bridge in the world. It was built in 1902 and measures 3,820 feet.

* The city of Beaver, Oklahoma, is the cow-chip-throwing capital of the world. Its annual competition is held in April.

* The 24-foot replica of Leonardo da Vinci's *Il Gavallo* in Grand Rapids, Michigan, is the largest equestrian bronze statue in the Western hemisphere.

* Middlesboro, Kentucky, is built entirely within a meteor crater.

* John Hancock was the only man to actually sign the Declaration of Independence on the Fourth of July. Most others signed on August 2, 1776.

* In the United States, there are more statues of Lewis and Clark's Native American guide Sacagawea than of any other woman.

* The world's longest shared border is the 3,987-mile boundary between the United States and Canada.

* Try this on your next vacation: If you stand at the point known as Four Corners in the southwestern United States, you can reach into four states—Utah, Colorado, New Mexico, and Arizona—without moving your feet.

* Chittenango, New York, is the childhood home of *The Wonderful Wizard of Oz* author L. Frank Baum. The town has yellow brick-inlaid sidewalks that lead to Oz-styled businesses. The yearly highlight is the "Oz-stravaganza," featuring a Munchkins parade.

* Hawaii is the most isolated population center on Earth. It is 2,390 miles from California, 3,850 miles from Japan, and 4,900 miles from China.

* Texas is the only state in the country that has had the flags of six nations flying over it. They are: Mexico, Spain, France, the Confederate States, the Republic of Texas, and the United States.

* The eruption of Mount St. Helens in 1980 was a disaster for many, but not for Idahoans. The great clouds of ash from the eruption drifted into Idaho and increased crop yields by an average of 30 percent throughout the 1980s.

* Maine is the only state that shares a border with only one other state—New Hampshire.

* Niagara Falls State Park in New York is the oldest state park in the United States. Approximately 140 of the park's 400-plus acres are under water.

* The state of Florida is larger than England.

* An earthquake on December 16, 1811, caused parts of the Mississippi River to flow backward.

* Honolulu is the only place in the United States that has a royal palace.

* The only letter in the alphabet that does not appear in the name of a U.S. state is Q.

* The only mobile national monuments are the cable cars in San Francisco.

* The "First Thanksgiving" was little more than a harvest feast. Thanksgiving was not an official holiday until Abraham Lincoln proclaimed a national day for giving thanks in 1863.

* The diary of King George III of England carried this entry on July 4, 1776: "Nothing of importance happened today."

* Three of the first five presidents died on Independence Day. John Adams and Thomas Jefferson died on the same day—July 4, 1826. James Monroe died on July 4, 1831.

* Although officially the 17th state in the Union, Congress forgot to vote on the resolution to make Ohio a state until August 7, 1953, which technically makes it the 47th state.

Diplomacy 101

International diplomacy is a risky business. Trying to reach an agreement between two nations—or the leaders of two nations—is sometimes dangerous, always difficult, and often impossible. Here are a few of the more challenging examples.

✳ ✳ ✳ ✳

THE JOB OF crafting a diplomatic agreement, of bringing both sides to the conference table, is entrusted to political leaders and diplomats. In modern times, when there is a breakdown in international relationships, diplomatic immunity usually brings embassy staff home safely. But it wasn't always that way.

A Brief History of Diplomacy

Certain touchy rulers in the Middle Ages, such as Attila the Hun or the Mongol Khans of the Golden Horde, would show their displeasure with more "civilized" nations by holding their diplomats for ransom or by sending said diplomats home in pieces. This seldom prevented wars, but it certainly got the point across.

One form of diplomatic blunder with great consequence often appears in the interaction between government and religion. Roman governor Pontius Pilate was responsible for deciding between the pardon or crucifixion of Jesus of Nazareth. Against his own judgment, he allowed the crowd to persuade him to have Jesus executed. If Pilate had thought it over, he would have perhaps allowed Jesus to live. After all, Jesus preached peace, not rebellion. A living Jesus might have become a great rabbi and advanced the cause of Judaism—but then Christianity would not have existed.

Likewise, Holy Roman Emperor Charles V could have sent Martin Luther to the stake for heresy, but due to political commitments to Frederick of Saxony, Luther's patron, Charles allowed the renegade monk to escape. Had Luther been executed, Protestantism might have remained a minor cult in a largely Catholic world.

But religion isn't the only stumbling block to diplomacy. In 1443, a blunder by the Ming emperor of China changed the world forever. Admiral Zheng's gigantic fleet had explored everywhere from China to Africa. It was poised to explore Europe and, eventually, the Americas. But a dispute in the Ming court caused the emperor to forbid any further voyages, break up the fleet, and finance agrarian programs instead—and for 500 years China was a land of peasant farmers, exploited by its neighbors.

World War I

"The War to End All Wars" featured some great diplomatic blunders. Preceding the war in 1908, Kaiser Wilhelm II gave an interview to the *Daily Telegraph* newspaper in an attempt to improve British-German relations. Instead, he managed to offend the British, annoy the Russians and French, and imply that the build-up of the German navy was targeted against Japan. All four of those nations would go to war against Germany six years later.

Another of the war's goofs was the Zimmerman Telegram, sent by Germany, offering a chunk of the American Southwest to Mexico for attacking the United States. However, the telegraph cable routed through London. The British read the telegram and passed it on to the enraged Americans. The telegram, coupled with the sinking of the passenger ship *Lusitania,* pushed America into the war.

But Germany's biggest diplomatic foul-up was to send the dangerous agitator Vladimir Lenin in a sealed railway car from Switzerland to St. Petersburg in an attempt to destabilize the Russian war effort. It worked far better than ever intended—Lenin became the leader of the Bolsheviks, led the Russian

Revolution, and became the first head of the USSR. Germany did get its intended result of Russia pulling out of the war, but the unintended consequence of this German act came much later—28 years later—when Soviet troops marched into Berlin during the next war.

World War II

Britain and France were far less concerned about Adolf Hitler and his remilitarization of Germany than they should've been. The führer clearly intended to expand his country's borders, and he did so with little resistance. Going against the Versailles Treaty that ended World War I, Germany annexed Austria in 1938. Franco-British apathy encouraged Hitler to go further, seeking to take over a part of Czechoslovakia called the Sudetenland. To keep a lid on potential conflict, Britain and France signed the Munich Agreement with Germany, granting the territory to the Third Reich. British Prime Minister Neville Chamberlain triumphantly returned to London, proclaiming "peace in our time." Well, peace for another 11 months, anyway, until German tanks rolled into Poland in September 1939.

France based much of its foreign policy on a chain of forts called the Maginot Line. The line was considered impregnable—until the Germans just went around the end of the chain.

Adolf Hitler allied with Benito Mussolini, who not only couldn't hold up his end of the war effort but also dragged the Germans into Africa, Yugoslavia, and Greece and weakened the Russian campaign. Finally, Hitler had to rescue Mussolini from his own troops.

Blunders in the Modern Age

After World War II, Chiang Kai-Shek's army had driven the Communists under Mao Zedong into Manchuria. They were about to destroy the Reds when American Chief of Staff George C. Marshall persuaded Chiang to enter into peace talks with the wily Mao. This gave the Reds time to regroup and retake mainland China.

When the French were losing in Vietnam, they asked President Dwight Eisenhower for help. He sent weapons and B-29 strikes, but the French effort failed. The United States somehow wound up continuing the war.

To defeat the Russians in Afghanistan, America armed and equipped the Taliban, including Osama bin Laden.

Diplomats still commit blunders every day; even small ones are not insignificant. When the president of Romania dined at the Pentagon in October 2003, U.S. officials put flags on the table: American—and Russian. It's an easy mistake—after all, Romania is next to Russia on the list of nations.

In another example, President George W. Bush, attempting to placate the Russians in 2007 about the construction of a U.S. missile base in the Czech Republic, invited Russian troops to be stationed there—without asking the Czechs.

Diplomacy is said to be the art of the possible. But if it's possible to win your opponents over, it's also possible to make some serious blunders.

✳ The British royal family changed its name from "Saxe-Coburg and Gotha" to "Windsor" in 1917, during World War I, because its original name sounded too German. It would have been difficult to fit onto a business card, as well. The royals are still known as the House of Windsor.

✳ Before the outbreak of World War II, Winston Churchill was informed that the Italians intended to fight on the side of Germany. After consideration, Churchill responded: "That's fair; we had them last time."

Origins: The History of Things

These intriguing stories offer insight into the history of some everyday items, expressions, and endeavors—stuff you never think to think about.

✳ ✳ ✳ ✳

The Latin Alphabet

PEOPLE HAD BEEN writing hieroglyphics (symbols that stood for objects) for at least a millennium before the first glimmer of an actual alphabet appeared. Around 2000 B.C., a group of Egyptian slaves (the Semitics) figured out how to communicate with one another using symbols that represented sounds, not just things. From this system, we eventually got the Phoenician and Aramaic alphabets, as well as the Greek and Latin alphabets. Early Greek was written right to left, before the "ox-turning" method (in which the direction of writing changed with every line) was adopted. By the fifth century B.C., the left-to-right method was in place.

The Evil Eye

From Europe to the Middle East, from Mexico to Scandinavia, folktales have long warned people against the power of the "evil eye." Essentially, the evil eye is an unintentional look of envy from a person who covets what the recipient possesses. At the very least, it's a bad vibe; at its most potent, the evil eye is blamed for bad luck, disease, and even death in the person who receives the look. Cultures that fear the evil eye have developed various means of protection: A common European custom is to wear a locket containing a prayer. In India, small mirrors are sewn into clothing to deflect an evil gaze and reflect back to who gave it; similarly, the Chinese use a six-sided mirror called a *pa kua*. The Italians have developed various hand gestures for protection. Sometimes the defense is more elaborate: Folk healers in Mexico smear raw chicken eggs over someone's body to keep him or her safe from the evil eye.

The Face-lift

Contrary to popular belief, the "plastic" in "plastic surgery" doesn't refer to the use of petroleum-based materials; rather, it's from the Greek word *plastikos*, meaning "to mold or shape." The first facial plastic surgeries date back to ancient Rome, when they were probably performed to fix ears and noses that had been torn off during Coliseum scuffles. It wasn't until the 1900s that face-lifts, or rhytidectomies (literally, the surgical removal of wrinkles), were performed for cosmetic reasons. These days, plastic surgeons in the United States perform facelifts at the rate of approximately 150,000 a year.

The Jump Rope

Skipping and jumping are natural movements of the body (especially for kids), and the inclusion of a rope in these activities dates back to A.D. 1600, when Egyptian children jumped over vines. Early Dutch settlers brought the game to North America, where it flourished and evolved from a simple motion into another elaborate form: double Dutch. With two people turning two ropes simultaneously, a third, and then fourth, person jumps in, often reciting rhymes.

Vampires

The word "vampire" is rooted in the Hungarian word *vampyr*, a spirit who feasts on the living. The vampire archetype we recognize today (fanged, bloodsucking monsters who otherwise look normal) seems to have originated in 18th-century Eastern Europe. In the early 1700s, Serbian police investigated dozens of claims of vampirism after people died in strange, inexplicable ways—and sometimes allegedly came back to life. Most scholars attribute these claims to premature burials or rabies; nonetheless, most of Europe was already caught up in Dracula drama. Vampire lore is thousands of years old and exists in many cultures around the world. In the Old Testament, Lilith (who, according to Hebrew legend, was Adam's first wife) is described as a bloodthirsty demon. Ancient Greeks told tales of a vampire-like creature called Lamia, who was fond of the blood of children. India is rich in vampire lore. The beautiful and terrible goddess known as Kali had fangs and four arms and drank the blood of her enemies to prevent them from coming back to destroy her. Vampires in Romania are called *strigoi* (from the Latin term for screech owl), and Romanians believe that these creatures are reanimated corpses who return to suck the blood of humans and livestock. In some Eastern European regions, cemetery workers would exhume bodies years after burial to check for vampirism. If the corpse wasn't decomposed, had one foot in the corner of the casket, and had a ruddy face, it was thought to be a vampire and was quickly decapitated.

Quiche

Although similar concoctions date back to ancient Roman cheesecakes and medieval European tarts and pies, the modern quiche recipe comes from the Lorraine region of France. The original quiche Lorraine was an open-face pie filled with eggs, cream, and bacon. Cheese was later incorporated, along with any number of additions, from shallots to shellfish, depending on one's preference. In North America, quiche enjoyed its greatest popularity as a trendy 1970s food, joined by other such notable offerings as fondue and Caesar salad.

Taxicabs

Think of Cleopatra being carted around on a sedan chair, and you have the origins of the modern-day taxicab. Rickshaws replaced sedan chairs as a means of transporting people from one place to another, followed by horse-drawn carriages, which finally gave us poor humans a rest. At the end of the 19th century, automobiles started to fill the streets, and with the invention of the taximeter (an instrument that measures both the time and distance a vehicle has traveled), transport by cab became increasingly popular. Throughout the world, cab companies have painted their taxis particular colors, both for identification purposes and to cut down on the number of unofficial drivers. Today in New York City alone, taxis drive more than 200 million passengers almost 800 million miles every year.

Clarifications on Columbus

Aside from the Pilgrims, Christopher Columbus is one of the most misunderstood figures in U.S. history—in fact, there's question as to whether he was even a notable part of it.

✳ ✳ ✳ ✳

Columbus was not Spanish. He was likely born in Genoa, Italy, of mixed Mediterranean heritages (including Greek). Scholars of medieval Spanish are quick to tell us that Spanish wasn't even his first language.

Columbus did not prove the world was round. This presupposes that any educated person still believed the earth was flat, and by 1492, few did. Of course, most people were uneducated, and because they seldom traveled farther than ten miles from the place they called home, few of them cared.

Columbus did not discover America. Native Americans were already well aware of the continents they had inhabited for millennia. But Columbus didn't even discover America for Europe. West African, Afro-Phoenician, and Viking explorers all show evidence that they'd visited the Americas centuries earlier.

What's more, Columbus never landed in the continental United States or even Mexico. His four voyages took him through the Caribbean islands and to the coasts of South and Central America. In the United States, we make a great fuss over someone whose only sighting of future American soil was Puerto Rico and the U.S. Virgin Islands.

Columbus was never hopelessly lost. Mariners of his day could easily determine latitude but not longitude. It was thus difficult to make accurate landfalls, but Columbus consistently did. Columbus was among the few European navigators who possessed the geographical aptitude of the Polynesians, Arabs, and Chinese. He did believe that he was near India, China, and Japan, but only because he misjudged Earth's circumference.

Rumors of War

Plenty of myths have come out of World War II, but few are as unfounded as the claim that President Franklin Delano Roosevelt allowed the Japanese to attack Pearl Harbor so the United States could enter the conflict.

✳   ✳   ✳   ✳

UNFORTUNATELY, THIS RUMOR has followed FDR's legacy almost from the moment of the attack, and many people continue to believe it today. But countless investigations and studies have failed to uncover a "smoking gun" that proves the president could have engineered such a huge act of treason.

Coded Knowledge

Conspiracy theorists frequently note that the U.S. military had successfully broken Japanese codes and thus knew in advance of the attack. This is partially true—Japanese codes had been broken, but they were diplomatic codes, not military ones. The military *had* received notice from other sources, including the British, that an attack was pending. What wasn't known was where the attack would take place. Almost everyone assumed it would be against the Philippines or some other Pacific territory, and no one had reason to believe that the target would be the military base at Pearl Harbor.

Another common assumption is that Roosevelt had the Pacific Fleet moved from San Diego to Pearl Harbor to lure the Japanese into attacking. However, it wasn't Roosevelt who made that decision. Rather, it was the State Department, which hoped to deter Japanese aggression with a show of naval force.

Ships at Sea

Many conspiracy theorists also like to claim that the American aircraft carriers based at Pearl Harbor had been sent on maneuvers prior to the attack as a precaution, so the attack wouldn't be as damaging as it could have been. In fact, the

Japanese devastated the Pacific Fleet, sinking four U.S. battle-ships and severely damaging four others. In addition, three light cruisers, three destroyers, and four smaller vessels were demolished or heavily damaged, and 75 percent of the island's military air fleet was annihilated before the planes could take to the sky. The value of the aircraft carriers that survived because they were on maneuvers wouldn't be realized until months later, at the Battle of Midway.

An Excuse to Fight

Perhaps most important is that Roosevelt didn't need a Japanese attack to bring the United States into the war. Though officially neutral at the time, the country was actively engaged in fighting the Axis by providing war materials to Great Britain and other Allied nations via the Lend-Lease Act. Furthermore, antiwar sentiment was waning dramatically as Americans grew increasingly angered by Japanese and German aggression. It was just a matter of time before the United States took off the gloves and waded into the war that was engulfing the world.

In FDR's Defense

It's a huge disservice to one of the nation's greatest presidents to assume that FDR would intentionally sacrifice the lives of thousands of troops and civilians, as well as cripple the coun-try's most vital Pacific naval base, just for the opportunity to enter a war that a growing number of Americans were starting to see as inevitable. Japan was intent on aggressively expanding its sphere of influence in the Pacific—territories that included American allies and interests. But as the drumbeat of war grew louder around the world, there was no way the United States could let that happen, despite the country's publicly stated neutrality. What's more, Roosevelt already had the required number of congressional votes for war when the time came. It's important to note that several major investigations were conducted to find what went wrong at Pearl Harbor, including an inquiry ordered by Roosevelt just 11 days after the attack. None found cause to suspect the president of any wrongdoing.

They Helped Kill Lincoln: Booth's Coconspirators

John Wilkes Booth is well known for his assassination of President Abraham Lincoln, but the rather lengthy list of his coconspirators has not been quite so memorable.

✳ ✳ ✳ ✳

A POPULAR SHAKESPEAREAN STAGE actor who traveled the country performing, John Wilkes Booth could have kept busy enjoying his notoriety and fame. Instead, inspired by the Civil War, he was firmly entrenched in his racist beliefs and loyalty to the Confederacy. Once Lincoln freed the slaves in the rebelling states, Booth branded the abolitionist president his archenemy. Dead set on bringing down Lincoln and preserving the Confederacy and slavery, Booth began to plot his attack. Initially, he planned to kidnap Lincoln and then ransom him for captive Confederate soldiers, but the conspiracy evolved, of course, into the first presidential assassination in U.S. history.

The Accomplices

Booth, who was charismatic and persuasive, had no trouble forming a gang of like-minded conspirators. Samuel Arnold, George Atzerodt, David Herold, Lewis Powell, John Surratt, and Michael O'Laughlen all joined with Booth to design various plots that would achieve victory for the South.

Meeting regularly at a boardinghouse run by Mary Surratt, the mother of one of the conspirators, the club decided to kidnap Lincoln in early 1865. They would snatch him from his box at a play and then ransom him for imprisoned Confederate soldiers. It would be a twofold victory, as they would cause grievance for their nemesis and bring the Confederacy closer to victory. Their plan was thwarted, though, when Lincoln failed to appear at the scheduled event. Similar plans were hatched, but for various reasons, none came to fruition. Frustrated with his inability to capture Lincoln and spurred by Lincoln's continued attempts to dismantle the system of slavery, Booth determined that kidnapping was simply not enough: Lincoln must die!

Arnold, John Surratt, and O'Laughlen later swore that they knew nothing of the murder plot, but Atzerodt, Herold, and Powell certainly did. They each had their own roles in the assassination scheme, even though they were unsuccessful. Atzerodt was slated to assassinate Vice President Andrew Johnson, while Powell and Herold were scheduled to kill Secretary of State William Seward. All three killings were planned for the same time on the evening of April 14, 1865.

Going into Action

Only Booth found complete success in the mission, however. Atzerodt apparently backed down from his assignment in fear. Powell cut a path of carnage through the Seward mansion, stabbing the secretary of state in the face and neck and wounding two of Seward's sons, a daughter, a soldier guarding Seward, and a messenger, although no one was killed. Herold had been with Powell but ran away when the mission didn't seem to be going smoothly. Booth shot Lincoln in the back of the head. The president died on the morning of April 15.

Booth immediately fled the scene, injuring a leg. He met up with Herold, and the pair ran for two weeks before being discovered on a small farm. The fugitives were holed up in a barn—Herold surrendered, but when Booth refused to do the same, soldiers set the barn on fire. In the ensuing melee, Booth was shot in the neck; he died a few hours later. Atzerodt, Herold, and Powell were hanged for their crimes, as was one more purported coconspirator, Mary Surratt. She ran the boardinghouse in which much of this plot was hatched, a plot which definitely included her son. Her specific involvement and knowledge of the affair, however, has frequently been challenged. The rest of the coconspirators, as well as others with suspicious ties to the group, were sentenced to jail time.

Early Vice Presidents

Some vice presidents have played key roles in state affairs; others have been primarily marginal figures.

✽   ✽   ✽   ✽

✽ John Adams (1789–1797, V.P. under George Washington): Here's what Adams had to say about his job: "My country has in its wisdom contrived for me the most insignificant office that ever the invention of man contrived or his imagination conceived."

✽ Thomas Jefferson (1797–1801, John Adams): He became vice president by coming in second to Adams in electoral votes, making the Adams administration the only one in history divided between two political parties. He was considered a good V.P., but was a bad money manager. After his death, his executors sold his remaining slaves to square up the large debts he left.

✽ Aaron Burr (1801–1805, Thomas Jefferson): After Burr killed Alexander Hamilton in a duel, he was indicted but not seriously pursued. He ran off to New Orleans, where he allegedly intended to raise a private army, conquer the Southwest, and become its leader. In 1834, Burr suffered a stroke and was debilitated until he died in 1836.

✽ George Clinton (1805–1812, Jefferson, then James Madison): He opposed ratification of the Constitution in 1788, stating that it gave the federal government too much power. He also disagreed with creation of the office of V.P., but that didn't prevent him from taking it. He was the first vice president to die in office.

✽ Elbridge Gerry (1813–1814, Madison): This vice president gets dubious credit for "gerrymandering"—redrawing legislative districts for optimum political advantage. After he died in office, the vice presidency remained vacant for three years.

✻ Daniel D. Tompkins (1817–1825, James Monroe): After years of litigation with the federal and New York state governments over loans and money, Tompkins sought stress relief from the bottle. He survived his term by a little more than three months.

✻ John Calhoun (1825–1832, John Q. Adams and Andrew Jackson): During the 1760s, he was a Regulator—a member of a vigilante group attempting to impose law and order in the Carolina backwoods. While serving in James Monroe's cabinet, he urged court-martial for Andrew Jackson—under whom he would later serve as vice president. Ravaged by tuberculosis, Calhoun was the first V.P. to resign the office.

✻ Martin Van Buren (1833–1837, Jackson): He spent a lot of time fighting former Speaker of the House Henry Clay. Van Buren was elected president, but the Panic of 1837 began within weeks of his inauguration. In his run for re-election, he didn't even carry his home state, New York.

✻ Richard M. Johnson (1837–1841, Martin Van Buren): He was the first and only vice president chosen by the Senate, as the 12th Amendment dictated; also the first Baptist V.P.

✻ John Tyler (1841, William H. Harrison): Tyler was vice president for only 33 days when Harrison died, and as president, he didn't appoint a V.P. at all. He sired 15 children by 2 wives and was elected to the Confederate House of Representatives not long before his death.

✻ George Dallas (1845–1849, James K. Polk): After being informed of alcohol abuse in Senate chambers, Dallas told the sergeant-at-arms to ban liquor on the Senate side of the Capitol, except for medicinal purposes.

✻ Millard Fillmore (1849–1850, Zachary Taylor): Fillmore had been an indentured servant in his youth. During his short term as vice president, he had the joy of presiding over a raucous Senate in which the senior senator from

Mississippi once drew a pistol. He later ran for president on the Know-Nothing Party ticket.

* William R. King (1853, Franklin Pierce): King wore a wig long after they'd gone out of style. As senator, he once challenged Henry Clay to a duel, but the confrontation never took place. The only bachelor V.P., King took the oath of office in Cuba and died 25 days later, so he didn't accomplish a lot.

* John C. Breckenridge (1857–1861, James Buchanan): Breckenridge was elected V.P. when he was just 35, and as a result, Buchanan mostly ignored him. While serving in the House, Breckenridge almost dueled another legislator with rifles, but the diplomats resolved their grievance in proper congressional style: They shook hands and had a chew together.

* Hannibal Hamlin (1861–1865, Abraham Lincoln): A former governor of Maine, Hamlin found the Senate boring and often didn't bother presiding. Lincoln didn't select him for his second term, or he might have become President Hamlin. He did try, as had Dallas, to sober up the Senate.

* Andrew Johnson (1865, Lincoln): The morning he took the oath of office, he drank whiskey to fortify himself, then launched into an anti-Southern rant. Lincoln suddenly began to appreciate the outgoing Hannibal Hamlin (who finally managed to shut Johnson up). The new V.P. was too intoxicated to swear in the new senators; a Senate clerk had to handle it.

* Schuyler Colfax (1869–1873, Ulysses S. Grant): Nicknamed "Smiler," he was always cordial and urbane. He was involved with the Know-Nothing Party (a movement hostile to immigrants and Catholics) but also campaigned actively against slavery. Late in his term, the Crédit Mobilier railroad scandal turned his public name to mud.

The Golden Age of Piracy: 1500–1835

The golden age of piracy spawned some of the most feared and bloodthirsty individuals to ever sail the seven seas.

✳   ✳   ✳   ✳

ALTHOUGH PIRACY GOES back to ancient times, historians consider 1500–1835 to be its golden age. These three-plus centuries of infamy spawned some of the world's most feared cutthroats—nemeses of all nations whose ships sailed the seven seas while engaged in exploration and commerce. These notorious buccaneers have become legendary in the annals of high seas adventure, daring, and cruelty.

Blackbeard

Take, for example, Edward Teach, whose glistening black beard established the pseudonym by which he became more popularly known. Probably the best-known pirate in history, Teach, aka Blackbeard, was the scourge of the Caribbean and the western Atlantic. His end came at the hands of English Lieutenant Robert Maynard in a cove off the coast of North Carolina. Blackbeard's treasure is still rumored to be buried somewhere on Ocracoke Island.

Captain Kidd

William Kidd was a privateer hired to rid the seas of marauders; instead, he became a pirate himself, stealing the plunder from the pirates he was sent to vanquish and sailing to New York with his ill-gotten gain. The authorities noticed his treachery, especially the powerful British East India Company, to whom the booty belonged. Kidd was captured and sent to England to be hanged—three times. The rope broke twice during Kidd's execution, but the third time was the charm.

Henry Morgan

Dubbed "The King of Pirates," Henry Morgan was as much
a scourge on land as he was on the high seas. Greatly feared
by the Spanish, Morgan once attacked the Cuban stronghold
Puerto Principe, as well as Panama's treasure city, Porto Bello.
The Spanish dubbed him "Morgan the Terrible." He was
probably the most ruthless of all the buccaneers. Morgan was
eventually knighted and hired by the English to rid the world
of piracy.

And the Rest

There were many pirates who diligently plied their trade in
terror and were considered scourges in their own right, though
not of the legendary status of a Henry Morgan. Some of the
lesser-known pirates of the golden age were Stede Bonnet,
Charles Vane, Edward England, Christopher Condent, Ben
Hornigold, the dapper Black Bart, Henry Jennings, Pierre
LeGrand, and Calico Jack Rackham. Calico Jack, however, was
overshadowed by the exploits of his wife, the most famous
of all female pirates (and there were several), Ann Bonney.
Disguised as a man, Bonney fought alongside her husband and
his crew, even when she was pregnant with Rackham's child.
When finally captured, Bonney used her condition to plead
for mercy and received a temporary stay of execution. Her fate
from that point is unknown. Some believe she was ransomed
by her father and returned to her native Ireland.

Life on the High Seas

Why anyone would become a pirate in the first place boggles
the mind. The ships were filthy and diseased; life was harsh.
Cramped quarters, rats, foul water, scurvy, weevil-infested food,
dangerous weather, and backbreaking work were as much a part
of buccaneer life as plundering and killing. Most pirate crews
consisted of men between the ages of 17 and 27; anyone older
or younger was not expected to survive. During the golden age
of piracy, there were said to be more than a million noncombat
deaths among the buccaneers.

Let's Settle This: History's Shortest Wars

As wars grow costlier and transportation gets faster, battles compress the same level of tragedy into shorter durations.

❋ ❋ ❋ ❋

Anglo-Zanzibar War (9:02–9:40 A.M., August 27, 1896, Great Britain versus Zanzibar): The British liked it when the Sultan of Zanzibar (an island off modern Tanzania) engaged in battles. When a new sultan named Khalid bin Barghash refused to, the Royal Navy gave Zanzibar a taste of British anger. Bin Barghash tapped out after just 38 minutes of shelling in what is the shortest recorded war.

Spanish-American War (April 25–August 12, 1898, United States versus Spain): Spain once had an empire, some of which was very near Florida. After months of tension, the battleship USS *Maine* blew up in Havana harbor. Though no one knew why it exploded, the United States declared war anyway. A few months later, Spain had lost Cuba, Guam, the Philippines, and Puerto Rico.

Nazi-Polish War (September 1–October 6, 1939, Nazi Germany and Soviet Union versus Poland): After Russian and German negotiators signed a secret agreement in August for the division of Poland, the Nazis invaded in vicious armored thrusts with heavy air attacks. Polish forces fought with uncommon valor, but their strategic position was impossible. Russian troops entered from the east on September 17, and Poland became the first European nation conquered in World War II.

Nazi-Danish War (4:15–9:20 A.M., April 9, 1940, Nazi Germany versus Denmark): Arguably the biggest mismatch of World War II (unless one counts Germany's invasion of Luxembourg). Sixteen Danish soldiers died before the Danish government ordered the resistance to cease.

Suez/Sinai War (October 29–November 6, 1956, Israel, Britain, and France versus Egypt): The Egyptians decided to nationalize the Suez Canal, which seems logical given that it is entirely in Egypt. British and French companies operating the canal didn't agree. The Israelis invaded by land, the British and French by air and sea. The invaders won a complete victory, but the rest of world got so mad that they withdrew.

Six-Day War (June 5–10, 1967, Israel versus Egypt, Syria, and Jordan): Israelis launched a sneak attack on the Egyptians, destroying the Egyptian air force on its airfields and sending the Egyptians reeling back toward the Suez Canal. Jordanians attacked the Israelis and immediately regretted it. The Israelis attacked Syria and seized Golan Heights.

Yom Kippur War (October 6–25, 1973, Egypt and Syria versus Israel): Egyptians and Syrians, still annoyed and embarrassed over the Six-Day War, attacked Israelis on a national religious holiday. Israeli forces were caught napping at first but soon regained the upper hand—they struck within artillery range of Damascus and crossed the Suez Canal. The United Nations' ceasefire came as a major relief to all involved, even the Israelis, who had no desire to administer Cairo and Damascus.

Soccer War (July 15–19, 1969, El Salvador versus Honduras): Immigration was the core issue, specifically the forced expulsion of some 60,000 Salvadorean illegal immigrants from Honduras. When a soccer series between the two Central American nations fueled tensions, a bloody yet inconclusive war followed.

Falklands War (March 19–June 14, 1982, Argentina versus United Kingdom): Argentina has long claimed the Falkland Islands as Las Islas Malvinas. In 1982, Argentina decided to enforce this claim by invading the Falklands and South Georgia. Although the Argentines had a surprise for the Royal Navy in the form of air-launched antiship missiles, the battle for the islands went heavily against them. Its survivors, including most of its marines, were shipped back home minus their weaponry.

The Lady with the Lamp: Florence Nightingale

Did she really invent modern nursing and then take to her bed and become reclusive?

✳ ✳ ✳ ✳

✳ Florence was born in Florence (Tuscany, Italy) in 1820 to William and Fanny Nightingale.

✳ Fanny's idea was to marry off her daughter to a good "catch," but young Florence turned down all the acceptable suitors.

✳ Her commitment to nursing stemmed from her deep Unitarian Christianity, emphasized by a sense of divine calling from the time she was in her late teens.

✳ She had to go to Germany to study nursing. Her main encouragement came from Dr. Elizabeth Blackwell, the first officially qualified female doctor in the United States.

✳ Florence Nightingale was an outstanding mathematician and statistician. She didn't invent the pie chart, but she used it and other innovative methods of data presentation.

✳ Only in recent generations have military hospitals become survivable; for most of history, disease was more deadly to soldiers than war itself. During the Crimean War, where Florence earned her nursing stripes, cholera and malaria ran far more rampant than rifle balls and shell fragments.

✳ Ever heard of World War I "donkey generals"? Florence dealt with donkey doctors. The wounded came in caked with battlefield filth, suffering from disease and malnutrition, and instead of being given anesthesia and compassion, they were encouraged to keep stiff upper lips. Believe it or not, the donkey doctors resented Florence's objections; in so many words, they told her to buzz off and bake some biscuits.

* Only after media reports of the soldiers' misery did doctors relent and let Florence organize a hospital her way. Incredibly, disease and death increased! This wasn't her fault; there was a major cholera and typhus outbreak among the troops. Some nurses and doctors died as well. With major support from the British War Office, better sanitation was emphasized, and death rates from disease decreased.

* Feminist irony: Florence, who had rejected a traditional gender role, ended up helping soldiers by organizing other women to bake biscuits and do laundry. One of her key complaints about military medical care was the horrid food and filthy clothing. Her kitchen and washing operations remedied that pestilential situation.

* Even as she was reforming and defining nursing, Florence Nightingale was human enough to have a considerable ego. Another enterprising woman, Mary Seacole, was also concerned about the soldiers—and she, an expert on cholera, traveled to the front to help Florence, who responded by hogging the limelight and declining Mary's help. The spurned volunteer set up her own treatment program financed by profits from a soldiers' restaurant she operated.

* Florence really did walk around with a lamp. She was the only woman allowed in the wards at night, when male orderlies were in charge of the hospital floor.

* Florence herself took ill in Crimea. It was called Crimean Fever back then; medical analysts now believe this was brucellosis—a chronic disease that also affected livestock. She recovered, but photos of her on return to England show a gaunt shadow of the vibrant young crusader she had been.

* Once back in England, Florence Nightingale campaigned for better nursing care. A meeting with Queen Victoria and Prince Albert led to the foundation of a nurse-training program. Before this, from a social standpoint, "nurse" had

barely been recognized as an occupation available to women. Now it was a legitimate and honorable profession.

* Even as an invalid—which she was for a quarter century, because of her brucellosis—she advised, watched, and assisted the growth of her profession. Never a paragon of tact, however, she became distant from family and suffered frequent depression most likely related to her illness.

* Believe it or not, she was accused of laziness after she returned home. One wonders if any of her accusers ever spent a quarter century dealing with a disease (perhaps more than one) that produced symptoms such as nausea, insomnia, depression, rapid heartbeat, weakness, inability to walk, intense spinal pain, and severe headache.

* When Florence was 60 years old, her illness and depression seem to have disappeared. The side effects of 25 years of relative isolation from humanity, except on her own terms, didn't clear up so easily. By this time, Nightingale nurses (as her program's graduates were known) were becoming authorities on the subject in their own right, and several brought their knowledge to the United States.

* Though Florence was an ardent women's rights advocate, some feminists felt she didn't do enough to support women who sought to make the leap from nursing to doctoring. She didn't approve of women's public speech-making, for instance, preferring instead to work behind the scenes.

* Florence had 15 years of relatively good health until her eyesight and mind began to fail in the 1890s. It is widely speculated that she suffered from Chronic Fatigue Syndrome. Today, her birthday (May 12) is International CFS Awareness Day.

* She lingered as a blind invalid under nursing care until she died in 1910, too early to see what her efforts wrought for military medicine in World War I.

Paul Revere: The Truth is Coming!

It's hard to get the straight story on Paul Revere, thanks in large part to Henry Wadsworth Longfellow's poem about the allegedly lone midnight rider. Let's sort through some of the misconceptions.

✳ ✳ ✳ ✳

Revere was half French. True. His mother was a Bostonian, and his father was a French immigrant named Apollos Rivoire, Anglicized to "Revere."

Revere was a brilliant silversmith. Not quite. He was certainly competent, and a good metalworking businessman, but he was no Michelangelo of silver. When history started venerating Paul Revere, it was a package deal: All his activities were magnified, logic and proportion aside.

Revere hung signal lanterns in a church tower. False. He had others hang them. Paul excelled at getting people to help his underground communications network. By the way, the actual signal was two dimly lit lanterns, which meant that the British army would take the Charles River route.

Revere yelled, "The British are coming!" False. That would be like someone from Pittsburgh yelling, "The Americans are coming!" Like nearly all colonists, Revere considered himself British. His warning specified that the "regulars" (i.e., the regular British army) were on the march—which they were. Furthermore, it's unlikely that Revere "yelled" anything, because British army patrols were everywhere.

Revere rode directly to Lexington and Concord. False. Revere was a key organizer of many riders in an informal, early-warning network (much like a primitive phone tree), and he often carried news from point A to point B for the colonial cause. On April 18, 1775, Revere was first in the chain of many riders who went forth to mobilize the militia and protect colonial munitions stores and leaders from surprise seizure. Fellow rider William Dawes soon joined him, and they later picked up Samuel Prescott.

Revere fought at Lexington. False. You can't fight while helping another guy lug a chest of documents around town. Revere was close to the fighting, though, with muskets being fired around him. Plus, he was doing more preserving a trunk of secrets than he might have with a musket, especially since the colonial militia broke and ran for it.

Revere was convicted of cowardice in the 1779 Penobscot Expedition. False. Commanding the expedition's artillery, Revere stood accused of disobeying orders. Rightfully offended, after the war he demanded a court-martial—and it exonerated him. Although his military career was underwhelming, the evidence of Revere's life hurls any hint of cowardice out the window.

Revere has always been considered a national hero. False. He was always a regional hero in Massachusetts, but it was Longfellow's poem that got him into history texts and the memories of schoolchildren everywhere. The poem overstates Revere's role at the expense of many others', but its mid-Civil War timing was impeccable in capturing public emotion. As often happens, history's heroes can be either forgotten or exaggerated, but they're rarely remembered as they truly were.

---

* Paul Revere probably did not own a horse at the time of his famous ride. In fact, he likely rode a borrowed horse.

* Civil War Colonel Paul Joseph Revere of the 20th Massachusetts, grandson of Revolutionary War hero Paul Revere, was mortally wounded at Gettysburg, Pennsylvania.

Military Blunders 101

Many of military history's biggest blunders have resulted from inexperience, negligence, diplomatic indifference, incompetence, lack of discipline, overconfidence, or poor information. Some would be laughable, if they hadn't resulted in the loss of human lives.

✳   ✳   ✳   ✳

The Battle of Karansebes (1788)

WHAT WAS MEANT to be a decisive engagement against the Ottoman Empire during the Russo-Turkish War turned out to be a self-destructive defeat. Two contingents of the Austrian army—one scouting the enemy, the other setting up camp—converged; each thought the other was the enemy, and a battle ensued. The scouting party had been imbibing a little schnapps, and discipline fell apart. The Austrians killed 10,000 of their own troops while the enemy was still a two-day march away.

Hitler Declares War on the United States (1941)

Even the mighty führer blundered big time when he declared war on the United States immediately following the sneak attack on Pearl Harbor. He walked right into President Franklin Roosevelt's web. The president had been waiting for a reason to enter the war in Europe. With the addition of the United States, the combined Allied forces were a little too much for Hitler, who just might have achieved his objective of dominance if he'd played the right card at the right time.

The Bay of Pigs Invasions (both of them)

Yes, there were two. The first one was in August 1851, when former Spanish officer and Cuban sympathizer Narciso López recruited a band of American mercenaries and landed at the Bahía de Cochinos (Bay of Pigs) to engage Spanish forces. The invaders were handily defeated and most were executed, including López and Colonel William Crittenden, nephew of

American Attorney General John Crittenden. According to experts, the attack was a tactical error. The Bay of Pigs is too easily defended against an invasion from the sea.

Although President Kennedy voluntarily took the heat for the failure of the second Bay of Pigs debacle (which consisted of CIA-trained Cuban exiles, who expected but never received American support), the reason for the second failure was much the same as the first: The Bay of Pigs can be defended much too easily. In this case, however, contrary to the expectations of the Cuban exiles, many in the local population took up arms against the invaders who were there to liberate them. Fidel Castro was still a popular hero to many.

The Spanish-American War (1898)

SNAFU and FUBAR are both acronyms that originated in the military—Situation Normal All Fouled Up and Fouled Up Beyond All Recognition. At the start of the Spanish-American War, General William Rufus Shafter's troops were issued woolen winter uniforms. The tropical climate in Cuba took a greater toll on the troops than the fighting did—even the 375-pound Shafter was a victim of heat prostration. Additionally, the troopship set to transport the Rough Riders to Cuba was not large enough to carry the troops and their horses. Only one man was mounted in the "cavalry" charge up San Juan Hill: Lieutenant Colonel Theodore Roosevelt, who was allowed to bring his favorite horse, Little Texas. The other horses were left behind. The Rough Riders became the "Tough Trekkers" when they hoofed it up the hill.

Custer's Last Stand
(The Battle of Little Bighorn, 1876)

No list of military blunders would be complete without this infamous cavalry catastrophe. It was mostly Custer's impatience and arrogance that caused the massacre of the Seventh Cavalry unit he led into battle. Custer's scouts also underestimated the size of the enemy force, an amalgamation of Cheyenne,

Arapaho, and Sioux, consisting of nearly 2,000 warriors. Custer's force numbered 263. If he'd waited a little longer, Custer would have linked up with the rest of his command and had a fighting chance.

The Charge of the Light Brigade
(The Battle of Balaklava, 1854)

This is another obvious choice. The Battle of Balaklava was one of the key engagements of the Crimean War. Major General Cardigan misunderstood the orders of his superior commander, Lieutenant General Raglan, and led his 670-strong cavalry unit to attack a Russian artillery bastion of more than 5,000. They went at it head-on, resulting in the deaths of 118 attackers (127 more were wounded). Cardigan survived long enough to become a field marshal—and have a sweater named after him. The battle itself was considered indecisive.

Invasion of Russia (1812 and 1941)

Perhaps the best known tactical errors involve Russia; both Napoleon and Adolf Hitler were helped to defeat by their unwise attacks on its vast, cold expanse. In Napoleon's case, his foolhardy 1812 invasion was foiled by strategic Russian retreats and the onset of the bitter winter. This failure was the beginning of the end for Napoleon, who ultimately abdicated the French throne in 1814.

Not learning from Napoleon's mistake, however, Hitler invaded the USSR in 1941, violating the 1939 nonaggression pact between Nazi Germany and Russia and exposing the Third Reich to a two-front war. The element of surprise and superior German equipment brought early success to Hitler's forces, but delays brought his army face-to-face with the brutal Russian winter. Mother Nature decimated the German troops, proving that the "master race" was no match for her biting cold.

George Washington's Hatchet Job

For 200 years, schoolkids have been taught that George Washington couldn't tell a lie. Considering the endurance of this story, today's political flacks could learn a thing or two from the man who made up the tale.

✳   ✳   ✳   ✳

ACCORDING TO LEGEND, six-year-old George tried out his hatchet on everything within reach, including his father's beloved cherry tree. When his father saw the remains of his tree, he asked George if he knew who had chopped it down. The boy famously cried, "I can't tell a lie, Pa; you know I can't tell a lie. I cut it with my hatchet." Father embraced son, declaring that his honesty was worth more "than a thousand trees, though blossomed with silver, and their fruits of purest gold."

Although the first U.S. president was renowned for his honor, virtue, and sense of duty, he often came across as cold, dull, and uninspiring—hardly the stuff of legend. Mason Locke Weems, a fiery pastor and bookseller, took it upon himself to spice up Washington's image. His book *The Life and Memorable Actions of George Washington* was first published in 1800, a year after Washington's death. It was an instant hit and was republished several times, with each edition boasting additions to a section titled "Curious Anecdotes Laudable to Himself and Exemplary to his Countrymen." The fabricated cherry tree story was included in the fifth edition (1806) and every edition thereafter.

The damage done by Weems's well-intentioned tale is immeasurable. First, he set the bar uncomfortably high, both for six-year-olds who are naturally inclined to fib and for parents pressured to value a misbehaving child's honesty above retribution. But the real harm comes in hoodwinking children into ignoring their sense of self-preservation. In 200 years, how many miscreants have bravely told the truth and received nothing but a sound scolding?

The Creation of Kwanzaa

When the holiday season arrives in the United States, offices and shopping malls are decked with posters that celebrate Christmas, Hanukkah, and Kwanzaa. Yet many don't realize how recently the secular holiday of Kwanzaa originated.

✻ ✻ ✻ ✻

I T DOESN'T TAKE long to trace the birth of Kwanzaa—one need only go as far back as Los Angeles in 1966, when Ron Karenga, a young political activist and scholar, invented the holiday. Karenga was a leader of the wide-ranging Black Nationalist movement. He intended Kwanzaa to be a replacement for Christmas, which he and his followers perceived as a vehicle of white power and commercialism.

Kwanzaa was officially inaugurated on December 26, 1966, when Karenga and his family and friends gathered together to light a candle that represented unity. According to Karenga, Kwanzaa "was chosen to give a Black alternative to the existing holiday and give Blacks an opportunity to celebrate themselves and history, rather than simply imitate the practice of the dominant society." Over time, Karenga reinvented Kwanzaa as a holiday meant to supplement, rather than replace, other holidays. The official Kwanzaa Web site states that Kwanzaa "is not an alternative to people's religion or faith but a common ground of African culture."

Kwanzaa is observed each year from December 26 through January 1. The symbols and practices of the holiday derive from a conglomeration of various African religions. Each day of celebration is devoted to one of the seven principles, or *Nguzo Saba*, which are unity, self-determination, collective work and responsibility, cooperative economics, purpose, creativity, and faith. The seven candles of the candleholder, or the *Kinara*, represent these seven principles. During Kwanzaa, African heritage and identity is discussed and celebrated through artwork.

The word *Kwanzaa* means "first fruits" in Swahili, an East-African language. The colors of Kwanzaa are black, red, and green: black for the people, red for the struggle, and green for the future and for the hope that comes from struggle. Many Kwanzaa traditions are inspired by the first harvest celebrations of Africa. Kwanzaa is a time for family and friends to gather in celebration, thus strengthening community and cultural bonds. Celebrants typically have one large feast, and the final day of Kwanzaa is reserved for reflection and self-evaluation.

Some controversy surrounds Kwanzaa, as it is tied up with the actions and political views of Karenga. He spent four years in prison for the 1971 assault and torture of two women who were involved with The Organization Us, a Black Nationalist group that Karenga founded in 1965. It was after Karenga was released from prison in 1975 that he repudiated some of his more extreme views. Today, Karenga remains the leader of The Organization Us. According to this organization's Web site, the heart of their project is "the continuing quest to define and become the best of what it means to be both African and human in the fullest sense."

It is difficult to gauge the popularity of Kwanzaa among African Americans and other groups worldwide. The majority of African Americans do not celebrate the holiday at all; some celebrate it as a replacement for other religious holidays, whereas others incorporate it to varying degrees into Christmas celebrations. A 2004 study by the National Retail Foundation found that 13 percent of African Americans celebrate Kwanzaa. Most celebrants value Kwanzaa as a vehicle for uniting disparate African American identities and as a way to reaffirm, revive, and study African, African Diaspora, and African American cultural traditions.

Silly Presidential Nicknames

From "Wobbly Warren" to "His Accidency,"
here's the wacky roll call.

✳   ✳   ✳   ✳

President	Nickname
James Monroe	Last Cocked Hat
John Quincy Adams	Old Man Eloquent
Martin Van Buren	The Little Magician; Martin Van Ruin
John Tyler	His Accidency
Zachary Taylor	Old Rough and Ready
Millard Fillmore	His Accidency
James Buchanan	The Bachelor President; Old Buck
Andrew Johnson	King Andy; Sir Veto
Ulysses S. Grant	Useless; Unconditional Surrender
Rutherford B. Hayes	Rutherfraud Hayes; His Fraudulency
James Garfield	The Preacher; The Teacher President
Grover Cleveland	Uncle Jumbo; His Obstinacy
Benjamin Harrison	Little Ben; White House Iceberg
William McKinley	Wobbly Willie; Idol of Ohio
Woodrow Wilson	The Schoolmaster
Warren Harding	Wobbly Warren
Herbert Hoover	The Great Engineer
Harry Truman	The Haberdasher
John F. Kennedy	King of Camelot
Lyndon B. Johnson	Big Daddy
Richard M. Nixon	Tricky Dick
Gerald Ford	The Accidental President
Jimmy Carter	The Peanut Farmer
Ronald Reagan	Dutch; The Gipper; The Great Communicator
George H. W. Bush	Poppy
Bill Clinton	Bubba; Slick Willie; The Comeback Kid
George W. Bush	Junior; W; Dubya

News That's Fit to Print

Often biased and sometimes downright wrong, journalism during the U.S. Civil War did offer some new innovations, including bylines and wire reports from the field.

✳   ✳   ✳   ✳

L IFE WAS CHANGING rapidly during the mid-19th century as modern technology enabled journalists to report news faster than had been possible during earlier wars. Previously, it took days or weeks for news from the front to be read in print. Now, faster travel and the widespread use of the telegraph meant that news could be printed immediately. Unfortunately, speed did nothing to improve upon accuracy—and perhaps even thwarted it. But the news had to be published, even if it was wrong.

Credit Where Credit Is Due

General Irvin McDowell thought journalists in the field should dress in white uniforms to show their purity and integrity. Of course, many journalists possessed neither virtue. In fact, printing a byline—displaying the name of the correspondent who wrote a particular article—came about as a response to objections over inaccurate or biased reporting. General Joseph Hooker insisted that if reporters were going to lie about him, they needed to sign their work.

General William Tecumseh Sherman, General George Meade, and others had even lower opinions of journalists. Sherman, upon being informed of the death of three special correspondents in battle, said, "Good. Now we shall have news from hell before breakfast!" Meade had a reporter drummed out of camp in humiliation—forcing him to ride away backward on a mule to the jeers of the soldiers—and the response of many journalists was to get revenge on the general for the rest of the war. In fact, many news reports about Meade were biased against him for the rest of his career.

The Business of News

Newspapers covered the war extensively. Larger papers sent multiple staff writers and artists into the field. Obviously, this became an expensive endeavor. The *New York Herald* used 63 people in the field during the war at a cost of about $1 million. Smaller papers shared reporters, who gladly wrote for several sources to make up for the low salaries each paper paid.

Newspaper publishers used various strategies to attract readers. Often, this meant slanting the news toward the views of the intended readership or focusing on readers whose views matched those of the publisher. Other publishers focused on getting the news first. Telegraph lines and special couriers helped news travel quickly to the newspapers, but some journalists would sabotage their competitors. One reporter sent in his own dispatch and then tied up the telegraph lines by also transmitting a hefty chunk of the New Testament to make sure his competitors couldn't get through with their own reports. Speed was at such a premium that battle news was often sent in incomplete form, which sacrificed accuracy for timeliness. Since most battles transpired in hours, while travel took days, many "eyewitness" reports were written by reporters who weren't even at the scene. Journalists sometimes did not arrive at a battle site until after the fighting had ended.

The glaringly incorrect early battle results from Bull Run and similar events caused readers and editors to demand more accurate reporting. Of course, this still didn't mean that articles were totally accurate or unbiased. All a reporter had to do to alter public impressions was to give credit selectively for victories or defeats. Even letters to the editors could affect public opinion. An example of this is a letter from a writer who used the pen name "Historicus." After the Battle of Gettysburg, the writer praised General Dan Sickles at the expense of General Meade. Despite the likelihood that Sickles wrote the letter himself, it colored the public understanding—and even the historical record, to a degree—against Meade.

Political Agendas

In the North, papers and politics went hand in hand. Horace Greeley's *New York Tribune* was strongly abolitionist, criticizing President Lincoln for being too moderate. (Greeley himself ran for president in 1872.) In the South, it was deemed unpatriotic to report any bad news accurately. So, bad news was sugar-coated, disguised, or omitted entirely. Even foreign correspondents working in the South found it hard to accurately report. Charles Mackay, Southern correspondent for *The Times of London*, repeatedly submitted inaccurate reports, even writing about Lee's "impending capture of Washington" in July 1863.

The Birth of the War Correspondent

William Howard Russell was the first well-known war correspondent. He wrote the earliest widely published news account of what we now know as "The Charge of the Light Brigade." His work in the Crimean War led *The Times of London* to assign him to cover the American Civil War. Because of his reputation, Russell traveled widely and interviewed major participants on both sides. Russell's views sided with the Union. His editors were pro-Confederacy, due to the English cloth industry's ties to the South, and since his opinions of the war did not match those of the paper, he was ultimately reassigned.

Successful journalists traveled with the armies in hopes of witnessing direct action. This upset General Sherman and others, who felt that reporters often gave away military information. The most memorable reporters, including T. M. Chester, an African American correspondent for *The Philadelphia Press*, had distinctive styles. At the siege of Petersburg, Chester wrote: "The enterprising managers of the firm of Grant & Lee take pleasure in announcing to the public in and around Petersburg that they are now prepared, and will continue until further notice, to give every evening a grand exhibition of fireworks for the benefit of their respective employees." The flamboyant Chester and other writers often brought a lighter touch to the otherwise grim news of war.

Did Custer Make a Stand?

"Custer's Last Stand" evokes notions of a war hero fearlessly advancing in a doomed battle. What really happened remains unclear.

✳ ✳ ✳ ✳

Custer's last stand, the legendary designation for the Battle of Little Bighorn, occurred during the climax of the Indian Wars of the 1860s and '70s, when the U.S. government corralled the western Native American tribes onto small reservations. In 1874, when gold was discovered in the Black Hills of South Dakota, the government sent troops to make sure Native Americans steered clear of the jackpot.

Such was the backdrop for the Battle of Little Bighorn. In June 1876, word spread that a large number of Native Americans had gathered under the auspices of Lakota (Sioux) leader Chief Sitting Bull. Army units throughout the Montana Territory planned to converge on and attack the gatherers, and General George Armstrong Custer led the Seventh Cavalry in this effort. At the time, Custer was already a Civil War hero known for his reckless yet successful military campaigns. On June 25, he and his cavalry stumbled upon the encampment. Fearing that Native American scouts were aware of his movements, he decided to attack before waiting for reinforcements.

A Story with No One to Tell It

The truth of Custer's Last Stand remains unclear because everyone under his direct command died in battle. With the intention of surrounding the native encampment, Custer divided his approximately 600 men into four battalions. Custer's doomed group numbered around 260 men.

Historical evidence suggests that when Custer's battalion attacked, they thought there were mostly women and children in the village. The plan may have been to take them hostage or use them as a shield. Lakota, Cheyenne, and Arapaho warriors had been fighting with another Seventh Cavalry battalion but quickly moved on to Custer's when they learned it had gotten closer to the women and children. The number of Native Americans involved in the attack is uncertain, but estimates range from 900 to 1,800. It is likely that the encounter lasted less than an hour; all of Custer's men were killed. Estimates of Native American deaths range from 36 to 300. The remaining battalions of the Seventh Cavalry fought into the following day, though they did not suffer in the same numbers and were shocked to learn of Custer's crushing defeat.

The Evolution of a Myth

The Battle of Little Bighorn created a popular sensation. At this stage in the war, a devastating rout at the hands of Native Americans was unexpected. Despite scattered calls of criticism against Custer's tactics, he was eulogized as a hero. Books, plays, paintings, and eventually movies depicted Custer as the last to die, surrounded by the remaining soldiers who, in the final moments of combat, organized an epic "last stand."

The reality of this scenario is contested. Based on the positions of bullet shells and fallen soldiers, it is likely that Custer's men quickly and unexpectedly realized they were in a hopeless situation. The last men to die possibly gathered for a final effort at the top of Custer Hill, where they'd retreated.

In recent decades, the saga of the Battle of Little Bighorn has slowly replaced the myth of Custer's Last Stand. Native Americans and others have sought to revise the battle's legacy, which at the time was used to fuel anti-Native American sentiment. A multicultural history of the United States would not see the Battle of Little Bighorn as simply a devastating defeat epitomized by the heroic "last stand" of a fallen national hero—it was most certainly a fleeting victory for Native Americans.

Daily Life in England, A.D. 1100

Think it's rough nowadays? Step back 900 years, and you'd see a whole new definition of hard living. Life was completely different in A.D. 1100: People believed the earth was flat; serfs were tied to the land, not quite slaves and not quite free; and the first Crusaders had sailed for the Holy Lands, but had not yet returned with new knowledge from the Islamic world. It wasn't obvious, but the Dark Ages were coming to an end. Here's a look at what daily life was like back then.

✳   ✳   ✳   ✳

FROM KING TO SERF, everyone was born into a set position, and every rung of the feudal social ladder was defined by a complicated exchange of rights and services. The only social mobility was in the church. Men and women from all walks of life could join a religious order and train for a position based on ability rather than birth. Even the poorest country priest could usually read and write—skills the lord might not have.

Living conditions were, well, *rustic.*

Most people lived in small rural settlements and never went more than a few miles from where they were born. With the exception of the local manor, houses were no sturdier than those built by the Three Little Pigs: made of turf, or straw-reinforced mud, with thatched roofs. Floors were beaten earth that were covered with rushes.  Instead of a fireplace, open fires burned on a raised hearth in the middle of the room; smoke found its way out a hole in the ceiling that also let in wind and rain. Furniture was at most a rough table and some stools. People slept on straw pallets on the floor.

Basically, everyone smelled horrible.

The only way to wash yourself, or anything else, was to carry water inside and heat it over the fire. Even nobility, who had servants to haul and heat water, did not bathe regularly. Clothing was not designed to be washed. Peasants often had only one set of rough wool garments, while nobles' clothing was embroidered with jewels and trimmed with fur. The rich hung their most expensive clothing on hooks in the privies (basically, the bathroom) that were built into the walls of manors and castles, believing the fumes would kill lice and other vermin. However, doing so did nothing to improve the smell of unwashed velvet.

Sanitation was primitive, especially in the towns. London had only 16 public latrines for a population of 30,000. People emptied slop jars into the streets, even though it was illegal. Many private homes had cesspits underneath the floorboards; when the pit filled up, the householder paid a "gong farmer" to dig it out. (Part of his pay was anything valuable that he found in the pit as well as the right to use the sewage as fertilizer.)

The food was a bit bland.

The potato, which later became the staple diet of the poor, would not reach Europe from the New World for another 400 years. Instead, peasants relied on grain for both food and drink: bread, porridge, and home-brewed ale. Most peasants lived on barley and oats, supplemented with vegetables from the garden and roots, nuts, and berries from the woods. Honey was the only sweetener. Most families could afford to keep chickens and a pig, but animals often had to be sold for cash to pay rent or taxes. Only the wealthiest could afford pepper or other spices, which came overland from the East—a trip that took more than a year. It was a hungry time, made hungrier by frequent crop failures and a growing population.

＊ **The flour used to bake and cook was so gritty it would wear down tooth enamel over time.**

The Iroquois Theater Fire of 1903

In the 21st century, it's easy to take for granted safety measures such as well-lit exits, unlocked doors, and fire escapes. But these precautions weren't always available—even when they were most sorely needed.

✳ ✳ ✳ ✳

A Spooky Premonition

Twenty-eight years prior to the fateful 1903 fire, a *Chicago Times* article titled "Burned Alive" spoke of the state of the current poorly designed buildings and predicted that because of the unsafe conditions, a building fire would take the lives of hundreds of people. Years later, an event occurred at Chicago's Iroquois Theater that would eerily mirror the article.

A "Completely Fire-Proof Theatre"

Advertisements and playbills for the Iroquois Theater, which opened on November 23, 1903, claimed the building was impervious to fire. Much like the infamous "unsinkable" *Titanic*, the theory was untested. Sure, it was easy to think all was well while sitting underneath the ornate, 60-foot-high ceiling and among the white marbled walls and grand staircases. The owners even planned 30 exits, which they claimed would help evacuate the entire building in five minutes. (They only built 27 exits, however.) They also had a special glass skylight built over the stage that could vent flames upward and out of the building instead of inward and toward the audience.

But, before the theater's opening, Chicago fire inspectors found exit signs were either missing or obscured by thick drapes, there were no backstage phones, no fire alarm system was in place, no sprinklers or fire buckets, and there lacked a sufficient number of hoses. In fact, the only firefighting equipment in the theater was six metal canisters containing a dry chemical product called Kilfyre. Little did the inspectors know that the owners had even skimped on the stage's asbestos safety curtain, which was only part asbestos—the rest was made of wood pulp. Other sources say the curtain jammed on its rod, rendering it ineffective.

The Inferno

A little after 3:00 P.M. on December 30, an overfilled theater of nearly 2,000 patrons was enjoying a matinee of the comedy *Mr. Bluebeard*. During the performance of the song "Pale Moon Light," the main spotlight began burning. Bits of curtain and the front of the stage caught on fire first, and embers fell onto the increasingly nervous singers below. Initially, the audience wasn't aware of any trouble, but in moments, flames began to lick the stage curtain. Finally, the audience was alarmed.

To avoid a rush of panicked patrons, the orchestra and performer and Chicago native Eddie Foy came out onstage and tried to calm the crowd. But the fire was out of control; hundreds leapt up and headed for what they thought were exits. In some corners, large mirrors were hung, which disoriented the crowd. In other corners, they were met with locked accordion gates (to prevent people from sneaking to better seats on other levels), doors that opened inward, or even gaping holes where unfinished fire escapes forced person after person to fall to their death as the crowd rushed in from behind. Then, the theatre went black; hundreds were trampled on the grand staircases as they tried to escape. All told, 602 people were killed that day at the Iroquois Theater, and all within only 20 minutes.

One for the Record Books

As a direct result of the Iroquois Theater fire, the self-releasing fire exit bolt, or "panic bar," was invented and installed as a mandatory safety improvement. As of 2008, according to National Fire Protection Association records, it is still the worst single-building fire in U.S. history in terms of fatalities. In comparison, the New York City Triangle Shirtwaist Factory fire claimed 148 lives, the Great Chicago Fire killed 250, and the Boston Cocoanut Grove fire killed 492.

Do the Tighten Up: A Brief History of the Corset

The medieval period was paradise for women's clothing: The flowing lines of women's gowns were comfortable and followed the natural figure. But it was too good to last. From the middle of the 15th century through the beginning of the 20th, with only brief respites, women forced their bodies into the shapes demanded by fashion.

✳   ✳   ✳   ✳

THE FIRST ANCESTRESS of the corset, worn from the mid-15th through the late 16th centuries, was a heavy under-bodice that laced up the sides or the front. A tapered "busk" of horn or whalebone was inserted in the front of the bodice to keep it rigid. At some point, whalebone was added to the sides and back. Interestingly, scholars report that the corset-wearers of the period were not necessarily uncomfortable—the infamously painful period of corsetry occurred later during the 19th century.

Boned bodices became fully boned stays in the late 17th century, when the preferred silhouette was long and narrow rather than broad and stiff. Stays that produced a slender line required more seams, tapering down to the waistline.

By the middle of the 18th century, extra shaping bones were sewn into stays to give the breasts some *oomph* and keep the back flat. Whalebone strips were laid diagonally on the sides to make the body long and narrow. Pregnant women were given a break—their stays laced at the sides, allowing more room.

Changing Styles

Women could breathe a little easier at the end of the 18th century. The popularity of fine cottons from India created a looser style using the natural drape of the fabric. Sashes narrowed and waistlines rose.

At first, women wore lighter stays under the new styles, made with more pliable materials and fewer bones. By the beginning of the 19th century, however, draped Greek statues were the ideal. Light muslin dresses clung to the body and underclothes that could spoil the silhouette were abandoned—at least in theory. In practice, even slender women often wore a cotton lining with two side pieces that fastened under the breasts, providing some support; heavier women experimented with stays that came down over the hips and tightly-fitted knitted silk body garments.

The respite was brief. A new silhouette emphasizing full skirts and narrow waists came into fashion with the end of the Napoleonic War, bringing the first true corset with it and ushering in the tight-lacing fad. Victorian women wanted tiny, wasplike waists, and the new corsets could give them that desirable figure. Usually laced up the back, the corset had a broad busk in the center front and narrow strips of whalebone at the back and sides. Gussets on the front at the top of the corset and on each side at the base produced roundness at the bust and the hips, emphasizing the smallness of the waist.

Over time, corsets became heavier and more restricting. Rubber-coated steel replaced the lighter, more pliable whalebone. Further changes in silhouette, including the bustle in the 1870s and the "S-curve" of the early 1900s, all exaggerated and distorted the natural female shape, requiring more heavily boned corset designs.

Women's underwear underwent a change in the 20th century. Steel shortages during World War I and the introduction of rubberized elastic allowed women some freedom from tight stays. Finally, the free-for-all loose fashions of the '20s marked the end of the corset.

Influential First Ladies of the United States

First ladies have had a lot of things in common. Nearly all have ambitiously boosted their husbands' careers and had input into public affairs. Nearly all have entertained, set trends, and promoted social causes. Here are some of the women who helped strengthen and expand the platform on which their successors would stand.

✳ ✳ ✳ ✳

Martha Washington (First Lady 1789–1797): No one elects a president's spouse, nor has she ever received a salary for hosting dinners, tolerating fools, and supporting her husband—but that's tradition, not law. This ethic originated with down-to-earth Martha, who established patterns of duty and dignity in the new republic's executive residence.

Abigail Adams (1797–1801): It's not clear if Martha Washington was involved in public policy, but Abigail Adams certainly was. As John Adams's key political advisor, she wrote letters to newspapers (the era's genteel approach to public discourse), listened to congressional debates, and tried in vain to get her husband to write women's rights into the Constitution. In fact, she threatened him with a women's rebellion.

Dolley Madison (White House Hostess 1801–1809; First Lady 1809–1817): Dolley was widely considered the most influential woman in the United States in the 1800s. As widower Thomas Jefferson's official White House hostess (a role filled by someone other than the president's wife) and then James Madison's first lady, Dolley was always graceful, valiant, and patriotic. She rescued national treasures from the White House in 1814 as the British army approached and the militia fled.

Dolley stayed relevant to the roles of hostess and first lady for half a century. She mentored White House hostesses Angelica

Van Buren and Priscilla Tyler, then first ladies Julia Tyler and Sarah Polk. When Dolley died in 1849, Congress adjourned immediately to mourn a beloved heroine.

Louisa Adams (1825–1829): The only foreign-born first lady (she was born in London), Louisa was the first to be directly involved in her husband's election campaign (she actually managed it). Without her political savvy, John Quincy Adams likely would not have won the presidency.

Julia Tyler (1844–1845): Julia married widower and president John Tyler, taking over for his daughter Letitia and daughter-in-law Priscilla, who had held the fort as White House hostesses. Julia was the first presidential wife to use a press secretary to manage the media. She was also the first to have the marine band play "Hail to the Chief" for her husband.

Sarah Polk (1845–1849): The wife of James K. Polk was arguably the first co-president—a full political partner in her husband's administration. She was a speechwriter, press secretary, political tactician, hostess, and confidante, integrating the varying roles laid out by her predecessors into a dominant political force.

Harriet Lane (White House Hostess 1857–1861): Niece of James Buchanan (the only president who remained a bachelor), Harriet was best known for championing her personal causes. She worked hard on behalf of Native Americans and also supported the movement to establish a national art gallery. Harriet blazed the trail of social activism among first ladies and White House hostesses.

Eliza Johnson (1865–1869): What can one say about a first lady with enough political pull to influence her husband's stay in office? When the sharks circled Andrew Johnson, Eliza overcame fragile health to lead the anti-impeachment effort. Since this process also determined future interpretation of the Constitution, Eliza helped establish the rights of the presidency itself.

Lucy Hayes (1877–1881): When a president is elected, favor-seekers swarm, looking for jobs and perks. When they tried to approach President Rutherford B. Hayes, his wife, Lucy, handily dismissed them, creating a policy that dovetailed with her husband's merit-based reform of civil service. She also picked up a torch long fallen from Abigail Adams's hands: women's rights. Her quiet activism inspired and fueled the growing political voice of women.

Edith Wilson (1915–1921): Edith was the first full presidential gatekeeper. A stroke (or possibly encephalitis) felled Woodrow Wilson in September 1919; he never fully recovered and was incapacitated until early 1920. Edith (not Vice President Thomas Marshall) determined what and whom her husband would see, delegating anything she considered unimportant.

Florence Harding (1921–1923): Not all groundbreaking is admirable. Many know that Warren G. Harding's administration was full of monkey business; few realize how well Florence manipulated the media to maintain the administration's popularity. Other first ladies had guided the media expertly, but no one had yet managed so well to hide corruption. Florence must take credit (or perhaps blame) for her strong effort to shield herself and her husband from retribution.

Lou Hoover (1929–1933): Lou was the first presidential spouse to broadcast by radio, to appear in public while pregnant, and to invite an African American woman for tea. (Just ten years earlier, Woodrow Wilson had supported the Ku Klux Klan.) Lou valued White House history, turning much old "junk" into treasured heritage. More practically, she got Herbert to issue an executive order that reduced civil service barriers for women.

Eleanor Roosevelt (1933–1945): Far more a political partner than other presidents' spouses had been, Eleanor connected the presidency with the people as no first lady ever had. It's doubtful FDR could have pressed his full domestic agenda without Eleanor, even considering his advanced political skills.

Jacqueline Kennedy (1961–1963): Like most first ladies, Jackie had been a tremendous help during her husband's rise. Once established in the White House, her multilingualism proved a foreign relations asset. The widest furrow Jackie plowed, though, was in the realm of sheer popularity—she was the most glamorously visible first lady in history. Not even Eleanor publicized the presidency as well as Jackie did. When she led a nation in mourning after her husband's assassination, she sealed her place in history.

Claudia "Lady Bird" Johnson (1963–1969): Lady Bird was all that most first ladies were, with one more thing: She changed the very look of the nation. By the 1960s, highways in the United States were a clutter of billboards overlooking ditches full of trash. Lady Bird declared war on ugly. Down came most of the billboards, and people adopted a national ethic against litter.

Elizabeth Ford (1974–1977): Betty Ford started to shatter Puritanical taboos when doctors diagnosed her breast cancer. Betty spoke publicly about her mastectomy, hoping to encourage more women to get checked. She admitted suffering from depression and seeing therapists, though she kept her substance abuse private until Gerald Ford left office. Even then, she turned her battle into a way to help others by establishing the Betty Ford Center.

Hillary Clinton (1993–2001): Like most politically active and visible first ladies, Hillary was controversial in the role. She was the first to use it as a ramp to build her own independent political base, becoming the first former first lady to be elected to the U.S. Senate in her own right and the first to run for the office of president. She also took the office of Secretary of State.

✳ Abigail Adams was the first of many esteemed first ladies to live in the White House.

✳ Dolley Madison initiated the inaugural ball.

✳ Lou Hoover spoke fluent Chinese.

Utopian Societies

In 1516, Sir Thomas More coined the term "utopia" in a book of the same name. In it he refers to an ideal, imaginary island where everything is lovely all the time. For centuries since then, groups of people (often led by fanatical figures) have broken off from society to develop their own communities intended to bring peace, harmony, and spiritual enlightenment to all their citizens—and ultimately the whole world. Unfortunately, utopian societies seldom work out as planned.

✳   ✳   ✳   ✳

Founder: Charles Fourier

Plan: In the mid-19th century, Fourier contacted out-of-work New Englanders with the proposition of joining communal-living groups he called "phalanxes." These groups would be arranged hierarchically according to members' trades or skills. Children are good at digging, for example, so they would be in charge of maintaining the garbage dumps. Group members would be compensated for their contributions to the community.

Outcome: Fourier died in Paris before he saw the development of any phalanxes. In the early 1840s, a group of devotees, or Fourierists, founded the North American Phalanx and kept it going until disputes over women's rights and abolition drove many away. A fire destroyed the site in 1854.

Founder: Robert Owen

Plan: Owen called his version of utopia New Harmony and hoped his "empire of goodwill" would eventually take over the planet. His attempt at communal bliss began in Indiana in 1825.

Outcome: Hundreds of devoted followers lived according to Owen's ideals, with individual members plying their crafts and contributing to the community (even if that meant there was no one with the ability to spin the wool shorn by an abundance of sheepshearers). With no sound economic plan, New Harmony was in chaos from the start. There were five constitutions drafted in the first year alone.

Founder: The Spiritualists

Plan: The Mountain Cove Community was the Spiritualists' attempt to create their own idea of harmony. They founded their group in Virginia in 1851 on a spot once considered to be the Garden of Eden. The group insisted that no one individual would be allowed to dictate to others; all the direction anyone needed would come from "the spirits."

Outcome: As part of their introduction into the community, members were required to give up all their possessions, again leaving issues such as finances to the spirit world. Not surprisingly, the experiment lasted less than two years.

Founder: Etienne Cabet

Plan: Cabet's *Voyage en Icarie*, written in 1840, depicted an ideal society, the Icarians, in which an elected government controlled all economic activity as well as social affairs. Cabet decided to make his dream a reality and set sail for America.

Outcome: The group landed outside New Orleans on swampland not fit for settlement. Malaria and starvation took many of this group of Icarians, and the rest deserted.

Founder: The Shakers

Plan: The Shakers were an 18th-century religious denomination of Protestants who decided to leave the immoral world behind and create a pious place in which to live and serve God.

Outcome: By the mid-1800s, the Shakers had built 19 communal settlements that attracted some 200,000 followers. Their numbers gradually dwindled, but their simple way of life continues to attract widespread interest. The Shakers are generally considered to be one of the few successful utopian societies.

Building the Colosseum

With recently deceased dictator Nero out of the picture, Rome's new ruler, Vespasian, sought to show the ravaged populace that he wasn't like his self-serving predecessor. He proved to be the ruler who could finally bring the people out of their long-lasting troubles—all it took was an architectural triumph designed to house 50,000 roaring Romans thirsty for an entertainingly gruesome battle.

✳ ✳ ✳ ✳

DURING HIS REIGN as emperor in the first century A.D., Nero had repeatedly proved himself a ruthless ruler, stealing everything he could from the Roman people and killing anyone who got in his way. In the year between Nero's forced suicide and the rise of Vespasian (born Titus Flavius Vespasianus), three other emperors took brief turns ruling Rome, but Vespasian became the man who mattered. He chose to launch his reign with a monumental gesture meant to cause the people to forget Nero. He initiated construction of the most substantial arena of the time, a structure that became the cultural nucleus of Rome—and remained so for the next 450 years.

Putting a Bad Ruler Behind Them

During Nero's reign, which marked the end of the long-running and brutal Julio-Claudian dynasty, land and resources were absorbed into his extravagant estate, the Domus Aurea. Set in the heart of Rome, Nero's grandiose property featured a lake, a mansion with more than 300 rooms, and hundreds of acres of land. The opulent interior of the house showcased unrivaled luxuries, from expansively marbled floors to a slave-driven revolving dome ceiling that would intermittently release mists of perfume and flutters of rose petals over the frequent assemblages of partygoers. Ever the egotist, Nero commissioned a towering bronze statue in his own image, the

Collossus Neronis, and ordered it to be erected at the palace steps to greet—or perhaps intimidate—visitors.

As an apt show of goodwill to the Roman people, Vespasian confiscated the land for his building project from Nero's lavish estate. The great Flavian Amphitheater eventually resided beside the lake Nero had built to complete his posh property. Historians suggest that it is from Nero's statue that the Flavian Amphitheater drew its eventual name, the Colosseum.

A Massive Undertaking

The arena was built with a multitude of materials and mirrored Greek architecture, despite the lack of experience the Romans had with such technology. Adapting to the task, the Romans used travertine stone to make up much of the exterior of the elliptical building; wooden floors covered in sand (which was good for absorbing blood) spread across the entirety of the interior. Tiers of seats allowed for massive seating capacity, and mazes beneath the main floor kept wild animals contained in preparation for events. Trapdoors to surprise gladiators, as well as a retractable roof to provide shade for patrons, completed the structure. Upon its opening, the Colosseum was the perfect meeting place for the Roman community.

The construction of the Colosseum lasted ten years and extended through two reigns. Upon Vespasian's death, his son Titus ascended to the position of emperor in A.D. 79 and sought to finish the arena. Titus brought thousands of slaves from Jerusalem to speed up the work, and the Romans celebrated in A.D. 80 with inaugural games that included the slaying of 9,000 wild animals, noonday executions, and gladiatorial brawls. This introductory series marked the beginning of a 450-year stretch of ongoing community celebrations and the creation of traditional Roman-style entertainment.

The Boston Tea Party

*We've all learned that our colonial forebears helped touch
off the American Revolution by turning Boston Harbor into
a big tea caddy to protest "taxation without representation."
In fact, wealthy smugglers set the whole thing up.*

✳ ✳ ✳ ✳

IS THE ORIGINAL not a great tale of democracy? Angry
patriots, righteously fed up with burdensome taxes and
British oppression, seize a British ship and spoil the cargo. In
reality, there's much more to the story.

The Backdrop

This tale begins with the 1765 Stamp Act, eight years before the
start of the Revolution. Because it cost Britain money to defend
the colonies, the king wanted help paying the bill. This would
happen through tax stamps, similar to modern postage stamps,
required on various documents, printed materials, goods, etc. For
the same reason that proclaiming "I will raise taxes" is the same as
saying "Don't elect me" 12 generations later, this caused an outcry.
Then, as now, most Americans would rather part with their life-
blood than pay an extra dime in taxes.

The colonists resorted to various forms of terrorism. Mobs
tarred and feathered government officials, burned them in
effigy, and torched their homes and possessions. Within
months, the horrified British gave up on the Stamp Act fiasco.

What's the Price of Tea?

Next the British tried the Townshend Act (1767), imposing
customs duties and hoping the average citizen wouldn't notice.
Tea, much loved in the colonies, was among the taxed imports.
Of course, Britain lacked the resources to patrol the entire colonial coastline against enterprising Dutch smugglers, who snuck
shiploads of tea past customs officials. Seeing opportunity,
clever colonial businessmen bought and distributed smuggled

tea; like teen-clothing branders two centuries later, they marketed their product by associating it with defiant rebellion. It worked: Colonials boycotted legally imported tea, often refusing to let it be unloaded from ships.

The Boston Massacre of 1770 (a shooting incident that escalated from heckling and a snowball fight) didn't help. The British realized that the Townshend Act wasn't working, but they maintained the tea tax as a symbol of authority. The British East India Company (aka John Company), which monopolized the importation of Indian tea to America, was losing a lot of money. In response, Parliament passed the 1773 Tea Act, which relaxed customs duties and allowed John Company to bypass costly London middlemen. It was a brilliant idea: John Company could unload ruinously vast inventories of tea while pacifying the tax-hating, bargain-hunting colonials.

Tea and Cakes in the Harbor

In November 1773, three British merchant ships anchored in Boston Harbor with the first loads of tea. Amid much social brouhaha, the smugglers roused mobs that prevented the tea from being unloaded. But by December 16, it was clear that the ships would land their tea the next day.

One group of protestors fortified itself with lots of liquor, dressed up in "Indian" costumes, and staggered toward the wharf in an outrage. Those who didn't fall into the water along the way boarded the British ships and began dragging the cargo up from the holds, cracking open designated cases and heaving tea leaves into the water. By the end of the night, approximately 45 tons of tea had been dumped overboard, and tea leaves washed up on Boston shores for weeks.

Afterward, the Sons of Liberty wandered home, proud of their patriotic accomplishment. Similar tea "parties" occurred in other colonial ports. The colonies had successfully impugned King George III and maintained a healthy business climate for smuggling activities.

The Royal Canadian Mounted Police

Is there an icon as visibly Canadian as the red-serge-and-Stetson uniform of the famous Royal Canadian Mounted Police?

✳ ✳ ✳ ✳

✳ The RCMP's legal establishment began in 1873 as the North-West Mounted Police (NWMP), assigned to bring law and order to western Canada. Their motto is French: *Maintiens le droit* ("Maintain the right").

✳ One of the Mounties' first jobs was to banish troublemakers. By 1874, whiskey peddlers from the United States had infested southern Alberta. The Mounties believed that the native First Peoples had suffered enough without rotgut booze, and most whiskey men abandoned their fort well ahead of the arrival of the NWMP.

✳ Along with a force of civilian volunteers from Prince Albert, the Mounties lost a battle in the snow to the Metis at Duck Lake, Saskatchewan, in March 1885 during the Northwest Rebellion. The government forces were lucky not to be wiped out—a decision for which they could thank Metis leader Louis Riel, who urged against further bloodshed.

✳ The NWMP began to operate in the Yukon in 1895. Good timing, considering the characters coming up from the United States to pan, hack, dig, and sift for gold. In Skagway, NWMP constables at the Canadian border, turned back undesirables and made sure the rest brought enough food.

✳ They became the Royal North-West Mounted Police in 1904, receiving that designation from King Edward VII. The RNWMP became the RCMP with the absorption of the Dominion Police, with law enforcement authority in every square yard of Canada (later every square meter).

* The Depression years were a time of modernization for the RCMP. The marine division was created in 1932. Police dogs became part of the force in 1935, and it began using aircraft in 1937.

* RCMP schooner *St. Roch* was the first vessel to navigate the entire Northwest Passage (through Canada's Arctic islands from Pacific to Atlantic, or vice versa) in one season (1944).

* An era ended in 1966. Universal RCMP training in horse-back riding and horse care was discontinued, though the Musical Ride carries on those equine traditions ceremonially.

* Only in 1969 did the RCMP discontinue use of dogsled patrols in the North.

* Women first became uniformed Mounties in 1974.

* Until 1984, the Mounties were responsible for Canada's internal counterintelligence function. The agent of change was the revelation of some unlawful covert operations concerning Quebec separatists.

* Canada has about half a million Sikh citizens and residents. Male Sikhs wear turbans, not Stetsons or billed police caps. In 1990, after a national controversy, Sikh RCMP constables were allowed to wear their turbans in uniform.

* Though a police force, the RCMP was also a regiment of dragoons (mounted rifles). It had a guidon with battle honors from the Northwest Rebellion, South Africa, and World Wars I and II.

* The Musical Ride dates back to the NWMP days. This ceremonial equestrian drill team shows off all over Canada from spring to fall. The 32 members of the Musical Ride perform in uniform (red serge and Stetson) and are armed with white lances.

Red Sun Rising

The Russo-Japanese War was a pivotal point of development for post-feudal Japan and its fledgling empire, with European nations finally having to accept the power of the East.

✳   ✳   ✳   ✳

A MERE 200 YEARS ago, Japan was a feudal state where disputes were settled with samurai swords and the penalty for dishonor was ritual suicide. Yet, the nation saw unification under Emperor Meiji in 1869. He decided that Japan must modernize and become open to the West, which it did with a vengeance. Industry boomed, and German and British advisors arrived—the former to train the army, the latter to build a navy. But Japan was still resource poor. The country needed coal and iron, oil and rice. It needed an empire.

Imperial Dreams

China had rice. China also had Korea. Japan wanted both, so it invaded and smashed China's primitive army and navy. However, building an empire wasn't going to be easy. Other countries had interests, as well. To keep Japan in check, Russia, France, Germany, and Britain jumped in to gobble up areas of economic influence in China. Russia irritated Japan when it grabbed Manchuria, which had coal and iron mines and the naval base at Port Arthur. These were some of the spoils for which Japan had gone to war in the first place. Russia had to go.

While Russia had a huge army in Europe, it was at the other end of the 5,500-mile, single-track Trans-Siberian Railway. Only about 130,000 troops were stationed in the far eastern part of the country, and reinforcements would arrive slowly. Russian naval strength, mostly at Port Arthur, was comprised of old and second-rate ships. Against this, Japan had developed a fast, modern navy and 283,000 troops, with 400,000 reserves. On February 8, 1904—without a declaration of war—Japan struck at Russia.

Japanese torpedo boats attacked the Russian fleet anchored at Port Arthur, causing severe damage. The next day, after sinking two Russian ships at Chemulpo (Inchon), Korea, the Japanese First Army began to come ashore. The general plan was to move the armies from Korea into Manchuria. From there they would split, some turning north to cut the Trans-Siberian Railroad while others simultaneously headed south to capture Port Arthur. The plan was simple, and the Russians probably should have known what to expect.

But Russia was plagued with bad leaders, bad equipment, and bad luck. As an example of the latter, only a couple of months into the war, their best admiral, Stepan Makarov, launched a series of energetic raids against the Japanese, but while returning to Port Arthur, his flagship *Petropavlovsk* sailed into a field of mines surreptitiously set by the Japanese and sank with all hands onboard.

Leadership Nightmares

Though Russian General Aleksei Kuropatkin had a sound defensive plan that would take into account the Russian soldiers' strengths, Czar Nicholas II put the incompetent General Mikhail Alekseev in charge of the war. Alekseev ordered an immediate offensive—which went completely against Kuropatkin's well-laid defense plan. While the Japanese troops attacked north toward Mukden and Harbin, the Russian army was pulverized in a series of foolish counterattacks and fell back in disarray. It is an understatement to say things were not going well for Russia.

In the south, Japan had begun the siege of Port Arthur. Surrounded by three rings of defensive fortifications and well supplied, Port Arthur should have been able to hold out for a year. But the fortress commander was another incompetent who wasted valuable defensive time in inaction and worry. By the end of July, Japan had 80,000 troops and almost 500 guns in position around the fort.

Russian Admiral Wilgelm Vitgeft took over and tried to fight a defensive campaign in support of Port Arthur, but the czar ordered him to break out and take his fleet to Vladivostok. However, when Vitgeft tried, Admiral Heihachiro Togo's hyper-modern battleships caught him in the Yellow Sea on August 10. Vitgeft was killed and most of his ships wound up back in Port Arthur. Time was definitely running out. Then began one of the strangest episodes in naval history.

A Dubious Idea

Thousands of miles away, back in the Baltic Sea, lay extra elements of the Russian navy—eight battleships, eight cruisers, and nine destroyers. Someone got the none-too-brilliant idea that they should cruise around the world to save Port Arthur. On October 15, they brashly set sail under the command of another incompetent, Admiral Zinovy Rozhdestvenski.

After mistakenly attacking British fishing ships they thought were Japanese torpedo boats and nearly starting a war with Britain, the hodgepodge of new and very old Russian ships went sailing off around Africa. Around this time, on January 5, Port Arthur surrendered to Japan. Unaware of that development, the fleet continued across the Indian Ocean, plagued by mutinies, fever, rotten food, and problems finding coal.

A Day Late and a Dollar Short

On May 14, the haggard ship crews approached Tsushima Island, situated between Korea and Japan. Opposing them was Togo's fleet. With a six-knot speed advantage, the Japanese pulled ahead of and around the Russians, bringing all of Togo's guns to bear. The Russian vessels were quickly encircled and 11 were destroyed.

Ironically, by then the land war had been over for two months, following Port Arthur's surrender. Later, through the efforts of U.S. President Theodore Roosevelt, negotiations led to the Treaty of Portsmouth on September 6, 1905, and an uneasy accord ensued—that would later erupt into World War II.

The Not-So-Coded Code Name

When rumors emerged that Nazi Germany was developing an atomic bomb during World War II, the United States quickly initiated its own program, the Manhattan Project. Where did this name come from?

❋ ❋ ❋ ❋

THE VENTURE CULMINATED in the detonation of the first atomic weapon in the New Mexico desert on July 16, 1945, and then the strikes on Hiroshima and Nagasaki that ended the war. Many people assume that the top-secret plan was given the cover name the Manhattan Project simply to confuse the enemy. In fact, the New York borough played a key part.

In 1942, General Leslie R. Groves, deputy chief of construction for the U.S. Army Corps of Engineers, was appointed to direct the top-secret project. The United States needed to build an atomic weapon before Germany or Japan did. Groves established three large engineering and production centers at remote U.S. sites in Oak Ridge, Tennessee; Hanford, Washington; and Los Alamos, New Mexico. The project's headquarters, however, was situated at 270 Broadway, New York City, home to the Army Corps of Engineers' North Atlantic division.

Standard Operating Procedure

The first proposed cover name was the Laboratory for the Development of Substitute Materials. That hardly rolls off the tongue, and Groves also felt that it would draw unwanted attention. Instead, he opted to follow Corps procedure and name the unit after its geographical area. The initial cover name of Manhattan Engineer District soon was shortened to the Manhattan Project. In 1943, the headquarters moved to Oak Ridge, Tennessee, and while much of Manhattan's role in the project has been forgotten, there is a poignant reminder on Riverside Drive outside the New York Buddhist Church: It's the statue of a monk that survived the bombing of Hiroshima.

Chapter 9

Villains, Kooks, and Crazies

The Moors Murderers: Britain's Most Hated Couple

A killing spree fascinated and horrified England in the 1960s. Saddleworth Moor always had an ominous air to it, but tensions suddenly got much, much worse.

✳   ✳   ✳   ✳

BURYING A BODY in highly acidic soil is smart—the flesh decays faster, making it harder for police to tell exactly what happened to the victim. That's what Ian Brady and Myra Hindley were counting on when they buried their victims in an acidic grassy moor.

Normal and Abnormal Childhoods

Myra Hindley was born in 1942 just outside of Manchester. She was a normal, happy girl and even a popular babysitter among the families in her neighborhood. At age 15, she left school. Three years later, she secured a job as a typist for a small chemical company. There she met Ian Brady, a 23-year-old stock clerk.

Born to a single mother, Brady was given to a nearby family at a young age when his mom, a waitress, could no longer afford to take care of him. In school, he was an angry loner who bullied younger children and tortured animals.

At the chemical company, Hindley became enamored with Brady, an intense young man fascinated with Nazis and who read *Mein Kampf* in German. In her diary, Hindley gushed that she hoped he would love her, although Brady was decidedly distant. It wasn't until a year after they met that he asked her on a date at the company's Christmas party.

An Off-kilter Romance

Brady's preoccupation with Nazism, torture philosophies, and sadomasochism didn't bother Hindley, and as the couple became closer, they began to photograph themselves in disturbing poses. It became evident that Brady had found a companion to help turn his twisted fantasies into reality: Between 1963 and 1965, the pair murdered five children and buried their bodies in the Saddleworth Moors, leading the gruesome acts to be called "The Moors Murders."

The Murders Begin

Their first victim, 16-year-old Pauline Reade, was on her way to a dance on July 12, 1963, when a young woman offered her a ride. Assuming that it was okay to take a ride from another female—Myra Hindley—Reade accepted. Along the way, Hindley suddenly pulled the car over to look for a missing glove; Reade helpfully joined Hindley in the search. Meanwhile, Brady had followed the car on his motorcycle. He snuck up behind Reade as she was looking for the glove and smashed her skull with a shovel. Reade's body was later found with her throat slashed so deeply that she was nearly decapitated. Unfortunately, hers wasn't nearly the grisliest death in the Moors Murders.

Four months later, on November 23, 1963, at a small-town market, Hindley asked 12-year-old John Kilbride to escort her home with some packages. He agreed. Brady was hidden in the backseat, and Kilbride became victim number two.

Keith Bennett had turned 12 only four days before June 16, 1964, when he encountered Hindley. While walking to his grandmother's house, he accepted a ride from Hindley, who again claimed to need help finding a glove. This time, instead of waiting in the car, she watched as Brady murdered the boy.

As the murderous couple stalked their fourth victim, their bloodlust swelled. On Boxing Day, an English holiday that falls on December 26, the couple lured ten-year-old Lesley Ann Downey to their home. Sadly, their youngest victim suffered the most gruesome and memorable fate. The couple took pornographic photos of the gagged child and recorded 16 minutes of audio of Downey crying, screaming, vomiting, and begging for her mother.

Expanding the Circle

But their treacherous ways reached a pinnacle when, perhaps bored with each other, they tried to get Hindley's 17-year-old brother-in-law, David Smith, in on the act. Like Brady, Smith was a hoodlum, not at all liked by Hindley's family. Smith and Brady had previously bonded by bragging about doing bad things, including murder. Until October 6, 1965, however, Smith assumed it was all a joke.

The couple invited Smith to their house, and he waited in the kitchen while Hindley went to fetch Brady. Upon hearing a scream, he ran to the living room to see Brady carrying an ax and what he perceived to be a life-size doll. It wasn't a doll, of course, but 17-year-old Edward Evans. Smith watched as Brady hacked the last bit of life out of the boy. Afraid that he would be next, Smith helped the couple clean up the mess as if nothing had happened. He waited, terrified, until early the next morning and then snuck out and went to the police.

Facing the Consequences

This wretched crime spree shook Great Britain. The trial of Myra Hindley and Ian Brady lasted 14 days, during which dozens of photos were submitted as evidence, including pictures of the couple in torturous sexual poses. Hindley claimed that she was unconscious when most of the photos were taken and that

Brady had used them to blackmail her into abetting his crimes. However, that claim was quickly dismissed, as police investigators who examined the photos testified that she appeared to be fully aware of what was going on and even seemed to be enjoying herself.

At the time of the trial, the bodies of Lesley Ann Downey, John Kilbride, and Edward Evans had been discovered, all buried in the moor. Great Britain had just revoked the death penalty, so Ian Brady was instead sentenced to three sequential life sentences for the murders. Myra Hindley was charged with two of the murders as well as aiding and abetting and sentenced to life in prison.

The couple suffered miserably behind bars. After serving nearly 20 years, Brady was declared insane and committed to a mental hospital. Hindley was so viciously attacked that she had to have plastic surgery on her face. In the 1980s, the couple admitted to the murders of Pauline Reade and Keith Bennett and led police to Reade's grave. Hindley claimed remorse and appealed many times for her freedom. She received an open degree from a university, found God in prison, and even enlisted the help of a popular, devout Roman Catholic politician, Lord Longford, in her bid for release. But the high court of England denied her requests. Although she fought for her freedom up until her death in 2002, perhaps Hindley knew deep down that she'd never be free—she even called herself Britain's most hated woman. The BBC agreed and ran the quote, along with her infamous mug shot and jail photos, as her obituary.

* Wild West legend Bill Hickok was holding two pair—aces and eights—when he was killed playing poker. These cards are now known as a "Dead Man's Hand."

* Herod the Great was identified in the New Testament Gospel of Matthew as having massacred all boys up to two years old in Bethlehem. There is no historical evidence of such a slaughter.

The Cottingley Fairy Hoax

It was a story so seemingly real that even the creator of the world's most intelligent literary detective was convinced it was true.

✳ ✳ ✳ ✳

Pixie Party

I T WAS SUMMERTIME in the English village of Cottingley in 1917 when cousins Elsie Wright and Frances Griffiths borrowed Elsie's father's camera. When he later developed the glass plate negatives, he saw a photo of Frances with a group of four tiny, winged fairies. A prank, he figured. Two months later, the girls took another photo. This one showed Elsie with a gnome. At that point, her father banned them from using the camera.

A few years later, Wright's wife mentioned her daughter's fairy photos within earshot of theosophist Edward Gardner, who was so taken with them that he showed them to a photographic expert. After study, this man declared the photos genuine. They caught the attention of spiritualist Sir Arthur Conan Doyle, author of the Sherlock Holmes series, who published a magazine article announcing the Cottingley fairies to the world.

A Delusional Doyle

In 1922, Doyle published *The Coming of the Fairies*. The book argued for the existence of fairies and contained the original photos along with three new pictures that Elsie and Frances had produced. Both the article and book ignited a pitched battle between believers and doubters. Many thought Doyle's fertile imagination had finally gotten the better of him.

Fairy Tale?

As years passed, people remained fascinated by the story. In 1981, Elsie admitted that the whole thing was a hoax taken too far, and that the fairies were actually paper cutouts held up by hatpins. Frances, however, maintained the fairies were authentic even up to her death.

Mothers of Atrocity:
The Women of the SS

Hitler's infamous Nazi Schutzstaffel force, better known as the SS, was responsible for countless war atrocities, including the annihilation of six million Jews during the Holocaust. They wore black uniforms with a skull on their hats and committed horrible crimes with merciless ease. But Hitler's racist ideology attracted not just brutal men, but women as well.

✳   ✳   ✳   ✳

Germany's Women Enlist

As WORLD WAR II dwindled, many German men were diverted to the front lines. To fill their positions, many German women were forced to join the SS-Gefolge, the SS female auxiliary, and serve as guards at concentration camps. However, plenty of other women volunteered, eager to show their love for the Reich. Most female guards were trained at the infamous Ravensbrück women's concentration camp in Northern Germany, where it's estimated that more than 130,000 female prisoners died. Female guards were called *Aufseherin*; as war crimes trials later revealed, they were every bit as cruel as their male counterparts. Here are the grisly stories of just four of the approximately 4,000 female SS guards.

Irma Grese:
The Most Notorious Female War Criminal Ever

Twenty-year-old Irma Grese worked at Ravensbrück before transferring to Auschwitz in 1943. There she rose to the rank of Senior SS-Supervisor, the second highest rank attainable in the SS-Gefolge, and she oversaw about 30,000 Jewish and Polish female prisoners. As well as selecting women for the gas chamber, Grese carried a whip and pistol with which she would frequently either beat prisoners to death or randomly shoot them. She also enjoyed watching prisoners being savaged by her pack of well-trained (and half-starved) dogs.

When Allied forces liberated the concentration camp, they made a ghastly discovery in her hut: Grese had the skins of three prisoners fashioned into lampshades. She was tried by a British war crimes court at Lüneburg, and to the end Grese was remorseless. She was sentenced to death by hanging. Famously, Grese refused a hood, and her last words commanded, "*Schnell*," German for "quick." Grese was executed on December 13, 1945.

Ilse Koch: The Bitch of Buchenwald

The wife of Karl Koch, the commandant of the Buchenwald camp, Ilse Koch's sadistic behavior earned her the moniker "Bitch of Buchenwald." She enjoyed riding around the camp on her horse, whipping any prisoners that caught her eye. She also shared Grese's depraved taste in home furnishings. As she rode around Buchenwald, Koch would select any prisoners with distinctive tattoos. SS guards would then kill and skin the selected prisoners and Koch would fashion the tattooed skins into such items as lampshades, book covers, handbags, or gloves.

Koch was sentenced to life imprisonment by an American military tribunal in 1947. She was pardoned two years later, but was then arrested and tried before a West German court. More than 20 years later, she committed suicide in a German prison.

Herta Oberheuser: A Doctor of Death

Dr. Herta Oberheuser was the only female defendant at the 1946 Nuremburg Medical Trials. Like the infamous "Angel of Death" Dr. Josef Mengele, Oberheuser conducted horrific human experiments on prisoners. In some experiments, Oberheuserwould brutally wound prisoners—without anesthetic—to replicate the injuries suffered by soldiers in battle. She would then contaminate the open wounds, scouring them with glass, sawdust, or rusty nails to study the body's reaction.

Having conducted some of the most gruesome human experiments on record, Oberheuser received a 20-year prison term. Yet, she was released in 1952 for good conduct and became a family doctor in Stocksee, Germany. Her license was revoked in

1958 after outcry from the Association of Former Ravensbrück Concentration Camp Prisoners. She died in 1978.

A Nazi Among Us

In 2006, 84-year-old Elfriede Rinkel was deported from her home in San Francisco back to Germany. For more than 60 years she had managed to hide her horrific secret, from both U.S. immigration officials and her Jewish husband. In truth, Rinkel had worked as one of Hitler's women of the SS, a guard at a Nazi concentration camp during World War II.

Born Elfriede Huth, Rinkel worked for ten months at the infamous Ravensbrück camp after responding to a want ad for guards. She worked with an SS-trained attack dog, brutalized female inmates, forced them to march to slave labor sites, and subjected them to inhumane conditions. During Rinkel's time at the camp, nearly 10,000 women died in the gas chambers, during medical experiments, or from malnutrition and disease.

When Rinkel moved to the United States in 1959, she managed to hide her concentration camp service from immigration authorities. She met her late husband at a German-American club in San Francisco. A German Jew, he fled to the United States to escape the Holocaust. He was an active member of the Jewish organization B'nai B'rith until his death in 2004. Friends say that he never suspected his wife was hiding such a dark secret; after all, they pointed out, she used to attend the synagogue with him and even contributed to Jewish charities. In a 2006 interview with the *San Francisco Chronicle*, Rinkel offered little explanation for why she kept her past hidden from her husband for 42 years. "That was my business," she said.

The Justice Department's Office of Special Investigations, formed in 1979 to find Nazis in the United States, revealed Rinkel's history by comparing guard rosters with immigration records. Rinkel was the first woman prosecuted by the office. She now lives in Willich, Germany. Due to Germany's statute of limitations, she is unlikely to be prosecuted.

Crime and Punishment: When Mobsters Screw Up

Not everything goes off without a hitch. In fact, it rarely does. Here are some examples of some of the most-botched crime jobs in history.

✳   ✳   ✳   ✳

ORGANIZED CRIME IS serious business. After all, it usually involves violence, weapons, other people's money, the law, and prison. With those pieces loose on the chessboard, it's really easy to mess up. Take the two New York mobsters who agreed to do a little job: hit Al Capone. They had a nice trip on the Twentieth Century Limited train, but in Chicago they were met at the train, taken someplace quiet, and beaten to death. Pieces of them were sent back to their bosses with a note: "Don't send boys to do a man's job."

Don't Mess with the Wrong Guy

There's also the mistake of not knowing who you're dealing with. Faced with debts in his electrical business, Florida businessperson George Byrum borrowed $50,000 from a mob loan shark. He was able to make $2,500 payments on the interest, but he couldn't pay off the principal, so he decided to go into the crime business himself. He tipped off a burglary gang about a house that he had wired, in exchange for a cut of the take. The burglars broke in, but the home owner was there, and they beat him up. The owner was Anthony "Nino" Gaggi, a Gambino family mobster.

Gaggi found out that Byrum had planned the burglary. On July 13, 1976, Byrum received a call from the Ocean Shore Motel from someone claiming to pitch him a lucrative wiring contract. When Byrum arrived at the motel, Gaggi and some friends were waiting, and that was the last anyone heard from Byrum.

If You're Laying Low, Lay Low!

Often criminal bungling is humorous. Enrico "Kiko" Frigerio was a Swiss citizen, and when the famed Pizza Connection—a scheme to push heroin through pizza parlors in New York—was broken by the FBI in 1984, he fled to Switzerland. Frigerio stayed there for years, until a documentary film crew decided to do a movie about his life. As technical advisor, he decided to give them a tour of his old New York haunts, but when he got off a plane onto U.S. soil, he was immediately arrested. Frigerio hadn't realized that he was still under indictment. Oops!

A Continuing Comedy of Errors

Jimmy Breslin once wrote a comic novel called *The Gang That Couldn't Shoot Straight*. He must have been thinking about New Jersey's DeCavalcante crime family, the only one never given a seat on the Mafia's ruling commission. Vincent "Vinnie Ocean" Palermo ruled the DeCavalcante family like a bad Marx Brothers movie. Once, Palermo's men were given free cell phones—supplied by the FBI to tap their conversations. Palermo also put a .357 Magnum to the head of a mechanic to force him to admit that he'd ruined the motor on Palermo's speedboat. "I was so mad, I bit his nose," Palermo said.

Then there was the time that Palermo and the missus went on vacation, and he decided to hide the family jewelry—$700,000 worth—in the bottom of a trash bag. "My wife took the garbage out for the first time in 20 years, and that was the end of the jewelry."

In 1999, Palermo was arrested and agreed to turn informant in exchange a lenient sentence. He helped to put away such stalwarts as Frankie the Beast, Anthony Soft-Shoes, and Frank the Painter. Palermo himself admitted to four murders, including that of newspaper editor Frank Weiss. He said that it was a good career move: "I shot him twice in the head. They made me a captain."

One List You Don't Want to Be On

With the Most Wanted List, the FBI came to rely on the vigilance of good citizens for its most dangerous work.

✳   ✳   ✳   ✳

URING THE MID-20TH century, nothing was cooler than a G-man. Tough, dogged, honest, and dedicated to rounding up America's worst criminals, agents of the FBI enjoyed wide and largely unwavering public support. This approval stemmed as much from the agents' heroic efforts as from the notorious reputations of the outlaws they hunted: criminals such as Pretty Boy Floyd, John Dillinger, and Bonnie and Clyde.

In 1949, a reporter capitalized on the public's interest in the agency by writing a wire story on the "toughest guys" the FBI was pursuing. The article was wildly popular, and Bureau Director J. Edgar Hoover, a master of public relations, created the Ten Most Wanted Fugitives List in response. When the list first appeared in 1950, it included bank robbers and car thieves, but over time, the types of criminals on the list changed. The 1970s saw a focus on organized crime figures; more recently, emphasis has shifted to terrorists and drug dealers.

Criminals must meet two criteria in order to become candidates for the list. First, they must have an extensive record of serious criminal activity or a recent criminal history that poses a particular threat to public safety. Second, there must be a reasonable likelihood that publicity from their presence on the list will aid in their capture. Criminals are only removed from the list for three reasons: They are captured, the charges against them are dropped, or they no longer fit the criteria for the list.

Over the years, the program has proved remarkably effective. Nearly 500 criminals have appeared on the list, and more than 90 percent of them have been captured. About a third of these fugitives were caught as a direct result of tips from the public.

The Men on the Moon

On July 20, 1969, millions of people worldwide watched in awe as U.S. astronauts became the first humans to step on the moon. However, a considerable number of conspiracy theorists contend that the men were just actors performing on a soundstage.

✳ ✳ ✳ ✳

THE NATIONAL AERONAUTICS and Space Administration (NASA) has been dealing with this myth for nearly 40 years. In fact, it has a page on its official Web site that scientifically explains the pieces of "proof" that supposedly expose the fraud. These are the most common questions raised.

If the astronauts really did take photographs on the moon, why aren't the stars visible in them? The stars are there but are too faint to be seen in the photos. The reason for this has to do with the fact that the lunar surface is so brightly lit by the sun. The astronauts had to adjust their camera settings to accommodate the brightness, which then rendered the stars in the background difficult to see.

Why was there no blast crater under the lunar module? The astronauts had slowed their descent, bringing the rocket on the lander from a maximum of 10,000 pounds of thrust to just 3,000 pounds. In addition, the lack of atmosphere on the moon spread the exhaust fairly wide, lowering the pressure and diminishing the scope of a blast crater.

If there is no air on the moon, why does the flag planted by the astronauts appear to be waving? The flag appears to wave because the astronauts were rotating the pole on which it was mounted as they tried to get it to stand upright.

When the lunar module took off from the moon back into orbit, why was there no visible flame from the rocket? The composition of the fuel used for the takeoff from the surface of the moon was different in that it produced no flame.

Bonnie and Clyde's Final Showdown

From the time Bonnie Parker met Clyde Barrow back in 1930, it seemed as though they were always running from the law. At first, the press and general public had looked upon this unlikely couple with something resembling starstruck eyes. True, they were outlaws. But they were also desperately in love with each other, which made for a rather twisted romantic tale.

✳ ✳ ✳ ✳

IN JANUARY 1934, Clyde made a fatal mistake while carrying out what he called the Eastham Breakout. The plan was to help two Barrow Gang members, Raymond Hamilton and Henry Methvin, break out of jail. The plan worked, but during the escape, a police officer was shot and killed. As a result, an official posse, headed by Frank Hamer, was formed with the sole intent of tracking down Bonnie and Clyde.

Wanted: Dead or Alive

In the month after the Eastham Breakout, Hamer studied Bonnie and Clyde's movements. He discovered that the pair kept to a fairly regular pattern traveling back and forth across the Midwest. Hamer also learned that Bonnie and Clyde used specific locations to meet should they be separated from the rest of the Barrow Gang. Upon hearing that the pair had recently split off from other gang members during a chase, Hamer checked his maps for the nearest rendezvous point, which turned out to be the Louisiana home of Methvin's father, Ivy. Hamer quickly told the posse they were heading south.

By mid-May, the posse had arrived in the tiny town of Gibsland, Louisiana. Finding that Bonnie and Clyde hadn't arrived yet, Hamer decided to set up an ambush along Highway 154, the only road into Gibsland. The posse picked a wooded location along the road and began unpacking the dozens of guns and hundreds of rounds of ammunition they had brought with them, which included armor-piercing bullets. The only thing left to figure out was how to get Bonnie and Clyde to stop their car so arrests could be made (or a clear shot could be had if they attempted to run).

Setting the Trap

Hamer came up with a solution: Ivy Methvin's truck was placed on one side of the road as if it had broken down, directly opposite from where the posse was hiding in the trees. Hamer hoped that Bonnie and Clyde would recognize the truck and stop to help Ivy. This would put the pair only a few feet away from the posse's hiding place. As for Methvin's role in all this, some say he willingly helped the posse in exchange for his son getting a pardon. Others claim the posse tied Methvin to a tree and gagged him before stealing his truck. Either way, the truck was put in place, and the posse took its position in the trees along the road on the evening of May 21.

Working in shifts, the posse waited all night and the following day with no sign of Bonnie and Clyde. They were about ready to leave on the morning of May 23 when, at approximately 9:00 A.M., they heard Clyde's stolen car approaching. At that point, Hamer and the other five men present—Texas ranger Manny Gault, Dallas deputy sheriffs Bob Alcorn and Ted Hinton, and Louisiana officers Henderson Jordan and Prentiss Oakley—took cover in the trees.

So Much for a Peaceful Surrender

The official report said that Clyde, with Bonnie in the passenger seat, slowed the car as it neared Methvin's truck. At that point, standard procedure would have been for the posse to give the couple a chance to surrender peacefully. Hamer, however, gave the order to simply fire at will.

The first shot was fired by Oakley, which, by all accounts, fatally wounded Clyde in the head. The rest of the posse members weren't taking any chances, and they all fired at the car with their automatic rifles, using up all their rounds before the car even came to a complete stop. They then emptied their shotguns into the car, which had rolled past them and come to a stop in a ditch. Finally, they all fired their pistols at the car until all weapons were empty. Approximately 130 rounds were fired.

When it was all over, Bonnie and Clyde were both dead. Upon examination, it was reported that the bodies each contained 25 bullet wounds, though some reports put that number as high as 50. Unlike Clyde, who died almost instantly, it is believed that Bonnie endured an excruciating amount of pain, and several members of the posse reported hearing her scream as the bullets ripped into her. For this reason, many people to this day question the actions of the posse members and wonder why they never gave the pair a chance to surrender.

The Aftermath

Afterward, members of the posse removed most of the items from Bonnie and Clyde's car, including guns, clothing, and even a saxophone. Later, they supposedly allowed bystanders to go up to the car and take everything from shell casings and broken glass to bloody pieces of clothing and locks of hair. Allegedly, two different people had to be stopped from removing parts of Clyde's body (his ear and his finger) as grisly souvenirs.

Despite Bonnie and Clyde's wish to be buried alongside each other, Bonnie's parents chose to bury her alone in the Crown Hill Memorial Park in Dallas. Clyde Barrow is interred at another Dallas cemetery, Western Heights.

Even though it's been more than 70 years since Bonnie and Clyde died, they are still as popular as ever. Every May, the town of Gibsland holds its annual Bonnie and Clyde Festival, the highlight of which is a reenactment of the shootout, complete with fake blood. If you're looking for something even more morbid, Bonnie and Clyde's bullet-riddled car and the shirt Clyde wore on that fateful day are both currently part of a display at the Primm Valley Resort and Casino in Nevada.

Cross-Dressing Across History

People dressing as the opposite gender, whether for fun or for necessity, is nothing new. In fact, cross-dressing dates back hundreds, if not thousands of years. Here are some famous—and often surprising—cross-dressers.

✳   ✳   ✳   ✳

✳ Frances Clayton (aka Francis Clalin) was a Minnesota woman who disguised herself as a man named Jack Williams. Along with her husband, Elmer L. Clayton, the disguised Clayton enlisted in a Union Missouri regiment in the Civil War in 1861. She learned to swear, drink, and chew tobacco, to better hide her true identity. The ruse went on for many months, and the couple fought together in several battles until Elmer was killed in the Battle of Stones River in Tennessee on December 31, 1862.

✳ Ellen Craft was the Georgia-born daughter of a slave woman and her white master. Born into slavery, Craft was light-complected enough that she was able to escape in 1848 by disguising herself as a white man while her husband, William, acted as her black servant. In order to make this daring getaway, Craft had to pretend to be a man because at the time no white woman would have traveled alone, with or without a servant. Eight days after their departure from Georgia, the Crafts arrived in Philadelphia as a free man and a free woman—albeit in men's clothing.

✳ French artist Marcel Duchamp was one of the leaders in the Dada and Surrealism art movements of the early 20th century. Under the name Rrose (or Rose) Sélavy (thought to be a pun on the phrase, *"Eros, c'est la vie"*), Duchamp made several photographic appearances in women's clothing for photographer Man Ray. Duchamp later used Rose as attribution for a number of written works and at least one of his sculptures, *Why Not Sneeze, Rose Sélavy?*

* Fifteenth-century French heroine Joan of Arc wore men's clothing while she traveled, as well as armor when she went into battle. Unfortunately, this fact was noted many times during her trial for heresy, of which she was ultimately convicted and burned at the stake.

* Dorothy Lawrence, an English reporter living in Paris at the outbreak of World War I, hoped to report on the conflict, but was aware that as a woman she would be unable to access the front lines. So Lawrence got a military-style haircut and a soldier's uniform and enlisted with the British Expeditionary Force. After ten days of service, she revealed her identity and was promptly arrested. Upon release, she promised not to tell or write of her experiences in the army—the original intent of her pretending to be a man. Sadly, she was eventually institutionalized and remained so far the rest of her life.

* Edward Hyde, the Third Earl of Clarendon, served as governor of New York and New Jersey from 1701 to 1708. Hyde, whose governorship was tainted by charges of corruption, is remembered as one of the worst American colonial governors. He is also noted for his reported penchant for women's clothing. It is said that he opened the 1702 New York General Assembly dressed as Queen Anne of Great Britain.

* Ed Wood, the man behind cult favorites such as *Plan 9 from Outer Space,* is often considered the worst motion picture director of all time. While that distinction guarantees him a place in the history books, it turns out that in addition to directing ghastly movies, he also enjoyed dressing as a woman. In fact, Wood wrote, directed, and starred in *Glen or Glenda,* a semiautobiographical movie about transvestitism, in which he appeared in a blonde wig and fuzzy angora sweater. "If you want to know me, see *Glen or Glenda,* that's me, that's my story. No question," said Wood.

Brainless Bad Guys

Even crime has its dimmest moments. Here's a collection of crime-related gaffes that put the "dumb" in dumbfound.

❋   ❋   ❋   ❋

Digitized Dummy

THEY SAY A picture is worth a thousand words. Sometimes it's worth even more. In 2003, when a Wal-Mart in Long Island, New York, discovered that $2,000 worth of digital cameras had been lifted from their store, they went straight to the videotape. There they found images of a male and female suspect but couldn't identify either due to the tape's grainy nature. Then they spotted something of interest: At one point during the heist, the female accomplice had taken pictures with a demonstration camera. Her subject? Her partner in crime, of course. When the digital information was fed into a printer, out popped a high-quality color image of a balding man with a mustache. The 36-year-old crook was subsequently identified through a tip line and charged with grand larceny. Like Narcissus, the love of his own image brought him down.

Leave Only Footsteps

Sometimes, ambition can impede the job at hand. According to prosecutors, in 2005, a 23-year-old man filled out a job application while waiting for a pie at a Las Vegas pizza parlor. Then, out of nowhere, the man flashed a gun and demanded that the cashier give him all the money inside her cash drawer. He fled the scene $200 richer. A witness recorded his license plate, and the robber was arrested at home shortly thereafter. But this lucky break wasn't really necessary—he'd jotted down his real name and address on the job application.

Statute of Style Limitations

A security guard working at Neiman Marcus in White Plains, New York, apprehended a young woman in 2007 for shoplifting. He caught up with the 19-year-old outside the store and accused her of stealing a pair of $250 jeans. While he waited for police to arrive, the accused railed bitterly against the guard. According to the police report, she was convinced that she was immune from prosecution based on a legal technicality, stating triumphantly, "It's too late. I already left the store!"

Big-Time Loser

Some criminals just don't know when to stop. In 2007, a New York man was pulled over for a traffic stop and racked up a mountain of criminal infractions in the process. He was intoxicated; not wearing a seat belt; driving toward oncoming traffic lanes with an open beer container by his side; driving with an expired inspection sticker and with license plates from another car; operating an uninsured vehicle; and transporting his two-year-old daughter without the benefit of a car seat or a fastened seat belt.

Indiscriminate Crook

In 2007, an ex-con pulled a fake handgun on two victims and demanded their cash. The only problem was, they were two uniformed New York City police officers. The officers responded by drawing their real weapons, and the mugger surrendered after a brief, but tense, standoff.

Crime Doesn't Pay

In 2007, a thief entered a Fairfield, Connecticut, Dunkin' Donuts. Intent on snaring the contents of its cash register, the would-be crook handed the clerk a note stating that he was carrying a gun and a bomb, and he would use both if he didn't receive cash. With that, the robber grabbed the entire machine from the counter and made his getaway. But there was one significant problem: The hapless criminal had made off with an adding machine instead of the cash register.

✳ Like fingerprints, all tongue prints are unique.

Women You Wouldn't Want to Mess With

As the stories of these legendary "ladies" attest, class and distinction doesn't necessarily mean an elevation over evil. Read on for horrifying tales beyond imagination.

✳ ✳ ✳ ✳

Wu Who?

EMPRESS WU, CHINA'S sole female leader, displayed a talent for ruthlessness and cruelty that belied her station as a member of the so-called "weaker sex." Born in A.D. 624, she became a fifth-level concubine to Emperor Taizong at age 14. Educated, beautiful, and gifted, she quickly caught the emperor's eye and earned the pet name "Charming Lady."

"Cunning lady" would have been more appropriate. Wu soon learned attention equaled power. Elevated to "second grade" concubine under Emperor Kao Tsung, Wu still wanted more. After securing the new emperor's favor by bearing him two sons, she devised a plan to eliminate her competition by strangling her own infant daughter and blaming the baby's death on the jealous actions of the empress and head concubine.

The emperor sided with Wu and elevated her to the throne. Empress Wu then ordered the "murderers" to be executed, allegedly first having their hands and feet amputated and then having them drowned. That level of cruelty set the tone for the rest of her reign. When a stroke incapacitated the emperor, she took over his duties and dispatched any opposition by means of exile, murder, or forced suicide.

After her husband died, Wu installed her weakest son as emperor so that she could continue to rule through him. When he proved difficult to manage, she facilitated his abdication and formally assumed the crown. But while Wu was inarguably brutal, she was also brilliant. The empress is credited with elevating the stature of women in Chinese society and with advancing agriculture and lowering taxes.

Bloody Bathory

Though born into nobility in A.D. 1560, Erzsebet (aka Elizabeth) Bathory was anything but noble. Known as "Hungary's National Monster," she was a sadistic serial murderess who is rumored to have tortured and killed up to 650 women, aided by a motley crew consisting of her children's wet nurse, a dwarflike manservant, and a brawny servant woman rumored to be a witch.

Frankly, Bathory's cruelty sounds like the stuff of legend. She reportedly began torturing peasant girls for entertainment by lashing and bludgeoning them. She moved on to dragging the women naked through the snow, and then drenching them with water until they froze to death. After Bathory's husband died, she moved to their castle at Cachtice. There she befriended Anna Darvulia, a sadist like herself (and rumored to be her lover, as well).

The relationship with Darvulia emboldened Bathory to engage in even more atrocious behavior. Legend has it that once Bathory was too weak to partake in more vigorous torture activities, she had a servant girl delivered to her bedside so she could bite the flesh from her. Other rumors persist that Bathory bathed in the blood of virgins to maintain her skin's youthful appearance.

It's hard to point to an exact cause for her outlandish actions. Bathory's parents were cousins, part of Hungary's elite aristocracy. Some believe this inbreeding caused her madness; others attribute Bathory's heinous crimes to her volatile temperament and unrestrained sense of upper-class privilege.

Since Bathory's victims were peasants, the ruling class (who mainly consisted of Bathory's relatives) tended to turn a blind eye to her vicious pastimes. But things changed after Darvulia died in 1609. Bathory then met Erszi Mjorova, the widow of one of Bathory's tenant farmers. It was Mjorova who may have encouraged Bathory to refine her tastes toward more upper-class victims.

When it was discovered Bathory's appetite had changed to girls of noble birth, her cousin the King of Hungary ordered her arrest. Convicted of 80 counts of murder, Bathory's noble heritage protected her from the death penalty. Instead, she was sentenced to be walled up alive in her castle. Unrepentant to the end, she lived in such a state for four years, until she was discovered dead by a guard in 1614.

LaLaurie the Gory

Delphine LaLaurie is another woman who has inspired countless tales and ghost stories. The wife of a prominent New Orleans dentist (her third husband, whom she married in 1825), she led a dual life. Publicly she was a gracious hostess, well known for her lavish parties and charmingly flirtatious disposition. But to the servants at the family's mansion in the city's French Quarter, Madame LaLaurie was a brutal mistress capable of unspeakable evil.

LaLaurie's life was by all accounts privileged and perfect. Eventually, however, the malevolent side of her behavior surfaced publicly. One night, a neighbor reported seeing a young servant girl fall (some say jump) to her death from the top of LaLaurie's three-story home while being chased by her hostile mistress. As a reprimand, the authorities removed the house slaves and fined the couple $300. The servants were then auctioned off to the highest bidders—who, coincidently, were LaLaurie's relatives. She repurchased the slaves and returned them to her service.

Things appeared to settle down at the LaLaurie home until a fire broke out in 1834. When firefighters arrived to put out the blaze, they discovered two slaves chained to the stove.

Apparently, the servants had set fire to the kitchen on purpose in order to attract attention to the atrocities taking place inside the mansion.

This is where it gets ugly. Implored by the servants to look in the attic, the rescuers uncovered horrifying evidence of LaLaurie's evil. Although no one's entirely sure what was found, there are stories of horrifying experiments being done on the slaves. Some describe more than a dozen naked bodies, both dead and alive, chained to the walls or strapped to operating tables. One man had a hole cut in his head with a stick inserted to stir his brains. A caged woman had her arms and legs broken and reset at angles to resemble a crab. Body parts were scattered everywhere.

Although Dr. LaLaurie is rumored to have known about his wife's grisly hobby, he was not thought to be a participant in her gruesome experiments. His wife, meanwhile, escaped the city before she could be brought to justice. However, a marker in Alley 4 of St. Louis Cemetery No. 1 indicates her body was returned to New Orleans from Paris for burial following her death in 1842.

✴ Nero attempted to kill his mother, Agrippina, four times before his guards stabbed her to death. Before she died, she requested to be stabbed in the womb, where Nero was conceived.

✴ A powerful woman you haven't heard of: Diane de Poitiers, Duchesse de Valentinois (1499–1566). Mistress of King Henri II of France, she more or less ran the realm while Henri did his own thing. Odd detail: Her personal emblem looked very much like the modern biohazard symbol.

✴ Caesar entered Egypt with his armies as the young Queen Cleopatra struggled with her younger brother over the throne. Both sought Caesar's support to secure power. The night before the scheduled meeting, Cleopatra smuggled herself into his headquarters rolled up in a carpet that was presented to him as a gift. Caesar was smitten.

Wanted: The Few, the Proud, the Foolhardy

Looking for a career change? Here are some job descriptions to (re)consider before your next interview.

✳ ✳ ✳ ✳

Floating Cities

JUST OFFSHORE FROM any wartime conflict are floating cities populated with more than 5,000 men and women: aircraft carriers. Twenty-four hours a day, seven days a week, the crews on aircraft carriers risk their lives by being blown overboard by jet blasts as they launch multimillion-dollar fighter planes from runways that are less than 1,000 feet long. Add to that four steam-powered catapults that are able to send a 49,201-pound F/A-18 into the air at 165 miles per hour in less than 2 seconds, and you have all the makings of one of the most dangerous workplaces on Earth.

The Big Snow Job

The next time you're enjoying a ski vacation, take a moment to remember the avalanche crew. While you're still slumbering under your down comforter, members of the resort's ski patrol avalanche crew have already made their way up to the top of the mountain to inspect the ski runs and to set off avalanches before the snow has a chance to slide.

The primary purpose of setting off avalanches at popular ski resorts is to prevent heavy accumulations of snow from endangering the lives of guests. This often means hiking up slippery mountain ridges long before dawn, rappelling off precarious cornices, and tossing dynamite charges into unstable areas. In places where the snow is ready to slide, avalanche crewmembers will "ski cut" a run and try to set off the snow before the first guests have finished their lattes.

Down You Go

If you're looking for hard, dirty, and dangerous work, then you've come to the right place. The business of coal mining has a long history of wall failures, vehicle collisions, collapsed roofs, and gas explosions. Even under the best circumstances, coal mining is highly unpredictable work— especially in underdeveloped countries where miners are forced to endure unsafe working conditions, shoddy material, and outdated machinery.

However, even with sophisticated monitoring devices, gas drainage, and improved ventilation techniques, miners are constantly threatened with suffocation due to carbon monoxide, methane, and sulfur accumulations.

Hide and Seek

It's the middle of the night, and the sheriff's department needs your help—a boy is missing from his Scout camp and it's beginning to snow. Search and Rescue crews are volunteers who save the lives of those who have lost their way in rugged terrain, fallen from steep ledges, need emergency medical treatment, or all of the above. Most volunteers are trained mountaineers and emergency medical technicians, but it's rarely enough training when it's just you against the elements. During the summer months, crews contend with bears, mountain lions, and snakes. In the winter, the worry is getting lost in a snowstorm or being buried by an avalanche while battling frostbite.

Take a Left on 45th Street

Perhaps one of the most dangerous places to be on a Friday night is the front seat of a taxicab. Working long hours for relatively low pay, many taxi drivers voluntarily put themselves at risk from any form of passenger violence. Although many cabs are fitted with cages that separate drivers from their customers, it's almost impossible to prevent an attack.

What's in the Closet?

Often fans will acquire an item that their favorite star once owned. Here are a few of the more outrageous examples.

✳ ✳ ✳ ✳

What Gall

Barton Lidicé Bene, noted celebrity-relic collector, was a fan of J. R. Ewing (Larry Hagman)—the cutthroat yet charming baron from the television series *Dallas*. Demonstrating his continued devotion, Bene had one of Hagman's gallstones placed in a setting, creating a handsome ring.

Enterprising Barber

Elvis Presley's personal hair stylist, Homer Gilleland, so loved the King that he saved a fist-size ball of Presley's hair clippings. He later gave them away to a friend who put them up for auction. Starting bid? $10,000!

Prime Sucker

If you prefer presidential memorabilia, a half-sucked throat lozenge from President Bill Clinton might fit the bill.

Heads, You Lose

Following Sir Walter Raleigh's beheading in 1618, his wife was presented with his embalmed head. She kept it for 29 years, and upon her death, the rotting heirloom was inherited by the couple's son Carew. The head was buried with Carew in 1666.

Einstein's "Computer"

Albert Einstein was one smart cookie. So it comes as no surprise that after his death in 1955, his brain was retained for examination to see what made it so far above average. Sliced into 240 sections for distribution, Einstein's gray matter was compared against other brains and found to be some 15 percent wider than the norm. Today, the bulk of Einstein's brain rests at Princeton Hospital in New Jersey.

Pretentious Pee

In November 1996, a souvenir-hunting art dealer saw a grand opportunity. While dining at a celebrity-filled Los Angeles bistro, the man happened upon Sylvester Stallone in the men's room. Noticing that the muscular star had neglected to flush his urinal, the man leaped into action. He hastily emptied a pill bottle and scooped out a few ounces of Sly's urine.

A Leg Up on the Competition

Some people save their own body parts as souvenirs. Such was the case with Union General Daniel Sickles. After having his right leg amputated after the Battle of Gettysburg, the unfazed warrior donated the limb to the National Museum of Health and Medicine in Washington, D.C. Reportedly, the enterprising officer escorted lady friends to see the relic, regaling them with tales of his bravery.

Pint-sized Phallus

Although the cause of Napoleon Bonaparte's May 1821 death is still open to debate, a certain part of his anatomy is thought to have been removed during his autopsy. Yes, *that* part! A priest by the name of Ange Vignali is said to have taken home the souvenir.

In 1916, Vignali's heirs sold the item. The pint-sized appendage (approximately one inch in length) has since gotten around—perhaps even more than during the famed general's life—and it currently resides with an American urologist.

Proud Appendage

The "Mad Monk" Rasputin is said to have left behind more than his legacy after being murdered in 1916. Tales of his castration have circulated since his death, and his surviving body part is purported to be of uncommon size. In 2004, the Russian mystic's alleged organ was placed on display at a St. Petersburg museum. "We can stop envying America, where Napoleon Bonaparte's is now kept," bragged the museum about their massive find. "Napoleon's is but a small 'pod'; it cannot stand comparison to our organ of 30 centimeters (11.8 inches)."

Doomed Cults and Social Experiments

On the upside, cults have the possibility of offering people acceptance and a sense of community when they would not otherwise have it. On the downside, if you join a cult, you could die.

✳   ✳   ✳   ✳

The People's Temple

The Leader: Jim Jones started his People's Temple with the idea that social justice should be available to all—even the marginalized, the poor, and minorities. He established a commune outside San Francisco in 1965 with about 80 people. Jones capitalized on the rising tide of activism in the 1960s, recruiting affluent, Northern California hippies to help the working-class families who were already members. The People's Temple helped the poorer members of their group navigate the confusing social welfare system. The temple opened a church in an impoverished section of San Francisco that provided a number of social services, such as free blood pressure testing, free sickle-cell anemia testing, and free child care for working families.

The Turning Point: Not all was as it appeared inside the People's Temple. A perfect storm of complaints from disaffected members, media reports that questioned the temple's treatment of current members, and an IRS investigation led Jones to move the People's Temple to Guyana, on the northern tip of South America. In the summer and fall of 1977, the People's Temple started what was supposed to be a utopian agricultural society, which they called Jonestown.

The Demise: In November 1978, U.S. Representative Leo Ryan of San Francisco led a fact-finding mission in response to concerns that members of the Temple were being kept in Guyana against their will. He offered to help anyone who wanted to leave.

A few members joined him, but as the congressional party was waiting on a landing strip for transportation, attackers drove out of the jungle and shot at them. Ryan and four others were killed.

Apparently worried about the closer scrutiny all this could bring, on November 18, Jones ordered his followers to commit "revolutionary suicide" by drinking Fla-Vor-Aid laced with cyanide. More than 900 members of the People's Temple died.

The Family

The Leader: Charles Manson was worried about pollution and environmental damage. Unfortunately, he manifested his concern by brainwashing teens and sending them on murder sprees. Manson had a hard life—spent mostly in juvenile halls, jail, and institutions. In 1967, he wound up in San Francisco, surrounded by young women, most of whom were unstable and in love with him. With a group of these girls, he headed to Los Angeles.

The Turning Point: After moving into the Spahn Ranch north of L.A., where Manson and his followers survived by scavenging discarded food, he started to polish what he considered his philosophy—an Armageddon in which race wars, called "Helter Skelter," would break out. According to this philosophy, Manson would be the one to guide the war's aftermath and rule the world.

Reportedly in an attempt to spark these race wars, the Manson Family staged a series of mass murders, most famously those of Sharon Tate and her guests on August 9, 1969. Because of orders from Manson, four members of the Family killed Tate and her three friends.

The Demise: Bragging to others about their murder sprees ultimately ended up undoing the Family. But the problem wasn't exactly finding the culprits, the problem was proving that members of the Family were responsible for the murders Manson ordered them to perform. Ultimately, a grand jury took only 20 minutes to hand down indictments for members of the family.

Branch Davidians

The Leader: David Koresh joined the Branch Davidians in 1981. The group had been in existence since 1955, having broken off from the Davidian Seventh-Day Adventists, which itself was a group that split with the Seventh-Day Adventist church more than 20 years before that. Koresh was amiable and flamboyant, easy-going and intelligent. After a face-off with the son of the leader of the Branch Davidians, Koresh ultimately ended up as the group's leader and spiritual guide. As all serious cult leaders know, it was important not only to establish himself as a demi-god, but also to impress upon his flock the impending apocalypse and the absolute necessity of following the rules he created.

The Turning Point: Koresh stockpiled weapons in anticipation of inevitable attacks. He taught his followers that they should prepare for the end. He questioned their loyalty and expected them to kill themselves for the cause. On February 28, 1993, the end began. Based on reports of illegal arms sales, child abuse, and polygamy, federal agents raided the Mount Carmel Center near Waco, Texas, setting off a gunfight that ultimately set up a 51-day siege of the Branch Davidian compound.

The Demise: On April 19, 1993, federal agents, in an attempt to force the Davidians out, launched tear gas into the compound. Koresh and the Davidians began shooting. The agents injected more gas, and the exchange continued for several hours. About six hours after the gassing began, fires erupted in the compound. This was followed by more gunfire within the compound, and agents on the scene reportedly believed the Davidians were either killing themselves or shooting one another. Firefighters came to the scene but were not allowed to combat the flames for some time out of fear of gunfire. After the smoke cleared, 75 people within the compound were found dead. Koresh was identified by dental records—he had been killed by a gunshot to the head. Later, accusations were made as to which side was responsible for the fires, but later investigations concluded that they had been set by the Branch Davidians.

Joseph Pujol, King of Farts

Most musical performers produce sound by vibrating the upper part of the digestive tract, but French entertainer Joseph Pujol gained great notoriety in the early 20th century for "singing" from his system's lower end.

✳ ✳ ✳ ✳

GOING BY THE stage name of Le Petomane, or "The Farting Maniac," Pujol wowed audiences with the sheer scope and variety of sounds he was able to create on command. He could mimic everything from earthquakes to cannons.

The Start of the Fart

Pujol attributed his bizarre ability to an incident in his early teens. Born in 1857 in Marseille, France, at the prophetic address of 13 Rue des Incurables, Pujol's life was unremarkable until he took a dip in the ocean one day. While holding his breath underwater, he experienced a strange, freezing sensation in his colon. He swam gasping to the shore, where he discovered water inexplicably gushing from his rear. He consulted a doctor who told him if he wished to avoid repeating the strange phenomenon, he should simply stay out of the ocean.

The experience taught Pujol that he possessed the ability to suck water into his anus and then forcefully expel it as far as ten feet away! With practice, he soon progressed from taking in water to "inhaling" air, which could be ejected in different amounts and pressures by controlling his sphincter muscles.

Pujol first showed off his talent to fellow soldiers in the French Army. When he became a civilian again, he apparently provided customers in his bakery with a performance that involved the imitation of various musical instruments. The act was such a hit that he began performing on stage, first in Marseille and then Paris in 1892. Even the king of Belgium covertly attended his show.

Floating Fluffies for Fun and Profit

The first thing Pujol did on stage was assure his audience that gas masks would not be necessary because his toots were odorless. He even joked that his parents had gone broke paying for perfume for his intestines. Impeccably dressed in a red coat and black breeches, he broke wind in the classic position: leaning forward, knees slightly bent, rear turned to the audience for maximum effect. His repertoire was varied—he could mimic the lengthy rip of a merchant tearing a bolt of fabric or sound off the grunts, barks, and moos of a menagerie of farm animals.

Although gentlemanly in public, Pujol was not too prudish to exhibit more of himself for private gatherings. Instead of his elegant satin breeches, he would perform wearing pants with a wide opening in the back seam so that the truly curious could observe the "art of petomanie" as well as hear it.

Extreme Emissions

Not content with his own nonamplified equipment, the enterprising Pujol strategically inserted a three-foot-long rubber tube for the second part of his act. With the aid of the tube, he could anally smoke a cigarette, play a flute, and blow out candles. Soon he was collecting almost three times the daily pay of famed actress Sarah Bernhardt.

But with success came imitation. After Pujol's gig at the Moulin Rouge ended over a minor legal flap, the theater began advertising a female "flatulist." But she was no match for Le Petomane as she was soon found cheating with a bellows placed under her wide skirt. A Paris newspaper criticized her act, and a flurry of lawsuits followed. The lady's career was blown.

How It All Came Out

Pujol started his own traveling show and, until World War I, farted his way from Algeria to Belgium. When his tour ended, Pujol became a baker in Marseille once more. And until his death in 1945 at age 88, the only cheese he cut in public was as a side dish for his pastries.

Beauty: The Long and Short of It

Throughout history, women have felt obligated to alter what Mother Nature dealt them by plucking, waxing, dying, painting, injecting, cinching, and lifting their natural assets to attract a mate.

⁂ ⁂ ⁂ ⁂

Head Binding

THE PRACTICE OF reshaping the head was popular on several continents, although in different forms. In Africa, the Mangbetu people bound their babies' heads with raffia to create an elongated shape. Women exaggerated their profile by coiffing their hair around baskets for an even more elongated look.

In the South Pacific island nation of Vanuatu, head binding is still practiced. Oil is used to soften babies' skulls, which are then tightly wrapped in a soft bandage made from banana bark and topped with a basket bonnet. Vanuatans prefer cone-shaped noggins and believe that this skull silhouette is not only beautiful, but also helps to increase the brain's capacity for memory. A 17th-century French textbook also reportedly advocated head binding as a memory enhancer.

Lip Stretching

Collagen-injected lips seem tame by comparison to the beauty regimens of some African tribes. When a young Mursi girl reaches age 15 or 16, she begins a lifelong lip-stretching process.

The process begins by puncturing the girl's lower lip and inserting a wooden plug into the cut. Gradually, larger plugs are inserted until the lip can accommodate a disc with a diameter up to five inches. Sometimes the lower teeth are removed to allow room for a larger plate. A woman reportedly has the right to decide when she has been stretched to her limit.

Neck Elongation

Swan-like necks are prized in many cultures, but a tribe who lives along the Thai-Burma border called the Padong (a subsect of the larger Karen group) has carried this ideal to the extreme. Their women begin their beautification routine around age six by having brass rings clasped around their necks. Each year brings a new ring or two, until the women eventually are adorned from chin to clavicle with 20-some neck rings. The more the better—one woman is known to boast 37 rings!

This practice appears to stretch the neck, but in reality the heavy brass rings press down on the collarbones to create this illusion. Since the rings are worn continuously, the neck muscles become too weak to support the women's heads if the rings are removed. However, on her wedding night, a Karen Padong woman takes off her rings for a neck-washing ritual.

Foot Binding

For the Chinese, less was considered more. There, teeny-tiny feet were treasured for many centuries. Foot binding is said to date as far back as the Shang dynasty (1700–1027 B.C.), when a club-footed Empress ordered that her court was to be hobbled like her. Another tale attributes the origin of foot binding to the Song dynasty, around A.D. 960, when a Chinese concubine seduced a ruler with her bound "lotus" feet.

The foot binding procedure generally began before age six, when a girl's bones were still flexible and her arch was not fully developed. The process began soothingly, with a sort of pedicure, but ended with eight of the girl's toes broken; the toes were then secured tightly to the heel with long bandage strips.

The binding process was repeated for many years until the young woman's feet were permanently contorted to a length of four inches or less. This disfigurement was appealing to men because it rendered the woman frail, dependent, and less likely to stray from home. Apparently, it was also a turn-on, since tiny feet feature prominently in ancient Chinese erotica.

Al Capone's Empire

Al Capone, one of the world's most notorious criminals, focused his efforts on a relatively small area.

✳ ✳ ✳ ✳

New York

ALPHONSE GABRIEL CAPONE was born on January 17, 1899, in Brooklyn, New York. He was the fourth son of Italian immigrants who moved to the area near the Navy yard upon first arriving in the United States. By all accounts, Capone's childhood was a normal, if rather harsh, one. The neighborhood by the Navy yard was tough. But soon, Capone's father moved the family to an apartment over his barbershop. The new neighborhood had greater diversity than the one in which they had previously lived. Capone was a typical child, hanging out with friends and doing fairly well in school. Or at least until he reached the sixth grade. The story is rather simple: a teacher hit him, he hit back, and he was expelled—never to return.

Shortly after this, the family moved again, and the new neighborhood had quite an effect on the young Capone. He met the people who would have the most influence on him throughout his life. Johnny Torrio, the "gentleman gangster," taught him how to have what seemed like an outwardly respectable life while simultaneously conducting business in the numbers racket and brothels. Capone also met Frankie Yale, who was on the opposite end of the gangster spectrum from Torrio. Yale was a muscle guy who used aggression and strong-arm tactics to build a successful criminal business. In the midst of all this lawless learning, Capone met Mae Coughlin, a middle-class Irishwoman. They had a son in 1918 and married shortly after.

Capone made an attempt to earn a legitimate living—moving to Baltimore after he was married and doing well as a bookkeeper. But when his father died in 1920, Capone followed Torrio to Chicago to start his infamous career in crime.

Chicago

Torrio had taken over the underworld business in Chicago, and with the coming of Prohibition in 1920, he ended up controlling an empire that included brothels, speakeasies, and gambling clubs. Torrio brought Capone on board as partner. Capone moved his family into a house on Chicago's Far South Side. But after a reform-minded mayor was elected in the city, Torrio and Capone moved their base of operations southwest to suburban Cicero, where the pair essentially took over the town. Frank Capone, Al's brother, was installed as the front man of the Cicero city government and was fatally shot by Chicago police in 1924.

By this point, Capone had made a name for himself as a wealthy and powerful man. He was also a target. When gangland rival Dion O'Bannon was killed, Capone and Torrio easily took over O'Bannon's bootlegging territory—but they also set themselves up for a lifelong war with the remaining loyalists in O'Bannon's gang.

Capone and Torrio survived many assassination attempts. In 1925, when Hymie Weiss and Bugs Moran attempted to kill Torrio outside the crime boss's own home, Capone's partner finally decided to retire. He handed the empire over to Capone. Capone adapted to his role as the head honcho very easily. He actively cultivated a public persona, showing up at the opera, Chicago White Sox games, and charity events. He played politics with the smoothest politicians. And he dressed impeccably.

From 1925 to '29, Capone simultaneously polished his public persona and meted out violence to retain his superior gangland status. In New York in 1925, he orchestrated the Adonis Club Massacre, killing a rival gang leader and establishing his influence outside of Chicago. In 1926, he is believed to have had public prosecutor Billy McSwiggin. When public perception turned against him, Capone stepped up his community involvement. He frequently told the press that his motto was "public service." In fact, because he provided jobs for hundreds of Italian immigrants through his bootlegging business, he genuinely thought himself a public servant. Knowing PR is everything, he also ran a soup kitchen to provide free meals. When it came to his employees, Capone could be generous to a fault. He also cultivated relationships with jazz musicians appearing in his Cicero nightspot, The Cotton Club. In 1926, Capone organized a conference to stop the violence among gangs.

The crime boss was wildly successful in creating his public image—so successful, in fact, that he caught the attention of the president of the United States. After the St. Valentine's Day Massacre in Chicago in February 1929, in which seven members or associates of a rival gang were killed, the government initiated a focused attempt to put Capone behind bars. In 1930, Capone was listed as Public Enemy Number One; by 1931, he was convicted on multiple counts of tax evasion and was sentenced to 11 years behind bars. He was ultimately transferred to Alcatraz, where he was unable to use money or personal influence to carve out the kind of pampered life he had hoped to live while in prison.

Florida

Because of intense media scrutiny in Chicago, Capone bought an estate in Palm Island, Florida, in 1928. Though the residents of the town were chilly to his family's arrival, the Capones established a home and a retreat in this small community. Capone returned there when he looked to avoid the glare of his public profile in Chicago, and it was at this estate that he died. While in prison, Capone suffered from neurosyphilis and was confused and disoriented. He was released from prison in 1939 and briefly stayed in a Baltimore hospital, but he returned to Palm Island, where he slowly deteriorated until his death on January 25, 1947. The man who took the world by storm with his organized and brutal approach to crime was survived by his wife, son, and four grandchildren. Though he occupied only a small corner of the world, Al Capone left a huge mark on it.

Great Achievements in Medical Fraud

Have you fallen for pills, ointments, and gadgets that swear to make you thinner or more muscular, with thicker hair and rock-hard abs? Well, you're not alone. Read on for a look at some of history's medical shams and charlatans.

✳ ✳ ✳ ✳

To the Rescue

IF YOU WERE diagnosed at the turn of the century with lumbago, puking fever, black vomit, consumption, decrepitude, falling sickness, milk leg, ship fever, softening of the brain, St. Vitus's dance, trench mouth, dropsy, or heaven forbid, dyscrasy, then chances are you were in big trouble. Not only did the "modern" medical community misunderstand most of these diseases, they were also clueless as to how to treat them.

Facing a life of interminable pain, many sufferers of these diseases resorted to hundreds of unfounded medical treatments, which sometimes worked and sometimes didn't. Here's a brief list of some of the more popular medical treatments and the claims by their originators:

✳ **The Battle Creek Vibratory Chair:** Many people who enjoy a bowl of Corn Flakes in the morning are familiar with their inventor, Dr. John Harvey Kellogg of Battle Creek, Michigan. Dr. Kellogg also designed a number of therapeutic devices, including the Battle Creek Vibratory Chair. After strapping the patient in, the chair would shake violently and "stimulate intestinal peristalsis" that was beneficial to digestive disorders. Prolonged treatments were also used to cure a variety of maladies from headaches to back pain.

✳ **The Toftness Radiation Detector:** If the Toftness Radiation Detector looks suspiciously like the PVC piping and couplings found at a hardware store, that's because it is. By passing PVC tubing outfitted with inexpensive lenses over the patient's back, chiropractors listened for a high-pitched "squeak" that meant that the device had detected areas of neurological stress, characterized by high levels of radiation. The device was widely used until 1984 when it was deemed worthless by the Food and Drug Administration.

* **The Foot-Operated Breast Enlarger Pump:** In the mid-1970s, silicone breast implant technology was still in its infancy. Instead, many women pining for larger breasts spent $9.95 for a foot-operated vacuum pump and a series of cups that promised "larger, firmer and more shapely breasts in only 8 weeks." As it turned out, more than 4 million women were duped into buying a device that produced nothing more than bruising.

* **The Crystaldyne Pain Reliever:** In 1996, one of the most popular pain relievers on the market was nothing more than a gas grill igniter. When the sufferer pushed on the plunger, the device sent a short burst of sparks and electrical shocks through the skin to cure headaches, stress, arthritis, menstrual cramps, earaches, flu, and nosebleeds. After being subjected to FDA regulations, however, the company disappeared with thousands of dollars, falsely telling their consumers that "their devices were in the mail."

* **The Prostate Gland Warmer and the Recto Rotor:** Even someone without the slightest bit of imagination would cringe at the idea of inserting a $4^{1}/_{2}$-inch probe connected to a 9-foot electrical cord into their rectum to soothe their ailments. However, for thousands of adventurous consumers in the 1910s, the Prostate Gland Warmer (featuring a blue lightbulb that would light up when plugged in) and the Recto Rotor promised the latest in quick relief from prostate problems, constipation, and piles.

* **The Radium Ore Revigator:** In 1925, thousands of unknowing consumers plunked down their hard-earned cash

for a clay jar that was impregnated with low-grade radio-active ore. The radioactive material was nothing more than that found in the dial of an inexpensive wristwatch, but the Revigator still promised to invigorate "tired" or "wilted" water that was put into it—"the cause of illness in one hundred and nine million out of the hundred and ten million people of the United States."

* **Hall's Hair Renewer:** For as long as there's been hair loss, there has probably been hair-loss cures. One of the better-known snake oils in the 19th century was Hall's Vegetable Sicilian Hair Renewer, which Reuben P. Hall began selling in 1894. According to the inventor, an Italian sailor passed the recipe to him; the results promised hair growth and decreased grayness. The first version was composed of water, glycerine, lead sugar, and traces of sulfur, sage, raspberry leaves, tea, and oil of citronella. Eventually, the formula was adjusted to include two kinds of rum and trace amounts of lead and salt. Of course, lead is poisonous, and the ingredients had to be changed once again. Still, the product sold into the 1930s. Perhaps it was its promise that "As a dressing it keeps the hair lustrous, soft and silken, and easy to arrange. Merit wins."

* **The Relaxacisor:** For anyone who hated to exercise but still wanted a lithe, athletic body, the Relaxacisor was the answer. Produced in the early 1970s, the Relaxacisor came with four adhesive pads that were applied to the skin and connected by electrodes to a control panel. The device would deliver a series of electrical jolts to the body, "taking the place of regular exercise" while the user reclined on a sofa. All 400,000 devices were recalled for putting consumers at risk for miscarriages, hernias, ulcers, varicose veins, epilepsy, and exacerbating preexisting medical conditions.

The Royal Dirt

Queens, kings, and mistresses—in the backstabbing world of royal courts, people got into all sorts of crazy things.

✳ ✳ ✳ ✳

✳ After his first wife died, King Louis XIV secretly married his longtime mistress, Madame de Maintenon. But because of her low social status, she never became queen.

✳ Edward III's notorious mistress, Alice Perrers, is said to have stolen the rings off the king's fingers as he died.

✳ Elizabeth I lost a fortune in gold and jewel decorations that came loose and fell off her clothes as she went about her daily business. This was a common problem for nobles at the time, and attendants were often charged with watching for fallen ornaments and discretely retrieving them.

✳ King Charles VI of France supposedly sent young Henry V of England a bunch of small balls, saying his age was more suited to games than to battle. Henry was not impressed and declared that he would soon play a game of ball in the French streets. He invaded France not long after.

✳ Jane Seymour, third wife of Henry VIII, picked out her wedding dress on the day her predecessor, Anne Boleyn, was executed.

✳ King Louis XV's longtime mistress, Madame de Pompadour, wielded so much power over the king she was known as "the real Queen of France."

✳ King Henry IV of England was a childhood friend of King Richard II, whom he later deposed.

✳ "Divorced, beheaded, died; divorced, beheaded, survived" is a popular rhyme used to remember the fates of Henry VIII's six wives.

* Edward III was the first English king to claim the French throne. His claim was through his mother, Queen Isabella, and had been included as part of her marriage contract to Edward II. The French king's refusal to honor the contract was the spark that started the Hundred Years' War.

* Egyptian pharaohs often married their siblings because it was believed that pharaohs were gods on Earth and thus could marry only other gods.

* Queen Cleopatra of Egypt was the first ruler in 300 years who actually spoke Egyptian. The Ptolemaic pharaohs were Greeks descended from Ptolemy, one of Alexander the Great's generals, so Greek was the dominant language of their court. Cleopatra also spoke several other languages, including Latin, Hebrew, and Aramaic.

* Richard II was so upset over the death of his first wife, Anne of Bohemia, that he had the house she died in destroyed.

* Edward I grieved the death of his wife, Eleanor of Castile, by building a stone monument at each place her funeral procession stopped en route from Lincoln to London. Three of the twelve original structures, known as Eleanor crosses, still stand today.

* On several occasions, Cleopatra dressed as the goddess Isis to play up the common belief that Egyptian kings and queens were the incarnations of gods.

* Henry VI of England suffered periodic mental breakdowns, during which he would respond to no one. One lasted more than a year.

* In Tudor England, being beheaded instead of hanged was considered a "favor" granted to condemned nobles.

* Emperor Augustus attempted to reform what he considered loose Roman morals. Unfortunately, he then had to banish his daughter Julia for committing adultery.

Odd Egg Rituals

Throughout the world, the egg is used for more than whipping up omelets. Here are some traditional charms, potions, and spells that make use of this seemingly innocuous breakfast staple.

✳ ✳ ✳ ✳

✳ In Macedonia, an egg can mean the difference between life and death. According to local lore, if you share a birthday or even a birth month with a dying relative, your days are likewise numbered. The only way to cheat fate is to share the yolk of an egg with this relative while standing on opposite sides of a stream. Similarly, a dying man might save himself if he finds someone to share a sugared egg on the threshold of a house.

✳ In Mergentheim, Germany, if someone falls gravely ill, that person ties a white thread around an egg and places it into a fire. If the shell turns black in the flame, death is not far off.

✳ Swamped at work? Beset by bad luck? Craving undead company? Sneak into a Jamaican churchyard at night and visit the grave of a friend or relative—one's mother would be the most suitable. Break an egg and offer it to the deceased with some rice and rum. The ghost will rise, eat the food, and offer you help and good luck in return.

✳ In Morocco, a woman who has a very young son and is preparing to give birth again keeps an egg close to her during labor. After the birth, the egg is given to the newborn's brother to ensure that the siblings will like each other. But if the egg should happen to be eaten by someone other than the baby's brother, the baby will grow up to hate the mother.

✳ All across Europe, eggs are used to tell fortunes. The most popular method is to carefully pierce the shell and catch drops of the egg white in a glass of water. The shapes that form in the water are examined and interpreted by an unmarried woman who is looking for clues to her future husband's profession. A ship means marriage to a sailor, a shoe means she'll wed a cobbler, and so on.

* The Scottish variant of this fortune-telling technique is called "drap glasses." A group of women get together, and each one brings an egg and hands it to the woman in charge. She then separates out the whites, drops each one into a glass of water, seals the rim with her hand, and inverts it. When everyone is done interpreting the shapes, the eggs yolks are used to bake "dumb cakes," so called because the fortune-telling is done in silence.

* In rural Russia, eggs can help you make friends with supernatural forces. The house sprite (*domovoi*), a ubiquitous if usually invisible presence in every home, is said to occasionally assume the shape of a snake. If the owners of the house find this snake, they would do well to offer it egg pancakes (*blini*). If the gift is accepted, the *domovoi's* benevolence is secured and the household will prosper; a rejection means the house will burn down.

* Occasionally, hens lay eggs with imperfect shells or without shells altogether. In England, such eggs are traditionally called "wind eggs," from the belief that the hen laying them had been impregnated not by the rooster but by the wind. In parts of Hungary, if a black hen lays a soft-shelled egg, it is destroyed upon discovery, for it signifies the worst of omens: that the earth is softening beneath a member of the family, which is a metaphor for impending death.

* Many cultures consider unusual eggs—misshapen, empty, yolkless, shell-less, or ones with the yolk and white merged—to be laid not by hens but by roosters. This belief is likely derived from the fact that the bodies of aged roosters (seven years or older) are often found to contain a white egg-shaped globule.

Entrepreneurs of Death: The Story of Murder, Inc.

Following the rise of the National Crime Syndicate, or what people now call the Mafia, a group of enterprising killers formed an enforcement arm that the press dubbed "Murder, Incorporated." Officially, they were known as "The Combination" or "The Brownsville Boys," since many of them came from Brooklyn's Brownsville area.

* * * *

THE COMBINATION BEGAN their mayhem-for-money operation around 1930 following the formation of the National Crime Syndicate. Until their demise in the mid-1940s, they enforced the rules of organized crime through fear, intimidation, and murder. Most of the group's members were Jewish and Italian gangsters from Brooklyn; remorseless and blood-thirsty, murder for money was their stock-in-trade. The number of murders committed during their bloody reign is unknown even today, but estimates put the total at more than a thousand from coast to coast. The name "Murder, Inc." was the invention of a fearless *New York World-Telegram* police reporter named Harry Feeney; the name stuck.

Filling a Need

The group was the brainchild of mob overlords Johnny Torrio and "Lucky" Luciano. The most high-profile assassination credited to the enterprise was the murder of gang lord Dutch Schultz, who defied the syndicate's orders to abandon a plan to assassinate New York crime-buster Thomas Dewey. The job went to one of Murder Inc.'s top-echelon gunsels, Charles "Charlie the Bug" Workman, whose bloody prowess ranked alongside such Murder, Inc., elite as Louis "Lepke" Buchalter, the man who issued the orders; Albert Anastasia, the lord high executioner; Abe "Kid Twist" Reles, whose eventual capitulation led to the group's downfall; Louis Capone (no relation to Al); Frank Abbandando; Harry "Pittsburg Phil" Strauss, an expert with an ice pick; Martin "Buggsy" Goldstein; Harry "Happy" Maione, leader of the Italian faction; Emanuel "Mendy" Weiss, who is rumored to have never committed murder on the Sabbath; Johnny Dio; Albert "Allie" Tannenbaum; Irving "Knadles" Nitzberg, who twice beat a death sentence when his convictions were overturned; Vito "Socko" Gurino; Jacob Drucker; Philip "Little Farvel" Cohen; and Sholom Bernstein, who like many of his cohorts turned against his mentors to save his own life. It was an era of infamy unequaled in mob lore.

Loose Lips

Many of the rank and file of Murder, Inc. appeared to enjoy killing, including Reles, a former soda jerk. Known as "Kid Twist," Reles was just as bloodthirsty as some of his contemporaries, but he was also cursed with a huge ego and a big mouth, and he wasn't shy about doing his bragging in front of cops, judges, the press, or the public at large. The little man with the big mouth would eventually lead to the unraveling of the Combination and greatly weaken the power of the National Crime Syndicate. When an informant fingered Reles and "Buggsy" Goldstein for the murder of a small-time hood, both men turned themselves in, believing they could beat the rap just as they had a dozen times before, but this one was ironclad. Reles sang loud and clear, implicating his peers and bosses in more than 80 murders and sending several of them to the electric chair, including the untouchable Buchalter. He also revealed the internal secret structure of the National Crime Syndicate. Reles was in protective custody when he "fell" to his death from a police-protected hotel room on November 12, 1941. By the mid-1940s, Murder, Inc., was a thing of the past, and the National Crime Syndicate was in decline. When it came to singing like a canary, only Joe Valachi would surpass the performance of Reles, once the most trusted member of the Brownsville Boys.

Jersey Jumper

With enough ingenuity, a person can get famous in all sorts of ways. Just ask Sam Patch.

✳   ✳   ✳   ✳

Factory Boy

SAM PATCH WAS born circa 1807 in Rhode Island. As a young boy, Sam worked in the Pawtucket mills, often for 12 hours a day. It was dull, hard work, but he found something to keep him occupied and his friends entertained: waterfall jumping. Waterfall jumping was an art. Jumpers dove in feet first, and they sucked in a deep breath just before hitting the water. Once underwater, they stayed under long enough to start frightened spectators buzzing. Finally, they burst out of the water, much to the delight of a relieved audience.

In his mid-20s, Patch left Pawtucket for Paterson, New Jersey. Beside being a factory town, Paterson was also home of Passaic Falls, an idyllic waterfall with a 70-foot drop that was second only to Niagara Falls on the East Coast.

Taking the Plunge

On September 30, 1827, Patch dove off a cliff and into the swirling waters of the falls. He emerged from the waters with a gasp; the "Yankee Leaper" had been born. Patch realized that he could either work for pennies in a hot, sweaty factory or parlay his jumping skills into fame and possibly fortune.

Patch developed a routine. He would lay out his coat, vest, and shoes on the ground, as if he may not need them again. He gave a speech containing one, or both, of his favorite sayings: "There's no mistake in Sam Patch," and "Some things can be done as well as others."

Soon, word of Patch's jumps got around. He attained celebrity status, and with fame's siren song ringing in his ears, Patch set out to jump whenever and wherever. On August 11, 1828, he jumped 100 feet from a ship's mast into the Hudson River at Hoboken, New Jersey. Patch's antics earned him much publicity, as hundreds of onlookers would gather to watch him jump from increasingly tall heights. In addition to being the "Yankee Leaper," he also became known as "Patch the Jersey Jumper."

On October 7, 1829, Patch leaped into immortality by jumping 85 feet into Niagara Falls from a platform off Goat Island. As an onlooker recorded: "Sam walked out clad in white, and with great deliberation put his hands close to his sides and jumped." Ten days later, he jumped Niagara again from 120 feet, netting a cool $75.

In November, Patch, now accompanied by a pet black bear, showed up in Rochester, New York, to jump the thundering Genesee Falls. He performed the jump on November 6, 1829; some reports say he threw the bear over the side as well. Showing that there was "no mistake in Sam Patch," he decided to repeat the plunge on Friday, November 13.

He may have chosen an ominous date to jump the Genesee, and he may or may not have been drunk, but he was certainly tempting fate. Sure enough, a third of the way down, he lost his form and hit the water like a sack of potatoes. One report later said that he had ruptured a blood vessel on the way down. Either way, thousands of spectators anxiously watched the water, but Patch never resurfaced.

Post-Patch

Even in death Patch was controversial. Some say his body wasn't found for months, while others say that it was found two days later. After his body was found, he was buried in a grave with a marker reading: "Here Lies Sam Patch. Such Is Fame."

But death did not stop Patch. He lived on for years in novels, comics, and popular plays such as *Sam Patch* and *Sam Patch in France.* There was a Sam Patch-brand cigar, and President Andrew Jackson even named his favorite horse Sam Patch.

Chapter 10

Weird Facts

Contrary to Popular Belief...

Just because something is common knowledge doesn't mean it's based in fact. Here are some popular perceptions that are just plain wrong.

✳   ✳   ✳   ✳

A Lead Pencil Hath No Lead: The Romans were crazy about lead. They drank from lead cups, painted their faces with lead makeup, and used lead rods as writing utensils. As most people know, all that lead went to their heads and caused health problems to no end. Fortunately, lead hasn't been used in pencils for hundreds of years, thanks to the discovery of graphite, which is mixed with clay and formed into small rods that are then wrapped in wood.

You Say Tomato, I Say Fruit: If you ask a scientist, you'll likely be told a tomato is a fruit. After all, fruits are classified as such because they develop from the ovary of flowers and contain the seeds of the plant from which they sprouted. A tomato is a perfect example of this process. But in 1893, the Supreme Court ruled that the tomato is legally a vegetable. The case reached the high court because of a tax and tariff problem—people paid more taxes for imported vegetables than fruits. The Supreme Court ruled that even though a tomato is a "fruit of the vine," in the "common language of the people" it's a bona-fide vegetable.

Food Fantasies: Ever wonder why your fast-food hamburger looks smashed and dried-out when you unwrap it, while the same type of burger unwrapped on TV looks thick and juicy? The difference can be attributed to food stylists who spend hours making sure that their products are picture-perfect. Stylists cook burgers just enough to brown them, which also keeps them plump and moist. And the glistening tomato and crispy lettuce covered in drops of dew? The effect is created with spray-on gelatin, which makes food shine under hot studio lights. Unblemished buns are hand-chosen, and sesame seeds are individually glued into place. Buns are lined with waxed paper to prevent that soggy look.

India Ink Is Homesick: It was the Chinese, not the people of India, who perfected what we understand today to be India ink. Originally, the ink was made by mixing soot from pine smoke with lamp oil, then adding gelatin derived from donkeys. These days, India ink is made from a blend of natural and synthetic materials and is manufactured around the world.

The Identity Crisis of the Horny Toad: The *Phrynosoma*, or horned lizard, is usually referred to as the horny toad or horny frog. The reptile isn't even related to frogs, but its short, wide body and froglike visage have wrongly convinced people of its identity. Call a horned lizard a toad at your own risk—when these critters get angry, they shoot blood out of their eyes.

The Panda: Barely a Bear?: It's official! The panda may or may not be an actual bear. Opinions vary on the matter. Scientifically speaking, the panda is a member of the Carnivora order, the family that comprises dogs, bears, raccoons, weasels, mongooses, hyenas, and cats. The panda's ancestors were bears, but there is disagreement about whether certain types of pandas (e.g., the red panda) should belong in the bear, or Ursidae, category. Some suggest they be grouped with the raccoon family, the Procyonidae, or in an entirely new all-panda family, the Ailuridae.

Where You'd Least Expect It

You'll be amazed to learn the whereabouts of these things.

✳   ✳   ✳   ✳

✳ A stolen painting by Mexican artist Tamayo was retrieved from an unlikely place: the trash. Out on a stroll, Elizabeth Gibson spotted it nestled among some garbage. After finding the painting posted on a Web site four years later, Gibson received a share of the one million dollars it fetched at a Sotheby's auction.

✳ John Wilkes Booth's body is buried in a Baltimore cemetery, but his third, fourth, and fifth vertebrae can be found on display in the National Health and Medicine Museum in Washington, D.C. They were removed for investigation after he was shot and killed while on the run following President Lincoln's assassination.

✳ Normally on display at the Elvis After Dark Museum, a handgun once owned by the King was stolen during a ceremony on the 30th anniversary of his death. Soon thereafter, the missing gun was found stashed inside a mucky portable toilet only yards from where the gun's exhibit case sat.

✳ Egypt, which receives less rainfall than most places on Earth, doesn't seem like the kind of place where you'd find sea creatures. Yet, it was there that geologists discovered the nearly complete skeleton of a *Basilosaurus,* a prehistoric whale. During the whale's lifetime, 40 million years ago, Egypt's Wadi Hitan desert was underwater.

✳ *Femme nue couchée,* a racy female nude painted by Gustave Courbet in the 19th century, turned up on a Slovakian doctor's wall in 2000, nearly six decades after it disappeared during World War II. It was believed to have been stolen by members of the Russian Red Army, but the country doctor claimed that he received the art as payment.

You Can't Teach an Old Flea New Tricks

Glitz, glamor, and fleas? Here's a different take on the entertainment biz—the age-old tradition of flea circuses.

✳ ✳ ✳ ✳

The Birth of an Industry

FLEA CIRCUSES HAVE long been a form of entertainment. The earliest flea circuses date back to 14th-century Asia, although they didn't hit their peak in popularity until the 16th century in Great Britain. While there are over 2,500 species of fleas, 19th-century flea circus ringleader Louis Bertolotto (whom one Web site dubbed the "Andrew Lloyd Webber of flea-biz") found only the females of the *Pulex irritans* species worthy of a place in his lineup: "I have found the males to be utterly worthless, excessively mulish and altogether disinclined to work." Perhaps some things never change.

In the beginning, finding fleas to audition for the circus was fairly easy—largely due to poor hygienic standards and the number of mangy dogs running free in the streets of London. But as people began to bathe regularly, circus owners had to pay as much as half a crown per flea. Considering that the average life span of a flea was only 30 to 90 days, this represented a very poor return on their investment.

The Casting Couch

Circus owners had to determine which entertainers were best suited for the individual roles. The larger fleas with their superior strength and stamina were chosen to power the merry-go-rounds. The flightiest were chosen as dancers, and the fleas with the strongest legs were made kickers, jugglers, or chariot racers. Center-ring performers had to audition by demonstrating how high they could jump and showing if they could stick to the inside of the casting director's jar.

In addition to the thrill of entertaining countless circus fans, flea trainers enjoyed working with their artistes because they never complained, were easy to house, and cost almost nothing to feed: Twice a day, the trainer would roll up his shirt sleeve and let his entertainers sink their fangs into his forearm. After 15 minutes of feeding, it was showtime.

The Show Must Go On

Although the fleas were ready, willing, and able to work, it was no easy feat capturing them for their performances. At only several millimeters in length, it took someone with an eagle eye to tie a tiny noose made of glass silk around the performer's neck. The trick was to secure the knot tight enough to restrain the flea but not cut off their circulation during mealtime. Trainers with poor eyesight or who lacked patience permanently glued the flea's feet to the stage.

As employees, fleas turned out to be tireless performers. They were inexpensive to feed, could be depended on for several shows a day, and were capable of jumping over 140 times the force of gravity—the human equivalent of leaping over the Statue of Liberty a thousand times an hour.

While some fleas were permanently attached to their posts, others were "trained" to play football or juggle. After securing a flea on its back, the trainer would toss them a small pith ball that was coated with citronella oil or other insect repellent. The flea was so repulsed by the oil that it would "kick" the ball away to the delight of the audience.

Like any other popular moneymaker, flea circuses were not immune to shysters, scalawags, and imposters who attempted to entertain their audiences with fake flea circuses. Since the performers were often too small to be seen with the naked eye, a number of proprietors cashed in by devising clever stages that were operated with a series of foot-operated machines and clickers. These ruses made it appear that the fleas were providing the show—when in fact they were still home on Fido.

Things You Never Knew About the Penny

We collect them in jars, make them appear magically behind people's ears, and long for the days when a handful would get us a candy bar at the corner store. We handle thousands of them every year, but how much do we know about the familiar penny?

✳ ✳ ✳ ✳

✳ Since they were introduced in 1787, more than 300 billion pennies have been produced. Today, there are about 150 billion pennies in circulation, enough to circle the earth 137 times.

✳ Since 1909, Abraham Lincoln has been the star of the penny, but it wasn't always that way. There have been 11 different designs, including the popular Indian Head penny introduced in 1859.

✳ The princess on the Indian Head penny was neither a Native American nor a princess. She was, in fact, the sculptor's daughter, Sarah Longacre.

✳ On the 200th anniversary of Lincoln's birth in 2009, the U.S. Mint introduced pennies that depict four different representations of his life. These replaced the Lincoln Memorial on the penny.

✳ Examine the faces on a penny, an original Jefferson nickel, a dime, and a quarter. All the presidents except Lincoln are facing left. People have long imagined a secret meaning behind this, but Victor David Brenner, the sculptor of the Lincoln penny, explained that he had worked from a photo of Lincoln facing to the right. Simple as that.

✳ If you have a strong magnifying glass, you can see the initials of the sculptors who designed the pennies. Since 1959, the initials of Frank Gasparro have been near the shrubbery to the right of the Lincoln Memorial. Pennies dated 1918 to 1958 have the initials VDB (Victor David Brenner) under Lincoln's shoulder.

* Pennies haven't been made of pure copper since 1864. During World War II, the U.S. Mint helped the war effort by recycling: It melted shell casings to make pennies. To conserve further, it considered creating plastic pennies but settled on zinc-covered steel. After the war, the Mint returned to a zinc-and-copper combination.

* Pennies have become a popular souvenir thanks to the penny-press machines at museums, amusement parks, and family vacation spots. These machines, introduced at the Chicago World's Fair in 1893, flatten and elongate a penny between two rollers and imprint a new image—anything from an octopus to the Liberty Bell to Mickey Mouse. Each year these machines roll out more than 12 million pennies into fun oval shapes.

* Money is shrinking—and not just in value. When the penny was introduced in 1787, it was about twice the size of today's version. The penny didn't reach its current size until 1857.

* See a penny, pick it up. There are about forty 1943 copper pennies in existence. One sold in 1999 for $112,500.

* You can't use pennies to pay at tollbooths—unless you're in Illinois. Lincoln's home state has a soft spot for pennies.

* A coin toss isn't a game of luck if you use a penny and call heads. The penny is the only coin with the face of the same person on both sides. A magnifying glass will reveal Lincoln sitting inside the Lincoln Memorial.

* Could the penny be relegated to the endangered-coin list? Because the price of metals is rising, it now costs more than a cent to make a penny. It costs only about four cents to make a $100 bill.

What Do You Mean by That?

Here are the fascinating origins of some well-known terms.

✳ ✳ ✳ ✳

Blue Bloods

In the Middle Ages, the veins of the fair-complexioned people of Spain appeared blue. To distinguish them as untainted by the Moors, they referred to themselves as blue-blooded.

Rob Peter to Pay Paul

In the mid-1550s, estates in St. Peter's, Westminster, were appropriated to pay for the new St. Paul's Cathedral. This process revived a phrase that preacher John Wycliffe had used 170 years before in *Select English Works*.

Humble Pie

While medieval lords and ladies dined on the finest foods, servants used leftovers (the "umbles," or offal) when preparing their meals. To eat humble pie means to exercise humility or self-effacement.

Men of Straw

In medieval times, men would hang around English courts of law, eager to be hired as false witnesses. They identified themselves with a straw in their shoe.

White Elephant

Once upon a time in Siam, rare albino elephants were to receive nothing but the best from their owners. Therefore, no one wanted to own one.

Touch and Go

English ships in the 18th century would often hit bottom in shallow water, only to be released with the next wave. The phrase indicated that they had narrowly averted danger.

What Exactly Is Mensa?

Almost everybody, it seems, has heard about Mensa—the club for really, really smart people—but nobody is sure exactly what it is. Or how to get in. Or what the standards are for membership.

✳ ✳ ✳ ✳

MORE THAN 50,000 Americans are part of the international society called Mensa. They're just people who have scored in the top 2 percent in one of more than 200 acceptable standardized tests. (Although spokespeople won't say exactly what the magic number happens to be, the standard measurement for "very superior" intelligence is an IQ of 130 or above.) About one in 50 Americans—six million in total—qualify for Mensa membership, whether they realize it or not (you can see for yourself at www.us.mensa.org/testscores).

Currently, American Mensa's youngest member is just 3 years old, and the oldest is 103. Mensa boasts 134 local chapters that offer a variety of activities, including movie nights at a member's home and dinners out with others. The group's name, which is related to three Latin words meaning "mind," "table," and "month," would seem to suggest meeting and eating every four weeks.

Brilliant Origins

The group, originally founded in Great Britain in 1946, with the American branch beginning in 1960 in Brooklyn, New York, currently boasts 100,000 members worldwide. There don't appear to be any scary, arcane rituals involved, or any need to keep proving oneself once "inside." One of the organization's main tenets is to provide intellectual company for like-minded individuals (in America, the membership is 65 percent male). While the club protects members' privacy, there are some notable folks who are or were willing to be identified, including actors Geena Davis and Alan Rachins, sci-fi writer Isaac Asimov, and NASA astronaut Bill McArthur.

College Mascots

College sports brim with colors, birds, wildcats, tigers, and bears in some form or other. Common canines abound, from bulldogs to wolves. There are numerous ancient warriors, such as Spartans and Trojans. Some mascots deserve high marks for originality.

✳ ✳ ✳ ✳

Aggies (Texas A&M, New Mexico State, Utah State, and others): It's worth remembering that many land-grant schools early on taught mainly agriculture, so their students—and sometimes their teams—were called Farmers. "Aggies" grew as slang for this, and many of these schools now embrace the name.

Banana Slugs (University of California-Santa Cruz): If a slug suggests a lethargic or reluctant team, that's just what students had in mind when they chose the image as a mascot. The bright yellow banana slug lives amid the redwoods on campus and represents a mild protest of the highly competitive nature of most college sports.

Boll Weevils/Cotton Blossoms (University of Arkansas-Monticello, men/women): When cotton ruled Dixie, the boll weevil was more fearsome than any snake. Evidently, the women's teams didn't care to be named after an invasive insect, and who can blame them?

Cardinal (Stanford): It's the color, not the bird. That sounds odd until you consider the Harvard Crimson, Dartmouth Big Green, Syracuse Orange, etc. The university's overall symbol, however, is a redwood tree. A person actually dresses up as a redwood mascot, but the effect is more like a wilting Christmas tree than a regal conifer.

Crimson Tide (University of Alabama): The school's teams have always worn crimson, but the term "Crimson Tide" seems to have been popularized by sportswriters waxing poetic about epic struggles in mud and rain.

Eutectics (St. Louis College of Pharmacy, Missouri): "Eutectic" refers to the chemical process in which two solids become a liquid, representing the school's integration of competitive athletics and rigorous academic programs. ESPN recognized the Eutectic—a furry creature dressed in a lab coat—as one of the most esoteric mascots in the country.

Governors (Austin Peay, Tennessee): This one made sense, as the school is named for the Tennessee governor who signed the bill establishing it. At least "Governors" is more inspiring than the old nickname, "Normalities." One wonders how the eminent statesman would react to the popular student cheer today: "Let's go Peay!"

Ichabods (Washburn University, Kansas, men): An Ichabod would be, at the least, a generous man. The university was established as Lincoln College, but it ran out of money. When philanthropist Ichabod Washburn bailed out Lincoln, the grateful school renamed itself. This may disappoint everyone who references the headless ghost in *The Legend of Sleepy Hollow*, but Washburn University's version is still a worthy tale. The women's teams are the Lady Blues.

Jennies (Central Missouri State, women): A jenny is a female donkey, but this name makes sense only when put in context: The school's men's teams are the Mules. Both are a big improvement on "Normals" and "Teachers," the names used before 1922.

Nanooks (University of Alaska-Fairbanks): *Nanuq* is Inupiaq (northern Arctic Eskimo) for a polar bear. Many UAF students insist that it refers to a character in the 1922 silent ethnography film *Nanook of the North*, but to avoid controversy, perhaps, the school administration sticks firmly to the *nanuq* story.

Paladins (Furman University, South Carolina): A paladin is a pious, righteous knight. The title originally belonged to the 12 peers of Charlemagne's court.

Poets (Whittier College, California): If opponents don't exactly tremble with fear when the Whittier mascot takes the field, it's because he's a big-headed figure who dresses in colonial garb and carries a pen and pad. The school was named for poet John Greenleaf Whittier.

Ragin' Cajuns (University of Louisiana-Lafayette): The name refers, of course, to the region's feisty Cajun ethnic heritage. Fans hold up signs saying "Geaux Cajuns!" Although decidedly not French, it certainly gets the message across.

Rainbow Wahine (University of Hawaii, women): Hawaii has an interesting situation because it chose to let its teams name themselves by sport. Some men's teams are the Warriors, some are the Rainbows, and some are the Rainbow Warriors. The women have been more consistent, all using Rainbow Wahine (wahine is Hawaiian for "women").

The Rock (Slippery Rock University, Pennsylvania): Some believe this school is imaginary, but it's not. There is no mascot; all teams are called "the Rock." Fans nationwide have embraced the school as a sort of cult favorite, giving it perhaps the largest honorary alumni body in college sports. When reading scores, numerous football announcers will read the Slippery Rock score last—and can expect irate phone calls if they don't.

Stormy Petrels (Oglethorpe University, Georgia): The name refers to a plucky shore bird that dives straight into heavy surf to find its food.

Tarheels (University of North Carolina): There's a lot of history at UNC, the nation's first state university. A Tarheel is a North Carolinian, though some use the term to refer to rural folk in general. The legend says that North Carolinian soldiers in Civil War Confederate service remained "stuck" to the ground as if they had tar on their heels. Inexplicably, the school uses a live ram as its mascot.

Odd Beer Names

You're thirsty, so you decide to stop in your local pub for a drink. The "Menu of Indecision" is literally jam-packed with hundreds of beers. Some are recognizable, but most have names that make you chuckle aloud. Here's a short list of a few oddly named American and Canadian brands.

✳   ✳   ✳   ✳

* Arrogant Bastard Ale
* Oliver's Hot Monkey Love
* Bourbon Barrel Lower da Boom
* Flying Frog Lager
* Satan's Pony Amber Ale
* Butt Monkey Chimp Chiller Ale
* Squatters Emigration Amber Ale
* San Quentin Breakout Stout
* Aroma Borealis Herbal Cream Ale
* Kill Ugly Radio
* Old Knucklehead
* Alley Kat Amber
* Money Shot Cream Ale
* Oatmeal Breakfast Stout

* 3 Stooges Beer
* Moose Drool
* Stone Double Dry Hopped Levitation Ale
* Demon Sweat Imperial Red
* Monk in the Trunk
* Dead Frog Ale
* Tongue Buckler
* Bitter American

Some Good Old Earth Sense

Ask anyone what they'd like to accomplish in their lifetime—chances are they'll say that they'd like to make an impact on the world, that they'd like to be remembered for their contributions. No one says, "I'd like to leave behind 67 million tons of trash."

✳ ✳ ✳ ✳

An Enduring Legacy

DURING THE COURSE of producing consumer products such as plastic bottles, newspapers, disposable diapers, and aluminum soda cans, we create a veritable ocean of waste for future generations to contend with. The sheer amount of garbage being thrown away is mind-boggling: The average American family consumes more than 182 gallons of soda, 104 gallons of milk, and 26 gallons of bottled water, with most of the empty containers being tossed in landfills or the ocean. One-third of the water Americans use is literally flushed down the toilet. Meanwhile, rainforests are being destroyed at a rate of 100 acres per minute, and 20 species of plants and wildlife are disappearing every week due to the impact of human waste on the environment. Nice legacy, huh?

Paper or Plastic? How About Neither?

Despite the fact that we can get our news in various ways, including television, radio, or online, many Americans still have a daily newspaper habit: Each day, more than 44 million newspapers are tossed! Although we now have more acres of forest than we did in 1920, it's still wise to keep in mind that more than 25 million trees a year are used to create these newspapers—valuable trees that eliminate carbon dioxide. By dispensing with a single run of just one major metropolitan Sunday paper, more than 75,000 trees could be saved. If all else, recycling the newspapers is the next best thing.

Junk mail is a pain to receive, but it's also a massive waste: The average U.S. household discards more than 13,000 pieces of junk mail per year—44 percent of which goes into the trash without ever being opened.

Another source of trash is the supermarket. Before we've wheeled our grocery cart to the car, we've loaded up with dozens of paper and plastic bags that are destined for landfills. Even with the shift to plastic bags, each supermarket could go through more than 700 paper bags an hour—more than 60 million bags across the United States. Unrecycled plastic bags often end up in the ocean where they kill as many as one million creatures a year. Bringing your own grocery bags is clearly the way to go. And those plastic rings that come with a six-pack of soda? They certainly don't make good necklaces for curious otters and other water-dwelling creatures, yet many birds and animals die from strangulation or drowning as a result of those plastic rings. Simply cut up the rings before throwing them away—look at that, you just saved an otter!

Add It Up

Consider this: Every year, the United States goes through 16 billion disposable diapers, 2 billion pens, enough car tires for 220 million vehicles, and 2 billion razor blades. Americans constitute only 5 percent of the world's population but generate more than 40 percent of the planet's trash, creating two to three times the waste of other industrialized countries. The answer, of course, is recycling. Recycling is nothing new: New York City introduced recycling programs back in 1890, and the city built its first recycling plant in 1898. By 1924, 83 percent of American cities were making at least minimal efforts to separate and recycle trash.

DROP OFF
RECYCLABLES
HERE

There's been progress, but it's estimated that more than 90 percent of our trash could be recycled. The energy saved from recycling one glass bottle could run a 100-watt lightbulb for over four hours. If each person recycled one aluminum can, it would save half a gallon of gasoline.

Seventeen Silly and Unusual Motorcycle Names

Many companies hire expensive marketing firms to come up with catchy names for their products. Others just wing it. The following is a list of motorcycles burdened with monikers seemingly conjured up during a hallucinogenic road trip.

❋   ❋   ❋   ❋

1. **Adonis:** Adorn your product with the name of a handsome Greek god and you better design something striking. A good place to start would be somewhere other than this 48cc, early 1950s motorbike, essentially the 98-pound weakling of the motorcycle universe.

2. **Anker:** Here's an idea: Name your sporty motorcycle after an object used to render vehicles stationary. At least this 1950s German company didn't make boats.

3. **Stahl:** Perhaps this was not the best choice of name for an American bike built during the motorcycle's formative— and typically unreliable—years, in the early 1910s.

4. **Satan:** The name of these big single-cylinder bikes from the late 1920s may have been acceptable in its native Czechoslovakia, but it didn't go over well on this side of the pond. Since the make only lasted one year, they apparently had a devil of a time selling them.

5. **Thor:** Name a bike after the Norse god of thunder, and it better live up to its name—and the Thor did. First produced in 1907, Thors were big 76-cubic-inch (about 1250cc) V-twin brutes that rivaled contemporary Harley-Davidsons for speed. But due to the competitive environment, Thor ceased motorcycle production by 1920.

6. Honda Dream: Japanese manufacturers have always leaned toward whimsical names for their machines, so it was hardly a surprise when the Honda Dream became reality in the early 1960s. When this 305cc bike arrived on American shores with its skirted fenders, stamped-steel frame and forks, and somewhat bulbous bodywork, typical '60s names like Venom, Tiger, or Commando hardly seemed appropriate, so the Dream was born. The Dream was a surprising success and sold under the Honda emblem for nearly ten years.

7. Snob: This 1920s German bike sported a lowly 155cc single-cylinder engine that really gave it no reason to brag.

8. New Motorcycle: A midsize bike built in France during the 1920s, one can't help but imagine an Abbott and Costello-type routine:

"What's that?"

"A New Motorcycle."

"Duh ... I know it's a new motorcycle. But what is it?"

"I just told you."

"All I know is it's a new motorcycle."

"Then why did you ask?"

9. Silver Pigeon: From 1946 to 1964, these scooters were quite popular in Japan, but it's hard to imagine the name would fly in the States.

10. Génial-Lucifer: Like jumbo shrimp, the two words just don't seem to go together. Nevertheless, this French builder of small-to-midsize motorcycles managed to tough it out for 28 years (1928–1956), which is more than can be said for most upstarts of the period.

11. **Juncker:** Blame it on the language barrier, but there's no way this small French bike of the 1930s would have sold very well in the States.

12. **Sissy:** An Austrian company chose this name to grace a mini-scooter that lasted only one year (1957). What were they thinking?

13. **RIP:** Seemingly doomed from the start, this English motorcycle company was born in 1905 and gone by 1909. May it rest in peace.

14. **Flying Merkel:** Ridiculous as its moniker sounds, this big American bike of the early 1900s lived up to its billing, as Flying Merkels set several speed records thanks to their advanced V-twin engines.

15. **Harley-Davidson Fat Boy:** One of Harley-Davidson's best sellers, the Fat Boy is a beefy motorcycle, originally offered in 1990 on the company's big softail frame with a large, 1340cc V-twin engine and unique solid wheels. This bulky bike is still sold today in an even "fatter" 1584cc form.

16. **Whizzer Pacemaker:** In the years after World War II, Whizzer offered a three-horsepower engine that could be bolted to a conventional bicycle to turn it into a rudimentary form of motorized transport. "Put a Whizzer on it!" trumpeted the ads, and thousands did. The company soon came out with a complete motorbike, the Whizzer Pacemaker, which some credit with starting the scooter revolution that led to the company's demise in the mid-1950s.

17. **Wackwitz:** Perhaps in its native Germany the name isn't so amusing, but this early '20s maker of small "clip on" engines (much like those sold by Whizzer) lasted only two years. And one can imagine why: "Put a Wackwitz on it!" just doesn't have the same ring.

Former Day Jobs

Not everybody started at the top of their profession—in fact, pretty much no one did. Here's what a few people were up to before they became household names.

✳   ✳   ✳   ✳

✳ Actor Rock Hudson, cartoon tycoon Walt Disney, and crooner Bing Crosby worked for the post office: Hudson as a letter carrier, Disney as an *assistant* letter carrier, and Crosby as a postal clerk.

✳ Legendary lover Casanova founded the French state lottery.

✳ Actor/director Clint Eastwood was a firefighter, lumberjack, steel mill furnace stoker, and lifeguard, so he comes by those craggy, manly good looks honestly.

✳ Speaking of craggy good looks, actor Robert Mitchum was a heavyweight boxer, and actor Lee Marvin was a plumber and a U.S. Marine.

✳ Singer Rod Stewart was a grave digger.

✳ Actor Harrison Ford was, famously, a carpenter, who installed kitchens and such for moguls who would later pay him much more handsomely for his theatrical labors.

✳ Actor/sex symbol Jayne Mansfield was a concert pianist and violinist before she became what some people labeled "the poor man's Marilyn Monroe."

✳ Actor Dustin Hoffman was once a janitor, but even that had to be easier than his other job, that of attendant in a mental hospital.

✳ Actor Greta Garbo toiled as a latherer in a men's barbershop.

✳ Actor Al Pacino was variously employed as a theater usher, porter, and superintendent of an office building.

Where Did That Name Come From?

Good question. And we, of course, have the answers.
Now you can use this info to stump your friends.

✳   ✳   ✳   ✳

WD-40: In 1953, the Rocket Chemical Company began developing a rust-prevention solvent for the aerospace industry. The name WD-40 indicates what the product does (water displacement) and how many attempts it took to perfect it.

Starbucks: *Moby-Dick* was the favorite book of one of the three founders of this coffee empire. He wanted to name the company after the story's fabled ship *Pequod*, but he and his partners reconsidered and settled instead on the name of the ship's first mate, Starbuck.

Google: In the 1930s, mathematician Edwin Kasner asked his young nephew to think of a word that could mean a very large number (1 followed by 100 zeros). The boy, Milton Sirotta, came up with Googol. The creators of the world's most popular search engine varied the spelling and adopted it to represent an infinite amount of information.

M&Ms: Chocolate pellets coated in sugar were popular in Britain for decades under the brand name Smarties. When Forrest Mars (son of the founder of the Mars candy company) saw soldiers eating them during the Spanish Civil War, he and his partner, R. Bruce Murrie, bought the U.S. rights. But there was already an American candy product called Smarties, so Mars and Murrie used their initials to form the new brand name.

GAP: Don and Doris Fisher opened their first store in 1969 to meet the unique clothing demands of customers between childhood and adulthood, identified and popularized then as "the generation gap."

Popular Hairstyles Through the Ages

Humans are the only animals to willingly and consciously cut their hair, and although this ability definitely has its perks, it's also been the source of many woes and bad decisions. Here are some of the more extreme, time-consuming, gravity-defying looks that have graced our crowns throughout the ages.

✳ ✳ ✳ ✳

Mohawk

ORIGINALLY WORN IN Native American cultures, the mohawk reappeared sometime in the 1970s, along with the punk rock movement. At its most extreme, the mohawk, called the mohican in the UK, featured a stripe of hair sticking straight up and running down the middle of the head, with the sides of the head shaved. It made a statement about not giving in to social standards. However, with the "fauxhawk" (small spike, not shaved on sides), the mohawk of today is much more watered-down.

Mullet

Also appearing sometime in the 1970s, the mullet soared to popularity in the '80s among rockers and rednecks. But the origins of the short-on-the-top-and-sides, long-and-free-in-the-back look are a bit mysterious. Some say that hockey players originated the 'do, and others think it's an offspring of rock 'n' roll (David Bowie was an early adopter)—but most agree that it should be retired.

Pompadour

In a pompadour, the hair is gelled back, giving it a sleek, wet look, and the front is pushed forward. The look is often associated with the 1950s, when it was worn by the likes of Elvis

Presley and Johnny Cash. But Madame de Pompadour, a mistress to King Louis XV and a fashionista in her time, originally donned the look in the 1700s. The style is still worn by retro rockabilly types, including Brian Setzer.

Beehive

This is another style with origins that date back to the 18th century. During the outlandish wig phase, when the bigger and more extravagant the piece, the more money and social status it carried, 'hives were very popular. Women allegedly even used them to house trinkets, such as small caged birds. In the 1960s, the beehive surged in popularity, and today, the crown of the beehive queen belongs to cartoon character Marge Simpson, who sports a tall blue updo.

Afro

Birthed by the black pride movement, the afro represents a time when African Americans stopped applying harsh chemicals to their hair in order to achieve something close to Caucasian texture and style. In the 1960s, the afro was a political statement, but today it is worn as fashion. Anyone with extremely curly hair can also adopt the style.

Powdered Wigs

In the 18th century, hygiene was hardly what it is today, and head lice were a rampant problem, so wigs were worn to cover shaved heads. But powdered wigs themselves were hotbeds for lice, roaches, and other critters. Still, wigs were worn until the end of the 18th century, when an expensive tax on white powder made the trend die down.

✳ Got a headache? In Tudor England, you'd use willowbark tea (naturally containing aspirin). If your head hurt too much to scrounge around for willowbark, you could resort to hair and urine. You'd take a lock of your hair, and boil it in your urine. Then you'd toss the hair into the fire. Headache cured!

✳ According to Guinness World Records, the longest hair on record (more than 18 feet) belongs to Xie Quiping of China.

Famous First Lines

The first line of a book is often its most important, having the potential to either intrigue or irk a reader from the start. Here are a few of the best first sentences from some noted novels.

✳ ✳ ✳ ✳

"Marley was dead, to begin with. There is no doubt whatever about that."

CHARLES DICKENS, *A CHRISTMAS CAROL*

"It is a truth universally acknowledged, that a single man in possession of a good fortune, must be in want of a wife."

JANE AUSTEN, *PRIDE AND PREJUDICE*

"You don't know about me without you have read a book by the name of **The Adventures of Tom Sawyer;** *but that ain't no matter."*

MARK TWAIN, *THE ADVENTURES OF HUCKLEBERRY FINN*

"When he was nearly thirteen, my brother Jem got his arm badly broken at the elbow."

HARPER LEE, *TO KILL A MOCKINGBIRD*

"One morning, when Gregor Samsa woke from troubled dreams, he found himself transformed in his bed into a monstrous vermin."

FRANZ KAFKA, *METAMORPHOSIS*

"On the first Monday of the month of April, 1625, the market town of Meung, in which the author of 'Romance of the Rose' was born, appeared to be in as perfect a state of revolution as if the Huguenots had just made a second La Rochelle of it."

ALEXANDRE DUMAS, *THE THREE MUSKETEERS*

"If I am out of my mind, it's all right with me, thought Moses Herzog."

SAUL BELLOW, *HERZOG*

"Happy families are all alike; every unhappy family is unhappy in its own way."

LEO TOLSTOY, *ANNA KARENINA*

"In the country of Westphalia, in the castle of the most noble Baron of Thunder-ten-tronckh, lived a youth whom Nature had endowed with a most sweet disposition."

VOLTAIRE, *CANDIDE*

"At a village of La Mancha, whose name I do not wish to remember, there lived a little while ago one of those gentlemen who are wont to keep a lance in the rack, an old buckler, a lean horse and a swift greyhound."

MIGUEL DE CERVANTES, *DON QUIXOTE*

"I was leaning against the bar in a speakeasy on Fifty-second Street, waiting for Nora to finish her Christmas shopping, when a girl got up from the table where she had been sitting with three other people and came over to me."

DASHIELL HAMMETT, *THE THIN MAN*

"He was an old man who fished alone in a skiff in the Gulf Stream and he had gone 84 days now without taking a fish."

ERNEST HEMINGWAY, *THE OLD MAN AND THE SEA*

"It was a pleasure to burn."

RAY BRADBURY, *FAHRENHEIT 451*

"We are at rest five miles behind the front."

ERICH MARIA REMARQUE, *ALL QUIET ON THE WESTERN FRONT*

"It was a bright cold day in April, and the clocks were striking thirteen."

GEORGE ORWELL, *1984*

Nine Types of Angels

Did you know that according to theories created by medieval Christian theologians, there are a variety of angels, each with distinct duties? Drawing on the Bible, they outlined nine types of angels within three major groups known as choirs. Some are clearly modeled after humans, while others are certainly not.

✳ ✳ ✳ ✳

The first choir, in its celestial form, is represented by wavelengths of light and force fields and frequencies of sound. These entities emanate vibrations, or waves, of devotional love into the universe.

1. **Seraphim:** These are the angels who are closest to God. They encircle his throne and emit an intense fiery light representing his love. Seraphim are considered "fiery serpents" and not even the other divine beings may look at them. There are only four of them and each has four faces and six wings. When they come to Earth, they leave their serpent appearance behind, preferring tall, thin, clean-cut human embodiments.

2. **Cherubim (Plural of Cherub):** These angels are the keepers of celestial records and hold the knowledge of God. They are sent to Earth with great tasks, such as expelling humankind from the Garden of Eden. Ancient art depicts cherubim as sphinxlike, winged creatures with human faces, not the fat babies with wings that now grace greeting cards and book covers. Ophaniel, Rikbiel, and Zophiel are cherubim, as was Satan before his fall to evil.

3. **Thrones:** Thrones' appearance is perhaps the most bizarre of the first grouping. They are said to look like great glowing wheels covered with many eyes. They serve as God's chariot and dispense his judgment in order to carry out his desires for humankind.

The angels in the second choir can exist in a state of transition between the celestial and human worlds. They are considered heavenly governors, attempting to strike a balance between matter and spirit, good and bad.

4. **Dominions or Dominations:** Think of dominions as middle management. They receive orders from seraphim and cherubim, then dish out duties to the "worker bee" angels of the lower orders. Their main purpose is to make sure that the cosmos remains in order by sending down power to heads of government and other authority figures on Earth. Zadkiel (sometimes called Hashmal) is the chief of this order.

5. **Virtues:** Shaped like sparks of light, virtues are in charge of maintaining the natural world, and they inspire living things in areas such as science. They also take orders from the angels above and convert them into miracles for those deserving them. When they make themselves known to humans in their earthly form, they are musicians, artists, healers, and scientists who work with the power of love, as well as through the seemingly alternate area of physics. The two angels described at the ascension of Jesus are believed to have been virtues.

6. **Powers:** In their celestial form, powers appear like brightly colored, hazy fumes. Powers are border patrol agents between heaven and Earth. They are also the angels that preside over birth and death. Some believe that they also preside over demons who wish to overthrow the world, while others, namely St. Paul, thought the powers themselves were the evil ones. In any case, powers are a group of experts who serve as advisers in the fields of religion, theology, and ideology.

The third choir is best known to us because they are most like humans with their vulnerability to the act of sinning.

7. **Principalities:** These angelic beings are shaped like rays of light. Just like a principal in school, it's the principalities who oversee everything. They guide our entire world—nations, cities, and towns. What's more, they are in charge of religion and politics. As if their plate isn't full enough, they are also in charge of managing the earthly duties of the angels below them.

8. **Archangels:** They, along with the angels, are guardians of people and all things physical. But don't call on them to help you personally; archangels respond best when dealing with matters involving all humankind. They are the first order of angels that appear only in human form. As such, they function among us as pioneers for change in the form of explorers, philosophers, and human rights leaders. This order is most commonly known because they are mentioned by name in the Bible—Michael, Gabriel, and Raphael.

9. **Angels:** Angels are the true intermediaries between God and individual people. Angels don't watch over nations; they safeguard households and individuals who believe in God in order to keep them safe from demons. They nurture, counsel, and heal. When people speak of a "personal angel," better known as a guardian angel, they are describing this type.

Who Knew?

Odd tidbits that you can use to show how smart you are.

✳ ✳ ✳ ✳

Too Much Web Surfing

STUDIES SUGGEST THAT Internet addiction is becoming a growing concern in the United States. One report found that one out of every eight people is "addicted" to being online. Addiction, in this case, is defined as a behavior-altering, habit-forming, compulsive, physiological need to use the Internet.

Not So Mobile

The world's largest functioning mobile phone is the Maxi Handy, which measures 6.72 feet tall by 2.72 feet wide by 1.47 feet deep. This phone was installed at the Rotmain Centre in Bayreuth, Germany, on June 7, 2004, as part of the "Einfach Mobil" (simple mobil) informational tour. Constructed of wood, polyester, and metal, the fully functional phone features a color screen and can send and receive text and multimedia messages. But just don't expect to slip it into your pocket.

Mining for Diamonds

It's finders keepers at the Crater of Diamonds State Park in Murfreesboro, Arkansas—the world's only public diamond-producing site. Visitors can keep any stones they dig up! The visitor center features exhibits and an audio/visual program that explains the area's geology. The center even offers tips on recognizing diamonds in the rough.

Against the Tide

In almost every country around the globe, the creation and selling of child pornography is illegal. Despite this, the possession of child pornography is not illegal in the Czech Republic. Political leaders cite as one of their primary reasons for not passing laws a fear of "entrapment," in which child porn can infiltrate innocent computers through unwanted spam e-mail.

Mush-ruminations

Everything you always wanted to know—
and more—about the mushroom.

✳ ✳ ✳ ✳

✳ France was the first country to cultivate
mushrooms, in the mid-17th cen-
tury. From there, the practice spread
to England and made its way to the
United States in the 19th century.

✳ In 1891, New Yorker William Falconer
published *Mushrooms: How to Grow
Them—A Practical Treatise on Mushroom
Culture for Profit and Pleasure*, the first book on the subject.

✳ In North America alone, there are an estimated 10,000
species of mushrooms, only 250 of which are known to be
edible.

✳ A mushroom is a fungus (from the Greek word *sphongos*,
meaning "sponge"). A fungus differs from a plant in that it
has no chlorophyll, produces spores instead of seeds, and
survives by feeding off other organic matter.

✳ Mushrooms are related to yeast, mold, and mildew,
which are also members of the "fungus" class. There are
approximately 1.5 million species of fungi, compared with
250,000 species of flowering plants.

✳ An expert in mushrooms and other types of fungi is called a
mycologist—from the Greek word *mykes*, meaning "fungus."
A mycophile is someone whose hobby is to hunt edible wild
mushrooms.

✳ Ancient Egyptians believed mushrooms were the plant of
immortality. Pharaohs decreed them a royal food and forbade commoners to even touch them.

* White agaricus (aka "button") mushrooms are by far the most popular, accounting for more than 90 percent of mushrooms bought in the United States each year.

* Brown agaricus mushrooms include cremini and portobellos, though they're really the same thing: Portobellos are just mature cremini.

* Cultivated mushrooms are agaricus mushrooms grown on farms. Exotics are any farmed mushroom other than agaricus (think shiitake, maitake, oyster). Wild mushrooms are harvested wherever they grow naturally—in forests, near riverbanks, even in your backyard.

* Many edible mushrooms have poisonous look-alikes in the wild. For example, the dangerous "yellow stainer" closely resembles the popular white agaricus mushroom.

* "Toadstool" is the term often used to refer to poisonous fungi.

* In the wild, mushroom spores are spread by wind. On mushroom farms, spores are collected in a laboratory and then used to inoculate grains to create "spawn," a mushroom farmer's equivalent of seeds.

* A mature mushroom will drop as many as 16 billion spores.

* Mushroom spores are so tiny that 2,500 arranged end-to-end would measure only an inch in length.

* Mushroom farmers plant the spawn in trays of pasteurized compost, a growing medium consisting of straw, corncobs, nitrogen supplements, and other organic matter.

* The process of cultivating mushrooms—from preparing the compost in which they grow to shipping the crop to markets—takes about four months.

* September is National Mushroom Month.

Chapter 11

Around the World

You Live Where?

Ever hear of Boring, Maryland? How about Nimrod, Minnesota, or Boogertown, North Carolina? Many of the small towns that dot the United States have interesting stories (true or not) behind the oddball names. Here are a few stops to put on your next cross-country road trip.

✳   ✳   ✳   ✳

✳ Peculiar, Missouri: As the story goes, 30 miles south of Kansas City was a small community needing a name. The folk put off naming their town—they didn't want to name it until their post office actually required it. The postmaster wrote the U.S. government requesting the regal-sounding name "Excelsior." Unfortunately, the name was already taken. The postmaster wrote time and time again for permission, using different names each time. Finally, in his exasperation he told them, "We'll take any name you have available as long as it's peculiar." Apparently it stuck!

✳ Wide Awake, Colorado: One night when a group of miners were sitting around a campfire, they were trying to come up with a good name for their new settlement. After passing a bottle around late into the night, someone finally said, "Let's just turn in and talk about it more when we're wide awake." "That's it!" shouted one of the miners. "Let's call it Wide Awake!"

✻ Toad Suck, Arkansas: Before the Army Corps of Engineers completed a highway bridge over the Arkansas River in 1973, the most reliable way over the river was by barge. Next to the river stood an old tavern where many of the bargemen would pull over to drink rum and moonshine. As one version of the story has it, it was at this tavern that they would "suck on bottles until they swelled up like toads."

✻ Accident, Maryland: The town of Accident traces its history to 1750 when a local named George Deakins accepted 600 acres from King George II of England in relief of a debt. Deakins sent out two independent surveying parties to find the best 600 acres in the county—neither of which was aware of the other. By coincidence, they both surveyed the same plot, beginning at the same tree. Confident that no one else owned the property, Deakins named the tract the "Accident Tract."

✻ Hell, Michigan: There are several competing stories as to how Hell got its name. One story suggests that two traveling Germans stepped out of a stagecoach and remarked, "*So schön und hell!*" which loosely translates to "So beautiful and bright!" Hearing this, the neighbors focused on the latter part of the statement. Another story is that one of the early settlers, George Reeves, was asked what they should call the town. Ever the eloquent gentleman, Reeves replied, "For all I care, you can name it Hell!"

✻ Ding Dong, Texas: Despite evidence to the contrary, the town of Ding Dong was not named because it's located in Bell County. Nor was it named after Peter Hansborough Bell, the third Governor of Texas, nor for the Hostess snack cake. Back in the 1930s, Zulis and Bert Bell owned a country store, and they hired a sign painter named C. C. Hoover to put up a new sign. Hoover suggested that he dress up the sign by painting two bells on it with the words, "Ding Dong." The surrounding community quickly took to the name.

* Tightwad, Missouri: During the town's early days, a local store owner cheated a customer (who just happened to be a postman) by charging him an extra 50 cents for a watermelon. To get back at the proprietor, the postman started delivering mail to the newly dubbed town of Tightwad, Missouri.

Other Oddball Town Names:

* Muck City, Alabama

* Goobertown, Arkansas

* Squabbletown, California

* Yeehaw Junction, Florida

* Oblong, Illinois

* Toad Hop, Indiana

* What Cheer, Iowa

* Bugtussle, Kentucky

* Dry Prong, Louisiana

* Frankenstein, Missouri

* Hot Coffee, Missouri

* Truth or Consequences, New Mexico

* Tick Bite, North Carolina

* Knockemstiff, Ohio

* Bowlegs, Oklahoma

* Short Pump, Virginia

* Embarrass, Wisconsin *and* Minnesota

Abandoned Amusement Parks

From crumbling midways to rusting and rotting rides, there's something creepy yet intriguing about an abandoned amusement park. Here's a sampling of defunct venues that currently await their uncertain fate and others that have completely disappeared.

✳ ✳ ✳ ✳

Six Flags New Orleans

THOUGH AN ABANDONED amusement park is a sad spectacle in itself, Six Flags New Orleans bears stark, physical reminders of Hurricane Katrina. When the hurricane blew through in August 2005, it forever altered the landscape and robbed citizens of far more than their summer amusements. Squeals of delight were once plentiful at Six Flags. Now, howling winds are all that whistle past rides such as the classic wooden coaster, Mega Zeph. Ninety percent of the park was under water during the catastrophe, and now any hope of rebuilding the operation has been lost to time.

Perhaps it's just as well. Six Flags is situated well away from the French Quarter and other popular tourist areas. As a result, it had always been an under-performer by the company's lofty standards. A sign reading, "Have a Great Day…" still welcomes urban explorers and curiosity seekers to the grounds, which are now officially cordoned off. A dingy mark of the flood-line rises halfway up the sign, serving as a reminder of how quickly laughter can be replaced by despair.

Pripyat Amusement Park, Ukraine

Though some abandoned amusement parks were once able to bring joy, there is one that never had the chance to do so. Pripyat Amusement Park never sold a puffy plume of cotton candy, or cranked a white-knuckled rider up the steep hill of a roller coaster, because this park had the misfortune of being located within the "hot zone" of Chernobyl, Ukraine.

The brand-new amusement complex at Pripyat was scheduled to open May 1, 1986. But that happy moment never came. Just days before, on April 26, an explosion at the nearby Chernobyl Nuclear Power Plant flooded the atmosphere with deadly radioactive particles, resulting in scores of deaths in the months and years that followed. Effects continue to this day. The notorious event is regarded as the world's worst nuclear disaster.

Viewed from a distance, Pripyat's amusement park seems relatively normal. A large yellow Ferris wheel stands motionless beside a bank of high-rise apartment buildings, suggesting that the operation has simply closed for the day. But closer scrutiny reveals that the giant wheel's frame has decayed to a point of instability, and its round cars have dropped to the ground. Swings located adjacent to the wheel are rotting, rusting hulks, no longer whimsical conveyances of mirth and merriment. And everywhere, an oppressive stillness permeates.

No one will ever ride the park's amusements, test their skill on the carnival games, or walk the midway. Once a vibrant city of about 50,000, Pripyat is now a radiation-tainted cast-off from the nuclear era. And it will remain as such until levels of Caesium-137 and Strontium-90 reach a point safe for human habitation, which could take many generations.

Palisades Amusement Park

Say "palisades" to most anyone in the New York area, and they'll likely envision an amusement park, not a line of cliffs overlooking New York City. New Jersey's Palisades Amusement Park ranked as one of America's most famous parks for much of its existence between 1898 and 1971. With rides like the Cyclone (a wooden roller coaster) and the Lake Placid Bobsled (a ride so intimidating that its lift hill was enclosed to prevent riders from looking down), Palisades packed them in. Throw in the world's largest outdoor saltwater pool and free entertainment from Diana Ross and the Supremes, Tony Bennett, the Jackson 5, and more, and it's easy to see why.

Despite its success, Palisades Amusement Park was demolished in 1971. Ironically, this occurred because the park had become too popular and was causing congestion and noise problems in the surrounding suburban area. Today, high-rise condos stand where people once let loose their cares and worries, and a monument marks the spot where the park once stood. It reads: "Here we were happy, here we grew!"

Old Chicago

In 1975, an amusement park with a twist opened 30 miles southwest of Chicago in Bolingbrook, Illinois. Old Chicago featured two roller coasters and a Ferris wheel, but it did so inside of a shopping mall. Despite the uniqueness of the operation and early success, Old Chicago was plagued with troubles.

The cavernous building, which contained the 73-foot-tall "Chicago Loop" coaster, was the victim of cost overruns that nearly flattened the operation. Then, adding insult to injury, another theme park—Marriott's Great America—opened in 1976 in Gurnee, 40 miles north of the Windy City, funneling a significant number of visitors away from Old Chicago.

But in the end, it was a lack of popular anchor stores that stopped the crowds from coming. The amusement park portion of Old Chicago closed in 1980, and its rides were sold off to other parks. The shopping center closed soon after in 1981. Nevertheless, its central idea lived on. Eventually, the vast West Edmonton Mall in Alberta, Canada (the world's largest mall), would feature a successful indoor amusement park, as would Minnesota's huge Mall of America. Today, a car auction lot sits where the unique amusement park once stood.

Cascade Park

Opened in May 1897 for the New Castle Traction Company trolley line, Cascade Park was named for the picturesque waterfall that tumbled beside it. In many ways, the New Castle, Pennsylvania, park typified the contemporary amusement ventures that would endure well into the 20th century. It featured a picnic grove, a wooden roller coaster (the Comet), a merry-go-round, a dance pavilion, and an assortment of eateries and concession stands. It also offered a 15-acre lake for swimming and a tourist camp with room for more than 2,000 campers.

The park was turned over to the city of New Castle in 1934, and became a public recreation area. Attendance waned when trolley service to the park was discontinued in the 1940s, but picnickers continued to support the park. Nevertheless, by the mid-1980s, the rides were removed and a chapter in amusement park history was closed.

Nostalgia seekers can still find numerous reminders of past glory at the old site. The carousel building, dance pavilion, and refreshment stands are all intact, as are the loading stations for the Tumble Bug ride and the park's train. Concrete footings that once supported the Comet roller coaster can also be found. Annual community events are now held at the park.

Circus World

Circus World lived a strange life as far as amusement parks go. Opened as the Circus World Showcase in Haines City, Florida, in 1974, the park was originally envisioned as a museum to document the history of the circus industry. But the venture faced stiff competition from two nearby theme parks: Disney World in Orlando and Busch Gardens in Tampa. To better compete, the operation added full-scale amusements, such as the Zoomerang (a steel looping coaster) and the Roaring Tiger (a wooden colossus known for its prodigious "airtime").

But by 1986, the circus-themed park had not lived up to expectations and was sold. It reopened in 1987 as Boardwalk and Baseball, a turn-of-the-century styled oceanfront boardwalk coupled with baseball memorabilia. Despite being a first-class effort, this too floundered and finally closed in 1990. By 2003, all traces of the park were gone. Today, visitors will find condos, hotels, and offices standing where a quirky amusement park once entertained wide-eyed children and adults alike.

Pass the Salt

When tourists float in the curative waters of the Dead Sea, they likely believe they are relaxing in the world's saltiest body of water. This is understandable, because just about every travel guidebook makes this claim—erroneously.

* * * *

Are you determined to soak in the world's saltiest lake? If so, you should skip the Dead Sea and head to Lake Asal in the tiny East African country of Djibouti. Lake Asal's salinity measures 400 grams per liter—more than the Dead Sea's 340 grams per liter.

Why is Lake Asal so salty? Salt lakes form in locations where water cannot flow away to the sea and is lost only through evaporation. Lake Asal was formed somewhere between 1 million and 4 million years ago, likely the result of volcanic activity and the resulting shift of Earth's surface. A crater lake 500 feet below sea level, Asal is fed only by underwater springs and is depleted only by evaporation. Consequently, the mineral salts have nowhere to go. Saline levels are so high that crusts of salt up to 13 inches thick accumulate at the lake's edge and are strong enough to withstand the weight of a car. There is no plant or animal life in the lake—nor on the land surrounding it.

Is that much salt a good thing? Lake Asal is not only extraordinarily salty but has the added distinction of being one of the least hospitable places on the planet. While the Dead Sea's buoyant, mineral-rich waters attract thousands of visitors annually, it is unlikely that Lake Asal will ever be a tourist destination. The air temperatures there are said to be unbearable and the glare from the salt blinding, and the lake itself emits a sulfurous stench. If you still want to take a plunge, do so with your shoes on, because the salt-crystal crusts can rip bare feet to shreds. What's more, you'll come out of the water coated in a thick, salty film. Lake Asal is surrounded by a salt pan that is mined, and the salt is exported by caravan to Ethiopia.

The Saga of Owens Valley

At the beginning of the 20th century, Los Angeles was a bustling city of only 250,000. Any development was dependent on one simple but important commodity: water. How it got the water it needed remains controversial today.

✳ ✳ ✳ ✳

RAINFALL IN THE city of Los Angeles was insufficient to keep the watersheds full enough for the city's rapid growth. New residents were migrating west to take advantage of the climate, but the city couldn't sustain the expansion—it was a desert, after all. In 1913, the Los Angeles Department of Water and Power, under the direction of Superintendent William Mulholland, completed construction on a 220-mile-long aqueduct, which diverted water from the Owens River in eastern California. This enraged residents of Owens Valley, a small agricultural community near the Nevada border, and led to one of the longest and fiercest water wars in U.S. history.

Life-giving Water

Water from the Owens River spurred the growth of Los Angeles and turned the arid lands of the San Fernando Valley into a virtual oasis, sending property values soaring and making fat cats out of favored politicians, bankers, and realtors—all cronies of Los Angeles Mayor Frederick Eaton. Like the mayor himself, all of them invested on the basis of privileged insider information. Although Eaton promised Owens Valley residents that the water would only be for domestic use in Los Angeles proper, the original aqueduct flow was ultimately diverted to the San Fernando Valley for agriculture. The subterfuge led Owens Valley residents to claim that the water rights had been obtained through deception, and the valley became a hotbed of violence. Sections of the water system were sabotaged; farmers who sold their property to Los Angeles at allegedly subpar rates were considered traitors, pitting neighbor against neighbor.

Livelihoods Lost

Los Angeles obtained a large portion of water rights from Owens Valley farmers, but the demand from San Fernando Valley investors was so great and so much water was diverted that the once-fertile Owens Valley was fast becoming a desert. In the meantime, the formerly arid San Fernando Valley was becoming a lush paradise. In 1924, Owens Lake, into which the river once flowed, dried up, and a group of armed farmers used dynamite on the Alabama Gates spillway section of the aqueduct, releasing water back into the Owens River. The desperate farmers tried everything from violence to lawsuits—all to no avail. By 1928, 90 percent of the water rights belonged to Los Angeles; agriculture in Owens Valley came to a halt.

In 1970, a second aqueduct was completed. Lack of an environmental impact report led to the overuse of groundwater, which dried out springs and seeps. Vegetation that depended on underground water began disappearing—a loss that caused further devastation to Owens Valley. Inyo County sued Los Angeles, but the water continued to flow while Los Angeles filed environmental impact reports that the courts ultimately found inadequate. In 1991 and 1997, agreements were signed between Inyo County and Los Angeles that called for the rewatering of the Owens River by 2003. But once again, Los Angeles was remiss in its promise. New lawsuits were filed, new agreements were reached, and deadlines were revised, but on December 6, 2006, Los Angeles Mayor Antonio Villaraigosa finally opened a valve sending a flow of water back to the Owens River. Unfortunately, the rate of underground pumping of Owens Valley water far exceeds the rate of replenishment, and the degradation and biodiversity of Owens Valley land continues. Under deteriorating climactic conditions, reversing desertification can be very difficult, but the Los Angeles Department of Water and Power has made a strong commitment to restoring the Owens Valley watershed and can even boast of several small successes in restoring the ecosystem.

The Eiffel Tower

Here's the skinny on one of the world's most iconic structures.

✳ ✳ ✳ ✳

✳ Gustave Eiffel designed his monument to the French Revolution in 1887 as a grand entryway to the 1889 International Exposition in Paris. The tower draws more than 6 million visitors per year.

✳ Eiffel and his crew of 300 workers assembled the tower's 18,000 pieces of iron in 2 years, 2 months, and 5 days. They finished on time and came in under budget.

✳ Every 7 years, at least 25 workers use approximately 60 tons of paint to rustproof the tower.

✳ On a clear Parisian day, a person at the top of the Eiffel Tower can see about 42 miles in every direction.

✳ In just one year, the tower recouped nearly the entire cost of its construction—thanks to elevator ticket sales. The tower was one of the first tall structures in the world to use passenger elevators.

✳ The Eiffel Tower is 989 feet tall and weighs approximately 10,000 tons.

✳ On the 4 sides of the tower, the names of 72 French scientists and engineers are engraved to honor their contributions.

✳ There are 2.5 million rivets in the Eiffel Tower.

✳ There are 1,665 steps to the top of the tower, though it's widely thought there are 1,792, representing the year of the First French Republic.

✳ Heat from the sun can cause the tower to expand up to three-fourths of an inch. During the cold winter months, the tower shrinks approximately six inches.

Going Green with the Zabbaleen

In Cairo, garbage is gold.

✳   ✳   ✳   ✳

AS THE WORLD'S cities scramble to find solutions to overflowing landfills, Cairo, an Egyptian city of 18 million people, is one of the few places that may never have that problem. For generations, the Zabbaleen (Cairo's garbage people) have been collecting and recycling trash. They are so efficient that only 20 percent of the collected trash ends up in a landfill.

The Zabbaleen have to be thorough; their lives and those of their families depend on it. For them, going home after a hard day's work isn't a long commute. More often than not their homes are built from construction and demolition site refuse, literally in the dump. Still, it is here that the Zabbaleen have forged a community 50,000 strong.

Work starts at dawn. Fathers and sons in small trucks and donkey carts make their way into the narrow city streets for the day's collections. Each unit has a separate route and pickup schedule. Laden, they return to their community, where women and children begin the task of sorting, often in their front yard.

Waste Not, Want Not

Plastics, glass, metals, textiles, paper, batteries—all are separated and sold either to middle men who deal in volume or small manufacturers, many of whom are also Zabbaleen. Animal bones are collected and sold to fertilizer plants. Food waste is fed to the 40,000 pigs and donkeys raised in the community's backyards. Their waste, in turn, along with inedible food, is composted. Then it too goes to the fertilizer plant.

The Zabbaleen have built paper compactors, cloth grinders, and aluminum smelters. Some of the profits from collecting provide community services, such as literacy programs, schools, and medical facilities. An immunization program has dramatically cut infant mortality rates and eliminated tetanus. Financed by the community, some Zabbaleen have trained as doctors and lawyers and come back to serve their benefactors.

Political Waste Mismanagement

At the turn of the century, city politicians in Cairo, Alexandria, and Giza decided to modernize their waste management systems by contracting European companies to carry out garbage collection. In Cairo alone the contract was worth $50 million. Suddenly, the Zabbaleen way of life was threatened. But citizens protested the substantial hike in garbage collection fees. The contractors weren't happy either. Their trucks were too big to negotiate the narrow crowded streets of the ancient cities.

Eco-Egypt

The Zabbaleen prevailed. They spent little time on celebration, however, as a new project has seized their enthusiasm—they are going green. With assistance from an organization called Solar Cities, the Zabbaleen are installing solar-powered water heaters on their rooftops. Moreover, they are building the heaters from salvaged materials. Previously, gas was used for heating water, but in Egypt, as elsewhere, the price of gas has gone up.

The water heaters could not be more prominent. "Garbage City" is located in the Moqattam district, a barren limestone terrain at Cairo's highest point. On a clear day the Giza pyramids are visible. Moqattam was quarried to build the pyramids, then abandoned as a wasteland until the arrival of the Zabbaleen, who were originally poor Coptic Christian farmers driven into the city from southern Egypt by drought.

Within Moqattam, the Coptic faith remains strong. Their church is a limestone cavern known as the "Cave Cathedral." Not only is it equipped with a state-of-the-art sound system and closed-circuit television with seating for 20,000 people, it is the largest church in the Middle East. Father Sami'an, the church leader in Moqattam was once asked what the poor could teach. He replied, "Simplicity."

Grand, Incomplete Structures and Monuments Around the World

Sometimes people decide to build something huge but then get tired of it and quit. Here are some of the greatest unfinished monuments, including a few that lingered long enough to make the incomplete phase part of their legacies.

✳ ✳ ✳ ✳

Crazy Horse Memorial (Crazy Horse, South Dakota): In 1948, the Ziolkowski family of South Dakota embarked on a multigenerational project. Having helped sculpt nearby Mt. Rushmore, Korczak Ziolkowski promised Native American leaders that he would undertake a similar monument in the state in honor of the brilliant Oglala war leader known as Chief Crazy Horse. Ziolkowski kept that commitment until his death in 1982, and his family carries on the sculptor's work to this day.

As of 2007, only the chief's head was complete, measuring 87 feet high. Assuming eventual completion, the result will tower at 563 feet, depicting Crazy Horse's outstretched arm pointing over his horse's mane. As long as things progress at the current rate, that will likely take centuries.

Washington Monument (Washington, D.C.): Yes, it's finished now, but the nation took a 27-year break during which it conducted a Civil War, ran low on funds, and politicized the project. The original 1848 plan called for a flat obelisk surrounded by a pillared ring (ghosted by today's flag circle), styled much like the front of the later Lincoln Memorial. Work ceased in 1856 because of money problems and a political takeover of the Washington Monument Society by the "Know-Nothing" Party. They put down only 26 feet of masonry before the Civil War.

In 1876, planners decided to resume work but settled on a tall, sharp-pointed obelisk. The finished structure was dedicated in 1885 and still stands today. It is 555 feet tall, and if you look carefully about 150 feet up, you'll see a difference in the color of the stone that marks the interruption in construction.

Germania (Berlin, Federal Republic of Germany): If you're a big thinker, maybe a big statue of yourself isn't enough. Maybe your entire capital should be a monument. After he subjugated the world, Adolf Hitler intended to transfigure Berlin into a monumental world capital, modestly renamed Germania. He got the Olympic Stadium built and had avenues widened to accommodate his vision. An egotistical Reich chancellor must have a humongous chancellery, so Hitler built a new one twice as long as the French Hall of Mirrors at Versailles. Soviet artillery flattened it at the end of World War II.

The rest of Germania never got past plans and experiments. Hitler wanted a triumphal arch more massive than the French Arc de Triomphe. The flawed assumption, of course, was that Hitler would keep triumphing. Then there was the proposed Volkshalle (People's Hall), a dome intended to hold 180,000 people. Besides the Olympic Stadium and the street renovations, the only remnant of Germania is a big concrete pylon that was poured to see how far into the earth these structures might sink. Good thing it was tested first: The pylon sank three times deeper than Hitler had hoped.

Ollantaytambo (Ollantaytambo, Peru): Why would people build with pink granite blocks 15 feet high by 6 feet wide by 6 feet deep? Maybe the ancient Incas knew that one day invaders would come. Maybe they wanted to honor their gods. Either way, they were still working on Ollantaytambo's immense structure when Hernando Pizarro's Spaniards showed up in 1536.

The Spaniards spent a lot of time fighting with each other, but they took a break to attack Ollantaytambo. Hernando and his men encountered a multiterraced fortress made of 15-foot pink blocks, with determined defenders raining missile weapons down on them. The Spaniards regrouped and took Ollantaytambo, ensuring that the Incas would never finish the citadel. The big blocks they left lying around indicate that more would have been in store for Ollantaytambo had the Incas survived.

Maginot Line (border of Germany/Luxembourg/Belgium/France): Though this lengthy series of interlocking forts and bastions was built after World War I to ensure that Germany could never again threaten France (and we all know how that turned out), it was also something of a monument. It embodied static defensive thinking—the notion (true enough in World War I) that the military defense had utterly outgrown the offense.

France originally planned to extend the Line all the way to the English Channel, but the monstrous structure had already consumed a large part of the defense budget. It was well-built, modern, engineered to take advantage of terrain—and militarily worthless. When the Germans invaded in 1940, they just went around the Maginot Line.

Great Wall of China (northern China): Occasionally, people will build something so vast it can't really ever be finished. The Great Wall began as a humble series of regional walls eventually linked together during the Qin Dynasty (around 221 B.C.). By the time one part was "done," some other part had eroded or fallen into disrepair. Most of the Wall was rammed earth packed between wooden frames, and the rest was made of stone.

Emperor Qin called this the Wan Li Chang-Cheng—roughly translated, the "10,000-Mile Wall." The actual length varied depending on which part had fallen down or been added to. For the next 2,000 years, numerous Chinese rulers ordered different degrees of repair, expansion, and upgrade work. The Ming Dynasty (1368–1644) built much of what survives today. It is impressive that Chinese leaders had enough resources to continue building and improving the Wall for so many centuries; it also illustrates how greatly they dreaded invasion from the north.

Stay Away if You Don't Like Crowds

You'll find plenty of people in Tokyo, as well as lots of other stuff. Here's some trivia.

✳   ✳   ✳   ✳

✳ There are 35 million people living in Greater Tokyo, making it the most populous metropolitan area on the planet.

✳ Large men known as *oshiya* ("pushers") are employed to cram commuters onto the city's overcrowded subways and trains.

✳ If you need to call 911 in Tokyo, you'll have to reverse the digits. To report a fire or call an ambulance, dial 119.

✳ Disneyland Tokyo opened in 1983, the first Disney park outside the United States. More than 17 million people visit the park each year, making it the most successful theme park in history.

✳ Built in 1958, the 1,100-foot Tokyo Tower is the world's tallest self-supporting iron structure. The tower is painted orange and white to be clearly visible to wayward airplanes.

✳ In 1923, a massive earthquake and subsequent fire destroyed most of Tokyo and killed more than 100,000 people. Most of the city had been rebuilt by 1930, only to suffer destruction again during World War II.

✳ The literacy rate in Tokyo is 99 percent, and the city has more than 150 institutions of higher learning.

✳ Tokyo hosted the 1964 Summer Olympics, the first time in history the Games were held in a non-Western nation.

✳ Tokyo boasts the world's first public monorail line, built to coincide with the 1964 Olympics. It runs between downtown and Haneda International Airport.

A House Is Not a Home...
Unless It's Haunted: The
Winchester Mystery House

*Sarah Winchester was one incredibly eccentric woman.
She was heir to her husband's rifle fortune, but her fear of
ghostly reprisals drove her to build one of the strangest
homes ever—the Winchester Mystery House.*

✳ ✳ ✳ ✳

The Tale of Sarah Winchester

S HE WAS BORN Sarah Lockwood Pardee in New Haven,
Connecticut, in 1839. At age 23, she married William
Wirt Winchester, owner of the Winchester Repeating Arms
Company. The Winchester rifle, with its ability to quickly load
and fire as many as 15 bullets in rapid succession, became the
favorite of pioneers as they crossed the growing country. As the
settlers helped blaze new trails into the frontier, the Winchester
protected them from bandits, wild animals, and other wilder-
ness dangers. It would be remembered as "the gun that won the
West." It also made William Winchester a very wealthy person.

In 1866, Winchester and his wife had a baby girl they named
Annie, but she died when she was only a few weeks old. The
infant's death pushed Sarah into a deep depression. William
developed tuberculosis and died in 1881, leaving Sarah alone
at only 42 years old. She also inherited her husband's wealth
and business, which provided her with an income of more than
$1,000 a day.

Proving that money alone can't buy happiness, the sullen Sarah
consulted a medium, who told her that her family was cursed
by the souls of those killed by Winchester rifles. When Sarah
asked what she could do, she was told that she must move West
and build a house to soothe those spirits. But, the medium

warned, construction on the house must never end—hammers and saws must work around the clock to keep the tormented souls at bay. (There is no record of what the medium was paid for such "sage" advice.)

Way Out West

Sarah trekked across the country in 1884—no doubt without a deadly Winchester rifle at her side—and arrived in San Jose, California, where she quickly purchased a small farmhouse and nearly 162 acres of land. Construction began immediately, entirely without the aid of blueprints or plans. Instead, Sarah selected an area of the house as her "séance room." Each night, between midnight and 2:00 A.M., she would "receive" building instructions from the ghosts that haunted the house. In the morning, she would give the carpenters her own hand-drawn sketches of what work would be done next.

What an "Interesting" Place You Have Here

As a result, the mansion took on some unusual features. Stained-glass windows, made by the world-famous Tiffany Stained Glass company, gave views of inner walls or closets. One window was set into the floor. Twisting staircases led back into themselves, or nowhere at all. One set of stairs ascended straight up to the ceiling. Another had steps that rose only two inches at a time. Dozens of closets were installed, ranging from the size of a three-bedroom apartment to one inch deep.

Although Sarah refused to entertain visitors, she designed the mansion to have two ballrooms. The Grand Ballroom was given rich parquet flooring, fine oak panels, and a silver chandelier with 13 candles. One evening, she threw a lavish dinner party, complete with grand golden plates, fine wine, tuxedoed musicians, and dancing far into the night. However, there was only one attendee—Sarah.

She Must Be a Triskaidekamaniac

Sarah was very fond of the number 13. Many of the windows and doors had 13 panes or panels. A number of staircases had

13 steps, and some rooms contained 13 windows. Chandeliers in the mansion had 13 candles apiece. Many of the trees planted around the landscape were arranged in groups of 13. Even one of the sink drains had 13 holes.

Not all of Sarah's eccentricities were superfluous, however. At times, she could be quite inventive: She once created a novel call box for her servants, complete with a number system and ringing bells. The mansion had a clever and intricate system of button-operated gaslights, as well as indoor toilets and showers. She even took a significant portion of her garage and installed a large oil-burning boiler that fed hot water to a rotating spout on the ceiling. As a result, Sarah invented the first car wash for the three cars she owned—a Renault, a Buick, and an extravagant Pierce-Arrow. All were chauffeur driven.

By 1906, the enormous mansion towered seven stories and had scores of rooms. The San Francisco earthquake of that year, however, caused the top three floors to collapse. They were never rebuilt, even though work still continued around-the-clock. In fact, the earthquake trapped Sarah for more than an hour under debris, where she yelled to her servants for rescue.

The Final Count

On September 5, 1922, construction stopped, as Sarah Winchester passed away peacefully in her sleep. In all, the Winchester House has 160 rooms, although it has been estimated that a total of 600 had been built, removed, revamped, or somehow changed in the 38 years of construction. It has more than 1,200 windows and some 10,000 windowpanes. There are more than 450 doorways and 900 doors, not including cabinet doors. The mansion holds 47 fireplaces and 17 chimneys, along with 5 or 6 kitchens. There are approximately 40 bedrooms and 2 basements. It takes more than 20,000 gallons of paint to coat the entire manor—in fact, once painters finish, it is time to start again. Even though building has ceased, in this way, work on the house will never end.

Birthplaces of the Rich and Famous

Was someone famous born in your hometown?

✳   ✳   ✳   ✳

BROOKLYN, NEW YORK is the birthplace for hundreds of celebrities. Perhaps the reason is that Brooklyn natives are street-smart and savvy. Comedians Eddie Murphy, Zero Mostel, Curly and Moe Howard of the Three Stooges, Charlie Callas, Jackie Gleason, Buddy Hackett, Joan Rivers, and Jerry Seinfeld all hail from Brooklyn.

On the other end of the artistic spectrum, composers Aaron Copland and George Gershwin were born in Brooklyn. It also gave us actors Tony Danza, Martin Landau, Veronica Lake, Susan Hayward, Mary Tyler Moore, Mickey Rooney, Barbara Stanwyck, Eli Wallach, Mae West, and Barbra Streisand.

Many stars who are household names in the United States were born in Canada, including Michael J. Fox of Edmonton, Dan Aykroyd of Ottawa, William Shatner of Montreal, Martin Short of Hamilton, Fay Wray of Alberta, Peter Jennings of Toronto, Lorne Michaels of Toronto, Mack Sennett of Quebec, Donald Sutherland of Saint John, Art Linkletter of Saskatchewan, Guy Lombardo of London (Ontario), Mary Pickford of Toronto, and Neil Young, also of Toronto.

Alabama contributed several civil rights leaders to history, including Ralph Abernathy from Linden, Coretta Scott King from Marion, and Rosa Parks from Tuskegee. Country music, singer-songwriter Hank Williams was born in tiny Mount Olive West, Alabama.

Sally Ride of Encino, California, has the perfect name for an astronaut. Born in Hollywood, California, Leonardo DiCaprio may have been destined to become a movie star.

Unusual U.S. Attractions

When the world-renowned, mouse-themed amusement parks lose their appeal, load your family into the car and check out some of these unique bits of Americana.

✳ ✳ ✳ ✳

Casa Bonita
Lakewood, Colorado

Said to be the largest restaurant in the Western Hemisphere (at 52,000 square feet), Denver's Casa Bonita is one of the last vestiges of a regional chain of Mexican theme restaurants. The exterior, clad in pink stucco with a gilded dome tower that houses a statue of the Aztec Emperor Quahuatomec, masks an even more outrageous interior: faux cliffs, faux caverns, and long lines for cafeteria-style Mexican dinners.

The Great Stupa of Dharmakaya
Red Feather Lakes, Colorado

Tucked in the mountains northwest of Fort Collins, Colorado, this is the largest stupa—a monument to a great Buddhist teacher—in North America. Dedicated to the late Chogyam Trungpa, the 108-foot spire is a work of ornate and symbolic art. It was built with a special formulation of concrete designed to last more than 1,000 years.

The Beer Can House
Houston, Texas

What do you do with 50,000 beer cans (which, on a six-pack-a-day regimen, took 18 years to save)? You cut off the ends, flatten the sides, and rivet them together to make colorful aluminum siding. That's how John Milkovisch sided his modest home at 222 Malone Street. Fortunately, the motif complemented his yard, which he had already paved over with concrete embedded with marbles and pieces of metal. Soon, however, the hammering Houston sun assailed the siding and overheated the house. So John recycled the lids and pull-tabs, creating curtains, mobiles, and fences to shade the house. When a warm Texas breeze blows, it's like a giant wind chime.

Bishop Castle
Beulah, Colorado

Jim Bishop is a man on a mission. Using rocks from the surrounding forest, he started building a one-room stone cottage in 1969 and never stopped. He now has what he describes as "the largest one-man construction project in the country, quite possibly the world!" Highlights include a tower that ascends high into the sky and a fire-breathing steel dragon that crowns the main structure.

Forbidden Gardens
Katy, Texas

Built by a Hong Kong tycoon as a testament to Chinese history, this Houston-area attraction features a one-third-scale model of one of China's greatest archeological finds: Emperor Qin's tomb and its resident army of 6,000 terra-cotta soldiers. The Gardens also include an elaborate model of the Forbidden City in Beijing.

World's Third-largest Fire Hydrant
Beaumont, Texas

Painted white with black spots to promote the video release of Disney's *101 Dalmatians*, this 24-foot-tall hydrant was a gift from the movie studio to the Fire Museum of Texas, where it is on permanent display. The waterworks within the mottled shell are capable of blasting 25 gallons a second. Just two years after the Beaumont hydrant was erected, a 29½-foot fire hydrant was unveiled in Elm Creek, Manitoba, Canada, taking over honors as the world's largest.

Coral Castle
Homestead, Florida

After his fiancée called off their wedding at the last minute, Ed Leedskalnin spent 28 years building an ornate castle as a monument to his lost love. Leedskalnin used only hand tools to cut massive blocks of coral—1,100 tons in all—that form the castle walls. Between moving and carving the coral, Leedskalnin gave visitors tours and sold pamphlets expressing his famously eccentric views on love, politics, and magnetic currents. Three days after leaving a note on the castle door—"Going to Hospital"—he passed away in 1951, leaving the castle to his nephew. His nephew sold it, and the new owners found Ed's life savings soon thereafter: thirty-five $100 bills, collected a dime (later a quarter) at a time—the price of admission.

Carhenge
Alliance, Nebraska

To memorialize his father, engineer Jim Reinders organized a project that became the stuff of legend: the construction of a scale model of Stonehenge using junked cars instead of slabs of stone. With the help of a backhoe, Reinders and his kin put together this lasting tribute to a much more mysterious landmark halfway around the world.

The Also Ran Gallery
Norton, Kansas

The mezzanine of Norton's First State Bank is home to the only museum in the United States dedicated to those who lost presidential elections, with a framed picture and a short biography of each person. The gallery features such famous faces as Thomas Jefferson and John Kerry alongside distinguished lesser-known losers as General Lewis Cass and Rufus King.

Forevertron
North Freedom, Wisconsin

Dr. Evermor (retired junk collector Tom Every) started building the Forevertron in 1983, and the 320-ton curiosity is now considered the world's largest sculpture. Evoking a Victorian view of the far future, Evermor used scrap metal of all kinds to build the monolith with the hope of using it to personally rocket into the cosmos.

Fountain of Youth
St. Augustine, Florida

The site of a natural spring that Spanish explorer Juan Ponce de León mistook for the legendary Fountain of Youth in 1513 is now a kitschy attraction with touristy diversions of all kinds. The spring's water is free for the taking—but you have to buy the souvenir bottle in which to take it home.

World's Largest Ball of Paint
Alexandria, Indiana

In 1977, Mike Carmichael started applying layer after layer of paint to an ordinary baseball. Since then, the ball has seen an average of two coats a day, earning the title "The World's Largest Ball of Paint." After more than 20,000 coats, the ball measures about 3 feet in diameter and weighs well over 1,300 pounds.

House on the Rock
Spring Green, Wisconsin

Capping a 60-foot geological formation named Deer Shelter Rock is one of the best-known architectural oddities in the United States. The House on the Rock (a parody of Frank Lloyd Wright's work) is the creation of Alex Jordan, who started building it in the 1940s as a vacation home. He kept on building, furnishing it with art, a three-story bookcase, and anything else that captured his fevered imagination. Jordan sold the house in the late 1980s, but subsequent owner Art Donaldson has since made the place bigger and stranger than it has ever been. The structure now has 14 lavishly decorated rooms—including the Infinity room, which has 3,264 windows—and a surrounding complex that houses a miniature circus, one of the world's largest carousels, and a resort.

My Folks Went to Athens and All I Got Was This Lousy Peplos

Tourism works like this: You go to a place, and the people in charge of the place take all your money. And you're okay with that. It's a peculiar setup, with roots that trace back to the ancient world.

✳ ✳ ✳ ✳

"On Your Left, the Hanging Gardens..."

WHAT DID THE very earliest tourists—if there were any at all—enjoy? Cuddly saber-toothed kittens at the petting zoo? Tar-pit paddle boat rides? Well, that was prehistory, and tourism wasn't yet an industry, but with the passing of many centuries, city-states and empires became sophisticated enough that tourism was feasible. Visitors couldn't enjoy Six Flags over Carthage, but that's only because it hadn't been invented. There were other places to go and things to see, but travel beyond one's own borders was nevertheless a risky proposition.

By the first millennium B.C., Near Eastern empires had developed waterways, roads, lodging, and systems of commerce sufficient to encourage tourism. Even better, there was a mass of potential tourists to make added investment in infrastructure worthwhile. Then with the rise of the Persian Empire around 500 B.C., two additional key elements—peace and effective government—made tourism not just possible but relatively pleasant for those involved.

The earliest tourist destinations evident in the Western historical record are Babylon (present-day Iraq) and Egypt. Both destinations had neat things to see: the Hanging Gardens, pyramids, temples, festivals, and street markets. The ancient world also had museums, lighthouses, religious celebrations, and a lively system of commerce to lure well-heeled visitors.

Going Greek

When Greece caught the attention of curious travelers around 500 B.C., visitors favored the sea route rather than brave the wilds of Asia Minor (modern Turkey). At about the same time, the Levantine ports of what are now Syria, Lebanon, and Israel flourished. In the 400s B.C., Greeks wrote travel guides that evaluated locations and facilities—a little like *Lonely Planet*.

Greek and Levantine destinations attracted visitors, but tourists still had to remain on guard. In those days, people carried cash (no credit cards, right?), which attracted the attention of swindlers, pickpockets, and cutthroats. Seas around favored ports were controlled well enough to allow local and regional commerce to thrive, but a ship full of people wearing the ancient equivalent of Bermuda shorts was easy prey for pirates. Until things became safer and easier, tourism couldn't grow.

Roamin' Romans

With its seafaring rival Carthage put out of the way by 202 B.C., Republican Rome began its rise to undisputed dominance of the Mediterranean Sea. By the time Rome had a bona fide empire (about 27 B.C.), well-laid Roman roads encircled *Mare Nostrum* ("our sea"), with inns spaced just a day's travel apart. Armed patrols ensured the security of land routes. The Roman fleet aggressively hunted down pirates, making sea travel safer than ever before. Roman maps told travelers where they might go; chroniclers offered details about the sites.

Many would-be travelers had the hardy soul that was required, but serious travel was for the affluent. Most Romans were too poor to enjoy the diversions of new places. And even for those who could afford visits to Athens, Judea, and Egypt, the land route meant overpriced food and uncomfortable lodging.

The Mediterranean's sea lanes may have been swept of pirates, but nothing could be done about storms and other nautical hazards. Mindful of this risk, Romans struck bargains with the gods before travel, promising to do this or that in return for a safe voyage. Of course, even the most attentive Roman gods couldn't guarantee a *pleasant* trip.

Fun and Games for Grownups

So what was there to see and do around *Mare Nostrum*? For the simple joys of gluttony and sin, one might try the western Italian coast. Sparta was some 300 years into decline by A.D. 1, but travelers were drawn there by the echoes of its martial past and by the quaint Spartan notion of equality between the sexes.

Athens reached its peak around the fifth century B.C., and was in decline by the first century A.D., but the city's art and architecture still drew crowds. In Egypt, the Pyramids were a major attraction, and Alexandria had a fabulous library bursting with the world's knowledge. Then there was Novum Ilium (New Troy or Troy IX). The site had been destroyed, abandoned, and reborn many times over the centuries. In 85 B.C., the Romans rebuilt it as a living memorial to their supposed Trojan heritage, with Greek and Persian touches to lure travelers.

Other Mediterranean destinations and diversions included zoos, freak shows, prostitutes, exotic foods—and above all, bragging rights for having undertaken a pleasure trip in the first place. The ancient traveler was nothing if not cosmopolitan.

Two-way

Because "Rome" signified a vast empire by the first century A.D., the city not only provided tourists who traveled from the city, but hosted countless citizens who came to Rome from across the empire. Visitors were impressed—and intimidated—by the city's sprawl, grime, and confusion. More than a million people lived in Rome, and the effect of the city upon visitors from quieter realms must have been breathtaking—and not always pleasantly. Still, any provincial who returned from *Roma Eterna* was hailed as a sophisticate, just as a Roman who could speak gracefully about the ancient route of the Greek poet Homer enjoyed an elevated social status. As Rome declined, so did tourism, but it's clear today that pleasure travel never died out.

Odd Items for Sale in Japanese Vending Machines

Japan seems to have a yen for selling unusual products via vending machine—they sell more than any other country. Aside from the usual candy, gum, and cigarettes, here are some of the more obscure items available for purchase in Japanese vending machines.

1. Fresh eggs

2. Bags of rice in various sizes

3. Fishing line, fish hooks, and fish bait

4. Toilet paper in small packets—most public restrooms in Japan charge a fee for toilet paper

5. Fresh flowers

6. Frequent flyer miles—Japan Air Lines (JAL) has a machine that reads a credit card and boarding pass and issues miles

7. Beer in cans or two-liter jugs

8. Film and disposable cameras

9. Pornographic magazines

10. Designer condoms

11. Batteries

12. Live rhinoceros beetles—a popular pet for Japanese kids

13. Kerosene—for home space heaters

14. Dry ice—sold at supermarkets for keeping frozen food cold until the customer gets home

15. Sake in preheated containers

California's Two Valleys

Some of the most significant real estate in California is its valleys. Here are two: one is a natural valley, while the other is more metaphorical.

✳   ✳   ✳   ✳

S AN FERNANDO VALLEY in Southern California and Silicon Valley in Northern California are like polar-opposite siblings. They're not just on the opposite ends of the spectrum geographically but also in terms of their industry, weather, and population. Still, both are still very much part of California.

San Fernando

The San Fernando Valley encompasses 260 square miles in and around Los Angeles. It is bordered by the Santa Susana Mountains to the northwest, the Simi Hills to the west, the Santa Monica Mountains to the south, the Verdugo Mountains to the east, the San Gabriel Mountains to the northeast, and the Sierra Pelona Mountains to the north. The area was inhabited by the native Tatviam and Tongva cultures for thousands of years before the Spanish settled there around 1797. When the Mexican-American War ended in 1847, the land was ceded to the United States.

Secession issues are a theme in the valley's life—in the 1970s and again in 2002, the residents of the city of Los Angeles voted on a proposal to allow the San Fernando Valley to secede and become an independent city. The proposal came from the suburban communities of the valley, which argued that their resources should be separate from those of Los Angeles. But the city wouldn't let them leave: The proposal failed both times.

The San Fernando Valley is blessed with dry, sunny weather. Smog is a particular problem—the surrounding mountain ranges trap it in the sunken valley—though recent environmental regulations have improved the suffocating pollution levels.

Speaking of residents, they're mostly an equal percentage of Latinos and whites. The valley has a reputation for sprawling subdivisions, despite the fact that there are many apartment complexes, as well. Though a handful of valley communities have at least one in five residents living in poverty, the valley overall still has lower poverty rates than the rest of the county. Prominent aerospace-technology companies were once based in the San Fernando Valley, but they have since moved. The motion picture industry is a predominant economic force in the area—including the multibillion-dollar pornography industry.

Silicon Valley

Like the older sister who ignores her pesky younger brother during passing periods at school, Silicon Valley sits just south of the San Francisco Bay area and seems to share with the San Fernando Valley only the name of their home state.

Once this area was covered with orchards. The influx of various technology-related companies and research firms caused one journalist to coin the term "Silicon Valley," and the name stuck. Since the early 1900s, the area has nurtured the growth of the electronics industry. It became the hub of innovation for many industries, including radio, television, military electronics, and computers. An early radio station—the first one in the nation to carry regularly scheduled programming—was started in San Jose in 1909. Nearby Stanford University has also been a huge contributor to the evolution of area industry.

Silicon Valley weather is moderate, quite similar to that of the Mediterranean. It's estimated that 44 percent of residents have college degrees (compared to 27 percent nationwide). People who live here mostly work in area's industries—technology, computer software, and venture capitalist firms. Some of the biggest names in business reside in Silicon Valley: Apple, Intel, and Yahoo!, among others. The term "Silicon Valley" has entered the pop-culture lexicon as a reference to the high-tech sector in general.

Castles, American Style

Castles aren't just for Europe anymore. Here are some of the best castles in the good ol' U. S. of A.

✳ ✳ ✳ ✳

Boldt Castle, Heart Island, New York

IN 1900, GEORGE BOLDT, owner of the luxurious Waldorf-Astoria Hotel, purchased one of the Thousand Islands in the St. Lawrence River and began construction on a six-story castle in honor of his wife, Louise. Hundreds of workers were employed in building the 120-room castle, as well as the Power House, the Alster Tower, the Hennery, the Arch, and a stone gazebo. But when Louise died suddenly in 1904, a broken-hearted Boldt lost interest in his dream. He never returned to the island, and the castle was abandoned for 73 years until the Thousand Islands Bridge Authority purchased it in 1977, restored it, and opened it to the public.

Herreshoff Castle, Marblehead, Massachusetts

Built in the 1920s by artist Waldo Ballard, the castle was patterned after Erik the Red's castle in Greenland. Local legends say that Ballard found buried treasure in his basement, which enabled him to build his dream castle, complete with parapets and rumors of a secret stairway and dungeon. The small castle has only a few rooms but includes a grand ballroom and a rooftop deck overlooking the Marblehead harbor. Ever the artist, Ballard painted details all over the castle, including medieval patterns, family crests, and even an oriental rug on the floor. The castle changed hands a few times, picking up the Herreshoff name from a previous owner before being purchased by the current owners, who converted the adjacent carriage house into a bed-and-breakfast.

Bishop Castle, Beulah, Colorado

Jim Bishop was not planning to be in the castle business when, in 1969, he began building a cabin out of local stone. A visitor commented that it looked like a castle, so a castle it became. Since then, Bishop has designed and built nearly every inch of the 160-foot-tall castle by himself, complete with precarious wrought-iron balconies and a basket-lift. Perhaps the most memorable feature is perched on the roof—a metallic dragon that shoots real smoke and fire through its nose.

Loveland Castle, Loveland, Ohio
Château Laroche ("stone castle") was the vision of Harry Andrews, an eccentric with a mission to propagate modern-day knighthood. Designed as a full-scale replica of a 10th-century French castle, Andrews worked on the project single-handedly from 1929 until his death in 1981. Even unfinished, the castle is a true fortification with 17 rooms, including an armory, banquet hall, chapel, master suite, great hall, and dungeon, as well as seven holes above the front door for pouring boiling oil upon invaders. Today, the castle is owned by a group of "knights"— medieval reenactors who uphold Andrews's vision. It is also reportedly home to a few resident ghosts.

Kracht's Castle Island, Junction City, Kansas
Don Kracht's castle began with a pond. After an excavation, the small island in the middle made the pond look more like a moat, so in 1988, Kracht designed a fantasy castle and began building. A retired schoolteacher, Kracht works on his unusual project, adding to it every day. Although the castle, which is partially based on Neuschwanstein Castle in Germany, has only three actual bedrooms, it features a drawbridge, bell tower, hot tub, amphitheater, waterfall, Italianate gardens, turrets, cannons, and a dungeon.

Biltmore Castle, Asheville, North Carolina
Tucked into the rolling hills of the Blue Ridge Mountains near Asheville, North Carolina, lies Biltmore Castle, America's largest privately owned home. Construction of the country home of George Washington Vanderbilt and his wife, Edith, began in 1889, and it officially opened on Christmas Eve 1895.

The 175,000-square-foot castle, which was modeled after three 16th-century French châteaus, has 250 rooms, including 34 bedrooms, 43 bathrooms, 65 fireplaces, and a basement that houses a swimming pool, gymnasium, and bowling alley. The Gilded Age estate boasted the latest amenities of the day, such as an elevator, fire alarms, mechanical refrigeration, and central heating, plumbing, and electricity. In 1930, at the request of town officials, the Biltmore estate was opened to the public in an effort to boost local tourism during the Great Depression, and today, more than a million guests tour the palatial estate and its magnificent gardens each year.

Iolani Palace, Honolulu, Hawaii

Located in downtown Honolulu, Iolani Palace is America's only official state residence lived in by royalty, serving as the home to Hawaii's last two monarchs—King Kalakaua and his sister, Queen Lili'uokalani, who succeeded him. As the first monarch to travel around the world, Kalakaua envisioned building a majestic palace like those he'd seen on his journeys. Built between 1879 and 1882, Iolani Palace featured the most modern technology of the time, such as indoor plumbing, telephones, and gas lighting.

When the U.S. government overthrew the Hawaiian monarchy in 1893, Queen Lili'uokalani was forced to abdicate her throne and was imprisoned in the palace for months. Although it was neglected for several decades, renovation of Iolani Palace took place in the 1970s, and it opened to the public in 1978, restored to its historic grandeur.

As an interesting side note, on April 30, 2008, a group of native Hawaiians, who do not recognize Hawaii as a U.S. state, occupied Iolani Palace to protest what they view as the illegal rule of the U.S. government.

New Uses for Dead Malls

In the 1970s, the heyday of shopping malls, a new one opened every three or four days. Today, many existing enclosed malls are slated to close or be demolished, and few are being built. But whether we see shopping malls as self-contained fantasy worlds or climate-controlled prisons, they are a constant presence in our urban landscape and part of our cultural identity.

✳ ✳ ✳ ✳

Dixie Square Mall, Harvey, Illinois

DIXIE SQUARE MALL is the mall emeritus of dead malls—it's been abandoned longer than many other malls have been in existence. The 800,000-square-foot mall opened in 1966, in a great location 20 miles from downtown Chicago and minutes from three interstates. During its heyday, it was anchored by Montgomery Ward and JCPenney and was full of shoppers. But by 1978, neighborhood crime and competition from other malls forced it to close.

The lights came on once more in 1979, when Universal Pictures partially renovated the structure to film Jake and Elwood Blues leading police on a merry car chase through the mall in *The Blues Brothers*. The mall has sat empty ever since and has been the site of frequent vandalism and even a rape and murder. Although there have been several attempts to demolish the mall, they've all fallen through due to shady contractors, the expense of asbestos removal, and questions of ownership. Too expensive to tear down, the mall currently sits in limbo.

Bell Tower Mall, Greenville, South Carolina

This 300,000-square-foot mall was built in downtown Greenville in the late 1960s, complete with the brick walls and carpeted floors that were hallmarks of the era. Although it enjoyed a few years of prosperity, it suffered as the suburbs pulled shops and shoppers away from the center of town. By 1982, Woolco, one of the anchor stores, had closed, and by decade's end, the four-screen movie theater had closed as well. The space has since reopened as County Square, housing a collection of county government offices. The former movie theater now serves as a family courthouse.

The Galleria, Sherman Oaks, California

Located in the San Fernando Valley, the Galleria was the epicenter of mall culture during the Valley Girl craze of the early 1980s. In 1982, it made two pop-culture appearances: in the teen movie *Fast Times at Ridgemont High* and in the lyrics of Frank Zappa's song "Valley Girl." It was later used in the films *Commando* (1985) and *Chopping Mall* (1986).

In 1999, the mall closed because of declining business and damage from a 1994 earthquake. After a major renovation, it reopened in 2002, sans roof, as an open-air town center, with a few stores, a 16-screen theater, restaurants, and offices, including the headquarters for Warner Bros. Animation.

Indian Springs, Kansas City, Kansas

This 700,000-square-foot, two-level mall has been resurrected several times, each time with a new purpose that locals hope will keep the wrecking ball from its walls. It opened in 1971 with three solid anchor stores, but a depressed economy, suburban growth, and competition forced it to close in 2001. The mall then repackaged itself as a mixed-use space with vendors, restaurants, and offices. The Kansas City School District leased the former JCPenney site for administration and classroom space, and the U.S. Postal Service used the former Dillard's store as a customer service center. The mall's tenaciousness touched some local filmmakers, who made a documentary entitled *I Saw You at the Mall* about the struggle to resurrect the dead mall. Nevertheless, Kansas City declared the mall a "blighted" property in 2006, and the city is currently planning to demolish it and redevelop the land for office buildings, a hotel, shops, housing, and athletic fields.

Pyramids Aplenty

Ask most people what they consider the oldest,
most magnificent architecture in the world, and the
pyramids of Egypt are sure to be part of the answer.
Magnificent they are, but they are not the oldest.

✳ ✳ ✳ ✳

✳ The Pyramids of Giza are the most famous monuments
of ancient Egypt and the only structures remaining of the
original Seven Wonders of the Ancient World. Originally
about 480 feet high, they are also the largest stone structures
constructed by humans. They are not, however, the oldest.

✳ What's older than the pyramids? That glory goes to the
prehistoric temples of Malta—a small island nation south of
Sicily. The temples date from 4000 to 2500 B.C. At approximately 6,000 years old, they are a thousand years older than
the pyramids. Not much is known about the people who
built these magnificent structures, but they were likely farmers who constructed the temples as public places of worship.

✳ Because the Maltese temples were covered with soil from
early times and not discovered until the 19th century, these
megalithic structures have been well preserved. Extensive
archaeological and restorative work was carried out in the
early 20th century by archaeologists to further ensure the
temples' longevity. The major temple complexes are now
designated as UNESCO World Heritage Sites.

✳ Which pyramid is the oldest? That would be the Step
Pyramid at Saqqara. It was built during the third dynasty of
Egypt's Old Kingdom to protect the body of King Djoser,
who died around 2649 B.C. It was this architectural feat that
propelled the construction of the gigantic stone pyramids of
ancient Egypt on a rocky desert plateau close to the Nile—
known as the Great Pyramids.

The Boneyard: Where Military Aircraft Go to Die

Many call it "The Boneyard," but Davis-Monthan Air Force Base in Tucson, Arizona, could be called "The Aerospace Hospice" or "Aerospace Death Row." The U.S. Air Force's 309th Aerospace Maintenance and Regeneration Center (AMARC) handles aircraft retired from active service. A few will fly again; most will not. Either way, "The Boneyard" is a surreal place.

✳   ✳   ✳   ✳

L ET'S SUPPOSE THAT you need somewhere to stash hundreds of old warplanes long enough to find a use for them. Maybe a Third World dictator or a parts dealer will come shopping; perhaps a tech zillionaire always wanted his own jet fighter. Rain or humidity would mean corrosion, which is no good. And unless you want to pour thousands of acres of pavement, you'll need dry, compact soil. Otherwise, the heavy bombers and stratotankers would sink into the earth. And you'd look incompetent if the Tanzania People's Defence Force bought some used fighter planes and you had to tell them that they could have them as soon as they shoveled them out of the mud.

So, what's your best option? A blistering hot desert no one else wants. The Army Air Corps searched for such a spot after World War II, and they settled on Tucson.

What Lives There?

What sleeps at "The Boneyard" has a value of many billions of dollars—probably equal to several years of defense budgets adjusted for inflation. In fact, Davis-Monthan pastures most of the U.S. military's retired aircraft from the last 50 years.

For example, you could find enough F-4 Phantom fighters to equip an air force, enough F-14s to shoot down that air force, and enough A-4 Skyhawks to wipe out the air force on the ground. Add to that enough naval strike and anti-sub aircraft to outfit several aircraft carriers and sink a main battle fleet, and enough KC-135 aerial tankers to refuel them all in flight. Other treasures include an old NASA "Vomit Comet" astronaut training plane; artifacts such as B-57 Canberras and B-58 Hustlers, remembered only by aircraft geeks and the air force itself; and Death Row—dozens of B-52 intercontinental bombers scrapped, or awaiting scrapping, by a huge guillotine.

Airplane Guillotine and Ghost Planes

When U.S. warplanes leave active service or Uncle Sam promises other countries that he'll destroy their airplanes, pilots fly them to Davis-Monthan and land them in the desert where crews render them inoperative or dismember them using a huge mobile guillotine with a six-ton blade. For the B-52 fleet (being destroyed in compliance with the 1991 Strategic Arms Reduction Treaty, known as START I), that means slicing off each bomber's wings, nose, and tail. The wreckage lies there so the Russians can verify the destruction by satellite photo.

Another Davis-Monthan oddity is the ghost A-10s. Perhaps to deceive against possible enemy attacks, on one runway, the Air Force has painted several A-10 shapes visible from the air.

Diamonds in the Rough

"The Boneyard" really shines when someone needs spare parts. Salvaging engine guts from old aircraft is cheaper than ordering new ones from Boeing, so the AMARC crew extracts the necessary parts and sends them where they're needed.

There are other U.S. aircraft graveyards, mainly in the Southwest, but Davis-Monthan is the largest and most interesting for one reason: If all the aircraft at AMARC took to the air with trained pilots, they could easily whip the vast majority of the world's air forces.

Alaskan Stories

"The Great Land," as Alaska's name means in Aleut, spawns stories to match its size. "Sourdough" Alaskans love to see if cheechakos ("tenderfeet," or non-Alaskans) will fall for them. But some big Alaska tales don't exaggerate.

✳   ✳   ✳   ✳

Most of Alaska cannot be reached by roads. True. You can drive a car to Anchorage, the Kenai Peninsula, Fairbanks, the oil fields at Prudhoe Bay (if you have official business), the Yukon border with Canada, and Haines and Hyder in southeastern Alaska (via Canada). Anything in the western half of the state is inaccessible by road, so high school sports teams often must fly to away games.

Surf's not up in Alaska. False. There are plenty of opportunities to hang ten in Alaska, which has close to 47,000 miles of tidal shoreline. On Turnagain Arm near Anchorage, surfers put on wet suits and paddle out to ride the single daily bore tide.

You get paid to live in Alaska. True. The state has invested vast mineral royalties in the Permanent Fund, which pays each man, woman, and child roughly $1,100-$1,800 per year. However, to get the dividend one must live in Alaska for a full calendar year and have no felony convictions. Before you start packing your bags, though, remember that the freight expense for goods makes the Alaskan cost of living higher than that of the lower 48 states. The dividend doesn't fully compensate.

Alaskans live in igloos. False, of course. Alaskans live in anything from ritzy condos to trailers to bush cabins. However, if you go adventuring in the bush, study up. In Alaska, almost everything is done a little differently, and you're mostly on your own in the bush. The penalty for ignorance can be death at the hands of nature, so it would behoove you to learn how to build a snow shelter.

For fun, Alaskans get tossed into the air on blankets. True. However, this custom is Inupiaq (northwestern Alaska Native, formerly referred to as Eskimo) and originates from the practice of tossing hunters into the air so they could see across the horizon. Now it's mostly part of spring festivities. If you had to spend the winter in Barrow, which goes without sun an average of 84 days per year, you'd be in the mood to celebrate the arrival of springtime, too.

Moose regularly wander into Anchorage. True. Moose can show up nearly anywhere in Alaska (including most towns) at any time of year. They aren't playthings; they are wild animals that can be very grumpy and dangerous, so don't toy with them. By definition, the worst location in Alaska is between a grizzly sow and her cubs. The second worst is between a cow moose and her calf, and moose are far more numerous than bears.

Everyone huddles inside during Alaskan winters. False. Alaskans know cabin fever in ways few "outsiders" do, but they also make a point of going on with life and having fun all year. Anchorage's outdoor Fur Rendezvous (which everyone calls "FurRondy") in February has ice sculptures, a Miners and Trappers Ball with a prize for the best beard, and FurRondy police who will throw you in a mobile jail if you're caught without a Fur Rendezvous pin. Anywhere else, there'd be lawsuits; in Alaska it's all in the spirit of the festival. FurRondy coincides with the ceremonial start of the famed Iditarod dogsled race to Nome.

Mosquitoes in Alaska are twin-engined. True. They are enormous and voracious in summer, and the blackflies are just as bad. Alaskan lore says that mosquitoes always feast on "sourdough" Alaskans before they resort to *cheechakos*.

Alaskans don't like outsiders. False. Alaskans often feel ignored and misunderstood by outsiders, but they're like any other group: They generally welcome visitors who embrace and respect Alaskan style, culture, and natural beauty. The main thing to pack for a trip to Alaska is an open mind.

Italian City-states: Art, Commerce, and Intrigue

Life in 15th-century Florence or Venice or any one of the countless city-states that once occupied most of Italy was sophisticated, fast-paced, and exciting.

✳   ✳   ✳   ✳

S OME TIME AFTER the fall of the Roman Empire in the fifth century, the country now known as Italy dissolved into individual communities called city-states. Devastated by long years of war and disease, each city remained a self-governing body that for generations did not bow to a centralized government. Most of them evolved into powerful entities that, by the 14th century, influenced many cultures of the Western world.

Life at the Top

The city-states were usually run by wealthy aristocrats—sometimes the same family remained in power for generations. But that was no guarantee things would run smoothly. Family members could be killed or exiled when another relative attempted to usurp more wealth or power. Many leaders employed diplomacy, caution, and a taste tester to make sure their food wasn't poisoned. When negotiations broke down, a dose of arsenic was a favorite bargaining tool—it often cast the deciding vote as to who would remain in charge.

Science and the Arts Flourish

Florence is widely considered the birthplace of the Renaissance, a period known for the study of humanist philosophy and new schools of art. Humanism, which would affect religious beliefs throughout Europe, was an ancient Greek concept stating that human life was valuable not just in relation to God but in general. The rebirth of this idea generated changes in art—which had long been used almost exclusively for religious images—and supported disciplines such as astronomy and science.

For many years, Florence was ruled by Lorenzo de' Medici, a patron of the arts who encouraged the work of some of the greatest thinkers and artists of the day, including Leonardo da Vinci, Michelangelo Buonarroti, and Sandro Botticelli.

Venice, on the Adriatic Sea, was one of the wealthiest cities in all of Europe by the late 13th century. The city-state was ruled by a great council, whose upper echelon chose a "Council of Ten." From their ranks, one member was chosen to serve as "Il Doge" (the duke), the ceremonial head of the city. Known internationally for its handcrafted Murano glassware, Venice was also a major shipping port that imported and sold goods from both the Eastern and Western worlds. The government practiced relative religious tolerance at a time when torture and killing were commonly used elsewhere by the Catholic Church to weed out nonbelievers.

Rigid Roles

Like the residents of many other city-states, the people of Florence and Venice lived in an unbreakable caste system, where few ever changed their social position. Although some historians today believe that the opposite was true because the people lived so closely together, on the whole, the working class did not socialize with the nobility. The contained surroundings did offer one benefit to the workers, however. Although they often struggled to pay their taxes and feed their families, the poor and the working class were exposed to humanist philosophies and had the opportunity to enjoy public displays of art. The standard of living for aristocrats would seem primitive by modern standards, but Italy's city-states contained palaces filled with gold tableware and beautiful artwork as well as residents who dressed in silk and satin. Women—no matter what their social standing—had few, if any, legal rights. Their life choices were limited to either marrying or becoming nuns in the Catholic Church.

Chicago's Green Mill

A little bar on Chicago's North Side holds a century's worth of history and lore.

✳   ✳   ✳   ✳

CHICAGO MAY BE one of only a few contemporary American cities where drink specials run all day long and bars serve liquor until 5:00 A.M., but in the 1920s, Prohibition reigned supreme—well, sort of. The city has plenty of stories from this era, but there are few landmarks that still resonate with Chicago's mob heyday like the Green Mill jazz club.

In 1910, Tom Chamales bought the club and turned it into one of Chicago's swankiest spots. In the Roaring Twenties, one of Al Capone's mob cronies, "Machine Gun" Jack McGurn, became a co-owner after a manager hired him to "persuade" a popular Green Mill performer not to take his act to a competitor (persuade meant "slice his throat and cut his tongue").

The club has drawn a diverse crowd of music lovers, mob aficionados, and locals. Everyone from Charlie Chaplin to Frank Sinatra has partied here. They might even have sat at the famed table where Al Capone once watched both entrances, lest he needed to exit through the secret door behind the bar, which opened to a tunnel that led to a nearby building.

Crowds come and go, but good music remains the same. To this day the Green Mill is the go-to spot for jazz on Chicago's North Side. Harry Connick Jr., Branford Marsalis, and Brazilian jazz guitarist Paulinho Garcia have all graced its stage. In the 1980s, the Green Mill started one of the first poetry-slam nights in the country, Uptown Poetry Slam. The Uptown Poetry Slam is still popular at the Green Mill today.

Chapter 12

Fascinating People

The Ida B. Wells Story

*Almost a century before Rosa Parks made her stand, activist
Ida B. Wells made a similar point on a train in Tennessee.*

*   *   *   *

LITTLE KNOWN TODAY, Ida B. Wells should certainly be
included among the most famous Americans. She was born
in 1862 to slave parents who were freed along with the rest of
the slaves in 1865. When Wells was 16, her parents and youngest sibling died during a yellow fever epidemic. In order to keep
her family together, Wells showed her budding strength as she
took a job as a schoolteacher and raised her younger siblings.

Wells moved her family to Memphis, Tennessee; it was here
that she experienced the act of racism that launched her career.
Wells bought a first-class train ticket for a "ladies'" car, but was
told to move to the "colored" car to make room for a white man.
Wells refused and the conductor tried to forcibly move her. As
Wells later explained, "the moment he caught hold of my arm
I fastened my teeth in the back of his hand." It took two more
men to drag her off the conductor and off the train.

Lashing Out Against Lynching

Wells sued the railroad company; she won the case in lower
courts but lost the case in appeals in Tennessee's Supreme
Court. The case instigated the fight for equality. Wells became

the co-owner and editor of *Free Speech*, an anti-segregationist Memphis newspaper, and focused her energies on revealing the horrors of lynching. In her book, *A Red Record: Tabulated Statistics and Alleged Cause of Lynching in the United States*, she showed how horrifyingly common the practice was, picking apart one popular excuse used to justify it: A black man's rape of a white woman. "Somebody must show that the Afro-American race is more sinned against than sinning," Wells said.

Wells argued that whenever the rape defense was brought into a lynching case, the truth was that it usually was a voluntary act between a white woman and a black man. Wells traced the history of this rape defense, and pointed out that white slave owners would often leave for months at a time, leaving their wives under the care of their black male slaves. In fact, she argued, white-black sexual liaisons were typically the other way around, with white owners sleeping with or raping female slaves.

Wells was the first scholar of note to unearth the hypocrisy behind this so-called protection of white women's honor through lynching: "To justify their own barbarism," Wells wrote, "they assume a chivalry they do not possess . . . no one who reads the record, as it is written in the faces of the million mulattoes in the South, will for a minute conceive that the southern white man had a very chivalrous regard for the honor due the women of his own race." Wells concluded that lynching was really the result of fear of economic competition, combined with white men's anger at voluntary liaisons of white women and black men, along with racism.

Continuing the Fight

Wells' work continued until her death in 1931. She married fellow activist and writer F. L. Barnett in 1895. The couple had four children and worked to help African Americans in Chicago. Wells also was a founding member of the NAACP and the first president of The Negro Fellowship League. In 1930, shortly before her death, she ran for the Illinois Senate.

Shemptastic!

There are those who always seek the path less traveled—they like vanilla ice cream instead of chocolate, prefer Lou Gehrig to Babe Ruth, and think Star Trek *superior to* Star Wars. *Likewise, when it comes to the Three Stooges, they may be decidedly pro-Shemp.*

✳   ✳   ✳   ✳

DECLARING A FAVORITE Stooge is dangerous. You can argue politics or religion with someone for hours on end, but to mess with a person's favorite Stooge is to toss down the gauntlet. As one of the boys themselves might have said, "Them's fightin' woids!"

Sure, there's no denying that Curly is a great clown. Before the role of Moe's punching bag dissolved into a succession of Curly Joes, Curly was the first to suffer the lead Stooge's abuse. Fingers in the eyes, pliers to the nose, punches to the stomach, and ice down the pants were all absorbed without much protest by Curly, who could always be counted on to respond "Soitenly!" to any crisis and "Nyuk, nyuk, nyuk," when he was particularly pleased with himself. And who can forget that it was Curly who pioneered the unique art of running in circles while lying on the ground?

In Praise of Shemp

But Shemp didn't need any funny sounds or exaggerated movements. With a squashed potato for a nose, sad basset hound eyes, and a hangdog expression that rivaled professional clown Emmett Kelly, Shemp just naturally looked funny, as if somebody had worked him over and he had simply forgotten to get fixed up again.

Shemp, with his lank, jet-black hair, oddly resembled Moe. Indeed, when Moe was beating on Shemp he might well have been beating on himself, a fact that psychiatrists probably see as awfully telling—that is, until a lobster rises out of a soup bowl at some swanky dinner party and clamps a claw onto Shemp's nose. So much for social commentary.

A Bit of Backstory

All Stoogephiles know the story of Samuel "Shemp" Howard. As Moe and Curly's brother, Shemp had been part of the act early on, when the trio performed in vaudeville with Ted Healy, as "Ted Healy and His Stooges." In 1932, Shemp left for Hollywood to try his hand at a solo career. There he carved out a successful path for himself as a character actor. But when Curly was debilitated by a stroke in 1946, Shemp loyally returned to the group to save the Stooges from folding. Thereafter, Shemp became the main target of Moe's wrath. On November 22, 1955, Shemp died of a heart attack while lighting a cigar and telling a joke.

As a Stooge, Shemp hung in there and gave it his all. While it was accepted that Curly would never really get the best of Moe, Shemp could and did successfully fight back. That is, until Moe played his trump card—the fluttering hand going up and down in front of Shemp's face. Once he did that, poor Shemp was mesmerized, and never seemed able to remember that a slap was the inevitable conclusion.

Shemp managed to be a great clown without any of the typical clown tricks. He played it straight, and in doing so he extended the tradition forged in the time of Chaplin, Keaton, and so many others: the clown as everyman. Perhaps that's why, when Moe looks at Curly and utters his menacing, "Oh, a wise guy huh?" we watch to see what type of torment is about to be unleashed. But when Moe threatens to "moiderlize" Shemp, we turn away, fearful that the agony Shemp is about to feel will be felt by us all.

How Do You Like Them Apples?

Johnny Appleseed is often depicted as a happy-go-lucky farmer who roamed the American frontier barefoot, wearing a pot on his head and scattering apple seeds. Although this image fits comfortably with folklore, Johnny Appleseed was actually a real person.

✳ ✳ ✳ ✳

JOHNNY APPLESEED WAS born John Chapman on September 26, 1774, in Leominster, Massachusetts. He made his name by moving west ahead of the first pioneers, mainly in and around western Pennsylvania, Indiana, and Ohio. He traveled with a supply of apple seeds that he used to plant orchards (some of which exist to this day). By the time the first settlers arrived, he had fully grown apple trees ready to sell to them, along with nutritious fruit and the intoxicating beverage of choice among weary travelers—hard cider. Chapman quickly became known for his friendly, outgoing nature, and settlers welcomed him into their homes both for his liquid refreshments and his entertaining stories. They nicknamed him Johnny Appleseed, and along with his popularity, legends about him began to spread.

Although there's no evidence to support the idea that Johnny Appleseed wore a cooking pot on his head, he was known to remain barefoot—even in ice and snow. He preached a liberal Christian theology called Swedenborgianism, befriended Native Americans, and espoused a deep love of nature. He believed it was a sin to chop down trees or kill animals, and he often used his apple tree profits to buy lame horses and save them from slaughter.

Johnny Appleseed died in 1845, but his reputation continued to grow. In 1871, a story about his life appeared in *Harper's New Monthly Magazine*, and the depiction served to elevate him from eccentric tree planter to "patron saint of horticulture."

Henry Ford and the Automobile Empire

Founded in 1903, the Ford Motor Company was an extremely innovative manufacturer. Henry Ford is known as the father of the modern assembly line used in mass production, and his Model T automobile revolutionized transportation in America and around the world.

✳   ✳   ✳   ✳

BORN IN DEARBORN, Michigan, Henry Ford developed an early dislike of farm life. Looking for a different kind of future, he took a job as an engineer with the Edison Illuminating Company in 1891. Two years later, he completed his own self-propelled vehicle, which he called the Quadricycle. Ford's second car, the 999, drove one mile in 39.4 seconds (91.4 mph), a new land speed record. The development of the 999 inspired Ford to found the Ford Motor Company.

In 1908, Ford introduced the Model T, a car that featured such innovations as the left-sided steering wheel along with an enclosed engine and transmission. The Model T's best selling points were that it was easy to drive and easy to repair. Its original price of $825 fell substantially when Ford introduced the continuous moving assembly belt in all of his plants—after that, the basic touring car cost $360. By 1912, there were 7,000 Ford dealerships in the United States; by 1918, half of all cars sold in America were Model Ts.

Payday

During this time, Ford introduced a significant change in his factories that would forever alter the American workforce: the welfare capitalism program. Ford reduced his employees' workday from nine to eight hours and doubled their salaries from $2.34 to $5.00 per day. Though he was sharply criticized by Wall Street, Ford defended the move, claiming that not only did the $5.00 workday alleviate Ford's employee turnover problem, but it also allowed his workers to afford the cars they were building, thus boosting the economy.

World War I was a turbulent time for Ford. He was denounced by the Anti-Defamation League for owning an anti-Semitic newspaper, *The Independent*. After several libel lawsuits, he stopped its presses for good in 1927. Adolf Hitler, who was fascinated by automobiles, hung Ford's picture on his wall.

Rolling Along

By 1927, all steps in Ford's manufacturing process—from refining raw materials to final assembly of the auto—took place at the vast Rouge plant in his hometown of Dearborn, Michigan. At capacity, this plant employed more than 81,000 people and became the world's largest industrial complex. Ford's dream of producing a vehicle from scratch without reliance on foreign trade became a reality. Two years later, Henry had successful dealerships on six continents; by 1932, Ford was producing one-third of the world's cars.

In 1938, Ford turned over the running of the day-to-day business to his son, Edsel Ford. Edsel's unexpected death five years later brought Henry out of retirement until he ceded the presidency to his 28-year-old grandson Henry Ford II in 1945. Ford died two years later, and Henry Ford II ran the company until 1982. In 1999, 41-year-old William Ford Jr., became chairman.

Little-Known Facts About Ford

＊ Ford was one of the early backers of the Indianapolis 500.

＊ Ford helped develop charcoal briquettes under his brother-in-law's name: E. G. Kingsford. Kingsford charcoal was made from wood scraps from the Ford auto factories.

Famous Simply for Being Famous

Today's 24-hour news cycle, and the machinery of fame that accompanies it, demands constant feeding. Some people achieve fame by actually accomplishing something. Other people achieve fame because ... well, they just do.

✳   ✳   ✳   ✳

ONE TRIED-AND-TRUE METHOD of achieving celebrity without really having to do anything is to be born into the right circumstances. The United States, with no aristocracy of its own, has always been deeply fascinated by those who have won life's lottery without even trying—that is, those born into fabulous wealth.

Brenda Frazier

Socialite Brenda Diana Duff Frazier (1921–1982) became famous when she appeared as a debutante on a 1938 cover of *Life* magazine, which went on sale when the country was still grappling with the Great Depression. Frazier, a banking and grain heiress, was an attractive teenager at 17 and a has-been by 29. No particular scandal marked her decline; rather, she became a recluse, addicted to drugs and alcohol. Unwittingly, she set another trend by suffering from anorexia and bulimia long before those eating disorders became household words.

Barbara Hutton

The sad-eyed heir of the Woolworth five-and-dime retail fortune, Barbara Hutton (1912–1979) came to be known as the "Poor Little Rich Girl." Her mother committed suicide when Barbara was six, and the lonely only child was abandoned by her father and raised by a series of relatives and nannies. Hutton inherited almost $50 million at age 21 and went on to wed seven times—primarily coupling with abusive fortune hunters, playboys, and dubious European "royalty." Her 1942 marriage to debonair film star Cary Grant led the press to cynically dub them "Cash and Cary," although Grant was the only one of Hutton's mates who never took any money from her (they divorced in 1945). As Hutton grew older and more disappointed in life, she was reportedly often seen intoxicated, bestowing expensive gifts on younger men. Devastated by the death of her only child, Lance Reventlow, in a 1972 plane crash, Hutton died of a heart attack seven years later. She reportedly left an estate worth only $3,000.

Gloria Vanderbilt

Born in 1924 into a grand old American fortune—her paternal great-great-grandfather, Cornelius Vanderbilt, "The Commodore," made his money in railroads—Gloria Vanderbilt didn't necessarily have the best that money could buy. Her father died when she was just 15 months old, and her mother (known as "Big Gloria") controlled the child's $4-million trust fund but lacked maternal instincts. Big Gloria much preferred gadding about with a decadent set of international high society.

Gertrude Vanderbilt Whitney, scion of the Whitney fortune and the sister of Little Gloria's father, sued for custody in a 1934 court case that riveted the nation with its lurid details (women sleeping until mid-afternoon, seen in bed together, and so on). After sculptor/philanthropist Whitney was granted custody, she left Gloria pretty much to her own devices, which included marrying very old men quite early in life. After a string of high-profile romances and poor-choice weddings, her fourth and final marriage to Wyatt Cooper was actually happy, producing two sons (in addition to two sons she had from a previous marriage). However, the happiness ended when her husband died during open-heart surgery at age 50, and their son Carter committed suicide in front of his mother by jumping from a high-rise apartment window. Vanderbilt's surviving son, Anderson Cooper, is a successful CNN reporter/anchor. Gloria Vanderbilt, an accomplished collage and watercolor artist, made a fortune of her own by licensing her name to lines of accessories and clothing, most notably denim jeans, in the 1970s and '80s.

Edie Sedgwick

A cousin of actor Kyra Sedgwick, Edie Sedgwick (1943–1971) was descended from a family that could trace its roots back to the American Revolution. Unfortunately, while the family possessed the requisite wealth and bloodlines, it also hid some very dark secrets, including madness, suicide, and alleged incest. A vivacious, photogenic charmer, art student Edie had already been institutionalized before she came to New York City and met Andy Warhol, who reimagined the stylish waif as a "superstar" in a Faustian bargain that served them both—for a while. Edie's name and connections got her into *Vogue*; editor Diana Vreeland declared Edie the "It Girl" of the early 1960s. Sedgwick bleached her cropped hair silver to match Warhol's wig and flittered through glittering nights before a series of bad love affairs and a serious drug addiction sent her speeding back home to California. Although she tried her best to get clean and happy, Sedgwick's demons caught up with her when she died from a barbiturate overdose. However, she remains a fashion icon decades after her untimely passing.

Paris Hilton

All of this brings us to the latest installment in the famous-for-nothing game: Paris Hilton, who has made herself a cottage industry through her family name and hotel fortune, a relentless pursuit of publicity, an Internet-peddled sex video, and a starring role in a reality television series. Paris's underwear-free dances on club tables, affairs with other heirs, tiny accessories such as dogs and "frenemies," and total self-absorption have already held the world's interest far beyond any reasonable sell-by date. The fact that Hilton finally served prison time for one of several infractions after a DUI arrest actually incited glee in many quarters.

Fore! The Story of Jeanne Carmen

Bottle-blonde Jeanne Carmen enjoyed a wild life. She was a '50s-era pinup model, earned the crown "Queen of the B-Movies" for her film work, and boasted friendships with Marilyn Monroe and Elvis Presley. What many people don't know, however, is that Carmen was also the first professional female trick-shot golfer.

✳ ✳ ✳ ✳

DISILLUSIONED WITH LIFE on an Arkansas cotton farm, 13-year-old Jeanne Carmen ran away from home with dreams of becoming a movie star. She landed a job as a burlesque dancer in New York before becoming a model. In 1949, she took an assignment to model golf clothes for a Manhattan store. During the shoot, she discovered she had a natural ability for the game of golf. She began honing her various golf tricks—eventually using them to gain wealth and notoriety.

Carmen's tricks included stacking three golf balls on top of each other, then driving the middle ball over 200 yards without disturbing the bottom ball. She could also hit the flagstick from 150 yards away one out of every three attempts. Her most popular trick, though, was to drive a golf ball off a tee that was clenched between the teeth of a prone (invariably male) volunteer without so much as grazing his whiskers. Carmen became so adept at these tricks that she demonstrated them for President Dwight D. Eisenhower and gave golfing lessons to Hollywood celebrities such as Jayne Mansfield.

Hustling for the Mob

Carmen put her modeling career on hold and spent the early '50s traveling the East Coast, earning up to $1,000 a day performing trick shots. It was during this time that she met Chicago mobster Johnny Roselli, one of Sam Giancana's crew.

He took her to Las Vegas and set her up hustling naive tourists on the links.

The hustle was simple: Roselli would find wealthy hotel guests and point to the curvy, glamorous Carmen and bet them that they couldn't beat her. For the first few holes she'd play like the ditzy blonde people expected and let them get ahead. Suddenly, she'd make an amazing improvement. Roselli never lost a bet. Carmen eventually tired of the lifestyle. When one of her opponents refused to pay, Roselli dangled him from the top of a Vegas hotel, threatening to drop him. It was time to move on.

Marilyn's Buddy

By 1952, Carmen was on the cover of the *Esquire Girl* calendar, living in Hollywood, and was neighbors with Marilyn Monroe—with whom Carmen claimed to have shared some wild nights in the company of Elvis Presley, Frank Sinatra, Clark Gable, Errol Flynn, and John and Bobby Kennedy. Carmen also landed roles in a host of forgettable B-movies such as *Guns Don't Argue* and *The Three Outlaws*, a western that was later remade as *Butch Cassidy and the Sundance Kid*.

Carmen's hopes of graduating to A-list movies perished on August 5, 1962—the night Monroe died. Carmen had spoken to Monroe earlier that evening, and she always refuted the idea that the pop icon had committed suicide, believing Marilyn was murdered by the mob. Carmen's old friend Roselli called her up soon after and advised her to dye her hair brown and leave Los Angeles. Carmen followed his advice and began a new life in Scottsdale, Arizona, where she married and started a family. She kept her colorful past a secret, but continued to play golf—although never for money.

In 1976, Carmen returned to California with her family after Roselli informed her that mob boss Sam Giancana was dead and she was finally safe. Carmen died in 2007, only chipping distance from a golf club where the older members still talk about the blonde beauty who could hit any trick shot.

Who Was Roget?

If there ever was any truth in the saying "The best things happen when you least expect them," then the story of Peter Mark Roget might just illustrate that point perfectly. And if it doesn't illustrate it, then it may well demonstrate, exemplify, or even illuminate that point.

✳   ✳   ✳   ✳

USING THE SAME word more than once can be an effective technique, or it can plunge the thought into an unwanted abyss. The world may never know if Dr. Peter Mark Roget suffered from *monologophobia*, the obsessive fear of using the same word twice, but he did spend his life compiling a classed catalog of words to facilitate the expression of his ideas. His thesaurus, he claimed, would "help to supply my own deficiencies." Roget's definition of deficiencies might conflict with most, since he was an accomplished scientist, physician, and inventor before he became one of the world's most famous lexicographers.

Birth, Genesis, Nativity, Nascency, the Stork . . .

Roget was born in 1779 and became a physician at age 19. As a young doctor, he influenced the discovery of laughing gas as an anesthetic and published important papers on tuberculosis, epilepsy, and the medical care of prisoners. As a scientist, he invented a log-log slide rule to determine roots and powers of numbers (which was used for more than 150 years—until the invention of the calculator) and began a series of experiments about the human optic system that would later aid the development of the modern camera.

While watching the wheels of a carriage through the blinds of a window, he realized that the image of an object is retained on the retina for about one-sixteenth of a second after the object has gone out of view, a point he subsequently proved. This conclusion helped lay the groundwork for a shutter-and-aperture device he developed, an early prototype for the camera.

Roget also helped with the creation of the London sewage system and was an expert on bees, Dante, and the kaleidoscope. Great achievements for a man who thought himself deficient!

The Logic and the Idea

It was only when Roget was 70 that he began putting together his first thesaurus (he borrowed the Greek word for "treasure house"), which would later bear his name. Roget's system, compiled from lists he had been saving most of his life, instituted a brand-new principle that arranged words and phrases according to their meanings rather than their spellings.

The thesaurus, now nearly 160 years in print, has sold more than 30 million copies worldwide and has become an institution of the English language. Despite critics' complaints that this reference book plunges people into "a state of linguistic and intellectual mediocrity" in which language is "decayed, disarranged, and unlovely," Roget set out to create a tool that would offer words that could express every aspect of a particular idea rather than merely to list potential alternative choices. He also believed that people often just forgot the precise word they wanted and that his book would help them remember.

"A Rose by Any Other Name"

* In 1852, Roget's first thesaurus contained 15,000 words; the sixth edition, published 149 years later in 2001, includes a whopping 325,000 words and phrases.

* Anyone can use the name *Roget* on their thesaurus, but only HarperCollins has trademark-protected *Roget's International Thesaurus*.

* New editions of the thesaurus are greeted by the press and public as a mirror of the times in which we live. The 1980s brought into vogue such terms as *acid rain, creative accounting, insider trading,* and *bag lady.* The '90s ushered in new terms such as *eating disorder, double whammy, zero tolerance, air kissing, focus group, spin doctor, road rage,* and *bad hair day.*

What's That in Your Hair?

A Midwestern hairdresser enters a magazine contest and creates an iconic look.

❋ ❋ ❋ ❋

WHEN MARGARET VINCI-HELDT set out to win a contest run by a beauty magazine in 1960, the 42-year-old hairdresser from Elmhurst, Illinois, had no idea she was about to create a look that would be adopted by women all over the world. With just a few hours of teasing and *lots* of hairspray and bobby pins, she unleashed one of the biggest fashion trends of the decade—the beehive hairdo. Also known as the B-52 for its resemblance to the bulbous nose of the famous World War II aircraft, her distinctive design piles the hair into a high dome resting on the crown of the head. Famous fashionistas of the era, including Brigitte Bardot and Jacqueline Kennedy Onassis, began sporting the elaborate 'do for the cameras, and women throughout the United States and Europe began rushing to the beauty salon on a weekly basis to get theirs.

Why All the Buzz?

It's difficult to pin down why the style became so popular. Some say it's the classic look; others point to the fact that the piled-high coif makes the wearer look taller; and still others note that it requires relatively little maintenance (though sleeping in one does involve some elaborate preparation). Whatever the reason, the beehive quickly became the iconic look of the pre-counterculture 1960s. Audrey Hepburn famously sported a beehive in what was unquestionably her most famous role—Holly Golightly in *Breakfast at Tiffany's*. The look was also seen regularly on *Star Trek*, worn by the secondary character Yeoman Janice Rand, and it even became the centerpiece of an episode of *The Flintstones*.

Though the style's popularity waned toward the late '60s, it remained a familiar part of pop culture for decades. The sassy Southern waitress Flo on the sitcom *Alice* was never seen without her trademark beehive, and virtually all of the matronly women who populated Gary Larson's world-famous *The Far Side* cartoons wore one. The style was the trademark look for arguably the worst TV mom in history, Peg Bundy of *Married . . . with Children*, as well as for everyone's favorite cartoon mom, Marge Simpson. The B-52's, a popular 1970s New Wave band, took their name from the slang term for the hairstyle—two of the band's female singers were known to sport the 'do. And John Waters lovingly put the beehive at the center of his 1988 cult movie *Hairspray*. More recently, British singer Amy Winehouse created her distinctive look in part by wearing elaborate variations of the beehive, which has actually led to a resurgence of the style in Britain and Australia.

Hairy Moments

While some have touted the beehive as "the last great hairdo" to be invented, the style has also had its share of low moments. In a survey sponsored by a British hair products company in 2005, the beehive was voted the third-worst hairstyle of all time, behind only the Mohawk and the mullet. A year later, an American woman traveling from Amsterdam to Cork was arrested by Irish customs officials for smuggling cocaine, which she had stashed in her beehive. Even at the height of the craze in the 1960s, there was a degree of backlash against the style. Persistent urban legends told of spiders or ants nesting in women's highly piled hair. Hatmakers of the era were also not fans of the beehive—many of them blamed the popularity of the new hairstyle for driving women's hats out of vogue.

Although the beehive may have had its detractors, it remains a thoroughly distinctive and original look that will forever be recognized as a symbol of its era.

If I want to knock a story off the front page, I just change my hairstyle.

—HILLARY CLINTON

The Biting Wit of Winston Churchill

Winston was witty, but he could also coat the literary dagger with 15-molar nitric acid. Here are some colorful quotes you may never have read.

✳   ✳   ✳   ✳

✳ In 1916, after a social meeting with Admiral John de Robeck, whom Churchill held responsible for the Gallipoli fiasco: "Get me a stiff whisky and soda, and get it quick. I have just done something I hoped I would never have to do. I have shaken hands with de Robeck."

✳ A memo to Admiralty in 1939: "Kindly explain the reasons which debar individuals in certain branches from rising by merit to commissioned rank. If a telegraphist may rise, why not a painter? Apparently there is no difficulty about painters rising in Germany!"

✳ Lady Astor's caustic comment at a dinner party: "Winston, if I were your wife I'd poison your coffee." Churchill's reply: "Nancy, if I were your husband, I'd drink it."

✳ Churchill didn't spare himself. Young Winston preparing for an important dinner party: "I must be upon my best behavior: punctual, subdued, reserved—in short display all the qualities with which I am least endowed."

✳ In 1940, when the German and Soviet foreign ministers met in Berlin, Churchill sent them scrambling for shelters with a bombing raid. Asked about it, he said: "We had heard of the conference beforehand, and though not invited to join in the discussion did not wish to be entirely left out of the proceedings."

✳ In 1941, on embracing Stalin as a new ally: "I have only one purpose, the destruction of Hitler, and my life is much simplified thereby. If Hitler invaded Hell I would make at least a favourable reference to the Devil in the House of Commons."

* In an Admiralty memo: "Is it really necessary to describe the Tirpitz as the Admiral von Tirpitz in every signal? This must cause a considerable waste of time for signalmen, cipher staff, and typists. Surely Tirpitz is good enough for the beast."

* In the North African desert, referring to the famously ascetic politician Sir Stafford Cripps: "Here we are, marooned in all these miles of sand—not one blade of grass or drop of water or a flower. How Cripps would love it."

* Another jab at poor Cripps, who had just given up stogies: "Those cigars were his last contact with humanity."

* At the White House, Franklin D. Roosevelt wheeled in one day and caught Churchill buck naked. Winston smiled and said: "The prime minister of Great Britain has nothing to hide from the president of the United States."

* Describing U.S. Secretary of State John Foster Dulles: "The only bull who brings his own china shop with him."

* In 1944, refuting complaints on issuing captured German arms to the Free French forces: "It is almost like saying, 'Don't shoot that German with a German-made pistol now. Far better be shot yourself by him and have a thoroughly harmonious type of armament developed on a scientific scale a few years after your funeral.'"

* In a cabinet meeting, ranting about needlessly long reports: "This paper, by its very length, defends itself against the risk of being read."

* Winston's style caught on. During World War I, he was first lord of the Admiralty. Said a subordinate: "We have made a new commandment. The seventh day is the Sabbath of the First Lord, and on it thou shalt do all manner of work."

Hallelujah!: Celebrities Who Found God

These famous folks got the call—and answered it.

* * * *

Sam Kinison: It may be hard to believe that this loudmouth (and often vulgar) comedian once commanded a pulpit, but before he graced the stages of the late night TV shows, he was an evangelical preacher (just like his Dad).

Kirk Cameron: He started out as lovable Mike Seaver on the TV show *Growing Pains*. But at age 18, the teen heartthrob did a little soul searching and became a part of the Christian evangelical ministry, The Way of the Master. Now he focuses his acting efforts on Christian productions such as the *Left Behind* series.

Run (from Run-DMC): This rap superstar asked us to "Walk This Way" with Aerosmith in 1986. Now the Reverend Joseph "Run" Simmons dispenses spiritual wisdom as a Pentecostal preacher.

Reggie White: The football star came by his nickname honestly—the NFL's "Minister of Defense" was an ordained evangelical minister.

Ralph Waldo Emerson: This famed poet graduated from Harvard University in 1821 and began his studies at Harvard Divinity School. Although he didn't graduate, he became a Unitarian minister in 1829. He resigned a few years later over a dispute with church officials but went on to publish a number of well-known essays and poems, including "Nature," which laid the foundation for the philosophy of Transcendentalism.

Mister Rogers: This kind neighbor with a closet full of cardigans was the real deal. Fred Rogers was a graduate of the Pittsburgh Theological Seminary and a Presbyterian minister before he followed the trolley to the Neighborhood of Make Believe in *Mister Rogers' Neighborhood*.

Walt Disney: FBI Man or Mouse?

It seems that Walt Disney, whose entertainment empire was as pure as Snow White, may have protected and shielded other facets of his life from public view—ones that might have darkened his squeaky-clean image.

✳ ✳ ✳ ✳

WALT DISNEY WAS born in Chicago on December 5, 1901, to parents Elias and Flora. His father was a farmer and carpenter, running the household with an overly firm hand. After a move, Walt and his siblings, worked the Disney land near Kansas City. They often found themselves on the receiving end of dad's strap. As a young boy, Walt took advantage of his infrequent free time by drawing, using a piece of coal on toilet paper. When the Disneys moved back to Chicago in 1917, Walt attended art classes at the Chicago Academy of Fine Arts.

Armed with forged birth records, Walt joined the American Red Cross Ambulance Corps and entered World War I in 1918, just before it ended. He returned to Kansas City, where two of his brothers continued to run the Disney farm. Although he was rejected as a cartoonist for the *Kansas City Star*, Walt soon began to create animated film ads for movie theaters, working with a young Ub Iwerks, who eventually became an important member of Disney Studios.

In 1922, Disney started Laugh-O-Gram Films, producing short cartoons based on fairy tales. But the business closed within a year, and Walt headed to Hollywood, intent on directing feature films. Finding no work as a director, he revisited the world of film animation. With emotional and financial support from his brother Roy, Walt slowly began to make a name for Disney Brothers Studios on the West Coast. The company introduced "Oswald the Lucky Rabbit" in 1927 but lost the popular character the next year to a different company. Disney had to create another cute and clever cartoon animal.

The Tale of the Mouse

According to Disney, the Kansas City office of Laugh-O-Gram Films was rampant with mice. One mouse was a particular favorite of Walt. This rodent became the inspiration for Disney's next cartoon character. Working with Iwerks, and borrowing copiously from Oswald, Disney Studios produced *Steamboat Willie* in November 1928 and Mickey Mouse quickly became a hit. The animated star introduced additional Disney icons, including girlfriend Minnie Mouse, the always-exasperated Donald Duck, faithful hound Pluto, and dim-but-devoted pal Goofy. Disney's cartoons won every Animated Short Subject Academy Award during the 1930s.

A Dark Side of Disney

As Disney Studios moved into animated feature films, Walt began to wield the power he'd gained as one of Hollywood's most prominent producers. Yet, his strict upbringing and harsh bouts of discipline had left him with a suspicious, ultraconservative mind-set. Bad language by employees in the presence of women resulted in immediate discharge. Disney was prone to creating a double standard between himself and his employees. For example, although Walt kept his dashing mustache for most of his life, all other Disney workers were prohibited from wearing any facial hair. While he considered his artists and animators "family," he treated them in the same way Elias Disney had treated his family—unfairly. Promised bonuses turned into layoffs. Higher-paid artists resorted to giving their assistants raises out of their own pockets. By 1941, Disney's animators went on strike, supported by the Screen Cartoonists Guild. Walt was convinced, and stated publicly, that the strike was the result of Communist agitators infiltrating Hollywood. Settled after five weeks, the Guild won on all counts, and the "Disney family" became cynically known as the "Mouse Factory."

An Even Darker Side

Disney was suspected of being a Nazi sympathizer; he often attended American Nazi Party meetings before the beginning of World War II. When prominent German filmmaker Leni Riefenstahl tried to screen her films for Hollywood studios, only Disney agreed to meet her. Yet, when World War II began, Disney projected a strictly all-American image and became closely allied with the FBI.

Disney was recruited by Hoover in late 1940 to flag potential communists in Hollywood. In September 1947, Disney was called by the House Un-American Activities Committee to testify on Communist influence in the motion picture industry. He fingered several of his former artists as Reds, again blaming much of the 1941 labor strike on them. He also identified the League of Women Voters as a Communist-fronted organization. Later that evening, his wife pointed out that he meant the League of Women Shoppers, a consumer group that had supported the Guild strike. Disney's testimony contributed to the "Hollywood Blacklist," which included anyone in the industry suspected of Communist affiliation. The list resulted in many damaged or lost careers, as well as a number of suicides. Included in the turmoil was Charlie Chaplin, whom Disney referred to as "the little Commie."

The FBI rewarded Walt Disney for his efforts by naming him "SAC—Special Agent in Charge" in 1954, just before his first amusement park, Disneyland, opened. Disney and Hoover continued to be pen pals into the 1960s; the FBI made script "suggestions" for *Moon Pilot*, a Disney comedy that initially spoofed the Bureau. The bumbling FBI agents in the screenplay became generic government agents before the film's release.

After a lifetime of chain-smoking, Disney developed lung cancer and died in December 1966. His plans for Disney World in Florida had just begun—the park didn't open until 1971. Upon his passing, many remembered the man as kindly "Uncle Walt," while others saw him as the perfect father for a mouse—since he had always seemed to be a bit of a rat.

Noteworthy Canadian Women

Kim Campbell was Canada's first female prime minister. Jeanne Sauvé was the first governor-general. What have other Canadian women done lately?

✳   ✳   ✳   ✳

Susan Aglukark: an Inuk who once worked as a linguist for the Department of Indian and Northern Affairs. This uplifting northern Manitoban musician plays guitar and sings in Inuktitut and English to inspire all people toward self-respect and strength.

Madame Louise Arbour: born in Montreal and one of Canada's most distinguished judges. She is a former prosecutor for the United Nations International Criminal Tribunal and former Justice of the Supreme Court of Canada. In 2004, Arbour became the U.N. High Commissioner for Human Rights, raising Canada's world profile in an area important to Canadians.

Jean Augustine: born in Grenada, emigrated to Canada in 1959. Augustine represents the level of opportunity available to immigrant Canadians: She started as a maid in Ontario, then became a teacher and later a principal. In 1993, she became Canada's first African Canadian member of Parliament for the Etobicoke-Lakeshore Riding (similar to a congressional district in the United States).

Dr. Roberta Bondar: from Sault Ste. Marie, Ontario. A noted researcher and professor, she began training as an astronaut in 1984. In January 1992, she became the first Canadian woman to leave the planet, spending eight days in space aboard *Discovery*.

The Honorable Jocelyne Bourgon: born in Papineauville, Quebec. As the first woman to serve as Clerk of the Privy Council, she was Canada's chief civil servant. Her reforms trimmed Canada's large civil service payroll by 47,000 jobs. She is now a member of the Queen's Privy Council for Canada (the monarchy's Canadian advisory body).

Major Deanna Brasseur: from Pembroke, Ontario. She entered the armed forces as a dental clerk and rose to become one of the first female CF-18 fighter pilots. Impressive, but perhaps more difficult was her courageous decision to tell her story of sexual abuse in the Canadian military, leading to reforms.

Rosemary Brown: emigrated to Canada from Jamaica and became the first African Canadian woman to serve in any Canadian legislature (British Columbia). Later she served on the board overseeing the Canadian Security Intelligence Service, Canada's national intelligence agency.

Major Maryse Carmichael: from Quebec City, Quebec, she became a pilot in her teens. Little did she know then that she would become the first woman to fly with the Canadian Forces' elite Snowbirds aerobatic team. She has also flown with the Forces' VIP transport squadron, trusted to fly the prime minister and governor-general around the world.

Françoise David: from Montreal, Quebec. David is one of Canada's most outspoken Francophones and feminist activists. Through La Fédération des femmes du Québec (Quebec Women's Federation), she has campaigned tirelessly for women's rights and against poverty in Canada.

Right Honorable Ellen Fairclough: from Hamilton, Ontario. She marched in the vanguard of Canadian women assuming roles in national leadership. As Canada's immigration minister, she did away with racial discrimination in Canadian immigration in 1962.

Barbara Frum: a U.S. immigrant from Niagara Falls. She became one of Canada's most highly regarded television journalists. Her empathy and sense of humor endeared her to the viewing public. After battling leukemia for 18 years, her adopted nation mourned her loss in 1992.

Pauline Julien: born in Trois-Rivières, Quebec. One of Canada's most successful musicians was a passionate crusader for Quebec separatism. She wove her ideals and dreams for her province into her music, even declining to perform for the queen.

Chantal Petitclerc: born in Saint-Marc-des-Carrières, Quebec. Although Petitclerc was paralyzed from the waist down when she was 13, she took up swimming, then wheelchair racing. At the Athens 2004 Paralympics, she broke three world records and earned Canada five gold medals to become Canadian Female Athlete of the Year.

Dr. Buffy Sainte-Marie: a Cree from Saskatchewan. Sainte-Marie was orphaned in infancy. Her guitar and voice talent surfaced in her teens, and she became a folk-rock balladeer in Canada. She has used her fame and resources to help First Nations at every opportunity, and like most on this list, she is a member of the Order of Canada.

Muriel Stanley Venne: born in Lamont, Alberta. This Metis Canadian founded the Institute for the Advancement of Aboriginal Women. A lifetime of hard work has made her a nationally admired human rights activist and the winner of numerous awards.

Hayley Wickenheiser: born in Shaunavon, Saskatchewan. This tough, physical hockey player has helped Canada win two Olympic gold medals. Wickenheiser was only 28 when she was Canada's top forward in 2006 at the Olympics in Torino, Italy.

Sharon Wood: born in Halifax, Nova Scotia, but raised in Vancouver. She climbed Canada's highest peak, Mount Logan (in the Yukon Territory), in 1977. After successfully climbing other challenging mountains in many countries, she became the first North American woman to conquer the world's highest peak, Mount Everest.

Julie Payette: born in Montreal. Being Canada's second female astronaut is quite an honor, but Payette's many talents make her an outstanding Canadian. She speaks six languages, is an accomplished singer and pianist, and is certified in deep-sea diving.

Frederick Law Olmsted and Central Park

Because Central Park is a staple of New York City and an outstanding example of what a public park should be, it's hard to believe there was ever a time when Central Park didn't exist. It's also hard to remember that its creation was the result of one man with a marvelous vision.

* * * *

NEW YORK CITY's Central Park is one of the most famous parks in the world. It often makes cameo appearances in books and movies and has long been the model of a restful retreat for harried urbanites.

We Want Green

By 1850, the outcry from citizens in New York City had reached an all-time high—people clamored for the creation of a large, central park to alleviate the crowded conditions of the rapidly growing city. A series of influential essays by Andrew Jackson Downing, a landscape designer, were published in *The Horticulturist*. Editorials in the *Evening Post* insisted that the subject of a public park should be brought to the forefront of civic discussion. In that year's mayoral election, both candidates included the creation of a public park in their campaign platforms. When Ambrose C. Kingsland was elected mayor of New York in 1851, he recommended that the Common Council set aside funds to purchase property for the park. The land for Central Park, in the area between the city and the village of Harlem, was bought in 1853.

Bridges, Metaphorical and Literal

In 1857, New York City held a design competition to create the layout of the park. Officials were looking for a design that would rival parks in London and Paris. The winners of the competition were Frederick Law Olmsted and Calvert

Vaux, who together created the Greensward Plan: a park that would contain separate circulation systems so that park users were not exposed to crosstown traffic. Pedestrians, horseback riders, and carriages followed

their own series of paths through the park; thoroughfares were concealed by dense shrub walls. A potpourri of bridges was installed throughout the park—no one identical to another.

Culturally, Central Park was an example of an idyllic design that welcomed people from all classes. At the time, the concept of a public park being open to everyone was not the self-evident idea that it is today. Olmsted's social consciousness led him to envision a green space that would be accessible to all citizens.

Portrait of the Artist

Olmsted was named the architect in chief of the Central Park project. As such, he was able to bring his vision of social equality to one of the largest parks in the country. A public park, he felt, should provide a restful place for those who did not have the means to vacation at country houses in other states.

Before designing parks, Olmsted led a varied life—traveling through the American South from 1852 to 1857, writing essays about slavery's impact on Southern culture for the *New York Daily Times*; sailing to England and hiking more than 300 miles; cofounding *The Nation*.

Olmsted is known for much more than just Central Park. He left behind a wealth of letters and writings, and he is considered the pioneer of landscape architecture in the United States. He was the driving force behind the majority of urban parks across the country. He designed the grounds for the 1893 Columbian Exposition in Chicago; the grounds that surround the U.S. Capitol; and even the grounds for McLean Hospital in Belmont, Massachusetts, where he died on August 28, 1903.

Real-Life Superheroes in Michigan

Crime-fighting men in tights, masked ladies in catsuits, and superheroes making the world safer one step at a time—these are not only the stuff of comic books. The town of Jackson, Michigan, has its own prowling super man, woman, and girl: Captain Jackson, the Queen of Hearts, and Crimefighter Girl.

✳   ✳   ✳   ✳

IN 1999, WHEN a Detroit man in his early forties moved to the city of Jackson for a new job, he became concerned that local police were not visible enough to deter crime in the city's aging downtown streets. The brand-new maximum-security prison on the outskirts of town seemed to be admitting all too many native sons. As he pondered the problem, it occurred to him that perhaps all it might take to turn things around was someone to serve as a middleman between law enforcement agencies and the town's citizens. He nominated himself for the position and phoned a local radio talk show to let them know that Captain Jackson had just arrived to save the city.

Custom Costumes

Captain Jackson, a man of average size who prefers to remain anonymous, devised his own costume, using Batman as a rough model. He dons a black hood and eye mask, a gray shirt and briefs, and of course, black tights. A round chest logo and flowing purple cape complete his dashing look.

But Jackson wasn't the only would-be caped crusader shopping for spandex. When his daughter began joining him on his rounds as Crimefighter Girl, she chose a yellow mask and cape to cover her black leotard and tights.

Then one evening in downtown Jackson, a woman with long blonde hair, a red heart on her chest, and a gold metallic belt showed up and introduced herself as the Queen of Hearts. Together, the three call themselves the Crimefighter Corps.

Here They Come to Save the Day

Once Captain Jackson had his costume, he began walking the city's streets every evening, stopping in taverns and other businesses to check in. Reactions ranged from amusement to relief that someone was keeping an eye on things. But the new "caped crusader" was careful not to overstep his bounds. Captain Jackson quickly developed a working relationship with the police and fire departments, and in 2005, Jackson's chief of police said the once crime-ridden downtown area patrolled by the Captain had become the most crime-free part of the city.

In addition to making Jackson a safer place, the Captain hopes to inspire people in other places to take back their streets. The Queen of Hearts, a martial arts expert, aspires to help mend broken hearts by fighting domestic violence.

Unmasked

In comics, Clark Kent and Peter Parker live in fear that their alter egos (Superman and Spider-Man, respectively) will be unmasked and their true identities revealed. Captain Jackson is no different in his desire for privacy, but in 2005, his name was revealed to the public when, off-duty, his alter ego was arrested for impaired driving. Jackson police had always known the Captain's identity but agreed to keep their ally's name a secret. Captain Jackson showed true superhero fortitude in riding out the flurry of publicity and continued making nightly rounds.

Future-Man

Although Crimefighter Girl is going off to college after logging thousands of public service hours, Captain Jackson plans to go right on checking the back doors of downtown businesses and discouraging panhandlers for as long as he is able. An Australian filmmaker has visited Michigan to showcase the Captain going about his duties, and he continues to make news as a superhero that actually does crime-fighting work. And as Captain Jackson said in a recent interview, "Time flies when you're saving the world."

Sacagawea's Untold Story

There aren't many tour guides as famous as Sacajawea, but in truth, she wasn't a guide at all—she had no idea where she was going, and she didn't even speak English!

✳ ✳ ✳ ✳

MERIWETHER LEWIS (a soldier) and William Clark (a naturalist) were recruited by President Thomas Jefferson to explore the upper reaches of the Missouri River. Their job was to find the most direct route to the Pacific Ocean—the legendary Northwest Passage. Setting out in 1803, they worked their way up the Missouri River and stopped for the winter to build a fort near a trading post in present-day North Dakota. There, they met a pregnant Shoshone teenager named Sacagawea.

Actually, they met her through her husband, Toussaint Charbonneau. He was a French fur trader who lived with the Shoshone (he is said to have purchased Sacagawea from members of another group who had captured her, so it may be inaccurate to call her his "wife"). Although Sacagawea is credited with guiding Lewis and Clark's expedition to the Pacific, the only reason she (and her newborn baby) went along at all was that her husband had been hired as a translator.

Pop Culture Icon

The myth of Sacagawea as the Native American princess who pointed the way to the Pacific was created and perpetuated by the many books and movies that romanticized her story. For example, the 1955 movie *The Far Horizons*, which starred Donna Reed in "yellow-face" makeup, introduced the fictional plotline of a romance between Sacagawea and William Clark. Over time, she has evolved to serve as a symbol of friendly relations between the

U.S. government and Native Americans. In 2000, she was given the U.S. Mint's ultimate honor when it released the Sacagawea Golden Dollar. At the same time, though, the Mint's Web site incorrectly states that she "guided the adventurers from the Northern Great Plains to the Pacific Ocean and back."

The Real Sacagawea

The only facts known about Sacagawea come from the journals of Lewis and Clark's expedition team. According to these, we know that she did not translate for the group—with the exception of a few occasions when they encountered other Shoshone. But because she did not speak English, she served as more of a go-between for her husband, the explorers, and members of other tribes they encountered in their travels. Concerning her knowledge of a route to the Pacific, Lewis and Clark knew far more about the land than she did. Only when they reached the area occupied by her own people was she able to point out a few landmarks, but they were not of any great help.

This isn't to say that she did not make important contributions to the journey's success. Journals note that Sacagawea was a great help to the team when she rescued essential medicines and supplies that had been washed into a river. Her knowledge of edible roots and plants was invaluable when game and other sources of food were hard to come by. Most important, Sacagawea served as a sort of human peace symbol. Her presence reassured the various Native American groups who encountered Lewis and Clark that the explorers' intentions were peaceful. No Native American woman, especially one with a baby on her back, would have been part of a war party.

There are two very different accounts of Sacagawea's death. Although some historical documents say she died in South Dakota in 1812, Shoshone oral tradition claims she lived until 1884 and died in Wyoming. Regardless of differing interpretations of her life and death, Sacagawea will always be a heroine of American history.

Strange and Unusual Talents

And you thought swallowing swords was pretty cool.

✳ ✳ ✳ ✳

Rubberboy: Daniel Browning Smith

NICKNAMED "RUBBERBOY," DANIEL is unique, even among his peers. Most contortionists are either forward benders or backward benders, but rarely both. Daniel, who is able to contort and dislocate his 5'8" body into almost any formation, is that rare exception, so much so that he holds three Guinness World Records. Daniel's opening and closing acts are especially awe-inspiring—he emerges from a tiny 19.5"×13.5"×16" box to begin and manages to fold himself back into the box before being carried off stage at the finale.

The Ayala Sisters

When Michelle, Andrea, and Alexis Ayala enter the circus ring, the petite sisters juggle fire, twirl, and spin—all while hanging by their long locks. Traditional hair suspension acts go up and down more than the stock market, never leaving the performer suspended for more than a half minute. But the Ayala sisters, like their mother before them, remain aloft for nearly six minutes, only coming back to the circus floor long enough to gain momentum for their final dizzying, high-speed spin.

The Wolf Boy

Take one look at Danny Gomez and you'll realize there's something different about him. Born with a condition called hypertrichosis, his entire body, including his face, is covered with thick black hair. But Danny is about much more than his unusual physical appearance. He's been performing since he was a small child—more than 20 years—and his amazing skills include juggling, trampoline, trapeze, and even daredevil motorcycle stunts. Danny's warm personality and quirky sense of humor make him a favorite with audiences, especially children. Danny and his older brother, Larry, who is also afflicted with hypertrichosis, frequently performed together as the Wolf Brothers until recently when Larry retired from showbiz.

Tim "Zamora the Torture King" Cridland

Audience members may cringe while watching Zamora perform, but they never forget him. Using martial arts techniques combined with Eastern teaching, hypnosis, and an extensive knowledge of anatomy, Zamora astounds and shocks his fans with feats of mind over matter—jumping on and eating glass, sword swallowing, electrocution, and body skewering—only to emerge intact and unscathed. That can't always be said for the more squeamish members of the crowd.

George "The Giant" McArthur

At 7'3", George McArthur stands out among performers but not just because of his imposing size. This multitalented gentle giant holds a Guinness World Record for having the most weight—1,387 pounds from slabs of cement—broken on his body while lying on a bed of nails. George started in the circus business as a fire-eater, a skill he learned while determined to rid himself of a fear of flames. Since then he's added sword swallowing, walking on broken glass, and straitjacket escapes to his performing repertoire.

Mighty Mike Murga

A supermarket of unique talent, "little person" Mighty Mike Murga works as a strong man, fire-eater, unicycle rider, and juggler. Though these might seem like typical circus skills, at 4'3", Mike has to work harder to overcome the challenges of his size and low center of gravity to perfect the skills his taller peers take for granted. Recently, Mike completed a tour with Mötley Crüe, whose heavy metal fans immediately fell in love with the diminutive star.

The Intriguing Life of Lady Randy

Wife of a British aristocrat and the mother of Sir Winston Churchill, Lady Randolph Churchill was an American-born socialite who both scandalized and fascinated British society with her lust for life—and her life of lust. Vivacious, flirtatious, charming, and disarming, she used her beauty and wit not only to advance her own social status, but also to further the legendary political careers of her husband and son.

* * * *

An Early Influence

JENNIE JEROME WAS an American princess long before she married into the British upper crust. The second daughter of Clara and "Wall Street King" Leonard Jerome was born in upstate New York on January 9, 1854, with a silver spoon firmly entrenched in her mouth.

Her father's leisure pursuits ranged from opera to horse racing and he was instrumental in founding the American Academy of Music and the American Jockey Club. Jerome also had an eye for the ladies: Jennie is rumored to have been named for Swedish nightingale Jenny Lind, who sang at the Jeromes' private theatre in their Madison Square residence.

Although Jennie moved to Paris with her mother and sisters in 1867, her father's philanthropic and philandering ways may have influenced her character. A champion of countless charitable causes and staple of the London social scene, Jennie was also noted for her parade of paramours—possibly up to 200.

Romance with Randolph

Lord Randolph Churchill, the third son of the 7th Duke of Marlborough, fell madly in love with the young, raven-haired American beauty he met at the Cowes Regatta in August 1873. Jennie accepted his proposal, but it took time for both sets of parents to acquiesce. They married the following April.

Seven and a half months later, their son, Winston Churchill, was born—with various justifications for his premature birth. Lord Randolph recalled Jennie's labor was hastened by a fall; her sister explained her nephew's early arrival as triggered by spirited dancing at the St. Andrew's ball. Sir Winston later quipped, "Although present on that occasion, I have no clear recollection of the events leading up to it."

Roller Coaster Social Status

Displaying a lively wit, a keen political intellect, and a talent for the piano, Lady Randolph was accepted into London's society, forgiven of her unfortunate American breeding. Dubbed "Lady Randy," her popularity soared when she was branded a "professional beauty," or P. B., a status equivalent to today's supermodel. A fashion icon, Jennie was noted for cinching her waist to a remarkable 19 inches.

Lady Randy's popularity with major political figures reportedly extended beyond the parlor into pillow talk. She is reputed to have dallied with kings and counts, which some historians credit as the impetus for her husband's (and later, Winston's) political successes. The Churchills were included in the Prince of Wales' inner circle until an unfortunate attempt by Lord Randolph to blackmail the prince backfired, and the couple and Winston were exiled to Ireland for seven years. During this time, Jennie gave birth to a second son, John Strange Spencer Churchill. Six years Winston's junior, he was reputed to be the love child of Irish nobleman Colonel John Strange Jocelyn.

Maternal Misfit to Political Manager

Restored to the prince's favor, the Churchills resumed their A-list social life, which left little time for parenting. Winston and John were raised by a nanny, then packed off to boarding school. Although Jennie's mothering skills are often disparaged, young Winston appears to have felt a bond with her. In an 1887 letter imploring her to spring him from school to attend the Queen's jubilee, Winston addresses her "My dear Mamma" and writes, "I love you so much dear Mummy and I know you love me too much to disappoint me."

As Winston grew older, their relationship morphed. It was not quite the traditional mother-son connection, but rather a friendly, supportive partnership. Realizing his potential, Lady Randolph encouraged her son's ambitions and ardently campaigned on his behalf.

The Marrying Kind

Following a protracted period of physical and mental decline, Lord Randolph died in 1895 at age 45. It is widely believed his death resulted from the latent effects of a syphilis infection he contracted at age 21, but this fact is disputed since neither Lady Randolph nor her sons were infected.

Jennie married twice more—both times to men young enough to be her sons. In July 1900, she married British army officer George Cornwallis West. Reportedly the handsomest man in Britain, he was 20 years her junior and only 16 days older than Winston. If this bothered her son, it didn't show. The Churchills attended the wedding; however, the groom's parents did not. Their marriage ended in divorce in 1914. In 1918, Jennie wed Montague Phippen Porch, a British civil servant. She was 67; he was 44—three years younger than Winston. Apparently the old girl still had it, commenting, "He has a future and I have a past, so we should be alright." She remained married to Porch until her death three years later.

Brought Down by Vanity

In the end, it may have been Jennie's vanity that was her downfall. Sporting a new pair of Italian shoes, she slipped and broke her ankle on her way to tea. Gangrene quickly set in, necessitating an above-the-knee amputation. While she was recuperating, an artery burst and she slipped into a coma and died June 29, 1921, with both sons at her side. Retaining the name Lady Randolph despite her subsequent marriages, she was laid to rest beside her first husband.

Liberace: Predestined to Play

Like his singing counterpart Elvis Presley, Liberace entered the world with a stillborn twin. But Liberace, christened Wladziu Valentino Liberace and usually called "Lee" or "Walter," was born with part of the birth sac over his head. Throughout the ages, the birth sac (or caul) has been seen as a mystical portent of special talents or powers, and in this case, the old wives' tale got it right: Few human beings have possessed Liberace's magical power to enthrall a crowd.

✳ ✳ ✳ ✳

Born to Beguile

BORN IN 1919, in West Allis, Wisconsin, young Walter was a sickly boy. He spoke with an odd accent that he later compared to Lawrence Welk's, although it may have come from seven years of childhood speech therapy. Nevertheless, he could joyously pound out accurate piano tunes by the time he was three, and, at age seven, he won a scholarship to the Wisconsin School of Music.

As a teen, Liberace soloed with the Chicago Symphony, as he originally wanted to be a classical concert pianist. He also hammered the ivories in silent-movie houses in the Milwaukee area. In 1939, he had a revelation after being asked to play a popular song, "Three Little Fishes," at the end of a classical concert in LaCrosse, Wisconsin. When the crowd went wild over the way he hammed up the song, he realized his destiny lay in entertaining the masses with humor and glitz.

By the early 1950s, Liberace was playing Carnegie Hall and Madison Square Garden. On May 26, 1954, he grossed a record $138,000 at the Garden. He was also a hit on TV with *The Liberace Show*. He received many awards—two Emmys, six gold albums, Entertainer of the Year, and two stars on the

Hollywood Walk of Fame (one for music and one for television). He was over-the-top, and people loved him for it.

The Gatherer of Glitz

Liberace began wearing flashy clothing so he could easily be seen in huge auditoriums. He soon discovered that the glitzier he became, the more audiences loved him. His wardrobe progressed from a simple gold lamé jacket to such unparalleled items as a blue fox cape that cost $300,000 and trailed 16 feet behind him, a sequined red-white-and-blue drum major suit that substituted hot pants for trousers, a sparkly silver cape garnished with mounds of pink feathers, and a black mink cape lined with rhinestones. One of his most outrageous getups was a King Neptune costume that weighed 200 pounds.

Liberace loved to surround himself with luxurious symbols of his music. The best-known example was his piano-shaped pool. He loaded his house with diamond- and crystal-studded candelabras and other objects—lamps, planters, bookends—fashioned in the shape of a baby grand. Today, much of his fabulous collection can be seen at the Liberace Museum in Las Vegas. The massive stash includes 18 pianos, such as the famed concert grand completely surfaced with tiny squares of mirror, and a Baldwin glittering with rhinestones.

Liberace's legendary wardrobe is there, too, along with his famous jewelry. He often wore five or six huge rings on each hand while performing, such as the behemoth adornment shaped like a candelabra, with diamond flames dancing over platinum candlesticks. Many of his jewelry pieces were shaped like pianos, including his wristwatch, which was studded with diamonds, rubies, sapphires, and emeralds.

Even his cars were decorated: He had a Roadster coated in Austrian rhinestones and a Rolls-Royce covered in mirror tiles.

The Liberace Museum also includes a re-created version of Liberace's lavish bedroom from his Palm Springs home. It features examples of his collection of exclusive Czech Moser crystal and a desk once owned by Russian Czar Nicholas II.

Nunsense?

Despite his great wealth (*The Guinness Book of World Records* once listed him as the highest-paid musician and pianist), Liberace was often prone to illness. In November 1963, he was near death from kidney failure caused by breathing toxic fumes from his costumes. He was calling relatives and friends to his hospital bed so he could say goodbye and give away his earthly goods, when he was suddenly and inexplicably cured. His explanation for the miracle was that a mysterious white-robed nun had come into his room and told him to pray to St. Anthony, patron saint of missing things and lost persons, then she touched his arm and left. Liberace never discovered who the nun was or where she came from, but he did recover.

Although raised Catholic, Liberace was very superstitious and was a great believer in numerology and fate. He insisted that his success was due to his favorite book, *The Magic of Believing*.

He Who Plays in Vegas, Stays in Vegas

Liberace eventually found a perfect venue for his talents in Las Vegas, where he bought a supper club just off the Strip called Carluccio's Tivoli Gardens. With its piano-shaped bar and lavish decor, it was pure Liberace.

After Liberace's death from complications of AIDS on February 4, 1987, at least two psychics claimed that his spirit remained at the restaurant. Staff reported floating capes, doors mysteriously opening and closing, and unexplained electrical disturbances. A magazine reporter, who accompanied investigators on a ghost hunt at Carluccio's almost two decades after "Mr. Showmanship's" death, wrote in a February 2005 article that the pair snapped a photo of a restaurant employee that revealed a ghostly form standing next to her. If ever there was a chance for one last photo op, Liberace would certainly find it very hard to resist showing his big smile for the camera.

Chapter 13

Love and Romance

Love Can Make You Crazy

Joan Crawford once said, "Love is a fire. But whether it is going to warm your heart or burn down your house, you can never tell." Oh, how right she was.

✳   ✳   ✳   ✳

L OVE: THE SWEETEST and sourest of the four-letter words. Sweet murmurs and soaring emotions can easily give way to angry shouts and irrepressible rage. And in some cases, burning houses, stabbings, and gunshot wounds also result. The violent outcomes of sexual jealousy are so common that they're an age-old and worldwide phenomenon. You don't have to read very far into the literature from any country from any time period, and the motivations behind the characters' violent and self-destructive acts will often boil down to a single factor: love gone bad.

A complete listing of love-motivated crimes would take longer to write than all the world's romantic sonnets combined. But here's a brief rundown of some of the more famous and bizarre cases of love's sociopathic side.

Normal Folks Made Famous

✳ Joey Buttafuoco was once an unknown Long Island auto repair shop owner with a knack for robbing the cradle. He began an affair with 16-year-old Amy Fisher, who tried to convince him to leave his wife. Apparently Fisher, who was given the nickname "Long Island Lolita" in the press, was displeased with his refusal to do so, because on May 19, 1992, she rang the doorbell of the Buttafuocos' home and shot Joey's wife Mary Jo point-blank in the head. Mrs. Buttafuoco miraculously survived the assault and went on to identify Fisher as her attacker. Joey Buttafuoco served four months in prison for statutory rape, while Fisher served seven years for aggravated assault. Both Fisher and Joey Buttafuoco seem to have recovered from the unfortunate event. Buttafuoco travels the talk show circuit, and Fisher wrote a book about her teenaged transgressions entitled *If I Knew Then*. They certainly know how to capitalize on a strange situation.

* During Thanksgiving weekend in 2002, failed real estate agent Richard McFarland of San Antonio, Texas, committed an elaborate, though badly planned, murder. His wife, Susan McFarland, intended to file for divorce. Richard, who had started shadowing her and even spying on her computer use, convinced himself that Susan was having an affair. He stole a Chevrolet Suburban, beat his wife to death, drove her in the stolen car to an abandoned farmhouse, and burned her remains. He was caught soon after and pled guilty to murder, receiving a 40-year prison sentence.

* Carolyn Warmus was a New York City elementary school teacher having an affair with her married colleague, Paul Solomon. On an ill-fated night in January 1989, Paul found his wife, Betty Jeanne Solomon, dead with nine bullets in her back and legs. It was later discovered that immediately after brutally murdering Betty Jeanne, Warmus met Paul for drinks and sex. While it appears that love drove Warmus to insanity, some claim that she was insane from the get-go—

several ex-boyfriends have come forward with disturbing tales of obsession, stalking, and restraining orders.

✳ The media developed a prolonged fascination with the exploits of NASA astronaut Lisa Marie Nowak, and with good cause. In February 2007, Nowak embarked on a 900-mile drive from Houston to Orlando National Airport. Her apparent plan was to harm Colleen Shipman, who was involved with Nowak's ex-lover, navy commander William Oefelein. It was alleged that Nowak wore diapers during the drive from Houston so that she wouldn't have to stop to use the bathroom, although Nowak denied this. Even stranger is what police found in Nowak's car: latex gloves, a black wig, a BB pistol with ammunition, rubber tubing, plastic garbage bags, a two-pound drilling hammer, pepper spray, and four brown paper towels containing 69 orange pills. One shudders at the possible uses of this grab bag of fun, but luckily Nowak's assault ultimately proved mostly harmless. She followed Shipman to her car and proceeded to tap on the window. When Shipman rolled the window down slightly, she received a dousing of pepper spray. She quickly drove off and contacted the police. Nowak later pled guilty to auto theft and misdemeanor battery in a plea deal with prosecutors. Nowak had previously been known as a smart, successful, and unusually caring woman. Her lawyers initially tried to plead insanity, which, oddly enough, is the only part of this saga that makes sense.

Famous Folks Made Infamous

✳ French actor Marie Trintignant experienced a horrible bout of jealousy-propelled carnage from her rock-star boyfriend, Bertrand Cantat, during the summer of 2003. In what he described as a fit of jealousy that put him out of his mind, Cantat beat Trintignant over the head while she was in Lithuania filming a movie. He'd convinced himself that Trintignant was currently embroiled in an affair with her ex-husband, or possibly in multiple affairs with multiple ex-boyfriends; she had four sons by four different men with whom she kept in contact. He was also jealous of her fictional affairs, having demanded that she stop acting in on-screen love scenes. By August 1, she was dead; pathologists liken the blows on her head to the impact of being thrown against a wall at 125 miles per hour. Cantat was charged with manslaughter and sentenced to eight years in prison. In October 2007, he was released on parole after serving four years. His early release set off an international debate about whether perpetrators of crimes of passion should be given more leniency than their more "cold and calculating" counterparts.

✳ When almost any American who owned a TV in the mid-1990s thinks of spousal murder, ex-football star O. J. Simpson immediately comes to mind. Sure, he was found not guilty of the crime. But if he had done it (which many people still believe he did, which the jury of the civil trial following the criminal case deemed so, and about which Simpson himself was prepared to speculate in a book that was ultimately canceled), the double homicide of ex-wife Nicole Brown Simpson and her friend Ronald Goldman would certainly be a prime example of romance leading to dark exploits down the road.

"Everything we do in life is based on fear, especially love."

—MEL BROOKS

"If you want to read about love and marriage, you've got to buy two separate books."

—ALAN KING

"Love is the answer, but while you are waiting for the answer, sex raises some pretty good questions."

—WOODY ALLEN

I Now Pronounce You Man and Dog

This Indian farmer took an odd path to release a curse.

✳ ✳ ✳ ✳

IN NOVEMBER 2007, a 33-year-old Indian farm laborer named P. Selvakumar married a four-year-old female dog named Selvi. There's no word as to where the couple registered.

The family of the groom had selected Selvi from an array of strays, then bathed the bride-to-be and dressed her in an orange sari and garland of flowers. In the style of a traditional Hindu marriage ceremony, the betrothed strolled at the head of a celebratory procession toward the Hindu temple in Manamadurai, a town in the Sivaganga District. There, Selvakumar formalized the marriage by tying the *mangal sutra*, or sacred string, around Selvi's furry neck.

Nearly 200 guests attended the reception—enough of a crowd to spook the bride into running. Selvi was later captured and placated with a bun and some milk. After all, arranged marriages can be difficult, and the ways of the heart are mysterious.

Star-Crossed

Selvakumar actually wed Selvi on the advice of his astrologer in an attempt to rid himself of a curse that had followed him for more than a decade and a half, ever since he had stoned two mating dogs to death and hung their bodies from a tree. The contrite farmer claimed that ever since the incident he suffered from hearing loss in one ear, paralysis of his legs and hands, and speech impairment. Medical doctors were unable to help him.

Such unions are not uncommon in the more rural areas of India, particularly to banish bad luck or evil spirits. After the curse is lifted, Selvakumar will be free to marry a human bride without filing for divorce or calling Animal Control.

Love Triangle, Celebrity Style

Director, actor, and screenwriter Woody Allen is famous for making movies that chronicle the bizarre trials and tribulations of his neurotic protagonists. But his public personal saga in the early '90s tops even the most convoluted of Allen's screenplays.

✳ ✳ ✳ ✳

WOODY ALLEN BUILT a career as a respected filmmaker with such movies as *Bananas, Sleeper, Manhattan,* and the Oscar-winning *Annie Hall.* His films were recognizably his own, and announcements of new projects were greeted with anticipation among critics and the public.

Setting the Stage

In 1980, Allen began a relationship with actor Mia Farrow, best known for her roles in the movie *Rosemary's Baby* and the TV series *Peyton Place.* Farrow already had six children, both adopted and biological, from her previous marriage to pianist Andre Previn. In 1987, Allen and Farrow had a son of their own, Satchel O'Sullivan Farrow (who later changed his name to Ronan Seamus Farrow). While she was with Allen, Mia also adopted a boy (Moses) and a girl (Dylan). Allen and Farrow never wed, but in 1991 Allen also adopted Dylan and Moses.

The Rising Action

Allen and Farrow spent 12 years leading what looked to be an idyllic, if somewhat peculiar, existence. The two never lived together, staying on opposite sides of New York City's Central Park. Farrow and her kids would trudge across the park with sleeping bags, to spend the night on Allen's side of the green.

This all ended in 1992, when Farrow discovered nude photographs Allen had taken of her adopted daughter, Soon-Yi Previn. It turned out Allen had been sleeping with Soon-Yi at least since her first year of college. Soon-Yi was 21 at the time of her mother's discovery, and Allen was 57.

Recognizing that Farrow was infuriated by this turn of affairs, Allen sued her for custody of their three children—Satchel, Moses, and Dylan. Farrow responded by accusing Allen of sexually abusing Dylan, who was seven years old at the time.

The press had a field day. The ensuing court-room drama was covered daily in news-papers in the United States and around the world. And the two stars of this media production didn't shy away from reporters. Allen was eager to emphatically deny the accusation of molestation, and he also revealed that he didn't regret his affair with Soon-Yi. When the story of the affair first broke, Allen responded, "It's real and happily all true."

Farrow, meanwhile, was more than open to depicting Allen as a small, sniveling, neurotic, and deeply creepy monster. Regarding Allen's relationship with their daughter Dylan, Farrow testified, "He would creep up in the morning and lay beside her bed and wait for her to wake up . . . I was uncomfortable all along."

Resolution—Sort Of

In the end, Farrow was granted full custody of the three chil-dren. The judge wrote a 33-page decision in which he described Allen as a "self-absorbed, untrustworthy and insensitive" father. He chastised Allen for not knowing the names of his son's teachers or even which children shared which bedrooms in Farrow's apartment. A state-appointed group of specialists con-cluded that Allen was not guilty of molesting Dylan, although the judge deemed the report "sanitized and . . . less credible."

Allen was disappointed to lose custody of his children, but he was happy to continue his relationship with their adoptive half-sister. After the suit, Soon-Yi and Allen were spotted at trendy restaurants across Manhattan. They married in 1997 and have adopted two children of their own. Farrow remains estranged from Soon-Yi but is busy with her current activities.

Love Bytes: The Origins of Computer Dating

What do four randy college students, a quiz show, and a Supreme Court nominee have in common? Computer dating!

✳   ✳   ✳   ✳

IN 1965, FRUSTRATED with the only easy means of meeting women—blind dates and mixers—Harvard undergrads Jeff Tarr, Vaughan Morrill, David Crump, and Cornell student Douglas Ginsburg came up with a plan to use computers to arrange dates between Ivy League students. This was decades before the Internet, so Tarr and Vaughan hatched a plan to complete compatibility questionnaires and feed them into a computer, which would then provide the names and telephone numbers of well-matched couples.

Fill in the Blanks

After conferring with business executives, lawyers, and computer scientists, Tarr was assured that his plan could actually work. The four matchmakers began writing a questionnaire that would be available for $3 each. Here's a sample question:

1. Your roommate gets you a blind date for the big dance. Good-looking, your roommate says. When you meet your date, you are sure it's your roommate who is blind—your date is friendly, but embarrassingly unattractive. You:

(a) Suggest going to a movie instead.

(b) Monopolize your roommate's date, leaving your roommate with only one noble alternative.

(c) Dance with your date, smiling weakly, but end the evening as early as possible.

(d) Act very friendly the whole time and run the risk of getting trapped into a second date.

National Attention

Several months later, the group realized that they had under-estimated the number of questionnaires it would take to keep the venture afloat and began looking for outside financing. Luckily, the popular TV quiz show *To Tell the Truth* and a 19-year-old coed from UCLA happened to save the day.

Producers from the quiz show contacted Morrill and asked him to appear on the air as one of their "mystery personalities." The spot netted the matchmakers free national publicity. At the same time, the guys invited Vicki Albright, Harvard law school's "Woman of the Year" and recent cover subject in *Newsweek*, to participate in their dating service and ostensibly to find her the ideal date. The results named a lucky bachelor. The Associated Press picked up news of the computer match; the story was printed in newspapers from coast to coast.

Speed Bumps

Even with early success, financing continued to plague the group. Finally, Tarr talked a New York-based data processing firm into keeping the business going by forming a new company called Compatibility Research. But computer time was expensive in the 1960s—even with outside resources. Tarr paid a fellow classmate $100 to write a computer program that would read the completed questionnaires, transfer the answers to punch cards, and set up the compatible matches. Since the only affordable computer time was between 2:00 A.M. and 4:00 P.M. on Sundays, it took nearly six weeks to produce a single list of compatible partners.

Despite these problems, computer dating continued to grow. By 1968, Operation Match had become a cultural phenomenon with over a million respondents, some of whom even went on to marry their computer-made match. Today, computer dating has become a multimillion-dollar industry, fueled largely by the popularity of the Internet. Match.com, eHarmony.com, and dozens of other services compete for the attention of singles.

A Chronicle of Kissing

Smooching, necking, spit-swapping, lip-locking—whatever you call it, kissing can be one of life's more pleasurable experiences. We've uncovered the history and naughty little secrets of the kiss.

✳ ✳ ✳ ✳

The First Kiss

ALTHOUGH HUMAN NATURE suggests that the first kiss would have been shared much earlier, anthropologists have traced the first recorded kiss to India in approximately 1500 B.C. Early Vedic documents report people "sniffing" with their mouths and describe how lovers join "mouth to mouth."

"With This Kiss, I Thee Wed"

The tradition that inspired the now-familiar phrase "You may kiss the bride" probably originated in ancient Rome. To seal their marriage contract, couples kissed in front of a large group of people. The Romans had three different categories of kisses: *osculum*, a kiss on the cheek; *basium*, a kiss on the lips; and *savolium*, a deep kiss.

The Holy Kiss

In the early Christian church, congregants would greet one another with an *osculum pacis*, or holy kiss. This greeting was believed to transfer spirits between the kissers. In the 13th century, the Catholic Church provided something called a "pax board," which the congregation could kiss instead of kissing each other. Until the 16th century, the holy kiss was part of the Catholic mass, though kissing the Pope's ring is something that's still practiced.

Butterfly Kiss

The strange but sweet butterfly kiss is named for its similarity to a feeling of butterfly's fluttering wings. Simply put your eye a whisper away from your partner's eye or cheek, and bat your lashes repeatedly.

Performance High

The adrenaline rush you get when you jump out of a plane or run a marathon is essentially the same rush you get from kissing. The neurotransmitters that fire when you're kissing cause the heart to beat faster and the breath to become deeper.

Kissing Competitions

Sideshows at the Olympic games of ancient Greece included kissing competitions. How one would have judged such a thing is hard to know, but similar competitions still crop up from time to time, usually for fund-raising purposes or simply for spectacle's sake.

Germ Theory

The human mouth is coated with mucus that is chock-full of microscopic bacteria. When you lock lips with someone, between 10 million and 1 billion bacterial colonies are exchanged. The good news: Saliva also contains antibacterial chemicals that neutralize the spit, preventing the transfer of harmful germs.

❋ The scientific name for kissing is *philematology*.

❋ More than 5,300 couples kissed for at least ten seconds in the Philippines on Valentine's Day in 2005.

❋ The first on-film kiss occurred between John C. Rice and May Irwin in the movie *The Kiss* (1896).

❋ In the 1927 movie *Don Juan,* Estelle Taylor and Mary Astor received a total of 127 kisses from John Barrymore.

❋ People spend an average of two weeks of their lives kissing.

❋ In Hartford, Connecticut, it's a crime for a man to kiss his wife on Sunday; in Indiana, a man with a moustache is forbidden to "habitually kiss human beings"; and in Cedar Rapids, Iowa, it's illegal to kiss a stranger.

Sit, Honey! How to Train Your Sweetheart

Men are often called dogs when it comes to their dating habits. So what if you could "train" your significant other the same way you train your canine? Turns out, it's not as far-fetched as it sounds.

✳ ✳ ✳ ✳

Behavioral Basics

I T'S A FACT: The science of psychology is the basis of most animal training. It's no secret that humans are animals, and, sure enough, the same kinds of techniques that work on pets can be used on people.

Behavioral psychology is the study of observable actions and responses. Most theories assume animals are born as "blank slates"; they are later shaped by their interactions with the environment. In its most basic form, this means we tend to repeat actions with positive consequences and avoid actions with negative consequences.

Seems simple enough, right? This sort of thinking is nothing new: For years, spouses have taken this approach to change their loved ones' behavior. Sandra Dee takes this approach with her husband, played by Bobby Darin, in the 1963 movie *If a Man Answers*. In it, her mother hands her a dog training manual and advises that what will work for the pooch will work for the hubby. Now, let's break down the core principles and see how they can work for you.

Understanding Reinforcement

The foundation of most animal training starts with the idea of reinforcement—something that increases a desired behavior. It could be positive: the addition of something to the environment, such as food or a belly rub. It could also be negative: the removal of something desirable from the environment, or a loud noise or disapproving look. Either can work, as long as the animal learns to associate the reinforcement with the behavior you're trying to teach. Now, let's put it into action.

Learning a Behavior: The Lazy Dog

In our first example, let's say we have a dog that won't go into its doghouse. Our initial thought might be to put a treat in the doghouse doorway to coax it inside. This, however, isn't likely to work; the dog will just grab the treat and dart away. Why? Because it's bribery, not reinforcement. Remember, reinforcement has to be linked with a specific behavior.

The trainer's answer is to ignore the dog while it's avoiding the house, and then reinforce it with the treat when it finally ventures inside on its own. The pup now knows a treat appeared because of what it did, and the behavior has been learned.

Learning a Behavior: The Lazy Boyfriend

Put this into a relationship setting: Let's say you want your boyfriend to dress up more often. Nagging him about it isn't likely to work in the long-term. The trick, then, is to avoid complimenting him or giving him extra attention on the nights he dresses like a slob. Then, on a night when he dresses nicely, you lay on the praise. Tell him with enthusiasm how great he looks, and—if you want to really reinforce it—give him some kind of special reward as soon as you get home. We'll leave it up to you to decide what the reward should be.

Maintaining a Behavior: The Dancing Dolphin

All right, the behavior's been learned—now it's time to maintain it. You may think the best thing would be to present a reward every time you see the behavior, but animal trainers have learned otherwise. They've found the more effective technique is what's called a variable schedule of reinforcement.

Think about it: A dolphin trainer won't usually give the animal a treat after every trick. Instead, the trainer will randomly reinforce the good behavior, giving the dolphin a treat on, say, the first, third, and sixth trick. That way the dolphin is more likely to keep working hard for the reward, since it doesn't know when it'll come, as opposed to thinking it can get lazy and do the absolute minimum to get the treat that comes every time.

Maintaining a Behavior: The Dancing Husband

It's no surprise that many men don't favor the dance floor. But once you've helped your husband learn the behavior (using the technique you learned above), you can keep him boogying by using the same kind of variable reinforcement used with the dolphin. In a similar scenario, after the second night of dancing, go easy on the compliments and rewards. Like the dolphin, if you lay it on thick every time, your hubby is going to realize he doesn't have to work hard to get his reinforcement. But if on, say, the third, fifth, and eighth nights, you deliver the full reward again, you'll enjoy continued success.

Stopping a Behavior: The Barking Dog

A barking dog is really annoying. But by using negative reinforcement, a trainer can teach it to keep quiet. Animals don't like having bright lights shone in their faces, so a trainer might use that as the unwanted addition to the environment. Every time the dog barks, he or she shines a bright light at it. As soon as the barking stops, the light goes off. Give it enough time, and the dog will learn what's happening and modify its behavior accordingly.

Stopping a Behavior: The Barking Boyfriend

Tired of your mate's horrible mood when he comes home from work? Try the same concept, but with more subtle tactics. When he starts getting cross, leave the room or stop responding to his mood. When he takes on a more pleasant tone, return to normal. He'll subconsciously make the connection.

That's just the start of how you can put animal training techniques to use in your personal life. Take the time to understand motivation and you can, within reason, have a lot more pull over people than you realize. Remember, it's all about reinforcement, no matter how small the gesture. Speaking of which, you looked really intelligent buying this book. Everyone noticed.

Beauty Is Pain

For thousands of years, human beings (especially women) have tried to change or improve their appearance by applying cosmetics—sometimes with deadly results.

✳ ✳ ✳ ✳

Back Then

IN THE OLD world, limited scientific knowledge prevented awareness that toxic and lethal chemicals were being coated on people's skin in the name of good looks. In fact, in the second millennium B.C., Old Kingdom Egyptians took makeup so seriously that they invented the science of chemistry to produce it. Chemists at France's Louvre Museum and a leading cosmetics manufacturer recently analyzed ancient stores of kohl, or mesdemet, a darkening agent (black, or less commonly, green) that Egyptians applied to both upper and lower eyelids to protect vision from the glaring sun. (Not incidentally, kohl also created a sexy, "smoky" eye.) The scientists found that kohl contained a dark sulfide of lead extracted from a mine near the Red Sea, synthetic compounds, and 7 to 10 percent animal fat to make the mixture creamy—the same percentage manufacturers use today, though modern cosmetics usually contain vegetable fat.

Cleopatra and her contemporaries also wore "lipstick" made of carmine, obtained from crushed beetles, in a base made from ant's eggs. Ancient Egyptians and Romans used other cosmetics containing mercury and white lead. Tattoos? Those are nothing new to either the Egyptians or the Indians. For centuries, they have used the reddish vegetable dye henna to create temporary tattoo patterns on the skin and to color hair, as well. Like the Egyptians, Hindu culture also used kohl as eye makeup.

Pale Beauty

Women in Roman Britain used a tin-oxide cream to whiten their faces. In 1558, Queen Elizabeth I started a fad by doing the same with egg whites, vinegar, and white powdered lead, a deadly mixture that caused poisoning and, ironically, scarring. By the 1700s, black "beauty spot" patches became necessary accessories to cover the scars.

Throughout Europe beginning in the Middle Ages and lasting up to the Industrial Revolution, having darker skin was considered a no-no; light skin meant luxury because you could stay inside. Upper-class people lightened their skin using white lead that often contained arsenic. In the 1800s, face-whitening was still a common practice. A mix of carbonate, hydroxide, and lead oxide was the norm. Used often, this could cause muscle paralysis or death.

And Now?

Of course, in modern times, we've learned our lesson. Or have we? In today's nail polishes, the reproductive toxin dibutyl phthalate, known as DBP, is a common ingredient. Other ingredients in nail polishes include formaldehyde (a carcinogen) and toluene, which has been linked to birth defects.

In 1992, an epidemic of papular and follicular rashes broke out in Switzerland, caused by vitamin E linoleate in a new line of cosmetics. In 2000, an outbreak of skin boils infected hundreds of pedicure customers in a California salon. Most recently, phthalates have hit the radar. Phthalates are a class of chemicals added to many consumer products, notably cosmetics and scented substances such as perfumes, soaps, and lotions. Some research shows that phthalates have the unfortunate distinction of causing cancer, birth defects, and sexual dysfunction.

In autumn 2007, runway shows featured a revival of the "Cleopatra" eye made famous by Elizabeth Taylor in the 1963 biopic. At the same time, the covers of various fashion magazines featured pale skin and deeply reddened lips—none of which, fortunately, are necessarily "to die for" anymore.

Reno: Divorcetown, USA

*Regret that wedding? If so, you might
consider a visit to Reno, Nevada.*

✳ ✳ ✳ ✳

RENO HAS BEEN known as the place to get a "quickie divorce"
for more than a century. In the 1800s, many people sought
riches in the mining, agricultural, and fur-trapping industries
that spread across Nevada and California. What better place to
put a town than in the path of those fortune seekers? By 1868,
Reno had become an important freight and passenger center.
Soon, there were plenty of restaurants, hotels, and lively entertainment venues. Good times for all? Well, not quite.

Making the Best of an Iffy Economy

Mining and agriculture were feast-or-famine industries. To off-
set those low points, Reno decided to host legal brothels. The
city also became the place to go for illegal gambling and easy
divorces. In the 1860s, Reno law called for divorce seekers to
reside in the town for six months and, at one point, a full year.
This was still much less time than required elsewhere.

"Divorce ranches" appeared overnight. These extended-stay
motels gave couples a temporary place to live in order to fulfill
the residency requirements. People flocked to Reno for release
from their marital bondage. Enter the nickname "Sin City."

Time Is Money

When the Great Depression hit, times got hard. Remembering
the cash generated from couples seeking divorces—attorney
fees, hotel stays, gambling houses, restaurants, and shopping—
Reno officials decided to reduce residency requirements to a
mere six weeks. As a result, more than 30,000 divorces were
granted in the county courthouse between 1929 and 1939. By
1940, 4.9 percent of all U.S. divorces were filed in Nevada. To
this day, Reno maintains a six-week residency requirement.

Love on the Set:
The Bergman-Rossellini Scandal

It didn't take much to rock the staid conventions of society shortly after the end of World War II. A movie director and his leading lady found that out the hard way.

✳   ✳   ✳   ✳

IT STARTED WITH a fan letter sent in 1949. "I saw your films . . . and enjoyed them very much," the letter began. It was addressed to Italian film director Roberto Rossellini and written by none other than actress Ingrid Bergman, who wrote it after seeing Rossellini's movie *Open City*. Bergman's letter also suggested that he direct her in a film. Their resulting collaboration was 1950's *Stromboli*. That movie, however, was eclipsed by the controversy that swirled around the couple when it became known that the married Bergman was having a baby by Rossellini, who was also married. The ensuing scandal engulfed Bergman in a scarlet torrent of vitriolic hatred.

A Hollywood Success Story

Since taking America by storm in 1939's *Intermezzo*, the talented Swedish-born Bergman had costarred with Humphrey Bogart in *Casablanca*, been menaced by Charles Boyer in *Gaslight* (her first Oscar-winning role), and been romanced on-screen by Cary Grant, Gary Cooper, and Gregory Peck. Audiences loved her in *The Bells of St. Mary's*. In fact, Bergman was Hollywood's top box-office female draw three years in a row. To the public, the beautiful actress had it all: a fabulous career, an adoring husband, and a devoted daughter. But privately, Bergman's marriage was rocky, and she was looking for new acting challenges after the failure of her film, *Joan of Arc*. The idea of working with Rossellini—the director being hailed for his mastery of Italian neorealist cinema—was appealing. Bergman later admitted, "I think that deep down I was in love with Roberto from the moment I saw *Open City*."

On Location

Stromboli was filmed on location in Italy, and rumors of an affair between Bergman and Rossellini soon reached America. Bergman received a letter from Joseph Breen, head of America's stentorian Production Code office—which enforced morality in motion pictures—asking her to deny rumors of the affair. Instead, on December 13, 1949, Bergman admitted she was carrying Rossellini's child. A flurry of negative press followed.

Bergman was reproached by Roman Catholic priests and received thousands of letters denouncing her—she was warned not to return to America. On February 2, 1950, Bergman and Rossellini's son, Robertino, or Robin, was born. *Stromboli* was released in the United States to bad reviews and scant business.

The Storm Grows

The scandal reached critical mass on March 14, when Senator Edwin C. Johnson railed against Bergman on the Senate floor. Johnson proposed a bill that would protect America from the licentious scourge that film stars of questionable "moral turpitude" such as Bergman threatened. He suggested future misconduct could be avoided if actors were licensed, with the license being revoked for bad behavior. This idea was met with derision, but Bergman's career in Hollywood was all but dead.

After divorcing their spouses, Bergman and Rossellini wed in Mexico on May 24, 1950. The couple continued to make films together in Italy and had twin girls Isabella (who went on to her own film stardom) and Isotta Ingrid in 1952. By the time Bergman was hired to star in *Anastasia* in 1956, America was ready to forgive her, and the actress was rewarded with both the New York Film Critics Award and her second Oscar. By that point, her marriage to Rossellini was nearing an end.

Bergman would go on to another marriage and further acclaim in her career, but she was always quick to point to the importance of her relationship with Rossellini, and the two remained devoted. Bergman died in 1982 of breast cancer.

Don't Bother Saving the Date!

A lot of outrageous Hollywood couples have gotten hitched over the years, but Jim Nabors and Rock Hudson? That rumor was rampant in the 1970s, and Hudson went to his grave trying to live it down.

✳ ✳ ✳ ✳

THE STORY APPARENTLY began as a joke that quickly became an urban myth. According to Rock Hudson, the instigators were a gay couple living in California who often promoted their annual parties with wacky invitations. One year the notice read: "You are cordially invited to the wedding reception of Rock Hudson and Jim Nabors." A lot of people took it seriously.

The obviously whimsical invitation was distributed all over the country and eventually found its way into a movie magazine. Other publications picked up on it, and off it went.

The joke took a jarring toll on Hudson and Nabors, who were friends but nothing more. In fact, once the rumor started to spread, the men realized they could never again be seen in public together without giving it legitimacy.

Hudson was especially hard-hit. He had always made an effort to keep his true sexual preference a secret, lest it negatively affect his career. In fact, at the time the rumor surfaced, Hudson was just beginning a long and successful stint on the television show *McMillan & Wife* (with Susan Saint James), a gig that depended on his "wholesome" reputation. It wasn't until he was diagnosed with AIDS that Hudson went public with his homosexuality.

Nabors, too, had a lot to lose. He had been horribly typecast because of his role as Gomer Pyle on *The Andy Griffith Show* and *Gomer Pyle, USMC*, and was struggling to reinvent himself. Scandalous rumors of an alleged marriage to a man were the last things he needed.

Spoken For: Commitment Customs

There are plenty of "engaging" practices that publicly express a couple's commitment without taking it all the way to the altar.

❋　❋　❋　❋

Rings...

RINGS ARE A time-honored symbol of love and commitment. However, different rings signify different things. Back in the day, high-schooler Biff would announce his intention to enter into an exclusive relationship with Susie by giving her his senior class ring. Susie would display this token by wearing it on a chain around her neck or lovingly wrapping it with yarn to secure it on her slender finger. Without the benefit of this "upper classman" advantage, younger Romeos resorted to cigar bands and even adhesive bandages to express their ardor.

A promise ring was the next stop on the love train. More feminine and mature than a class ring—not to mention custom-fit—a promise ring held the pledge of a future engagement and signified the first tentative step toward the aisle.

...and Things

Letter sweaters, jackets, and ID bracelets also symbolize a "going steady" status. Some college men present their sweethearts with lavalieres, necklaces with their fraternity letters, to signify their relationship. But the ultimate Greek act of commitment occurs when a frat boy "pins" his intended life partner.

The Catholic Church took a dim view of the monogamous trend that began among youth in the 1950s. In 1957, *TIME* magazine reported on a Catholic high school in Connecticut that expelled four students for going steady. An article in a Paulist Fathers publication warned it was "impossible" for a young boy and girl in an exclusive relationship to be alone together "without serious sin." (Amen.)

Gestures of Love

Exchanging trinkets is not the only way to express commitment. Some couples feel the need to memorialize their undying affection for each other by publicly linking their names for all to see. Whether scrawling their names on trees, water towers, bathroom stalls, or their own skins via tattooing, the whole world is a canvas for young lovers.

In Rome, the Eternal City, couples often express their commitment in a "novel" way. In life-imitates-art fashion, recently young lovers have been mimicking a scene from *I Want You*, a best-selling-book-turned-movie in which the protagonist padlocks a chain around a lamppost on a bridge; he then tosses the key into the Tiber river to signify his everlasting love. Since then, so many love locks have been wrapped around lampposts over Rome's Ponte Milvio bridge that the authorities have had to install special steel posts to preserve the light posts.

Commitment Ceremonies

Ceremonies are sometimes used to signal commitment without entering into a contract. Handfasting, an ancient Celtic ritual where the couples' wrists were symbolically tied together, was practiced by the upper class as an engagement of sorts, to signify a promise of marriage before dowry details were worked out. For the peasant class, for whom dowries often weren't an issue, handfasting was kind of a trial marriage signifying that the couple would stay together for a predetermined length of time, generally a year, and then reevaluate their relationship. The phrase "tying the knot" reportedly came from handfasting.

"Jumping the broom," in which couples literally jump over a broom, is another non-wedding commitment ceremony, although today many African weddings incorporate this practice into the traditional rites. The origins of this ceremony are thought to have begun during America's slavery era. Since slaves were not allowed to marry, the broom-jumping ritual was a way for the couple to publicly vow their fidelity.

Love in the Time of Art: The Complex Affair of Frida Kahlo and Diego Rivera

Even a typical, run-of-the-mill love affair is prone to ups and downs. But the relationship between artists Frida Kahlo and Diego Rivera gives the typical love story a run for its money. Jealousy, disloyalty, and short tempers along with a hefty dose of adultery, bisexuality, physical disability, artistic genius, and fame all play a part in one of the most fascinating love stories of modern times.

✳ ✳ ✳ ✳

Meet the Girl

FRIDA KAHLO WAS born in 1907 in Coyoacan, Mexico, a small town near Mexico City. Kahlo contracted polio at age six; as a result, her right leg and foot were thin and stunted, a deformity that embarrassed her through childhood. At age 15, Kahlo enrolled in the National Preparatory School in Mexico City, where she became known for her personality and academic ability. In 1925, Kahlo was on the brink of graduating when she was seriously injured in a bus accident. She was bedridden for several months and sustained injuries to her back, pelvic bone, and spinal column that would affect her for the rest of her life.

But great pain can bring great fortune, as it was during this time that Kahlo began to paint. Although she had received little formal training in painting, Kahlo proved to have natural skill. She continued as an artist even after physically recovering from the accident.

Meet the Boy

Diego Rivera was born in 1886 in the small town of Guanajuato, Mexico. He began his formal artistic training at age 10, and by 20 he was a successful artist. During his 20s, he traveled internationally. He became known as a huge (six feet tall, 300 pounds), outspoken, womanizing, politically liberal, and morally questionable example of a man.

Rivera was also known for political influence in his art. In the early 1920s, the liberal Mexican government decided to reclaim the indigenous heritage of pre-Columbian Mexico. The minister of education appointed artists to adorn public buildings with murals depicting the lives of contemporary Amerindians and telling ancient stories of the past. In 1921, Rivera began the first of his murals, in the auditorium at the National Preparatory School in Mexico City.

Girl Meets Boy

Even the most ardent cynics can't deny that the meeting of Kahlo and Rivera was hopelessly romantic. Kahlo was a student at the National Preparatory School when Rivera painted his mural. She admired Rivera because he continued to paint his controversial mural despite the right-wing students who rioted against him. She hid in the back of the auditorium to watch him paint.

Years later, Kahlo encountered Rivera at a party held by a mutual friend. At one point during the party, the boisterous Rivera took out a pistol and shot the phonograph. Kahlo was intrigued by the artist.

Soon after, Kahlo learned that Rivera was creating a new mural at the Ministry of Education in Mexico City. She gathered up some of her own paintings, boarded a bus, and walked right up to Rivera while he was painting. She showed him her work, and asked what he thought. He told her that she had talent, and thus bloomed the beginning of their relationship.

They were married in 1929; Kahlo was 22 and Rivera, 42.

Boy Hurts Girl, Girl Hurts Boy

It's no surprise that this relationship was headed for stormy waters. In 1930, Rivera was commissioned to paint in San Francisco, and Kahlo came along for a sojourn in the States. During this period, she developed her own art but was known as Rivera's young wife. Kahlo believed in recapturing her indigenous heritage and dressed in bright colors, large jewelry, and flowing skirts. Rivera shared Kahlo's cultural views but nonetheless dressed in European suits.

This tension between the theory and practice of the couple's radical views was a recurring theme in their relationship. Kahlo once boasted, "I was a member of the Party before I met Diego and I think I am a better Communist than he is or ever will be." While they both denounced capitalism, Rivera admired the industrial progress of the West and hoped to reconcile it with Communism. This belief got him in trouble in 1933 when he included a depiction of Stalin in a mural he painted in New York City's Rockefeller Center. The mural was supposed to pay homage to the possibilities of industrial progress, and John D. Rockefeller himself insisted that Rivera remove Stalin. When Rivera refused, the mural was destroyed.

Girl Paints Her Reality

Kahlo, meanwhile, hated the United States and what she considered its advanced state of social decay. Her unhappiness inspired some of her best work. Her beautiful, dreamlike landscapes reflect a sense of personal anguish and divided identity. She also used imagery and symbolism to make political and sociocultural statements. Her works have been called surrealist, although Kahlo rejected this designation, explaining, "I never painted dreams . . . I painted my own reality."

After the Rockefeller debacle, Rivera and Kahlo moved back to Mexico. Rivera's repeated infidelities strained their relationship, but in 1934, Frida discovered that Rivera was having an affair with her younger sister. This ruptured their marriage, and things would never be the same—Kahlo initiated various love affairs with both men and women. Her most notorious lover was Leon Trotsky.

Kahlo and Rivera's relationship continued to deteriorate, and they divorced in 1939. Seemingly unable to be happy together or apart, they remarried in 1941.

Boy Loses Girl

Throughout the 1940s, Kahlo's career took off, while Rivera's stagnated. But this decade also marked a decline in her health. Kahlo underwent several operations on her back and leg, but each operation only did more damage. However, Kahlo's fierce spirit and inextinguishable love for Rivera never diminished. Less than two weeks before her death, the couple took part in a demonstration against the American intervention in Guatemala—despite protests from her doctors.

Kahlo died on July 13, 1954. Her body was taken to the foyer of the Palacio de Bellas Artes in Mexico City. Rivera sat by her side the whole night, refusing to believe that she was dead. For better or worse, Rivera had been an unending inspiration to Kahlo's art, and it seems that Kahlo was as integral to Rivera's spirit. Rivera's health steadily declined after his wife's death, and he passed away in 1957.

* Kahlo's last name is German and in fact, her father was born in Germany and immigrated to Mexico.

* Following his exile from the Soviet Union, Leon Trotsky lived with Kahlo and Rivera in Mexico City. He moved out of Kahlo's home shortly before he was assassinated in 1940.

* Rivera's full given name was Diego María de la Concepción Juan Nepomuceno Estanislao de la Rivera y Barrientos Acosta y Rodríguez.

* Kahlo and Rivera's relationship was portrayed in the 2002 movie *Frida*. Salma Hayek portrayed Kahlo and Alfred Molina played Rivera in the film.

Chapter 14

Pop Culture

Anarchy in the USA: The Birth of Punk

Punk rock exploded onto the international music scene in 1977 with a distinctively British bent— overshadowing the music's American origins.

✳ ✳ ✳ ✳

THEY WERE A British rock 'n' roll band that crashed through the United States, playing a brash, stripped-down, and rough-edged style of music. Their lyrics angrily denounced the Queen and British society and nihilistically declared that their generation had no future. Menacing, vulgar, and confrontational, they were the complete antithesis of The Beatles and they made The Rolling Stones look like choir boys.

They were the Sex Pistols—and with their seminal 1977 recording *Never Mind the Bollocks, Here's the Sex Pistols* and a short, chaotic, and highly publicized U.S. tour in January 1978, they introduced mainstream America to the furious, frenzied sound of punk rock.

"(I'm Not Your) Stepping Stone"

But the music the Sex Pistols were importing wasn't all that new, nor did it originate in Britain. Known for its bare-bones, primal musical form and antiestablishment lyrics, punk rock actually germinated in the United States.

Punk rock emerged in the early 1970s at a time when rock 'n' roll seemed to be veering a million miles from its simple original form and rebellious spirit. Progressive rock—popularized by groups such as Pink Floyd, Yes, and Genesis—featured long, opuslike compositions that were artistically complex and heavily layered. The mainstream rock churned out by performers ranging from the Eagles, Doobie Brothers, and James Taylor was safe and tame. These two genres dominated the American rock music scene at the time.

"Today Your Love, Tomorrow the World"

On the fringes, however, was a different sound created by a new generation of American bands who scolded contemporary rock as pompous, excessive, and lame. They were heavily influenced by garage rock—a raw and unpretentious musical style rooted in rock's original form. Garage rock had been around since the early '60s, and although it gained some prominence through bands such as The Kinks and The Who, it generally remained underground. Now, groups such as The Velvet Underground, MC5, the New York Dolls, and the Stooges (fronted by Iggy Pop) were stripping the music back to basics—and influencing others to do the same.

Among those feeding off the gritty new sound were two New York City musicians named Tom Verlaine and Richard Hell, who in 1973 formed the band Television. In March 1974, Television began playing a regular Sunday night gig at a seedy, hole-in-the-wall club on the edge of New York's East Village called CBGB.

Television quickly gained a loyal local following that gravitated to the band's thoroughly antiestablishment style and demeanor as much as to their music. Band members sported short cropped hair, T-shirts, tight jeans, leather jackets, and bondage gear—completely rejecting the hippie-influenced look of their rock contemporaries (Richard Hell later added a unique accessory to the look: the safety pin). They brandished an edgy, screw-the-world attitude that resonated with their audiences.

Throughout 1974, numerous bands followed in Television's footsteps at CBGB, including the Patti Smith Group, Blondie, and the Talking Heads. The Ramones also played at CBGB, and their short, three-chord, ultrafast songs would come to characterize the provocative new sound people were labeling "punk rock." CBGB became Ground Zero for the burgeoning—albeit still mostly underground—punk movement.

One man attuned to the vibrant punk scene and subculture was a London entrepreneur named Malcolm McClaren. Hanging around New York in 1974, McClaren met several artists spearheading the new movement. Inspired, he returned to London in May 1975 and began managing a little-known local band called The Strand, which he reinvented in the punk style and renamed the Sex Pistols.

A year later, The Ramones played in London—an event that galvanized the nascent U.K. punk scene led by the Pistols and such future British punk icons as The Clash, The Stranglers, and the Buzzcocks.

Punk was about to turn the rock establishment on its ear.

❋ The Sex Pistols' final concert on January 14, 1978, ended with singer Johnny Rotten leaving the stage after asking the audience, "Ever get the feeling you've been cheated?"

❋ CBGB remained open from 1973 until higher rent costs forced it to close in 2006.

❋ Richard Hell had a nonspeaking role in the 1985 movie *Desperately Seeking Susan,* which starred Madonna.

❋ All members of The Ramones adopted the last name, "Ramone" though none of them were related.

Wacky TV Horror Hosts

In the early days of television, these colorful and offbeat hosts of horror movie shows became local celebrities.

✳ ✳ ✳ ✳

AFTER *KING KONG* was broadcast on television in 1956, horror movies exploded in popularity, and the TV "horror host" became an icon closely associated with this era. Although many horror hosts were local figures—sometimes weather reporters or news anchors pulling double duty—some became known nationally.

Vampira

One of the most-loved horror hosts was Vampira. This character was born when Maila Nurmi was discovered by a producer at the 1953 Bal Caribe Masquerade in Los Angeles. Nurmi attended the ball wearing a slinky black dress inspired by a character in Charles Addams's *New Yorker* cartoons. *The Vampira Show* premiered in 1953, and at the height of her fame, Vampira was known worldwide.

The Cool Ghoul

Another well-known horror host was John Zacherle. After playing several characters in a TV Western, Zacherle was offered a chance to host a horror show in Philadelphia called *Shock Theater* in 1957. This show was gorier than its contemporaries and used elaborate props, such as severed heads dripping blood made from chocolate syrup.

Morgus the Magnificent

One classic horror host still on the air in the 21st century is Morgus the Magnificent, portrayed by actor Sid Noel. Morgus debuted in 1959 on *House of Shock* in the New Orleans local television scene. After a nearly 20-year hiatus, in October 2006, *Morgus Presents* debuted.

Memorable TV Theme Songs

A great TV theme song can tell you everything you need to know about a show in less than a minute. Here's a behind-the-scenes look at some memorable theme songs.

✳ ✳ ✳ ✳

1. **"Where Everybody Knows Your Name" (*Cheers*):**
   Written by Judy Hart Angelo and Gary Portnoy (and sung by him, too), this comforting tune conjures up images of a place where the lonely and downtrodden can find a friend to lean on, where people can forget about their troubles for a while, and, yes, "where everybody knows your name." And that's exactly what *Cheers* provided for 275 episodes from 1982 to 1993.

2. **"Love Is All Around" (*Mary Tyler Moore*):** Songwriter Sonny Curtis wrote and performed the empowering theme song for this trailblazing show about women's lib and the single life of spunky career woman Mary Richards. The opening sequence shows a fresh-faced Mary as she arrives in her new city and tosses her beret into the air out of the pure excitement of starting a new life. The original lyrics contemplated "...you might just make it after all," but after the first season, when it was clear that *Mary* would be a success, the lyrics were changed to "...you're gonna make it after all!" The bubbly and upbeat song has even been covered by Joan Jett & The Blackhearts and Sammy Davis Jr.

3. **"Theme Song from *The Brady Bunch*" (*The Brady Bunch*):** Series creator Sherwood Schwartz collaborated with composer Frank DeVol to come up with this famous theme song that describes what happens when a second marriage merges two families and six children under one roof. The song alone is memorable, but so is the opening sequence, which divided the screen into nine squares, one for each family member, including the housekeeper, Alice.

On the left, we saw the three daughters "All of them had hair of gold, like their mother. The youngest one in curls." The right side introduced the three sons, who with their father made "...four men, living all together. Yet they were all alone." Who sang the song, you ask? The cast, of course!

4. **"Ballad of Gilligan's Isle"** (*Gilligan's Island*): Here's the plot in a coconut shell: Five passengers go on a boating expedition that was supposed to last only three hours, but there was a storm, and their boat, the S.S. *Minnow* shipwrecked. The Skipper, his goofy first mate, Gilligan, and the passengers set up house on an island and make various futile attempts to be rescued. True *Gilligan's Island* aficionados know that there were two versions of the theme song, which was written by George Wyle and the show's creator Sherwood Schwartz. The first version specifically mentions five of the cast members, then lumps two other characters together, referring to them as "the rest." But Bob Denver (aka Gilligan) thought the song should be rewritten to include "the Professor and Mary Ann." Denver may have played the doofus on camera, but he used his star power to get equal billing for his fellow cast mates. He truly was everyone's "little buddy."

5. **"Meet the Flintstones"** (*The Flintstones*): Surprisingly, there was no theme song for this cartoon during its first two seasons. Then show creators William Hanna and Joseph Barbera wrote lyrics for a tune by Hoyt Curtin. The show, which took place in the prehistoric town of Bedrock, was a parody on contemporary suburbia. There were no brakes on cars, just bare feet to slow things down. Cameras were primitive—birds feverishly chiseled slabs of rock to capture various images. And instead of a garbage disposal, people just kept a hungry reptile under the sink. Still, it was a "yabba-dabba-doo time. A dabba-doo time." In fact, it was a "...gay old time!"

6. **"I'll Be There for You" (*Friends*):** Written and performed by The Rembrandts, "I'll Be There for You" pretty much sums up the premise of these loyal friends who supported each other through life's ups and downs. The intensely popular sitcom showed just how funny it is to be in your twenties (eventually thirties), single, and living in New York City. Three guys and three girls formed a special bond as they roomed together, sometimes dated each other, and always entertained audiences worldwide. The song wasn't intended to be a full-length track, but eventually the band went back into the studio and recorded a longer version of the song, which topped U.S. charts and reached number two in the UK.

7. **"Those Were the Days" (*All in the Family*):** Longing for a less complicated time, "Those Were the Days" was written by Charles Strouse and Lee Adams and was performed at the family piano by bigoted, blue-collar Archie Bunker and his screechingly off-key "dingbat" wife Edith. In the show, which aired from 1971 to 1979, staunchly conservative Archie is forced to live with a liberal when his "little goil" Gloria and her husband Michael move in with the Bunkers. The resulting discussions shed light on two sides of politics and earned Michael the nickname "Meathead."

8. **"Theme from *The Addams Family*" (*The Addams Family*):** TV and film composer Vic Mizzy wrote the music and engaging lyrics that helped to describe the "creepy... kooky... mysterious... spooky... and all together ooky" Addams Family. The show takes a peek at the bizarre family: Gomez and Morticia, their children Pugsley and Wednesday, Cousin Itt, Uncle Fester, and servants Lurch and Thing, who all live together in a musty castle. The show lasted only two seasons, but it lives on in pop culture through reruns, cartoons, movies, and video games.

9. **"Theme to *Happy Days*" (*Happy Days*):** Bill Haley and His Comets recorded a new version of their hit "Rock Around the Clock" for the theme song of the show about the middle-class Cunningham family and their life in Milwaukee in the 1950s and 1960s. After two seasons, the song "Theme to Happy Days," composed by Charles Fox and Norman Gimbel and performed by Truett Pratt and Jerry McClain, moved from the show's closing song to the opener. The song was released as a single in 1976 and cracked Billboard's top five. The final season of the show featured a more modern version of the song led by Bobby Avron, but it was unpopular with fans.

10. **"Making Our Dreams Come True" (*Laverne & Shirley*):** Factory workers never had so much fun! Laverne and Shirley were two kooky girls who were introduced to TV audiences on *Happy Days* and ended up with their own hit show. They got into all kinds of trouble but always made it look like fun. The upbeat theme song was written by Charles Fox and Norman Gimbel and sung by Cyndi Grecco. The lyrics were empowering, but perhaps the most repeated line over the years was a mix of Yiddish and German words: "Schlemiel! Schlemazl! Hasenpfeffer Incorporated!"

11. **"Sunny Day" (*Sesame Street*):** *Sesame Street* was the first TV show to merge entertainment and learning for the preschool set and is largely responsible for children starting kindergarten knowing their letters, numbers, and colors. The show, which airs in more than 120 countries, has won more than 100 Emmy Awards, making it the most award-winning TV series of all time. The cheerful and idyllic theme song was written by Joe Raposo, Jon Stone, and Bruce Hart, but the singers are all children. Or at least they were when the show debuted in 1969!

12. **"Theme from *The Monkees*" (*The Monkees*):** Here they come . . . The original "prefab" four, The Monkees were a mix of zany actors and musicians cast as a rock band for the 1960s TV show of the same name. "Theme from *The Monkees*" was written by Bobby Hart and Tommy Boyce, and once the band members were cast, they recorded the song. The band was so successful that they went on tour and three of their songs reached number one on U.S. charts. The show only lasted two seasons, but The Monkees are now best known for their musical success and occasionally get together for reunion tours.

13. **"The Fishin' Hole" (*The Andy Griffith Show*):** When *The Andy Griffith Show* debuted in 1960, Sheriff Andy Taylor became one of TV's first single dads when his wife died and left him to raise their young son Opie in the small town of Mayberry. Aunt Bea came to town to help out, and Deputy Barney Fife helped keep small-town crime at bay. The result was an endearing slice of Americana that still lives on in syndication. The show's theme song was written by Earle Hagen and Herbert Spencer and is memorable but not for the lyrics—there are none! The melody is carried by a lone whistler (Hagen) and accompanies footage of Andy and Opie heading off together for some quality fishing time.

14. **"The Love Boat" (*The Love Boat*):** *The Love Boat* was just one of producer Aaron Spelling's offerings that dominated TV sets in the '70s and '80s. Love was definitely exciting and new every week when the Pacific Princess cruise ship set sail with a new set of passengers and a new set of challenges! Paul Williams and Charles Fox wrote the theme song, and for the first eight years, Jack Jones provided the vocals, but in 1985 Dionne Warwick recorded her version for the show. With lyrics such as "Set a course for adventure, your mind on a new romance . . ." people were hooking up all over the Pacific seaboard.

15. **"Ballad of Jed Clampett"** (*The Beverly Hillbillies*): When hillbilly Jed Clampett struck oil while hunting on his land, he packed up his family and moved where the other rich people lived—Beverly Hills, California, of course! His beautiful and usually barefoot daughter Elly May attracted a lot of attention as did pretty much everything about the Clampett family. Series creator Paul Henning wrote the "Ballad of Jed Clampett," which was performed by bluegrass musicians Flatt and Scruggs. After the show debuted in 1962, the song made it to number 44 on the pop charts and all the way to number one on the country charts.

16. **"I Love Lucy"** (*I Love Lucy*): One of the most popular TV shows ever produced, *I Love Lucy* starred Lucille Ball as zany redhead Lucy Ricardo and Desi Arnaz as her husband, Cuban bandleader Ricky. Lucy and her reluctant neighbor and best friend, Ethel Mertz, were always involved in one harebrained scheme or another during this classic's six-year run. The show's theme song, written by Harold Adamson and Eliot Daniel, is most recognizable in its instrumental version, but the song does have lyrics. During a 1953 episode in which Lucy believes everyone has forgotten her birthday, Ricky croons "I love Lucy, and she loves me. We're as happy as two can be . . ."

17. **"A Little Help from My Friends"** (*The Wonder Years*): Set in the late 1960s and early 1970s, *The Wonder Years* chronicled the life of teenager Kevin Arnold as he grows up in suburbia in a middle-class family during this turbulent time. During the opening credits, the theme song, "A Little Help from My Friends," plays alongside "home movies" of Kevin and his family and friends. Hardly recognizable as the classic Beatles tune, Joe Cocker's cover of the song is much slower and in a different key, but was reportedly loved by the Fab Four themselves.

Saying How You Feel
Without Saying a Word

With the right stroke of keys, you can add emotion and personality to your e-mail message—without using those irritating exclamation points and CAPITAL LETTERS!!!!

✳   ✳   ✳   ✳

Emoticon Primer

EMOTICONS ARE USUALLY read sideways and use the punctuation keys to elaborate on a smiley face.

(1) The colon key makes a set of eyes **:**

(2) The semi-colon creates a wink **;**

(3) A dash is a nose **-**

(4) Parentheses indicate smiles **)** or frowns **(**

Combine (1) or (2) with (3) and (4), and you have a face **:-)**

Use these variations, or create your own and express yourself.

8-)	sunglasses	**:-Y**	side comment
0:)	smiling angel	**;-D**	winking and laughing
>-)	evil grin	**=O**	surprised
{:-)	person with a toupee	**:,(**	crying
:*)	drunken smile	**[:-)**	wearing headphones
:-&	tongue-tied	**l(**	trying to stay awake
:-($)	put your money where your mouth is	**l-D**	big laugh
		}:[	angry
#-)	partied all night	**8-P**	yuck
:-X	kiss	**:-E**	buck teeth

:-#	braces on teeth	!:-)	I have an idea!
@>---	rose	:-x	I'm keeping my mouth shut.
~:-/	Elvis		
=):-)=	Abraham Lincoln	:-P	tongue sticking out
*<B>	Santa Claus	;-)	wink
:-<	pouting	?:-|	curious
:-}	embarrassed	O:-*	pretending innocence
|-)	daydreaming	:-(	frowning/unhappy
=:-O	scared		

Unrotated Emoticons

You can read these messages straight on, without getting a crick in your neck.

>_<	troubled	^*^	kiss
#^.^#	shy	O_O	shocked
^_^	smiling	<.<	look left
^o^	happy/laughing	>.>	look right
-_-;	sweat	>.<	d'oh!
T-T	crying	=^-^=	happy kitty
\^.^/	Yay! (arms up)	~_~	tired
O.o;;	bug-eyed/weirded out		

A Sampling of Fad Inventions

If we could figure out the next fad, we'd all be millionaires, right? Here are some seemingly crazy ideas that turned out to be both lasting and lucrative.

✴   ✴   ✴   ✴

✴ Hacky Sack: Mike Marshall created this version of the foot-bag in 1972 to help his friend John Stalberger rehabilitate an injured leg. After they marketed it, the Hacky Sack rehabilitated their bank accounts as well. In Oregon in 2006, Tricia George and Paul Vorvick set a doubles record of 1,415 foot-bag kicks in ten minutes.

✴ Hula Hoop: Its origins date back some 3,000 years, when children in ancient Egypt made hoops out of grapevines and twirled them around their waists. Wham-O introduced the plastic version of the toy in 1958, and 20 million were sold in the first six months.

✴ Pet Rock: Its genesis makes sense when you consider the occupation of its inventor. In the mid-1970s, advertising executive Gary Dahl packaged ordinary beach stones in an attractive box and sold them with instructions for their care and training. They cost a penny to manufacture and sold for $3.95, and though the fad lasted less than a year, it made Dahl millions.

✴ Rubik's Cube: Enrico Rubik introduced his puzzle cube in 1974, and it became popular in the 1980s, confounding millions of people worldwide with its 43 quintillion (that's 43 followed by 18 zeros) solutions.

✴ Sea Monkey: It was Harold von Braunhut who came up with a simple three-step kit that allowed youngsters to breed their own aquatic creatures. The wee primates are actually a unique species of brine shrimp.

* Slinky: In the early 1940s, a torsion spring fell off marine engineer Richard James's desk and tumbled end over end across the floor. He took it home to his wife, Betty, who gave it the cute name. Since then, more than a quarter billion Slinkys have been sold worldwide.

* Super Soaker: The giant water gun was invented in 1988 by aerospace engineer Lonnie Johnson. An intriguing feature was the incorporation of air pressure, which enabled more water to be sprayed at greater distances. Some of today's pump-action models can "shoot" water accurately as far as 50 feet.

* Twister: The Milton Bradley Company released this unique game in 1966, and it was the first one in history to use the human body as an actual playing piece. Worldwide, approximately 65 million people have become entwined in the game of Twister.

* View-Master: The View-Master is a device for viewing 3-D images, presented on reels that contain 14 small slides of film. It was introduced at the New York World's Fair in 1939 as a "modernized" version of the scenic postcard. The View-Master was so prevalent during World War II that the U.S. military purchased 100,000 viewers and more than 6 million reels for training purposes.

* Yo-Yo: The first historical mention of the yo-yo dates to Greece in 500 B.C., but it was a man named Pedro Flores who brought the yo-yo to the United States from the Philippines in 1928. American entrepreneur Donald Duncan soon bought the rights from Flores. Sales of the toy peaked in 1962, when more than 45 million units were sold.

The Secret Origin of Comic Books

Today's graphic novels have a long history that stretches back to newspaper comic strips.

❋ ❋ ❋ ❋

IN THE 1920S and '30s, comic strips were among the most popular sections of newspapers and were often reprinted later in book form. Generally, these were inexpensive and looked like newspaper supplements, though other formats were tried (including "big little books" in which the comic panels were adapted and text was added opposite each panel).

These so-called "funny books" were often given away as premiums for products such as cereal, shoes, and gasoline. Then, in 1933, a sales manager at the Eastern Color Printing Company in Waterbury, Connecticut, hit on a winning format: 36 pages of color comics in a size similar to modern comics. *Famous Funnies: A Carnival of Comics*, considered the first true comic book, featured reprinted strips from comics such as *Mutt and Jeff*. It was a giveaway, but it was a hit. In 1934, Eastern Color published *Famous Funnies #1* and distributed the 68-page comic to newsstands nationwide with a cover price of 10 cents.

As the demand for reprinted strips outpaced supply, publishers began introducing original material into comic books. One publisher, searching for features to fill the pages of a new book, approached a young creative team made up of writer Jerry Siegel and artist Joe Shuster, who had been trying for years to sell a newspaper strip about an invincible hero from another planet. Siegel and Shuster reformatted the strips into comic book form, and Superman debuted in *Action Comics #1*. It was an instant hit. The "Golden Age" of comics followed, introducing many of today's popular heroes, including Batman, Wonder Woman, Captain America, and The Flash. In the 1960s, the "Silver Age" introduced new, more emotionally flawed heroes such as Spider-Man, Iron Man, and the Hulk.

The A to Z of IM-ing

Interpersonal communication keeps getting faster. Writing letters took too long, so people became adept at the quick phone call, which was largely replaced by e-mail. Instant messaging offers the speediest way to express yourself, but only if you know the lingo.

✳ ✳ ✳ ✳

ADN: Any day now

AFK: Away from keyboard

AYTMTB: And you're telling me this because?

BRB: Be right back

BTA: But then again

BTDT: Been there, done that

CRBT: Crying really big tears

CU: See you

CUL8R: See you later

DEGT: Don't even go there!

DIKU: Do I know you?

DQMOT: Don't quote me on this

EG: Evil grin

EOM: End of message

FICCL: Frankly, I couldn't care less

FWIW: For what it's worth

FYEO: For your eyes only

GD/R: Grinning, ducking, and running

GGOH: Gotta get outta here

GMTA: Great minds think alike

HB: Hurry back

H&K: Hugs and kisses

H2CUS: Hope to see you soon

IB: I'm back

IDTS: I don't think so

IMHO: In my humble opinion

JIC: Just in case

JK: Just kidding

JMO: Just my opinion

KIT: Keep in touch

KOTL: Kiss on the lips

KWIM: Know what I mean?

LOL: Laughing out loud

LTNS: Long time no see

MOS: Mother over shoulder

MTFBWU: May the force be with you

NM: Never mind

NMU: Not much, you?

NOYB: None of your business

OMG: Oh my God

OTH: Off the hook

OTTOMH: Off the top of my head

P911: My parents are in the room

PRW: Parents are watching

PU: That stinks!

QIK: Quick

QT: Cutie

RME: Rolling my eyes

ROTFLUTS: Rolling on the floor laughing, unable to speak

SH: Same here

SMHID: Scratching my head in disbelief

SSIF: So stupid it's funny

TIC: Tongue-in-cheek

TMI: Too much info

TNSTAAFL: There's no such thing as a free lunch

UCMU: You crack me up!

UV: Unpleasant visual

VEG: Very evil grin

VSF: Very sad face

WH5: Who, what, where, when, why?

WOMBAT: Waste of money, brains, and time

X: Kiss

XLNT: Excellent

YG2BKM: You've got to be kidding me

YKWYCD: You know what you can do

ZUP: What's up?

Zzzz: Bored

Presto! Change-o! Wham-O!

In 1948, Richard Knerr and Arthur "Spud" Melin developed a slingshot specifically designed to hurl bits of meat into the air to feed hawks and falcons. Their new company's name was a stroke of onomatopoeia—Wham-O was the sound the slingshot made.

✳ ✳ ✳ ✳

CALIFORNIAN FRED MORRISON fashioned a small plastic disc toy he called the Pluto Platter, noting America's fascination with flying saucers. In 1955, Knerr and Melin saw it and purchased the design. But Knerr wasn't pleased with the name. While traveling the East Coast, he noted the recent closing of the Frisbie Baking Company. He had heard stories of pie-plate tossing as a sport at nearby Yale University in the 1920s. Intrigued, he quickly changed the name to Frisbee.

Loop the Hoop

In 1957, a visiting Australian told of native children who exercised by twirling bamboo hoops around their waists like Hula dancers. The concept was not lost on Knerr and Melin. Using a tough but lightweight plastic, they fashioned a large hoop, and the Hula-Hoop was born. At a cost of $1.98 each, Americans purchased 25 million hoops in the first four months of 1958. Worldwide sales topped 100 million by the end of the year.

Bouncing into History

In late 1964, chemist Norman Stingley concocted a synthetic rubber compound that had a lot of bounce to the ounce. His employer saw no commercial potential, but Wham-O picked up Stingley's idea, creating the Super Ball. At just under two inches in diameter, the Super Ball was no ordinary orb: Once the ball bounced, it continued to bounce... and bounce.

Wham-O also made its name by creating crazy toys such as the Slip-N-Slide, Monster Magnet, Silly String, and the Air Blaster—guaranteed to blow out a candle at 20 feet.

Origins of Modern Icons

Who knows what makes some characters endure while others slip through our consciousness quicker than 50 bucks in the gas tank? In any case, you'll be surprised to learn how some of our most endearing "friends" made their way into our lives.

✻ ✻ ✻ ✻

1. **The Aflac Duck:** A duck pitching insurance? Art director Eric David stumbled upon the idea to use a web-footed mascot one day when he continuously uttered, "Aflac... Aflac... Aflac." It didn't take him long to realize how much the company's name sounded like a duck's quack. There are many fans of the campaign, but actor Ben Affleck is not one of them. Not surprisingly, he fields many comments that associate his name with the duck and is reportedly none too pleased.

2. **Betty Crocker:** Thousands of letters were sent to General Mills in the 1920s, all asking for answers to baking questions. Managers created a fictional character to give the responses a personal touch. The surname Crocker was chosen to honor a retired executive, and Betty was selected because it seemed "warm and friendly." In 1936, artist Neysa McMein blended the faces of several female employees to create a likeness. Crocker's face has changed many times over the years. She's been made to look younger, more professional, and now has a more multicultural look. At one point, a public opinion poll rating famous women placed Betty second to Eleanor Roosevelt.

3. **Duke, the Bush's Baked Beans Dog:** Who else to trust with a secret recipe but the faithful family pooch? Bush Brothers & Company was founded by A. J. Bush and his two sons in 1908. The company is currently headed by A. J.'s grandson, Condon. In 1995, the advertising agency working for Bush's Baked Beans decided that Jay Bush

(Condon's son) and his golden retriever, Duke, were the perfect team to represent the brand. The only problem was that the real Duke is camera-shy, so a stunt double was hired to portray him and handle all the gigs on the road with Jay. In any case, both dogs have been sworn to secrecy.

4. The California Raisins: Sometimes advertising concepts can lead to marketing delirium. In 1987, a frustrated copywriter at Foote, Cone & Belding was working on the California Raisin Advisory Board campaign and said, "We have tried everything but dancing raisins singing 'I Heard It Through the Grapevine.'" With vocals by Buddy Miles and design by Michael Brunsfeld, the idea was pitched to the client. The characters plumped up the sales of raisins by 20 percent, and the rest is Claymation history!

5. Joe Camel: Looking for a way to revamp Camel's image from an "old man's cigarette" in the late 1980s, the R. J. Reynolds marketing team uncovered illustrations of Old Joe in their archives. (He was originally conceived for an ad campaign in France in the 1950s.) In 1991, the new Joe Camel angered children's advocacy groups when a study revealed that more kids under the age of eight recognized Joe than Mickey Mouse or Fred Flintstone.

6. The Coppertone Girl: It was 1959 when an ad for Coppertone first showed a suntanned little girl's white buttocks being exposed by a puppy pulling on her bottoms. "Don't be a paleface!" was the slogan, and it reflected the common belief of the time that a suntan was healthy. Artist Joyce Ballantyne Brand created the pig-tailed little girl in the image of her three-year-old daughter, Cheri. When the campaign leapt off the printed page and into the world of television, it became Jodie Foster's acting debut. As the 21st century beckoned, and along with it changing views on sun exposure and nudity, Coppertone revised the drawing to reveal only the girl's lower back.

7. The Gerber Baby: Contrary to some popular beliefs, it's not Humphrey Bogart, Elizabeth Taylor, or Bob Dole who looks up from the label of Gerber products. In fact, the face that appears on all Gerber packaging belongs to mystery novelist Ann Turner Cook. In 1928, when Gerber began its search for a baby face to help promote its new brand of baby food, Dorothy Hope Smith submitted a simple charcoal sketch of her four-month-old neighbor, Ann Cook—promising to complete the drawing if chosen. As it turned out, that wasn't necessary because the powers that be at Gerber liked it the way it was. In 1996, Gerber updated its look, but the new label design still uses Cook's baby face.

8. Mr. Whipple: The expression "Do as I say, not as I do" took on a persona in the mid-1960s—Mr. Whipple. This fussy supermarket manager (played by actor Dick Wilson) was famous for admonishing his shoppers by saying, "Ladies, please don't squeeze the Charmin!" The people at Benton & Bowles Advertising figured that if, on camera, Mr. Whipple was a habitual offender of his own rule, Charmin toilet paper would be considered the cushiest. The campaign included a total of 504 ads and ran from 1965 until 1989, landing it a spot in *The Guinness Book of World Records*. A 1979 poll listed Mr. Whipple as the third most recognized American behind Richard Nixon and Billy Graham.

9. The Pillsbury Doughboy: Who could resist poking the chubby belly of this giggling icon? This cheery little fellow was "born" in 1965 when the Leo Burnett advertising agency dreamt him up to help Pillsbury sell its refrigerated dinner rolls. Originally devised as an animated character, agency producers instead borrowed a unique stop-action technique used on *The Dinah Shore Show*. After beating out more than 50 other actors, Paul Frees lent his voice to the Doughboy. So, if you ever craved dinner rolls while watching *The Rocky and Bullwinkle Show*, it's no wonder . . . Frees was also the voice of Boris Badenov and Dudley Do-Right.

Check Out These Really Super Heroes

The most recognizable superheroes aren't just preternatural crime fighters. Born in the pages of comic books decades ago, these powerful and popular icons are as beloved as ever.

✳   ✳   ✳   ✳

Superman: The definitive superhero debuted in *Action Comics #1*, published in 1938. Kal-El, the only survivor of the planet Krypton, escapes its explosion after his father, Jor-El, puts him in a spaceship that crash-lands near Smallville, USA. Kal-El, named Clark Kent by his adoptive parents, has superpowers of all kinds on Earth. Cocreator Jerry Siegel said he came up with Superman on a sleepless night in the early 1930s, but it took him several years to actually sell the pitch.

Batman: The alter ego of millionaire Bruce Wayne first appeared in *Detective Comics #27* in 1939. In response to his parents' murder at the hands of a thief, Wayne pushes his body and mind to their limits and becomes a mysterious vigilante. Batman was actually born in 1938, after Bob Kane created a birdlike prototype for a superhero. Comic book writer Bill Finger collaborated with Kane and decided that a "Bat-Man" would be more sinister.

Spider-Man: Premiering in *Amazing Fantasy #15* in 1962, Spider-Man was teenager Peter Parker, who'd been bitten by a radioactive spider. The incident gave Parker spiderlike characteristics, such as the ability to cling to walls, as well as superhuman agility and speed. Marvel Comics' Stan Lee and Steve Ditko created Spider-Man as the first superhero with real problems, such as dating and paying rent.

Wonder Woman: The first major superheroine, Wonder Woman made her comic debut in 1941 in *All-Star Comics #8*. One of a race of warrior women called Amazons, Wonder Woman was given mega-strength and otherworldly powers by a cadre of Greek goddesses and gods. She was created by psychologist William Marston, who criticized comics for their "blood-curdling masculinity." Marston used Wonder Woman's golden manacles (a symbol of female subjugation by the patriarchy) to convey that war could be eliminated if women took control.

The Hulk: In *The Incredible Hulk #1* (1962), Dr. Bruce Banner saves teenager Rick Jones from rays emanating from a gamma-bomb test, but in the process, he gets irradiated. After that, whenever Banner becomes angry, he transforms into the green-skinned, seven-foot, 1,000-pound Hulk. Drawing on the Atomic Age for the Hulk's origin, co-creator Jack Kirby said he was also inspired by a news account of a woman lifting a car to save her child.

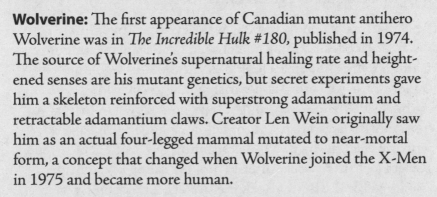

Wolverine: The first appearance of Canadian mutant antihero Wolverine was in *The Incredible Hulk #180*, published in 1974. The source of Wolverine's supernatural healing rate and heightened senses are his mutant genetics, but secret experiments gave him a skeleton reinforced with superstrong adamantium and retractable adamantium claws. Creator Len Wein originally saw him as an actual four-legged mammal mutated to near-mortal form, a concept that changed when Wolverine joined the X-Men in 1975 and became more human.

Invisible Girl: Along with teammates Mr. Fantastic, the Human Torch, and the Thing, the Invisible Girl (aka Susan Storm) was introduced in *Fantastic Four #1* (1961). After the superhero team was exposed to cosmic radiation on a spaceflight, Marvel's superheroine could turn invisible at will, make others invisible, and generate invisible force fields. When artist and writer John Byrne took over the series in 1981, he felt that the Invisible Girl was too passive—a damsel in distress who had to be rescued by her teammates. As Byrne expanded the Invisible Girl's powers, she became more assertive and was renamed the Invisible Woman.

The Bikini: Scandal on the Beach

Bikinis are such a common sight on public beaches that it's hard to believe the skimpy, two-piece bathing suits were considered scandalous when first introduced in France at the end of World War II. It's important to note, however, that French designers didn't actually invent the bikini; that honor goes to the ancient Romans.

✳   ✳   ✳   ✳

EONS-OLD MOSAICS AND murals suggest that a two-piece bathing suit—a pre-bikini, if you will—was commonly worn by Roman women at the beach or poolside. Some historians believe two-piece swimwear may date back even further. Recently discovered cave drawings show Minoan women wearing primitive bikinis as far back as 1600 B.C.

The bikini as we know it today was developed by fashion designer Jacques Heim, who debuted his daring creation in a Cannes swim shop in 1946. He called the suit the "Atome" in honor of the tiny atom and christened it "the world's smallest bathing suit." The Atome might have gone down in history as just another fad were it not for fellow designer Louis Reard, who unveiled his own two-piece suit on the fashionable French Riviera just three weeks after Heim. He called his suit the "bikini" after the Bikini Reef, the site of atomic bomb tests.

The bikini arrived in the United States in 1947 to a lot of curiosity but few sales. Conservative Americans found the bathing suit a little too risqué, and some communities even banned it. Two decades passed before American sexual attitudes loosened up enough for the average woman to feel comfortable baring her navel (and sometimes much more) at the beach.

The bikini has gone through some wild variations over the years, including the daring monokini of the freewheeling '60s, but today it is one of swimwear's most popular styles.

The PEZ Candy Craze

How much would you pay for a small plastic candy dispenser? PEZ has inspired legions of obsessive fans who are willing to shell out thousands for a rare find.

✳   ✳   ✳   ✳

EDUARD HAAS COULDN'T have known what kind of monster hit he was creating when he built the first PEZ prototype in Austria in 1927. After all, it seems like a simple enough idea: a cute character with a tilting head that spits out candy.

Haas first conceptualized PEZ as a smoking alternative, which may be why the dispensers look like lighters (the first batch of PEZ came in metal tins). The candies were first made only in peppermint flavor. In fact, the name PEZ is derived from *pfefferminz*, the German word for peppermint. Legend has it that Haas's product was shot down when he first tried to market it in America. He then got the idea to put a playful face on the dispenser and sell it as a children's toy. PEZ had found its place.

These days, PEZ is made in Orange, Connecticut. The plant is said to run 24/7, churning out crunchy little candies and colorful dispensers around the clock. And boy howdy, are people ever eating them up.

Most Expensive Dispensers

PEZ is a collector's dream. While there's no official list, PEZ dispensers can fetch a pretty penny. Some collectors report a transparent 1950s Space Gun model selling for more than $11,000. The original Locking Cap model is said to have sold for $6,575, and the Big Top Elephant dispenser is believed to have pulled anywhere from $3,600 to $6,000 at auction.

Rarest Dispensers

Many collectors seem to agree the rarest dispenser is the elusive Mr. Potato Head model. The design, like the Potato Head toys, has a blank head with attaching face pieces. But this smiling spud didn't last long; PEZ pulled it off the shelves after a few months over concern of kids choking on the detachable pieces.

The Original Head

The first head to appear on PEZ is a source of debate. Some say it was Mickey Mouse; others insist it was Popeye.

The Most Popular PEZ

The dispenser designs most commonly named as top sellers are Santa Claus and Mickey Mouse.

The Most Featured PEZ

The Tweety Bird PEZ makes regular primetime appearances, thanks to its immortalization in an episode of the TV show *Seinfeld*. In "The Pez Dispenser," the crowning moment occurs when Jerry places the dispenser on Elaine's lap during a piano recital, causing her to burst out in laughter.

The Tallest Dispenser

Marge Simpson's model takes the cake here with an impressive $5^1/_8$-inch-tall stature. Other tall orders include Bugs Bunny, Asterix, Yosemite Sam, Uncle Sam, and Goofy.

PEZ-tastic Facts

＊ Americans eat more than 3 billion PEZ candies every year.

＊ There is a Bullwinkle dispenser, but no Rocky.

＊ The only real people to ever be featured on dispensers are Betsy Ross and Daniel Boone. Some say Paul Revere has a model as well, but its title was simply "Captain." The matter has become another PEZ controversy.

＊ An Elvis dispenser was shown in the 1994 movie *The Client*, but it was created as a prop by the filmmakers and was never an official PEZ issue.

＊ PEZ is available in Kosher flavors.

＊ There are two widely recognized PEZ museums: one in Burlingame, California, and one in Easton, Pennsylvania.

A Literary Archaeology of *MAD*

*For those who know it only by reputation, MAD is a
satire magazine that makes fun (of the PG-13 variety) of
anyone or anything, from Saddam Hussein to pop culture
to the British royal family. It's a thick-skinned reader's
hoot and a touchy reader's cerebral hemorrhage.*

✳   ✳   ✳   ✳

MAD HAS BEEN *MAD* since the early 1950s, but its prehitory extends back to the Great Depression. Its emblem, Alfred E. Neuman, dates back even further.

Contrary to popular belief, iconic publisher William "Bill" Gaines didn't invent *MAD*. His father, Max Gaines, pioneered newsstand comic books in the mid-1930s as cheap, commercially viable amusement for children. Son Bill was an eccentric prankster, the type of kid peers might label "Most Likely to Publish an Iconoclastic Satire Mag." Upon his father's tragic death in 1947, Bill inherited the family comic book business, Educational Comics (EC). He steered EC to stand for Entertaining Comics: a publisher of garish horror comics veering into sardonic social commentary.

In 1952, Bill's early collaborator Harvey Kurtzman proposed a new comic called *MAD*, which would poke fun at just about anything. Kurtzman's brainchild was a success, and in 1955 Bill allowed Kurtzman to convert *MAD* from comic book to magazine. Kurtzman left EC shortly thereafter, but their creation still thrives more than a half century later.

MAD Under Fire

The assaults on *MAD* came early and often from two predictable directions: 1) *MAD* corrupted America's youth; 2) *MAD* violated some copyright. In *MAD*'s natal McCarthy era, mocking traditional American anything meant painting a target on one's own back; it could even suggest Communist leanings.

MAD's shameless irreverence, gory imagery, and refusal to kowtow sent Bill Gaines before a Senate subcommittee. An interrogator would show Gaines a gross image from an EC comic like *MAD* and ask, "Surely you think this is too disgusting for children?" "Nah," Gaines would reply, reveling in the indignant sputters. Gaines and *MAD* didn't back down.

The intellectual property issues generally came from heavy hitters like National Periodical Publications (*Superman*) and composer Irving Berlin. The core question was *MAD*'s legal right to poke fun at pop culture: songs, cartoon characters, ads. *MAD* won most such challenges. Its dopey mascot, Alfred E. Neuman, came to symbolize the right to parody.

What, Us Worry?

MAD first depicted its wing-eared emblem as "The What, Me Worry? Kid" and "Melvin Coznowski" in 1954. The image reportedly came from an old postcard. In 1955, the staff began calling him "Alfred E. Neuman," a name evidently nicked on a lark from successful film composer Alfred Newman. *MAD*'s bright, talented staff never fatigues of telling the reader how stupid and mediocre the magazine is, and Alfred's vacant gaze appears to bear them out. But *MAD* didn't invent him. We don't know who did, but *MAD* had to go to court to keep him.

In 1965, *MAD*'s use of Alfred withstood two serious legal challenges from plaintiffs alleging previous copyrights. In the end, *MAD*'s lawyer located advertising and artistic images of proto-Alfred dating back to 1895, undermining both claims. Alfred still grins his vacuous smile on most *MAD* covers.

MAD's Evolution

Like any publication that celebrates a 50th birthday, *MAD* has changed. By the late 1950s, it had abandoned horror motifs in favor of increased contemporary political satire. *MAD*'s content has grown saltier and more risqué but is now far less sexist and homophobic. Fear not: *MAD*'s still as stupid as ever—as they advise every subscriber with each subscription renewal offer.

Where No Show Had Gone Before: The Origin of *Star Trek*

Star Trek is so integrated into modern American geek culture that it's hard to believe the original series more or less flopped. In fact, the series almost wasn't made at all.

✻ ✻ ✻ ✻

Concept

SCIENCE FICTION WASN'T new in 1960, as any Edgar Rice Burroughs devotee will tell you, but it was on the brink of going mainstream. A creative producer named Gene Roddenberry wanted to produce a science-fiction TV series about space exploration, loosely based on C. S. Forester's classic *Hornblower* seafaring novels. Roddenberry didn't have much luck selling the concept until 1964, when he pitched it to Herb Solow, a senior production executive at Desilu Studios.

Early fact: Comedienne Lucille Ball was a key part of *Trek*, though she never appeared in an episode. She owned Desilu.

A Tough Sell

Solow and Roddenberry tried to sell the networks a pilot (in TV-speak, a sample episode). Only NBC bought. The episode, "The Cage," bore modest resemblance to the later series and was in fact later melded into another episode as a backstory. NBC didn't buy *Star Trek* based on "The Cage," but some aspects of it impressed them. Other details, such as the "guy with the pointed ears" (Leonard Nimoy's Mr. Spock), didn't go over quite as well. The network ordered a second pilot.

Early fact: For a brief time, the series concept was called *Gulliver's Travels*, and the captain was Gulliver.

In 1965, Desilu produced the second pilot, "Where No Man Has Gone Before." Most of the cast was new. NBC still had misgivings about the Spock character: They felt he looked diabolical enough to alienate devout Christians. Nonetheless, the network ordered a season of *Trek* for 1966–67. The U.S.S. *Enterprise* was finally spaceworthy.

Early fact: *Trek* actresses' scanty costuming was inspired partly by pulp magazines and partly by Roddenberry's vast libido.

"These Are the Voyages..."

Trek presented a huge challenge to prop, costume, and set designers. As a result, it was chronically overbudget. The show depended on heroic improvising by the crew, making salt shakers into surgical tools and Styrofoam into futuristic fixtures.

Early fact: Due to the high cost of union labor, the crew maintained a nonunion costume sweatshop nearby.

Trek also showed up at precisely the right time to find a following. In those days of civil rights strife, antiwar protests, the space race, and Cold War fear, *Star Trek* portrayed humanity unified behind high ideals. Their United Federation of Planets refused to interfere with other planets' cultures. The crew's ethnic and gender mix supported the impression. *Enterprise* officers included an African woman, a Japanese man, and a Russian man. While the *Enterprise* ran on naval lines, it acted more like an exploration ship than a heavy cruiser. *Star Trek* was what the late 1960s counterculture wanted to see.

Early fact: *Trek's* third and final season depicted the first interracial (white/black) kiss on American TV.

Downfall

Unfortunately, *Trek* never earned stellar ratings. The third season aired in the "banana peel" slot: 10 P.M. Fridays. Not even a massive letter-writing campaign could save the show.

But its fans wouldn't let go, and in 1979 came *Star Trek: The Motion Picture*. Then came scores of novels, more movies, and even several new *Trek* TV series. In 2009, yet another new *Star Trek* movie was released to the delight of fans everywhere.

MTV: A Cultural Monolith

Screaming out of about a half-million television sets on August 1, 1981, was something most people hadn't seen before: an entire cable channel dedicated to broadcasting music videos. The channel was named, aptly, Music Television, or MTV.

✳   ✳   ✳   ✳

USING A MONTAGE of images from the Apollo 11 moon landing, MTV began at 12:01 A.M. with the introduction, "Ladies and gentlemen, rock and roll." The first video played? "Video Killed the Radio Star" by the Buggles. The format of the first days of MTV was similar to Top 40 radio at the time—hosts introduced song after song, but instead of playing a song on the radio, the hosts played a video. The first hosts, called VJs—video jockeys—were Nina Blackwood, Mark Goodman, Alan Hunter, J. J. Jackson, and Martha Quinn.

The Evolution

Early programming at MTV con-sisted almost entirely of videos made for cheap or cut together from other sources, such as concerts. As MTV started to stake its claim in popular culture, however, videos started to become more slick and developed.

Record companies soon realized the marketing potential that came with having a video on MTV, so they began to finance the creation of videos. Videos became more elaborate and highly stylized, oftentimes with story lines and character development. Many directors who would later find success directing feature films started their careers directing music videos. Many new rock groups hit it big with videos that ultimately gained a huge following among the MTV audience. Eventually, programming at MTV branched out into award shows, animated shows, and reality shows, gradually moving away from music videos.

In the mid-1980s, Viacom bought MTV (among other channels) and created MTV Networks. Shows hosted by VJs slowly lost airtime in lieu of more conventionally formatted programs. Programs such as *MTV News* and *MTV Unplugged*, which featured acoustic performances, were worked into the lineup. In the early 1990s, animated shows, including *Beavis and Butthead* and *Celebrity Deathmatch*, were introduced. By 2001, reality programming, such as *MTV's Fear* and *The Osbournes*, was added. Almost all of MTV's music programming had been moved to other channels. In addition, the network had channels across the globe, taking over airwaves in Europe and Asia.

The Youth

MTV's audience has always been a young group—people between 12 and 24 years old. "The MTV Generation" became a term to define those growing up in the 1980s. But as that generation aged, the channel continued to change its programming and identity to match the interests of the next group of 12–24-year-olds. As a result, videos were gradually replaced with reality shows. Series such as *The Real World* and *Road Rules* became staples in MTV's rotation. But as MTV continued to gain popularity and became a huge dictator of taste for the youth generation, it also came under fire for its impact.

Groups such as the Parents Television Council and the American Family Association have criticized MTV frequently, arguing that the channel advocates inappropriate behavior and lacks moral responsibility for its programming targeted at kids. Of course, MTV hasn't always been its own best advocate, as seen in controversies such as the 2004 MTV-produced Super Bowl halftime show, in which Justin Timberlake tore off part of Janet Jackson's wardrobe and exposed her breast; as well as MTV's problematic coverage in July 2005 of the Live 8 benefit concert, when the network cut to commercials during live performances and MTV's hosts repeatedly referred to the show incorrectly. Given that they were broadcasting the show to the very fans who wanted to see the bands they were interrupting, this may have marked a milestone in cultural politics, where the typically liberal youth culture was just as annoyed with the channel as the conservative groups were.

Social Activism

While full recovery from such snafus is probably unlikely, MTV has tried to respond to criticism about its programming. The network has a long history of promoting social, political, and environmental activism in young people. During election years, the network has invited presidential candidates to discuss their platforms. MTV has also initiated annual campaigns addressing a variety of issues affecting the youth culture—hate crimes, drug use, violence. In addition, MTV started branching out into various social activities, most notably the Rock the Vote campaign, which encouraged young people to vote.

The Meaning

MTV's effect on popular culture has been enormous. Some call it a reflection of youth culture today, but others say it dictates what's happening. Still, MTV has stayed the course like any solid corporation. Its mission has always been to appeal to youth culture. So, while the gradual decline in the airing of music videos may be bemoaned by older viewers, the young people in the 21st century want reality shows about rich people in Southern California. The target demographic has stayed the same, but the people in that demographic have changed.

One critique the network can't seem to dodge is its effect on the music industry. First, MTV has a tendency to remember only its own history as opposed to musical history in general. Older artists influential in the creation of genres and styles are left out of the MTV world, despite the fact that so many artists on MTV are obviously in debt to them. Second, by playing only those artists who fit into a prescribed image and are backed by big money from music companies, the network has aided the consolidation of the music industry and narrowing choice. MTV is still screaming out from televisions around the world.

Fantastic Fads of the 1990s

In the 1990s, the World Wide Web was born, grunge reigned over the music scene, and O. J. took off in his Bronco. For many, the 1990s were a golden era. The tech boom made many people rich, the fashion scene was much less ridiculous, and hip-hop hit the mainstream. Despite the slacker attitude, the last decade of the 20th century had its fair share of fads, too. Here are a few that stand out.

1. **Grunge:** After the glitz and glamour of disco and the excess and pomp of hair bands, it was inevitable that the music pendulum would swing. That shift created grunge— a genre of music categorized by dissonant harmony, lots of guitars, and cynical lyrics. Grunge was initially delivered by young men and women from the Pacific Northwest who dressed in flannel shirts and ripped jeans. Groups like Nirvana and Pearl Jam were the first to emerge on the scene around 1991, but when the indie scene exploded into the mainstream, groups like Soundgarden, Alice in Chains, and Stone Temple Pilots became household names.

2. **Hypercolor T-shirts:** Clothing manufacturer Generra created these fad-ready T-shirts in the late '80s, but they really caught on in the '90s. The shirts were dipped in temperature-sensitive pigment, which meant that when heat was applied to the fabric, the color changed. Shirts would turn vague shades of blue, yellow, pink, and gray depending on the level of heat they received, working much like the body-heat activated fad of a previous decade—the mood ring.

3. **The Macarena:** "Macarena," a catchy tune from Spanish group Los del Rio, became a worldwide phenomenon in 1996, smashing records by staying at number one on Billboard's Hot 100 chart for an astonishing 14 weeks. The jovial, bouncy tune (that repeats itself over and over and

over again) had its own dance, making it two fads in one. The group remains popular in their home country, but once the Macarena had played itself out a year later, the song and the group were only a distant memory in America.

4. **The Waif Look:** While they weren't exactly "full-figured," 1980s supermodels like Cindy Crawford were zaftig compared to the half-starved, heroin-chic look embodied by models like Kate Moss, who weighed in at barely 100 pounds. The super-skinny look was a worldwide trend in fashion and came with some serious backlash. Girls everywhere were literally starving to look like the women in the fashion magazines. The waif look garnered much criticism and controversy, but it only fueled the fire. Not until the 2000s did the pendulum begin to swing to the "real women are beautiful" direction.

5. **Tattoos and Piercing:** Human beings have many pierceable body parts: ears, noses, lips, tongues, eyebrows, and bellybuttons, just to name a few. In the last decade of the 20th century, no cartilage was safe from the needle of a piercing gun. If you had your fill of metal rings and studs, you could move on to some ink and round out your counterculture look. Both tattooing and piercing were all the rage in the 1990s and many people today have the tats and scars to prove it.

6. **Hip-Hop Fashion:** When hip-hop music became more mainstream in the early '90s, its fashion style became a trend as well. Rappers such as The Fresh Prince, Kid 'N Play, and Left Eye of TLC sparked a trend in wearing brightly colored, baggy clothing and baseball caps. Often the jeans were so baggy that they hung down several inches below the waist, making the question, "Boxers or briefs?" irrelevant. An offshoot of the hip-hop fashion was the fad of wearing clothes backwards, which was popularized by teen rappers Kris Kross.

The Reality of Reality TV

Reality television has been around as long as the old Candid Camera, *but it experienced a sensational explosion in the 2000s. It may not have much scripting, but it does have a lot of fiction.*

✳ ✳ ✳ ✳

Faking is big Hollywood business. Production crews are professional hoaxers who can produce flying garter snakes, imitate the bellow of a water buffalo in rut, and make up Oprah Winfrey as E.T. They can then make E.T./Oprah seem to emit that bellow while marveling at the reptiles. Just a day at the office for Hollywood—but it means anything we see *might* be fake.

Meet Dr. Frankenbite. A "frankenbite" is a deceptive clip. It may be several out-of-context bits welded together; it may even be one moment's sound matched to another moment's video. If Hollywood wants a contestant to utter something ridiculous, it'll create the necessary frankenbite. Imagine writing a history paper and being allowed to lift and commingle any sentences from your sources, regardless of context. Think of how clever you'd appear—until you got caught, that is.

They only showed the contestants' mean/dumb/weird side. A reality TV show has, on average, four film-worthy group activities happening at a given time. Because they also film nighttime activities, sleeping hours count, so that's 672 hours of footage per filming week. Distilling those 672 hours into 42 minutes of TV means you see no more than a fraction of what occurs. If they chose the boring parts, would you watch?

Don't be fooled by that soundstage. The *Big Brother* "house" is a soundstage. Donald Trump's boardroom is a set; so are the apartments on *The Apprentice.* How did the *Amazing Race* dolly grip ride along to get that shot of the contestant on the back of a yak? No matter how real it looks, all the Hollywood apparatus is just off camera.

Many contestants are actors. More reality contestants have acting backgrounds than the producers would like to admit. People who have done some acting know how to play the show-biz game, and many would like to play more of it and may be more easily manipulated. That contestant who's constantly singing copyrighted lyrics to spoil the live Internet feeds gives producers headaches.

Reality shows have draconian nondisclosure agreements. These alone reveal how much there is to hide. Reality show participants are required to sign nondisclosure agreements ("snitch, and our lawyers will visit"). Contestants on *Kid Nation* had to sign agreements that extended three years beyond the end of the 13-episode cycle. On other shows, between their elimination and the program's wrap, participants are sequestered at resorts. *The Amazing Race* contestants even made "red herring" appearances around the world to throw off viewers.

Kudos to the contestants. Not that reality TV producers fake or control everything. They may nudge the process toward a gripping final showdown, but the contestants still have to engage in competition. An *American Idol* finalist always gets a chance to wow the judges and the voting public. Contestants suffer real accidents and injuries. Stagehands didn't push Michael Skupin into the fire on *Survivor IV: The Australian Outback,* nor were his third-degree burns merely makeup. Who doubts that *Fear Factor* contestants authentically vomited the giant cockroaches and other disgusting things they consumed?

What drives this reality craze? Profit. Reality contestants cost less than big stars. What's more, most show formats offer golden product-placement revenue options. Suppose *Big Brother* contestants win soda in a food competition. Why not make a promotional deal with a top-brand beverage company? The excited contestants produce a free commercial—and all the revenue goes to the network! In the end, the dollar sign makes reality TV.

The Real Origin of the Barbie Doll

*It didn't take long for the Barbie doll to become not only
an iconic toy, but a symbol of adult style and ambition,
as well. Where exactly did Barbie come from?*

✳   ✳   ✳   ✳

W HEN BARBIE APPEARED in 1959, she was the first adult-
styled plaything for young girls. Previously, girls were
offered stuffed animals and vinyl baby dolls, presumably meant
to evoke maternal instincts. Barbie was a creature to which a
young girl could *aspire*—albeit a statuesque one.

German Influences

Before Barbie, there was a doll called Bild Lilli, a provocative
copy of a cartoon character in the German newspaper *Bild*.
Clad only in a short skirt and tight sweater, Bild Lilli was sold
to grown men through tobacco shops and bars.

Ruth Handler, the genius behind Barbie, instinctively understood that young girls wanted to enter the adult world early.
Handler had noticed her own daughter, Barbara, assigning her
paper dolls grown-up roles while playing with them. When
Handler spotted Bild Lilli in Europe during a family vacation,
she recognized the doll's possible commercial potential and
purchased several examples, each in a different outfit.

Barbie's earliest appearance, although toned down from Bild
Lilli, still owed much to her forerunner: She was pale, with
pouty red lips and heavily made-up eyes casting a sidelong
glance, not to mention her absurd measurements (which, on
a human counterpart, would equal 38"-18"-32"). Barbie was
also a protofeminist icon, holding at least 95 different careers.
Her original job description, "a teenage model dressed in the
latest style" (even though she looked older), later evolved into
nonspecific "career girl," with astronaut, ballerina, doctor, pilot,
attorney, paleontologist, and presidential candidate versions.

The Barbie Empire Grows

Millions of baby-boom children grew up imagining themselves as Barbie, who went on to acquire boyfriend Ken, close friend Midge, little sister Skipper, and a wardrobe that any Hollywood star would envy. Actually, "acquire" could have been Barbie's middle name (although it was really Millicent). She needed everything. At first, it was just a trunk to hold her detailed clothes and teeny accessories. Then came furniture and a beach house, accessed via luxury cars (pink Cadillac, red Porsche). Her features and hair softened; her other friends (Stacey, a British pal; and Christie, her African American friend) came and went; and, after a long engagement, she finally dumped Ken (named after Handler's son).

During the past half-century, Barbie has reflected both fashion and social history. Charlotte Johnson, who originally dressed the doll, took her job seriously, interpreting the most important clothing trends of each successive era. Barbie also inspired top designers, including Armani, Christian Dior, Dolce & Gabbana, John Galliano, Gucci, Alexander McQueen, and Vivienne Westwood, to create exclusive originals for her; Philip Treacy designed her hats, and Manolo Blahnik her shoes.

The Decline of the Barbie Era

What was once shocking has now become rather staid. Little girls nowadays seek the hypersexualized, even more cartoony-looking Bratz, who come off as even poorer role models. In comparison, Barbie looks square and has lost market share. Her future seems to be as a nostalgic collectible for adults—a complete collection of early Barbies, plus friends and outfits, was auctioned for record prices in late 2006; a single doll, Barbie in Midnight Red, sold for $17,000. In order to retain value, collectors keep limited editions in their original boxes. In a way, Barbie has come full circle: From her sordid start as Bild Lilli, Barbie has once again become a toy for grown-ups only.

Chapter 15

The Kitchen

Weird Theme Restaurants

When good food and service are just not enough, it's comforting to know that there is a plethora of new experiences for the discriminating (and adventurous) diner.

✳   ✳   ✳   ✳

Moscow

LOOKING FOR A thrill? Gogol is an underground restaurant located in the heart of downtown Moscow. Designed to look like a wartime bunker, guests are alerted when their order is ready to be picked up by an ear-shattering air raid siren.

If that doesn't suit you, try The Real McCoy. In order to find the entrance to the restaurant, diners must find the secret door identified by a small plaque. After knocking, a doorman confirms your identity by peering through a small peephole. Inside, The Real McCoy looks like a 1930s Prohibition-era speakeasy, complete with a brass still.

Taiwan

If you long to relive that night spent in the hospital getting your gallbladder removed, you'll simply love the D.S. Music Restaurant. Borrowing from the ever-popular medical theme, guests are seated around a hospital bed. Visitors can also order cocktails (called "medicine") served in IV bags administered by sexily clad "nurses."

Think you've seen it all? The Modern Toilet restaurant offers its clients the very best in lavatory cuisine. It "seats" 100 guests on porcelain commodes instead of chairs, where they feast from a menu of items served on miniature toilet seats. Can't find the napkins? Just reach to your side and grab some toilet paper.

The Jail captures all of the memories of your last incarceration. From the moment that you enter the solid steel doors, you'll thrill at the feel of your wrists being shackled as you're escorted to an intimate table behind bars. Fortunately, The Jail features reasonably priced Chinese cuisine instead of prison rations.

Tokyo

Also known as the Shibuya Medical Prison, guests at the restaurant Alcatraz are shackled from the moment they enter the bar. Inmates in black-and-white striped jailhouse uniforms lead you to a cell where you can order drinks like the "Influenza" and hover over your meal—served in a stainless steel basin.

Why grow up when you can dine at the Alice in Wonderland Café? From the moment you enter, you are made to feel like you belong at the Mad Hatter's tea party by an all-female staff of waitresses dressed in skimpy French maid costumes. While the main courses are on par with other restaurants, guests love the White Rabbit crepes and Tweedle Dee and Dum parfait.

United States

Leave it to the Americans to come up with a restaurant that's built around bowls of cereal. Cereality is a franchise with cafés located in Ohio, West Virginia, Minnesota, Florida, Texas, and Arizona. With the assistance of pajama-clad "cereologists," customers can choose from a wide variety of hot or cold cereal.

When you've had enough of healthy cuisine, it's time to take the plunge at the Heart Attack Grill in Chandler, Arizona. The restaurant sports a high-fat, high-cholesterol menu, touting the great taste of their Quadruple Bypass Burger and Flatliner Fries (fried in lard). Wash it all down with Jolt Cola or beer.

The Humble Beginnings of America's Favorite Dessert

Whether you love it or hate it, there's no denying that JELL-O is one of the world's best-known products—not to mention America's best-selling dessert.

✳ ✳ ✳ ✳

JELL-O DATES BACK to 1845 when an inventor and philanthropist named Peter Cooper obtained a patent for a flavorless gelatin dessert. Cooper packaged the product in convenient boxes—complete with instructions—but did little to promote it. As a result, most people continued to make gelatin the old-fashioned way, which was very labor-intensive.

In the 1890s, Pearl B. Wait, a carpenter and cough medicine producer from Le Roy, New York, perfected a fruit-flavored version of Cooper's gelatin dessert. Wait's wife, May, called the product JELL-O and offered it in lemon, orange, raspberry, and strawberry flavors. But Wait had little luck selling the stuff. In 1899, Wait sold the business to his neighbor and owner of the Genesee Pure Food Company, Orator Frank Woodward, for $450. Woodward's company was best known as the manufacturer of a popular coffee substitute called Grain-O.

A savvy promoter, Woodward advertised JELL-O in such magazines as *Ladies' Home Journal*, calling it "America's Most Famous Dessert." Sales soared. In 1904, Woodward introduced the iconic JELL-O Girl, the brand's first trademark. Usually depicted playing with boxes of JELL-O, the character was based on Elizabeth King (the daughter of Franklin King, an artist for Genesee's advertising agency) and was drawn by Rose O'Neill. JELL-O ads featuring Kewpie dolls, another O'Neill creation, debuted in 1908.

Competitors tried to stop JELL-O's rising popularity but to no avail. One competing gelatin maker even ridiculed the "sissy-sweet salads" made with JELL-O, apparently unaware that it was JELL-O's reputation as an easy-to-make, nonthreatening, tasty dessert that made it popular across ethnic and social lines.

JELL-O quickly became a must-have on American tables. And since it cost only ten cents a box, it was within everyone's budget. In 1912, a booklet was published featuring JELL-O recipes from six of America's most famous cooks. Later booklets, which numbered in the hundreds, included *Thrifty JELL-O Recipes to Brighten Your Menus; JELL-O, Quick Easy Wonder Dishes*; and the oddly titled *What Mrs. Dewey Did with the New Jell-O!* One booklet even included recipes from celebrities such as Ethel Barrymore and opera singer Madame Ernestine Schumann-Heink. JELL-O was so popular that during the first quarter of the 20th century, samples of it were given to immigrants arriving at Ellis Island as a special "welcome to America."

JELL-O slowly expanded from its original four flavors and is available today in a taste-tempting array that includes apricot, cherry, cranberry, lemon, lime, watermelon, and even margarita, piña colada, and strawberry daiquiri.

Indeed, new and daring flavors have done much to maintain JELL-O's reputation as America's favorite dessert. And its amazing versatility hasn't hurt either. In addition to enjoying JELL-O as a dessert unto itself, fans often jazz it up with mixed fruit, whipped cream, crushed cookies, and other goodies. Some home cooks even make it a dinner side dish by adding a medley of mixed vegetables. (Serve this at your own risk.)

Today, JELL-O is owned by Kraft Foods, which has expanded the JELL-O brand with a huge array of JELL-O pudding products (famously advertised by comedian Bill Cosby) and other items. But it is JELL-O gelatin that remains the company's biggest seller, moving about 300 million boxes a year—a true testament to the world's fascination with desserts that jiggle.

SPAM: Revolution in a Can

*The story of how a "miracle meat" swept
the nation—and the world.*

❊ ❊ ❊ ❊

IN 1926, Geo. A. Hormel & Co. came out with the
nation's first canned ham. Eleven years later, the company
unveiled something even more revolutionary: a canned meat
product that didn't require refrigeration. Developed by Jay C.
Hormel, the son of the company's founder, it was marketed
under the name "Hormel Spiced Ham" to public apathy.

Indeed, to say that Hormel Spiced Ham didn't exactly set
the canned meat market on fire would be an understatement.
Adding to the problem was the fact that many other canned
meat lunch products were being produced by competitors,
which cut sharply into Hormel's market share. In an effort to
generate greater public interest in its product, Hormel offered
a $100 prize for a catchier name. The contest winner suggested
SPAM, which may have been a shortened form of "shoulder of
pork and ham." Of course, over the years, people have had fun
with the name, suggesting it stands for "Something Posing as
Meat" or "Spare Parts Animal Meat."

Hormel reintroduced its canned luncheon meat and its new
name in mid-1937 with a national advertising blitz that touted
SPAM as appropriate for any meal, including breakfast. In
1940, Hormel started advertising SPAM with what some
experts consider the first singing commercial. The lyrics were
simplicity itself: "SPAM, SPAM, SPAM, SPAM/Hormel's
new miracle meat in a can!/Tastes fine, saves time/If you want
something grand/Ask for SPAM!"

In a brilliant move, Hormel also became a major sponsor of an
extraordinarily popular radio show starring George Burns and
Gracie Allen. Ad spots during the radio program introduced

the public to "SPAMMY the Pig" in 1940. Almost immediately, Americans took to SPAM, and sales skyrocketed.

SPAM Goes to War

SPAM was especially popular during World War II, both at home and on the front lines. It wasn't subject to wartime rationing like beef, so it became a dinner staple in many American households. The military liked SPAM because it required no refrigeration. SPAM fed many an Allied soldier throughout the war and was even credited by Soviet Premier Nikita Khrushchev with helping save the starving Soviet army.

Here to Stay?

Decades later, SPAM still sells well and has achieved a certain cultural panache. And while Americans consume their share of the spiced canned meat, SPAM has developed an even bigger following in South Korea, where it is sold in gift packs and used as an ingredient in a variety of traditional Korean dishes.

In recent years, of course, *spam* has also become a universal word for unsolicited e-mail. Understandably, this negative connotation does not sit well with Hormel Foods, which has gone to court to keep companies that deal in the prevention of unwanted e-mail from using its trademark. "It's really important that SPAM doesn't get confused with anything else," Vice President Julie Craven told ABC News. "I think any time [the name is] used inappropriately, it is under assault."

This is not to suggest that Hormel Foods doesn't have a sense of humor when it comes to SPAM. The company has expressed appreciation for a popular *Monty Python* sketch that extols the product at length and is even a sponsor of the musical *Monty Python's SPAMALOT*, a stage play based on the movie *Monty Python and the Holy Grail*, which includes a SPAM reference.

Such allusions only prove SPAM's long and far-reaching cultural influence—a heady accomplishment for a product originally developed as a quick meal for harried housewives.

Some Clear-Eyed Liquor Logic

Sit back with a glass of your favorite adult beverage and ponder some of the many misconceptions about alcohol.

✳ ✳ ✳ ✳

Red wine is made from red grapes and white wine is from white grapes. "White" grapes, of course, are more yellow or green than white. Most white wine is produced from these grapes, but some varieties are in fact made from black grapes. The skins of black grapes are varying shades of purple or red, but the pulp is actually gray. White wines are made only from the juice of grapes, whereas red wines include the crushed skins and stems. During fermentation, the pigment from the grape skins colors the wine red. This also infuses the wine with the tannins that create each particular flavor of red wine.

Rosé or blush-colored wines, such as White Zinfandel, are produced from black grapes either by allowing limited contact with the grape skins during the fermentation process or, more likely, by simply adding a specific amount of red wine to the finished white wine.

"Liquor before beer, you're in the clear; beer before liquor, you'll never be sicker." Anyone who has been to a college party has probably heard similar drinking tips, but the fact is that mixing different types of alcohol will not make you more intoxicated. It's possible that combining a variety of different-flavored cocktails will upset your stomach and make you feel sick, but it will not make you any drunker. A unit of alcohol is a unit of alcohol, whether it is consumed in the form of beer, wine, or liquor, or is disguised in a sweet fruit punch or a puddle of cream.

A standard drink is the equivalent of a 12-ounce bottle of beer, a 4-ounce glass of wine, a 3-ounce glass of fortified wine such as sherry or port, or a 1-ounce shot of hard liquor. Each drink contains the same amount of alcohol, so whether you consume four of the same standard drinks or four different ones, you will have swallowed the same amount of alcohol and will therefore be equally drunk.

The misconception that mixing drinks will make you more intoxicated stems from the fact that flavored shots of hard liquor are often consumed much faster than a beer or glass of wine. Drink a couple of beers and throw back a few watermelon shots in an hour and, yes, you could end up on the bathroom floor while your friend who nursed just beer stands over you. She's able to hold your hair and laugh at you simply because she consumed fewer units of alcohol. And if you think that a sandwich and a cup of coffee will get you sober, you've got a few more things coming—up.

Alcohol evaporates when it's heated. Many cooks who add spirits or wine to a dish do so with the belief that all of the alcohol burns off in the cooking process. In fact, the amount of booze that remains in the dish depends on how—and how long—the ingredients are exposed to heat. For example, if you deglaze a pan by adding wine to a boiling liquid and then remove the dish from the heat source, about 85 percent of the alcohol will be retained. If you flambé a crepe or plum pudding by dousing it in brandy and then lighting it, the flame will die out within a minute or so—but as much as 75 percent of the alcohol will remain. Baking and stewing are the most effective ways to remove the booze from a dish, but depending on the length of time the food spends in the oven or on the stovetop, it will still retain some alcohol. Bake a rum cake for an hour, and about 75 percent of the alcohol will cook out, whereas simmering a beef bourguignonne for two and a half hours will burn off 95 percent of the wine.

A Savory Sampler of Food Phrases

*It seems that food and the English language
go together like peanut butter and jelly.*

✳   ✳   ✳   ✳

There's No Such Thing as a Free Lunch: In the 1840s, bars in the United States offered anyone buying a drink a "free lunch." It was really just a bunch of salty snacks that made customers so thirsty, they kept buying drinks.

Hair of the Dog that Bit You: Medieval doctors believed if a rabid dog bit you, your chance of recovery was better if a hair was plucked from the dog and placed on your wound.

The Big Cheese: In 1802, a cheese maker delivered a 1,235-pound wheel of cheese to President Thomas Jefferson. Citizens declared it the "big cheese," referring to both the wheel and its important recipient.

In a Nutshell: This saying, which indicates a lot of information conveyed succinctly, is so old that Cicero used it. He said that Homer's *Iliad* was penned in such small handwriting that all 24 books could fit "in a nutshell."

Cool as a Cucumber: Even on a warm day, a field cucumber stays about 20 degrees cooler than the outside air. Though scientists didn't prove this until 1970, the saying has been around since the early 18th century.

Bring Home the Bacon: The Dunmow Flitch Trials, an English tradition that started in 1104, challenged married couples to go one year without arguing. The winners took home a "flitch" (a side) of bacon.

Spill the Beans: In ancient Greece, the system for voting new members into a private club involved secretly placing colored beans into opaque jars. Prospective members never knew who voted for or against them—unless the beans were spilled.

Egg on Your Face: During slapstick comedies in the Victorian theater, actors made the fall guy look foolish by breaking eggs on his forehead.

Gone to Pot: Dating to pre-Elizabethan England, this phrase refers to pieces of meat that were hardened, on the verge of spoiling—and good only for the stew pot.

Cook Your Goose: In 1560, a town attacked by the Mad King of Sweden, Eric XIV, hung up a goose—a symbol of stupidity—in protest. The furious king threatened, "I'll cook your goose!"

Easy as Pie: Making a pie from scratch isn't easy; the phrase is a contraction of the late-19th-century phrase "easy as eating pie."

In a Pickle: From the old Dutch phrase *de pikel zitten*, which means to sit in a salt solution used for preserving pickles—sure to be an uncomfortable situation.

With a Grain of Salt: To take something "with a grain of salt" is to consider the subject in question with skepticism or suspicion. Salt was once believed to have healing properties, and to eat or drink something with a grain of salt was to practice preventive medicine against potential poisoning or illness.

Happy as a Clam: The original phrase was "happy as a clam at high tide." Because clam diggers are able to gather clams only at low tide, the clams are much safer (and happier) when the tide is high and the water is too deep to wade into.

Take the Cake: The phrase originated at cakewalk contests, where individuals would parade and prance in a circle to the audience's delight. The person with the most imaginative swagger would take home first prize, which was always a cake.

A Baker's Dozen: Medieval English bakers would dupe customers by making loaves that contained more air pockets than bread. By 1266, authorities enacted a law that required bakers to sell their bread by weight. To avoid heavy penalties, bakers started to add an extra loaf for every dozen: hence the number 13.

Craziest Coke Claims:
Fact vs. Fiction

Coca-Cola is a staple of the All-American diet.
It's also a regular in the rumor mill.

✳ ✳ ✳ ✳

For a common can of soda, you'd never guess all the strange claims about Coke. Most are no more than myth. A few, however, are the real thing. Time to separate fact from fiction!

Coke was originally green in color.

'Fraid not. The kind folks at Coca-Cola say their bubbly beverage has been brown since the first bottle was produced in 1886. However, the glass of the bottle was green in the early days, which may have led to the rumor.

Coke once contained cocaine.

Believe it or not, this one's true: The original Coke formula used leaves from the coca plant. No one is entirely sure how much cocaine was used in a bottle of Coca-Cola, but some estimates place it at approximately two percent. Early ads even promoted the drink as a "brain tonic" that could cure headaches and chase away depression.

Once health experts began to realize the negative effects of cocaine, Coca-Cola modified its formula to use "decocainized" coca leaves with the same flavor—a process still in place today. A company called Stepan actually has a factory where workers remove the cocaine from the leaves and ship the drug-free product to Coca-Cola. Surgeons use the leftover cocaine, which is legal as a local anesthetic for minor surgeries. Stepan is the only legal U.S. supplier of cocaine for these purposes.

Coke can be used as a household cleaner.

True—and your kitchen counter will never taste better. The Coca-Cola Company says the acidic drink could theoretically hold the power to clean. Coke points out, however, that many other acidic agents—vinegar, for example—are considered completely safe as food ingredients. As far as any health implications, Coke notes that "rubbing something in a cloth soaked in a soft drink is not at all like drinking a soft drink" because "people don't hold soft drinks in their mouths for long periods of time." Also, Coke says, your saliva neutralizes the acid before it moves any lower in your body.

Coke will dissolve corrosion.

This statement also has some truth to it. Because of the acidic level mentioned above, the drink could theoretically knock some rust off of corroded metals. The Coca-Cola Company, however, recommends instead using a product actually designed for that purpose.

Coke gives you kidney stones.

False, the soda sellers say. Coke claims its product has never been shown to cause stones and may, in contrast, help prevent them. Not having enough liquid in your diet can contribute to the problem, and Coke, its reps say, provides a "pleasant and refreshing way to consume part of [your] daily fluid requirements." These people are good.

Coke works as a spermicide.

We hate to be the ones to break the news, but no. The myth started after the debut of New Coke in 1985, when scientists began to notice an increase in birth rates in parts of Africa. As the story goes, two Harvard researchers looked into it and found women in the villages had, in fact, been using the drink as a contraceptive. The scientists decided to test both New Coke and the original Coke to see what was going on. They found New Coke was five times less effective than original Coke as a spermicide, which explained the increased rate. Both drinks, though, had too mild an effect to be considered even remotely practical.

Those Arches are Golden: The McDonald's Kingdom

In the restaurant industry, there is probably no greater success story than McDonald's. Today, McDonald's has become synonymous with fast food around the world.

✳ ✳ ✳ ✳

IF YOU THOUGHT Ray Kroc opened the first McDonald's, you'd be wrong. In 1940, two brothers, Dick and Maurice (Mac) McDonald, opened the first McDonald's on Route 66 in San Bernardino, California. As was common at the time, carhops served hungry teens with made-to-order food. But that all changed in 1948, when the McDonalds fired the carhops and implemented their innovative "Speedee Service System," a technique that streamlined the assembly process and became the benchmark for premade hamburgers. Additionally, this process allowed profits to soar . . . they could now sell hamburgers for 15 cents, or half what a dinner would cost.

In 1953, Dick and Mac decided to franchise their restaurant, and the second McDonald's opened in Phoenix, Arizona. It was the first Mickey D's to sport the famous golden arches. A year later, an entrepreneur and milkshake-mixer salesman named Ray Kroc visited. He was impressed with the McDonalds' enterprise, and he immediately joined their team. In 1955, he founded the current McDonald's Systems, Inc., and opened the ninth McDonald's restaurant in Des Plaines, Illinois. Six years later, Kroc bought the business from the McDonald brothers for $2.7 million. The poorly constructed deal stipulated that Dick and Mac could keep the original restaurant but somehow overlooked their right to remain a McDonald's franchise. Because of this error, Kroc opened a restaurant down the block from the original store, and within a short time he drove the brothers out of the hamburger business.

Two All-Beef Patties

Kroc's many marketing insights included Hamburger University—where the graduates are presented with bachelor's degrees in Hamburgerology—ads targeting families, and the introduction of Ronald McDonald and "McDonaldland." Feeling the need to adapt, the company altered the menu for the first time in 1963, adding the Filet-O-Fish (prompted by Catholics who didn't eat meat on Fridays), followed by such famous additions as the Big Mac and apple pie.

McDonald's spread quickly and, in 1967, the first McDonald's restaurant outside the United States opened in Richmond, British Columbia. Ten years later, McDonald's operated on four continents. It completed its world domination in 1992 by opening an African restaurant in Casablanca, Morocco.

In 1974, along with Fred Hill of the Philadelphia Eagles, McDonald's founded the Ronald McDonald House, an organization that caters to families of critically ill children seeking medical treatment. As of 2008, there were 259 outlets.

Hold the Mayo

All has not gone smoothly for the Mc-empire over the past several years, however. In 2000, Eric Schlosser published *Fast Food Nation*, a critical commentary on fast food in general and McDonald's in particular. This was followed by several lawsuits: one on obesity (claiming McDonald's "lured" young children into their restaurant with their playgrounds) and others claiming damaged health due to saturated fats.

A huge sensation followed the 2004 release of the film *Supersize Me*. This documentary accused fast-food restaurants of ignoring America's escalating obesity crisis. Later that year, in response to the public's desire for healthier food, McDonald's did away with its super-size meals and implemented more chicken and fish options. In 2005, they added a range of salads and low-sugar drinks and agreed to put nutritional information on all their packaging.

A Bagful of McUrban Legends

If you're one of the more than 100 billion served at McDonald's restaurants, you've probably heard at least one shocking (but ultimately untrue) rumor about the fast-food giant.

✳   ✳   ✳   ✳

IN THE 1980S, word began circulating that McDonald's had implemented an interesting recycling program at its restaurants. Employees secretly rifled through the garbage to reclaim still-intact food-serving packages, which were then reused for subsequent orders. Those "in the know" who ate at McDonald's made sure to crumple their packages to thwart the company's nefarious money-saving scheme.

This garbage-picking anecdote is one of many outrageous urban legends about McDonald's. Why are the Golden Arches the subject of such scandal? To start, there's the ever-present public suspicion of unscrupulous corporations that seek to maximize profits at the expense of quality and safety. And as a high-profile multinational company perceived as spearheading the globalization movement, McDonald's is a favorite target of antiglobalization Davids looking to slay McGoliath.

Here's a brief look at some of the tastier McDonald's myths that have been served up over the years.

Mmm ... worm burgers. A long-standing rumor in the 1970s and '80s was that McDonald's used ground worms as filler in its hamburgers. McDonald's has always maintained that its burgers are 100 percent beef and has gone to great lengths to prove it, including procuring a letter from the U.S. Secretary of Agriculture backing the claim. Besides, McDonald's officials are quick to add, worm "meat" costs a lot more than beef, making its use in patties economically unfeasible. A similar tale was circulated in the 1990s. This time the filler ingredient was cow eyeballs, which are actually in high demand for scientific research. Consequently, their use in Big Macs would be even more cost prohibitive than worms.

What's in the shakes? It has long been alleged that McDonald's calls its milkshakes simply "shakes" because there isn't any milk or dairy products in them. The fact that they can be safely consumed by lactose-intolerant persons, say myth mongers, proves it. Among the ingredients that McDonald's has purportedly substituted for milk over the years are styrofoam balls, pig fat, and the fluid from cow eyeballs (that way, nothing is wasted!). But according to McDonald's ingredient lists, its shakes do contain milk—specifically, whole milk and nonfat milk solids.

Near-death by bird feathers. One of the more bizarre legends ever conjured up involves an unnamed girl in an unnamed location who had a near-death experience after eating a McFlurry (an ice cream concoction with fruit, candy, or cookie bits whipped in). The girl, according to the story, almost died from a violent allergic reaction to bird feathers. Doctors traced her dietary consumption leading to the reaction and pinpointed the McFlurry. It seems that they discovered through someone at McDonald's headquarters that one of the ingredients in the frozen treat is indeed bird feathers. In all versions of the tale, the girl and her whereabouts are unnamed because she doesn't exist, and the "feather" reference likely derives from the airy consistency of the product, not the mix-ins.

I'll have a hot choko pie. Another McDonald's falsity perpetrated by e-mailers is that McDonald's apple pies lack one key ingredient—apples. Rumor spreaders in the United States claim that potatoes, pears, and crackers are substituted for apples, while their Australian counterparts offer even more imaginative surrogates, such as ostrich eggs and something called *chokos*—a cucumberlike fruit that costs significantly more to import to Australia than the Granny Smith apples that are actually used in the handheld dessert.

Fugu About It

People who love sushi and sashimi say these Far Eastern delicacies are to die for. Although they don't mean that literally, consuming some raw fish truly is dangerous.

✳   ✳   ✳   ✳

THE MOST NOTORIOUS and celebrated of the Japanese sashimi selections is the pufferfish, called fugu in Japan. The flesh of the pufferfish can be lethal if prepared incorrectly, and only specially licensed chefs are allowed to sell it. Even so, a number of people die every year from eating it (often, they are untrained enthusiasts who catch, prepare, and consume their own pufferfish and accidentally kill themselves). The poison paralyzes the person, who stays fully conscious before dying from asphyxiation.

Most Japanese cities have several fugu restaurants, which are usually clustered together because regulations once placed limits on where they could operate. And though closely monitored, not all fugu restaurants are equal. People seek out the best-quality fugu, which supposedly still has nonlethal amounts of the poison remaining in its flesh and produces a tingling sensation on the tongue.

Sushi Safety

Although fugu remains an almost exclusively Japanese delicacy, sushi ranks among the most wildly popular "exports" from Japan. If you've hesitated to try it, you may have good reason. Raw fish can be infected with parasites, and every year there are hundreds of cases of illness caused by them. In the United States, however, you are more likely to become ill from eating cooked beef or chicken than raw fish. That's because commercial fish intended for raw consumption must be frozen for at least 72 hours at -4 degrees Fahrenheit in order to kill dangerous parasites and their larvae.

A Wormy Problem

The most common infection is tapeworm, a relatively benign parasite that many people don't realize they have until they pass it. Tapeworms, as well as flukes or "flatworms," can cause abdominal cramps, diarrhea, nausea, fatigue, and weight loss, but are usually easy to treat. Of much greater concern is the roundworm, also known as *anisakis*, which can bore into the lining of a person's stomach or intestines and cause severe abdominal inflammation and pain, often within an hour of eating. Surgery may be required to remove it. The worm can taint the flesh of a fish with toxins, and eating it could cause a severe allergic reaction.

A Food and Drug Administration (FDA) study of Seattle-area restaurants found that one in ten samples of salmon contained roundworm. Fortunately, virtually all were dead because the fish had been flash frozen. As in the United States, most countries now require that all types of commercial fish intended for raw consumption be deep frozen. However, researchers with California Health Services (CHS) continue to place raw fresh fish on its list of seven risky foods that can carry infection-causing viruses, bacteria, and parasites (other foods on the list include rare-cooked ground beef, uncooked egg yolks, unpasteurized milk, and alfalfa sprouts). According to CHS, properly prepared, handled, and frozen sushi-grade fish is safer than other raw fish, but it still is not as safe as cooked fish.

The Case for Dining Out

The bottom line is that it is safest to eat cooked seafood. But if you can't resist sushi, make sure it is prepared by trained, experienced chefs who know what they're doing. The FDA suspects most illness is caused by the consumption of homemade sushi. Satiate your sushi cravings at reputable restaurants and ask whether the fish has been deep frozen. The safest bet is to order sushi dishes made with cooked fish, such as California rolls. And if you go to Japan, get your fugu fix only from a reliable dealer.

Who Put the PB in the PB&J?

What goes equally well with jelly, bacon, marshmallow fluff, chocolate, and banana? Peanut butter, of course. And most schoolkids think that George Washington Carver is the man behind that magic.

∗   ∗   ∗   ∗

THE MYTH THAT George Washington Carver invented peanut butter has spread as easily as this spreadable favorite. But by the time Carver was born in 1864, peanuts were being crushed into a paste on five continents. Peanuts have been grown for consumption in South America since 950 B.C., and the Incas used peanut paste in much of their cooking. Fifteenth-century trade ships took peanuts to Africa and Asia, where they were assimilated into local cuisines, often as a paste for thickening stews. In the 18th century, peanuts traveled back across the Atlantic Ocean to be traded to North American colonists. In 1818, the first commercial peanut crop was produced in North Carolina. Today, there are approximately 50,000 peanut farms in the United States, and 50 percent of the peanuts produced on these farms are turned into peanut butter.

A Popular Nut Paste

So the Incas, not Carver, must be credited with first grinding peanuts into a paste. But the forefather of modern-day peanut butter was an anonymous doctor who, in 1890, put peanuts through a meat grinder to provide a protein source for people with teeth so bad they couldn't chew meat. A food-processing company saw the potential in the doctor's product and started selling the nut paste for six cents per pound. Dr. John Harvey Kellogg (the inventor of corn flakes) had been feeding a similar paste made from steamed, ground peanuts to the patients at his sanatorium in Battle Creek, Michigan. In 1895, he patented his "process of preparing nut meal" and began selling it to the general public.

The nut paste caught on, and peanut-grinding gadgets became available, along with cookbooks with recipes for nut meals, pastes, and spreads. In 1904, visitors at the St. Louis World's Fair bought more than $700 of peanut butter. In 1908, the Krema Nut Company in Columbus, Ohio, began selling peanut butter, but only within the state because of spoilage problems.

Carver's Contributions

So how did George Washington Carver get into this story? Carver was an agricultural chemist and inventor who had a strong interest in peanut production and a firm belief that it could benefit American agriculture. Born to slaves, Carver worked and studied hard. He earned master's degrees in botany and agriculture from Iowa Agricultural College (now Iowa State University), and became the director of agriculture at the Tuskegee Normal and Industrial Institute for Negroes in 1897.

At Tuskegee, Carver researched and developed approximately 290 uses for peanuts, incorporating them into foods, cosmetics, ink, paper, and lubricants. He didn't patent any of these, believing that the earth's crops and their by-products were gifts from God. Although he published several works about the benefits of peanuts in agriculture, industry, and cuisine, he became associated with the crop only late in his career.

Influential Nonetheless

The story of Carver's humble beginnings, talents, and professional success took on mythic proportions. A number of authors generously (and erroneously) credit him with everything from inventing dehydrated foods to rescuing the South from poverty by promoting peanut products. At some point, the invention of peanut butter was attributed to him.

Schoolchildren everywhere are entranced by Carver's personal success story and his contributions to American agriculture. He is a role model despite the fact that he didn't invent peanut butter. Giving credit where it's due—to the Incas—does not diminish the value of Carver's accomplishments.

Vodka: More Than Just a Drink

Here are a few shots of info regarding the popular liquor.

✳ ✳ ✳ ✳

✳ What do screwdrivers and Bloody Marys have in common? Vodka! This colorless alcohol hails from Russia, where its original name, *zhiznennaia voda,* means "water of life."

✳ To make vodka, vegetables (such as potatoes or beets) or grains (barley, wheat, rye, or corn) are put through a process of fermentation, distillation, and filtration. Grain vodkas are considered to be of the highest quality.

✳ The most expensive vodka in the world is Diaka, which comes in a crystal bottle that also contains crystals. The makers of Diaka attribute the vodka's quality to its filtration—it goes through 100 diamonds up to a carat in size.

✳ Vodka seems to have provided a distraction for a couple of notorious Russian czars. In 1540, Ivan the Terrible stopped fighting long enough to establish the country's first vodka monopoly, and in the late 17th century, Peter the Great improved methods of distillation and means of export.

✳ During the reign of Peter the Great, it was customary that foreign ambassadors visiting the court consume a liter and a half of vodka. Lightweight ambassadors began to enlist substitutes for the deed so the actual official could discuss important matters with a clear head.

✳ The Russian phrase *na pososhok* is a toast to the last drink given to a departing guest. It derives from the tradition that visitors traveling from afar would often facilitate their trip with a walking stick called a *pososh,* which had a hollowed-out hole on top. At the end of the visit, a glass of vodka was placed in the hole, and if the visitor could drink the vodka without touching the glass, he was likely able to get home.

Chill Out: The Popsicle Story

As luck would have it, some of the best inventions actually happened by accident. The world would be a sadder place without penicillin, microwave ovens, ice cream cones, Post-it Notes, potato chips, Super Glue, Slinkies, or heaven forbid—Popsicles.

❊　❊　❊　❊

THE POPSICLE WAS "invented" by an industrious 11-year-old boy named Frank Epperson on an unseasonably cold San Francisco evening in 1905. After accidentally leaving his drink in a cup on the front porch overnight, Epperson discovered that the drink had frozen around the wooden stir stick. The next morning, he pulled the frozen drink out of the cup by the stick and voilà . . . the Popsicle was born.

Epperson's frozen invention originally took the neighborhood by storm as the "Epsicle." It wasn't until 1923 while running a lemonade stand at the Neptune Beach amusement park in Oakland, California, that he realized the money-making potential of his discovery. His own children loved the cool treat, begging him for one of "Pop's 'sicles." In 1924, Epperson applied for the first patent of the "Popsicle," the first "drink on a stick."

The Popsicle Goes Big Time

A year later, Epperson sold the patent and rights to the brand name "Popsicle" to the Joe Lowe Company in New York. As it turned out, he made a wise business decision—during the first three years, he earned royalties on the sale of more than 60 million Popsicle ice pops. Popsicles soon began to appear all over the world—they were affectionately known as "Ice-lollies" in Great Britain and "Icy Poles" in Australia.

Popsicles grew in popularity with kids and adults alike. As soldiers returned home from World War II and began building families, the average breadwinner could afford the convenience of having their own refrigerators and freezers. That meant that busy homemakers could buy large quantities of Popsicles in "multipacks" and store them indefinitely in the freezer, dispensing them to the kids whenever they deserved a treat (or needed a bribe). In the mid-'40s, cartoonist and adman Woody Gelman created the "Popsicle Pete" mascot to help market the product in magazines, comic books, and television commercials. Eventually, cardboard advertisements were distributed to the company's vendors touting the new marketing slogan, "If it's Popsicle, it's possible."

Popsicle Spin-Offs

The treats continued to sell well and, in 1965, they became part of the Consolidated Foods Corporation lineup. At that time, 34 different flavors were offered by the company. Several years later, "Creamsicles" (a sherbet pop on a stick with a vanilla ice cream center) were sold in orange and raspberry flavors. The new item became so popular that "National Creamsicle Day" is now celebrated every August 14.

The Popsicle continued to make the corporate rounds when the Gold Bond Ice Cream Company purchased the U.S. operations of Popsicle Industries; it was purchased three years later by Unilever. In 1993, the Popsicle underwent another change when the Unilever company name was changed to the Good Humor-Breyers Ice Cream Company, where the brand remains a fixture today.

* Popsicles also are used in craft projects, as children, adults, and just about anyone who goes to camp uses the sticks in craft projects. But the "stick bomb" is one of the more notorious creations made from used Popsicle sticks. After weaving five sticks together in a specific pattern, the stick bomb is thrown to the floor, where it "explodes" with a loud pop.

* Popsicle Pete creator Woody Gelman was also the writer and co-creator of the Bazooka Joe comics found in Bazooka gum, as well as the sci-fi trading card series Mars Attacks.

Candy That Time Forgot

Between the First and Second World Wars, there were almost 6,000 candy companies in the United States. Then, in the 1970s and '80s, the big companies—Mars, Hershey's, and Nestlé—started snapping up the competition. Suddenly, candy became less varied and more streamlined. Here are some of the candies of yesteryear.

❉   ❉   ❉   ❉

Choco-Lite

DON'T BE FOOLED by the name of this candy bar—Choco-Lite wasn't guilt-free chocolate, though it *was* slightly smaller than most bars. The "lite" likely referred to the dozens of small holes that were punched through the bar, making it seem airier.

Marathon

Mars made this funny-looking, awesome-tasting candy bar in 1973. It featured eight inches of braided caramel covered in milk chocolate. At that length, it was much longer than most of the other candy bars on the shelves. Sadly, it wasn't popular enough to go the distance. Mars discontinued it in 1981.

Chicken Dinner

The Sperry Candy Company created the Chicken Dinner Bar in the early '20s and no, it didn't taste like chicken. The bizarre name was meant to convey the feeling of well-being and prosperity associated with "a chicken in every pot." Instead, the bar was chocolate-flavor caramel rolled in nuts, similar to today's Nut Roll. The candy was phased out in the '60s.

Forever Yours

This confection, created in 1923, was distributed as two bars in one pack—one chocolate, one vanilla. In 1936, the vanilla bar (which was covered in dark chocolate) left the pack and struck out on its own as the Forever Yours bar. It was discontinued in

1979, but it came back ten years later as the Milky Way Dark Bar. In 2000, it was renamed Milky Way Midnight.

Nestlé's Triple-Decker

This bar was discontinued in the early '70s, probably because it was too expensive to produce. The bar had three layers of chocolate: white, dark, and milk. Fans say that the bitter/creamy/sweet combo was unparalleled; there are more than a few online message boards where chocoholics swap recipes for homemade versions.

Bit-O-Choc

Many candy fans out there will recognize the Bit-O-Choc's successful brother, Bit-O-Honey. The latter candy, a sweet, almond-flavored nougat bar, is still being produced 80 years after the Schutter-Johnson candy company created it. Bit-O-Choc, on the other hand, didn't last long. By all accounts, the "molar-ripping" bar was only slightly better than another incarnation, Bit-O-Coconut. The candy was phased out after a few years on the market.

Fat Emma

In Minneapolis in the 1920s, nougat was big business. Pendergast Candy Company had developed a way to use egg whites to create lighter, fluffier nougat that folks loved. Though Frank Mars would eventually use the nougat recipe in his most popular bars (Milky Way and 3 Musketeers), Pendergast made a puffy candy called the Fat Emma, which, though discontinued, is still used in the industry when referring to a candy bar with fluffy nougat filling.

Caravelle

Fans of the Caravelle bar say that eating one was almost a religious experience. The creamy chocolate was wrapped around dark, moist caramel and malted-flavored crisp rice. When Cadbury acquired its producer, Peter Paul, in 1988, the Caravelle was discontinued.

The Making of a Jelly Bean

For a tiny candy, the making of a jelly bean is one enormous process.

* * * *

YOU MAY NOT know it to look at them, but a handful of jelly beans represent three whole weeks of work. Candymakers have the sugary treats' creation down to a science, and one thing's for sure: It's not simple.

Inside Out

Most jelly beans start with the inside. Confectioners stir up a boiling mix of flavors and colors to form the inner goo. Some companies even go as far as putting in real fruit puree. Afterward, it's time to cook up the middle and work toward the outside.

The liquid centers slosh to their next step, where machines squirt them out one pop at a time into starch-filled molds. That's where the candy gets their shape. After several hours of cooling, the soon-to-be beans are taken out and brushed with sugar. At this point, the candymakers set them aside for as long as 48 hours before moving forward with making the outer shells.

Shake, Rattle, and Roll

Finally, the beans are ready to be finished. Workers bring the tasty centers into a giant metal rotating pan. There, they shake the beans around for two full hours, letting them gather several layers of external goodness. But the job isn't done yet—the crews still have to pour glaze over the treats to give them their signature shine. A few more days of seasoning, and these little treats are ready to be branded and sent out. Many confectioners use a special kind of food coloring to stamp the company name directly onto the bean. Then machines move the jelly beans into boxes, seal them up for freshness, and finally ship them away—the last step in a long journey from the factory and into your stomach.

Wacky Jelly Belly Flavors

There was a time when root beer was considered an exotic flavor for a jelly bean. With locations based in California and southern Wisconsin, the Jelly Belly candy makers have raised the bar for strange flavors, especially with some of their most recent selections.

✳ ✳ ✳ ✳

✳ Pickle

✳ Black Pepper

✳ Booger

✳ Dirt

✳ Earthworm

✳ Earwax

✳ Sausage

✳ Rotten Egg

✳ Soap

✳ Vomit

✳ Sardine

✳ Grass

✳ Skunk Spray

✳ Bacon

✳ Baby Wipes

✳ Pencil Shavings

✳ Toothpaste

✳ Moldy Cheese

✳ Buttered Popcorn

✳ Dr. Pepper

✳ Jalapeño

✳ Margarita

✳ Spinach

✳ Cappuccino

✳ Peanut Butter

✳ Café Latte

✳ 7UP

✳ Pomegranate

✳ Baked Beans

✳ Mojito

✳ Grape Crush

✳ Chili Mango

✳ Peach Bellini

✳ Cotton Candy

✳ Toasted Marshmallow

✳ Caramel Corn

The Mystery of the Fortune Cookie

The fortune cookie may be the most famous symbol of Chinese food in America. But venture over to China and you won't find an advice-filled twist of dough anywhere in sight.

✳ ✳ ✳ ✳

A FORTUNE COOKIE IS to Chinese food as a stomachache is to a greasy-spoon joint: There's no question it'll follow the meal. It turns out, though, that the former is far from common in the actual country of China; in fact, you might be hard-pressed to find anyone there who's even heard of one. So where did this crunchy cookie come from?

The Chinese Theories

Some trace the cookie's creation to early Chinese immigrants in America using them as a means to carry on traditions from home. One story says the cookie's roots originated as far back as 12th-century China, during the rule of the Yuan Dynasty.

According to that tale, rebel monks started making a special kind of mooncake, into which they'd slip secret messages to their comrades without the invading Mongols finding out. Legend has it the men baked the cakes, messages and all, then sold them to Chinese families to spread their rebellion plans.

Another theory traces the first fortune back to ancient Chinese parlor games. In these sessions, men would write proverbs on paper and then place them inside twisted pastries.

Yet another hypothesis puts the cookie credit in the hands of George Jung, founder of Los Angeles's Hong Kong Noodle Company. Jung is believed by many to have cooked up the first fortune cookies as a way to add some happiness in the dreary post–World War I era. However, some speculate the cookies may have also served as a simple distraction for Jung's guests while their food was being prepared.

The Japanese Alternative

The other school of thought claims the Japanese actually invented the fortune cookie. Researchers have found family bakeries in the city of Kyoto that have been making similarly shaped fortune crackers since the late 1800s, long before the treat first surfaced in America around 1907.

Called *tsujiura senbei* (fortune crackers) or *omikuji senbei* (written fortune crackers), the Japanese cookies do have some differences: They are larger, darker in color, and have more of a sesame-miso flavor than the vanilla-butter combo of the Chinese variety. The fortunes are also presented within the fold rather than inside the cavity. Even so, fortune-cookie devotees insist the similarities are too great to ignore.

Some Japanese families theorize that the cookies first came over to the United States around 1890, when a man named Makoto Hagiwara helped build the Japanese Tea Garden in San Francisco's Golden Gate Park. A nearby bakery called Benkyodo, Makoto's family claims, served the cookies to visitors. It was from there, they say, that other Asian restaurants in California picked up the idea, leading to its popularity.

Fortune Resistance

Wherever it began, years later the fortune cookie still hasn't taken off within the nation of China. An American importer named Nancy Anderson is trying to change that, but the work isn't coming easy. Anderson imports fortune cookies from California to Hong Kong to sell to restaurants, mainly ones that cater to—surprise, surprise—foreign tourists.

With added packaging requirements, translation costs, and international taxes, the cookies end up costing more than double their worth. Anderson has found most restaurant owners wary of the desserts; her efforts have yielded little success. International disdain aside, though, the beloved cookie doesn't seem to be in any danger of disappearing from Chinese custom in America—and that's one fortune you can count on.

Chunks of Cheddar

Chew on these savory slices of trivia.

❋ ❋ ❋ ❋

❋ Until 2002, cheddar was the second most popular cheese in the United States (after processed American), but passion for pizza has bumped it to number three after mozzarella.

❋ Cheddar, England, a village in the southwestern county of Somerset, is home to the famous geological site Cheddar Gorge. Beginning in the 16th century, visitors to Cheddar Gorge tasted cheese at local inns and started taking home "cheese from Cheddar." The cheese was actually from cheese makers throughout Somerset County, not just in Cheddar.

❋ The production of cheddar involves "cheddaring"—the repeated cutting and piling of curds to create a firm cheese.

❋ Cheddar is so important to the English palate that during World War II, it was illegal to commercially produce any other variety of cheese in England.

❋ Traditional English cheddar is produced in wheels and aged in cloth for a minimum of six months.

❋ "Squeaky curds" refers to fresh young cheddar in its natural shape, before it's pressed into a block and aged. Fresh curds are considered a delicacy—and they actually make a squeaking sound when you eat them.

❋ Cheddar cheese is naturally white or pale yellow. These days, much of it is dyed orange with seeds from the annatto plant. Early cheese makers used carrot juice and marigold petals.

❋ Originally, cheese was dyed to prevent seasonal color variations. Traditional cheddars had a natural orange color derived from the carotene-rich grass cows ate during spring and summer. In winter, cows ate dry feed, and the resulting cheese was white. Consumers had the misperception that orange cheese was more nutritious, so cheese makers began coloring their cheeses a "healthful" shade of orange.

* As dry feed has become more commonly used year round, dyeing now depends on regional preferences and traditions. Wisconsin cheddar is usually dyed orange, while New England and Canadian cheddars are typically left white.

* Prior to 1850, nearly all cheese produced in the United States was cheddar.

* You can tell the age of cheddar by its taste. Young cheddar has a mild taste; the longer it ages, the sharper and more tangy it becomes.

* "American" cheese is a young, pasteurized cheddar that undergoes additional processing to become the familiar easy-to-melt variety.

* People in the United States eat more than nine pounds of cheddar cheese per person per year.

* The "World's Best Cheddar" is made in the United States: Cabot Creamery in Vermont took home blue-ribbon honors at the 2006 World Championship Cheese Contest.

* According to historians, President Andrew Jackson once served a 1,400-pound block of cheddar at the White House.

* In 1964, the Wisconsin Cheese Foundation created a 34,665-pound wheel of cheddar for display in the Wisconsin Pavilion at the 1964–1965 World's Fair in New York.

* In 1988, Simon's Specialty Cheese in Little Chute, Wisconsin, made a 40,060-pound wheel of cheddar known as the "Belle of Wisconsin."

* In 1995, a cheese maker in Quebec, Canada, claimed to have created the largest wheel of cheese—a 57,518-pound round of cheddar.

Like a Rock

Rolling Rock has long been one of Pennsylvania's favorite libations, and for years, barroom patrons have bickered over the significance of the number 33 on the beer's label.

✳   ✳   ✳   ✳

BEER DRINKERS LOVE beer labels almost as much as they love the yeasty, thirst-quenching nectar itself. Each word and turn of phrase is examined, disputed, and questioned in discussions that are usually helped along by concerted suds consumption. Consider, for example, the number 33 on bottles of Rolling Rock beer. Some lager analysts have theorized that the double digits denote the year—1933— that Prohibition was repealed and alcoholic beverages were once again allowed to flow freely. Others contend that "33" refers to the number of steps from the brewmaster's office to the brewery floor. Equine enthusiasts claim that a timely wager at the track—placing a $33 bet on horse number 33 on the third race on the third day of the third month—provided Rolling Rock's future owner with the funds necessary to buy his brewery. So which one of these tantalizing theses holds the answer?

The truth is, none of the above. In 1939, company executives developed a distinctive description of their product to adorn the label. To ensure that the manufacturer printed the pronouncement correctly, the number of words in the elongated adage—33—was added at the end of the text as a guideline. Only after the first bottles of Rock rolled off the line was it discovered that the number 33 had been mistakenly left at the end of the slogan. The text reads: "Rolling Rock. From the glass-lined tanks of Old Latrobe, we tender this premium beer for your enjoyment as a tribute to your good taste. It comes from the mountain springs to you. 33"

The Diabolical Fork

Using a fork was not always a demonstration of good manners. In fact, according to an anonymous writer, "It is coarse and ungraceful to throw food into the mouth as you would toss hay into a barn with a pitchfork."

✳ ✳ ✳ ✳

I N THE CASE of the fork, the tool preceded the utensil. The English word *fork* comes from the Latin *furca*, which means "pitchfork." Thousands of years ago, large bronze forks were part of Egyptian sacrificial rituals. By the seventh century A.D., Middle Eastern royal courts were using small forks to eat.

Venice and the Fork

Table forks appeared in noble Italian homes in the 11th century, and over the next 500 years, they slowly made their way onto the tables of Europe. The first forks came to Venice at the outset of the 11th century, when a Doge—the head of the government—wed a Byzantine princess. Her forks, however, were despised as an example of oriental decadence. According to John Julius Norwich, "Such was the luxury of her habits that she scorned even to wash herself in common water, obliging her servants instead to collect the dew that fell from the heavens for her to bathe in. Nor did she deign to touch her food with her fingers, but would command her eunuchs to cut it up into small pieces, which she would impale on a certain golden instrument with two prongs and thus carry to her mouth." People in the West associated forks with the devil, and it was considered an affront to God to eat with something other than the hands he had designed for the job. When the princess died young, it was widely regarded as Divine retribution.

Exotic Object to Mainstream Convenience

Stories describing forks and their use appear in documents from the 13th century onward. Cookbooks and household inventories, however, suggest that forks were rare, valuable, and esoteric items. When the Italian aristocrat Catherine de Medici married the future Henri II of France in 1533, her dowry included several dozen table forks wrought by famous goldsmith Benvenuto Cellini. In 1588, forks were removed from *La Girona*, a boat in the Spanish Armada that wrecked off the coast of Ireland. During the 17th century, forks became more common in England, although numerous writers of the period scoffed at the utensil and the class of people who used it.

During the reign of Charles I of England, the fork was relatively common among the upper classes; King Charles himself declared in 1633, "It is decent to use a fork." Soon, sets of forks and knives were sold with a carrying case, as only very wealthy households could provide eating utensils for everyone at the table. Travelers also had to provide their own knives and forks during stopovers at inns. Governor John Winthrop of the Massachusetts Bay Colony owned the first fork—and for some time, the only fork—in colonial America. George Washington was inordinately proud of his set of 12 forks.

Forks, Forms, and Fashion

The first dinner forks had two tines, which were often quite long and sharp. Eventually three- and four-pronged forks were made, with wider, blunted tines arranged in a flattened, curved shape. During the 19th century, forks became commonplace in the United States and were sometimes called "split spoons."

Silver from the Comstock Lode flooded the market after 1859, and the electro-plating process made silverware affordable to nearly all people. Middle-class families subsequently claimed social refinement by acquiring complicated table settings featuring a unique utensil for every food. These place settings expanded from a few pieces to hundreds. Finally, in 1926, then Secretary of Commerce Herbert Hoover decreed that there could be no more than 55 pieces in a silver service, reducing, among other things, the number of forks dedicated to a single purpose. Indeed, it was time to put a fork in it.

I Scream, You Scream, We All Scream for Ice Cream (Cones)

Germs and sheer chance prompted an American classic.

✳ ✳ ✳ ✳

THE STORY OF the first ice-cream cone has become part of American mythology. The stock story is that a young ice-cream vendor at the 1904 St. Louis World's Fair ran out of dishes. Next to him was waffle-maker Ernest Hamwi. Hamwi got the idea to roll his waffles into a cone, and now, more than a century later, we're enjoying his legacy.

The ice-cream cone wasn't just born of convenience or a vendor's poor planning. Germs played a role, too. Italian immigrants fostered the introduction of ice cream to the general public, first in Europe and then in the United States. Called "hokey pokey men" (a bastardization of an Italian phrase), street vendors sold "penny licks," a small glass of ice cream that cost a penny. The vendors wiped the glass with a rag after a customer was done and then served the next person. Forget that people occasionally walked off with the glasses. Forget that the glasses would sometimes break. This is about as sanitary as the space under your refrigerator. Unsurprisingly, people got sick. Ice-cream vendors needed a new serving method.

In the early 1900s, two people—Antonio Valvona and Italo Marchiony—independently invented an edible ice-cream cup. Still, the cone did not appear until 1904. Today, cones come in many varieties, but in 1904, Hamwi was making *zalabia*, a cross between a waffle and a wafer covered in sugar or syrup. He called his creation a *cornucopia* (a horn-of-plenty, a symbol of autumn harvest), and after the fair, he founded the Cornucopia Waffle Company with a business partner. A few years later, he started his own company, the Missouri Cone Co., and finally named his rolled-up waffles "ice-cream cones." How sweet it is!

Chapter 16

Death and the Macabre

Death ... Isn't It Ironic?

No matter who you are, it's inevitable your time on this earth will end. But some people have a way of shuffling off this mortal coil with a bit more ironic poignancy.

✳   ✳   ✳   ✳

✳ In 1936, a picture of baby George Story was featured in the first issue of *Life* magazine. Story died in 2000 at age 63, just after the magazine announced it would be shutting down. *Life* carried an article about his death from heart failure in its final issue.

✳ In the early 1960s, Ken Hubbs was a Gold Glove second baseman for the Chicago Cubs. The young standout had a lifelong fear of flying, so to overcome it, he decided to take flying lessons. In 1964, shortly after earning his pilot's license, Hubbs was killed when his plane went down during a snowstorm.

✳ While defending an accused murderer in 1871, attorney Clement Vallandigham argued that the victim accidentally killed himself as he tried to draw his pistol. Demonstrating his theory for the court, the lawyer fatally shot himself in the process. The jury acquitted his client and Vallandigham won the case posthumously.

* Private detective Allan Pinkerton built his career on secrecy and his ability to keep his mouth shut. However, biting his tongue literally killed him when he tripped while out for a walk, severely cutting his tongue. It became infected and led to his death in 1884.

* When he appeared on *The Dick Cavett Show* in 1971, writer and healthy living advocate Jerome I. Rodale claimed, "I've decided to live to be a hundred," and "I never felt better in my life!" Moments later, while seated on stage, the 72-year-old Rodale died of a heart attack. The episode never aired.

* South Korean Lee Seung Seop loved playing video games more than anything. His obsession caused him to lose his job and his girlfriend and eventually claimed his life as well. In August 2005, after playing a video game at an Internet café for 50 consecutive hours, he died at age 28 from dehydration, exhaustion, and heart failure.

* Jim Fixx advocated running as a cure-all, helping develop the jogging fitness craze of the late 20th century. However, in 1984, he died from a heart attack while jogging. Autopsy results showed he suffered from severely clogged and hardened arteries.

* Thomas Midgley Jr., was a brilliant engineer and inventor who held 170 patents. After contracting polio at age 51, he turned his attention to inventing a system of pulleys to help him move around in bed. In 1944, he was found dead, strangled by the pulley system that he had invented.

* At least two of the Marlboro Men—the chiseled icons of the cigarette culture—have died from lung cancer. David McLean developed emphysema in 1985 and died from lung cancer a decade later. Wayne McLaren portrayed the character in the 1970s, and was an antismoking advocate later in life. He contracted cancer and, despite having a lung removed, the cancer spread to his brain. He died in 1992.

What's New in Voodoo?

New Orleans is famous for many things, one of them being the voodoo shops competing to sell you a spell or two.

✳ ✳ ✳ ✳

NOT SURPRISINGLY, New Orleans boasts at least four shops that specialize in voodoo paraphernalia, along with an honest-to-goodness voodoo museum. Its Creole heritage allows New Orleans to bill itself as the voodoo capital of the world. Whether or not you're a believer in spells, love potions, and zombies, the items carried by these quaint shops are well worth the visit. It's an opportunity to inhale the essence that makes New Orleans unique among American cities.

Details, Details

The word *voodoo* is derived from the Fon word *voudoun* (spirit). Erzulie's, Bloody Mary's, Reverend Zombie's, and Voodoo Authentica are all voodoo shops located in the French Quarter of New Orleans. These shops offer a variety of items unique to the uninitiated, such as potion oils, gris-gris (lucky mojo bags), voodoo dolls, jujus (blessed objects that ward off evil), ritual kits (everything you need to perform your own voodoo ritual for less than $50), voodoo candles, handmade crafts, incense, jewelry (including chicken-foot fetishes and gator-tooth necklaces), voodoo spells, spiritual guidance, voo beanies, African power dolls, spiritual goat's milk soaps, T-shirts, and much more. You can even have a hex removed if someone has put one on you, or join a class to learn how to make a voodoo doll.

Most of the shops also feature ghostly tours, which usually include a visit to the grave of Marie Laveau, one of the world's better-known voodoo queens and a popular woman in New Orleans history. So, the next time you're in New Orleans, don't be a zombie—drop into one of the city's unique voodoo shops and visit for a spell, especially during Voodoofest, which takes place every Halloween.

Celebrity Haunts

It's not surprising that so many celebrity ghosts hang out near Hollywood. What other town could inspire such dreams and passions, highs and lows?

❋　❋　❋　❋

Marilyn Monroe

H OLLYWOOD'S ROOSEVELT HOTEL, home of the first ever Academy Awards in 1929, eternally hosts at least two celebrity spooks (along with a handful of other less famous specters). The ghostly reflection of silver-screen goddess Marilyn Monroe has often been seen in a wood-framed mirror that used to hang in the room where she frequently stayed. Today, visitors can simply visit the lower level, just outside the elevators, to get a glimpse of the mirror. Being a restless sort, Monroe's ghost has also been reported hovering near her tomb in the Westwood Memorial Cemetery and at San Diego's Hotel del Coronado.

Montgomery Clift

Marilyn Monroe isn't lonely at the Roosevelt. Her good friend, four-time Oscar nominee Montgomery Clift, has also never left the hotel that served as his home for more than three months in 1952 while filming *From Here to Eternity*. To commune with Clift, reserve Room 928, where he is said to leave the phone off the hook, pace the floor, and cause inexplicable loud noises. One of the room's guests even reported feeling an unseen hand tap her on the shoulder.

Rudolph Valentino

The ghost of romantic hero Rudolph Valentino has been spotted all over Hollywood, including near his tomb at the Hollywood Forever Memorial Park, floating over the costume department at Paramount Studios, and at his former Beverly Hills mansion. Throughout the years, owners of his former home have reported seeing "The Sheik" roaming the hallways, hanging out in his former bedroom, and visiting the stables (now turned into private residences). Others report seeing his specter enjoying the view of Los Angeles from the second-floor windows of the main house.

Ozzie Nelson

Bandleader and television star Ozzie Nelson can't seem to leave the Hollywood Hills home he shared with Harriet, David, and Ricky for more than 25 years. Reports of Nelson's ghost started circulating in Tinseltown soon after Harriet sold the house in 1980. Subsequent residents of the house have reported seeing doors open and close by unseen hands and lights and faucets turning on and off by themselves. One female homeowner even reported that the ghost pulled down the bed covers and got amorous with her.

Orson Welles

One of Hollywood's most respected writers, actors, and directors, Orson Welles still reportedly spends time at his favorite Hollywood bakery. Known as a man with gourmet tastes, it's no wonder Welles's spirit lingers at Melrose Avenue's Sweet Lady Jane, legendary for their extraordinary desserts. Tales of Welles's apparition have circulated among staff and guests of the restaurant for years. Visions of him seated at his favorite table are often accompanied by the scent of his favorite cigar and brandy.

John Wayne

Drive down the coast about an hour or so from Los Angeles, and you'll come to Newport Beach, home of the *Wild Goose*. The vessel served as a minesweeper for the Canadian Navy during World War II before actor John Wayne purchased her in 1965 and converted her into a luxury yacht. The ship was said to be "Duke's" favorite possession, and he put her to good use during countless family vacations, star-studded parties, and poker sessions with buddies such as Dean Martin, Bob Hope, and Sammy Davis Jr. Shortly after Wayne's death in 1979, new owners claimed to see a tall smiling man in various places on the yacht. Sightings of John Wayne's ghost on the *Wild Goose* have continued ever since. Those who want to try to see Duke's ghost for themselves can charter the *Wild Goose* for private events. But be prepared to bring your wallet—prices to charter the haunted boat start at $1,450 per hour.

Benjamin "Bugsy" Siegel

One ghost who can't seem to decide where to haunt is gangster Bugsy Siegel. Some stories claim that Siegel's ghost haunts the Beverly Hills home that once belonged to his girlfriend Virginia Hill, where he was gunned down in 1947. But the most prevalent Siegel sightings occur at the Flamingo Hotel in Las Vegas. Though the hotel has changed completely since Siegel opened it in the early 1940s, his ghost is said to still linger around the pool, as well as the statue and memorial to him in the hotel's gardens. Guests in the hotel's presidential suite have been sharing their lodgings with Siegel's spirit for years. He seems to favor spending time near the pool table when he's not in the bathroom.

Elvis Presley

Apparently, Elvis has NOT left the building, or so claim stagehands at the Las Vegas Hilton, formerly the International Hotel. Presley made his big comeback there and continued to draw sellout crowds in the hotel's showroom until his death in 1977. The most common place to spot the King's sequined jumpsuit-clad ghost is backstage near the elevators. Elvis is also known to haunt his Memphis home, Graceland.

Famous People Who Died Before Age 40

* * * *

Jessica Dubroff (7): Pilot, plane crash, 1996

Heather O'Rourke (12): Child actor, bowel obstruction, 1988

Anne Frank (15): Dutch-Jewish author, typhus in concentration camp, 1945

Ritchie Valens (17): Rock singer, plane crash, 1959

Eddie Cochran (21): Rockabilly musician, auto accident, 1960

Sid Vicious (21): Punk rock musician, suicide from heroin overdose, 1979

Aaliyah (22): R&B singer, plane crash, 2001

Buddy Holly (22): Rock singer, plane crash, 1959

Freddie Prinze (22): Comedian/actor, suicide, 1977

River Phoenix (23): Actor, drug overdose, 1993

Selena (23): Mexican-American singer, homicide, 1995

James Dean (24): Actor, auto accident, 1955

Otis Redding (26): Soul singer, plane crash, 1967

Brian Jones (27): British rock guitarist, drug-related drowning, possibly homicide, 1969

Janis Joplin (27): Rock/soul singer, heroin overdose, 1970

Jim Morrison (27): Rock singer, heart attack, possibly due to drug overdose, 1971

Jimi Hendrix (27): Rock guitarist/singer, asphyxiation from sleeping pill overdose, 1970

Kurt Cobain (27): Grunge rock singer/guitarist, gunshot and lethal dose of heroin, presumed suicide, 1994

Reggie Lewis (27): Basketball player, heart attack, 1993

Brandon Lee (28): Actor, accidental shooting on the set of *The Crow*, 1993

Shannon Hoon (28): Rock singer, drug overdose, 1995

Heath Ledger (28): actor, prescription drug overdose, 2008

Hank Williams (29): Country musician, Heart attack, possibly an accidental overdose of morphine and alcohol, 1953

Andy Gibb (30): Singer, heart failure due to cocaine, 1988

Jim Croce (30): Singer/songwriter, plane crash, 1973

Patsy Cline (30): Country music singer, plane crash, 1963

Sylvia Plath (30): Poet and author, suicide, 1963

Brian Epstein (32): Beatles manager, drug overdose, 1967

Bruce Lee (32): Martial artist/actor, possible allergic reaction, 1973

Cass Elliot (32): Singer, obesity-related heart attack, 1974

Karen Carpenter (32): Singer and musician, cardiac arrest from anorexia, 1983

Keith Moon (32): Rock drummer, medication overdose, 1978

Carole Lombard (33): Actor, plane crash, 1942

Chris Farley (33): Comedian/actor, overdose of cocaine and heroin, 1997

Darryl Kile (33): Major League Baseball pitcher, coronary heart disease, 2002

John Belushi (33): Comedian/actor, overdose of cocaine and heroin, 1982

Sam Cooke (33): Soul musician, homicide, 1964

Charlie Parker (34): Jazz saxophonist, pneumonia and ulcer, brought on by drug abuse, 1955

Dana Plato (34), Actor, prescription drug overdose, 1999

Jayne Mansfield (34): Actor, auto accident, 1967

Elliott Smith (34): Singer/songwriter, suicide, 2003

Andy Kaufman (35): Comedian/actor, lung cancer, 1984

Josh Gibson (35): Negro League baseball player, stroke, 1947

Stevie Ray Vaughan (35): Blues guitarist, helicopter crash, 1990

Bob Marley (36): Reggae musician, melanoma that metastasized into lung and brain cancer, 1981

Diana, Princess of Wales (36): British royal, auto accident, 1997

Marilyn Monroe (36): Actor, barbiturate overdose, 1962

Eric Dolphy (36): Jazz saxophonist, diabetic insulin shock, 1964

Bobby Darin (37): Singer/actor, complications during heart surgery, 1973

Lou Gehrig (37): Major League Baseball player, amyotrophic lateral sclerosis (ALS), 1941

Michael Hutchence (37): Rock singer, hanged, possibly suicide, 1997

Sal Mineo (37): Actor, homicide, 1976

Florence Griffith Joyner (38): Olympian/sprinter, possible asphyxiation during epileptic seizure, 1998

What It's Like: Crime Scene Decontamination Crew

Chances are, one TV show that will never make the lineup is CSD: Miami (Crime Scene Decontamination). *It seems unlikely that viewers would want to watch cleanup crews swab up buckets of blood while they eat their dinner.*

❋　❋　❋　❋

CLEANING UP AFTER someone dies is no picnic. Particularly if that person died in a violent way, say, a murder or suicide. Blood has pooled through the mattress and soaked into the floor below, bits of bone and brain matter are everywhere—that mess doesn't go away by itself. That's when Crime Scene Decontamination units (also called CTS—Crime/Trauma Scene-Decon crews) are called in.

CTS decon crews handle the worst of the worst. Hours or even days after a violent crime has occurred or a methamphetamine lab has been busted, CTS decon crews are contracted to come in and clean up. Sorry crime show fans: You won't find a slightly-grizzled-but-still-handsome detective tiptoeing through this scene in an Armani suit—this is dirty work that would make most people sick to their stomachs.

The Task at Hand

By the time the decontamination crew is called to the trauma scene, the police, fire department, and crime scene investigators have all done their jobs and left (*these* are the people you see on TV). A decontamination lead will be appraised of the situation and alerted to the risks involved. Some are worse than others, such as decomposing bodies. Bodies that are discovered hours, days, or even months after death are considered to be in a state of decomposition or "decomp." During decomp, the body swells, the skin liquefies, and maggots move in to feed off the body. But this all pales in comparison to the smell as ammonia gas from the body fills the room. And if this doesn't make you contemplate a new line of work, consider that all of the creepy-crawlies that made the body their home must be rounded up and destroyed to eliminate any biohazard threat.

Dressing for Success

After putting on disposable head-to-toe biohazard suits, cleaners will don filtered respirators, rubber gloves, and booties before entering the crime scene. They'll also bring tools of their trade. There are no microscopes, centrifuges, or fingerprinting kits; instead, there are 55-gallon plastic containers, mops, sponges, enzyme solvents, putty knives, and shovels.

Once the contaminated material has been cleaned off of the room's surfaces and the site has been returned to normal, the cleaners must properly dispose of the hazardous waste material. Since federal regulations deem even the smallest drop of blood or bodily fluid to be biohazardous waste, the cleaners must transport all matter in specially designed containers to medical waste incinerators—all at additional cost to the client.

The Big Business of Violence

To date, more than 300 companies provide professional decontamination of crime scenes. Each one of these companies typically handles up to 400 cases a year and is on call around the clock. Decontamination companies are contracted through police departments, insurance companies, or by the deceased's relatives. And there's big money to be made: Companies charge between $1,000 and $6,000 to clean up a crime scene and return it to its original condition. In addition to cleaning houses, decon crews often clean car interiors and busted meth labs. In the case of the meth labs, virtually all of the carpeting, furniture, cabinets, and fixtures—anything that can absorb dangerous chemicals such as methanol, ammonia, benzene, and hydrochloric acid—must be removed and destroyed.

The TV executives will probably never glamorize decontaminating crews. However, for those families in need of a CTS decon team, they provide a valuable service in helping them get their lives back to normal. It is important, sensitive work and in most cases, worth every penny the cleaners charge.

A Few Good Men (and Women)

A crime scene decontamination company is hardly going to have a booth at the local job fair. So, who on earth would get into this kind of work? Some decon workers find their way into the field from medical backgrounds (say, as an emergency room nurse) or the construction industry. The latter, in particular, proves helpful when dealing with jobs that require walls to be torn into or taken down. This is often the case in clean-ups that take place in meth labs.

And then there's the paycheck. Depending on the company and its location, decontamination cleaners can make as much as $35,000 to $60,000 a year and sometimes more. In metropolitan cities where caseloads are high, cleaners can earn as much as $100,000 a year—and that's without a college education. Of course, few actually see that much money; the average career of a decontamination cleaner is less than eight months.

One of the requirements for becoming a decontamination cleaner is a strong stomach and the ability to detach themselves from their environment but still have empathy for family members and friends of the deceased. If the thought of picking up dog poo grosses you out, this is not the job for you. It's also not for you if you are easily depressed or internalize human suffering. Decontamination cleaners must be able to handle the worst-case scenario as "just part of the job." Before crew members are sent on their first job, cleaners must go through training that includes performing heavy physical labor while wearing a biohazard suit, watching videos of prior crime scenes, or cleaning up a room strewn with animal remains—all without tossing their cookies.

The Late, Semi-Great *Titanic*

Many believe the sinking of RMS Titanic *to be the champion of all maritime disasters, but history tells a far different tale.*

❊   ❊   ❊   ❊

WHEN THE LUXURY liner *Titanic* slipped beneath the waves in 1912, people of the era witnessed a truly historic spectacle, as an estimated 1,500 souls had been quickly snuffed out. While the death toll was appalling, it was by no means the worst on record. Lesser-known shipwrecks before and since have claimed more lives. Here are a notable few.

The *Sultana*

On April 27, 1865—nearly 44 years before the *Titanic* received its first rivet in an Irish shipyard—the paddle-wheel steamer *Sultana* made its way up the mighty Mississippi River. Onboard were an estimated 2,300 passengers, a group primarily composed of Union soldiers returning home from the Civil War. Just after the ship cleared Memphis, Tennessee, one of its main boilers exploded. In an instant, hundreds of people and a sizable chunk of the superstructure ceased to exist. Seconds later, a raging fire threatened those who had survived the initial explosion. A horrific tragedy was in the making.

All told, approximately 1,700 perished in the incident. The culprit was determined to be an improperly patched boiler that never stood a chance against such elevated pressures. In the most heartbreaking of ironies, many of *Sultana's* victims were newly released POWs who had survived the notorious Cahawba and Andersonville Confederate prison camps.

The *Provence II*

Less than four years after the *Titanic* tragedy, another vessel surpassed the *Sultana* in total lives lost. On February 26, 1916, the French auxiliary cruiser *Provence II* was making its way across the Mediterranean Sea, transporting an enormous contingent of sailors from North Africa to Salonika. A torpedo launched by the German submarine *U-35* struck the craft, mortally wounding it. The damage caused an immediate and pronounced list that rendered most of the ship's lifeboats useless. Of the nearly 4,000 people onboard, 3,130 would perish.

The *Goya*

Even in such a macabre category as maritime disasters, there always seems to be another tragic event that will displace the "top dog." Consider the *Goya*, a German transport ship that was evacuating some 7,000 refugees and wounded soldiers from the Baltic states of East Prussia and Poland. On April 16, 1945, after setting out for Copenhagen, the ship tragically moved into the crosshairs of the Soviet minelayer submarine *L-3*. Locking on its quarry, the *L-3* fired two torpedoes at the ship. They found their mark, and the *Goya* split in two. The vessel sank in a blisteringly fast four minutes and took nearly everyone with it. Of the 7,000 onboard, 183 survived.

The *Doña Paz* and the *Vector*

It doesn't require icebergs or a world war to commit a vessel to the "worst of" category. Sometimes an innocuous ferry crossing can produce disastrous results. Such was the case with the Philippine passenger ferry *Doña Paz*. As the craft negotiated the Tablas Strait on December 20, 1987, it struck the oil tanker *Vector*. Nearly 9,000 barrels of petroleum ignited into a firestorm and spread onto the *Doña Paz*. In minutes, the blazing ship sank, taking nearly everyone onboard with it. Things were almost as bad on the *Vector*. Of the 13 crew members who went to work that fateful day, only two returned home.

So, if not an outright record, what was the death toll on the *Doña Paz*? Here's where things get interesting. The "official" toll was 1,565, but other sources place the number at 4,375. Then again, since the ferry was severely overcrowded, well-reasoned estimates reach as high as 9,000. If that's the case, the *Doña Paz* is the deadliest maritime disaster in history.

Mike the Headless Chicken

Chickens are known not for their intelligence but for their pecking, their much-emulated dance, and, in one special case, a chicken named Mike was known for losing his head.

✳ ✳ ✳ ✳

O N A FALL day in 1945, on a farm in Fruita, Colorado, chickens were meeting their maker. It was nothing out of the ordinary; Lloyd and Clara Olsen slaughtered chickens on their farm all the time. But this particular day was fortuitous for Lloyd and one of his chickens.

As Lloyd brought down his knife on the neck of a future meal, the head came off. The decapitated chicken flapped and danced around, which normally happens when a chicken loses its head.

But this chicken didn't stop flapping around. Most headless chickens only live a few minutes before going to the chicken coop in the sky, but this particular bird was alive and well several hours (then several months) after it had lost its, er, mind.

Open Mike

Lloyd was fascinated by this chicken that had somehow cheated death. The chicken continued to behave exactly like the other chickens on the farm—he just didn't have a head. Mike, as he was named, even attempted to cluck, although it sounded more like a gurgle since it came out of a hole in his neck.

Lloyd was starting to see the entrepreneurial possibilities that Mike had created—a living, breathing headless chicken was sure to be a goldmine. But Lloyd knew he had to devise a way for Mike to get nutrients or he would die. Using an eyedropper, a mixture of ground-up grain and water was sent down Mike's open esophagus, and little bits of gravel were dropped down his throat to help his gizzard grind up food.

That'll Be a Quarter

Mike the Headless Chicken was not some magical beast with the ability to cheat death; he was just an ordinary chicken that got lucky. Scientists who examined Mike determined that Lloyd had done a shoddy job of butchering him. Most of his head was actually gone, but the slice had missed Mike's jugular vein, and a blood clot prevented him from bleeding to death. Most of a chicken's reflex actions originate in the brain stem, and Mike's was pretty much untouched.

None of this mattered to the general public. When Mike went on a national sideshow tour in 1945, people lined up to see this wonder chicken and paid a quarter for the privilege. At his most popular, Mike was drawing in about $4,500 per month, which is equivalent to about $50,000 today. He was insured for $10,000 and featured in *Life* magazine.

What became of Mike's head is a mystery. Most photos show a chicken head alongside Mike, either at his feet or pickled in a jar. But rumor has it that the Olsens' cat ate the original head, and Lloyd used another chicken's head as a stand-in.

A Moment of Silence, Please

It's wasn't the lack of a head that was toughest on Mike—he had a problem with choking on his own mucus. The Olsens employed a syringe to suck the mucus out of Mike's neck, but one fateful night, Mike was traveling back home to Fruita, roosting with the Olsens in their motel room. Lloyd and Clara heard Mike choking in the middle of the night and reached for the syringe. Alas, they discovered they had left it in the last town where Mike had appeared. Mike finally succumbed to death that night in Phoenix in 1947.

These days, Fruita holds an annual Mike the Headless Chicken Day every third weekend in May to honor the memory of their most famous resident.

Back from the Dead

Nothing is certain but death and taxes... yet sometimes that's not so true. History is riddled with strange tales of people who just weren't content staying dead.

✳ ✳ ✳ ✳

✳ After a major automobile accident in 2007, Venezuelan Carlos Camejo was declared dead. The coroner had just begun the autopsy by cutting into Camejo's face when the man began to bleed. Immediately realizing that the crash victim was still alive, the doctor became even more stunned when Camejo regained consciousness as he was stitching up the incision. "I woke up because the pain was unbearable," Camejo told reporters after his ordeal.

✳ Ann Greene, a young servant in Oxford, England, was convicted of killing her illegitimate newborn child after the baby was stillborn in 1650. After she was hanged, Greene's body was cut down and transported to Oxford University where it was to be used for anatomy classes. As the lesson progressed, Greene began to moan and regained consciousness. The students helped revive her and treated her injuries. Eventually she was given a pardon, gained a level of celebrity, married, and had several children.

✳ In 1674, Marjorie Erskine died in Chirnside, Scotland, and was buried in a shallow grave by a sexton with less than honorable intentions. Erskine was sent to her eternal rest with some valuable jewelry the sexton was intent on adding to his own collection. After digging up her body, the sexton was trying to cut off her finger to steal her ring when, much to his surprise, she awoke.

✳ After being found unconscious and sprawled on the floor of her Albany, New York, apartment by paramedics in 1996, Mildred Clarke, 86, was pronounced dead by a coroner.

About 90 minutes later an attendant noticed that the body bag containing Clarke was, in fact, moving. Clarke recovered but unfortunately only lived for another week, giving into the stress of age and heart failure.

* When 19th-century Cardinal Somaglia took ill and passed out, he was thought to be dead. Being a high-ranking church official, embalming was begun immediately so he could lie in state, as was customary. As a surgeon began the process by cutting into the cardinal's chest, he noticed that the man's heart was still beating. Somaglia awoke and pushed the knife away. However, the damage was done, and he died from the embalming process.

* Oran was a devout sixth-century monk on Iona, a small island off the coast of Scotland. According to legend, he was buried alive by his own urging to sanctify the island but was dug up three days later and found alive. He told his fellow monks that he had seen heaven and hell and a host of other sights. "There is no such great wonder in death, nor is hell what it has been described," he claimed as he was pulled from the ground. The head monk, Columba, ordered that he be reburied immediately as a heretic. To this day, when someone in the region broaches an uncomfortable subject, people will tell that person to "throw mud in the mouth of St. Oran."

* In 1740, 16-year-old William Duell was convicted of rape and murder and sentenced to death by hanging. After his lifeless body was removed from the gallows it was taken to the local college for dissection. His body was stripped and laid out in preparation for the process when a servant who was washing the corpse noticed it was still breathing. After a full recovery, he was returned to prison, but it was decided that instead of being hanged again he would be exiled to the then-prison state of Australia.

* A victim of the horrors of war, three-year-old Lebanese Hussein Belhas had his leg blown off in an Israeli attack in 1996. Declared dead, the boy's body was placed in a morgue freezer, but when attendants returned he was found alive. After he recovered from his injuries, Belhas took a stoic stance on his fate. "I am the boy who died, and then came back to life. This was my destiny," he said.

* In late 1995, Daphne Banks of Cambridgeshire, England, was declared dead. On New Year's Day, 1996, as she lay in the mortuary, an undertaker noticed a vein twitching in her leg. Examining closer, the attendant could hear snoring coming from the body. The 61-year-old Banks was quickly transferred to a local hospital where she made a full recovery.

* As mourners sadly paid their last respects to the Greek Orthodox bishop Nicephorus Glycas on the island of Lesbos in 1896, they were met with quite a shock. Glycas had been lying in state for two days as preparations for his burial were being made. Suddenly, he sat up and looked around at the stunned congregation. "What are you staring at?" he reportedly asked.

* During the 16th century, a young man named Matthew Wall died in the village of Braughing, England. As pallbearers were carrying him to his final resting place, they dropped his coffin after one of them stumbled on a stone. When the coffin crashed to the ground, Wall was revived and went on to live a full life. When he actually did pass away years later, the terms of his will stipulated that Old Man's Day be celebrated in the village every October 2, the anniversary of his return from the dead.

---

* **It is considered bad luck to use areas of a cemetery for other purposes, and the disturbed deceased will likely haunt those responsible for the decision.**

Sin Eating: A Strange Profession

An ancient custom of "eating" a dying person's sins has made its way into contemporary culture—and brought with it a wave of questions about the unusual practice.

✳   ✳   ✳   ✳

IF YOU THINK you've had a rough lunch, wait until you hear about these guys: The so-called sin eaters were a group of people who would perform intricate eating rituals to cleanse dying people of their sins. The idea was to absolve the soon-to-be-deceased of any wrongdoing so they could die peacefully, without guilt or sin.

Much of the history of sin eating is based on folklore, particularly from Wales. Historians, however, have traced mentions of the practice back to early Egyptian and Greek civilizations, and references to sin eating can be found elsewhere in England as recently as the mid-1800s. *Funeral Customs*, a book published in 1926 by Bertram S. Puckle, refers to an English professor who claims he encountered a sin eater as late as 1825.

The sin-eating ritual is believed to have typically taken place either at the bedside of someone who was dying or at the funeral of one who had already died. Legend has it that for a small fee, the sin eater would sit on a low stool next to the person. Then, a loaf of bread and a bowl of beer would be passed to them over the body. Sometimes the meal would be placed directly on the body, so that the food would absorb the deceased's sin and guilt. The sin eater would eat and drink, then pronounce the person free from any sins with a speech: "I give easement and rest now to thee, dear man. Come not down the lanes or in our meadows. And for thy peace I pawn my own soul. Amen." Family members, it is believed, would burn the bowl and platter after the sin eater left.

Odd Job

Sin eating wasn't the most lucrative profession, nor were sin eaters highly regarded among their peers. Many of them were beggars to begin with, and most were considered scapegoats and social outcasts. They would live alone in a remote area of a village and have little or no contact with the community outside of their work. Some accounts say they were treated like lepers and avoided at all costs because of their association with evil spirits and wicked practices. It was also widely believed that sin eaters were doomed to spend eternity in hell because of the many burdens they adopted. The Roman Catholic Church allegedly excommunicated the sin eaters, casting them out of the Church.

Sin Eating Today

Interestingly enough, sin eating lives on—at least in spirit. The idea of the sin eater saw its most recent resurgence with the 2003 movie *The Order*. The film (titled *The Sin Eater* in Australia) starred Heath Ledger and focused largely on a sin eater who was discovered after the death of an excommunicated priest.

In 2007, Hollywood revisited sin eating with *The Last Sin Eater*. That movie, based on the 1998 novel of the same name by Francine Rivers, tells the tale of a young girl whose grandmother has just died. At the funeral, the girl makes eye contact with the sin eater—something suggested as a forbidden act. The girl then spends most of the story trying to figure out how to absolve herself of this act. Sin eating has also made its way into several comic book storylines, most often as the name of villainous characters. These characters have been featured in numerous Spider-Man storylines as well as in some of the Marvel Ghost Rider creations.

While the custom may have died out in modern society, one thing's for certain: The archaic legend of the sin eater is just too delicious to pass up.

Too Hot to Handle

Although the Great Chicago Fire garnered international headlines, an inferno that raged in Peshtigo, Wisconsin, burned brighter, longer, and deadlier.

✳ ✳ ✳ ✳

CONSIDER THE COLORFUL tale of Mrs. O'Leary's cow—yes, the one about the celebrated igniter of the Great Chicago Fire of 1871. Despite historical evidence that attempts to lay this fanciful tale to rest, many believe that a clumsy bovine tipped over the gas lamp that started the infamous fire. To go this myth one better, consider the "great" fire itself. Apparently, many believe that the Chicago fire was the most disastrous blaze in U.S. history.

To this misinformed if well-intentioned lot, we offer two words: Peshtigo, Wisconsin. In a bizarre twist of fate, the great Peshtigo fire occurred precisely when Chicago staged its little bonfire. In terms of total devastation and number of fatalities, the Peshtigo blaze leaves Chicago in its embers. To this day, it is considered the worst forest fire in North American history. Here's the backstory to the backdraft.

From Tinderbox to Tragedy

Unlike many large fires, Peshtigo's was a conglomeration of smaller blazes that joined into a firestorm. At the time, a prolonged drought had turned the usually lush countryside into a dry thicket. Slash-and-burn land-clearing practices (the cutting and burning of woodlands to create agricultural space) also presented a potential problem. With a slew of these fires burning on October 8, 1871, the area around Peshtigo had become a tinderbox, with conditions ripe for disaster.

According to some accounts, the great blaze began when railroad workers touched off a brush fire. But these reports are about as reliable as the fable concerning Mrs. O'Leary's cow. No one is sure of the fire's precise origin, but one thing is certain:

Once it started, the fire took on a life of its own. Survivors would compare its violent winds to those of a tornado. A firestorm had been born.

Extensive Losses

In one hour's time, Peshtigo was completely gone. Eight hundred lives were lost in the town alone. As the fire continued on its hellish mission, 16 other towns would succumb to its deadly, wind-whipped flames. The great blaze would destroy a 2,500-square-mile area (nearly 500 square miles larger than the state of Delaware) and wouldn't relent until its winds changed course, pitting the fire against itself and robbing it of its fuel source.

Damage estimates from the fire reached $169 million, which happens to be identical to the Chicago fire. But what stood out were the fatalities. The Chicago fire had snuffed out the lives of an estimated 250 people—no small number, of course—but the Peshtigo fire had claimed as many as 2,400 lives.

Since the greatest loss of life occurred in Peshtigo itself, the fire became closely associated with the town. Many wondered why the Peshtigo fire department couldn't do more to control the blaze. But the department was staffed about as well as any of that time, which is to say it was woefully understaffed. The fire company had a single horse-drawn steam-pumper designed to fight fires at its sawmill. Beyond that, it didn't have the technology to fight even the simplest structural fires, never mind an unprecedented vortex of flame. Peshtigo's citizens were sitting ducks as they awaited their fate amid dry wooden buildings and sawdust-strewn boulevards.

Perhaps the most troubling detail about the Peshtigo Fire is its near-anonymity. Most adults have never heard of it, and despite its well-documented impact, schools seem to overlook it. This undoubtedly speaks to Chicago's fame, which served to magnify the relative significance of its fire. But there's no need for enhancement when the fire being considered is the "Great Peshtigo Fire." Its sobering statistics say it all.

Robert Ripley: Master of Weird

In the world of the weird and unusual, there are few names more widely known than Robert Ripley. If you've ever read a Ripley's Believe It or Not! *book or magazine, been to a Ripley's Odditorium, or watched episodes of the old TV show, you know that his enterprise was a cultural zeitgeist for much of the 20th century.*

✳ ✳ ✳ ✳

T HOUGH SOME OF his contemporaries were less than compassionate regarding their bizarre subjects, Ripley was known for his intelligence as well as his reverence for the wondrous sights he brought to the masses for more than 30 years.

Believe It or Not Beginnings

Ripley was born in Santa Rosa, California in 1890. He dropped out of high school to support his family, but as a gifted artist, he discovered at age 16 that his cartoons were good enough to sell. In the early 1900s, while pursuing a brief stint as a semipro baseball player, Ripley sold cartoons to several San Francisco papers. By 1913, he was living in New York City, drawing cartoons for *The New York Globe*, and sending the money he earned home.

It was at the *Globe* in 1918 that Ripley drew his first "Believe It or Not!" cartoon, which portrayed oddities from the world of sports. The response was incredible. In the days before the Internet and flights to far-flung locales, the masses were hungry for news of the weird, and they definitely got their fix with the bizarre stuff featured in Ripley's drawings.

Ripley married in 1919 and began traveling the world a few years later. He knew that the more places he explored, the better his stories would be. In 1925, he published a travel journal as well as a how-to book about handball. In 1926, he became the handball champion of New York City—believe it or not.

The Most Popular Man in America

The *New York Evening Post* bought Ripley's wildly popular cartoon in 1923, then, in 1929, sold it to publishing magnate William Randolph Hearst for syndication. This brought Ripley immense fame—it's estimated that at its peak, 80 million people across the United States read his cartoon series every day.

In the 1930s, Ripley' radio show went on the air. He took a tape recorder with him on his world travels and reported from the road, much to the delight of listeners. Shortly after the radio program launched, Ripley did several film reels. Then, at the Chicago World's Fair in 1933, he opened his first Odditorium—a museum that housed collections (both authentic and replicated) of the strange and unusual things, such as mummified cats, sideshow performers, and scale models of sharks. By 1940, there were Odditoriums in New York, San Francisco, Cleveland, Dallas, and San Diego.

Ripley's radio show stayed on the air for more than 18 years, with extraordinary tales from inside caves, deep under water, and odd foreign locales. When television arrived, Ripley recognized the need to change formats, and the radio show ended. In 1949, the first broadcast of the *Believe It or Not!* TV show aired with Ripley as host. He only filmed 13 episodes due to his bad health, and he died of a heart attack on May 27 at age 58.

All-Around Decent Guy

People in the early part of the 20th century clamored for news of the odd and impossible. Ripley could have manipulated such a naive public, but he swore that he never made anything up and was willing to prove every statement he made. Norbert Pearlroth, his assistant of more than 25 years, worked tirelessly in the New York Public Library to verify his boss' wild reports. Today, Ripley's Believe It or Not! museums and attractions around the world still bring in more than 13 million visitors each year.

And for Your Sins: The Rock

When people discuss famous prisons, you can bet your bottom dollar that "The Rock"—Alcatraz Island, or just Alcatraz for short—is nearly always mentioned.

✳ ✳ ✳ ✳

FOR THOUSANDS OF years, Alcatraz Island sat peacefully off the coast of California—until Spanish explorer Lieutenant Juan Manuel de Ayala sailed into San Francisco Bay in 1775. For a long time, the island's only inhabitants were pelicans, rocks, grass, and more pelicans. Ayala named it Isla de los Alcatraces, which means "Island of the Pelicans."

A Less Peaceful Future

The island evolved into a military fortress, then during the Civil War, it served as a prison for enemy soldiers, insubordinate army personnel, and Confederate sympathizers, thus beginning its long and illustrious history.

A new prison complex was built on Alcatraz Island in 1912. The U.S. Army turned Alcatraz into a 600-cell military prison—the largest reinforced-concrete building in the world. But getting food, water, and supplies to the island became too expensive for the military.

New Trends in Lockups

Before long, a new kind of criminal emerged: mobsters. The public needed a place to put these feared lawbreakers, and "escape-proof" Alcatraz provided the perfect solution. In 1934, the federal government took over Alcatraz from the military and redesigned it to strike fear in the heart of any public enemy. Significantly fortified buildings, combined with the jagged rocks of Alcatraz Island and the icy waters and strong currents of San Francisco Bay, made escape seem virtually impossible.

James A. Johnston was hired as warden of Alcatraz. Under his administration, prisoners received only basic necessities. When extreme discipline was warranted, prisoners were placed in a "strip cell"—a dark, steel-encased room with a hole in the floor in which the inhabitant could relieve himself. Guards controlled the ability to flush. This institution took the concept of solitary confinement to a new level. The strip cell got its name because inmates were stripped naked before entry. They were also placed on severely restricted diets. The room was kept pitch-black. A mattress was allowed at night but taken away during the daytime.

Getting Out

No prisoners were sentenced directly to Alcatraz. Instead, the facility was populated with the worst inmates from other prisons. It was not until prisoners got in trouble elsewhere in the penitentiary system that they were sent to the Rock. People tried to escape over the years, but they failed miserably—until June 11, 1962, when Frank Lee Morris, Allen West, and Clarence and John Anglin executed a clever escape plan. The complex plot involved escape holes made with crude drills fashioned from kitchen equipment, human decoys, and a rubber raft made from raincoats. After a bed check, three of the inmates were never seen again, having escaped through utility corridors and ventilation shafts to the beach. Allen West, however, failed to make his escape hole large enough by the scheduled time and was left behind. The trio's escape was officially deemed to be unsuccessful—there was no evidence that any of the three survived the attempt—but the television show *MythBusters* proved that escape was indeed possible with the materials they had at hand.

Alcatraz closed in 1963. In 1972, Congress created Golden Gate National Recreation Area, which included the island. In 1973, Alcatraz reopened as a tourist destination and is now an ecological preserve.

Dinner with a Ghost

Next time you enjoy a meal at your favorite restaurant, know that you may be dining with some unseen guests. Here are a few eateries where a ghostly good time is always on the menu.

❋   ❋   ❋   ❋

Stone's Public House, Ashland, Massachusetts

Since 1834, Stone's Public House has been serving up food and drink to area residents and visitors alike. Should you choose to stop in for a bite, first take a good look at the photo of John Stone hanging over the bar's fireplace, so you'll be sure to recognize his ghost when it appears. Stone's spirit is said to be one of a handful that haunt the inn. Other spirits include a man that Stone accidentally murdered in an argument during a card game. According to the legend, Stone and several friends buried the man in the basement. The spirits make their presence known by breaking glasses, causing cold breezes, and appearing as shadowy figures.

Arnaud's, New Orleans, Louisiana

The ghost of a man dressed in an old-fashioned tuxedo is often spotted near the windows of the main dining room. But this ghost, believed to be that of Arnaud Cazenave, the first owner of the establishment, is not alone. A ghostly woman has been seen walking out of the restroom and moving silently across the restaurant before disappearing into a wall.

Country House Restaurant, Clarendon Hills, Illinois

As the story goes, many years ago, a woman who was dating one of the restaurant's bartenders stopped in and asked him to watch her baby for a while. When he refused, the woman put the baby back in her car, sped off down the road, and promptly crashed into a tree, killing herself and her child. That should have been the end to this sad tale, but apparently the ghosts of both the young woman and her baby found their way back to the restaurant. The young woman's ghost has been blamed for banging on walls and doors and the jukebox playing on its own. She has also been seen walking through the restaurant and sometimes people outside see the ghostly woman in an upstairs window. Patrons and employees have also reported hearing a baby cry, even when there were no babies present.

Poogan's Porch, Charleston, South Carolina

Originally built as a house in 1888, the building underwent major renovations and reopened as a restaurant in 1976. Perhaps it was those renovations that brought the ghost of Zoe St. Amand, former owner of the house, back to see what all the fuss was about. Zoe's ghost is described as an older woman in a long black dress who silently wanders through the establishment at all hours of the day and night.

Big Nose Kate's Saloon, Tombstone, Arizona

Named after Mary Katherine Haroney, thought to be the first prostitute in Tombstone, the building was originally known as the Grand Hotel. At this establishment, there are several ghosts who seem to enjoy passing the time touching patrons and employees, moving objects, and appearing in the occasional photograph. The most famous ghost, however, is that of a man known only as the Swamper. Legend has it that the man lived in the basement of the saloon and had dug a secret tunnel under the street and into a nearby silver mine. He would sneak into the mines late at night and make off with untold amounts of silver. The strange sounds and muffled voices still coming from this long-abandoned tunnel seem to prove that even in death, the Swamper continues his underhanded and illegal mining practices.

✳ When you experience a chill up your spine, it is said that someone has just walked across your future gravesite.

The Day the Music Died

Death comes to everybody and, whatever the circumstances, it is always tragic. Read further for stories of pop stars whose candles burned a little too brightly.

✳ ✳ ✳ ✳

Michael Hutchence, singer for INXS

ONE OF THE great inconveniences of death is that the deceased has no control over what happens immediately after death. In the case of Michael Hutchence, he had no opportunity to put on some clothes. Typically, those who choose to take their own life have the advantage of foreknowledge and can make certain arrangements, often including a note of explanation. Hutchence, however, was reportedly found nude with a belt nearby. That, and the absence of any written confession, has led many to conclude that the 37-year-old died as the accidental result of autoerotic asphyxiation—that is, choking oneself to achieve sexual gratification. His death, however, was officially documented as a suicide. An ignoble end to a man who fronted one of Australia's most successful bands.

Richard Manuel, member of The Band

Canadian singer and pianist Richard Manuel was just 18 years old when he joined veteran rock 'n' roller Ronnie Hawkins's band, The Hawks, in 1961. Manuel and his bandmates slogged through years of clubs and bars; in the process, they became good friends and built a reputation as one of the world's best road bands, working with music legends including Bob Dylan.

Eventually, The Hawks signed with Dylan's manager, changed their name to The Band, and recorded a series of albums that spawned years of critical and commercial success. Manuel was often named as the best singer of the group, and he had plenty of admirers, including Eric Clapton. But by 1976, Manuel had deteriorated from a creative, compelling performer to an addict crippled by drugs and alcohol. After the group broke up (their farewell concert was well documented in the film *The Last Waltz*, directed by Martin Scorsese), Manuel checked himself into rehab. Most of the members of The Band reunited at various times, with limited success. In January 1986, word of manager and longtime friend Albert Grossman's death sent Manuel back to his addictions. On March 14, 1986, Manuel hanged himself in a hotel room in Florida.

Herman Brood, Dutch rock star

He may not be a household name in America, but in Amsterdam the name Herman Brood carries the same weight as Elvis does in Memphis or Jerry Garcia does in San Francisco. Brood was a brilliant artist: a jack-of-all-trades who worked as a musician, painter, actor, and poet. Though he never achieved true international rock stardom, Brood's talent earned him the appreciation of music and art fans around the world.

With a reputation for excessive and unrestrained drug and alcohol abuse, Brood bounced through Dutch society with a buoyancy that defied reason but rarely seemed unmerited—after all, he had class, he had grace, and even his critics had to admit that he was talented. But by the summer of 2001, Brood was depressed and tortured by an intense addiction to heroin, which he kept at bay through a daily diet of alcohol and speed. On July 11, 2001, he threw himself off the rooftop of the Amsterdam Hilton at age 54—a site that now conjures the memory of Holland's most brilliant pop star.

Hank Williams Sr., country music icon

His professional career lasted just five years and he was only 29 when he died in 1953, but Hank Williams Sr. covered a lot of ground. His 1949 recording of "Lovesick Blues" catapulted him into national prominence and led to a string of hits that made him a country-music icon. Williams was just doing what came naturally. "A song ain't nothin' in the world but a story just wrote with music to it," he said. But by mid-1952, Williams's drinking was out of control and he was addicted to painkillers.

On December 30, Hank was driven from Montgomery, Alabama for a series of shows. Exactly what happened after that is still hotly debated. Some stories say that before leaving town, Williams had the driver stop at a doctor's office for injections of vitamin B-12 and morphine. After a night in a hotel, Williams and the driver made it as far as Knoxville, Tennessee, where they checked into a hotel. There, the reportedly inebriated Williams insisted on two additional shots of morphine.

Williams's promoter called to inform the driver that the star was expected to perform in Canton, Ohio, the next day. The driver had two hotel orderlies carry the now-unconscious singer to the car. Another driver later took over, with Williams apparently sleeping in the back seat. It wasn't until the next morning that the driver realized that Williams was dead. He was pronounced dead on January 1, 1953. Despite the rumors surrounding his death, Williams will always be remembered as having died on the way to a show he couldn't miss.

Nikki Sixx, bassist for Mötley Crüe (not dead, though not for lack of trying)

Born Frank Carlton Serafino Ferrana, the man who would become known to heavy metal fans as Nikki Sixx, learned to play rock bass in Idaho. In 1975, at age 17, he moved to Los Angeles and changed his name. Sixx went through bands, jobs, and drug habits before scoring big with Mötley Crüe. The band had a string of hits, mostly written by Sixx. Dazzled by success, Crüe members indulged in vice; Sixx later said that at the time he considered his body a "human chemistry experiment" and would mix narcotics and alcohol in search of a new high. Once, he claimed to have overdosed at a London heroin dealer's house and, after being beaten back to life with a wooden club, was deposited in a Dumpster. In December 1987, he overdosed again, and for two minutes was technically dead at an L.A. hospital. He revived after two shots of adrenaline were injected into his heart. Soon after, the band entered rehab, emerging drug free.

The Story of the Straitjacket

Don't get too tied up in the history of this confining device.

✳   ✳   ✳   ✳

BEFORE PROGRESSIVE PSYCHOANALYSIS and newer medications, doctors didn't know how to treat mentally ill patients, so they often restrained them in a jacketlike garment with overlong sleeves. The ends of the sleeves went far beyond a patient's hands, and they were secured to the patient's back, keeping his or her arms crossed close to the chest, restricting most arm movement. Many institutional straitjackets are made of canvas or duck cloth for strength, but modern jackets intended for fetish or fashion wear use leather or PVC instead. The establishment of asylums and the use of straitjackets gained momentum in the early 1800s. Doctors believed that patients had lost all power over their morals and that strict discipline was necessary to help patients regain self-control.

Get Me Out of Here

Escape artists have used straitjackets in their acts for years. Harry Houdini first thought of using the straitjacket in the early 1900s while touring an insane asylum in Canada. He amazed disbelievers by getting out of one in front of live audiences. Later, he turned it into a public spectacle by escaping as he hung upside-down, suspended from a towering skyscraper.

The Guinness Book of World Records reports that David Straitjacket escaped from a Posey straitjacket in 2005 in 81.24 seconds. This record was broken in succession by Jeremy Kelly and Ben Bradshaw. On July 4, 2007, Jonathan Edmiston, aka "Danger Nate," escaped from his Posey in an incredible time of 20.72 seconds. For the record, the Posey *is* considered to be the most difficult straitjacket from which to escape.

Visiting the Dead:
Captivating Cemeteries

Most of the world's cultures believe strongly in dignified, respectful care for the dead. The word cemetery comes from the Greek word for "sleeping place." Here are some popular and unusual burial grounds in the United States.

✳ ✳ ✳ ✳

✳ Almost 4 million visitors a year quietly walk through the grounds of Arlington National Cemetery in Arlington, Virginia. There are upward of 100 funerals each weekday throughout the year. More than 300,000 people are buried here, including presidents William Howard Taft and John F. Kennedy and Supreme Court chief justices Earl Warren, Warren Burger, and William Rehnquist. The cemetery is the final resting place for veterans from all of the nation's wars. Military personnel from the American Revolution through the struggles in Iraq and Afghanistan are buried here.

✳ The smallest national cemetery is located at the Veterans Administration Medical Center in Hampton, Virginia. This .03-acre site holds 22 bodies in 3 short rows and is currently closed to new interments. The burial ground was used as an emergency measure in 1899 during a yellow fever epidemic at the center.

✳ The National Memorial Cemetery of the Pacific on the island of Oahu in Hawaii offers a stunning view of Honolulu and is the resting place for the recovered remains of 13,000 World War II service personnel, as well as the unidentified remains of 800 servicemembers who died in Korea. Several Medal of Honor recipients from the Vietnam War are interred here. This cemetery has been a revered site since ancient times, when *alii* (royal) burials were held. Violators of *kapus* (taboos) were sacrificed here as well.

❋ There's a wagon wheel carved into the headstone of one of dozens of circus folk buried in Showmen's Rest, a section of Mount Olivet Cemetery in Hugo, Oklahoma. According to circus lore, it was a practice of the day for a local sheriff to remove the nuts from one of the wheels on the office wagon of any show coming to town. This would prevent the circus from leaving before all the bills were paid. Once accounts were settled, the nuts would be returned. Hence, the show business term "making the nut," or taking in enough money to break even.

❋ Another Showmen's Rest section is found in Forest Park, Illinois, in a 750-plot section of Woodlawn Cemetery. One of the most interesting features is a mass grave of more than 50 employees of the Hagenbeck-Wallace circus who were killed in a train wreck nearby on June 22, 1918. Sometimes, neighbors around the cemetery claim they can hear the sounds of elephants trumpeting, but they probably aren't hearing ghosts. The noises likely come from the elephants in a nearby zoo.

❋ Barre, Vermont, is known as the granite capital of the world, and its cemeteries feature some of the most remark-able headstones in the world. Artisans praise the city's gray granite because its fine grain reflects light well and is not weathered by the elements. In Barre's Hope Cemetery, unique tombstones depict life-size figures, a queen-size bed, an armchair, and a giant soccer ball.

❋ Mount Moriah Cemetery in Deadwood, South Dakota, is the resting place of cowpokes, gunslingers, dance hall veter-ans, pioneer preachers, and assorted politicians. Side by side are the graves of legends Wild Bill Hickok and Martha Jane "Calamity Jane" Cannary. After Hickok was shot to death in 1876, Calamity Jane regularly visited Mount Moriah. It's said that just before she died in 1903, she said, "Bury me beside Wild Bill—the only man I ever loved."

Writing What You Know

In 1994, fans of novelist Anne Perry's Victorian murder mysteries were shocked to learn that the best-selling writer knew her topic a little too well.

✳   ✳   ✳   ✳

I T STARTED OUT innocently enough: Juliet Hulme arrived in New Zealand in 1948, where she met Pauline Parker. Sixteen-year-old Parker and fifteen-year-old Hulme quickly became best friends, particularly over their shared experience of serious illness and its related isolation. As a young girl, Parker had suffered from osteomyelitis, an infection of the bone marrow that required several painful surgeries. Hulme had recurring bouts of respiratory ailments, culminating in tuberculosis.

Intelligent and imaginative, the two girls created an increasingly violent fantasy life they called the "Fourth World," which was peopled with fairy-tale princes and Hollywood stars they dubbed the "saints." They wrote constantly, sure their stories were their ticket to the Hollywood of their imagination. At night, the girls would sneak outside to act out stories about the characters they had created.

No Matter What

In 1954, Hulme's parents separated. As her father prepared to return to England, Hulme's parents decided to send Juliet to live with relatives in South Africa. Not only would the climate be better for her health, they reasoned, but also the move would bring an end to a relationship that both girls' parents felt had grown too intense. Ever fantasizing, Hulme and Parker convinced themselves that Parker was also moving to South Africa with Hulme. Not surprisingly, Mrs. Parker refused to allow it. Determined to stay together, the girls decided to kill Parker's mother and flee to America, where they planned to sell their writing and work in the movies that played such an important role in their fantasy life.

On June 22, the girls went on what they described as a farewell outing to Victoria Park with Mrs. Parker. There, they bludgeoned Mrs. Parker to death with half a brick tied in a stocking. The girls expected the woman to die after a single blow so they could blame the death on a fall, but they were wrong—it took 45 blows to kill her. The hysterical girls then ran back to a park kiosk, screaming and covered in blood. The girls' story that Mrs. Parker had fallen rapidly unraveled after the police arrived and found the murder weapon in the surrounding woods.

"Incurably Bad"

The trial, with its titillating accusations of lesbianism and insanity, grabbed international headlines, not only because of its brutality, but also because of the excerpts from Pauline Parker's diary that were used as evidence. The diary revealed the intensity of the relationship between the two girls and their fantasy world. The diary also made it clear that the murder, flippantly described in its pages as "moider," was premeditated. The entry for June 22 was titled "The Day of the Happy Event."

Parker and Hulme were found guilty in a six-day trial during which the Crown Prosecutor described them as "not incurably insane, but incurably bad." Because they were under 18, they could not be given a capital sentence. Instead, they were sentenced to separate prisons for an unspecified term. After five years, they were released on the condition that they never contact each other again. Hulme returned to England and later took her stepfather's name, Perry. She also changed her first name; as Anne Perry, she went on to write dozens of popular mysteries. Parker lives in obscurity in an English village.

The murders were fairly forgotten, at least for a time. Years later, Perry's true identity was uncovered as a result of the publicity surrounding the 1994 release of the movie *Heavenly Creatures*, directed by Peter Jackson. The film, starring Kate Winslet as Hulme, focused on the events leading to the murder. Understandably, Perry was upset about the film.

Chapter 17

Everything Else

The Buffalo Creek Flood

In 1972, a calamitous flood roared through mining towns in West Virginia, leaving utter destruction in its wake.

✳ ✳ ✳ ✳

BUFFALO CREEK WINDS its way through 16 mining communities in West Virginia and empties into the Guyandotte River. As part of its mining operations, the Buffalo Mining Company, a subsidiary of Pittston Coal Company, dumped mine waste—mine dust, shale, clay, and other impurities—into Buffalo Creek. The company constructed an impoundment dam in 1960. Six years later, it constructed a second dam. By 1972, a third dam was built.

The Precursors

A flood on Buffalo Creek should not have been much of a surprise. In 1967, the U.S. Department of the Interior warned West Virginia state officials that the Buffalo Creek dams were unstable and dangerous. This conclusion came from a study of state dams conducted in response to a mine dam break that killed nearly 150 people—mostly children—in Wales in 1966.

In February 1971, the third impoundment dam on Buffalo Creek failed, but the second dam halted the water, preventing damage. The state cited Pittston Coal Company for violations but failed to follow up.

A Wall of Water

A few days before the fatal flood, a heavy, continuous rain fell. By 8:00 A.M. on February 26, the water had risen to the crest of the third dam, which collapsed within five minutes. The force of the water then crushed the other dams, and water rushed down the creek. A black wave—anywhere from 10 to 45 feet high—gushed through the mining towns. The area of Buffalo Creek was smothered with 132 million gallons of filthy wastewater in waves traveling at more than seven feet per second. In all, the flooding left 125 people dead, more than 1,100 injured, and more than 4,000 homeless.

The Aftermath

It took only three hours for waves of mine waste to demolish the Buffalo Creek community, but it would take years for the area to recover. Three separate commissions concluded that the Buffalo Mining Company blatantly disregarded standard safety practices. The Pittston Coal Company, in a statement from its New York office, declared the disaster "an act of God." Citizens responded by saying they never saw God building the dams.

West Virginia Governor Arch Moore Jr. banned journalists from entering the disaster site, explaining that the state did not need any additional bad press. He promised to build 750 public housing units. Ultimately, 17 model homes and 90 apartments were constructed. A promised community center was never built. With the federal disaster funds, Moore tried to build a superhighway through Buffalo Creek. West Virginia's Department of Highways purchased hundreds of lots from flood survivors. A two-lane road was built, but no superhighway. Most of the property remained in state hands.

State and federal mine agencies passed laws to improve conditions in coalfields. In 1973, West Virginia passed the Dam Control Act, which regulated dams in the state. However, enforcement was lax, and in 1992, the Division of Natural Resources estimated the state had 400 hazardous dams.

Merger Mayhem! Or: How to Fail in Business Without Really Trying

As many businesses find out, what appears to be two plus two doesn't always equal four.

✳ ✳ ✳ ✳

SOME BUSINESS MERGERS don't turn out to be as feasible in reality as they may sound in theory. But these failures shouldn't come as a complete surprise: According to financial experts, 50 to 80 percent of all business mergers fail.

K-Mart Holdings Company and Sears Roebuck

This merger had financial experts scratching their heads. K-Mart, already bankrupt, paid $11 billion for Sears—which had its own share of financial troubles—to form a bastion against giant competitor Wal-Mart. The merger finalized in 2005 and spurred a layoff of more than 500 Sears employees.

Daimler and Chrysler

It was the largest corporate takeover of 1998: Daimler/Benz bought the Chrysler Group for $38 billion, forming the world's fifth-largest automotive company. However, the company was hard-pressed to make a profit, and the merger eventually failed. Daimler announced plans in 2007 to sell Chrysler to Cerberus Capital Management, and the partnership was dissolved.

AOL and Time Warner

In 2000, Internet giant AOL announced it would buy media giant Time Warner to become AOL Time Warner. A victim of the Internet business bust, the merger turned out to be such a debacle that today, even though AOL takes in more money than Yahoo!, Amazon, and eBay combined, its stock is practically worthless. The biggest loser in the merger was AOL: Most Time Warner divisions are still performing well. It wasn't long before the company quietly stopped using AOL at the beginning of its name and reverted back to Time Warner.

Curious Facts About Languages, Words, and Letters

Word geeks unite—here are some titillating tidbits.

✳   ✳   ✳   ✳

✳ The first three Greek letters—alpha, beta, and gamma—are etymologically equivalent to the Hebrew words for "ox," "house," and "camel." This is because both the Greek and the Hebrew alphabets evolved from ancient Phoenician script, in which each letter was named after the object originally represented by the Phoenician hieroglyph. Phoenicians were prolific maritime traders, and the Phoenician alphabet took hold along their trade routes across Europe, the Middle East, and North Africa, evolving over time into the Aramaic, Arabic, Hebrew, Greek, Cyrillic, and Latin alphabets.

✳ Before the 1917 Communist Revolution, letters of the Russian alphabet had names. For instance, the first three letters were called *az, buki,* and *vedi,* meaning "I," "letters," and "know." Read in order, the alphabet composed a message. Its precise meaning has not been clearly established, and the translations vary (primarily in details). It reads something like this: "Knowing all these letters renders speech a virtue. Evil lives on Earth eternally, and each person must think of repentance, with speech and word making firm in their mind the faith in Christ and the Kingdom of God. Whisper [the letters] frequently to make them yours by this repetition in order to write and live according to laws of God."

✳ The longest palindrome word in any language is the Finnish word *saippuakivikauppias*—"door-to-door salesman of lye for soap." If that job seems a bit specialized, consider the following outdated German term for a revenue agent: *Obertranksteuerdonativcautionszinsgelderhauptcassir,* meaning "first main cashier of duty on drinks and bail rent moneys."

* It is said that above the entrance to the temple of Apollo at Delphi, there were three inscriptions. The first read *Gnothi seauton,* or "Know thyself"; the second was *Meden agan,* or "Nothing in excess." The third was merely the letter *E:* a capital epsilon. Neither ancient philosophers nor modern scholars have been able to solve the mystery of this Delphic *E.* (One dubious but appealing explanation is that the person charged with writing these inscriptions got discouraged from completing the third one after rereading the second.)

* The ampersand is actually a ligature of the letters *e* and *t* in the Latin word *et,* meaning, predictably, *and.* This is why the phrase *et cetera* was often abbreviated as &c in various 18th- and 19th-century writings. The term "ampersand" itself is a convoluted corruption of "and (&) per se and," which literally means "(the character) & by itself (is the word) and."

* In early Russian, the pronoun *I* used to be *Az,* the first letter of the alphabet. However, at some point another letter started meaning *I:* the last letter of the Russian alphabet, *ya.* This is why Russian mothers sometimes rebuke boastful children prone to beginning sentences with *I* by saying "I is the last letter of the alphabet!"

* The plural of *octopus* is not *octopi;* the academically agreed-upon plural of this word is *octopuses.* However, if circumstances compel you to pluralize *octopus,* and the plain English way of going about it just doesn't satisfy, then write *octopodes.* *Octopus* is derived from the Greek—"eight legs"—and should be pluralized according to Greek rules, not Latin.

* Traditional Irish and Welsh have no word for the color blue—the word referring to that color, *glas,* also refers to certain shades of green and gray. The Navajo language also does not distinguish between blue and green but has two

words for the color black. However, none of these languages has anything on the ancient Greeks when it comes to odd color perception: Authors such as Homer and Euripides consistently describe the sky as bronze; the sea and sheep as wine-colored; and blood, tears, and honey as green.

* The word *butterfly* is one of the most persistent and baffling mysteries of linguistics. All European languages, even such closely related ones as Spanish and Portuguese, have completely different words for *butterfly* (in Spanish and Portuguese, it's *mariposa* and *borboleta*, respectively). This is in stark contrast to just about all other words for everyday objects and animals—the word *cat*, for instance, varies across European languages only in details of spelling.

* Many geographical features and locales bear tautological names. For instance, the Sahara Desert literally means "Desert Desert," since *sahara* is the word for "desert" in Arabic. Similarly, Mount Fujiyama translates from Japanese as "Mount Fuji-mount," Lake Tahoe means "Lake Lake" in Washo, and the Mississippi River is "Big River River" in Algonquin. The world's most extreme example of a tautological place-name is probably Torpenhow Hill of west England (locally pronounced Trup-en-ah). *Tor*, *pen*, and *how* all mean "hill" in different languages, the first two being Celtic and the last being Anglo-Saxon. Therefore, "Torpenhow Hill" literally means "Hillhillhill Hill."

* The word *and* can easily be used five times in a row within a single grammatically correct sentence. For instance, suppose a business owner were painting a sign to hang above the front door: "Stanford and Andrews." A passerby might offer this advice: "You should adjust the spacing between 'Stanford' and 'and' and 'And' and 'rews.'" Similarly, the verb *had* can be used 11 times in a row, given appropriate punctuation: "In his essay, James, where John had had 'had,' had had 'had had'; 'had had' had had a better effect on the teacher."

The Struggle to Borrow a Book

While libraries have been around almost as long as civilization, they've only recently become a public enterprise.

✳   ✳   ✳   ✳

MOST OF US take the library for granted. We rely on the fact that we can stroll into a building conveniently located in our neighborhood; browse thousands of books, movies, or audio recordings; and borrow the selection of our choice for a few weeks. But this wasn't always the case. Although libraries in one form or another have existed for thousands of years, public lending libraries are a relatively recent invention.

The Early Days

The earliest known library was actually more of an archive for government and public records. Housed in a temple in the Babylonian city of Nippur some 5,000 years ago, the collection included thousands of clay tablets stored in several rooms. The ancient Greeks took a long stride toward our modern notion of a library by creating collections of writings on literature, philosophy, history, and mathematics that were kept in the famous schools established by great thinkers such as Plato and Aristotle. Libraries also flourished during this same period in China, particularly around 206 B.C. under the Han Dynasty, which charged its extensive civil service system with collecting, storing, and categorizing their collections.

These early libraries were not open to just anyone, and the notion of lending out scrolls and tablets would have been preposterous. With everything handwritten, items were simply too precious to let them leave the building. The ancient world's crowning achievement in book collecting was the great library at Alexandria, Egypt. Established by the Ptolemy Dynasty, the collection included several hundred thousand scrolls. This library was known to lend out part of its collection to other institutions—but only with substantial security deposits.

The Roman Empire also had its share of libraries—though many of their works were actually pilfered from Alexandria when Julius Caesar conquered Egypt—that served scholars and scientists. Roman baths also often contained library rooms with small collections that were available for patron use on-site.

During the Middle Ages in Europe, various monastic orders, particularly the Benedictines, kept extensive libraries that focused on spiritual works. They commonly lent works to one another, initiating what was probably the first interlibrary loan system. The Middle East saw significant growth in libraries between 700–1000 B.C., and many classical works of Greece and Rome survived only in Islamic collections. With the coming of the Renaissance and its emphasis on learning and literacy, public and private libraries flourished beginning in the 1600s, particularly in the many new European universities.

The Newest Thing

The 1700s saw the rise of two new trends—circulating libraries, which were profit-seeking ventures run by printers and book merchants who essentially rented books, and social libraries, which were private clubs whose paid members shared books among themselves. The first social library in America was said to have been founded by Benjamin Franklin in 1731.

It wasn't until 1833, when the New Hampshire legislature agreed to support a library in the town of Peterborough, that the first publicly funded, open-access library appeared in the United States. Boston opened the first city libraries in 1854, and other local governments followed suit, though they often faced opposition. Many felt it was a waste of taxpayer dollars. Thankfully, industrialist Andrew Carnegie had a different view. The father of the American public library system, Carnegie was a self-made millionaire who believed that education and hard work gave anyone a shot at the American Dream. He began bankrolling public libraries in 1886 and eventually donated more than $40 million to build libraries around the country.

Garden Gnomes:
Here (or There) to Stay

How German statue makers became the kings of kitsch.

✳ ✳ ✳ ✳

GNOMES HAVE APPEARED in folktales and mythology for hundreds of years, and they've been showing up in people's gardens for almost as long. Traditionally, these short, gnarled, ageless creatures were said to dwell underground, where they served as protectors of the earth's treasures.

A Gnome by Any Other Name...

The first garden gnomes were likely produced as early as the 1800s by the world-renowned statue makers of the German town of Gräfenroda. Similar to the gnomes we see today, these terra-cotta *gartenzwerge* (garden dwarves) were adorned with bright red caps, probably modeled after the head gear of the region's miners. Sir Charles Edmund Isham of Britain became enchanted with them while visiting Germany and brought about 20 of them back to his estate in Northamptonshire in 1847, beginning a gnome migration that would eventually spread across most of the globe. One of Isham's statues has survived to this day: Six inches tall and jauntily leaning on a shovel, he's known as Lampy, and he occasionally leaves the grounds of the estate to make appearances at conventions.

Gnome Sweet Gnome

After Isham helped popularize the little figures, two German ceramic artists, Phillip Griebel and August Heissner, began mass-producing them for the world. By 1900, more than a dozen companies in and around Gräfenroda were churning them out. The industry saw its ups and downs during the first half of the 20th century but came back strong in the 1960s. Griebel's company is still in business and actually produces some models from its founder's original patterns and molds.

Roaming Gnomes

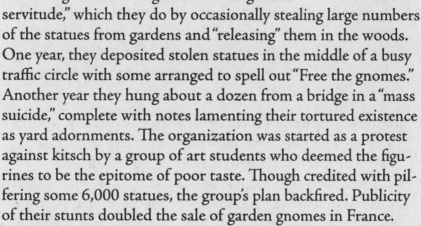

Today, there are as many people who love and collect gnomes as there are critics. The latter group includes a tongue-in-cheek organization known as the *Front de Libération des Nains de Jardins* (the Garden Gnome Liberation Front), which first appeared in France in the 1990s and has chapters in several countries. The stated goals of these pranksters are to end the evil of "gnome trafficking" and to free gnomes from "garden servitude," which they do by occasionally stealing large numbers of the statues from gardens and "releasing" them in the woods. One year, they deposited stolen statues in the middle of a busy traffic circle with some arranged to spell out "Free the gnomes." Another year they hung about a dozen from a bridge in a "mass suicide," complete with notes lamenting their tortured existence as yard adornments. The organization was started as a protest against kitsch by a group of art students who deemed the figurines to be the epitome of poor taste. Though credited with pilfering some 6,000 statues, the group's plan backfired. Publicity of their stunts doubled the sale of garden gnomes in France.

Another trick has more uncertain origins but a decidedly more playful motive. Gnome-napping victims are whisked to various locations around the world and photographed in front of famous landmarks. The owners receive pictures in the mail along with brief notes from their gnomes detailing their travels. The practice was famously documented in the 2001 French film *Amelie*, when the main character enlists a stewardess to play a prank on her father as a way to bring him out of his shell. But the roaming gnome phenomenon predates the film by at least 15 years. The earliest known incident involves a missing gnome from Sydney, Australia, who sent his owners a postcard claiming he was vacationing in Queensland. The gnome reappeared in the yard two weeks later with a light coat of brown shoe polish—apparently, he'd gotten a suntan at the beach.

Fifteen Tornado Safety Tips

The United States has significantly more tornadoes than the rest of the world because of low-lying geography and a climate that breeds strong thunderstorms. With wind speeds up to 320 miles per hour, tornadoes kill about 60 people every year in the United States when uprooted trees and debris turn into deadly missiles. Check out the list below and get prepared!

✳   ✳   ✳   ✳

1. **Determine the best locations for shelter at home and work.** The safest location is always a basement, below the deadly wind and projectile objects. If you can't go underground, find a small interior room or hallway on the lowest level of the building.

2. **Conduct tornado safety drills with your family.** Make learning quick and fun, and children will remember the basics of what to do, especially if you go through the motions several times. Just as most kids know what to do if their clothes are on fire, the same drill could be applied for tornado safety—instead of "Stop, drop, and roll" try "Run, duck, and cover!"

3. **Prepare an emergency supply kit.** Experts recommend that each person (and pet) has supplies for at least three days, including bottled water (two quarts per person, per day), nonperishable food, and a first-aid kit that includes prescription items as well as aspirin and antacids. Make sure you have tools such as a can opener, utility knife, wrench (for turning power valves), whistle, battery-powered radio, several flashlights, and batteries. Each person will need blankets, clothing, rain gear, and heavy-soled shoes or boots. Lastly, stash away some cash and a copy of credit cards, passports, social security cards, phone numbers, and insurance information. Once a year, check your supplies and determine if family needs have changed.

4. **Make an inventory of your possessions.** For insurance purposes, videotape or photograph everything you would need to replace in case you lose it all. When you're sure that you've included everything, keep the inventory somewhere away from the premises, such as a safe-deposit box.

5. **Know how your community sends its warnings.** If it's a siren, stay inside and take cover. Know where the designated shelters are in the buildings where you spend time.

6. **Know the difference between a "watch" and a "warning."** There's a big difference in the danger level between the two terms used during stormy weather. A watch simply means that conditions are favorable for a tornado to develop. Be alert, but you don't need to take shelter. If there's a warning, a tornado has been spotted. When a warning is posted for your area, take shelter immediately.

7. **Stay away from windows.** At 320 miles per hour, shards of glass can be deadly. You can eliminate this risk if you make sure your shelter area is free of windows. If this isn't possible, protect yourself with a heavy blanket.

8. **Don't bother opening windows.** It's true that air pressure equalizes when there's an opening in the building, but the American Red Cross says that it's far more important to get to safety than to open windows. If there's flying debris, the windows will most likely break on their own!

9. **Get in position.** Once you're in your shelter, find a sturdy piece of furniture, such as a workbench or table, and stay under it. Curl into a ball on the floor, and lock your hands behind your head to protect it from flying debris. If you can't find a table to get under, crouch under a door frame because the beams will offer some protection.

10. **Mobile home residents need to take extra precautions.** If you live in a mobile home, never try to ride out a severe thunderstorm at home; go to a prearranged shelter. As a

last resort, go outside and lie flat on the ground using your hands and arms to protect your head. It might be hard to believe that you're safer outside, but mobile homes are easily ripped from the ground.

11. **What if you're in a public building?** The first choice is a basement or lower level. If that isn't an option, avoid wide-open spaces such as cafeterias or auditoriums—there's not enough physical support for you there. Look for an inside hallway, or a small closet or bathroom (with no windows).

12. **What if you're in a vehicle?** Never try to outrun a tornado. Get out of your vehicle and try to get inside a building. If there isn't time, lie down flat in a ditch or any low-lying area away from the vehicle. (Hiding below an underpass isn't safe because you're still exposed to flying debris.) Use your hands and arms to protect your head.

13. **What if you're outdoors?** Finding a building is your best bet. If there's no time, follow the same instructions as above.

14. **What to do when the storm has passed.** Treat injuries with your first-aid kit, but don't attempt to move anyone who is severely injured. Use the phone only for emergencies, such as calling for an ambulance. Then, listen to the radio for emergency information. If the building you are in is damaged, beware of broken glass and downed power lines as you evacuate. Check on neighbors who might need assistance, but otherwise stay out of the way so that emergency crews can do their work.

15. **Beware of fire hazards.** Never strike a match until you're sure there is no leaking gas. Anything that holds gas can rupture and be vulnerable to explosions if you see (or smell) leakage after a storm. If you think there might be a gas leak, open all doors and get out of the house. Also watch out for severed electrical wires, which can spark debris piles. Check appliances to see if they are emitting smoke or sparks.

Primed to Be a Private Eye

Think being a PI is all high-speed chases and sultry suspects? Actually, for the most part, working as a private investigator can be a lot like any job—you stare blankly at a computer screen in a dimly lit cubicle for eight hours a day—only for less money. But the good news is that working in the private investigation field can be just about anything you make of it—just look at Thomas Magnum!

✳   ✳   ✳   ✳

THE FIRST PRIVATE eye on record was a French criminal and privateer named Eugene Francois Vidocq, who founded a private investigation firm in 1833. But Vidocq was hardly a man with a spotless record, and neither were his employees: Most of his investigators were his friends who were ex-convicts and others of questionable character. Vidocq was periodically arrested by the police on a series of trumped-up charges, but he was always released after they failed to produce enough evidence. Despite his questionable background, Vidocq made a number of significant contributions to the field of investigation, including record keeping, ballistics, indelible ink, and unalterable bond paper.

The Modern PI

Fast-forward to recent statistics from the U.S. Department of Labor, which state that in 2006, there were approximately 52,000 working gumshoes. While more than a third of working private investigators have college degrees, many have only high school diplomas or associate degrees, and some have neither. Those with college degrees come from varied backgrounds, such as accounting, computer science, business administration, or dozens of other majors that lend themselves to specific types of investigative work. Interestingly, most private investigators do not have a degree in criminal justice.

The Nature of the Work

Talk to anyone who's knowledgeable about the private investigation business and they'll tell you that the prerequisites for success are an unquenchable thirst for answers and the ability to root out details after everyone else has come up empty-handed. Superior communication skills and a special area of expertise, say, in computers, also come in handy. The most successful private eyes are people who can think logically, apply their unique knowledge to a problem, and consistently come up with creative means to their ends.

A Day in the Life

Depending on their background, private investigators can end up working for a variety of employers: individuals, professional investigative firms, law firms, department stores, or bail bondsmen. Many set up their own private practice. One place they can count on *never* working is for the local police department or the FBI. Government agencies rarely interface with private investigation firms. Unfortunately, that nixes the dramatic movie image of a lone-wolf PI getting a call in the middle of the night because the police are stumped.

The type of work private investigators do is largely dependent on the type of company they work for, the types of cases they take, and what their clients ask of them. The majority of cases have to do with locating lost or stolen property, proving that a spouse has been unfaithful, finding missing friends or relatives, conducting background investigations, or proving that a business associate absconded with the company cash.

Much of the work that private investigators do involves long hours sitting behind the wheel of their car doing surveillance with binoculars and cameras. Only the highest-profile cases involving investigative firms with large operating budgets can afford sophisticated surveillance vans loaded with high-tech equipment. Other cases require detectives to collect facts the old-fashioned way: by interviewing suspects, witnesses, and neighbors in person. Facts that can't be collected that way are often obtained by perusing public records by computer or researching tax records, business licenses, DMV records, real estate transactions, court records, and voter registrations.

The PI Paycheck

But how much can a private eye expect to make? Fortunately (or unfortunately, whatever the case may be), the entertainment industry has painted a rather broad picture of the private investigation business. For every television show about a PI living on a Hawaiian estate, there's another show about a PI living in a dilapidated trailer on the beach. The truth is, the median salary for private investigators in May 2008 was $41,760. The middle 50 percent earned between $30,870 and $59,060; the lowest and highest 10 percent earned $23,500 and $76,640, respectively. Not too shabby, but probably not the lap of luxury, either.

Still Want to Be a Private Eye?

For those who remain undaunted by the proposition of spending ten hours a day in a car or cubicle for $25,000 a year, here's some insight on how to pursue a career in private investigation:

Many private investigators have retired early from military, police, or fire department careers. Having pensions or retirement funds can help until the earnings as a PI increase.

Some states require specific schooling while others require new investigators to spend time completing on-the-job training before applying for their license. Most states have licensing requirements for becoming a PI, so it's important to look into what's required and how long it takes before one can expect to begin to make a decent living. If the type of work requires that private investigators carry a firearm, a private eye will need to look into the local ordinances for carrying a concealed weapon.

If nothing else, private investigation can certainly be a fascinating and challenging career choice that promises a break from the ordinary job doldrums.

Wicca: That Good Ol' Time Religion?

Until Wicca grew more popular in the 1990s, many people had never even heard of it. Even among Wiccans the debate continues to percolate: How old is this really?

❋ ❋ ❋ ❋

To STUDY THE genesis of the religious and magical practice of Wicca, one must be sure not to confuse "Wicca" with "witchcraft." Not all witches are Wiccan; Wicca is a nature religion that can involve the practice of witchcraft.

Antiquity

Throughout human existence, most cultures have had populations that might be considered "witches": esoteric specialists, such as midwives or herbalists, or people claiming spiritual contacts or divinatory skill. To believe someone is a witch is to believe that person is able to foresee or change outcomes. Some cultures fear and hate witches; others embrace them. We might call them folk practitioners, shamans, or witch doctors. Wicca cannot demonstrate descent from such stock, but it draws much inspiration from old Celtic and English folk practices.

During the medieval era, Christian leaders slew thousands of Europeans over witchcraft accusations. Many of that time's definitions of witchcraft were hardly credible because the persecutors themselves wrote them. They equated witchcraft with diabolism because if it wasn't Christian, it had to be Satanic.

Evidence suggests that the persecutions had little to do with witchcraft but much to do with vendettas, estate seizures (of affluent widows), and the governmental need for an enemy on which to focus public anger. Some Wiccans claim that Wicca endured in secret among the survivors of these persecutions. Unfortunately, there's no evidence that Wicca existed during "the Burning Times" in the first place, so survival is moot.

Victorian Renaissance

Interest in secret societies and the occult grew in Europe in the 19th century. Interest in ancient Greco-Roman philosophy grew along with admiration of ancient divinity concepts—including a feminine divine presence or, more bluntly, the idea of God as a woman. While that notion revolted many Judeo-Christian traditionalists, others found it appealing. By the early 1900s, several British occult organizations and movements drew upon and combined pre-Christian religious ideas and magical theory. Some simply gathered to party, whereas others formed study groups. While none were visibly Wiccan, they would later help to inspire Wicca.

Gardner

During the 1930s, an English civil servant named Gerald B. Gardner developed a strong interest in the occult. Some sources claim that socialite Dorothy Clutterbuck had initiated him into a witches' coven, but that's doubtful because Mrs. Clutterbuck was known as a devout Anglican. More likely, his initiation came from a woman known only as "Dafo," who later distanced herself from occultism. In the early 1950s, Gardner began popularizing a duotheistic (the god/the goddess) synthesis of religion and magic that he inititally called "Wica." Why then? Well, in 1951, Parliament repealed the 1735 Witchcraft Act, so it was now legal. Wicca borrowed all over the place, creating a tradition of eclecticism that thrives today.

Buckland

When Wicca came to America with Gardner's student Raymond Buckland in 1964, its timing was impeccable. For Wicca, the 1960s counterculture was rich soil worthy of a fertility goddess. Today, self-described "eclectic Wiccans"—Wiccans who essentially define their own Wicca to suit themselves—probably outnumber Gardnerians, a group one might fairly call "orthodox Wiccans." Rough estimates place the number of Wiccans in the United States today between 200,000 and 500,000.

The History of Birkenstocks

Birkenstock sandals may be icons of the 1960s, but the company that makes them is more than 200 years old.

✳ ✳ ✳ ✳

THE BIRKENSTOCK COMPANY traces its roots to the German village of Langen-Bergheim, where in 1774 Johann Birkenstock was registered as a "Shoemaker." In 1897, his grandson, Konrad Birkenstock, introduced the first contoured shoe lasts, which enabled cobblers to customize footwear.

At the time, there was a debate regarding whether it was healthier to train your feet to fit your shoes or to wear shoes made to support the foot's natural shape. The Birkenstock company worked to promote the second idea. By 1902, Birkenstock's flexible arch supports were being sold throughout Europe. During World War I, Birkenstock employees worked in clinics to design shoes especially for injured veterans.

It took the aching feet of a tourist to bring the Birkenstock to America. In 1966, Margot Fraser came across them during a visit to a German spa. The shoes soothed her foot ailments, and she was hooked. Fraser secured the distribution rights and set out to sell the strange-looking sandals back home.

At first, the only places that would carry her Birkenstocks were health food stores. In the 1970s, as health food became more popular, people discovered Birkenstocks at the same time that they discovered tofu and alfalfa sprouts. Birkenstocks' association with "granola" and "hippies" came directly out of this.

Although the company has attempted to bring its sandals into the realm of high-end fashion, the footwear has kept its "crunchy" connotations. Interestingly, researchers discovered shoes more than 8,000 years old in a cave in Missouri, and the modern shoe that they most resembled was the Birkenstock! Comfort never goes out of style.

Hot Ice

Antediluvian is highly pressurized carbon that began as dead plant and animal matter—hardly the stuff of romance, right?

✳   ✳   ✳   ✳

DIAMOND MINES WERE established near Kimberley, South Africa, around 1870, and soon after, British colonialist Cecil Rhodes began to poke around the area. He purchased various diamond claims, and in 1888 Rhodes merged his company with another, creating De Beers Consolidated Mines, Ltd.

From the outset, De Beers aimed for dominance of the African diamond trade. This was a very ambitious goal, not simply because of Africa's challenging geological and political nature, but because diamonds were considered just another gemstone, found only in riverbeds in Brazil and India. The few diamonds that were cultivated and sold justified a high price, but speculators were more interested in rarities such as gold and jade.

De Beers was nothing if not visionary. The company forged connections with miners, sellers, buyers, and cutters who were allowed to deal in diamonds only from De Beers and its affiliates. In structure and in practice, this was a cartel, which eventually had almost complete control over the trade. The key was manipulation of supply and demand. De Beers maintained a stockpiled inventory of unsold diamonds and purchased stones from other producers. By periodically withholding diamonds from the market, demand—and prices—escalated.

Sweet Romance

Meanwhile, Westerners fell prey to an ingenious marketing scheme that maintained diamonds were an ego-boosting signifier of discretionary income. Diamonds were also marketed as the only way a fella could hope to get his gal to blurt, "Yes! I'll marry you!" A copywriter named Frances Gerety devised the familiar ad line "A Diamond Is Forever" in 1947. By the second half of the 20th century, about 80 percent of the world's diamond supply was under De Beers's control. Almost all of those gems were mined in African colonies under shabby European control; the vast majority were sold in the United States.

An amusing irony to all this "commerce of romance" is that most raw diamonds are purchased cheaply by industry, because the real, practical value of diamonds is tied to the gems' extraordinary hardness and durability. Relatively simple contouring makes a diamond sharp and ideally suited for the grimy, dusty chores of cutting, drilling, grinding, and polishing.

Blood Diamonds

Western wholesalers, retailers, and buyers weren't concerned about where their rocks came from until the "blood diamond" scandal of 1998. The controversy began to brew in 1992, when a rebel group mixed up in the Angolan civil war created a complex diamond-smuggling network to finance arms deals. The strategy worked well and was adopted throughout the '90s by other troubled African nations, including Sierra Leone, Liberia, the Republic of Cote d'Ivoire (Ivory Coast), and the Democratic Republic of the Congo. The armies and militias that abused the populace of these countries, and stole boys and young men for duty as soldiers, would barely have been possible if not for the sale of rough diamonds.

The United Nations undertook an investigation of blood diamonds (or conflict diamonds) in 1998. Lurid news stories about atrocities financed by the West's desire for the gems were damaging embarrassments to De Beers and others in the diamond trade. The industry quickly distanced itself from the miserable nations involved. De Beers didn't have direct ownership of mines in any of these countries, but it did buy rough diamonds from war zones. The UN noted this and other facts, and initiated resolutions that prohibited the purchase of diamonds mined in conflict zones. In 1998, Angola was the first nation to be sanctioned by the UN on the diamond trade.

A Snag in the Process

By 2000, De Beers, other diamond concerns, and nonprofits formed the World Diamond Council. This body introduced the Kimberley Process Certification Scheme, to ensure that all rough diamonds are bought and sold in non-conflict zones. De Beers now claims that all of its diamonds are conflict-free.

The snag in the Kimberley Process is that while diamonds can be called conflict-free, to accurately trace the origins of many African diamonds is very difficult. It's a step in the right direction, but it may not be enough. Some observers are skeptical because the Kimberley Process is run from Kimberley, the very location of De Beers's earliest jackpot mines, and the home of De Beers–affiliated offices, mines, and distribution centers. Some may call the setup "practical." Others may call it "cozy."

Once the Kimberley Process was set in motion, an enormous number of diamonds were churned from mines that had supposedly been worked dry years before. The industry's toughest critics claim that the town is a way station that launders diamonds from questionable sources.

Is the Diamond Market Forever?

Recently, diamond-mining activity has increased in Canada, Russia, and Australia. Diamonds from these nations are certifiably conflict-free and are a growing presence on the world market. As for De Beers, its presence isn't as monolithic as before, but the company still controls about 40 percent of the world's diamond trade. However, the global economic recession that began in the fall of 2008 prompted De Beers to suspend mining operations in South Africa at the end of that year. In March 2009, De Beers temporarily shut down mines in Botswana, the most prolific of the company's African sources. As one diamond dealer in Johannesburg, South Africa, explained to *The Times* of London, "The bottom has fallen out of the market."

Statements on Stupidity

Fools, ignoramuses, dimwits—it's human nature to comment on stupid behavior, and we've gathered some interesting observations on a lack of intelligence.

✳ ✳ ✳ ✳

We are all born ignorant, but one must work hard to remain stupid.

BENJAMIN FRANKLIN, AMERICAN STATESMAN AND PHILOSOPHER

A person must have a certain amount of intelligent ignorance to get anywhere.

CHARLES KETTERING, INVENTOR

Two things are infinite: the universe and human stupidity; and I'm not sure about the universe.

ALBERT EINSTEIN, THEORETICAL PHYSICIST

He was distinguished for ignorance; for he had only one idea, and that was wrong.

BENJAMIN DISRAELI, BRITISH POLITICAN AND AUTHOR

In politics, stupidity is not a handicap.

NAPOLEON BONAPARTE, FRENCH EMPEROR

I do not believe in the collective wisdom of individual ignorance.

THOMAS CARLYLE, SCOTTISH ESSAYIST

A good man can be stupid and still be good. But a bad man must have brains.

MAXIM GORKY, RUSSIAN AUTHOR

Love is being stupid together.

PAUL VALERY, FRENCH POET

He was born stupid, and greatly increased his birthright.

SAMUEL BUTLER, POET

Anything too stupid to be said is sung.

VOLTAIRE, FRENCH PHILOSOPHER

When a stupid man is doing something he is ashamed of, he always declares that it is his duty.

GEORGE BERNARD SHAW, IRISH AUTHOR

A word to the wise ain't necessary—it's the stupid ones that need the advice.

BILL COSBY, COMEDIAN

Human beings can always be relied upon to exert, with vigor, their God-given right to be stupid.

DEAN KOONTZ, AUTHOR

Give me a smart idiot over a stupid genius any day.

SAMUEL GOLDWYN, MOVIE PRODUCER

If you're poor and you do something stupid, you're nuts. If you're rich and do something stupid, you're eccentric.

BOBBY HEENAN, PROFESSIONAL WRESTLING MANAGER

I'm not offended by dumb blonde jokes because I know that I'm not dumb. I also know I'm not blonde.

DOLLY PARTON, MUSICIAN AND ACTOR

I think there's a difference between ditzy and dumb. Dumb is just not knowing. Ditzy is having the courage to ask!

JESSICA SIMPSON, MUSICIAN AND ACTOR

If you think your boss is stupid, remember: You wouldn't have a job if he was any smarter.

JOHN GOTTI, MOBSTER

Some people think having large breasts makes a woman stupid. Actually, it's quite the opposite: A woman having large breasts makes men stupid.

RITA RUDNER, COMEDIAN

I may be dumb, but I'm not stupid.

TERRY BRADSHAW, NFL HALL OF FAMER

There is more stupidity than hydrogen in the universe, and it has a longer shelf life.

FRANK ZAPPA, MUSICIAN

When Oil Became an Industry

Today, oil is a well-established industry. But a little more than 100 years ago, oil took a backseat to coal when it came to energy.

✳ ✳ ✳ ✳

AT THE TURN of the 20th century, most, if not all, industrial and transportation equipment ran on coal. Used only for lubrication, lighting lamps, and sometimes for burning in stoves, oil wasn't a major energy source. The majority of America's oil was pumped in Pennsylvania. The Seneca nation in western Pennsylvania used oil that seeped from natural springs, and corporations realized that they could refine kerosene, used for cooking and lighting, from petroleum. Kerosene was in demand, as it was easier to obtain than whale oil.

Coal Is King

Why hadn't petroleum caught on? It had to do with the law of supply and demand. At the time, most oil rigs produced only about 50 barrels a day. There was no real indication that oil could be produced in large quantities. Coal, on the other hand, was plentiful and cheap. And gasoline? It was just a by-product of refining kerosene from oil. The internal combustion engine found in most cars today was little more than an experiment: The waste from refined kerosene made a good source of fuel for the engines. But gasoline wasn't plentiful enough to mass-market the new invention. Even so, one man believed that oil could be a major source of fuel. His name was Patillo Higgins.

Searching for a Gusher

Higgins, along with other investors, formed the Gladys City Oil Company in 1892. He was convinced that under the salt dome of Spindletop, Texas, was a large reserve of oil. After a couple of unsuccessful years, some of the partners—including Higgins—left the company. But in 1899, Higgins partnered with another man who shared his belief in Spindletop: Anthony F. Lucas.

A cable drilling tool was the industry standard for oil rigs in the 1800s. This tool dropped a wedge-shape bit into a hole, pulverizing the rock beneath. After a few drops, the debris was scooped out and the process repeated. When the team hit thicker rock, Lucas tried a new drilling system—the rotary drill. This drill used a cutting head similar to modern drill bits—teeth or sharp edges are rotated to cut through material. The rotary head attached to a long series of connected pipes.

Eureka!

Progress continued until January 10, 1901, when the drill reached depths between 1,000 and 1,140 feet, and workers suddenly had to run for their lives. It was raining pipes—tons of them! Up from the hole came a loud roar, followed by masses of steel drilling pipe shooting into the air. Shortly after, mud—lubricant for the drill—gurgled from the ground. Suddenly, the hole began to belch natural gas. Finally, the oil spewed out in a geyser more than 100 feet into the air. It took nine days to bring it under control.

Early on, Spindletop produced about 80,000 barrels of oil each day. Compare that to some modern oil rigs that produce about 100,000 barrels a day. However, the sudden abundance of oil wasn't the only success. Lucas had proved that rotary drilling could cut through deep, hardened layers of rock, and that these depths could contain large pockets of petroleum. With that, Higgins's prediction—that the world would demand oil instead of coal—soon came true.

By 1904, Spindletop—an area of about one square mile—hosted 400 oil rigs. Rigs soon spread across Texas and changed the landscape forever. With oil in abundance, industry quickly shifted, making room for the internal combustion engine to be further developed, which in turn helped fuel the demand for oil to make gasoline. The modern petroleum industry had begun.

How to Beat a Lie Detector Test

The polygraph or "lie detector" test is one of the most misunderstood tests used in law enforcement and industry.

MANY EXPERTS WILL tell you that lie detector tests are based on fallible data—regardless of how scientific the equipment appears, there's no sure way a person can tell whether or not someone is lying. Since the test is so imperfect, be suspicious of anyone who makes your fate contingent upon the results of a polygraph test. Still, here are a few suggestions on how to beat one:

1. Unless you're applying for a job, refuse to take the polygraph test. There are no laws that can compel anyone to take it.

2. Keep your answers short and to the point. Most questions asked of you can be answered with a "yes" or "no." Keep it simple.

3. During the polygraph test, you'll be asked three types of questions: irrelevant, relevant, and control questions. Irrelevant questions generally take the form of, "Is the color of this room white?" Relevant questions are the areas that get you into trouble. Control questions are designed to "calibrate" your responses during the test. See the next point.

4. Control questions are asked so that the technician can compare the responses to questions against a known entity. The easiest way to beat a lie detector test is to invalidate the control questions. Try these simple techniques when asked a control question:

   * Change your breathing rate and depth from the normal 15 to 30 breaths per minute to anything faster or slower.

   * Solve a math problem in your head, or count backward from 100 by 7.

   * Bite the sides of your tongue until it begins to hurt.

The Heart of Gander: Canadian Hospitality on 9/11

A calamity allowed a small town in Newfoundland to demonstrate its kindness and generosity to the entire world.

✳ ✳ ✳ ✳

W E LIVE UNDER a crowded sky. At any given moment, there may be a quarter of a million human beings in the air, in hundreds of airplanes, flying to and from the farthest corners of the planet. There may be a thousand transatlantic flights in the sky, half of them on their way to North America. And so it was on September 11, 2001.

The 9/11 Attacks

The story is familiar by now. That morning two airliners, commandeered by terrorists, struck the twin towers of the World Trade Center in New York City; another hit the Pentagon; and a fourth went down in Pennsylvania when the passengers and crew fought back against the hijackers.

At 9:45 A.M. eastern time, with about 500 flights coming in from Europe, the U.S. Federal Aviation Administration closed U.S. airspace. But those airliners high over the Atlantic Ocean had to go somewhere—and fast—because they only had so much fuel.

Unable to Enter the United States

The flights that were not far enough away from Europe to reach a "point of no return" were ordered back to the continent, but that still left more than 225 aircraft with no place to land but Canada. Canadian Transport Minister David Collenette gave orders to shut down Canadian airports to all outgoing flights except outgoing police, military, and humanitarian flights, and to accept incoming

U.S.-bound international flights. Action had to be taken immediately, because planes were coming into Canadian airspace at the rate of one or two per minute. There was a lot of sorting out to do in what the Transport Ministry called "Operation Yellow Ribbon."

Government officials in the United States and Canada didn't know what additional danger these incoming planes might contain, and they knew there was a very real possibility of another series of terrorist attacks—this time on the still-open Canadian cities. Therefore, planes were kept away from the busy airports in Toronto, Montreal, and Ottawa. They were instead diverted to airports in the Atlantic provinces of Nova Scotia, New Brunswick, and Newfoundland and Labrador. Halifax International Airport handled 40 flights, while other planes were sent to Greater Moncton International, Stephenville International, and the Canadian Forces Base at Goose Bay. Transpacific flights were mostly sent to land at Vancouver International Airport. Also, a total of 39 flights landed at Gander International Airport in the province of Newfoundland and Labrador.

The Edge of North America

Gander is located in the northeastern part of the island of Newfoundland. The area was chosen in 1935 as the site of a Royal Canadian Air Force Base, and a town began to grow up around it. During World War II, as many as 10,000 people lived near the base, which became an important fuel stop on flights to Europe, when aircraft couldn't carry enough fuel to make it from one continent to the other in a single bound. It was the last stop out and the first stop in for airplanes crossing the Atlantic Ocean. This earned the town the name: "Crossroads of the World."

After the war, the town was moved away from the expanded airport and became incorporated in 1958. Gander's orientation remained aeronautical, with many of its streets named for famous aviators such as Charles Lindbergh, Eddie Rickenbacker, and Chuck Yeager. Later, as improved aircraft made refueling in Gander unnecessary, the town's economy began to diversify, particularly with tourism.

Rising to the Occasion

In 2001, Gander had a population of roughly 9,000—it was about to get a great deal larger. As 39 wide-body jets began landing and filling the taxi-strips and parking aprons, thousands of crew and passengers were stuck on board, each one having to be screened before being deplaned and cleared through immigration. Not wanting to cause panic, the pilots of many of the aircraft had not told their passengers the reason for the stop. This had the unfortunate result of allowing rumor and fear to spread, so Canadian police and airport officials had to calm the jittery travelers as well as get them sorted out. Soon, Gander would have 6,600 additional mouths to feed and no word as to when U.S. airspace would reopen. What happened next has been seen by some as close to a miracle.

The town's citizens had been told of the situation, and they were waiting with food and blankets, ready to help. Some of those offering assistance had driven hundreds of miles from the other side of Newfoundland with stacks of sandwiches and kettles of soup. Gander had only 550 hotel rooms, so residents opened their schools, churches, and homes to the visitors, whom they called the "plane people." Even striking school bus drivers set aside their differences and bussed passengers to their temporary quarters. The phone company set up long-distance phone banks so the stranded could call home. High school students served as guides, and nurses and doctors saw to the passengers' medical needs. To help pass the time pleasantly, the visitors were given boat rides on the lake or excursions in the forest and were taken to restaurants. They were supplied with necessities like soap, deodorant, towels, tokens for doing laundry, and even underwear.

The residents of Gander opened their hearts and their homes to the stranded travelers and for three days housed, fed, and entertained them, until the interdict was lifted and the planes could continue on to U.S. airports. All across Canada people rose to the occasion.

An Honorable Legacy

On September 11, 2002, Canadian Prime Minister Jean Chretien, Transport Minister David Collenette, and U.S. Ambassador Paul Cellucci traveled to Gander to join 2,500 citizens at the airport for a memorial service to mark the first anniversary of the attacks. Chretien said, "9/11 will live long in memory as a day of terror and grief. But thanks to the countless acts of kindness and compassion done for those stranded visitors here in Gander and right across Canada, it will live forever in memory as a day of comfort and of healing." In summation he added, "You did yourselves proud, ladies and gentlemen, and you did Canada proud."

In gratitude, Lufthansa Airlines has named an airliner the Gander/Halifax. And the passengers have not forgotten the kindnesses shown to them. Though the citizens of Gander neither asked for nor expected anything in return, their guests have sent cards, gifts, and donations of more than $60,000 for the town. Some have returned to vacation there and once again enjoy Canadian hospitality.

✳ *TIME* magazine rarely deviates from the familiar red band on its covers. However, a black band commemorated the terrorist attacks of September 11, 2001, and a green band celebrated the environment on April 28, 2008.

The Beginnings of Braille

Once upon a time, a world without seeing meant a world without reading. This changed forever when Louis Braille, a precocious blind teenager, invented an ingenious system that finally enabled the blind to read with ease.

✳ ✳ ✳ ✳

THROUGHOUT HISTORY, MANY different remedies, inventions, and institutions have been developed to accommodate the blind. These usually develop in cities where the blind population is large enough to necessitate such programs. The first large-scale school for the blind, called the Quinze-Vingts hospice, was endowed in 1260 by Louis IX of France. The students there set off the extraordinary chain of events that ultimately led to Braille.

In 1771, brilliant French linguist Valentin Haüy watched men from the Quinze-Vingts hospice perform in front of a mocking crowd. Haüy was enraged that instead of receiving a good education, blind students were reduced to performing in the street. As the story goes, a few years later, Haüy gave a coin to a blind beggar, who determined the denomination of the money by feeling the bumps on its face. Haüy was inspired, and in 1784, he opened his own school for the blind, The Royal Institute for Blind Youth, in Paris. He made embossed, oversize books with raised letters, usually round and cursive, that the blind could feel, one by one, as they read. Embossed books made reading slow and difficult, but Haüy's students were grateful to be able to read at all.

Braille Enters the Scene

Around the same time Haüy was teaching his pupils in Paris, Louis Braille was born in Coupvray, a village located east of France's capital. Louis injured his eye at the age of three while playing with his father's tools. The injury became infected, and the infection quickly spread to the other eye. Eventually, young Louis went blind. It was clear to everybody in Coupvray that Louis was a special child—he showed a genius for music and craftsmanship, and in 1819, at the age of ten, he was awarded a scholarship to the school Haüy had founded.

Louis was amazed by the embossed books at his new school. Haüy's books were cumbersome and expensive, so there were only 14 in the library. Louis read them all, but the process was laborious: Each letter had to be felt individually, so by the time Louis finished a sentence, he could barely remember how it had begun. He began experimenting to improve on Haüy's method.

Braille Meets Barbier

Louis's moment of insight came from an unexpected source. Charles Barbier de la Serre, an entrepreneur and soldier in the French army, visited Haüy's school in the 1820s. Barbier had devised a system of touch-based communication while serving as a captain under Napoleon. During battle, it was necessary for officers to communicate quickly at night amid loud artillery fire. Barbier devised a technique called "night writing," in which pages were embossed with a system of dots rather than raised letters.

Louis was amazed. Raised dots would be easier to feel than raised letters, and if the dots were small, several of them could be felt at once against a fingertip. Louis set to work on his own dot-based alphabet. In 1824, at the age of 15, Louis perfected the system that is now known as Braille. Each Braille character is called a *cell*, and there are one to six dots in a six-position cell. The given letter or punctuation mark depends on which dot is raised, in which position, within the cell.

Louis taught his invention to his fellow students, who learned it quickly. The superiority of Louis's method was immediately obvious to anyone who used it. Louis also developed a Braille code for music. Today, standardized Braille codes have been developed for languages the world over, and it is the best and most popular form of reading for the blind.

Military Jargon Gets Mustered Out

These interesting military phrases have seeped into civilian life so successfully that many people don't realize they started out as soldier slang.

✳   ✳   ✳   ✳

Blockbuster: Today the word usually refers to a wildly successful movie, but during World War II it was a nickname used by the Royal Air Force for large bombs that could "bust" an entire city block. "Blockbuster" retired from military service in the 1950s when advertisers started using it as a synonym for gigantic.

Bought the Farm/Gone for a Burton: Because they face death daily, most soldiers try to avoid talking about it. During World War I, U.S. soldiers often said that someone missing or killed had "bought the farm"—what many families did with their loved one's death benefits. Heavy-hearted British soldiers in World War II would raise a glass—in this case a British beer called Burton—to a departed brother, saying he'd "gone for a Burton."

Push the Envelope: If you're tired of your boss urging you to "push the envelope," blame World War II test pilots. They listed a plane's abilities—speed, engine power, maneuverability—on its flight envelope and then did their best to get the plane to outperform its predetermined limits.

Bite the Bullet: During the Civil War, the "anesthetic" often used on wounded soldiers was a bullet or block of wood to bite down on. The patient, with no alternative, was forced to endure the procedure and excruciating pain so he could get on with the process of healing.

Show Your True Colors/With Flying Colors: Military regiments would end a victorious battle "with flying colors," or with their flag ("colors") held high for all to see. To "show your true colors," or to reveal your intentions, derives from early warships that would temporarily fly another nation's flag to deceive an enemy into feeling safe.

Over the Top: Nobody wanted to go over the top during World War I—that is, to charge over the parapets toward the enemy, a maneuver that resulted in high casualties. Soldiers who went over the top were considered incredibly—even excessively—brave.

Boondocks: In the early 1900s, U.S. troops in the Philippines fought guerillas hiding in the remote *bandok*—Tagalog (the primary language of the Philippines) for "mountains." Soldiers translated the word as boondocks.

Grapevine: Civil War soldiers likened telegraph wires to grapevines, the latter having a gnarled appearance. News that arrived by "grapevine telegraph" (or simply "grapevine") was eventually considered to be "twisted" or dubious.

Rank and File: Military officers lined up marching soldiers in "ranks," rows from side to side, and "files," rows from front to back. When the soldiers returned to their offices and factories after military service, "rank and file" came to represent the ordinary members of society.

"Veni, vidi, vici." (I came, I saw, I conquered.)

JULIUS CAESAR

"Never in the field of human conflict was so much owed by so many to so few."

WINSTON CHURCHILL

"I have not yet begun to fight."

CAPTAIN JOHN PAUL JONES

Common Misconceptions

Don't believe everything you read in the history books. Many events that for centuries have been passed down as true have eventually been proven false. Some were originally based on fact, but all became twisted and embellished as they were told and retold like a game of telephone. None of the following really happened.

✳   ✳   ✳   ✳

1. **Lady Godiva's Naked Ride:** Even if the Internet had existed during the Middle Ages, you wouldn't have been able to download nude pictures of Lady Godiva because she never actually rode naked through the streets of Coventry, England. Godiva was a real person who lived in the 11th century, and she really did plead with her ruthless husband, Leofric, the Earl of Mercia, to reduce taxes. But no records of the time mention her famous ride. The first reference to her naked ride doesn't appear until around 1236, nearly 200 years after her death.

2. **Sir Walter Raleigh's Cloak:** The story goes that Sir Walter Raleigh laid his cloak over a mud puddle to keep Queen Elizabeth I from getting her feet wet. Raleigh did catch the queen's attention in 1581 when he urged England to conquer Ireland. The queen rewarded him with extensive landholdings in England and Ireland, knighted him in 1584, and named him captain of the queen's guard two years later. But an illicit affair with one of the queen's maids of honor in 1592 did him in. He was imprisoned in the Tower of London and ultimately beheaded for treachery. The story of the cloak and the mud puddle probably originated with historian Thomas Fuller, who was known for embellishing facts.

3. **Nero Fiddled While Rome Burned:** When asked who fiddled while Rome burned, the answer "Nero" will get you a zero. Legend has it that in A.D. 64, mad Emperor Nero

started a fire near the imperial palace and then climbed to the top of the Tower of Maecenas where he played his fiddle, sang arias, and watched Rome flame out. But according to Tacitus, a historian of the time, Nero was 30 miles away, at his villa in Antium, when the fire broke out. Nero wasn't exactly a nice guy—he took his own mother as his mistress, then had her put to death. Despite this, historians believe that the fire was set by Nero's political enemies, who were right in thinking that it would be blamed on him. Actually, Nero was a hero, attempting to extinguish the blaze, finding food and shelter for the homeless, and overseeing the design of the new city.

4. **The Forbidden Fruit:** Both the apple and Eve get an undeserved bad rap in the story of Paradise. According to the Book of Genesis, Adam and Eve were evicted from Paradise for eating "the fruit of the tree which is in the midst of the garden." There's no mention of any apple! Some biblical scholars think it was a fig, since Adam and Eve dressed in fig leaves, while Muslim scholars think it may have been wheat or possibly grapes. Aquila Ponticus, a 2nd-century translator of the Old Testament, may have assumed that the apple tree in the Song of Solomon was the fruit-bearing tree in Genesis. Two centuries later, St. Jerome also linked the apple tree to the phrase "there wast thou corrupted" in his Latin translation of the Old Testament.

5. **Cinderella Wore Glass Slippers:** Ask anyone and they'll tell you that Cinderella wore glass slippers to the ball, but historians say that part of the legend isn't true. More than 500 versions of the classic fairy tale exist, dating back as far as the 9th century. In each account, Cinderella has a magic ring or magic slippers made of gold, silver, or some other rare metal, which are sometimes covered with gems but are never made of glass. In the earliest French versions, Cinderella wore *pantoufles en vair* or "slippers of white squirrel fur." In 1697, when French writer Charles Perrault

wrote "Cendrillon," his version of the tale, the word *vair* had vanished from the French language. Perrault apparently assumed it should have been *verre*, pronounced the same as *vair*, but meaning "glass."

6. **Witches Were Burned at the Stake in Salem:** Although there really were witch trials in Salem, Massachusetts, in 1692, and 20 people were put to death, none of the accused were burned at the stake. Hanging was the method of execution, although one victim was crushed to death under heavy stones. Moreover, there's no evidence these people were practicing witchcraft or were possessed by the devil. Historians now believe that they, along with their persecutors, were suffering from mass hysteria.

7. **"Let Them Eat Cake":** She probably said a lot of things she later regretted, but Marie Antoinette never suggested hungry French mothers who had no bread should eat cake. In 1766, Jean Jacques Rousseau was writing his "Confessions" when he quoted the famous saying of a great princess, which was incorrectly attributed to Marie Antoinette, Queen of France and wife of Louis XVI. But Marie Antoinette couldn't have made the statement because in 1766, she was only 11 years old. Historians now believe that Rousseau's "great princess" may have been Marie Thérèse, the wife of Louis XIV, who reigned more than 75 years before Louis XVI and Marie Antoinette.

8. **The Great Wall of China Is Visible from the Moon:** You can see a lot of things while standing on the moon, but the Great Wall of China isn't one of them. In his 1938 publication, *Second Book of Marvels*, Richard Halliburton stated that the Great Wall was the only human-made object visible from the moon. However, the Great Wall is only a maximum of 30 feet wide and is about the same color as its surroundings, so it's barely visible to the naked eye while orbiting Earth, much less from the moon.

A Bomb in a Bottle

You don't toast the bride with this cocktail.

✳   ✳   ✳   ✳

THE MOLOTOV COCKTAIL is a crude but effective hand-held weapon that can be put together as simply as a grade-school science experiment: Fill a slim, easily gripped bottle to about the three-quarter mark with gasoline or other flammable liquid (kerosene and even wood alcohol will do); push a wick-like shred of oily rag snugly into the neck of the bottle; and wait for the perfect moment. Then light the rag, fling the bottle, and watch for the red-orange explosion of fire. The ideal outcome is a panicked scramble of enemy troops, some of them ablaze and many out in the open, where they can be picked off by gunfire.

Originally known as the petrol or gasoline bomb, this simple but intimidating weapon took its most enduring name from Soviet Foreign Minister Vyacheslav Molotov, who claimed on radio broadcasts during his nation's brutal 1939–40 Winter War against Finland that the USSR wasn't dropping bombs on the Finns, despite all evidence to the contrary. The Finnish Army jokingly responded to the foreign minister's lie by calling the Soviet air bombs "Molotov breadbaskets." Finnish troops had already been using petrol bombs against the invading Soviets (the devices had been widely used in the Spanish Civil War of 1936–39) and soon dubbed them "Molotov cocktails."

During the Winter War, Finland's national alcohol retailing monopoly, Alko, manufactured 450,000 bottle bombs made from a mix of ethanol, tar, and gasoline—perhaps the only time the weapon has been professionally produced on a mass scale.

That winter, the Finns bloodied the Soviets far more seriously than the world anticipated, and although they ultimately lost the brutish little war, "Molotov cocktail" would shortly enter the popular lexicon. Cheers!

Zoot Suits: 1940s Hip-hop

In their time, zoot suits were more than a clothing fad.
They were the minority cultural statement of their day.

✳ ✳ ✳ ✳

T HERE'S NO WAY to know for certain who wore the first zoot suit—the fashion didn't get a name until lots of guys were wearing them. Reports exist of similar fashions as far back as 1907. To trace the fashion's early popularity, though, we must go back to Harlem in the 1930s, where the entertainment was swing or jazz, and young African American men hitting the nightspots wanted to look sharp. Like young people of any era, these cats adapted something and made it theirs.

In the early days, the zoot suit was called a *drape*. It would be as flashy as the cat could afford: plenty of color, padded shoulders, accessorized with a long watch chain and a hat. Many young zoot-suiters topped the look with a "conk," a style in which the hair is straightened with an agonizing lye treatment.

What It Was

For a description, let's consult a zoot-suiter who may be familiar to you. He was born to a Baptist minister and named Malcolm Little, but America knows him as African American activist Malcolm X: "I was measured, and the young salesman picked off a rack a zoot suit that was just wild: sky blue pants thirty inches in the knee and angle-narrowed down to twelve inches at the bottom, and a long coat that pinched my waist and flared out below my knees."

Naming It

Credit for the term "zoot suit" usually goes to Harold C. Fox, a clothier and musician from Chicago. But how? The language of zoot suits was a language of rhyme: "reet pleats," "reave sleeves," "ripe stripes," "stuff cuffs," and "drape shape." Fox claimed that he said "zoot suit" because in jive, "the end to all ends" was the ultimate praise, so he used the ending letter of the alphabet for a rhyme. The rest of the terminology is well documented, so Fox's claim isn't easy to dismiss. He continued to wear zoot suits for the remainder of his long life, and in 1996 he was buried in one. Now that's old-school.

Branching Out

The zoot suit caught on with young minority males, and more than a few whites, all across the country. In Southern California, the zoot suit became a cultural statement for stylish young Hispanic cats called *pachucos*. This was long before Hispanic America found a national political voice, so the *pachuco* culture was an early regional and cultural identity statement, and its drape was the zoot suit. Nor was it just for men. *Pachucas* wore short-skirted variants of the zoot suit, lots of makeup, and big hair.

Some claim that the term "zoot suit" came from street Spanish (called *caló* in reference to old Spanish gypsy slang), but Fox's Chicago version has clearer roots.

Pedroing Out

As the United States entered World War II, the zoot suit represented frivolity when the nation was in an austere, buckle-down mood. In June 1943, tension boiled over in L.A.'s Zoot Suit Race Riots, with civilians and servicemen attacking any zoot-suiter—typically Hispanic, Filipino, or African American.

By 1950, the fashion was in decline. Now it's part of history.

You got to be tricking yourself out like the dude ... look like a zoot, walk like a zoot, talk like a zoot."

—THOMAS SANCHEZ, FROM HIS BOOK *ZOOT SUIT MURDERS*

American Terms and Their British Equivalents

We're talking about two nations divided by a common language.

✳ ✳ ✳ ✳

	American Term	British Term
1.	ballpoint pen	biro
2.	toilet paper	bog roll
3.	umbrella	brolly
4.	fanny pack	bum bag
5.	cotton candy	candy floss
6.	french fry	chip
7.	plastic wrap	clingfilm
8.	zucchini	courgette
9.	potato chip	crisp
10.	checkers	draughts
11.	thumbtack	drawing pin
12.	busy signal	engaged tone
13.	soccer	football
14.	astonished	gobsmacked
15.	sweater	jumper
16.	elevator	lift
17.	restroom	loo
18.	truck	lorry
19.	ground beef	mince
20.	diaper	nappy
21.	mailbox	pillar box
22.	bandage (Band-Aid)	plaster
23.	baby carriage/stroller	pram
24.	collect call	reverse-charge call
25.	aluminum can	tin
26.	to go drastically wrong	to go pear-shaped
27.	complain	whinge

Satanic Marketing

What's behind the vicious rumor that put mega-corporation Procter & Gamble on many churches' hit lists?

✳ ✳ ✳ ✳

PROCTER & GAMBLE, one of the largest corporations in the world, manufactures a plethora of products, from pet food to potato chips. The company takes pride in its reputation as a trusted business, so it was a huge shock when, starting in the 1960s, Christian churches and individuals around the country spread the rumor that P&G was dedicated to Satan.

The Devil Is in the Details

How the rumor got started remains a mystery. According to one of the most popular versions of the story, the president of P&G appeared on *The Phil Donahue Show* in March 1994 and announced that, because of society's new openness, he finally felt comfortable revealing that he was a member of the Church of Satan and that much of his company's profits went toward the advancement of that organization. When Donahue supposedly asked him whether such an announcement would have a negative impact on P&G, the CEO replied, "There aren't enough Christians in the United States to make a difference."

There's one problem with this story—and with the variations that place the company president on *The Sally Jessy Raphael Show*, *The Merv Griffin Show*, and *60 Minutes*: It didn't happen.

Lose the Logo

Adding fuel to the fable was the company's logo, which featured the image of a "man in the moon" and 13 stars. Many interpreted this design to be Satanic, and some even claimed that the curlicues in the man's beard looked like the number 666—the biblical "mark of the Beast." By 1985, the company had become so frustrated that it had no choice but to retire the logo, which had graced P&G products for more than 100 years.

Speaking Out

Procter & Gamble tried to quell the rumors, which resulted in more than 200,000 phone calls and letters from consumers. Company spokespeople vehemently denied the story, explaining: "The president of P&G has never discussed Satanism on any national televised talk show, nor has any other P&G executive. The moon-and-stars trademark dates back to the mid-1800s, when the 'man in the moon' was simply a popular design. The 13 stars in the design honor the original 13 colonies."

In addition, the company turned to several prominent religious leaders, including evangelist Billy Graham, to help clear its name, and when that didn't work, it even sued a handful of clergy members who continued to spread the offending story. Talk show host Sally Jessy Raphael also denied the allegations, noting, "The rumors going around that the president of Procter & Gamble appeared on [my] show and announced he was a member of the Church of Satan are not true. The president of Procter & Gamble has never appeared on *The Sally Jessy Raphael Show*."

Senseless Allegations

Like most urban legends, this story falls apart under the slightest scrutiny. First, one must ask why the CEO of an international conglomerate (especially one that answers to stockholders) would risk decades of consumer goodwill—not to mention billions in sales—to announce to the world that his company was run by and catered to Satanists. Even if that were the case, he needn't bother announcing it, since any deals with the devil would be a matter of public record.

In 2007, a jury awarded Procter & Gamble $19.25 million in a civil lawsuit filed against four former Amway distributors accused of spreading false rumors about the company's ties to the Church of Satan. The distributors were found guilty of using a voicemail system to inform customers that P&G's profits were used to support Satanic cults.

Go Ahead—Speak Canadian!

There is, of course, no single "Canadian slang" in such a huge nation with people spread over thousands of miles. Canada has two official languages for ambitious slang-slingers to corrupt!

✳ ✳ ✳ ✳

✳ **Allophone:** someone whose mother tongue is other than English or French, usually an immigrant but sometimes an Aboriginal Canadian.

✳ **Biscuit:** something half of Canadians pursue and the other 49 percent watch—namely, a hockey puck.

✳ **Bloquiste:** a member of the Bloc Quebecois, a national political party advocating the independence of Quebec.

✳ **Bunnyhug:** same thing as a "hoodie," that is, a hooded sweatshirt with pockets in front for your hands (or other stuff). Seems to have originated on the Prairies.

✳ **Deke:** a fake out, from "decoy." The term began as hockey slang for putting a move on an opponent, then went from rinks to the mainstream.

✳ **Dépanneur:** Dep for short, this is a convenience store. The word comes from the term for a repairperson, someone who gets you out of difficulty—as a convenience store does. Common in both English and French in Quebec.

✳ **Eh:** tag question roughly meaning "you see?" Canadians' signature utterance is the one folks in the United States most often kid them about—in fact, they do it so often that it long ago grew old. Best not used by visitors to Canada.

✳ **Five-hole:** between a hockey goalie's legs. Could refer to anything passing through one's legs or to any situation where someone got away with something at your expense.

✳ **Garburator:** the garbage-disposal unit under a sink.

* **Grits:** the Liberal Party, a moderate-left national political party with its main power base in Ontario. As a rule, the Grits have to screw up pretty badly to be out of power.

* **Holy!:** expression of surprise. Emphasize the first syllable.

* **Hoser:** narrowly speaking, a clumsy, foolish, probably drunk person. Used to refer to anyone who can't cut the mustard. Thanks to Canadian comics Dave Thomas and Rick Moranis doing Bob and Doug McKenzie on SCTV, and much to Canadians' general chagrin, Americans have adopted it as slang for "Canadian."

* **Keener:** a brown-noser.

* **Molson muscle:** beer gut, apparent among sufferers of the condition known in the United States as "Dunlop's Disease" ("Your belly done lops over your belt").

* **Shebang:** a crude shelter or hut.

* **Shivaree:** a loud serenade for newlyweds, Acadian in origin, intended to chase away evil spirits.

* **Sieve:** more hockey slang, meaning a terrible goalie.

* **Skookum:** British Columbian slang for someone or something strong or sturdy, from the Chinook jargon spoken by most British Columbian and Washington state tribes of old.

* **Spud Island:** Prince Edward Island (called P.E.I.), which is essentially Canada's Idaho in terms of agriculture.

* **Tory:** used to refer to the Progressive Conservatives, Canada's moderate right wing before right banded together in hopes of winning federal power. Still used by some for its successor, the Conservative Party of Canada.

* **Touque:** rhymes with "Luke" and refers to a stocking cap, watch cap, etc. In most of Canada during winter, the term for one who does not wear a touque is "hypothermia fatality."

Index

✳ ✳ ✳ ✳

Mythical creatures, 24–27
"My Way," 205, 211

N

O'Rourke, Heather, 603
Orphans of the Storm, 190
Orr, Coby, 98
Orwell, George, 407
Osbournes, The, 554
Ostriches, 133–34
Oswald, Lee Harvey, 20, 21
Otello (opera), 246
Othello (Shakespeare), 218, 246
Ott, J. J., 19
Our Mutual Friend (Dickens), 231, 232, 233
Out: Stories of Lesbian and Gay Youth in Canada, 242
"Over the Rainbow," 176
Owen, Robert, 324
Owens Valley, 422–23
Oz, Frank, 176

P

Pacepa, Ion, 21
Pacino, Al, 188, 402
"Pale Moon Light," 317
Palermo, Vincent "Vinnie Ocean," 345
Palmer, Arnold, 98
Pantomime, 202, 203
Parker, Bonnie, 346, 348–50
Parker, Charlie, 605
Parker, Dorothy, 236
Parker, Pauline, 632–33
Parks, Rosa, 434
Parsons, Jack, 38–40
Particle beam weapons, 70–71
Pasternak, Boris, 220
Patch, Sam, 382–83
Patriot, The, 154
Paul, Les, 230
Paxton, Bill, 195
Payette, Julie, 482
Peanut butter, 580–81
Pearl Harbor, 286–87
Pearl Jam, 217, 556
Pearlroth, Norbert, 621
Peck, Gregory, 514
Pencils, 384
Pennies, 389–90
People (magazine), 139, 251
People's Temple, The, 363–64
Percy, Walker, 208

Perkins, Frank, 22
Perrault, Charles, 670–71
Perry, Anne, 632–33
Perry, Matthew, 166
Perry, William "The Refrigerator," 85
Persistence of Memory, The, 239
Peshtigo, WI, fire, 618–19
Peter, Laurence, 199–200
Peter Plan, The (Peter), 199
Peter Prescription, The (Peter), 199
Peter Principle, The (Peter), 199–200
Peter Pyramid: Will We Ever Get to the Point?, The (Peter), 199–200
Peter the Great (Czar of Russia), 582
Petitclerc, Chantal, 482
Pets of celebrities, 137–40
Peyton Place (TV show), 502
PEZ candy, 547–48
Pheidippides, 90–91
Phelan, Gerard, 94
Phenomena, unexplained, 19
Philadelphia Experiment, 13–14
Phil Donahue Show, The, 676
Phobias, 251
Phoenix, River, 603
Picasso, Pablo, 213, 224, 238, 240
Pickford, Mary, 189–90, 434
Pierce, Franklin, 292
Piercing, 68, 557
Pillow Talk, 188
Pincus, Gregory, 54, 55
Pinkerton, Allan, 598
Piracy, 293–94
Piranha, 135–36
Pirsig, Robert, 200
Pi-Sheng, 47
Piston Coal Company, 634–35
Pitt, Brad, 187
Plan 9 from Outer Space, 352
Planet of the Apes, 192
Planned Parenthood Federation, 54, 55
Plante, Jacques, 96
Plath, Sylvia, 604
Plato, 37
Plato, Dana, 605
Pliny the Elder, 133
Poe, Edgar Allan, 137
Poisons, 247–50
Polk, James K., 291, 321

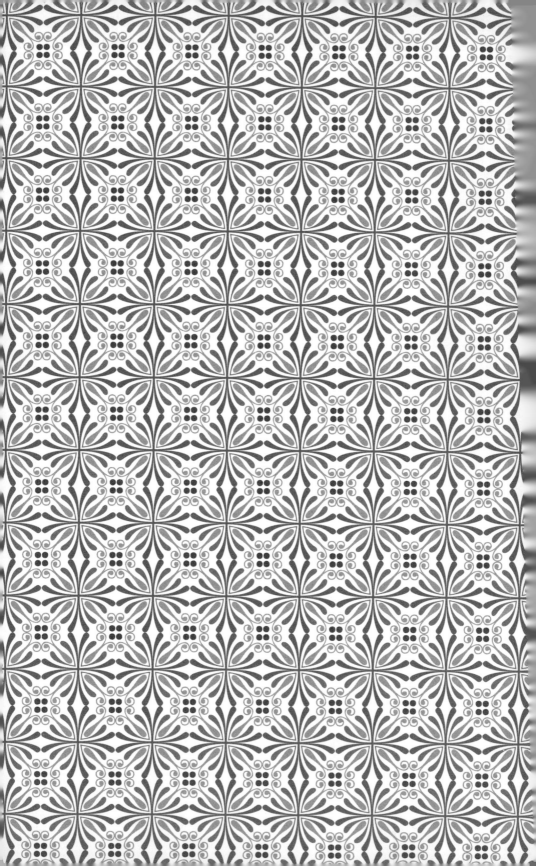